THE KING'S OWN L

In memory of my father

Paul Langer

holder of the Cross for Civil Merit in Wartime,
awarded to him in 1915 by the Emperor Francis Joseph
for his successful proposals for a method of pension payments
to the war widows of the War of 1914–18

promoted by the then President of Austria
to the second highest rank in the Austrian Civil Service
on 1 January 1938

dismissed by the Nazis ten weeks later
because he had been born a Jew. Set to work as a dustman in 1941,
deported to Theresienstadt in 1943, to Auschwitz in 1944.

He has not been heard of again.

Let this be his memorial.

THE KING'S OWN LOYAL ENEMY ALIENS

German and Austrian Refugees in
Britain's Armed Forces, 1939–45

PETER LEIGHTON-LANGER

Foreword by
the Right Reverend Dr Peter Selby
Bishop of Worcester and Bishop to Her Majesty's Prisons

VALLENTINE MITCHELL
LONDON • PORTLAND, OR

First published in 2006 in Great Britain by
VALLENTINE MITCHELL
Suite 314, Premier House, 112–114 Station Road,
Edgware, Middlesex HA8 7BJ

and in the United States of America by
VALLENTINE MITCHELL
c/o ISBS, 920 NE 58th Avenue, Suite 300
Portland, OR 97213-3786

Website: www.vm.books.com

British Library Cataloguing in Publication Data
Leighton-Langer, Peter
    The king's own loyal enemy aliens – German and Austrian
    refugees in Britain's armed forces, 1939–45
    1. Aliens – Great Britain – History – 20th century
    2. Political refugees – Germany – History – 20th century
    3. Political refugees – Austria – History – 20th century
    4. Political refugees – Great Britain – History – 20th century
    5. World War, 1939–1945 – Great Britain – Refugees
    6. Great Britain – Armed Forces – History – World War, 1939–1945
    I. Title
    940.5'4'008931'041

ISBN 0-85303-691-8 (cloth)
ISBN 978-0-85303-691-3 (cloth)
ISBN 0-85303-693-4 (paper)
ISBN 978-0-85303-693-7 (paper)

Library of Congress Cataloging-in-Publication Data
A catalog record has been applied for

X steht für unbekannt, by the same author, was published in German by
Berlin Verlag Arno Spitz GmbH (1999) now Berliner Wissenschafts-Verlag BWV

English manuscript first published in Germany by the author in 2003.
P. Leighton-Langer, Neumarkt 3, 64625 Bensheim, Germany.
Copyright © P. Leighton-Langer

Typeset in 11/13pt Janson Text by FiSH Books, Enfield, Middx.
Printed in Great Britain by MPG Books Ltd, Bodmin, Cornwall

Contents

List of Plates

The author thanks all those who provided photographs for their kind assistance. The Royal Pioneer Corps Association photographs are held at the Royal Logistical Corps Museum, Deepcut.

Foreword

To engage with history is to engage with paradox. The title of this book is about such a historic paradox: that the vast majority of the 'enemy aliens' in Britain during the Second World War were people whose loyalty to Britain was beyond reproach. They were aliens by birth, but sought with gratitude to make their home in Britain, not just physically but in many cases emotionally too. They were often among those with the strongest feelings of loyalty to the King. 'Enemy aliens' they were, because the country from which they came was one with which Britain was at war; but they were in every important sense friends of Britain. Their loyalty was beyond question.

To engage with history is sometimes also to engage with a detail of one's own life. My parents were not among those about whom this book is written, in that they did no military service: my father's occupation as a qualified engineer was deemed sufficiently important for him to be required to continue in that task as a civilian, after he had been interned as an 'enemy alien' and then quickly released. But as I read the many stories contained in this book I observe the same instincts – love for their new and adopted country and a determination to make it their home and play their part in securing its traditions and its liberties – that I recall from the conversations within my own family and with family friends, of whom Peter Leighton-Langer was one. The particular ways in which individuals and families served their new homeland and took their place within it varied, naturally; this book is valuable precisely for the detail in which that variety is presented, while holding before us the common thread of a courageous determination to make a new home, and support that new homeland in its fight against the evil from which they had fled.

Six decades on from the end of that war, we easily forget the emotional trauma such a determination involves, and the courage required to live it out. Deciding to take part in whatever way in a war effort directed against one's country of origin involves a special courage and conviction compared with what it takes to fight in defence of one's native land. The fact that the war had the outcome we now know it had cannot obscure what would have happened to these enemy aliens had victory gone to those who would have accounted them traitors. It is only recently that the resistance to the Nazis within Germany, mentioned in the author's preface, has begun to be written about seriously: certainly it was not taken seriously by British authorities at the time. As for the 'enemy aliens', their experience was in many cases internment by the authorities and suspicion among their neighbours.

The author invites us through these pages to remember and reflect, and not to allow those whom he describes in the title of the German original as the *Unbekannt* to remain unrecognised among us. After all, we live now at a time when there is more forced migration than at any time in human history. That means there are more people having to make painful decisions about where they belong and which is the cause to which they shall give their loyalty. It means that there are many whom we pass in the streets who are determined to be loyal citizens and even in some cases soldiers of their new land, but yet know themselves to be regarded with suspicion that they may be a danger.

In drawing that analogy I have no wish to imply that all those whom the author describes would take a similar step if they had to face the changed circumstances faced by the refugees of today. It is simply, and importantly, to make the point that the traumas, the decisions, the courage and the determination recorded here should not be allowed to pass unrecognised, and that we do well to assume that history will continue to demand the profoundly difficult decisions that are required in situations where resident aliens are from a country with which their new homeland is at war. Peter Leighton-Langer has ensured that the fate and achievements of a significant group of people are available to those in any generation who have similar challenges to face, and we should with gratitude read, reflect and remember.

Peter Selby:

The Right Reverend Dr Peter Selby
Bishop of Worcester and Bishop to Her Majesty's Prisons
December 2005

Introduction

Today, when anyone speaks of German resistance against Hitler, what is likely to be meant is the unsuccessful officers' coup of 20 July 1944, the leaflet action of Hans and Sophie Scholl, brother and sister, who were active at Munich university and paid for their impudence on the block, the men who formed the so-called Kreisau Circle, a group of high-powered intellectuals, who planned for a better Germany, and the sermons, speeches and writings of such men as Pastor Niemoeller, Bonhoeffer, Count Galen and a few others, who showed tremendous courage in publicly denouncing the evil policies of the Nazi government inside Germany. The *Gedenkstätte deutscher Widerstand* (Memorial to German Resistance), an official German government foundation, as well as other organisations, has publicised further stories giving details of what other brave people did or tried to do, giving their best to fight or at least to undermine the Hitlerite ideology and power structure in the time of the Nazis. The number of Germans whom Nazi judges sent to their deaths for political crimes speaks for itself.

Those who have written about specifically Jewish resistance to Hitler and his gangs concentrate largely on the revolt in the Warsaw ghetto. Some stories also tell of the resistance of other groups, who tried – generally for short periods only and under communist guidance – to resist Nazi efforts.

All these, however, have one thing in common. They were all completely unsuccessful and most of them perished pitifully. The history of communist resistance against Hitler is no success story either. Moreover it is blemished forever by the close co-operation of the communists with the Nazis in the period from August 1939 to June 1941.

The story of the German and Austrian refugees who bore arms in the forces of the British crown, however, is hardly known at all. Yet undoubtedly, the vast majority of these men and women joined these forces in order to fight against Hitler and his Nazis and not for any other motives. They remained German and Austrian nationals throughout the war and even if, at a later stage, the great majority decided not to return to the countries of their birth and gave up their previous nationality, their fight can be seen as part of German resistance against the forces of evil in Germany. There were about 10,000 of them in all, some 7,000 from the old Reich and about 3,000 from Austria, enough for a couple of divisions, if anyone had thought of forming them into such formations. In contradistinction to all other forms of German resistance, however, the great majority stayed alive and in the period immediately following the end of hostilities many of them were able and willing to help in restoring their countries of origin.

There are indeed some who know one or other of this band of men and women. On the whole, they are admired, thought to be interesting people and even honoured for having done what they have done. But the idea that they were not just a few exceptional cases, but part of a force of certainly no less than 10,000, is a matter of surprise to almost everyone, including many who were themselves part of it. And it is an interesting fact that even biographical stories of refugees, of which after all there are many, hardly mention this aspect of life in exile, which was the fate of so many Germans and Austrians at the time of the war.

I want to tell the story of these men and women. I was one of them and I think we deserve to be remembered. We did not realise it then, but now there can be no doubt that we were not nearly as unimportant as we thought and that, in fact, our contribution to the Allied war effort was such that it is well worth relating.

As far as Germany and Austria are concerned, we ought to be remembered with pride. When we left those countries and for many years afterwards we felt that we were Germans or Austrians, legally we were German nationals throughout the war and to a considerable extent we were treated as Germans by the British. In any case, all of us had had an education in the German language and to German or Austrian standards. We were recognised as good soldiers, some of us indeed as the best, as I shall show. Many of us have achieved renown in our careers since then. Our education – even that of the youngest – had started with a German or Austrian school and many had received all their education there. It stood us in good stead in our later lives.

Nevertheless this is not the first book on this subject by any means. In 1950 a group of men, who had organised themselves into the Ex-Service NB (Non-British) Association, asked Professor Norman Bentwich of London University, a man who had already done a lot for us during the war, to lend his name to the production of a book intended to preserve our memory. This book, *I Understand the Risks* (London: Victor Gollancz, 1950), was written with the assistance of several of those who had initiated it. David Eversley, previously Eberstadt, a native of Frankfurt, a renowned scientist and at one stage chief planning officer to the Greater London Council, was the chief instigator. The object was to produce a record of the basic facts and at the same time to demonstrate to the British public that the contribution to the British war effort by this fine body of men had been considerable. Bentwich's only paid assistant was Julius Carlebach, past rector of the High School for Jewish Studies at Heidelberg, who kindly wrote an introduction to the original German version of this book. For his labours then Carlebach received a weekly wage of £6.

A much more recent book, which also refers to our story, has been written by Dr Wolfgang Muchitsch. He is a young Austrian who now holds an important position under the provincial government of Styria. In *Mit Spaten, Waffen und Worten* (Vienna and Zurich: Europa Verlag, 1992) he tells the tale of the Austrians who served as pioneers, as fighting soldiers and as propagandists in the BBC.

In an article entitled 'German- and Austrian-Jewish Volunteers in Britain's Armed Forces 1939–1945' (Year Book XL, Leo Baeck Institute, London, 1995), Dr John P. Fox concentrated on the Jewish aspects of the story, which contains some interesting statistics.

A number of former colleagues have written their autobiographies. Some of these have been published, others were produced privately, for the use of their families, for the benefit of their grandchildren perhaps. In many of them, their days with the military play an important part. Peter Master's *Striking Back* (Novato, CA: Presidio Press, 1997) should be mentioned especially amongst these.

And, lastly, we are mentioned in unit and regimental histories, often indeed merely as 'men who spoke perfect German', but in some cases also with full particulars of our origins and status. The most important of these is Ian Dear's *Ten Commando* (London: Leo Cooper, 1987). Bryan Samain's *Commando Men* (London: Stevens & Sons, 1948) also is a most useful source.

Much of the information in this book is based on what has been published hitherto. Additional information, which is contained herein, originates from the National Archives (formerly the Public Records Office) in London. The war diaries of all units may now be inspected there. Whilst I have been able to study in full detail many of those which interested me particularly, Major Rhodes-Wood, who has written a comprehensive history of the Royal Pioneer Corps, had collected relevant excerpts from those of all companies throughout the war period. Those of the so-called Alien Companies and the complete war diary of No. 3 Pioneer Corps Training Centre have been put at my disposal by Lt. Col. John Starling of the Royal Logistics Corps, who has also been most co-operative in other respects.

The *Dokumentationsarchiv des Österreichischen Widerstands* in Vienna contains many documents referring to individuals. Some of these contain perfectly straightforward facts. Others however, require a lot of explanation. I shall refer to these later. A book entitled *Jüdische Schicksale, Berichte von Verfolgten*, published there, is also very interesting and some of its stories can be quoted.

However, both in London and in Vienna the result of a great deal of research is merely to establish that a certain person did or suffered a certain action on a particular day in a particular place. This means that the person existed, and it can always be established that he or she was Austrian or German. However, only rarely does it lead to a story which can be told.

The fact that in this book I have been able to go beyond what others have published and beyond the dry information to be gained in archives is due to the large number of former colleagues, their children and other relatives, who have written to me and told me their stories in the course of the years during which I conducted my researches. In most cases I have been permitted to use their own words and it is this which – I feel – makes this book more lively than it would otherwise be.

I am, of course, unable to guarantee that everything I have been told is perfectly true. But the fact that only very little of the information I have been given conflicts in any way with the experiences I have had, or seems incredible for any other reason, leads me to believe that what is contained herein is not very far from the truth, and where I have doubts I hope that I have expressed them sufficiently clearly for them to be obvious.

I am exceedingly grateful to those who have helped me by their kind co-operation. They are Werner E. Abraham, Mrs Lorraine Allard, Manfred Alweiss, my own former colleague at Marks & Spencer's Ken Ambrose, Martin Amson, Mrs Ruth Anderman, Herbert Anderson, my wife's cousin-in-law Klaus Anschel, Alice and Colin Anson, Mr and Mrs M.V. Arnott, C.C. Aronsfeld, Mrs Isabelle Avetoom, George Baer, Horace Norbert Barrett, Ken W. Bartlett, Harold Becker, Eric M. Beecham, Mrs Lieselotte Bier, Mrs Marion Blin, Peter Block, Rudolph Walter Boam, Gerhard Boehm, Frau Ruth Bratu, Mrs Lotte S. Bray, Bern Brent, Walter Brian, Allan Bright, Henry R. Brook, Sidney Edward Brook, Ernest Brown, Harold Bruce, F. Burnell, Richard Burnett, Rev. Erich Cahn, Professor Dr Julius Carlebach, John Carson, P.A. Carson, C.P. Carter, Mrs Ruth Cemach, who kindly put at my disposal all issues of the *Ex-Serviceman* between October 1948 and December 1956, Erich Clement, Hans Joseph Cohn, Professor Patrick Collinson, D.M. Compton, Michael Conway, Rev. Peter Crawford, Mrs Rita Curtis, Stephen Dale, William W. Dieneman, Professor Dr

E.W. Duck, Peter Eden, Albert Edwards, F.H. Edwards, Sidney Edwards, Bernhard F. Eibner, Leo Eisenfeld, Professor Walter Elkan, John Gordon Elting, Georg D. Engel, John Envers, who told me everything about the X Troop which was not told by Ian Dear, Mrs Ava M. Farrington, Dr Heinz D. Feldheim, Mrs M.E. Felix, William Field, Herbert N. Frank, my old chum Bryan Fisher, Ralph G. Fort, Walter Foster OBE, Ludwig D. Fried, Peter Howard Fry, John Gassman, Peter Harry Gayward OBE, Mrs Eva E. Gillatt, Martin Glenville, Werner Goerke, Franz Gockel, Dr Bill Godsey, Sidney Goldberg, Herbert Goldsmith, Professor Dr Ernest Goodman, Henry William Grenville, Sir Ronald Grierson, S.H. Gruber, Louis Hagen, Mrs Anna E.C. Harvey, Mrs Judith Headley, Howard Peter Hein, R.H. Hellmann, Ad Hermens, HRH the Princess Margaret of Hesse and by Rhine, Gunther P. Hirsch, H. Hoffmann, Frederick Hogan, Ms Joan Holden, Mrs Eva Holland, Paul Hollander, my old and newly rediscovered pal Walter Horn, John Horton, W.A. Howard, Miss Beata Hulsen, Richard Hyman, Alan Jackson, Ernest M. Jacobs, C.S. Jarrett, Peter W. Johnson, the Canadian ambassador in Bonn, Rudy Karrell, F.G. Katz, Eric J. Kennedy, Dr Eric Kenneth, Dr Eric A. Kirby, my wife's dear cousin Trudi King, Mrs Ilse Klein, Heinz Klingler, Eric Koch, Manfred Kory, Mrs Lilly Laker, Kurt Land, Alfred Thomas Lane, Jack Charles Lee, Mrs Jennifer Langer, Martin Lawrence, Ernest Lennard, Hans Leser, Mrs Bertha Leverton of the Reunion of *Kindertransport*, Frau Irma Levy, Karl-Ernst Levy, Frau Renate Loewenheck, Ian Lowit, F. Lustig, my wife's dear cousin the Lady McWilliam, Sascha Manierka, Walter Marmorek, Andrew Martin, Peter F. Masters, K.P. Mayer, Paul Yogi Mayer, Peter Mayer, M. Maynard, J.E. Melford, Peter Meyer, Leopold Michel, Mrs U. Miles, H.F. Miller, Frank Mond, Henry Lewis Morland, David J. Morrison-Wilpred, my daughter Joanna's father-in-law Henry P. Mortimer, Ernest Morton, Steve Nelson, S.K. Nelson, Group Captain Hans Neubroch OBE, my old friend George Newman, Harry Nomburg, H. Oden, Professor Dr Dietrich Oppenberg, Peter M. Oppenheimer, Dr Arnold Paucker, Geoffrey Phillips, Manfred Pinz, Henry Platt, Mrs Erica Prean, who enabled me to find out so much about the members of No.1 Allied Volunteer Platoon ATS, R. Pringle, Andy Rasp, Bob Reid, Mrs Helga Relation, my own dear cousin John D. Renner, Henry Rodwell, Garry R. Rogers, Mrs Lore Rosen, Heinrich Rosenkranz, Dr Werner S. Rosenthal, who went to no end of trouble to inform me about the men who finished up in the so-called German Democratic Republic after the war had ended, Herbert Paul Rosinger, Mrs A. Rosney, Ralph Sanders JP, Mrs Sarah Sanders, Heinz Schmoll, Henry Seaman, John Seaman, Mrs Laura Selo, R.W. Sherman,

Avraham Shomroni, Stefan-Helmut Simon, H. Peter Sinclair, Mrs Margot Smith, Mike Sondheim, who knows all about anybody who has ever been to Australia, Professor Keith Spalding, Alfred Spier, Ronald Stent, John Stanleigh, Bob Stenham, E. Stern, Frau Edith Stern, Dr Hans Sternberg, Harry Stevens, John Gordon Steward, Herman Straus, Steven Strauss, Ms Julia Stuart, E.J. Studley, Steven Summerfield, Ms L. Talbot, Otto Talsky, C. Teddern, Gerd Treuhaft, Dr Peter E. Trier CBE, Hans George Tuchler, Willi Usher, my wife's and my old friend Mrs Inge Lucy Verney, Ralf Wachtel, Sighard Wahlhaus, Ms Frances Waldek, Ron Walters, Eric Walters-Kohn, Mrs Irene Ward, Kenneth R. Ward, Fred M. Warner, Peter Wayne, Rolf Weinberg, Hans Paul Weiner, Konrad Weiss, H.E. the past President of the State of Israel Ezer Weizmann, Walter Wilson, E. Winter, G.V. Wolf, Dr H.G. Wolff, Frau Friedl Wollmerstedt, Hanno Zade and Eberhard Zamory, as well as some others, who have asked that their names should not be quoted.

My thanks are due also to Dr Siegwald Ganglmair, Mag. Peter Schwarz and others in the *Dokumentationsarchiv des Österreichischen Widerstands* in Vienna, the ladies and gentlemen of the National Archives in Kew, Professor Dr Friedrich T. Kahlenberg and Dr Lenz of the Federal Archives in Coblenz, Mr Richard Grunberger of the Association of Jewish Refugees in London, the Chief of the Staff Support Branch of the US Department of the Army Terrence J. Gough, Ms Elizabeth A. Berrio, Assistant Director, History Office of the US Department of Justice, and Major G.F. Crook of the Royal Pioneer Corps Association in London, who have given me valuable help, and Professor Hansjoachim Henning of the Gerhard-Mercator University at Duisburg, whose encouragement was much appreciated.

Lt. Col. John Starling, formerly Director of Land Service Ammunition of the British Army, historian of the Royal Pioneer Corps and currently on active service with the Royal Logistics Corps, has helped enormously, and it would be churlish not to mention that Dr Michael Meister, member of the German Parliament for the Hessian Christian Democratic Union, has given me his active and consistent support over a long period.

Stanley Foukes has checked my English and has taken a lot of trouble to ensure that it conforms to acceptable standards

Though my wife is last on the long list of people to whom thanks are due, my gratitude to her is most sincere. She has helped me to deal with all the difficulties, small and large, which arose whilst I researched, digested and wrote, she has put up with a lot of changes that became necessary, she has told me what she thought about my results and I should say that without her I could not have done it.

A last point concerning this book. The general structure of the events described is largely based on my own memory, but the detailed facts supporting it are the result of an enormous amount of intensive studies. My sources for these I have listed in the original German version (*X steht für unbekannt*, Berlin: Berlin Verlag Arno Spitz Gmb, 1999). It contains 600 footnotes and whoever wishes to check on them is welcome to do so. However, I do not consider it necessary to reproduce them here all over again.

Other than in the original German version I have made available the complete alphabetical register of names of ex-enemy alien members of the forces, as far as these are known to me at the date of publication. Excepted are those who have asked that their names should not be mentioned – some 50 or so. In many cases I know little more than just the name, but many others have permitted the publication of other facts concerning their lives. As a result, however, I do not have to tell what has happened to each of them in the body of the book. This has enabled me to concentrate on the military aspects only and I trust that, as a result, the English version will be thought more easily readable than the German original. The alphabetical register is necessarily incomplete, but new information comes to light regularly.

The Purpose of this Book

The generally accepted view in this simplifying age is that the Second World War was a war between nations. On one side there were the Germans and the Japanese and on the other there were the British and Americans, the Soviets, Poles, Greeks and Yugoslavs, and the French, although it is recognised that only de Gaulle's Free French were enemies of the Germans all the time. Most other countries were neutral, some – shame upon them – favouring Germany, but the majority were in favour of the Allies. The Italians changed front in the middle of the war. All the Germans were bad and all the others good, except possibly the Japanese, who were nasty Orientals and did unpleasant things to more or less everybody who was not Japanese.

This is a picture which is easy to paint. It is conveyed to us all in innumerable war stories, films and other media. Although their fathers and grandfathers went through it all and had personal experience of what really happened, a considerable part of the world's population believes that this is how it was.

Regrettably, I cannot agree. The fact is that after the First World War, which finished in 1918, the old world collapsed. In Germany, Austria, Russia, Czechoslovakia and Hungary republics were established and dynasties and aristocracies, which had been the basis of society for well over a thousand years, were abolished from one day to the next. Theorists came to power, who thought they knew all about bringing happiness to all mankind – or at least to their electors – but who, lacking experience, made a great, big hash of things. All these countries had lost the war one way or another and the victors imposed on them crippling reparations, as well as keeping them short of food and other essentials for several years afterwards.

Then in 1923 Germany and Austria tried to overcome the effects of all this by debasing their currencies, until every bit of money was completely worthless and everybody who had lent money to the government during the war – and there were lots of people who had done that – was in the poorhouse.

In 1929 the theories of government then in vogue led to a crash on the world's stock markets, in the wake of which millions of people lost their jobs and had to exist on what the not very generous governments doled out to them.

All this happened in the short period between 1918 and 1929 – a mere 11 years! For many people – good people, brought up with the right ideas, in the spirit of everything that was thought desirable: religion, patriotism, loyalty to the sovereign and so on – this was the end of a stable world, a world that had given their forefathers a living, which they understood, even if occasionally it was hard. What happened in those 11 years they did not understand, and it called into question all the precepts by which they had been brought up. The politicians who competed for their favours in the, for them, unusual climate of democracy, not subject to the stabilising influence of an established sovereign, were themselves at sea, did not know how to cope and pursued policies which were irrelevant and useless.

In these circumstances one must not be surprised if a large number turned to a man whose one great aim was to make them believe that, after all and in spite of what had happened, they were the greatest, and the only reason why they could not show their greatness was a conspiracy against them which the Jews, popular objects of hatred in any Christian country, had initiated.

Hitler was not the only one who gained a great following amongst his people in those years. Already in 1924 Mussolini had marched on Rome and become the *Duce* of the Italians. Lenin and Stalin in Russia were of the same ilk, even if ostensibly their philosophy was based on the internationalist precepts of Karl Marx. In other countries, too, movements like the Nazis and the Fascists came to the fore, and altogether the 1930s were a period when everywhere throughout Europe ruthless politicians presented themselves as saviours of their people and everywhere they gained a following. There was the Arrow Cross in Hungary, the Fiery Cross in France, the British Union of Fascists of Sir Oswald Mosley and quite a few others in other countries. Everywhere they tried to establish themselves as much by the force of thugs, which they used against all whom they disliked, as by the polling booth.

In those days, however, one did not have to be a hooligan to share at least some of the ideas which the Nazis and Fascists propagated. Many were confused. They did not know whom to believe. They knew, indeed, that circumstances had altered. They knew that war had impoverished their countries. They knew that the progress of science and technology was changing things. They knew that the order of society was not what it had been. But they were unable to understand why all this should affect them in their immediate environment, which did not show changes other than those resulting from their new inability to maintain it as it had been.

As nobody explained this to them in such a way that they could recognise the real reasons, many fell for Hitler and his kind. So they became prey to politicians who named innocent people as their enemies.

Many rejected the common standards of decency and morals. They reverted to old prejudices, fables and beliefs of earlier times. And they resurrected the myths that attached tribal bands to their leaders by bonds of blood and common soil to follow them to victory or death. In some countries there were more of them and in others there were fewer.

This is not an apology for the Germans. In Germany there were more such people than anywhere else and in Germany they gained control of the government by legal means. The opposition to them was lame and useless, essentially because many of the non-Nazi Germans believed even then that to take the law into one's own hands was wrong and that it was the organs of the state – the courts of law, the military and the police – who could and should be relied upon to maintain the law. The great majority of German Jews believed that too. It was not until some time after the Nazis had taken over that some at last realised that they had been wrong. Nevertheless it is not true that all Germans were Nazis and certainly it is not true to say that all Germans fought for Hitler until utter defeat stared them in the face.

When eventually the war came, when eventually the realisation had spread throughout Europe that Hitler and his minions had to be stopped, the countries which took sides with Hitler were those where parties who sympathised with his views formed the government, whilst in the countries which decided to fight Hitler the parties forming the government took the opposite view.

Each country was split, some down the middle and others somewhere along the edge of the political spectrum. In no country did the parties that disagreed with their government's stance rise against that government, but in every country people were found who, when circumstances made it possible for them, actively aided the side against which their own government and thus their own country was at war. The Second World War, therefore, was a European civil war, in which the forces of freedom, justice and enlightenment fought against those of oppression, sophistry and dictatorship, and these two forces were present to some degree in all European nations.

As regards the Germans, German nationals put on military uniforms on the side opposing their legal government before any others, and German and Austrian soldiers served in the British army virtually from the word go. Most of them were Jews and people whom the Nazi laws had turned into Jews, but a fair number also were gentiles, some of whom had left Germany for political reasons and others who were not politically minded at all, but who opposed the Nazis and wanted to fight for freedom.

It is their story I want to tell in this book.

1

Who Were These Germans?

For many hundreds of years Germans have come to England, worked here and have made this country their home. The fact that in many cases their background was not very dissimilar to that of the English enabled them, generally, to be assimilated rapidly. Only a few continued maintaining their ties with their homeland and remained strangers in a foreign land. This applied more often in areas where considerable numbers of German-speakers were together, than in areas where they were on their own. Such areas where many German-speakers congregated were the City of London, as well as parts of Bradford, Sheffield and Bristol – places, in other words, where foreign trade was done. Many of these people were Jews, but by no means all of them. The names of many important and well-known firms are a reminder of their commercial success.

After Hitler's assumption of power in 1933 refugees from Germany started streaming into England. At first it was a few hundred only, but with every year thereafter the numbers increased. However, not everybody was allowed to enter Britain and the much-desired British visa was granted only to those who could furnish proof that after their admission they would not become a burden on the state. Those who were granted the right of entry were either persons of means, or they possessed some skill which was in short supply in the United Kingdom, or they could prove that their stay would be of short duration only, because they had previously arranged to move on somewhere else.

In March 1938 Hitler occupied Austria and in September of that year, as a result of the Munich agreement, Czechoslovakia was forced to cede to Germany all the areas in which ethnic Germans predominated. As a result the German refugees were joined by Austrians and people from the Sudetenland, who had become German nationals as a result of these changes. In the same year both Jewish and Christian charities began to bring out of the Reich children whom the Nazis persecuted or were likely to persecute for religious or racial reasons.

Accordingly, the 72,000 who were in Britain on 3 September 1939 were a mixed bunch. Most probably more than half considered themselves members of the Jewish religion, but amongst these the number of orthodox Jews was fairly small. A majority had been members of 'reformed' communities in their homelands and quite a few had no great ties to the religion to which they nominally belonged. These were the sort of people who, when asked what religion they belonged to, said 'Jewish' because they had been born Jews and so that was what they were.

A further group, which was pretty numerous, consisted of people who were Jews or 'of Jewish admixture' only by the definition of the Nuremberg Laws, which the Nazis had brought into force for the preservation of 'the purity of the Aryan race', of which they considered the German people to be the best example. These, whom one might call Nuremberg Law Jews, were descendants of up to four generations of persons who had left the Jewish religious community and become baptised either as Catholics or as Protestants, in some cases more than 100 years earlier. In most cases these people had no ties with Judaism whatsoever and many had been most surprised when they found that officially they no longer belonged to the German people.

Then there were the political refugees. But these again were not all alike, for in many cases they too had no more in common than their dislike for what the Nazis were doing, the courage of having advocated political ideas which differed from those of the Nazis and the fear that, if they had stayed within reach of Hitler and his minions, they would have had some very unpleasant things happen to them. Apart from that they came from all parts of the political spectrum between the moderate right and the extreme left and included people with very conservative and even nationalistic views, as well as red-hot communists and all shades of opinion in between.

And lastly there also was a not inconsiderable number of Germans who were in England or for that matter in other parts of the British empire for reasons of business or family, or for any other non-political reason, who were neither racial nor political refugees, but just simply Germans living abroad. Amongst these, indeed, there were some who were loyal to Hitler and the Nazis, whom they held to be the legitimate German government, but by far the greater number rejected Nazism and saw themselves on the side of Hitler's opponents, on the side of freedom and justice.

One of the really surprising things about all these people, however, is that even according to the records of the then German government, which have come to light since the end of the war, there was no espionage organisation worth mentioning amongst them and what little existed was well known to British counter-espionage, who managed to turn the lot to Hitler's disadvantage. But, leaving out those very few who felt some sort of loyalty to Hitler, the rest had little in common other than their German nationality and an education in the German language.

The German nationals who were in the United Kingdom at the beginning of 1938 were mainly from the Reich, as it existed between 1919 and 1938. That means that they came from any part of what is today the Federal Republic of Germany, or from those parts east of the Oder–Neisse line which Germany ceded to Poland after the end of the Second World War and which, in the main, consist of Silesia, Pomerania and East Prussia. They came from all parts of this vast area and included natives of Prussia and of Bavaria, Rhinelanders, Hessians, Saxons, Palatines, Hamburgers, Stuttgarters and any amount of Berliners, as well as people from what other provinces there were.

In 1938 they were joined by Austrians, mainly from Vienna. The Sudetenlanders, who started to come after September of that year again were from all parts of the Bohemian and Moravian fringe territories, but already included some also from the inner Czech and Slovak areas, notably from Prague and from Brno (Brünn).

When they arrived in Britain and certainly for quite a while thereafter all the emigrants were German nationals in their own eyes and they were under no illusions about this status. At that stage few had any intentions of changing their nationality. They wanted to get away not from their identity, but from the Nazis, who had persecuted them or were threatening to do so. Some indeed envisaged that they might become British at a later stage, but in the first place they were German nationals on the run from the Nazis and all they wanted was to get away from them to somewhere safe, so that they could settle down and rebuild their lives without fear from their neighbours or the authorities.

Much later many of them became good British citizens, but this was only after they had endured the war at the side of the British and had had time to assimilate themselves to British ways and adapt their way of life to British ideas and traditions. The number of those who eventually became British citizens is considerably greater than those who emigrated further at a later stage or those who returned to Germany or other country of origin after the Nazis had been defeated.

The position of all these people in respect of their nationality was so complicated that it deserves to be looked at in some detail. Most of those, who came from the pre-1938 Reich had possessed German nationality from the time they were born, although in this context it must be remembered that they had not become German nationals because they were born in Germany, but rather as a result of their fathers having been German nationals. German law, then as now, took no notice of a person's place of birth; what mattered was the nationality of the father, provided the child had been born in wedlock. Otherwise it was the mother's nationality which determined the nationality of the child.

The laws of Austria were similar. However, in 1919 the Austro-Hungarian empire was broken up along more or less ethnic lines, as a result of which many who had held the nationality of the empire, but who had ties with more than one of the successor states, had to be permitted to opt for one or other of the new countries. The Viennese were particularly affected as Vienna, the empire's capital, had always attracted people from all parts of the empire. As a result quite a few of the Austrians were citizens of that country by virtue of the fact that they, or their parents, had opted to be Austrians in 1919, when they could also have decided to be Czechoslovaks, Poles, Hungarians, Rumanians, Ukrainians, Yugoslavs or Italians, depending on which part of the empire they had originally come from. A few of these, indeed, were the first in their families to speak German as their mother tongue and their parents and grandparents had been brought up speaking one of the other 12 official languages of the old monarchy. However, all who on 12 March 1938 held Austrian nationality became German nationals on that date by virtue of the incorporation of the Austrian republic into the German Reich, and this act of the German government was recognised by the United Kingdom after the Austrian plebiscite in May of that year.

As for the Sudetenlanders, they on the whole had Czechoslovak nationality, because in 1919 the German-speaking inhabitants of what then became Czechoslovakia had been given guarantees of equal treatment with the Czechs and Slovaks, as a result of which the vast majority of them, Jews and gentiles, had opted to become citizens of that country. Nevertheless, the history of the years following the foundation of the new republic shows that tensions arose between the nationalities, and it was not only the nationalistic Germans who felt that their treatment by the Czech majority was not as it should be. This led to quite a few of the Sudetenlanders preferring to think of themselves as Germans rather than as Czechoslovaks. After the incorporation of the Sudetenland into the Reich in September 1938 all German-speaking residents of those areas became German nationals and this, too, was recognised by the government of the United Kingdom.

Those Czechoslovak nationals who did not live in the fringe areas of Bohemia or Moravia, however, retained this nationality until March 1939, when Hitler occupied the whole of Czechoslovakia. Then the Bohemians and Moravians became nationals of the German protectorate there and the Slovaks became nationals of the new independent Slovakia; again, the British government accepted it all.

The 72,000 Germans in the United Kingdom in September 1939 included all of these, except, perhaps, the few who had come from Slovakia. At that moment in time the British government had accepted the position of the German government and there was practically no difference between the British and the German attitude towards the legal position of all these people as German citizens.

Until the British declaration of war against Germany on 3 September 1939 the British nationality acts had operated normally *vis-à-vis* the Germans. These acts had permitted foreigners without regard to their origins to apply for naturalisation after five years of residence and, as German emigration had started already in 1933, a few of the first German emigrants after Hitler's assumption of power just managed to become British subjects before the war began. Some time in 1939 they had taken the oath of loyalty and from that moment they were no longer foreigners as far as official Britain was concerned, but loyal British subjects. Others, who had come a little later, had applied and their applications were in various stages of completion, but on commencement of the state of war all naturalisation proceedings stopped and whoever had not taken the oath by that date was still a German.

Except for about 40 special cases, whoever was a German, and therefore an 'enemy alien' in Britain on 3rd September 1939, was still an 'enemy alien' in the eyes of the British authorities when the war ended on 8 May 1945 and for quite some time thereafter.

The special cases really seem to have been very special indeed. Thus there was the case of a girl of 17, the daughter of a divorced couple of Austrian origin. Their divorce had taken place in 1930 and since then both parents had become British, the father by naturalisation after the requisite period of residence in Britain, and the mother by means of a second marriage, this time with a British subject. On neither occasion, however, had there been an opportunity for their common daughter to become British, and this omission was rectified, wartime notwithstanding. Other such special cases are thought to have been on similar lines.

The position concerning the nationality of the refugees under German law, however, did not remain the same throughout the war. In 1941 all German nationals who were Jews according to the Nuremberg Laws and who had emigrated from the Reich (including, of course, Austria and the Sudetenland) had their German nationality revoked. After that such persons were stateless under German law, unless they had by then assumed the nationality of another country. However, this decree was not publicised outside Germany. As far as the British were concerned this measure was of no effect, because British law provides that no action of an enemy can have any legal effect within the United

Kingdom. As a result, those who were affected by this measure did not generally know anything about it and continued to regard themselves as German nationals. Germans who were not Jews under the above definition were not affected by the action of the German government and retained their German nationality also under German law.

However, the purpose of the German action had been to enable the Nazis legally to possess themselves of any parts remaining in Germany of the property of those whose nationality had been revoked, and the German authorities themselves took precious little notice of this revocation on several occasions, when persons who had been deprived of their nationality fell into their hands at later dates and were executed as traitors.

A further change occurred in 1943. By the Moscow Declaration of 27 November 1943 the Allies decided that they would recreate Austria as an independent state after the war. In Britain this led to the recognition that those who had been Austrians before 1938 and had become Germans as a result of the *Anschluss* should now be recognised again as Austrians. Accordingly all those affected were to be given the opportunity to have themselves registered as Austrians rather than Germans. However, as it was not envisaged that this measure should make any difference to the Austrians' status as enemy aliens, this had no practical effect. Thus the whole business appeared to be little more than a nuisance to many of those affected, especially as they were expected to complete a lengthy questionnaire in order to establish their status. The British, too, did not insist. It was all the same to the British authorities, some of whom had thought they were doing the Austrians a favour. The result was that most of the Austrians, even those who were very consciously Austrian rather than German, did not bother and took no notice of the whole business. This had no consequences for them. There were no positive consequences for those who claimed to be Austrians and no negative ones for those who failed to do so – merely the statistics became even more unreliable than they usually are anyway.

The great majority of the refugees and a fair number of those who do not fall under this description came from what might fairly be called a bourgeois background. Many had received the benefit of a university or other higher education and those who were not old enough yet to have completed such a course had in the main attended schools which led to higher education. They or their parents had been members of the professions, teachers, artists, established traders or other comparable classes of society in their countries of origin. Even when they had lost their property, their jobs and their income, their social position had not really changed, and they felt themselves to be and had the habits and appearance of members of the middle classes. For many this changed abruptly when they came to England. A foreigner, when landing in England, does not belong to any class at all. He is judged by his ability to pay and the ability to pay of most of the refugees on arrival was very limited. Many depended on charity or on subsidies granted to them by benefactors. As a result they did not have the status they were used to possessing. In many cases this state of affairs lasted for a long time. For people who were used to being independent, this was a terrible comedown and many, especially amongst the young, resented it bitterly. In some cases, indeed, their supposed benefactors turned out to require services for which they were mentally unprepared, and this served to deepen their resentment. In many cases this engendered revolutionary ideas. Many developed strong sympathies for the political left wing.

However different their origins might have been, however they differed from each other by background, religion, race or politics, what united the vast majority of people of German nationality in Britain in the years before and during the war was their common hatred of Hitler and his Nazis. In Germany the refugees had been at the mercy of those people. When they left Germany they wanted revenge. They wanted to pay back the indignities and the injuries to which they and theirs had been subjected. In their opposition to the Nazis they were prepared to accept any ally, as long as that ally's opposition to Hitler was as unequivocal as their own. They hoped that each of Hitler's foreign adventures in the years preceding the war would lead to his downfall, and when eventually his invasion of Poland led to the declaration of war against Germany by Britain and France they were amongst those who received this news most enthusiastically.

2

The Early Pioneers

At the beginning of 1939 it was recognised that accommodation would have to be found for quite a considerable number of refugees from Nazi persecution, for whom no other homes could be found. In England a Council for German Jewry had been formed as a kind of sub-organisation of the Jewish communities of Great Britain and the British Commonwealth. This sponsored the establishment of a transit camp for such people, and the site chosen for this was one of the 'mystery Q-ports' of the First World War at Richborough on the Kentish coast. This had not been used since then. After the buildings in the part known as Kitchener Camp had been made reasonably fit for human occupation by a small group of skilled refugees, some three and a half thousand men found temporary homes there. Of these about 2,000 had come from within the boundaries of the Reich, some 1,000 were Austrians and maybe 500 came from elsewhere, the majority of these mainly from what had been Czechoslovakia.

After the commencement of hostilities many of the inmates of this camp asked for permission to join the army in order to be able to participate in the fight against Hitler. Although at an inter-ministerial meeting approval for this was obtained within less than a fortnight after the war began, it took quite some time before anyone in the War Office took notice of this decision. The generals and other officers concerned were absolutely unprepared for anything like that. On the whole they were amazed that they should accept enemy aliens into the British army, and even after they had steeled themselves to accept what the Secretary for War had agreed to, they found the idea that they should issue arms to such people completely crazy.

However, good fortune came to their aid. On 17 October 1939 the Auxiliary Military Pioneer Corps had been created under Army Order No.200 as a mainly unarmed labour corps. The intention had been to absorb into this corps those men whom the normal fighting units and the corps of the army did not want on account of asocial behaviour, mental disabilities or criminal tendencies, or for other reasons, which made them less desirable than others. It was to be organised into 'Q' (queer) and 'C' (criminal) companies. The name of the officer who first suggested that 'A' (alien) companies should be added to this assortment is not known, but whoever he was, his proposal found support and was translated into immediate action. For more than three years thereafter the Auxiliary Military Pioneer Corps, later the Pioneer Corps and later still the Royal Pioneer Corps, was the only part of HM Forces in which a normal male enemy alien without special qualifications was able to serve.

Already at that time the war cabinet, blessed as it was with plenty of good will, prejudice and ignorance, laid down the lines of policy concerning the employment of enemy aliens in the forces. As it was felt that not enough was known about these men as individuals (and probably also because MI5 had taken a distinctly hostile attitude towards them), they were to be kept away from all secret weapons, plans and things of such kind. On the other hand, for their own protection and because, if taken prisoner, they might be subject to immediate execution by the enemy, they should not be allowed to get into positions where this could happen to them. And lastly, it was to be assumed that British soldiers would instinctively distrust men who spoke English with a German accent and that they should not, therefore, be admitted into normal British units.

In January 1940 No.3 Auxiliary Military Pioneer Corps Training Centre (3 AMPCTC) was formed at Richborough under the command of Brigadier the 2nd Marquis of Reading, the son of the famous advocate and Viceroy of India. By 6 January 905 of the refugees at Richborough had volunteered to join up and exchange their civilian quarters there for those in the military part of the camp, which, however, looked the same and were equally uncomfortable. In the course of the next two months another 600 or so were added to this total.

They were recruited under the following conditions:

> Refugee soldiers will not be used for front line service; the majority will remain in the United Kingdom; should any be sent to the British Expeditionary Force in France, they will remain behind the lines.
>
> They will receive the normal serviceman's pay of 2 Shillings per day.
>
> The wives of servicemen receive an allowance of 17 Shillings per week with additional allowances for each child. Half the servicemen's pay will normally be paid to their wives.
>
> The engagement will be for the duration of the emergency.
>
> Any decisions concerning permission to remain in the United Kingdom or possible naturalisation will be taken in respect of each man bearing in mind his behaviour and merit after the end of hostilities.

Many of those who reported for duty were well beyond the age at which they might have been considered to be young. Quite a few were veterans of the First World War, when they had fought on the side of the Central Powers, and many others had also passed the threshold to middle age. Many came although they were not in the best of health and got through their medicals by false pretences, because they felt it to be their moral duty to be amongst the soldiers taking part in the war.

In many cases these men were not able to do anything outstanding. They just did what they could and little is known about them. By chance a few names are known. They include *inter alia* Walter Bun, Ralph Sanders (previously Rudi Zweig), Ernst Werner Goerke, Andy Rasp and Hans Schwefel. Their stories appear in the register. But what is outstanding about these and all the others like them is the fact that they joined up at all, ignoring the facts and sacrificing their health, so as not to be left out.

When the war had ended many of the ex-pioneers joined together in the Ex-Service NB (non-British) Association. This Association issued a monthly journal, the *Ex-Serviceman*, the last copy of which appeared in December 1956. Reading this, one is struck by the number of obituaries concerning men who must have been in their early forties when they joined up. They died of all manner of illnesses. One is tempted to think that their strenuous service, at a time of life when the body is no longer as fit as once it was, might have been a common cause.

Older men had yet another way to serve the Allied cause whilst at Richborough. Using 58 radio receivers and a number of recording instruments, 150 of them at the behest of the Ministry of Information set up a listening watch which, during the first year of the war, was the only station which listened in to all German radio senders every day around the clock. Important broadcasts were recorded on tape.

When the new soldiers received their uniforms unexpected problems arose. The men turned out to be bigger than the average. As a result small men had the choice of dozens of uniforms, but clothing for the bigger ones was rare indeed. Caps in particular were awkward, and there were many men who had an awful job to keep their heads covered as required by King's Regulations. It took some time before everybody could be said to be properly dressed, and the tailors had quite a job. However, photos suggest that in the end they all looked quite reasonable.

A number of British officers and NCOs were posted to No.3 AMPCTC and the volunteers received their initial training under their command. Very soon new units were formed from amongst them which were then known as 'A' (alien) companies. The British army had not recruited soldiers in Europe outside the British Isles since the King's German Legion under Wellington's command, and so there was only the colonial army to serve as an example for the organisation of these companies. After all, the British had had plenty of experience of how to organise troops formed from odd kinds of people. Thus at the beginning the officers were British throughout, so was the company sergeant major (CSM) and so were the sergeants in charge of half the sections into which the companies were divided. The sergeants in command of the other half were non-British and taken from amongst the men who formed the company. All the lower charges, corporals and lance corporals were also non-British. As in all native units, the senior NCO from the nationality of the other ranks was the CQMS (company quartermaster sergeant), who was responsible for feeding the men and was expected, as far as possible, to provide what the men wanted.

This was the pattern in all the 'A' companies. Each of them was made up of ten sections of 30 men each. The sections with odd numbers had British, those with even numbers had German or Austrian sergeants. The CQMS wore the three stripes and crown of a staff sergeant and got the highest pay. The CSM and the four officers – a major commanding, a captain as second in command, and two lieutenants – were British. Only the British were armed, the sergeants carrying rifles, all others revolvers. Therefore the company's armament consisted of five .303in rifles and five 9mm Smith & Wesson revolvers.

The first such company was the 69th. Early in March 1940 this was sent to France as part of the British Expeditionary Force. It was followed in quick succession by the 74th, 87th, 88th and 93rd Companies, so that by May 1940, when the German blitzkrieg in the Low Countries and in France began, 1,500 Germans and Austrians were there wearing British uniform. One other company, the 77th, was also formed at Richborough at that time. This was not sent to France, however, but was stationed at Donnington in Shropshire.

As with all military units formed by people whose mother tongue is different from that of the country which they serve, this was also a problem for these companies, aggravated perhaps by the fact that their own language was that of the enemy. The language in which all commands and most of the instructions were given was English, of course. However, amongst themselves the men spoke partly English and partly German, which in many cases led to their communicating in a somewhat horrible mixture of languages then known as 'Emigranto'. Those who used English generally did so in order to perfect themselves in what they saw as the language which would become their main vehicle of communication in the future, whereas those who spoke mainly German often had the sense to realise that in public it was more acceptable to speak good German quietly than bad English loudly. Many of those who used English did so with a more or less pronounced German accent, and this led to uncertainty, even distrust, amongst Britons with whom they came into contact. There were occasions when these German soldiers in British uniform were thought to be spies or even German troops in disguise, and wherever the units were stationed it had to be explained to the local people just who they were and how they came to be where they were.

Inside the companies attitudes differed materially. There were companies in which it was definitely not done to speak German, whilst in others those who spoke English were given the impression that they were traitors to their heritage. An example of the difficulties which people made for themselves in this respect is the story of F.L. Meyer, who was posted from 229 Company to 93. In 229 Company English was the normal language for all, but when he first joined his new comrades, greeting them in English, someone called out to him, '*Verleugnest Du Deine Muttersprache?*' (Do you disavow your mother tongue?)

However, their language was not the only characteristic which marked out these men. The education which the vast majority had received was also quite different from that of soldiers in other units of the Pioneer Corps. Only very few of them had not completed an education of grammar school standard and maybe a third were university graduates. The older ones amongst them had almost all been members of the professions or had had jobs which marked them out as members of the middle classes. Had they not had the wrong nationality most would have been considered potential officers. The younger ones, too, had the same kind of background and brought with them much more than many others of their age groups. Of course, this showed and it was this which gave the A companies the excellent reputation which they enjoyed wherever they went.

In May 1940 the Allied troops in the Netherlands and northern France were routed by Hitler's armies. At that time the 87th and 88th Companies were stationed at Le Havre and at Harfleur. They were amongst the very few organised bodies of troops which could be used against the enemy in northern France after the Allied collapse. In expectation of a German attack, and although completely unarmed and almost completely untrained, they were placed in positions covering the road from Harfleur to Montvilliers. Only on the following day were they issued with one rifle per man. According to Heinz Schmoll's report below they were also given ammunition on the scale of five rounds between every two men.

Fortunately for them the question of whether they would have been able to use their arms to good effect was never tested. The men who had fought on the side of the Central Powers in the First World War had no difficulties with their weapons and could certainly handle them. Others, however, do not appear to have been quite as adept. According to one account, when members of 88 Company were first given their rifles and underwent weapon drill, it was more a case of 'rifles . . . falling all over the place' than a display of military efficiency. In the same vein R.H. Hellmann, who was in 87 Company, wrote: 'We actually had rifles for some time! Fortunately, we never used them, being quite untrained . . .'.

Nevertheless these men managed to impress one person – their brigade commander. Col. Arthur Evans MP had been entrusted with the command of the brigade hastily formed to cover Le Havre. He realised that these men had enormous potential, that their spirit was excellent and that all they needed was proper training to turn them into proficient soldiers. A few weeks later, on 10 July, he said so in the House of Commons. We shall return to this occasion later.

The positions in front of Le Havre were relinquished after only a few days so that no contact was made with the enemy. However, it would appear that after this experience in some places a little more confidence was placed in the 87th and 88th Companies, and possibly also in the 69th and 93rd which had also been armed in the meantime, for all four companies were brought to Rennes. This was to be the centre of a line for the defence of the Brittany peninsula, which was the point where after the evacuation of Dunkirk the British Expeditionary Force was to be reconstituted. It was intended to consist of the 52nd (Scottish Lowland) Division, the 3rd Infantry Division and a division of the Canadian Army.

According to Churchill's *The Second World War*, the movement of the 52nd Division to France, under earlier orders, was to have begun on 7 June. These orders were confirmed. The 3rd Division under the then General Montgomery was assigned to France and the leading division of the Canadian army, which was well armed, was directed to begin arriving there on 11 June. At that time the 51st Highland Division was also still in France holding a sector of front line near the Somme, and so was a composite force known as 'Beauman Force' which had been scraped together from bases and lines of communications. These should also have formed part of the new BEF.

However, all these plans were scrapped following the surrender of the greater part of the 51st Division and the French armistice. All British troops still in France were brought back to England in a further great

effort at evacuation on or around 16 June 1940. With them came the five
A companies of the Pioneer Corps, the 69th, 87th, 88th and 93rd being
evacuated through St Malo and the 74th from Brest. The 69th was
embarked in a Dutch collier. The 74th was in a convoy of three ships and
both the leading vessel and the one bringing up the rear were attacked
heavily. The 74th were lucky – they were on the one in the middle.
Nevertheless the journey from Brest to Plymouth took three days.

Before their evacuation all the companies had again to surrender
their arms. On this occasion the behaviour of the men of 88 Company
bordered on mutiny. When ordered to pile their arms they threw them
into a disorderly heap. But it appears that so far from being punished
for this they earned the respect of their officers.

On the quaysides the ladies of the Women's Voluntary Services
received the men with cups of tea and treated them as heroes. So it was
quite a comedown when they all got to Westward Ho! where No.3
AMPCTC had meanwhile been transferred, and Brigadier the Lord
Reading welcomed them with all the abuse he was capable of heaping
on them for being filthy dirty, unshaven and looking like no soldiers
should ever look. The men felt that after all they had been through this
was unjust but it pulled them together. In the end it did a lot for their
self-respect, as did the fact that they were kitted out anew and received
their arrears of pay.

Heinz Schmoll, a native of Haynau in Silesia was in 88 Company.
He had been with that company from the start and his story from the
point of view of the common soldier, taken from his autobiography, is
worth quoting:

> [At Richborough] we were billeted in wooden huts and it was bitterly
> cold. Most of the time the water taps were frozen and we had to bring
> in snow in buckets and thaw it on the cast-iron hut stove. We were
> issued with ill-fitting uniforms which had to be altered by the local
> tailor. There was a lot of square bashing but since we were not issued
> with rifles there was no arms drill. One day we were visited and
> inspected by Lord Reading, the founder of the corps. We were told
> that we were to join the British Expeditionary Force in France.
> Before embarkation we received inoculations against typhus and
> tetanus. After the last inoculation I became very ill and called for the
> Army doctor to visit my bunk. I quickly learned that if you could still
> walk you had to go on sick parade . . .
>
> Our instructor was Sergeant Major Bennison from the Durham
> Light Infantry and my Section Sergeant's name was Chamberlain.
> Our company was commanded by Major Woodcock and we also had

a Captain and two Lieutenants whose names I do not remember, but all of them were ex-Indian Army of the 'When I was in Poona' type.

Eventually we were transported to Southampton and then onwards by boat to Le Havre, to a camp in St. Addresse which consisted of Nissen huts. There was a good view from the cliff tops down to the harbour. An old naval gun was close by. The Nissen huts had no furniture whatsoever, not even bunks. We slept on groundsheets on the bare concrete floor. Eventually we hacked holes into the floor with the pickaxes we had been issued with, in order to accommodate our hips. Some of the men organised scraps of wood and made their own beds. Our officers got the message. Soon a truck appeared loaded with wooden bunks, palliasse covers and bales of straw. We filled the palliasses with the straw and made our beds.

Our job at Le Havre consisted of unloading boats bringing provisions for the troops. I remember carrying cases of Lee-Enfield rifles, boxes of ammunition and sacks of flour. In our free time most of the chaps streamed down town to the red light district in the Rue des Galleons, headed by most of the married men who had not got used to our monastic life. We heard about their experiences in great detail, the 'exhibitions' and 'gamme rouge' and more. In due course we had our first war casualties of various types of VD and several consequent hospitalisations. Condoms were now issued.

The German army started advancing and we experienced several severe air raids and strafings on Le Havre docks, where we took cover behind the unloaded crates. Our anti-aircraft defences were nil except for sporadic rifle fire. As the German armies advanced further into the Low Countries we were ordered out in the field to a place called Harfleur not far from Le Havre.

On the market place of Harfleur a truck arrived with crates of Lee-Enfield rifles and boxes of ammunition for our company. We unloaded and opened the boxes and proceeded to unblock the grease filled rifles by lowering the weights of pull-throughs which had been heated over a bonfire down the barrels. After this smelly exercise we were issued with one rifle each and five rounds of ammunition for every two men. Sergeant Major Bennison instructed us in the use of the weapons and the bayonet and also indicated the general direction from where the Germans might appear. Because most of our men were German Jewish refugees we were told to tear out the page from our Army Book 64 which indicated the names and addresses of next of kin, in case we were taken prisoner. Our main duty was to patrol road junctions and look for German parachutists and fifth columnists. While on guard duty we marched up and down the road day and night with stints of four hours on and four hours off. I once fell asleep while marching. In the distance we heard the detonations of the heavy bombing of Le Havre. We slept on groundsheets on the bare earth or in ditches. After a while we were ordered back to our camp in St. Addresse which we found completely looted by French civilians. We had to be re-issued with lost army kit, such as shirts, drawers cellular, socks, housewives (sewing needle kit), razors, palliasses and so on. We were now ordered to patrol docks at night and for the first time I felt like a real soldier carrying a rifle on the alert.

The German advance continued and the air-raids increased. We were put on a train going west, in cattle trucks which bore the legend: '40 hommes 8 chevaux'. During our journey west we saw thousands of civilians fleeing from the German advance with bicycles, carts, ancient motor vehicles (some with gas bags on the roofs), horses, dogs, cats and bundles of personal belongings. We arrived at Rennes railway station from where we were marched perhaps twenty kilometres to a camp at a place called Aquaduct. The Nissen huts there were familiar. We were told to hand in our rifles and there were angry scenes as the men threw their rifles on a heap. I was extremely upset to be disarmed, since my reason for joining the British Army had been to kill Nazis. I put in an application to my Commanding Officer to be transferred to an internment camp. This unprecedented application was not granted. Perhaps just as well.

We commenced building a huge circular reinforced-concrete bomb-proof army headquarters, which we referred to as the 'officers' funkhole'. As soon as it was completed we were ordered to blow it up, as word came that the BEF was being evacuated from Dunkirk. We did so and then we were marched in full kit, including greatcoats in the June heat, to the railway station at Rennes from where we went by train in the familiar trucks labelled '40 hommes 8 chevaux' to the port of St. Malo. By this time the bulk of the BEF had been evacuated from Dunkirk and the spearheads of the German army were closing in on us. My thoughts were that after letting me out of Buchenwald the Nazis were after all catching up with me.

We spent one week on the racecourse of St. Malo close to the beach, dumping all Army equipment into the sea in order to prevent it from falling into enemy hands. Trucks, bren carriers and motor cycles were started, put into gear and allowed to propel themselves into the sea. There was a lot of air activity, doubtless the fringes of the beginning Battle of Britain. Our officers decided to build a bonfire and burn all our company records, including the soldiers' pay details. All the time we tried to hitch a ride on anything that would float and take us back to Blighty. Eventually we managed to get a lift on a French tramp steamer. As there was only just enough room for us men we had to leave all our kit behind on the beach. This included kitbags and the greatcoats which we had carried in the heat of the season all the way from our camp. As soon as we were aboard a great number of the local population, who had earlier cursed us for leaving them, fell on our equipment like vultures and took everything away. There was nothing to eat on the boat except our emergency rations which consisted of a pack containing a mixture of chocolate and Marmite. The sanitary facilities were totally inadequate.

The boat proceeded on a zig-zag course all the way to the English coast. There was an alert out for submarines and dive-bombing of vessels leaving the French coast. One of the vessels, the 'Lancastria', received a direct hit and was blown out of the water in front of our eyes. Our boat was packed with soldiers including remnants of the fighting forces, as well as some civilians and probably some fifth columnists. It took us seven days to reach Southampton where we were met by the Women's Voluntary Services with buns and tea. While boarding the train bound for London we heard over the loudspeaker Churchill's famous speech, 'We shall fight them on the beaches . . . We shall never surrender'.

A happening, which was to remain singular in the history of the alien companies, occurred shortly after the five companies had returned from France. This was at the time of the internment of enemy aliens. The returned soldiers were exceedingly perturbed when they discovered that this included also their own dependants and other relatives. Especially in 88 Company resentment came to a peak and it is said that a mutiny was avoided only by the immediate despatch to the company of a senior official from Whitehall who assured the men that their relatives would be released immediately.

As a result of events in France, however, a further group of Germans and Austrians were recruited into the Pioneer Corps, people who had not originally emigrated to Britain. In France, too, refugees had asked to be allowed to join the forces in order to do their bit in the fight against Hitler. The French, however, had not been even as well intentioned towards them as the British and so they were given the choice between becoming foreign *legionnaires* or *prestataires*.

There can be no doubt that a very great deal of what has ever been written about the inhuman conditions of service in the French foreign legion is substantially correct. In an article which appeared in the *Ex-Serviceman* of January 1954 one of the *legionnaires* tells of the way in which people were treated and how they treated each other, even at the beginning of the war when he was in it. By the standards of today the conditions which then obtained seem almost incredible.

The *prestataires*, on the other hand, were a labour corps, similar to the British pioneers but without the pioneers' military status. During the winter of 1939–40 a number of both, *prestataires* and *legionnaires*, either came under British command or were used in the areas in which the BEF operated. As a result quite a few of them were in Dunkirk with the British army at the end of May.

During the evacuation from Dunkirk, when some 330,000 soldiers were shipped across the Channel in all sorts of ships and boats, most of the *legionnaires*, being military, were also taken across. The greater part of the *prestataires*, however, their status being doubtful, were left behind. After arrival in England the *legionnaires* were given three choices. They could either join de Gaulle's Free French, or they could elect to be shipped to Dakar in order to rejoin the Vichy French, or they would be allowed to join the British pioneers. No one was very surprised that the great majority preferred service with the pioneers to either of the two French alternatives. The unfortunate *prestataires*, who had been left behind, took off their uniforms and tried to get away. Quite a few were successful. However, a story by one Hans Sternberg, published in a German newspaper some years ago, confirms that some of them also succeeded in becoming pioneers eventually.

Sally Wachenheimer, a Jew from Zwingenberg an der Bergstrasse, a small town in southern Hesse, was one of those who had gone to the *prestataires*. His battalion had come under British command. It even had a British officer commanding it, one Major Scott. When the BEF retired onto Dunkirk this battalion marched with them as far as the coast, but there they were left. Scott, wearing British uniform, was evacuated. He took the nominal roll of his unit back with him to England. Like the rest of the battalion Wachenheimer remained on the other side. When enemy troops approached he and some Jewish comrades got together. Amongst them there were a number of other Hessians like himself: Dr Freudenthal, a dentist from the town of Schluechtern, Leo Kaufmann from Frankfurt, Alfred Stern from Mergentheim and a man named Zucker, who came from Kassel. They 'requisitioned' what civilian clothing they could find in the deserted villages round about and marched southwards.

After a lengthy journey they reached a fishing village called Pornichet, some miles west of St Nazaire. There they found a fisherman who said he was prepared to take them south along the west coast of France, until they might reach territory not controlled by the enemy. On the high seas they were stopped by a British torpedo boat, HMS *Imogen*, and taken to Plymouth. They were interrogated, after which they were interned. They had, however, mentioned Major Scott, as a result of which investigations were made and Major Scott was located. Basing himself on his nominal roll this gentleman was able to confirm what the men had said and recommended that they should be well treated. So they, too, finished up being pioneers. They were not the only ones.

The case of R. Schulze was yet of another type, but he, too, was probably not the only one of his kind. His father had been a communist and after Hitler had come to power had been imprisoned in a concentration camp. Schulze himself became a merchant seaman and in November 1941 he was on a German freighter when it docked at Boulogne. The proximity to England must have fired his imagination, for he deserted and fled. Via France, Spain and Portugal he eventually reached the United Kingdom. On 21 March 1942 he also joined 69 Company PC.

3

Later Companies

During the summer of 1940 the five companies which had been brought back from France were used in various ways. The danger of invasion made the erection of defences along the English south coast a matter of first priority. German and Austrian pioneers were used to build these mainly in the south-west of the country, for instance in Taunton, Chard and Yeovil, and also in Herefordshire. After the commencement of enemy air attacks on English cities some of them were drafted into the target areas, where they cleared the rubble and assisted the ARP (Air Raid Precautions). Muchitsch wrote:

> Night after night heavy attacks were flown against the British capital. In order to maintain the life of the town and to safeguard the most important lines of communication, military units were brought in, who could carry out the necessary work of clearing up and repair. In the first place those units were called upon which had the pick and spade as their cap badg... In November 1940 69 Company was ordered to London to undertake clearing and demolition work there.

88 Company also was stationed in London and was quartered in a girls' school in Bow Road. Heinz Schmoll wrote:

> Every morning we were marched to the bombed sites and proceeded to knock down damaged buildings after the ARP men had turned off the gas. The smell of gas and dead bodies of cats, dogs and people was everywhere. We became expert at flattening damaged houses. First the floorboards were removed and then the walls were knocked inwards. The remaining chimneys were cut at the base and felled like trees. At the end of the day we were marched to a nearby public bath to wash off the grime of our work...

On 29th December 1940 five alien pioneers were killed by a German bomb. Amongst the fatal casualties only one name is known, an Austrian, Private S. Buchsbaum; 19 others were badly injured. One of the wounded appears to have been Samuel Herschdoerfer, a Corporal of 137 Company PC. Gerd Treuhaft, a Viennese, described an incident which may or may not be the same. The number of dead quoted by him does not tally with the above report, but information concerning numbers is not always accurate. Here is his story, which was published in the *Watford Observer* on 29 December 1995:

The band leader at Lyons' Corner House announced that the alert had just sounded. Nobody took any notice. 'It's seven o'clock, let's go,' Hans said. I agreed, but then the band started to play my favourite tune 'J'attendrai'. 'I'll be with you in a second, I just want to listen to this song,' I shouted to Hans who was on the point of paying his bill. He made no objections as his new girl friend was going to see him off at the station. 'See you at Waterloo' he replied. I nodded.

A few minutes later the band finished playing 'J'attendrai'. I paid the bill and Lily and I went towards the exit.

Suddenly a fire bomb dropped 100 yards from the restaurant.

The people from the street pushed into the entrance and we couldn't move. The Charing Cross Road was mayhem and we had great difficulty reaching Charing Cross station from where I hoped to get a bus or train to Waterloo.

The bombardment of the City of London didn't seem to come to an end. 'No trains for the next 20 minutes' came over the platforms. I looked round hoping to see Hans, but he was nowhere to be seen. He probably caught the last train. Outside the RTO offices there was an endless queue of soldiers waiting to get their passes signed. I joined the end. Lily was with me. Neither of us realised that London was going through the heaviest night of the blitz. My only thought was what would the Major say? I had just finished my first year in the army and had never been up for punishment. Now I expected to be tried by the King's Rules and Regulations.

Lily and I sat on the tube stairs hoping it would soon be over. After a further 40 minutes the loudspeaker announced 'There will be no more trains tonight.'

'If only I hadn't listened to that song,' I said to Lily. 'Where am I going to sleep tonight now?'

'Come home with me,' she suggested.

I had only known her for six weeks and wondered what her mother would say. The clock struck midnight and there was nowhere else to go...

As we walked, the bombs still dropped uninterruptedly on the houses of London...

At six o'clock I got up with the rest of the family. My first train left Charing Cross at 8.30 a.m., so there was time for a good breakfast, which Mrs Jones kindly provided.

I was on my way back from the station to my billet, when I saw the Orderly Sergeant riding towards me on his bicycle shouting that I should report straightaway to the company office.

Now I was in for it, I thought to myself as I hurried along to see the Major. He was standing in the Orderly Room when I entered.

'I am so glad you are here,' said the CSM. 'So am I,' said the Major shaking hands with me. This was not the reception I had expected and I didn't know how to reply. Then he asked me if I had had enough sleep and suggested that I should retire to my billet for a couple of hours. I began to feel a bit confused.

When the Major left the office I learned that they all thought I had been killed. Feeling very bewildered I asked who had been killed. 'Don't you know?' said the Orderly Room Corporal. 'A bomb fell on our bus and eight of our men have been killed.'

'Hans too,' he added, knowing from another friend I had been with him...

In 137 Company, the first of the new companies which had been formed after the French collapse, there were a number of German and Austrian doctors who were not allowed to practise in Britain, not having passed their qualifying exams and who therefore served as pioneers. When this company also was stationed in areas targeted by the *Luftwaffe* these men ignored the law and observed the 'rules of humanity' by treating victims of the attacks as and when they came across them.

Several of the municipal authorities responsible for the areas in which the companies operated expressed their appreciation of the work of the alien soldiers by letters to their commanding officers. Such letters are attached to the war diaries of 69 Company from Erith and Bexley, of 87 Company from Bermondsey and Blackheath and of 88 Company from the Borough Councils of Bow, Poplar and Edmonton. Five alien soldiers were killed in attacks on Liverpool.

87 Company, then in Pembroke Harbour, lost its second in command, Captain Garratt, and four men. This, however, was due to Garratt's criminal negligence. He had wanted to demonstrate that under given conditions a hand grenade was quite safe. It was not. The enemy had no part in this.

In the course of the next two years nine more 'A' companies were formed. They consisted almost entirely of German and Austrian volunteers, so that the total number of companies rose to 15. As a result the overall strength then was over 4,500 men. No.3 Pioneer Corps Training Centre (3 PCTC), which had been formed at Richborough, was moved first to Westward Ho! and later to Ilfracombe in Devon. The great majority of the 'A' companies formed in Britain took their origin from there. About that time also two Czechoslovakian companies, Nos. 226 and 227, and one Italian company, No. 270, were formed. These were also termed 'A' companies, the same as the Austro-German ones.

The greatest part of the recruits for the later companies came from the internment camps for enemy aliens, which had been established after May 1940, mainly on the Isle of Man. Against the background of the general panic the government had not only acceded to the proposals of the secret service concerning the implementation of its internment policy, it had also stopped the recruitment of enemy aliens into the services. The Government's White Paper of 31 July 1940, however, indicated that government policy was again being reversed and so, after a while, every male internee between the ages of 16 and 50 was given the opportunity to volunteer for the Pioneer Corps. In many cases strong pressure was put onto the internees to follow this course of action – on 26 November 1940 Home Secretary Herbert Morrison even stated in the Commons that HM Government considered entry into the armed forces to be the normal way in which internees between the ages of 18 und 50 could expect to be released – but, nevertheless, every one of those who then reported to the colours was still a true volunteer, because every one of them could just as well have awaited his later release from internment. Naturally, many in fact did choose just this way. Amongst the older ones it was the majority who did so.

It is possible that boredom in the internment camps also contributed to people's decisions to join up. Walter Horst Nessler, who was young and did not fancy being cooped up in internment, is quoted as having said: 'We were simply too young just to sit about doing nothing.' The story of his recruitment into the pioneers and subsequent release from internment as told by Charles Carter sounds rather like a sick joke:

A few days before I was released from internment in the Isle of Man I had sworn my oath of loyalty as a soldier, had been accepted as such and had received the King's shilling. From that moment onwards I was legally a soldier and subject to military law. Nevertheless, when the day came on which we were to be released from internment and transferred to the recruiting depot, we had quite a shock. We were escorted to the ship by armed soldiers and from then on, on board ship and on the train after landing in England, we remained under armed guard.

After arrival at our destination we marched, still guarded by our escort with bayonets fixed, to the clothing and armaments depot. There we were given uniforms and full military equipment including arms and ammunition. And thus, in a matter of minutes, we were transformed from being dangerous or at least doubtful characters into soldiers of His Majesty the King.[1]

At this point it should be said that female internees were not at that stage given any opportunity to join the services. As a consequence there were a number of cases where the husband was in the forces whilst his wife remained in internment. This state of affairs is said to have continued for months in some cases.

About that time an attempt was made to separate the Austrian pioneers from the German ones. A considerable number of Austrian politicians, some prominent ones amongst them, had fled to Britain and so a government-in-exile could easily have been formed. The British government did not appear to view a project of this kind with any kind of disfavour. After all, the British had become hosts to quite a number of foreign governments by that time, and amongst all of them an Austrian government would not have been considered odd.

However, as is usual in Austria the politicians were completely at variance with each other. There were three main groups. First there were what might be described as the conservatives. Amongst these were the monarchists, those supporters of the former Schuschnigg government who had escaped Hitler, some Catholics, Christian socialists and suchlike. The monarchists were the most active. Important members of this group were Archduke Robert of Hapsburg and Sir George Franckenstein, who had been the last Austrian minister to the Court of St James. He had been naturalised and knighted by the King immediately after the *Anschluss*. The second group were the communists. Like all the rest of their kind they had begun by considering the war to be a game between hostile groups of imperialists and wanted to have nothing to do with it. However, the moment the Nazis attacked the Soviet Union they became the loudest critics of the Allied war effort until then, because, as they proclaimed, the Allied leadership had been so inefficient and ineffective. These people actually succeeded in the space of a single day to deny what they had strenuously maintained to be the truth until the day before and to declare the contrary to be true. Nevertheless, whatever they said was expressed in a tone of complete conviction and, as a result, they always found people who believed them. The third group were the social democrats, who were rather more serious in their ways, but nevertheless, could not bring themselves to co-operate with the conservatives. Moreover, a goodly part of them were not in the least convinced that they ought to be working for the post-war re-establishment of an independent Austria and that the country should not remain part of Germany, when this might again have a democratic government. They were not Austrians in the sense of an independent Austria but rather Austro-Germans in the sense of the Austrian parliament's resolution of 1919, when it was decided that Austria should be part of Germany. There was nothing illegitimate in this attitude, but it stopped them from doing anything to recreate an independent Austria. When attitudes diverged to that extent it must surprise no one if the result was a failure.

Despite this, however, Archduke Robert approached the British Foreign Office twice, at first in September 1940 and again in January 1941, with proposals to reorganise the Austrian members of the 'A' companies into an 'Austrian Legion', and it is remarkable that his proposal found enough support there to cause steps to be taken to transform it into reality. The 220 and 229 Companies were chosen to become Austrian units and in the course of late winter 1941 the non-Austrian soldiers of those two companies were exchanged for Austrians from other 'A' companies. To everyone's surprise and especially that of the Archduke this turned out to be very unpopular with the men concerned. By that time all companies had developed their own identity and the men felt a very definite loyalty towards them. Away from their original companies, bereft of their normal environments, they felt unhappy. A specifically Austrian separatist fervour was conspicuous by its absence. Moreover a rumour went round that it was intended to allow an Austrian Legion to be commanded by Prince Starhemberg, who in the 1930s had been boss of the *Heimwehr*, a right-wing, anti-Nazi political group with rather fascist leanings. This sufficed to make even the most enthusiastic supporters of an independent Austria wary of the project at hand. The experiment was observed closely by responsible quarters in the British government and the officers commanding the companies in question were required to put in reports concerning the reception of the proposals by their men, with the result that the whole of this episode is fairly well documented.

Muchitsch takes the view that the attitude of the Austrian social democrats had a considerable influence on the men at that time. This may be so, but as a great deal of his information is taken from social democratic sources and my own experience was different, I believe that he overestimates this. This, however, is the only point where I do not agree with any of his appraisals.

Anyway, it is a fact that, whilst 220 Company remained largely Austrian almost until the end of the war – when it was strengthened by a couple of sections consisting of East and Central Europeans – the changes which had been made in 229 Company were partly reversed as early as March 1941. Moreover, later reinforcements to 229 Company certainly did not consist of Austrians only.

A further point concerning the question of a separate Austrian consciousness should be mentioned at this point. During the whole of the war Britain was host to the armed forces of virtually all the countries which had at one time or another been overrun by Hitler and the Nazis. Together with their countries, however, the governments to whom these troops belonged had lost most of their sources of finance. Therefore, so that these very fine forces could be maintained as fighting units, the British government had to arm and equip them. As it was quite uneconomical to produce separate uniforms for each country, this meant that they were all put into British battle dress and looked superficially like British soldiers. Only their badges of rank and in most cases their headgear were different. To stress the fact that they were not British, however, they all wore immediately below the shoulder seam a strip of cloth, a kind of label, on which the name of their country was embroidered. Similar strips showing their national origin were worn by soldiers of the dominions and colonies, and at an early stage of the war anyone who had any foreign connection could wear the name of the country where he (or she) came from on the sleeve of his uniform. Had an Austrian Legion been formed the men of this formation would certainly have been expected to wear an 'Austria' band on their battle dress. 220 and 229 Companies never got that far, however. Yet the wearing of an 'Austria' ribbon certainly was not prohibited. Several people who had been members of Young Austria before joining up appear to have worn such tapes on their battledress sleeves, though there is only one case which was recorded at the time. That was Erich Goldhammer, and the article which mentions him says he wore it proudly.

Apart from the ex-internees additional recruits joined the 'A' companies in the period from 1940 to 1943. In the main they came from amongst young people who were reaching the age of 18. They volunteered without anyone having put pressure on them to do so. As author of this story and one of this group I may be permitted to tell of some of my experiences in the expectation that they were fairly similar to those of others who joined in that period and under similar circumstances.

From my arrival in England at the age of 15 in September 1938 I had worked officially as an 'agricultural trainee', but really I was a farmer's boy and the fancy title was only to stop the Ministry of Labour becoming upset on account of my not having a working permit. I did not like having to get up at a quarter to six every morning to milk the cows, seven days a week, 52 weeks in the year, three years on end, and so looked forward to joining the army as soon as I was 18. Even though it was perfectly clear to me that the pioneers had to work hard and often did not do the cleanest of jobs, I also had no doubt that few jobs could be dirtier than what I was doing anyway, so being a pioneer certainly seemed a step up.

Accordingly, on my eighteenth birthday I took the bus into High Wycombe, the nearest town, found the army recruiting office and told the astonished sergeant there that I was Austrian and wanted to become a pioneer. The man was delighted. I do not think that a real volunteer had come into his office for a long time, if ever, and I had the feeling that he might have kissed me, had it been the proper thing to do. But it was his job then to ask me a few questions, and when he asked my occupation I answered truthfully that I was a farm labourer. 'How old did you say you were?' he said, and when I confirmed that it was my eighteenth birthday he became very disappointed and very sad. 'You know,' he said, 'you are a bloody fool. If you had come yesterday I should have taken you and kissed your hand. But didn't you know that all agricultural work is a reserved occupation from age 18 onwards? As from today you are 18 and so I can't take you for the army. You'll just have to stay with your cows. Leave your address just in case there is a change.'

A reserved occupation was any job which was considered vital to the war effort and thus more important than service in the armed forces. Whilst otherwise the forces could recruit anyone provided he was fit, if the Ministry of Labour had declared anyone to be in a reserved occupation that was a final prohibition. Fortunately for me in December 1940 that ministry raised the age of reservation for agriculture from 18 to 21, and only three days later a buff envelope arrived in the mail instructing me to report to No. 3 PCTC (the 'AM' had by this time been dropped) at Ilfracombe as soon as possible.

I arrived on 21 December 1941. Christmas was looming and in the circumstances no one was in the least interested in making a soldier out of me, as a result of which I was given a battle dress and all the other bits which a soldier ought to have, including a suit of denims. Then someone told me to put these on and report to the cookhouse. The sergeant cook was pleased to see me, because he had an enormous heap of potatoes in a corner of the kitchen and I was just the right person to peel the lot. That day and in the week following I peeled more potatoes than I had ever seen before or since.

After four weeks' training in Ilfracombe – square bashing, arms drill, physical exercises and whom to salute and whom not to salute (very important) – a dozen of us were posted to 229 Company. We moved on 27 January 1942. At that time 229 Company was engaged in building a Nissen hut camp at the bottom of a disused quarry at Upton Lovell, along the main road (now the A36) from Wilton to Warminster, or more exactly between Codford St Peter and Heytesbury. By the time we arrived most of the huts had been completed and were useable. The roads and footways, including those leading to the huts, were as nature and hundreds of men's feet stomping over them month after month in a wet English winter had made them. And it was very cold.

The men of the company had been issued with rubber boots, but unfortunately the company quartermaster had received only the exact number for the men then present. He had no spares, so that the new intake had to make do with their leather boots. These were completely unable to keep out the wet for more than half an hour, when they were still relatively new, or for more than five minutes after having been force-dried nightly for a fortnight in front of the iron stoves, one of which was the sole means of heating each of the huts. These two weeks were amongst the most miserable in my life. It is just not at all nice to have one's feet in icy water all day and to be unable to warm them up even at night time.

In addition the 'beds' on which we were expected to sleep consisted of two trestles about three inches high at each end, across which three one-inch planks were laid, swinging freely in the middle. As the weight which the centre plank had to carry was greater than that on the outside planks it bent through further, with the result that the edges of the outside planks stuck into one all night, and no amount of stuffing straw into palliasses could avoid this.

That first fortnight was awful. There is no other word for it. Fortunately things got better. By the end of March the roads and even the footpaths had been finished and the job for which 229 Company had come to Codford neared its end. North of Marlborough a firing range was being built for the Royal Armoured Corps and on this a road had to be made up. This was the next job which 229 Company was entrusted with. On 27 April the company moved to Ogbourne Maisie, two miles north of Marlborough on the Swindon road (A338). There it was quartered in the stables of a country mansion, and as these had originally been designed to house horses they were much better built than the Nissen huts of Upton Lovell, which after all, were only intended for human beings. They were lovely and warm, dry and roomy. Where previously there had been one horse there was space for four soldiers, and we had bunk beds so that the space in the individual stalls was used in the best possible way.

As far as I remember, the group of four to which I belonged had got together quite accidentally and it is because of this, and because it seems to me that our 'racial' composition was fairly typical of that of 229 Company as a whole, that I want to go into this. Our senior was Freddie Raape, whose mother had been left a widow after his father's death. Subsequently she had married an Englishman, which was why Freddie, born at Darmstadt, had come to Britain. He was neither Jewish nor was he a political refugee. His best friend was George Popper from Vienna, as Jewish as Freddie was 'Aryan'. Willi Lutz and I, both of us also from Vienna, were 'racially mixed'. Willi had a Jewish mother and a Catholic father and I have three Jewish grandparents amongst my forbears. So between the four of us we had 62.5 per cent Jewish and 37.5 per cent 'Aryan' grandparents. The make up of the company as a whole may not have been very different.

The improvement in the conditions in which we lived allowed many of us to show our skills. The sergeants' mess was in a large, whitewashed room adjoining the stables. Corporal Portner, who had been not entirely unknown as an artist in his native Vienna and who was later to be killed in action, covered the walls with murals, which people came to look at.

Shortly after it had been formed the Company had had a wall newspaper, which had survived a few issues until it was closed on higher orders because of its impertinence. At the beginning of 1942 the production of such papers was encouraged by the War Office education department and so this paper was revived. 229 contained a dozen or so journalists with the result that *Foresight*, as it was called, became a very interesting and readable organ. The editor was Harry Cemach, Corporal in No.4 section. Charles Carter was our resident cartoonist. *Foresight* was published weekly and all its issues have been saved in the Imperial War Museum, where they may still be seen and read. It is the only such paper in the British army of those years which has been preserved.

The normal rations which our quartermaster sergeant drew from the RASC depot every day, and which the cooks of other units turned into the usual army grub, became delicious meals in the hands of our cook, who had been *chef de cuisine* at the Hotel Sacher in Vienna before his emigration. We ate so well that the officers of other units in the area invited themselves to eat with the men of 229 Company whenever there seemed to be a reasonable excuse.

What happened in 229 Company was not, of course, exactly the same as what happened in all the other alien companies of the Pioneer Corps. Each of these companies had its own image and was different from every other one. Walter Fast, later Walter Foster and secretary of the Anglo-Austrian Society, has written about his experiences in 251 Company:

> When I had finished square-bashing at Huyton I was sent to 251 Company AMPC, stationed outside Bicester and engaged in the construction of a vast Royal Ordnance Depot. The pioneers did the navvying. There we were in deep mud digging ditches (that was done with pick and shovel in those days), humping hundredweight bags of cement on our backs, trying to fit together large curved sheets of corrugated iron to make Nissen huts. The only skill I acquired was laying flagstones to provide mud-free paths. Work was at navvy pace with a lot of leaning on shovels and not too strenuous. For evening entertainment there were three dreary pubs at Bicester, but Oxford was only 12 miles on my bicycle. More often my goal was Aylesbury, a good hour on my bike, from where the Metropolitan Line ran into Baker Street. To go to London a soldier needed a pass and the military police were watching at Bicester and Oxford railway stations, yet there were no MPs guarding the London Underground!
>
> We were a motley crew of middle-European Jews and ex-French Foreign Legionnaires of all nationalities. We worked far more productively than the usual run of pioneers who were physically or mentally sub-standard rejects from other regiments, but we must have been a hard lot to command. Imagine the face of a nineteen year old public school orderly officer doing the rounds at dinner and asking in clipped tone the standard 'Any complaints?' and the burly foreign legion corporal slowly rising from his seat and growling 'Not today, Sir, but maybe tomorrow!' The officers clearly regarded a posting to one of the Alien pioneer companies as a punishment, and perhaps it was.

This last comment may not be quite justified. H.F. Miller who was a

British officer in 74 Company from 1942 to 1944 wrote: 'initially I found it rather strange having to be in charge of these aliens who... in so many cases were so unfitted for the jobs they were given, but I must confess that they always gave of their best and I was sorry to leave them...'.

Life in the 'A' companies was not, however, without its brighter side. There were any number of artists and others, who had connections to the cultural side of life, and this resulted in entertainments of the highest standards. Many of those to whom this description applies did not get to the companies at all, but remained with the entertainment section in Ilfracombe or were posted to the Southern Command Pioneer Corps Orchestra, officially a part of 229 Company, PC.

Sergeant Strietzel, previously a member of the Vienna Philharmonic Orchestra, had formed that orchestra from amongst the musicians in the pioneers. It could bear comparison with any other orchestra at that time. C. Aronowitz was first violin and W. Stiassny was a frequent soloist on the piano. F. Lustig was amongst its members. Originally it had been conceived as the Pioneer Corps' own orchestra, but because of its excellence it was soon taken over by a higher formation. It became the Southern Command Continental Orchestra and has entered the history of music under this name.

In Ilfracombe there was a theatrical section whose performance reached equally high levels. One of the most popular performers was Poliakow, known as Koko, previously clown in Bertram Mills' Circus. Other members of the troupe were Rudolf Jess, H. Karg Babenburg, Peter Land and Norbert Schiller. The well-known moderator and later BBC director, Carl Jaffe, was its original organiser. Others who should be mentioned were the author A. Perles and the Austrian lyricist Amon Rosenthal, who later changed his name to Arthur West.

In spite of the perils which marked the situation of the country after the collapse of France and in spite of the air attacks on British towns and installations, life was fairly peaceful for the majority of the alien pioneers in Britain in 1941 and 1942. They had to work hard and frequently they got exceedingly dirty. On the other hand none was near any front line and the danger to their lives was no greater than that to the civilian population. Yet they were soldiers and benefited from the status which soldiers have in wartime. They were sent on a week's leave regularly every quarter and during those periods and at weekends were permitted to move around the country relatively freely. Also they were looked after by all sorts of societies, charities and other agencies whose job it was to look after soldiers in general and see to it that they enjoyed reasonable comforts, often far in excess of those enjoyed by many civilians. Their evening and weekend entertainment was taken care of, and wherever any alien soldiers were stationed there were socials and theatres and dances, to which the local girls, civilian or in uniform, were invited and which they frequented in large numbers. It is obvious that, human nature being what it is, not all the relationships which resulted from this could be merely of a passing nature.

For many an alien soldier this was a first step towards his later naturalisation in the United Kingdom. All this getting-to-know-each-other and the warm sympathy which emanated not only from the girls one met – so different from the experience of many of the men until then – made Britain appear the most friendly and welcoming country they knew. Author Arthur Koestler, who served in 248 Company where, despite his fame (or perhaps because of it?) he was not especially popular, wrote that English people who come upon a needy foreigner tend to treat him like they would a friendly dog roaming the street in search of his master. They take him home, see that he is comfortable and give him a good dinner. After that they are pleased when he feels at home.

After his early release from the service Koestler wrote the book of the film 'Lift up your head, comrade'. This film came to be made at Chesil Beach near Weymouth under the auspices of the Ministry of Information in 1942. The actors were the men of 74 Company and they acted more or less what they did in their daily lives, for the film was about the fate of the German and Austrian refugees who had been accepted into the British army. The title was taken from 'Halte Schritt, Kamerad, Kopf hoch, Kamerad', the refrain of a song written by an Austrian, Jura Soyfer, when he had been imprisoned at Dachau concentration camp. As an example for the previous history of many of the soldiers Koestler chose the story of Bobby Spuner, another Austrian, who had once been European welterweight champion boxer. Spuner (later Spooner) had been taken to Dachau after the Austrian *Anschluss* and there had been badly maltreated by the Nazi SS. They broke both his hands and nearly killed him. The film was shown widely in British and American cinemas in 1942–43, as a result of which the public became aware of the contribution made by German and Austrian refugees. Many of Koestler's later writings show traces of his experiences with the pioneers.

Contacts with the people of the country were also made in other ways. So for instance, men of 249 Company, which was engaged in building camps for prisoners of war in the neighbourhood of Glasgow and later in the area of Sedburgh in the Lake District, gave German lessons at the local evening institutes in their spare time, whilst others did the same for a neighbouring unit of the Intelligence Corps and for the Home Guard. In 1943 CQMS Glas of 249 Company, who had made all the arrangements, was given a certificate of good service in recognition of his efforts. In other companies similar contacts were made.

Another way in which mainly Austrian pioneers were used in those days was as ski instructors. A whole group of them came to do this job in the winter of 1942. Muchitsch wrote:

> The 'Austrian instructors', as the group was termed, were intended to train the 51st Highland and 52nd Lowland Scottish divisions on the pattern of the French Chasseurs Alpins or the Italian Alpini. They were organised by Sergeant Pick, a former Austrian army instructor. In this job he had designed the winter uniform of the Austrian mountain divisions. The instructors included a number of men who later occupied senior positions in the British army of occupation in Austria. One of them was Major Schnabel, who remained in 52nd Division as divisional ski instructor and later became divisional intelligence officer. Another was the later Lieutenant-Colonel Lasky, a native of Vienna, who had taught the then Prince of Wales, the later Edward VIII, how to ski. The greater part of the pioneers went back to their units after having finished their jobs as ski instructors, but some were able to continue in this capacity at the Mountain Warfare Training Centre of the Middle Eastern Forces in the Lebanon.

This chapter cannot end without the story of the alien companies which were formed in North Africa. Refugees from Nazi oppression, who had fled to France, had not been well treated there. Even before the commencement of hostilities many had been interned and taken to camps in the Pyrenees and in North Africa. The younger ones could get out of this by joining the French foreign legion or the *prestataires*, but there again they felt that they were being treated as prisoners. After the French defeat, when France became a vassal of Hitler, the situation got even worse. Many of the *legionnaires* deserted, reached England and joined the pioneers. Many of the others got to North Africa where they were again interned. The *prestataires* were released and they too were immediately interned. After that they had to do forced labour in the coalmines and on the Trans-Sahara Railway, which was then being built. The resentment of the Germans and Austrians there against the French was exceeded only by their hatred of the Nazis.

After the Allied landings in North Africa on 8 November 1942 and the appointment there of Admiral Darlan as Governor General, there was at first no change in the fate of these people. Then, however, the French authorities once again proposed to the internees that they should rejoin the *prestataires*. At this point two Viennese, Karl Waldorf and Robert Feigl, were instrumental in attracting the attention of Major Brister, a former commander of 69 Company PC, who by then was on the staff of GHQ North Africa at Algiers. It was largely due to his efforts that eventually the British accepted these people into the army and in consequence a number of additional 'A' companies of the Pioneer Corps were formed. Amongst these 337 and 338 Companies consisted exclusively, 362 Company partly, of Germans and Austrians.

The following article was published in the August 1950 issue of the *Ex-Serviceman*, the journal of the Ex-Service NB Association over the initials 'H.C.':

> The suggestion to form Alien Pioneer Companies in North Africa came from a few former members of the French Prestataire Companies [attached to the British Expeditionary Forces in 1940 under the name of Foreign Labour Companies]. After Dunkirk about 100 had fled to North Africa, where they were interned in a camp approximately 100 miles from Algiers. I was one of them.
>
> We sent a messenger to Algiers a few days after the landing of the Allies in North Africa to communicate with the AFHQ [Allied Forces Headquarters] and to find a way by which we could be enlisted in the British Army. The reply did not come quickly. Before a result was achieved I went to Algiers myself and joined forces with the other negotiators already staying there. I heard there the full account of their negotiations. Their proposal of enlistment of all refugees living in the various concentration camps in North Africa had not been met with great enthusiasm on the part of the British authorities, until Major Brister and the political advisor of the British AFHQ, Mr. Harold Macmillan, MP [the later prime minister], had intervened and submitted the whole question to the War Office in London. There it was still pending.
>
> Algiers was full of soldiers, British and American. No-one really knew what was going to happen with the old Vichy officials. Darlan and Giraud were the heads of the French Algerian Government, and de Gaulle was not even allowed to come to Algiers. Little had changed in the French administration. The Vichy officials were still in power, hostile as ever to all foreigners and Jews in particular.
>
> Whilst we waited for the answer from London we contacted the Central European refugees then in Algiers and most of them agreed

to join the British Army, if authority were granted. Some, however, had already approached the Americans, who were willing to employ them as civilians in responsible positions; some had joined the Corps Franc of the de Gaulle forces. We did not know what to do really. We could not understand the British attitude. How could any power engaged in the most deadly fight against a common enemy refuse the services of men eager to assist? Just as we had given up all hope of a favourable outcome to the negotiations, two British officers appeared unexpectedly in the small hotel we were living in to announce that an affirmative reply had been received from London. An Alien Pioneer Company would be formed. Everyone willing to join should be at the Ecole des Ponts outside Hussein Dey at 9.30 a.m. on Wednesday, 16th December 1942.

They could give us no information as to our new status. They could not tell us what pay we would receive, if we would really be British soldiers with all their rights and duties. They could only repeat from the cable they had received, that we would be considered as British soldiers. This we understood to be quite different from our desire TO BE BRITISH SOLDIERS. Our fear that we would be misled again, that we would be used and then cast aside as before, was not relieved, but we were relying on British fairness and decided to risk it.

On Wednesday morning, 16th December 1942, sixteen men turned up at Hussein Dey. Very few were missing of the refugees then present in Algiers. The 337 (A) PC Company had started. The first number of enlistment was 13809000. The bearer was an Austrian count, the son of an adjutant of the late Emperor Franz Josef; the second was a Czechoslovakian engineer, the third a German doctor of philosophy.

The company grew very slowly. Most of the Central European refugees were in internment camps in Southern Algeria; they were in the coal mines of Kenadza, in the concentration camp of Djelfa, in Said and in the punishment camp of Hadjerat M'Guil. They provided cheap labour for the French who were not willing to let them go. It is due only to the hard work of Major Brister, Mr. Younger [later minister of state] and Mr. Macmillan that they finally succeeded in joining the British Army.

The British did not enlist any Spanish or Italian refugees at that time. Spain was neutral and was not to be offended. The reason for the initial refusal of the Italians is unknown to me. The arrivals of men were so few that by Christmas 1942 the Company did not number more than 36 pioneers.

After Christmas a detachment arrived from Suzzoni, where I had been interned, and then about 20 men from Kenadza, who looked very weak and aged. Most of them later became very good pioneers after they had been clothed and fed properly for a few weeks.

On New Year's Eve the Company's strength had grown to approximately 70. After being trained, they went daily to the various depots to load and unload food, ammunition, etc. for the front line, a few hundred miles away.

In February the company numbered approximately 150 men. Our barracks were moved to the town of Hussein Dey. Whilst we were already soldiers of the British Army, thousands of our comrades were still in the French concentration camps or in so-called French Labour Units. A few of these men arrived from time to time after having escaped from the camps. Most of them had enlisted in the French Foreign Legion or in the Corps Franc of General de Gaulle, to have the opportunity to get away from the camps. They had thrown their uniforms away and had then asked to be enlisted into the British Army. The 337 (A) PC Company was nearly at full strength by the beginning of April.

Mr. [then Major] Younger, Major Brister and Mr. Macmillan tried everything to obtain the release of all the internees from the French. Finally, they got authority to visit and enlist them in the camps themselves, so that they would pass from the French supervision directly under British Army discipline. The French authorities were so afraid that they did not want them to be a day free in Algiers.

By the end of March or beginning of April the refugees from the concentration camps arrived in Algiers. The first were enlisted into 338 (A) PC Company. A short time later, the 362 (A) PC Company was formed as well. These three companies were mainly composed of Central European refugees...

It is fair to assume that the enthusiasm for service in the British army in particular shown by these refugees was a further pointer to the doubting Thomases in the War Office that they might trust the anti-Hitler Germans and Austrians more fully. In particular, the emigrants to North Africa had clearly been more inclined towards France and the French way of life than towards the British originally, so that their conversion, as it might be called, could be deemed to be quite flattering to the British ego. As a result the members of these North African companies were given more responsible jobs for which only the most reliable people could be used, before the companies in England were treated likewise. Thus a former foreign *legionnaire*, Sergeant Morgenstern, was given the job of interrogating some most important prisoners of war, including even General Thoma himself.

Muchitsch related the stories of a number of men from 337 and 338 Companies:

> The life of the Austrian Corporal Schatzberger may serve as an example for the fate these men had been subjected to. This man had fled to France shortly after the Anschluss. There he was interned from September 1939 until April 1940. Having volunteered for the Prestataires he was posted to a unit under the command of the BEF. During the German advance into France he and his comrades were ordered to save themselves by flight. With the aim of getting to Britain they marched from Rennes via Bordeaux to Bayonne, but missed the last British ship by a very short space of time. Their only possibility of salvation now was North Africa. After arrival at Casablanca Schatzberger was accepted as a prestataire, but then he was demobilised and interned as a travailleur etranger. He only just managed to avoid being sent to either the coal mines of Kenadsa or the railway builders of Colomb-Bechor. After the Allied landings he reported to the British, who immediately issued him with an Army uniform and identity papers to protect him against the French.
>
> 338 Company was formed in Algiers in March 1943, after an Allied commission had succeeded in liberating the desert camps. 169 of the internees from the camps at Colomb-Bechar, Kenadsa and Bidon came to this unit. 95% of the men, many of them former Foreign Legionnaires, had been interned in Algeria and Morocco after the fall of France. The majority were Germans and Austrians, but there were also some Czechs, Poles, Romanians, Yugoslavs, Italians, Russians, Hungarians, Egyptians, Portuguese and Spaniards.
>
> The biography of the Austrian lawyer Dr. Friedrich[2] Schneck describes the horrors of the desert camps ... Dr. Schneck had been a trade union secretary in Vienna. He was also a member of the illegal Social Democratic party. 1938 he fled to France. In Paris he became a member of the Central Council of Austrian Emigrants. As prestataire his fate was similar to that of Corporal Schatzberger. He, too, got to North Africa but there he was interned at the Kenadsa camp, whose inmates were used as slave labour in the coal mines and for the construction of the Trans-Sahara-Railway. After the Allied

landings Schneck assumed a leading part in the organisation of the resistance by the camp inmates against their French guards, whereupon he was transferred to the notorious punishment camp at Hadjerat M'Guil. In tiny cells and with inadequate nourishment the inmates of this camp were at the mercy of the sadism of their French tormentors. Schneck used his time there to collect evidence against these. After the internees had been freed as the result of Allied intervention, he volunteered for the pioneers and was very soon promoted Sergeant. In the trial of the French guards of Hadjerat M'Guil, which took place in the summer of 1943, the evidence Schneck had collected ensured their conviction and punishment, which was the death penalty in the case of four of the accused. Later Sergeant Schneck was commended for his bravery, when his action after the explosion of an ammunition depot at Maison Carrée was instrumental in avoiding a greater catastrophe.

Daily Orders No.445 of the Officer Commanding Algiers Military District includes the following:

> The following courageous action has been reported to me. On 12 May 1943 during an air attack three barrels of petrol in the centre of a stack were set on fire by shrapnel. Without hesitation and with complete disregard for their safety the undermentioned men removed the burning barrels from amongst the remainder, as a result of which a much larger conflagration with potentially much greater losses was avoided. By their action the actual losses did not exceed fifty gallons of petrol.

One of the three men whose names were mentioned was Private Kurt Pleuse of 338 Company.

Members of these companies, whose names are known, are almost all Austrian. This not because the companies were entirely or even predominantly Austrian, but because many of the Austrians amongst them were later able to have their names registered by the Austrian government and are recorded in the *Dokumentationsarchiv des oesterreichischen Widerstands* in Vienna. They include Hans Bauer, Hans Escher, Johann Slawyk, Heinrich Fein, Erich Brings, Dr Hans Reif and a certain 'von S.', whose father is said to have been a senior naval officer in the German armistice commission at Algiers. The father tried to persuade his son to return to Germany, and had even visited him in his detention camp, but had remained unsuccessful. The number of Germans in these North African companies was certainly no less than that of Austrians. However, whilst the archives in Vienna contain a lot of information, there is no equivalent for this anywhere in Germany. The Germans, regrettably, are unknown and will probably remain so.

Like the 'A' companies in England the North African ones also had their share of artists and intellectuals. A band, 'the Pionian', and male choir, 'The Singing Pioneers', were formed from these units and entertained the troops during the Italian campaign. The 'Pionian' made a five-month tour visiting the units of the 8th British and the 5th US armies in the winter of 1944–45.

The British army rule that soldiers are discharged in the country where they joined up was changed in favour of the men of these companies. The great majority were released in Britain, but some elected to be discharged in Germany or Austria, and this also was permitted.

NOTES

1   What Carter said concerning arms and his having been issued with them is contrary to both the author's own experience and the reports of others. There really is no doubt that until the beginning of 1942 recruits joining 3 PCTC were instructed in the use of fire arms but were not actually issued with any.

2   In earlier accounts there had been some confusion as to whether what is described above happened to Johann or to Friedrich Schneck. However, new research by Dr Lebensaft of the Austrian Academy of Science has established that is was Friedrich.

4

A Change of Atmosphere

In the summer of 1942 the pioneers at last received the news that they were to be armed. The alien soldiers had proved themselves to be keen and reliable workers with a high disciplinary standard. Except only for their tendency to disappear from their camps and barracks at weekends – a practice which was officially prohibited, but to which in most units a blind eye was turned – their officers rarely had any reasons to complain about them. Insubordination and drunkenness, favourite military crimes elsewhere, were almost unknown amongst them. Their devotion to the central aim of all the Allies – the final destruction of Hitler and his Nazis – was absolute. That this was the true situation had been realised even in the War Office, and so those who took the view that it was dishonourable for soldiers not to be trusted with arms gained the upper hand.

As a result 229 Company, in line with all the other alien companies of the Pioneer Corps, was equipped with one brengun for each of its ten sections, a stengun for each of its sergeants and a P2 rifle with bayonet for each of its men. The fact that the P2s were the oldest rifles on issue in the forces – no P2 had been produced since the Boer War – did not disturb anyone. They fired .303in ammunition, the same as the Lee Enfields of the infantry and they were beautifully made. Their rate of fire was marginally slower, but who cared about minor details like that?

It would be wrong to state that there had been no disciplinary problems at all in the alien companies. Of what crime Private Fenner had been guilty is not known. The war diary of 229 Company merely records that he was court martialled on 26 January 1943, that he tried to commit suicide a day later, that he went on hunger strike the following day and that he was transferred to a detention camp on 1 February. Similarly there is a record in the war diary of 69 Company to the effect that on 23 August 1943 Private Ojola was sentenced to 28 days detention, but again there is no mention of his crime. However, cases of this kind were rare.

Often, when individuals failed to observe the letter of the law, they were too clever to get caught or they were covered by their comrades, for it was very rare for the men not to stick together and to let each other down. For a time a considerable part of the supply of American cigarettes to the London black market was in the hands of a group of soldiers of 229

Company, who made an awful lot of money that way, but were never caught. More serious than these matters was the case of a breach of trust on the part of a man, who had been with the pioneers since 1939 and who appears to have served in one of the first six companies. After the end of the war he served in the Allied Military Government of Occupied Territories AMGOT. A number of papers, none of which indeed seem to have been very important, but which bore the classifications 'confidential' or 'restricted', were found in the files of the Central Control Commission of the former East German Socialist Unity Party in Berlin in 1996. The name of the man who appears to have been responsible is mentioned in the files. However, there is no definite proof. Nevertheless for all these crimes the old jingle applies, that no one has ever been punished for what he has done, but only for being found out.

Already in December 1941 six NCOs of the 'A' companies were granted commissions in the Pioneer Corps. They were Ernst Bendit, Leopold Frankel, Ernest Goldstein, Wolfgang Rudolf Kochmann and Max A.F. Matros, all Germans from the Reich, as well as the Italian Paul Tumiati. Bendit is mentioned in the war diaries of 249, 246 and 137 Companies. He ended his service as a major commanding a pioneer company. Goldstein was sent to 219 and Kochmann to 229 Company. What happened to Frankel and Matros is not known at present. This appears to have been a trial and as the trial was successful it was extended.

Some time later another small group was sent to Officer Cadet Training Units (OCTUs) and after a short period of training they came back to their units as second lieutenants. From then on increasingly the subalterns in the 'A' companies were Germans and Austrians and after a while they were also transferred to other units of the Pioneer Corps. Most of their names are known. They included Second Lieutenants Jung, Andermann, Bischitz, Garai (later Garry), Pollack, Wiseman and Wisloch. A little later a few more were added. Amongst them were K.H. Barany, J. Blutstein, R.J. Falck, H.P. Langer and K.A. Jellinek. The last-named was one of those who did not survive the war. Second Lieutenants Calmon, H. Brettell, C.H. Costello, Dietrichstein (later Dickson), F. Goldschmidt, H.P. Goldsmith, F. Gross, R.E. Kingsley, E. Litvinoff, Peter A. Alexander, S.L. Pledge and Markstein were also in this batch. Beadle also was commissioned about this time and was posted first to 248 Company and then to 69. In June 1943 he was transferred to the RAC.

Before the end of 1942 a larger batch got their commissions. They included R.H. Engel and E.A. Saywood, both of whom were first posted to 77, after which they went on to 88 Company, A.H.H. Eppenstein went to 74, H.K. Frank to 248, Kurt Frankenstein and K.S. Warburg to 87, C.E.L. H.Reiche, H. Ringel, Springer (who later on was mentioned in despatches) and R. Herz to 219, Gondos and Müller to 93, F.C. Haarhans to 165, G.A. Wassermann to 137, A.R. Howritz and K. Scharf (Scarfe) to 88, and I.S. Milch, as well as F.G. Schulof to 249 Company. A.H. Ehrenfeld is mentioned in the officers' list of 246 Company on 1 February 1942 and as lieutenant on the strength of 77 Company on 30 June 1942. Leopold Kuh (later Kew), who had been CQMS of 219 Company, got to 74 Company as subaltern. Later on he became second-in-command of a company with the rank of captain. J. Weinstein-Rath, who has already been mentioned as one of the first sergeants of 69 Company, went to 219 Company. He dropped the 'Weinstein' at a later stage and called himself Rath only. After the end of the war he became officer commanding a company of the (by then) Royal Pioneer Corps with the rank of major. That was a company which had been recruited from amongst displaced persons.

At this point it should, however, be said that these officers who were given their commissions in the Pioneer Corps during 1942 and 1943 were not the first German and Austrian officers in HM Forces altogether. A small number of enemy aliens who had important qualifications in areas essential to the war effort were commissioned very much earlier. One such was Robert Kronfeld, the son of a Viennese dentist and a close relative of the Austrian ex-chancellor and future president Dr Karl Renner. Kronfeld was a renowned glider pilot, who had gained distinction in this art by flying his flimsy craft in the Alps and in the Rhoen mountains in Germany. He had held several world championships. Having got to England in 1934 he was welcomed there by the gliding fraternity, who enabled him to continue his hobby. This brought him to the attention of the War Office when they started to look into the possibility of using gliders for warlike purposes early in the war. One day in 1940 he was summoned to the War Office, walked in as a civilian enemy alien and came out as a British colonel. Later on he was also in the RAF, where his rank was that of a squadron leader. He was one of the principal planners and organisers of the use of gliders in the Normandy landings during the night of 5–6 June 1944. However, he and a few others like him were exceptional cases. Kronfeld met an early death. On 12 February 1948 he was flying a new type of glider designed by himself, when he went into a spin and crashed.

In March 1943 the War Office published an Army Order as a result of which all members of 'A' companies in the Pioneer Corps could apply for transfer to fighting units of the army, as well as to the ships of the navy and to the air force. The response to this was tremendous. In some cases the applications were delayed as there was insufficient staff in the departments responsible for dealing with them. At the same time most distinctions between British and enemy alien servicemen and women, which had obtained hitherto, were removed so that, at least theoretically, Germans and Austrians could be used in any capacity in all of HM Forces.

The ones who asked for transfers to fighting units were by no means only the younger ones. Naturally, there were relatively more younger men than older ones, but many of these also wanted to get to grips with their enemies at close quarters before the war ended. Those who did not volunteer were mainly men who felt themselves unable to do so on grounds of health or family. The number of those who preferred service behind the lines because it was less dangerous or maybe more comfortable was probably rather small. However, those who remained pioneers were the ones who at the end of hostilities were the bulk of the men who were most easily available to act as interpreters and sometimes as administrators when AMGOT was established. They were the ones who enabled the military government to communicate with the people of the conquered areas in their own language. As a result a not inconsiderable number received exceedingly quick promotion to high rank at that time. Several were demobilised with the rank of lieutenant colonel, a rank which was rarely reached by any who had volunteered to fight.

Those who had asked to be transferred to fighting units did indeed have to submit to a selection test in order to determine whether they were sufficiently intelligent to join the renowned regiments to whose membership they aspired. Most of the tests were held at a selection centre at East Croydon and were of the usual type, similar to what is used in education and industry to this day. No case of anyone failing to reach the required standard has been reported. As far as is known the majority were classed as possessing above average ability. The first transfer instructions started to arrive shortly afterwards.

According to Bentwich there were exactly 4,760 enemy aliens in the Pioneer Corps on 2 June 1943. He states that this figure has been taken from official statistics. Unfortunately he does not say how or where he obtained it. Nevertheless I think we may assume that it is accurate. For his assertion that out of these 4,760 a total of 2,664 were transferred to other regiments, he has given us his calculations. They seem reasonable, though probably not absolutely exact. If they are right a mere 2,096 remained in the original pioneer companies. As a result the alien companies were reduced to less than half their original strength. Some were converted to British companies, others were disbanded. On the whole it was the older companies which continued to retain their 'A' company status. The remaining aliens in the other companies were posted to them. The companies which had been formed in Algeria remained unchanged. The figures given by Bentwich are as follows:

(1) After 1941, to technical and specialist units,	
RAOC, REME, RASC, RAMC, RE	995
(of these about 400 were again transferred to other	
regiments included under (2) at a later date)	
Intelligence Corps	220
	1215
(2) After 1943, to combatant units:	
Armoured Corps	216
Royal Artillery	221
Infantry	174
Special Forces	116
Army Air Corps (Gliders)	17
Parachute Regiment	75
Commandos	110
Others	20
	949
(3) Outside the Army:	
Royal Navy	80
RAF	25
	105
(4) Special duties:	
to General Service Corps (War Crimes)	50
retained in Pioneer Corps	100
	150
(5) Commissioned and later transferred to fighting units	140
Pioneer Commissions in AMGOT	105
	245
Total transfers	2664

After that a further wave of enemy alien recruits joined the services. Quite a few, mainly amongst those who had come to Britain in the *Kindertransporte* in 1938 and 1939, had allowed themselves to be put off from volunteering earlier by the prospect of having to become pioneers. When this was no longer necessary they came forward and went straight into fighting units. The total number of those who joined at this stage is not known. Estimates vary between 1,000 and 2,000. Bentwich mentioned 1,390, but as this figure was arrived at by adding several items, one of which was 'about 1,000', this figure sounds much more accurate than, clearly, it is.

It should, perhaps, be mentioned that the German communists, who at that time maintained a small headquarter organisation at Manchester, also chose this moment to recommend to their members who were of military age to join the British forces, a decision which many of them were to have cause to regret at a later stage, when their past membership of the British army made them suspect to the authorities in the German Democratic Republic. However, at that time these people 'accepted the party directive with enthusiasm'. It is an interesting reflection, however, that they were so much under the sway of their party that they waited for a directive before doing something, which many really wanted to do and which they could have done without any difficulty for years beforehand.

248 Company was one of those disbanded. Their last task before this happened was the construction of a PoW camp at Otley. After completing the latrines a wag decorated the main wall there with a German language reminder to the future inmates 'We thank our *Führer* that we may shit here'. The originator of this gag was still there when, to his chagrin, the camp was occupied by Italian PoWs.

220 Company was the one which continued to exist the longest. After having been an almost purely Austrian company for most of its existence, it had acquired a Czech and a Baltic section and its remaining eight Austrian sections had included an admixture of a few Germans and Poles when it was sent to France some two months after D-day. There it was used for forestry work and in December 1944 it was doing just this in the Ardennes, divided into detachments with headquarters in St Hubert, when the last offensive of the *Wehrmacht* began. Without any warning the Company suddenly found itself right in the front line. They had frequent contact with enemy armoured forces and the whole Company had already been written off by British headquarters, which assumed that they had been destroyed. However, their officer commanding, Major Howard, directed them so skilfully that eventually they were able to extricate themselves from their predicament. The frequency of their movements led the enemy to assume that it was opposed by a much larger force than was in fact the case. The enemy offensive stopped short of the positions of 220 Company, as a result of which they were able to await the arrival of the British 2nd Armoured Division. Then they retired in good order. The Company was eventually disbanded at Kellen, a suburb of Kleve, in Germany in February 1946. A War Office brochure, which was published in November 1945, entitled 'The British Army's Foreign Legion', dealt almost exclusively with 220 Company. There it is said 'literally to have hacked its way from Normandy to the Reichswald'.

This may be the right place also to tell the story of Willy Usher, originally Uscherowitz, who was with 220 Company all the way, and of his elder brother Arthur. Arthur was born in 1921, Willy in 1923, both in Vienna. Arthur left Vienna shortly after the *Anschluss*. Via Czechoslovakia and Romania he made his way to Palestine. There he volunteered for the pioneers, with whom eventually he arrived on the Greek island of Crete. When Crete was invaded he just managed to escape being taken prisoner, and got to North Africa. There he remained for some time, before he was allowed to transfer to a marauder unit of the Jewish Brigade at Sfax. After fighting in Africa had ceased his unit was in action in Western Europe and finally in Germany. After it was all over they were stationed at Venlo, near the Dutch–German border.

In the meantime Willy, who had had some very unpleasant experiences at school in Vienna, had got to England with one of the *Kindertransporte*. In Leeds he was apprenticed to a tailor. In 1940 he was interned at Huyton and from there he was sent to Canada. In July 1941 he was sent back again and released from internment. As he was not yet 18 he could not join the proper army yet, but he reported to the Home Guard and served there until January 1943. Then he joined up, and was posted first to 219 Company in Northampton. From there he got to 69 and eventually to 220 Company in Sledmere, Yorkshire. Then he changed his name. With 220 Company he got to France and eventually took part in the fighting near St Hubert. Then he became an interpreter with the military government at Schilde. After fighting had ended he was able to go to Vienna, to try to find his parents, but his search was to no avail. His father had died, his mother and the rest of the family had been sent to Auschwitz. It was only following his return to his unit that he heard that Arthur was in Venlo only a few miles away. They met a few hours later, Arthur a corporal and Willy, who in the meantime had become a sergeant.

Other companies were also sent to France in 1944 and worked on various jobs. Eric Walters-Kohn, a sergeant in 69 Company wrote:

> in Normandy my Viennese accent proved to be a useful fighting tool. One September morning we received reports that three Germans had been seen near Breteville, not far from Caen. A heavily armed search party went out but, after several unsuccessful hours, returned empty-handed. At about 4 o'clock a French farmer came with the news of another sighting and he was able to explain exactly where the Germans had been seen. Without stopping to think of any heavy weapon I rushed off in the direction indicated

which led me to a barn. I stood outside and shouted at the top of my voice, in German: 'Come out and give yourselves up. I have only my pocket knife. You will not be harmed.' I did not have to call this many times before they did as they were told, over 20 of them appearing from the barn with their hands up, looking bewildered. It was the combination of my Viennese accent with my British uniform which did for them...

That summer we had been put to work in the ruins of Caen, where bodies still lay in the streets. Ordered to help build a bridge over the River Orne I detailed one of my corporals, a Viennese taxi-driver named Sonnenschein (anglicised to Sunshine), to take two six-wheeled lorries and shift the rubble we needed. It was a very hot day, there was a horrible stench everywhere and we were plagued by mosquitoes. Piled high with rubble and, with the by now shirtless party, the lorries set out on the return trip through the ruined town. They were stopped by two Redcaps.

'Who is in charge here?'

'I am,' said Corporal Sunshine.

'Who gave these men permission to take off their shirts?'

'I did,' said Corporal Sunshine.

'Why did you do that?'

'Because there is too much sunshine,' came the reply.

'What is your name, corporal?'

'Corporal Sunshine.'

Sunshine was put on a charge for insolence, but once it was established that he really was called Sunshine, the charge was withdrawn.

Later, Walters-Kohn was at a prisoner of war camp near Bayeux. Many of the prisoners were absolutely convinced of a German victory, particularly after the new German weapons had been introduced. However, the fact that that some also had different expectations is confirmed by the following conversation between two Viennese prisoners, overheard by Walters-Kohn:

'Did you know,' asked the first, 'that no one is allowed to go up to the top of the Stefanskirche any longer?' (The church of St Stephen, in the centre of Vienna, had the highest tower in the city.)

'Why not?' asked the second prisoner.

'Because you can see the front line from there.'

At the beginning of March 1945 Walters-Kohn was given the job of escorting a trainload of SS and Gestapo men from Normandy to Ostend. 'The train was held up at Bruges for half an hour, during which time some 60 Flemish workers gathered on the platform and attempted to attack the prisoners. I had to call on the escort party to form a cordon in front of the train with fixed bayonets'. The men he protected did not know that seven years earlier their escort commander had been taken to Dachau on board a train guarded by SS men, a journey on which not all who started had survived.

As this chapter deals with changes in the treatment of the enemy aliens in the United Kingdom during the war, their service in the Home Guard should also be mentioned. For those who do not know, it may be worth mentioning that the Home Guard, originally called the Local Defence Volunteers, was formed in 1940 from amongst civilians, who became spare time soldiers without giving up their normal jobs. They were formed everywhere throughout Britain and no one who volunteered, young or old, sick or healthy, was turned down. Except, of course, foreigners. However, even this changed and in 1943, according to his own statement, Gunther P. Hirsch, a Berliner, was commissioned as lieutenant in the Cumnor Platoon of the 1st Berkshire Battalion and later on in the University of Oxford Platoon of the Home Guard.

5

Name Changes

In the course of 1942 several alien companies of the Pioneer Corps were alerted for overseas service. Although such information was given to the officers commanding under strictly confidential cover, many even of the men in the ranks soon realised that something was going on and many started worrying what might be their fate in such circumstances and what would happen to their dependants. As most had signed a declaration at the commencement of their service to the effect that they knew of the danger of being executed as traitors in case of capture by the enemy, their worries seemed quite justified. But their worries went further. As most of the members of their families were legally Germans, they, too, had the status of enemy aliens. Whilst the head of the family served in the army they were given a special status, which protected them. But what would happen if the serving soldier, from whom this protection emanated, should die? Questions like these led to unrest.

Some of the men approached their officers and asked whether this was not the time when they should be granted British citizenship or some similar status, which would solve these problems. They found support for their points of view amongst the officers commanding the companies, as a result of which at least one of them, Major A.M. Richardson, commanding 229 Company PC, wrote to his Group Commander, the Commanding Officer of 36 Group PC, on 9 February 1943:

> The order, which has been received by this company to mobilize for service overseas has brought to the fore a question on which all my men feel very deeply.
>
> They are all enemy aliens and the great majority are Austrian and German refugees from Nazi oppression. Most arrived in this country in 1939, some earlier, and their antecedents were enquired into by the Home Office on arrival.
>
> On acceptance for the Army their bona fides was again gone into and they were accepted. They have been serving in the main for well over two years.
>
> They ask to be protected by being naturalized as British subjects and thus be put on the same status as all other belliger-

ents, i.e. under the protection of some government. At the moment they are enemy aliens and thus in fact either stateless or traitors, if they fall into the hands of the enemy.

Their second and greater concern is over the status of their families in England. These are likewise enemy aliens and subject, therefore, to the restrictions imposed on such people as regards movement, occupations, etc. What would be their state, if their menfolk are killed?...

May I ask that this subject be treated with the utmost urgency in view of the circumstances?...

Having been raised at this level, the problem was taken seriously in responsible quarters. The solution which was proposed to the soldiers was very different, however, from what they had requested. It was felt that the problem was not so much the nationality of the soldiers who were going to be exposed to contact with the enemy, but the possibility that the enemy might recognise them as German nationals. Therefore, and as a special measure, everybody who wanted it should be issued, as it were, with a false name and where necessary with a false identity.

In order to make this possible a War Office order was issued at the beginning of April 1943, more or less simultaneously with the decision to permit enemy aliens to enter into fighting units of the services. By this order German and Austrian soldiers who would now be serving in direct hostile contact with the troops of their countries of origin were advised to adopt, for their own protection and for the duration of the emergency, names which would hide their true identity and would thus protect them from being recognised as nationals of the enemy countries. The order was not worded so as to lead to the assumption that any permanent changes of name might be envisaged. It was simply a measure for the protection of soldiers who might fall into the hands of the enemy, and being recognised as the enemy's own nationals, might be accused of high treason and put to death as a result. There was no intention to do more than to replace the old names by new ones in the soldiers' pay books and on their identity discs.

Most of those affected were young and inexperienced. They could not imagine that a change of this kind might be a change for life. But when one arrives in a new unit with new documents, which show a new name, then one has ceased to be, as in my own case, Peter Langer. One is William Peter Leighton and all that has happened before is past. The experience of all who changed their names on that occasion was similar. Only a very few recognised the danger and at a later stage converted their names again, often into double-barrelled ones. An example for this course of action was Walter Friedenstein, who had been a well-known banker in Vienna and who, therefore, was aware of the need to protect one's name. He changed to Walter Foster in 1943. Soon after his release from the army in 1945, however, he made it known generally that from then on he wanted to be known as Walter Foster-Friedenstein. However, he was rather older than most of us and recognised the consequences of his change of name at an early stage.

The names which most of us adopted bear witness to the spirit of frivolity with which this matter was regarded. Heinrich Mosenthal, who had read his Shakespeare, is responsible for the fact that some of my descendants now sport the noble name of Mortimer. In 229 Company there was one whose name was Zobel. Many hours of queuing on pay-parades in alphabetical order had shown him the disadvantages of being last in the alphabet. He called himself Abingdon. A certain Tischler, a bit of a wag, wanted to call himself Thistethwaite and only changed his mind after it had been forcibly pointed out to him that he would have to pronounce this tongue-twister himself and that this – in view of his accent – might well in itself lead to his being denuded and discovered. Thus a lot of fun was had by all and a lot of names were adopted, which were not by any means such as many of the men wanted to be known by for the rest of their lives.

Perhaps the best – though not necessarily true – story has been told by James Leasor. He writes that a certain Finckelstein changed his name to Ferguson and later on again a second time to Findlay. The purpose of this double change is said to have been that Findlay might be able truthfully to say, that before he was called Findlay he had been called Ferguson.

There were also people whom their parents, full of family pride, had given high-sounding names at birth. Thus Claus Leopold Octavio Ascher became simple Colin Anson and Count Saloschin converted to the much more ordinary name of Saunders. Others again changed their names with the full intention of making the change permanent and people like that normally had good reasons for choosing the names they adopted.

Together with the men, their wives and children had to change their names as well. How this was to be done and how much influence the family had on the husband's decision was left to the individuals. In some cases, no doubt, there were difficulties. Certainly, Mrs Inge Vogel, the wife of Private Rudi Vogel of 220 Company, knew nothing about any new name until she received a curt letter from the War Office, 'Following your husband's change of name you will be known as Mrs Inge Verney in future'.

The most important result of all this was one that had not been intended at all. Certainly the British authorities had not intended it and most of the men had not either. For after their names had been changed these men no longer stuck out amongst their fellows in other regiments. To their comrades in their new units they seemed to be English, because their names were English and the fact that some of them spoke English with a peculiar accent became much less important. Lots of English people have peculiar accents, too. Thus they had taken an important step towards being anglicised.

More than half the men joined in this lovely game of change-your-name, and the name changes were not by any means restricted only or even mainly to those who bore obviously Jewish names. It seemed to be a good idea and very few thought of any consequences beyond the next weeks or months.

As a result the reader of this book may become uncertain when reading about what happened after the changes had been executed. Many of the names mentioned here from this point onwards will be English or even Scots or Irish. In many cases the previous names will be unknown, and until the relevant records become available in the Public Records Office in the year 2018, they will generally remain so.

The men's status as enemy aliens, however, was not touched by all this. They remained what they had been before. The normal procedures for naturalisation under the Aliens Acts were not restarted until 1947. Applications were admitted only then, but those who could prove to have served in HM Forces were given priority and were exempted from the need to insert notices in the press, advertising their wish to be naturalised, which is normal procedure in the case of all other such applications. Most of the pioneers and other German and Austrian members of HM Forces used this opportunity to acquire British nationality.

The British measures were effective. Very few of those taken prisoner by the Germans were recognised for what they were by their captors, and where this was the case they were protected by the very determined attitude of the British government, which through the intermediary of the Swiss made it quite clear to the Germans that any measures against British prisoners of German nationality would call forth immediate reprisals against German prisoners of war in British hands.

6

Technicians and Other Experts

At the commencement of the war the British forces had been barely adequate to defend and to safeguard order in the British Empire. However, compulsory military service was introduced almost immediately after the outbreak of war and this resulted in considerably greater numbers of men being under arms, but it also meant that the provision of arms and armaments to them became a matter of great difficulty.

In order to equip the new soldiers in accordance with the requirements of modern warfare, enormous industrial efforts had to be undertaken and for this purpose large numbers of people were needed. There was an immediate outcry for thousands of highly skilled technicians. Whoever had any claim to be a technologist, an engineer or a skilled technical worker was snapped up by industry, whilst those who had already joined the army were entrusted with the maintenance and repair of arms, equipment and vehicles. But nowhere were there enough such men, and so it was not surprising that the technicians amongst the enemy aliens serving in the Pioneer Corps were called upon to do their bit also at an early stage.

For a long time the supply of arms to the fighting units of the British army has been the job of the Royal Army Ordnance Corps, the RAOC. At the commencement of the war this corps had the full responsibility not only for the procurement and supply, but also for the repair and maintenance of all types of arms and armaments. It is, therefore, not surprising that it was the first part of the army other than the Pioneer Corps, which invited enemy aliens to join its ranks. This occurred in the autumn of 1940.

However, many of these men were not really very pleased with this invitation. They did not wish to serve behind the lines and looked upon the RAOC offer as a change which would get them no nearer to their objective of actually fighting the enemy. Many did not understand – and were not told – that at that stage the RAOC was more important to the prosecution of the war than any single fighting unit. They also failed to appreciate that with a transfer to the RAOC they would be put on an equal footing with their British comrades and, like them, they would be armed, which after all was a great step forward when compared to their unarmed existence in the pioneers. Instead of the expected flood of applications for a transfer, there was just a smallish trickle and even later there were probably no more than 200 to 300 men who got to the RAOC from the 'A' companies of the Pioneer Corps.

In view of the increasing complexity of the material used by the forces it soon became obvious that the RAOC in its then structure was not capable of dealing with the tasks of repair and maintenance. Its officers had the wrong background and education and its structure was insufficiently flexible. So a new corps was formed, the Royal Electrical and Mechanical Engineers (REME). The officers of the REME were recruited in small part only from the RAOC, a larger part came from the Royal Engineers (RE), but the greatest part were men who were recruited direct from outside the forces. This gave the REME a special image and service which then soon proved more popular than the RAOC had ever been. They, too, opened their ranks to the men of the 'A' companies, but set their sights somewhat higher than had been the case with the RAOC, and so in the end the number of transfers to the REME is not likely to have been higher. The Royal Army Service Corps (RASC), which is responsible for the supply of food and clothing as well as the provision of transport to the Army, was opened to enemy aliens in 1941.

According to Bentwich the total number of men of the 'A' companies who transferred to these three corps, as well as to the Royal Army Medical and Dental Corps and the Royal Engineers, was just under 1,000. In spite of all enticements, however, it took quite a while before all these 1,000 men had decided to apply for transfers. That this should have been so is based on an answer to a parliamentary question by Professor A.V. Hill in September 1942. According to this there were 61 scientists with higher university degrees, 75 men who had completed studies at technical high schools and 95 men with completed apprenticeships serving in the Pioneer Corps at that time. In particular, the employment of the last-named as labourers in the ranks of the pioneers should have been a source of annoyance to the technical corps (REME and RAOC). There is evidence, however, that at least some of them were transferred in the following year.

Many of those who did apply for transfer and were accepted had interesting careers. Thus M. Maynard, previously Moses, from Alsfeld in Hesse, had been apprenticed to a Jewish motor vehicle repair shop in his home town. In 1938, when he was 16, the Nazis imprisoned him in Buchenwald concentration camp. After his release he emigrated to England and got another apprenticeship with the Zipp Fastener Co. in

Edmonton. In May 1940 he was interned and was taken to the Isle of Man. From there he volunteered for service in the pioneers.

His technical education stood him in good stead when, after a very short sojourn in the Pioneer Corps, he joined the RAOC on 10 September 1940. He was employed as an armaments mechanic immediately. A short time later he became an instruments mechanic and having proved himself in this capacity also, he was sent for further studies to the Military College of Science. Having completed his course there successfully he returned to normal service, was promoted to sergeant and became responsible for a group of instrument repair shops in the south-east of England. One of these was at Dover at a time when the town was subject to regular bombardment by hostile artillery from the other side of the Channel. Later on, after the Normandy landings, he commanded the instrument repair shop of 30 corps in Holland and in Germany. Between the end of hostilities and his release from active service in 1947 he was responsible for the supply of locally produced motor vehicle spares to the British army in Germany. Upon his release he received a certificate for special services from the General Commanding the British Army of the Rhine.

A graduate of Vienna Technical University, who does not wish that his name be mentioned, was granted membership of the British Institute of Mechanical Engineers following his emigration. In the spring of 1940 he volunteered for service with the pioneers. As he was the man with the most technical knowledge in his company, he first of all became the company storeman. When it was eventually realised what qualifications he held, he was offered an immediate commission in the RAOC in 1941. This he accepted. By 1942 he had been promoted to major and became assistant director in the RAOC. Shortly after this he was transferred to the REME. He was posted to Headquarters First Army, where he was in charge of the planning and organisation of workshops for the landings in North Africa. Then he was responsible for the execution of these plans. He served in Algeria, Italy and lastly in Austria. Although he was offered promotion to brigadier on several occasions, he preferred to remain a major on the grounds that he understood the job he was doing, but had no idea of the additional duties which would be his if he accepted higher rank.

In addition to the responsibilities briefly described above, the RAOC also had other obligations. Amongst these was the provision of certain military statistics. A.T. Lane – previous name and origins unknown – was a statistician. Because of this he was transferred from the Pioneer Corps to the RAOC and eventually became responsible for the preparation of all technical statistics for submission to the War

Cabinet. In 1944 he was with HQ 21st Army Group when this moved to France and he ended his service, still a statistician, in the HQ of the British Army of the Rhine.

A further transferee from the pioneers to the ordnance was the well-known artist Mathaeus Johannes Koelz, who later adopted Kelts as his surname. He had been born at Mülldorf, Bavaria, on 5 April 1895. His family moved to Hohenbrünn at a later date. In the First World War he served in the German army as an officer. After that he became a policeman and, as luck would have it, was a member of the police squad which prevented Hitler's attempted *coup d'état*, the so-called 'beer hall putsch', in Munich in 1923. In his spare time he painted. His paintings were executed in a very conservative, traditional style and he was by no means one of those whom the Nazis victimised for their advanced ideas. So it came about that in spite of his having been on the 'wrong' side in 1923, in 1937 he was asked to paint Hitler's portrait. This was intended to be a great honour for him, but he made it clear that he had no intention of accepting. The news of this unheard-of impertinence was passed to a police official, who had been Koelz's colleague at some time earlier on. This man immediately realised that what Koelz had done could not remain unpunished in Nazi Germany and would have very serious consequences for him. Following this man's warning Koelz left Germany the same day and, after having fled first to Prague and then to Rotterdam, he finally came to England.

Being obviously German, rather than Jewish, Koelz and his family had a tough time at Oxted, where they settled. His daughter was the subject of an attack at school, which left her with a permanent injury, and there were other unpleasant incidents. He was interned and was one of the many who were sent to Australia on the Dunera. Nevertheless, after his return to Britain in 1941 he, too, volunteered for service with the pioneers, where he was one of the oldest. At first he was posted to 248 Company, then to 74. He was transferred to the RAOC on 18 June 1943 and was promoted to sergeant on 5 April 1945.

During his period of service Koelz portrayed several of his comrades in the pioneers, his officers and their wives. In the last hours before his flight from Germany he had cut up into several parts his masterpiece, a triptych, which he hid in various places. His daughter, who tried to restore this, now owns a few of the pieces. Others she is still looking for.

In the planning of the invasion of Normandy one of the most important aspects was that the bridgehead would not be established around one of the big harbours and that, therefore, harbour facilities for the unloading of heavy equipment would have to be provided on beaches, on which such operations would be exceedingly difficult. The problem was solved by means of floating caissons which were towed across the Channel and anchored as close inland as possible, forming artificial harbours. These were the so-called Mulberry Harbours. One of the first enemy aliens to be commissioned, Captain Kleinberg, a specialist in bridge building, had been transferred from the pioneers to the RAOC. He was posted to the War Office, where he took part in the design and construction of these harbours.

Others, who are known to have served in the RAOC are listed below. In many cases more may be learnt about them by reference to the register. They are:

> Boehm, Rudolph Walter, from Breslau and Berlin, alias Rudolph Walter Boam
> Breitbart, Horst Guenther, from Berlin-Charlottenburg, alias Alan Bright
> Cemach, H., ACA, from Vienna
> Feldheim, Dr Heinz Dietrich, 13804320, from Dortmund
> Hagen, Louis, MM, from Potsdam, alias Lewis Haig
> Hartmann
> Hayek
> Jung, from Vienna
> Korn, Frank, OBE, from Berlin
> Kuhnel
> Peyer alias Palmer
> Schmoll, Heinz, from Haynau, Silesia
> Sponer, Rudolf, from Czechoslovakia
> Weiss
> Wiener, Heribert, from Czechoslovakia

The Royal Electrical and Mechanical Engineers, being a wartime creation, were very different in their make-up from the rest of the army. As their job was to maintain the very modern arms and machines essential for fighting, there was no question of their being organised on the lines of traditional units. Engineers work in workshops and so workshops were their units. To work there a man has to know his craft and so the lowest rank in REME was that of craftsman, an honoured description in trade and industry.

We have met Heinz Lothar Schmoll as chronicler of 88 Company PC in France. He left the pioneers to be transferred to the RAOC in 1941. Concerning his experiences in RAOC and REME, he wrote:

I started working as a storeman in the extensive arsenal stores with thousands of bins and signposts at every crossroad of the stores. The work was rather boring.

After I had been there some time the REME were formed and artisans of the RAOC were invited to transfer. Because of my training in a locksmith's shop in Breslau I opted to become a fitter. I had to pass a trade test which required me to bench-make a steel hexagon shaft to fit into an even shaped aperture in a steel plate, with no more than a thousandth of an inch clearance. I passed the test and passed from private soldier to craftsman. In the workshops we plied our trade on 25-pounder field guns, pontoons, rocket launchers and armoured cars.

However, as workshops are often dirty places, and the gentlemen who were used to officers being clean and well turned out at all times did not want to have men in charge of such mucky places in the officers' mess, even some of the largest workshops were commanded by warrant officers. Yet their importance was considerably greater than that of many men who held commissions. This importance had to be recognised and so these men were promoted to warrant officer first class, equivalent to regimental sergeant major, men to whom even generals deferred in their areas of responsibility. They were called conductors or sub-conductors, paid as much and more than the colonels of some regiments and revered by all who came in contact with them. Amongst these demi-gods in uniform at least two were refugees. Both came from Berlin.

The very exciting story of how Bright, original name unknown, eventually got into the army will be found in the register. Having served in 165 Company, Pioneer Corps, as a private, in 1943 he was transferred to the REME and immediately sent to India. In the 25th Indian Division he was entrusted with the command of the divisional REME workshop and became warrant officer first class. He finished up in Malaya and was released from service there.

The other was Henry Louis Ward, previously Hans Ludwig Warwar. He transferred to the REME at an early stage. Having an engineering background he was sent on a six-month course to Lucas, the electrical firm in Birmingham, where he received further intensive training. In 1945 he was also posted to India, to Assam and Bihar. He was attached to the Indian army and put in charge of an Indian army workshop in the rank of sub-conductor.

An officer who eventually became second in command of a major workshop was R.S. Marmorek. At the beginning of the war he had studied technology at Cambridge. Like so many others he too was interned in May 1940 and sent to Canada. After his return from there he was asked to work as a civil engineer on important war work. In 1944 his job was incorporated into the army, as a result of which he was given an immediate commission in the REME. There he was responsible for waterproofing the canvas covers of the lorries used in the Normandy landings. Later on he was posted to Iraq, but he finished his service as deputy commander of the central repair shop at Benghazi, Cyrenaica. Others who are known to have served with the REME are listed below. Where known, further details concerning them are contained in the register. They are:

Baerwald, Ernst, from Munich
Baumgarten, Horst Norbert, 13807029, alias Norbert Barrett
Bruell, Egon, 14442497, from Austria
Burnell, F., from Berlin
Cohn, Hans, from Wolfenbuettel and Berlin, alias John Carson
Fast, Walter, from Vienna, alias Walter Foster, OBE
Feldheim, Dr Heinz Dietrich, from Dortmund
Foster, R., 16001269
Frey, Peter Hans, from Berlin, alias Peter Howard Fry
Goldschmidt, H.F., from Delmenhorst, alias Herbert P. Goldsmith
Gruber, S.H. (Schani), from Austria
Hagen, Louis, MM, from Potsdam, alias Lewis Haig
Holzhacker, K., P(AL)/6879, from Austria
Lederer, E.
Marx, F., 13301329, from Austria
Moses, M., 16001227, from Alsfeld in Hesse, alias M. Maynard
Pfeffer from Austria, alias Alan Peters
Prager, Guenther, from Austria
Reinisch, 13809617, from Austria
Rosenbluth, alias Eli Howell, MA
Rosenfeld, Georg Jakob, from Karlsruhe, alias George Jakob Rosney
Rosenkranz, Heinrich (Heini), from Vienna, alias Henry Robertson
Rosenthal, Heinz, from Fuerth, alias H. Rodwell
Simion, Ernst, from Berlin, alias Simeon
Spier, Alfred, from Rauisch Holzhausen, Kreis Marburg
Stern, Robert Eric, from Vienna, alias R.E. (Bob) Stenham
Strauss, Ulrich, from Berlin-Charlottenburg, alias Steven Strauss
Striem, Hermann, from Gross-Wartenburg (Sycow) near Breslau
Sussmann, Hans, from Vienna, alias John Gordon Steward, 13046364

Ward, G.
Zade, Hanno
Zeisler, Siegmar, from Berlin, alias Ralph Sanders, JP, MInstAM

The number of men who were transferred to the RASC probably exceeded the number of transferees to RAOC or REME.

Amongst those who were commissioned in that corps was Alberti, who had been a stationery manufacturer in Germany. An ex-pioneer, he was director of stationery in the RASC for a time. After the fighting had ended he was in Germany, controlling German printing shops, including the one which produced the *Soldier* magazine. He experienced his greatest satisfaction when a German general, von Blaskowitz, knocked at his office door before coming in, stood to attention, saluted and requested his permission to have something printed.

Salisbury had been one of the ski instructors of the 52nd Lowland Division. He was commissioned in the pioneers, after which he tried to get to another corps. He was successful with the RASC and was promptly posted back to 52nd Division. This time, however, he became officer commanding of one of the last horse-drawn units in the Corps.

'Captain E.' is the pseudonym used by Bentwich for a man whose connection with the RASC was full of ups and downs. Three months after volunteering for the pioneers he transferred to the RASC as a lorry driver. Then he was sent to OCTU. However, after he had been commissioned, the RASC decided it did not want him after all, although the OC of his old unit would have liked to have him back. So he was sent back to the pioneers instead. He stayed there for six months, after which the RASC changed its mind. He was posted to a troop transport company, with whom he took part in the battle of Falaise and with whom he stayed during the advance through northern France, Belgium and Holland. He got as far as Bremen. Following the German surrender he was sent to the Far East, where he served as second in command of an RASC company in Ceylon until released in 1946.

An other rank, W. Bingham, former name unknown, driver of an ambulance vehicle, evacuated wounded under heavy fire in Normandy. For this action he was awarded the Military Medal. It was one of 11 such medals which enemy aliens received in the course the war.

Hans Leser, on the basis of his service number the eighty-fifth enemy alien to have been accepted into the pioneers, went to France with 74 Company PC in January 1940. In 1942 he was transferred to the RASC at Aldershot. He remained a driver until someone noticed that he could speak German rather well and transferred him to the staff of General Eisenhower as sergeant translator.

Others who are known to have served with (or been attached to) the RASC are listed below. In many cases more may be learnt about them by reference to the register. They were:

Abraham, L.L., 13804777
Abraham, P.
Abraham, Werner Emanuel, from Duisburg
Berman, Rudolph
Bier, Herbert N., 13106759, from Frankfurt
Boehm, Rudolph Walter, from Breslau and Berlin, alias Rudolph
    Walter Boam
Bume, M., from Austria
Burnell, F., from Berlin
Dick, Ari, from Vienna
Eppenstein, Andrew, alias Andrew H.H. Elliott
Ettinger, Gerry S.
Goldberger de Buda, 13802043
Goldsmith, O.A.
Herzberg, E., P(AL)/32404, from Austria
Jacob, Ernst M., from Aldekerk, alias Ernest M. Jacob
Jaretzki, K.S., 13802733, alias C.S. Jarrett
Karpe, F.J., 13800363
Komaromi, Hans, PAL/1401, from Austria
Lasky, Wolf, OBE, from Vienna, alias Laszky
Lemberger, Hans Karl, 1441666 from Vienna, alias J.C. Lee
Lustig, Franziska, No.W/118218, from Vienna
Lustig, Lisl, from Austria, married Lustig
Odenheimer, Hans, from Heidelberg, alias H. Oden
Oppenheim, Herbert, from Querfurt near Halle
Oppenheimer, Rudolph, 13802972, from Fuerth
Paul, K., P(AL?)/32733, from Austria
Reichenberg, P.L.
Rosenstein, Ernst Zeno, PAL/1115, from Bensheim in Hesse
Rosenthal, Dr Erwin Isaak Jacob, from Germany
Rosenthal, Heinz, from Fuerth, alias H. Rodwell
Rothenberg, Henry R., 13802670
Schaechter, L., P(AL?)/31453, from Austria
Schoen, E.F., from Austria
Schornstein, Fritz, PAL/30942, from Vienna, alias S. Sharoni
Siegel, Hans Peter, from Munich, alias H. Peter Sinclair
Spielman, E.
Stern, Robert Eric, 16001118, from Vienna, alias R.E. (Bob) Stenham

Weiner, Hans Paul, from Trautenau, Czechoslovakia
Weiss, Eduard, from Austria
Westford, Harvey, from Austria
Wolff, Martin

Technicians and men with special skills were sought also by other corps. Professor Bernadelli, who held a Chair of Economics at the University of Cambridge, was a field cashier officer in the Pay Corps with the Burma Expeditionary Force through the grim campaign of 1942–43. Later he was a broadcaster in Delhi for the Ministry of Information. Other men in the Pay Corps were Sidney Brook, formerly Siegfried Josef Baruch, and for a short time at the end of his service also Harry Curtis, previously Helmut Cahn from Dusseldorf.

At least one man was in the Army Fire Service. Sergeant Sheldon lectured to thousands of men of that corps who went over to the continent, his subject being continental fire services and conditions in Germany and Austria. His qualification was that he had been an officer in the fire brigade of his Austrian home town before being exiled to England. He was in Ostend with the AFS when a fire broke out in tanks loaded with aviation spirit, the loss of which might have endangered the Allied defence against Rundstedt's offensive in the Ardennes in December 1944. When the army reached Germany he got the job of dealing with German fire-fighting equipment. Unfortunately, neither Sheldon's original name nor his home town are known.

At least four former pioneers were military policemen at one stage or another. Richard Hyman, originally Heymann, a Breslauer who had been to France with 69 Company in 1940, was transferred to the Corps of Military Police and was attached to the 51st Scottish (Highland) Division. In this capacity he travelled from Normandy via Brussels as far as Hamburg. There he had to liaise with the local police in the fight against venereal disease amongst British soldiers who used the facilities of the Reeperbahn, Hamburg's sinful mile. He was demobilised in March 1946. Yet another Sheldon, Walter, was also an MP, which in this case means Military Policeman. He went through the campaign in north-western Europe, was a member of a police unit in Germany training German police, and was with a group looking for Himmler. The other two are Rudolph (Rudy) Julian Falck and Paul Yogi Mayer, today an MBE, from Bad Kreuznach, temporarily Michael Frank.

The classical corps in which technicians are used, of course, is the Corps of Royal Engineers. Being one of the three ordnance arms and of ancient origin, the REs took a long time before permitting enemy aliens to join them, and when eventually they did so they tried to ensure that they got only the best. Amongst the Germans and Austrians who were thus honoured were Sergeant (later Captain) Hertz, who had been active already in the refurbishing work at Richborough Camp and ended up as architect for the NAAFI in Germany, and Walter Marmorek, who had been the chief at Richborough and had been to France with 69 Company, PC. Following his transfer to the sappers he was set to work clearing mines at Monte Cassino, repairing bridges over the River Arno and building army camps in Carinthia. His service culminated in his appointment as deputy commander, Royal Engineers, with the rank of major in his native Vienna.

Captain Keith was a younger man, who was commissioned in the sappers from the pioneers. He was attached to headquarters, Canadian army, but after the occupation of north-western Europe he had to deal with allied ex-prisoners after their release and shepherd them back to their original countries. He finished his service dealing with German army accounts concerning people who had been in forced labour camps during the war. Lance-Corporal Helmut Gordon, crane driver in the R.E., was mentioned in Army Orders and thanked by the Commander in Chief of the Home Forces for saving the life of a mate on a crane. Others who are known to have served as sappers are listed below. In many cases more may be learnt about them by reference to the register. They are:

Bischheim, Bernhard, from Frankfurt, alias Bernard Beecham
Bratu, Artur E., from Offenbach, alias George Bennett
Engel, Werner, alias Peter W. Eden
Kennedy, Eric J., from Austria
Kleinberg
Meller, Erich, PAL/45758, from Vienna
Mellinger, Lucas
Paucker, Dr Arnold, from Germany
Rosenthal, Klaus Walter, from Berlin, alias Walter Roberts
Schornstein, Fritz, from Vienna, alias S. Sharoni
Schwitzer J.G., 13802309, from Hungary, alias Tommy G. Swinton
Simon, Stefan Helmut, from Berlin
Stensch, Rudolf, from Berlin, alias Ronald Stent
Vulkan from Austria
Warwar, Hans Ludwig, from Berlin, alias Henry Louis Ward
Weiss

The Royal Army Medical Corps (RAMC) may perhaps object to its members being classed as technicians, as the title of this chapter suggests. But as medical men are certainly not ordinary soldiers and their job in the services is to repair people, where others repair weapons or machines, I hope that my reasoning may cause them to forgive me.

Thirteen medical men of German or Austrian origin, who had been at the University of Cambridge, are said to have received their commissions in the RAMC more or less simultaneously. Amongst them were Lieutenant Seelig, who was commissioned into the Indian Army Medical Corps (IAMC), and Flight-Lieutenant Katz, a Fellow of Trinity College, who was able to join the Australian Air Force as a medical officer, after having been deported there on HMT Dunera. Martin Strauss was in the RAMC and so were Lieutenant-Colonel Wiant, and Joachim. Major Goldstein was a medical specialist who served first in Nigeria, then in India and lastly in Rangoon. A Viennese, Major Fuchs, was chief surgeon of the 8th Army. His name appears in the roll of honour. In the same rank, that of Major RAMC, the later Professor Elias Lehmann of Beersheba University, a native of Nuremberg, accompanied the 8th Army all the way from Benghazi to Vienna. Dr Paul Rothschild made it to lieutenant-colonel and served in Persia and India. Major Schnitzer became chief medical officer of a British military hospital in his native city of Vienna and Captain Grueneberg, a scientist of many parts, was seconded to the War Office to carry out research in ballistics and the effects of shrapnel. It was upon his advice that British soldiers were not issued with chain mail vests, as had at one time been proposed. His last job was as chief pathologist to the army in the greater part of Italy.

The Viennese psychiatrists, renowned members of the Austrian medical schools, which had been teachers of the world, were met with a great deal of prejudice at first. However, they managed to overcome this and in the end were highly esteemed. Amongst them were Major Last and Major Fisher, who became the officer commanding the military wing of a mental hospital in India. Major Wittkower designed the psychological tests for the selection of officers used by the War Office.

Some 50 German and Austrian doctors, who were refugees in India, were able to join the Indian Army Medical Service. Most were engaged originally as civilian medical practitioners for the army, but after 1943 they received commissions in the IAMS. Among these were Colonel Weingartner, chief medical officer to the forces of the Sultan of Bikaner, Major H.A. Friedlander, Major H.R. Heldt, an ophthalmologist, Major M.V. Klein and Major H.G. Dunn. Others in or attached to the RAMC or IAMS were:

Buchanan, Mrs
Cohn, Susanne, from Breslau, married Lustig
Danziger, Dr Heinz G., from Leipzig, alias Dr Henry Dunn
Federbusch, E.H., from Austria
Gerber, Dr J.H.
Hamlin, Dr
Hess, Dr, from Vienna
Hoexter, Professor Dr, from Hamburg
Kaufmann, Dr
Margaret, S., from Austria
Sander, Gus, alias Saunders
Schotz, Dr
Schreuer, Rudy, from Berlin, alias R.W. Sherman
Schul, Pinkus
Sekler, Wolf Mesulem, from Kolomea
Strauss, Martin
Weissenberg, Werner, 13800300

It is not known whether Albert Stern was the only enemy alien to serve in the Army Dental Corps. No others have, however, come forward. Stern was born in Berlin on 4 May 1918, emigrated to Britain in 1935 and began his studies as a dentist at the Royal Dental Hospital in London the following year. Having volunteered for the army he was posted to 88 Company, Pioneer Corps, in February 1940. He went to France with them in 1940 and remained until in 1942 he was given leave to complete his studies. Having done so he reported back and was transferred to the Army Dental Corps. On 1 January 1945 he was commissioned as lieutenant and posted to the Scottish District. Then he was sent to Beirut and later moved to Gaza. He was released with the rank of captain in January 1947.

Dr Heilbronn was a physicist who became a member of the Royal Corps of Signals. The same applies to Dr (later Professor) Bernhard Herrmann Neumann. The Signals were out of bounds for enemy aliens even after 1943, so the transfer to that regiment was a signal honour for both. Both were mathematicians of note.

Unusual was the fate of Gunther Elting. Born in Berlin-Wilmersdorf, he was apprenticed as a toolmaker. Having reached England early in 1939 he immediately found a job in Lord Austin's tool room in the latter's motor car factory at Longbridge, Birmingham. However, because this was an industry of national importance, two days before war actually broke out, Austin's sacked him as an enemy alien at the behest of the Home Office. In May of the following year he was interned and was one of those sent to Australia on HMT *Dunera*. In the autumn of 1941 he returned to England, volunteered for service in the pioneers and was posted to 93 Company. However, in the following year it was at last realised that a knowledgeable engineer was wasting his time in the pioneers and so he was transferred to the reserve on condition that he would find suitable employment in the munitions industry. He was taken on by a firm in Coventry which manufactured rifle ammunition and employed him as an instructor for their work force. This he did for the rest of the war.

Cooking is an art, and it is agreed by all who experienced it that the food served to the men in the alien companies of the Pioneer Corps was much better than in the army generally. Most of the chefs in the 'A' companies' kitchens had previously cooked for the demanding public in one of the bigger Central European cities, a large number of them in Vienna. They included men from the best restaurants and hotels. Of course, even they could not get ingredients which were just not obtainable during the war, but what they produced from the raw materials which they could get hold of was remarkable. When the Army Catering Corps was created in 1940 the cooks of all the 'A' companies and of 3PCTC were transferred to it. Two of these, however, Russell (Heinz Reifenberg) and H. Gimpel, were mentioned in despatches not for the quality of the food they produced, but for bravery.

The Army Education Corps was a creation of the later years of the war. It was set up at the instigation of people who, rightly, contended that after six years of war and service many members of the forces had not received the education and training which would enable them to play a useful part in civilian life after their demobilisation. In the event, however, the members of the corps did not confine themselves to these objectives, but concentrated their efforts on political subjects, which, considering the background of most of them, was not at all surprising. It is probably no exaggeration to say that the activities of this corps did a lot to bring about the overwhelming victory of the Labour Party in the general election of 1945.

The aliens in the corps were no exception. Dr E. Rosenthal, who had taught at Manchester University, found a place there. Having been born in Heilbronn in 1904, he had lectured on oriental studies. After his service with the pioneers he was transferred to the RASC, then to Intelligence, before getting to the Army Education Corps. Ultimately he was responsible for the re-education of German prisoners of war in Cyrenaica.

The Education Corps also had Dr Walter Wodak in its ranks. Before the war he had been a lawyer and diplomat in Vienna as well as a leading member of the Social Democratic Party. Having fled to Britain he became a lecturer for the Workers' Educational Association. In August 1940 he volunteered for service as a private in the Pioneer Corps. His transfer to the Army Educational Corps took place in February 1942. The subjects of his lectures included international law, as well as British war aims and methods. After having been an instructor at the BAOR college for a time, he was promoted to staff sergeant and was one of the Austrian NCOs in the British Austrian Legal Unit, which was formed to assist the new Austrian government in the task of revising the Austrian legal code. He was politically active throughout the war and was demobilised on 26 November 1945. He became first secretary of the Austrian Embassy in London in 1948 and ended his professional career as secretary general of the Austrian Foreign Office in Vienna.

Another alien who served in the Army Education Corps was Company Sergeant Major Law. He too was qualified to lecture on international affairs. He was called on to speak to units of 21st Army Corps on the problems of Germany and broadcast, in German, commentaries on the course of the war. R. Fraeyhan and N.P. Richards were also members of this corps.

It is generally known that the number of scientists who emigrated from Germany and Austria because of the Nazis and came to Britain was very substantial. Most of them did not indeed join the armed forces, but many co-operated with them closely, for which reason it may be in order to mention at least some of them here. Winston Churchill observed in 1940: 'Since the Germans threw out the Jews and lowered their technical standards, our science is ahead of theirs'. Amongst the scientists who worked on the development of the atomic bomb there were 12 Germans and Austrians. Four more assisted the Air Ministry in research and development. Bigger groups were in the research departments, which concerned themselves with radar and with the development of new aircraft types. A project for fog dispersion which went under the codename Fido was virtually an Austro-German joint enterprise. Sir Alexander Fleming, the discoverer of penicillin, had Dr Chain as his assistant. Dr Gutmann, a medical man who had come to Britain from Germany in 1939, found new ways in the treatment of paralysis. The motivation of all these people was the same as that of the pioneers.

Dr Samuel, a Cambridge lecturer in political science, served in the Pioneer Corps for two years. Then, from one day to the next, he was transferred to the Political Intelligence Section of the Foreign Office. On his last night with the pioneers he slept on a straw paliasse in a tent. The next night he had a ducal bedroom at his disposal.

Otto Zarek's fate was similar. During his service in 249 Company he was attached to Sir Robert (later Lord) Vansittart, then under-secretary at the Foreign Office, for six months. He went back to the company in October 1941. Whilst there he wrote a book on German culture. In 1943 he was again attached to the Foreign Office and did work connected with psychological warfare. He finished up in the prisoners of war division and served there until it was closed down in June 1948.

An appropriate end for this chapter is the story of Hans Ornstein. He was in the British forces for a very short time only; most of the war he spent in the service of the French. He was neither a technician, nor was he a doctor, but he was a high-grade expert on petrol and petroleum products. Born 1892 in Vienna he was a relative of Carl Adler, the founder of 'Olex', a company which had its origins in Vienna at the turn of the century, transferred its operations to Germany before the First World War and still continues today under the name of Deutsche BP. As a relative of the boss Ornstein was given charge of the Dusseldorf office whilst still a young man. In 1914 he got his call-up papers and served in the Austrian artillery as an officer on the Russian and Italian fronts for four years. After that he went back to Germany. On Hitler's becoming chancellor in 1933, he emigrated. He reached Paris, where BP offered him a job. When war broke out in 1939 he volunteered for the French army, where he was commissioned, but as he was 47 by then, they posted him to the fortress artillery in Algiers. In 1940, following the collapse of France, he was released and immediately went back to BP in their Algiers office. He was there when the Allies landed in December 1942.

When the Free French also arrived in Algiers, Ornstein volunteered for service with them, was confirmed in his rank of *capitaine* and, being a petroleum expert with excellent connections to the British, was given the job of organising the supply of petroleum products to the Free French forces in the Mediterranean area. Getting bored with this administrative job, which he could do with his eyes shut, he still managed to get into the front line in the battle of Monte Cassino in 1944.

After the end of hostilities British Petroleum needed a reliable man to represent British interests in Germany. So the Free French released him and he was transferred to the British army. He was given the rank of a full colonel and sent to Hamburg. Some months later the board of Deutsche BP asked him to take on the job of managing director of that company. He remained in this position, becoming one of the leading figures in German industry, until he was pensioned off in 1958. For his services he received the CBE.

7

Commandos and Paratroopers

The alien companies of the Pioneer Corps were by no means the only units consisting almost entirely of German-speaking soldiers. There were others and the most remarkable of these was the 3rd Troop of the 10th Inter-Allied Commando. It is this troop and the pathfinder companies of the 1st and 6th Airborne Divisions which this chapter is about.

The story of how both paratroops and commandos were first formed is well known. Both are the result of Churchill's realisation that the war could not be won solely with units organised in the old traditions of the army, and that new forms of organisation were needed. In this he followed his illustrious predecessor, the Duke of Wellington, whose realisation that the British army needed a screen of skirmishers to fight Napoleon resulted in the formation of the Light Infantry and with it of the Rifle Brigade and the King's Royal Rifles. To fight Hitler men were needed who could be dropped from the air and others who would utilise British naval supremacy to raid the coasts held by the enemy. Like Wellington's skirmishers, so the commandos and paratroopers should be the elite of the army, capable of operating on their own or in small groups, thinking for themselves and being trained to perfection in the business of fighting.

The existence of many conflicting ideas in the War Office is borne out by the fact that the idea of using German speakers as parachutists was proposed and accepted almost from the beginning, at a time when the more fuddy-duddy parts of this ministry were still opposing the arming of the alien companies of the Pioneer Corps with anything more lethal than iron rods. Major B.A. Wilson, MC, had been Officer Commanding 87 Company PC in France in 1940 and had known his men. Presumably because of this experience and because he himself knew German he was placed in command of the newly formed 21st Independent Parachute Company, pathfinders of the 1st Airborne Division. Its job was the identification and marking of the dropping areas for the main force of the division, in other words, they were to be the people who would go in first on every occasion. Wilson recognised that a substantial part of this company and others like it should consist of Germans and Austrians, who would have the sort of basic knowledge which would be required. They could act as interpreters, interrogate prisoners and many a man might even have local knowledge of the areas of operations, based on his own past experiences. With this in mind Wilson approached the War Office, where his reasoning met immediate approval. As a result a circular was issued to all the officers commanding alien pioneer companies, in which they were asked to supply volunteers for the newly formed parachute units.

This circular did not have the desired effect everywhere. Quite a number of the company commanders to whom it was addressed decided not to publish it in their companies – at least not in its original form. They knew their men and realised that most of their best NCOs and men would respond immediately, leaving them with the problem of finding others to take their places. They did not, therefore, ask for volunteers, but sent to Wilson men of their own choice. In some cases these were people whom they wanted to get rid of, whilst some of the others had absolutely no intention of becoming parachutists, making it their business to get back to their units as quickly as possible.

Wilson and his colleague, Major Lander, saw about 80 men in the first batch. From these they selected 20. At a later stage they selected another 20. Each one had to be an excellent soldier. Naturally, the selection criteria for the aliens were higher than those for their British colleagues. As a result the aliens became an elite within the elite. In the end about one in five of the men of the 21st Independent Parachute Company was a German or Austrian.

Their maiden action was as advance guard of the 1st Airborne Division in the parachute drop at Bône in Algeria on 12 November 1942. On this occasion, however, their enemy was not the German *Wehrmacht* but the Vichy French troops of Admiral Darlan. Although these had vigorously opposed the Allied landings at Algiers, at Oran and in Morocco, they were not very numerous at Bône, so the landing was practically unopposed. Only some days later, when they had advanced to the Tunisian frontier, did they make contact with troops of the *Wehrmacht*.

Their next airborne action was planned to be the invasion of Sicily on 10 July 1943. This was the first major invasion where allied troops were to meet troops of the *Wehrmacht*. Unfortunately, and contrary to the enthusiastic reports which the Allied commands issued at the time, a lot of things did not work out and did not go as smoothly as they should have done and as they did in later similar operations. The paratroopers of the 1st Airborne Division were entrusted to badly trained and inexperienced crews of the US Transport Command. The weather also was bad and some of the navigators believed themselves to be over the dropping zones, when in fact they were still well out to sea. The parachutists who jumped from these aircraft were lucky if the ships of the Royal Navy managed to fish them out of the water. Many drowned. Also, by no means all of the division's gliders reached their destination. Generally the men of 21 Company were amongst those who were picked up under hostile fire.

After this their next job was the landing at Taranto, although in this instance they did not go in by air. Following the Italian surrender the Fifth US Army landed at Salerno on the morning of 9 September 1943, but was strongly opposed by German forces. Simultaneously the British Command had decided to use the 1st Airborne Division for the capture of the important Italian naval port of Taranto, which was full of ships of the Italian navy about whose intentions concerning the observation of the armistice nothing was known. As all transport aircraft were being used for the Salerno landing there were none available for this operation. Admiral Cunningham, the naval commander, therefore packed the 6,000 men of the division onto five British cruisers and one destroyer and steamed boldly into the harbour, depositing the troops on shore. The Union Jack which they hoisted there was the first Allied flag to be flown on the continent of Europe since the British expulsion from France in 1940.

From Taranto they advanced northwards rapidly. Already on 15 September they had reached Gioja and Bari and on 25 September they occupied the airfields at Foggia, from which the *Luftwaffe* had withdrawn that morning. Their last action in Italy was 'Operation Hasty', east of Rome. Amongst those who accompanied the 6th Welsh Parachute Battalion on this occasion was Peter Block, whose job was everything for which a knowledge of German was necessary or useful.

Whilst 21 Company was still in Italy its third platoon was separated from the company. It was turned into the 1st Independent Parachute Platoon, becoming the pathfinders of the 2nd Independent Parachute Brigade Group, which was formed out of the 1st Airborne Division at the same time. The withdrawal of these men from the division was compensated for by the transfer to it of US units of roughly equivalent strength, temporarily turning the division into an Anglo-American formation. Whilst the number of Germans and Austrians in the pathfinder platoon was small, nevertheless some remained.

On 15 August 1944 Allied troops landed on the south coast of France. In the preceding night an airborne landing had taken place near Le Muy. This time the 1st Independent Parachute Platoon was in the lead. They met little resistance and were able to join up with the troops of the 45th US Division, which had gone ashore at St Tropez, the next day. Thereafter their advance was speedy, reaching Grenoble on 24 August and entering Besançon on 8 September.

The 1st Airborne Division was brought back to Britain to be used in Montgomery's noble attempt to cross the Rhine at Arnhem and end the war in 1944. They were given the job of landing north of the river at Arnhem itself, to take the bridge by surprise and to hold it until the main body of the army coming up from the south should join them. The forces making up this main body, which at the beginning of the operation were still standing to the south of Eindhoven some 60km from Arnhem, were supposed to advance at high speed through enemy-held territory along the road through Eindhoven and Nijmegen to the Arnhem bridge. The road should have been captured and secured by parachutists and glider-borne troops. So the advancing army expected it, and particularly the bridges, including the very important one over the southern arm of the Rhine at Nijmegen, to be in British possession when they got there. It was a very daring concept, but the risk was justified, for the prize, a foothold on the other bank of the Rhine, could well have led to a much earlier end to the war. Its object was the immediate defeat of Germany.

In the early hours of 17 September 1944 21 Company, fulfilling its normal role as pathfinders, jumped into Oosterbeek and Wolfheze, northern suburbs of Arnhem, where they secured the division's landing area without meeting too much opposition from the enemy. The rest of the division followed them immediately. Having landed successfully they advanced upon the bridge, but found it to be more strongly held by the enemy than had been expected. They could not, therefore, occupy the whole of the bridge, but remained within a relatively small perimeter at its northern end. 21 Company remained in or near its landing point.

The units advancing northwards through Eindhoven and Nijmegen were held up during their advance and reached the southern end of the Arnhem bridge three days late. By that time the enemy had been reinforced and attempts to occupy the southern end of the bridge failed. For four days the troops which had come from the south tried to take the southern end of the bridge, or to help their comrades fighting desperately on the north shore by other means. Only on 25 September did Montgomery order the 1st Division to withdraw. The soldiers had to cross the fast-flowing river by night, swimming or in small boats. On the morning of the next day some 2,400 of the 10,000 men who had jumped into Arnhem a week earlier were on the south shore of the Rhine. The rest were dead or in enemy hands. The losses of 21 Company, though severe, were not that bad and, relatively, those of the aliens amongst them were lighter still. Nevertheless, Arnhem caused more losses amongst the Germans and Austrians in British service than almost any other single action.

Sergeant Martin Lewis, originally Lewin, was one of the men of 21 Company. He was a German who had come to Britain with one of the *Kindertransporte*. Having joined the pioneers he volunteered for service with the parachutists. With 21 Company he had served in North Africa and Italy. At Arnhem he was wounded. Later, after he had got back to his unit he still took part in the operation in Norway in 1945.

Another who was at Arnhem was Nicky Allington, also in 21 Company. The information concerning him is somewhat conflicting. Bentwich commented that 'Several Russian Pioneers had adventurous service in commando expeditions. Thus Sergeant Allington, who had also been in the Foreign Legion and interned in Oran, was in the Airborne Division which took part in the capture of Oran in 1943 . . .'. On the other hand D.M. Compton, the archivist of the 21st Club, the veterans' association of 21 Company, lists Allington with his original name of Bärblinger and the army number 13807673. If this is correct, and there is no reason to doubt it, he must have joined the pioneers through No.3 PCTC at Ilfracombe in the first half of 1942. Had he been in the French foreign legion, he could have transferred to the British either in 1940, immediately after Dunkirk, or after the occupation of North Africa in the early spring of 1943, but never at the time or place which his number indicates. Also, had he joined in North Africa, his number would have commenced with 13809. In addition one might venture to say that Bärblinger does not sound particularly Russian, nor even Russo-German, because of the 'ä'. However, there is no doubt that Allington attended the parachutist's course at Ringway from 26 April to 4 May 1943 and that he was a member of 21 Company. He may well have been involved in the capture of Oran in 1943. His Russian origins, his service with the foreign legion and his previous internment in Oran, however, come into a more doubtful category.

Corporal Anton Guttmann of 69 Company, PC, resigned his rank and chose the name Gordon when he transferred to the parachutists. He also took part in the parachute course at Ringway mentioned above. His report from there says he had been nervous, but that his jumps were good. From there he joined 21 Company. He was commissioned and from 1944 to 1945 he was ADC to the general officer commanding in Norway. After that, still in airborne, he served in India.

Lieutenant Pollack had been one of the first volunteers in Richborough, had been in 87 Company, PC, as a private soldier and was one of the first to be commissioned, still in the pioneers. His transfer to

the Parachute Regiment did not involve any reduction in rank and later
he gained the Military Cross for bravery. His later meeting with Harry
Cemach in Batavia has already been mentioned above.

Bernard Dawson, formerly Descarr, was also in 21 Company. He
had to be hospitalised after the company had returned from Italy; he
did not return. The same applied to Fenton, formerly Fenyce, and to
Ronald Grierson (now Sir Ronald), formerly Griessmann. The last
named was wounded in Italy after being mentioned in despatches.
Upon recovery he was transferred to the 1st Special Air Service, with
whom he was in Germany in 1945. There he was wounded for the
second time. Bob Kendall, formerly Kraus, was in 21 Company, as was
John Melford, formerly Mendelsohn, who eventually became captain
and taught at the BAOR college. Concerning Chris Blakeley, formerly
Bachwitz, it would appear that his parents, who were in the United
States, were able to arrange for his early discharge, after which he also
went to America. This may have taken place before the unit was sent
to North Africa. All that is known concerning Schlonovien is that he
was returned to his old unit after having been injured in a training
jump. Harold Bruce, formerly Schilling from Berlin, commanded a
section of the 21st at Arnhem. He later became a professional officer
and remained in the army until 1958. Others were George Bruce
(formerly Preger), Redferne (formerly Rosenthal), Schivern and
Sobotka. About them only their names are known. MacManus,
formerly Mertz, had been a pioneer since 1942.

John Stanleigh, formerly Schwartz from Brandenburg in what was
then Prussia, has written about some of his adventures himself, but
perhaps the most interesting fact about him is that after his retirement
he became one of the foremost leaders of the nuclear disarmament
movement in Britain.

Timothy Bleach was a scion of the Berlin bankers' family
Bleichroeder. According to Bentwich he was shot at Arnhem as he
asked his way back to the Rhine. D.M. Compton, however, is of the
opinion that he drowned trying to swim across the river.

Also amongst those killed at Arnhem was John Peter Rodley,
formerly Rosenfeld, who had been in North Africa and Italy. He had
broken a leg in a practice jump at the start of his parachutist's career,
but had been able to return to the 21st. Probably Rodley is identical
with the Corporal Rodney who is mentioned by Bentwich. According
to Bentwich's account, Rodney had been a mathematician in civil life
and had broken his neck during practice. Bentwich adds that he lost his
life while attacking enemy troops with hand grenades and challenging
them to surrender. Sugarman's information is that he was killed by a

ricochet. He even mentions that it happened in the garden of Stationweg 8, Arnhem. Morland has yet another version in that he maintains Rodley had been killed whilst still in the air, before he ever touched the ground. Maybe all these different stories are true, but in at least two cases it was another man to whom these things happened. Who can tell?

Walter Landon, formerly Landauer, son of a Jewish father and an Aryan mother, had been a member of 229 Company, PC. He came from Munich and was one of the very best who served in the pioneers. His death deprived the world of a most talented and decent young man, who would certainly have made his mark had he survived.

Almost the same name was chosen by Walter Levy-Lingen. When he joined 21 Company he called himself Walter Langdon. He, too, lost his life at Arnhem. Bentwich wrote:

> A German self-propelled gun was giving trouble...Langdon had a PIAT (projector infantry anti-tank), which is a heavy weapon for one man who has to crawl through mud to get within range. He crawled to within forty yards of the enemy gun, fired and put it out of action. But he was himself hit by a sniper. He had to be left on the field and was reported missing. In 1945 a notice in the Official Gazette announced that he had been posthumously awarded a Certificate of Gallantry...

He was the son of a Jewish judge of the German Supreme Court. After his parents had sent him to Britain they committed suicide. At the time of the commencement of the war he had been an undergraduate at Balliol College, Oxford, studying chemistry.

Lieutenant R. Falck, who has been mentioned above, had several things in common with Levy-Lingen. He also had studied at Balliol and he was a parachutist. He, indeed, had been commissioned in the Pioneer Corps, where he served in several different companies. He had retained his commission on transfer. He, too, came down by parachute at Arnhem, where he met his death.

Two other men who served in 21 Company are Private Fenner and Lance Corporal Mertz, later McManus. Both are mentioned in the nominal roll of officers and men who successfully completed the 61b and 62nd course of parachute training held at Ringway from 26 April to 4 May 1943, where they attained the necessary standard of proficiency. A complete copy of this roll exists. Whether Fenner is the same man as the Private Fenner who some months previously had been court-martialled in 229 Company, PC, and sentenced to detention, and had then attempted suicide (see above) is not known. This does not seem unlikely to me, but Fenner's former comrades in 21 Company reject the possibility on the grounds that no one with such a record could have been accepted for training as a parachutist. They think that there must have been two people, both of whom had adopted the same name.

Michael Compton, formerly Hans Günther Josef Hoffmann, and Peter Block were the two Germans who remained in the 1st Independent Parachute Platoon after this had been separated from 21 Company. They were with this platoon during the liberation of Greece in 1944. Eight days after British commandos had occupied Patras on 4 October, the *Wermacht* began to pull out of Athens. On the day after that the men of 1 Platoon jumped into the Athens airport at Megara, captured and held it until the rest of their brigade followed on the next day, 14 October. As the enemy left Athens, so their places were taken by men of the brigade.

Outside the capital, however, the situation became chaotic. This was used by the communist EAM and ELAS partisans for a rising against the legitimate Greek government, which had the active support of the British. Consequently the British troops in the centre of Athens were surrounded and had to fight for their lives. It was several weeks before reinforcements arrived and, together with the troops of the rightful government, they could become masters of the situation. This civil war, by which a communist take-over was only just avoided, ended on 15 January 1945, when an armistice between the warring parties was concluded. The 1st Platoon was there the whole of the time.

21 Company was not by any means the only parachute unit which had enemy aliens on its strength. The 22nd, which was the Pathfinder Company of the 6th Airborne Division, also had its complement. When on the night of 5–6 June 1944, before the invasion of the Normandy beaches, this division, partly by parachute and partly carried in gliders, landed in the rear of the enemy, Bob Stenham, formerly Stern of Vienna, earlier of 220 Company, PC, was the eighth man to touch down, and Werner Oppenheim, alias Ronald Michael King, of Berlin and earlier of 249 Company, PC, was right behind him. Following the landing the 6th Airborne Division held positions between the so-called Pegasus Bridge at Bréville and Trouville. They were taken out of the line only after the battle of the Falaise gap. Later on they were in action along the river Maas during the successful defence against Rundstedt's last offensive in the winter of 1944–45.

On 23 March 1945 the first British units crossed the Rhine west of Wesel. Led by commandos they moved round the enemy defences manned by about 2,000 troops, and on the morning of the next day they were in position to the east of the town, when they had to face an enemy counter-attack led by tanks. What happened then is best described in the words of Bryan Samain:

> At eleven o'clock that morning, dead on time, the Airborne troops came in. The sunny sky was filled with the drone of hundreds of aircraft, which we couldn't see at first, but which we eventually identified as hosts of Liberators and Dakotas, flying in from the north in rigid formation, about a mile east of Wesel.
>
> It was a wonderful sight; we could not help cheering, despite the fact that, somewhere well out of our range, the Germans were putting up an intense barrage of ack-ack fire. Nevertheless those planes never wavered an instant from their course. On and on they came, until they were right over the target. The gliders calmly banked to find their landing zones, whilst amid the tiny puffs of ack-ack fire in the distance, we could see thousands of white patches twisting and swaying in the sky, each patch a man, and no bigger than a thimble from where we were.
>
> These were the men we had been waiting for – the men of the British Sixth Airborne Division and the American Eighteenth Airborne Corps. We were very glad to see them...

Despite this euphoric description the German ack-ack gunners had at least one success. One of the leading Allied aircraft carrying men of 22 Independent Parachute Company was hit. Amongst those inside, waiting to jump, was Stenham. He was wounded in the arm, which had to be amputated. In this action Oppenheim was a member of a group of 16 men – eight British and eight American – who jumped before everybody else. Their job was to place smoke containers in the target territory for the orientation of incoming aircraft. This they did successfully.

Another parachutist was Sidney Edwards. He was not with the pathfinders. As Siegfried Eimerl he had been born in Vienna on 15 May 1925. He volunteered for the army in 1943 and at first was trained as a glider pilot. During Rundstedt's last offensive Edwards was in the Ardennes with the 5th Battalion of the Parachute Regiment and at the Rhine crossing at Wesel he was one of Samain's 'white patches' in the sky. After that, in the middle of a burning village, he accidentally met his cousin Albert Edwards, formerly Adalbert Eisner, of whom we shall hear more in the next chapter. The two cousins were still together when at Wismar the British first met Soviet troops. Later on Sidney was sent to India, Singapore, Java and Sumatra with his 5th Battalion, thence to Malaysia and eventually to West Africa. He was released from the service from there.

Lieutenant Pollack was amongst the men who had joined 88 Company, PC, at Richborough. He was commissioned whilst still a pioneer. He retained his commission on transfer to the parachutists. Whilst there he received the Military Cross.

Many gave their lives. One of them was Denby, formerly P.C. Dreyfuss, a student. He had been in France with 74 Company, PC, in 1940. He was one of the first to be killed in Normandy on D-day. Lieutenant R. Falck has been mentioned before. Having come to Britain he first went to Charterhouse School, after which he was at Balliol for two years. He joined the pioneers, was commissioned and served in several 'A' companies. He, too, transferred to the paratroopers, served with the 1st Airborne Division and was killed at Arnhem.

One of the men who jumped into Normandy with the 6th Airborne Division in the night of 5–6 June 1944 was Friedrich Gaensler, alias Gordon. He had been transferred to the Royal Scots Fusiliers from the pioneers and had become a parachutist only at a later stage. Later, in March 1945, he was in Norway. After the end of hostilities he served with the military government in Germany.

W. Hughes, original name unknown, was also amongst those who jumped into Normandy during the night before the landings. He had the misfortune of being taken prisoner. His captors soon realised that he was a Jew, but never doubted that he was British. They did not, therefore, find him particularly interesting. He was taken to a labour camp. There his problem was to hide his true identity from his fellow prisoners, some of whom quickly became highly suspicious of him. A very unpleasant situation arose at a parade, where all those who were not British were told to leave the ranks and form a separate group. A number of Americans and some French obeyed. Hughes was urged to join them by some of the British prisoners. A German NCO became aware that an argument was going on and came over to see what it was about. Somehow his attention was distracted and the danger passed.

Sergeant E. Simeon, previously Simion, a glider pilot, had previously been a parachutist. He sailed his glider into Arnhem, loaded with jeep, anti-tank gun and a two-man detachment on 17 September 1944. He was killed in action there three days later.

In the eyes of the public the commandos, established in 1940, had quickly achieved the status of an elite. At first all the members came from Britain and the Empire. But in the next two years the remains of a considerable number of various Allied armies, whose countries had been conquered by the Nazis, came to Britain. All wanted to have commandos of their own. Eventually Lord Louis Mountbatten, then chief of the commandos, agreed to this and as a result the so-called No. 10 Inter-Allied Commando was formed. Its sub-units were French, Dutch, Belgian, Polish, Norwegian and Yugoslav.

Mountbatten's father had been the German Prince Ludwig of Battenberg, a member of the reigning family in the Grand Duchy of Hesse. He had served in the Royal Navy and had been Admiral of the Fleet and First Sea Lord for some years before the outbreak of the First World War in 1914. Despite the fact that there was no doubt concerning his loyalty to the British, he was forced to resign from all his offices because of his background. His son had always felt this to have been a grave injustice. The formation of the Inter-Allied Commando allowed Mountbatten to take the initiative for the formation also of a German troop, to demonstrate that the British attitude towards Germans in Britain in the Second World War was very different from what it had been in the First.

Naturally, this proposal met with resistance within the War Office and the War Cabinet was called upon to consider the matter. There Churchill himself is said to have made the final decision. He demanded that every man should be checked and tested until there was not the slightest doubt concerning which side he was on; otherwise, however, he gave the proposal his full support. At the same time he is said to have given the troop the name by which it has since become known. 'Because they will be unknown warriors', he is alleged to have said, 'they must perforce be considered an unknown quantity. Since the algebraic symbol for the unknown is X, let us call them the X-Troop'. Members of the troop have cast doubt on the truth of this story, and certainly amongst them the troop never bore this name. But on the other hand, it is a good story and it sounds like the sort of thing Churchill could have said. So maybe it is true after all. At a later stage there were plans also for the formation of an Italian and a Japanese troop. A lack of suitable volunteers, however, prevented their establishment.

In order to protect its members the German troop, which was given the number 3, was formed under an especially dense veil of secrecy. This secrecy remained in force for a relatively long period and in some respects is still being maintained. The cover names, which other German members of the forces were permitted to have, were obligatory for this troop and in addition they were all given fake families and the whole of their background was remodelled. They were never known as the German Troop. Especially at the beginning they were referred to as the British Troop in the Inter-Allied Commando. Nevertheless the unit achieved a remarkable reputation, and stories which really did happen to its men have been woven into several novels to serve as a factual historical background.

No.3 Troop was first formed at Aberdovey, North Wales, in July 1942. Although the men were mainly of German and Austrian origin, the first eight all appear to have come from Czechoslovakia. Later the troop also included a few from Hungary, Russia and Denmark. Its war establishment was 80, but it does not appear ever to have reached that strength. Long before the eightieth man had reported, the troop had suffered severe casualties. These were always replaced, however. The names of 122 men, who are said to have served in the troop at one time or another are mentioned in the various sources, and it may be that this is the lot. They were:

Abramowicz, Richard, alias Arlen (Arnold?)
Aitcheson, original name unknown
Arany, Peter F., alias Peter F. Masters
Arenstein, Hans, alias Harry Andrews
Arnstein, A.V., alias Anderson
Ascher, Claus Leopold Octavio, alias Colin E. Anson
Auerhahn, W., alias Peter Vernon Allen Wells
Barth, Georg A., alias George A. Streets
Bate (or Bates), original name unknown
Bauer, Georg, alias Bower
Baum, Hans, alias C. Leslie Trevor,
Baumwollspinner, alias Robert Barnes
Bierer, F., alias Frederick Bentley
Billmann, alias Ken Bartlett
Blumenfeld, Ludwig, alias Michael Merton
Burnett, W., original name unknown
Carlebach, Peter, alias Peter Andrew Carson
Dändler (Dungler?) K., alias Keith Douglas
Dobriner, Max, alias Geoffrey Dickson
Eberstadt, Ernst Carl Eduard, alias David Edward Charles Eversley
Emmett, Bunny, a mystery man, origins unknown
Engel, Hanns-Günter, alias John Envers
Farago, Ladislas, alias Ford
Farley, original name unknown
Feder, E. Wolfgang, alias Bryan Fenton
Fleischer, F., alias Fletcher
Foster, R., original name unknown
Frank, M.G., alias G.M. (Mac) Franklin
Frey, H.C., alias Fraser

Freytag, E.H., alias E.H.(Tommy) Farr
Fürth, Hans G., alias Anthony Firth
Gans, Manfred, alias Freddie Gray,
Geiser, H.E.A., alias Henry Gordon
Glaser, Kurt J., alias John (or James?) Griffiths
Goldschmidt, K.J., alias (Hubert) Brian Groves, later Grant
Goldschmidt, V., alias Vernon (Ducky) Dwelly
Goldstern, K., alias R.K. Garvin
Gray, F., original name unknown
Gumpertz, K. Wilhelm, alias Kenneth W. Graham,
Guttmann, Hans-Julius, alias Ronnie Gilbert, MBE
Hajosch, alias Ian Harris, MM
Hansen, E.R., alias Jack Davies (Davis ?)
Heathcote, original name unknown
Henschell, Oskar, alias O'Neill
Herschthal, F., alias Freddy Hepworth
Herschthal, Walter, alias Walter Hepworth
Hess, Otto, alias Peter Giles
Hirsch, S., alias Steve K. Hudson
Hornig, Paul, alias Paul Streeten
Jacobus, Peter, alias Fred Jackson
Jessen (Jensen?), R., alias Rolf James
Kargerer-Stein, E. von, alias Didi Fuller
Karminski, Otto (Putzi), alias Simon
Kellmann, M., alias M.J. (Ernest) Kirby
Kirschner, André G., alias Andrew Kershaw
Knobloch, G.H., alias H. George (Nobby) Kendal
Kottka, Vladimir, alias Jones
Krausmann, Hans, alias Harry Aitchison
Kury, M., alias J.F. McGregor
Landau, E., alias E.R.F. Langley
Lanyi, Djury (Georg) H., alias George Lane
Lenel, Ernst R., alias Ernest R. Lawrence
Levin, H., alias Patrick Hugh Miles
Levy, Karl Ernst, alias Ken Lincoln, BEM
Lewinsky, Max, alias Max Laddy (Laddie?)
Lewis, original name unknown
Liebel, Peter, alias Peter Leigh-Bell
Litvak, Eugen, alias Leslie Dale
Loewenstein, O.J., alias Roger E. Kingsley
Loewy (Levy?), Moritz, alias Maurice Latimer,
Long, original name unknown

Lowy, Arthur F., original name unknown
Luchtenstein, alias Ludlow
Martin, W., original name unknown
Meyer, Kurt, alias Peter Moody
Mines, J., original name unknown
Monahan, original name unknown
Nathan, Eli, alias Ernest Norton
Nathan, Erich, alias Eric William Howarth (Howard?)
Nell, G.H.H., alias Gerald P. (Jerry) Nichols
Nomburg, Harry, alias Harry Drew
Peters, H., original name unknown
Peyer, alias Palmer
Platschek (Plateck? Platek?), alias 'Bubi' Platt
Pollaschek (Polatschek), O., alias A.C. Turner
Pratt, original name unknown
Reich, S.R., alias R.G. (S.?) Hamilton
Rice, original name unknown
Rosskamm, Stephan, alias Steven Ross
Rotschild, Freddy, changed name unknown
Sachs, H.P, alias H.A. (A.H.?) Seymour
Saloschin, Count Georg V. (Salinger?), alias George V. Saunders
Samson, A., alias A. Percy Shelley
Sauer, G.J., alias G.J. Sayers
Schloß, Yarlow, alias Jack Scott
Schwitzer (Schweizer?), J.G., alias Tommy Swinton
Smith, original name unknown
Smith, J., original name unknown
Spencer, Frederick, original name unknown
Spielman, E., original name unknown
Sruh, Gottfried C. (Friedl), alias Geoffrey M. Broadman
Stein, A., alias Tom Spencer
Steiner, Uli, alias Leslie Scott
Stevens, T., original name unknown
Stewart, J., original name unknown
Strauss, D., alias David Stewart
Theilinger, J., alias J. Taylor
Thornton, original name unknown
Tischler, Peter J., alias Peter J. Terry
Trojan, Richard W., alias Richard W. Tennant
Vogel, Egon, alias Egon Ernest Robert Villiers
Ward, G., original name unknown
Warren, H., original name unknown

Warwick, R., original name unknown
Wassermann, O., alias William J. Watson
Weikersheimer, L., alias L. Wallen
Weinberg, K., alias Gary Mason
Weinberger, E.G., alias E.G. Webster
Weiß, Ali, alias A. White
Wilmersdoerffer, H. J., alias John Geoffrey Wilmers
Wolf, Walter L., alias Allan W. Marshall
Zadik, W.G., alias W.G. Thompson
Zweig, Werner, alias Vernon Nelson

There is no doubt that the two Smiths were different persons. It cannot be said for certain whether, in addition to Erich Nathan, alias Eric William Howarth, there might have been an Eric Howard. The sources are somewhat contradictory, but I am of the opinion that most probably they refer to the same person.

In addition to the above-mentioned the following served in other units of the commandos:

Etzdorf, Baron Rüdiger Otto Ulrich, alias Attersley, in the 1st Commando, and Calman, C. (or Calmon) in the 2nd

Clarke, K.E., alias Goldschlager, in the 10th Commando, but possibly not in its 3rd Troop. He may have been a member of the Dutch Troop

Trepel, Charles, and Zivohlava, J., alias Gautier, Jean, in the French Troop of No.10 Commando

His tombstone describes Richard Lehninger, alias R. Leonard, as a commando and whilst it was a commando operation where he met his death, he was really an interpreter attached from another unit. Possibly Ulrich Hollander, alias Michael Alexander Thomas, and a German-Polish soldier by the name of Gellert were also commandos. And lastly James Leasor names two men as commandos whose existence, however, may be thought to be very doubtful indeed. They are Stephen Rigby, the hero of his tale, and Finckelstein, alias Findlay alias Ferguson.

However, another group should also at least be mentioned. The 51st Commando was a unit which was formed in Palestine. It is said that the great majority of its members also were of German and Austrian origin. Beginning with the Ethiopian campaign and the battle of Amba Alagi they were into most things in Africa, the Eastern Mediterranean and in Italy. Their story, however, will have to be told by someone else and it is to be hoped that they, too, will find a worthy historian soon.

The first officer commanding 3 Troop 10 Commando was Captain Bryan Hilton-Jones, a Welshman. He was the son of a medical doctor. He spoke excellent German and was an expert mountaineer. He was superbly fit and the training to which he subjected the first eight men – as well as all the others who came later – was tough and unrelenting. One of their first efforts was a memorable route march of 53 miles from Aberdovey to the top of Snowdon and back. Including three hours rest on the top they took 18 hours to cover this distance, an average of three and a half miles per hour.

It took some time for all the men to report. The criteria for entry were strict, but apart from this all men had to undergo the strictest of security checks. The selectors had more than 350 volunteers to choose from. A batch of 43 men reported on 26 October 1942 and a further 16 on 13 February 1943. The eightieth man did not come until 16 April.

Amongst the earliest entries was a Hungarian by the name of Djuri Lanyi. He had chosen to be known as George Lane. At the Olympic Games of 1936 he had been captain of his country's water polo team. As his English was marked by a strong Hungarian accent, he had been advised to describe himself as a Welshman. It was thought that a German would not be able to tell the difference. After leaving Hungary Lanyi had studied at Christ Church, Oxford, and at London University. Then he had tried to be a journalist. At the beginning of the war he volunteered for service with the Grenadier Guards, who accepted him as an officer cadet, only to chuck him out a little later because of his nationality. He went to the pioneers but was one of the first to be transferred to Special Operations and then to No.4 Commando. He became the first troop sergeant.

Under Hilton-Jones' expert leadership the men of X Troop became physically fit to equal the best anywhere. In addition they were taught the skills of their trade. They became specialists in the use of boats and parachutes, weapons and explosives; they became experts at opening locks; they learnt to drive railway engines, climb vertical cliff faces and recognise every hostile formation on sight. In *Ten Commando*, a very well researched history of that unit, Ian Dear takes the view that they were the best-trained unit of the entire British army. However, they were aware of it and there are suggestions that on occasions their attitude towards others was not entirely free of arrogance. Some of them are reported to have been very critical of the standards of other units and to have said so. This did not always make them popular.

The first action in which members of the 3rd Troop took part was the raid on Dieppe on 19 August 1942. This was carried out by two British commando units, the 2nd Canadian Division and the 4th

Canadian Armoured Brigade. The 10th Commando supplied 15 men of the French Troop and five of the X Troop. They had special tasks. The men of the X Troop were supposed to search for military documents and other information in the *Wehrmacht* headquarters situated in the town hall.

From the point of view of the participating troops the attack was a catastrophe. Although it had been reported that Dieppe was held by no more than a weak battalion, the attackers found the town well defended. The first allied troops, which landed at 06:05 hours, came under withering fire. Armoured landing craft came ashore so that hostile artillery could fire straight up their bows. Armoured vehicles inside were destroyed before they had even started their engines. In one sector a mere three tanks succeeded in landing. Two were destroyed almost at once and the third called back after having advanced just a few yards. The infantry was decimated and what remained was also called back, as far as this was possible. Out of the five separate task forces only that consisting of No.4 Commando under Lord Lovat was successful. They took and destroyed the enemy gun positions at Varengeville west of Dieppe and withdrew after completing the job.

Of the roughly 5,000 Canadians who took part in the raid 3,367 were lost. These included 1,946 who were taken prisoner, 568 of them wounded. The rest were killed or were missing. The Royal Navy lost some 550 men. Due to Lord Lovat's successful action the losses of the commandos, mainly British, were light – 'only' 175 men. The German casualties, dead and wounded, were in comparison a mere 600.

The five men from the X-Troop were Platt, Rice, Latimer, Bate and Smith. Although they seem to have reached land they were quite unable to carry out the task they had been given. Bate was killed, Rice and Smith were not heard of again. Platt was wounded in the leg. Only he and Latimer came back. Apart from their names nothing is known concerning Bate, Rice and Smith. The name of Bate does not appear in either Bentwich's roll of honour or in Peter Eden's list of the fallen. As both lists tend to give original names rather than changed ones, however, this does not lead to doubts concerning his fate. It is merely a question of under which name he appears. There are quite a few to choose from.

Both Latimer and Platt were of Czechoslovak origin. After Platt's wound had healed he came back to the X Troop and became the troop's storekeeper for the rest of the war. Latimer was the only one to come back intact. We shall meet him again in the attack on Walcheren in 1944, in which he played an important part.

Despite the ghastly losses, Churchill defended the decision to attack Dieppe. He himself had played a part in the planning. Later he wrote that due to the raid the German troops along the French coast had been reinforced, which had the effect of lessening German pressure on the Soviets. Therefore, he thought the losses were justified. Fortunately there does not seem to have been any other action afterwards during the entire war in which the British sacrificed so many men in such an irresponsible manner.

On the night of 12–13 September 1942 an attack took place on St Laurent-sur-Mer on the north coast of Normandy. This bore the code-name 'Operation Aquatint' and this, too, does not seem to have been very successful. The operation appears to have been carried out by commandos, although reports speak of a 'Small Scale Raiding Force'. It is possible that this had no connection with the commandos, but not very likely. At least three members of the raiding party were killed. One was Richard Lehniger, who had changed his name to Leonard. All three are buried in the village cemetery of St Laurent, near the later Omaha Beach. Lehniger's gravestone is remarkable in that it shows the badge of the Pioneer Corps and the German-language inscription '*Die Internationale wird die Menschheit sein*' (the international will become all of humanity). At the time of his death he was 42 years old. It appears that at one time during his service Lehniger was in one of the Czechoslovak companies of the Pioneer Corps. On his tombstone the word 'Commando' appears beneath 'Pioneer Corps', but in slightly smaller letters. If he was in the X Troop, he must have been the oldest member by far. However, it is more likely that he was not a regular member of the commandos at all, but had been attached to the Aquatint party direct from his pioneer company or from one of the many unusual units which at that time various generals entrusted to adventure-seeking officers under their command. Probably his case was similar to that of Private Nagel, alias Newman, who participated as interpreter in the Bruneval Raid, the first major action of the Parachute Regiment.

A further action which ended badly for the British troops who took part was the raid on the heavy water plant at Vemork in Norway in November 1942. A group of REs was landed by glider in the vicinity of the works, which they were expected to destroy. According to reports a member of the X Troop also participated. This may have been Broadman, originally Friedl Sruh. He is said to have been the only one who managed to return.

Yet another early operation was the raid on Herm, one of the Channel Islands, on 27 and 28 February 1943. X Troop men who took part were F. Bentley and Kenneth Miles, but possibly some others were there also. Bentley was a corporal at the time. We shall refer to Miles again later on.

From the beginning men of the troop took part in very small-scale actions. Again and again small groups of men landed on enemy-held coasts, spied out the land, took prisoners whom they questioned there and then, and disappeared into the dead of night. Terry and Webster tell of one such action which also goes back to that time. They landed on the French coast, met a group of Frenchman at a prearranged point and collected a suitcase from them. This they brought back to Britain. Another tip and run raid on the French coast was carried out by 12 Commando at some time in 1943. They were accompanied by Harry Drew as interpreter and expert for everything German.

On 26 May 1943 Kenneth Miles, Paul Streeten, Franklin and Colin Anson of the X Troop were sent to Troon in Scotland, and were attached to the marine commandos there. As Lance-Sergeant Miles was the senior and in charge of the detachment. Lance-Corporal Streeten was his deputy. Miles and Anson were attached to 40 Commando, Streeten and Franklin to 41. Again, their job was to accompany these units as interpreters, as interrogators of prisoners of war, and otherwise to assist them in any way of which they were capable.

During the night of 9–10 June 1943 they landed on Sicily. They went ashore shortly after midnight and came under machine gun fire right away. Nevertheless, during that night and during the following days the four men from the X Troop remained unharmed. They seem to have achieved what they set out to do, after which they awaited the Allied landings, which took place in the first days of July and resulted in the clearing of the enemy from the island.

The next allied objective was the southern tip of Italy. The men of 40 Commando were embarked on a ship, which was attacked by hostile aircraft whilst crossing the Straits of Messina. In this action Anson suffered a head wound, which made it necessary for him to be evacuated. Later, after his wound had healed, he came back to X Troop. Towards the end of the war he became its senior NCO.

41 Commando landed along the road and railway line from Catania to Messina. Their task was to block the enemy's retreat from Messina. With the object of establishing themselves in one of the local railway stations, a group of men including Streeten got onto one of the platforms. At that moment the platform hit by a shell from an 88mm gun. Shell splinters and ricochets flew about and Streeten was hit. In a letter dated 1984 he wrote to Ian Dear that tiny bits of shell were still abounding in his head and neck.

Vernon Nelson, who had not been one of the four at the Sicily landing but had joined them later, was also wounded whilst attached to 40 Commando in Italy.

The decision that the X Troop should not be used as a complete unit, but only in small detachments, must have been made about this time. Thus a further detachment of 11 men under the command of Lieutenant Emmet left Britain for Algiers. On 7 November 1943 they met up with the Poles and Belgians of 10 Commando. With them they moved to Taranto and on 4 December they were inspected at Molfetta. Following this the detachment was split into even smaller sub-units. Merton and Marshall came under command of the Poles, who were themselves attached to the 78th Division. Alan Marshall, originally Wolf, was known as 'SS-Wolf' amongst his comrades. Envers commented that he was 'a blue-eyed, fair-haired, Jewish youngster, whose bearing corresponded to everyone's idea of an SS-man'. Eventually they took possession of a deserted front-line village called Pescopennataro, above the river Sangro. It was bitterly cold. Most of the time the village was in the clouds. They could hardly ever see further than a hundred feet. Their supplies were brought up the hill by mule. The two X troopers slept on the steps of the altar in the village church. Already on the day after their arrival the Poles became engaged with nearby enemy troops and the fighting went on sporadically day after day. There were casualties on both sides. On the night of 21–22 December 1943 they succeeded in stopping an attempted breakthrough by the enemy.

Nobby Kendal, an Austrian, was attached to the Belgians. He managed to form the very first Allied ski patrol in Italy. They were at Montenero on the extreme left flank of the 8th Army. With the assistance of the local mayor Kendal found some cherrywood skis with frayed bindings, as well as some white cloaks, normally worn at funerals by the local fraternity. Equipped with these he and some of the Belgians trained for a couple of days, whereupon they tried their luck in the Luperian mountains. About 3,000 feet up they happened upon an Austrian patrol sheltering in a stone hut. The Austrians were in possession of a small mortar, which they used to fire with some accuracy upon the Belgians. Fortunately the snow was deep enough to absorb all the fragments so that this was about as ineffective as the Belgians with their rifle and machine gun fire on the walls of the hut. After everyone had had enough, Kendal and his patrol retired out of range thus ending this first memorable engagement without bloodshed.

Another X trooper, Groves, was with No.9 Commando when, during a diversion on the night of 30 December 1943, this unit engaged the enemy alongside the river Garigliano. On the following night he was to assist with the recovery of the dead and wounded. In doing so he stepped on a landmine, which exploded and tore off his foot. A similar fate befell Wells, attached to 40 Commando, who became victim of another such mine during the crossing of the Garigliano on 21 or 22 January 1944. Groves survived, Wells did not.

Nos.9 and 43 Commandos operated in the rocky hills near Monte Ornito. During an attack over open territory Barnes, attached to 9 Commando, was badly wounded by a mortar bomb. Subsequently he was given an award, which is variously described either as the British Empire Medal (BEM) or the MBE (Member of the Order of the British Empire). Neither award seems appropriate in the circumstances, but the fact that he received one or the other is confirmed by several sources.

Steven Ross was also with 9 Commando. He was wounded by artillery fire. His life was saved by a group of Czechs who, fortunately for him, had decided to change their status as soldiers of the *Wehrmacht* for that of prisoners of the British just at that time. They found Ross and wanted to surrender to him. He asked them to carry him down the hill to where there was a British first aid station. In the circumstances the language in which they communicated was German. The Czechs knew the area much better than Ross and got him to the first aid post at the double. Ross survived, only to be wounded again at a later date in the fighting alongside the river Arno. On 5 August 1944 the London *Zeitspiegel*, a paper run by Austrian emigrants during the war, reported that a soldier named Ross had given copies of that paper to Austrian prisoners whom he had known in the past. However it is very unlikely that this was the same man.

By and large, the other X troopers who had gone to Algiers in November 1943 remained with the 8th Army. They were joined by Shelley, David Stewart and Ken Bartlett, all of whom had been commissioned in the field. Bartlett later became the officer commanding the X Troop. These three officers, together with several others, arrived as reinforcements from Britain at the beginning of 1945. In April 1945 a number of them were involved in fighting in the area of Lago Comacchio near Ravenna.

At the beginning of 1944 five X troopers were with No.2 Commando, when they occupied the island of Lissa (Vis) alongside the Dalmatian coast. With them was Lieutenant C. Calmon, who was later promoted to major. He spoke several Slav languages and knew Dalmatia. Apparently, he had been commissioned before he was transferred to the commandos. He stayed on Vis for nine months, during which time he published an army newspaper with the title *Vis-a-vis*. The others who were on Vis were Miles, Scott, Merton and Kendal. At that time they all ranked as sergeants, but all four were commissioned before the end of hostilities. We shall hear more about Scott below.

Peter Giles was moved out of the X Troop in 1943. He was a reserved and good-looking young man. It appears that he was transferred to the SOE. He was parachuted into Yugoslavia to work with partisans. There he was captured, ill-treated and shot. A former comrade describes him as the bravest of the commandos.

As early as September 1943 planning for the invasion of France had advanced so far that Allied staffs began to think about the disquieting effect on enemy troops of continuous raids on the French coasts. It was decided to reduce these drastically, so as to induce a feeling of security and lack of attention. In spite of this, however, something happened, as a result of which a limited number of further raids became necessary.

In April 1944 a coastal battery in the vicinity of Houlgate was attacked from the air. A bomb went astray and fell into the water just offshore. This caused a series of explosions which ran along the whole length of the shoreline. The immediate assumption was that this might be a new method of defence about which nothing was known, and so the commandos were told to go and have a look at what it was.

Between 14 and 19 May 1944, therefore, four further small-scale raids took place. The objectives were the beach defences in front of the villages of Bray Dunes, Les Hemmes, Quend Plage and Onival. Bray Dunes lies between Dunkirk and the Belgian border, Quend Plage and Onival are either side of the Somme estuary. Apart from a few sappers, all the participants of the raids were members of 10 Commando. It is not known whether any X troopers were on the other raids, but the raid on Onival, the last one, was commanded by Lieutenant (formerly Sergeant) George Lane, whilst Jack Davies, the one Dane who served in the X Troop, was in charge of the boat which took them in to land.

Before they departed they were briefed. They were told that no one knew whether the devices they were looking for were magnetic or acoustic, electrically controlled or contact explosives. It could, so it was said, even be something completely new and unknown. According to Hilton-Jones, who was in charge of the whole operation, 'at the end we did not know whether the things might not even go off, if we just looked at them'. One man asked whether the starting of the boat's engine might cause it to explode. 'Why don't you try?' he was told.

By the time the raid on Onival took place the riddle had been solved. The commandos who had landed at Quend Plage had found one of the objects they were looking for and whilst they began, ever so carefully, to investigate it, one of the sappers slipped and held on to it. To their great surprise it did not go off at once. They were, therefore, able to take a good look at it and found that it was an ordinary Teller mine, which was joined by wire to other similar mines suspended from ordinary wooden sticks rammed into the sea bed.

Nevertheless the Onival raid was not cancelled. It appears that, for one thing, the men were all geared up to go and would have been most disappointed, and for another, there was something else, another object, in the area of Onival, which they might as well have a look at whilst they were there. What this was has not been recorded, but it was described as element C and became the ostensible reason for their going.

The group landed according to plan and was not noticed by the defenders. Lane and the RE officer, Lieutenant Wooldridge, and two NCOs went on land and made notes about the defences. They found neither mines, nor any element C. So they decided to go further inland and see what they could find. After a while the officers decided to proceed on their own and instructed the NCOs to go back to the small boat, in which the four of them had come, with orders to leave them – the officers – to their fate should they not be back by 3am.

A short while later the NCOs, looking in the direction which the officers had taken, saw something like the flashlight of a camera and heard someone calling, a shout and the sound of firing. Some Verey lights were fired into the air, canisters exploded along the shore and the whole area was lit up by flashes. The NCOs were discovered and shot at, but managed to hide and eventually reached their boat unscathed. However, they did not want to leave the officers without means of escape, so they swam out to the larger accompanying boat, which lay off the coast.

As a result of what they reported it was assumed that Lane and Wooldridge had found element C, had tried to take a photo of it and had been captured or killed in the attempt. This was not so, however. Lane and Wooldridge marched inland for about three-quarters of an hour and were completely oblivious to all the excitement which went on behind their backs, and which possibly the two NCOs had caused themselves. They found nothing of any interest, however, and so decided to return. When they got back to the beach they were discovered and a hostile patrol started to fire at them. They succeeded in taking cover just as another patrol on their other side also opened up. Not seeing them any longer the two patrols then fired at each other over their heads for a time, but eventually this bit of excitement also came to an end.

All this had held them up and it was some time after 3am before they got back to where their companions had left the boat for them.

They succeeded in getting this out to sea, but by the time they did so, the accompanying boat had gone. They dumped all their gear into the sea and shortly after six in the morning they were discovered by an enemy patrol vessel, which came alongside and arrested them. They were taken to Cayeux, where they were locked up and interrogated. At first they were threatened with shooting and with being handed over to the Gestapo but then they were imprisoned in separate cells, apparently in the local jail. As was to be expected, opening the lock presented little difficulty to Lane. He got out fairly quickly, but as he crept out of the cell he fell over a sentry who had been asleep in the corridor. The man woke up and told Lane in quite a friendly manner that it would be better if he went back again, as round the corner 'there was another one, anyway'.

For some days the interrogations went on. Lane's interrogators believed him when he said that he was Welsh. Then one day they were blindfolded and handcuffed before being put into a car and driven away. His blindfold was not very good and so Lane was able to read a signpost which indicated a place called La Petite Roche Guyon. This was the ancient home of the Dukes de la Rochefoucauld, and at that time the headquarters of Field Marshal Rommel, but of course Lane did not then know all that.

After their arrival Lane and Wooldridge were again locked up in separate rooms, but shortly afterwards an officer came and told them that they would presently be taken before a very high-ranking officer and would they please behave like officers and gentlemen. He then took them to an adjoining room, where they were introduced to a German general. This was the Chief of Staff of Army Group B, General von Tempelhof. He told them that they were about to be taken before Rommel and this was done almost immediately afterwards.

Rommel sat at a desk at the other end of an enormous room. He did not let them walk all the way to him, however, but got up and came towards them. With an interpreter, a Captain Lang, they all sat down at a table, whereupon Rommel opened the conversation, addressing Lane with 'So you are one of these commando gangsters?' Lane answered, saying that indeed he was a commando, but certainly not a gangster and indeed, the commandos were the best soldiers anywhere. Rommel seemed to like that and said he would not disagree with Lane, but the two of them had been captured in peculiar circumstances. After all, they might be saboteurs and he assumed they knew what would await them if that was so. Lane replied that he would hardly have been invited to meet Rommel, if that was what they thought of him.

'You look upon this as an invitation?' was Rommel's next question and Lane said that indeed he did and he was very honoured. This broke the ice and after that the conversation became quite friendly and turned largely on the question of whether and when an Allied invasion would take place. Lane and Wooldridge said they had read in *The Times* that such plans were being made and after a few more questions the interview was over. It ended by Rommel assuring them that they had nothing to fear.

After this they were taken to Fresnes, where they were interrogated further. Some time later they arrived at Oflag 9 AH. There Lane had to tell the truth about himself to the senior British officer. After all it was quite clear that no Englishman would ever accept his story that he was Welsh. Having made his confession, however, the other prisoners treated him as one of themselves and the secret of his origins remained undiscovered by his captors. Lane was awarded the Military Cross for his part in this business.

The invasion became reality during the night of 5–6 June 1944. As had happened in Italy, the X troopers who had remained in Britain were split up into small detachments and attached to other units. Most of these detachments consisted of four men. Their skills and abilities were summed up in a memorandum sent to commando headquarters, as follows:

(a) Interrogation and identification.
Experience shows that because 3 Troop personnel speak the German language perfectly (i.e. both colloquially and in dialect) prisoners enjoy talking to them. Consequently much information is forthcoming which is unlikely to be disclosed through ordinary interrogation methods.
(b) Treatment and exploitation of prisoners.
If tactical information required urgently is to be received in time it is essential that the interrogating personnel should be right forward. This is necessary not only to obtain information but also to ensure proper treatment and search of prisoners from the moment of capture. In this connection, with 3 Troop personnel right forward, it was found possible in Italy to use prisoners as guides walking ahead, thus avoiding minefields, to make them assist in evacuating wounded, and to help in carrying equipment.
(c) Interpretation of captured documents.
The following example indicates some of the uses that can be made of a trained interpretation of captured documents.
In Italy, on one occasion, a sketch of minefields and defensive positions, expressed in tactical signs, was found in the tunic of a

captured NCO. The sketch was immediately interpreted by a 3 Troop man and life undoubtedly saved.

Similarly in raids on HQs 3 Troop personnel know what to look for.

(d) Patrols.

An important offensive function for which 3 Troop is specially trained is to operate with fighting patrols, as specialized recce troops with particular reference to roadsigns, vehicle markings, military abbreviations on signposts and enemy weapons...

The war diary of No. 3 Troop, 10 Commando shows that one officer and 43 other ranks were amongst the first Allied troops to land on the Normandy beaches. In general the men remained with the units to which they were attached for the entire period from D-day until after the Allied breakout from Normandy in the battles of the Bulge and the Falaise gap in August. In some cases the attachments seem to have been continued even beyond that time.

Except for the party attached to 6 Commando, the man in charge of each detachment was a sergeant. The NCO in charge of the 6 Commando detachment was Nicholls, a corporal. His deputy was Lance-Corporal Masters. The commandos were organised into two brigades of four complete commando units each. The First Brigade was commanded by Brigadier the Lord Lovat and consisted of Nos. 3, 4, 6 and 45 Commandos, the Fourth Brigade was under command of Brigadier Leicester and was made up of Nos. 41, 46, 47 and 48 Commandos. All except 46 Commando landed on D-day – 46 followed a day later. The commandos with numbers from 41 up were units of the Royal Marines, which had not until that date seen action to anything like the same extent as the others, and here the men of the X Troop received a more cordial welcome than in the three older units.

The First Brigade was given the task of landing at Ouistreham and securing the bridges over the river Orne and the Orne canal on the left flank of the invading force. The job of Fourth Brigade with two commandos was to destroy enemy defences between Lion-sur-Mer and St Aubin, whilst its 47th Commando was to take Port-en-Bessin independently of the others.

As is well known the landings were strongly opposed by the enemy. The troops which were first to land generally had the heaviest casualties. The men of the X Troop were no exception. Franklin, Webster and Laddy died on the beach or before they had even got that far. The detachment with 4 Commando was put out of action within days. Howarth, the sergeant, was wounded whilst still on the beach,

Graham was killed on 13 June, Sayers wounded the next day and Thompson taken prisoner during the night of 19–20 June.

The X troopers with 45 Commando were Arlen, Hepworth, Saunders, Shelley and Stewart. The day following the landing this commando was involved in heavy fighting inside the village of Franceville-Plage. Arlen made an attempt to put an end to this. Carrying a white flag and unarmed he walked into the enemy positions and demanded their surrender, 'as three more divisions were following on behind the British and that, therefore, any further fighting would result in needless losses to both sides'. This demand was answered by machine gun fire and a counter-attack. Arlen, clearly furious, doubled back to where he had come from, grabbed his Tommy gun and ran towards the enemy position from which he had been fired on. He was killed before he got there.

On the morning of 8 June Saunders was wounded in the leg by a grenade. In the course of this action both sides suffered casualties. What happened later was related in the Berlin *Tagesspiegel* newspaper of 1 February 1998:

> On 8 June 1944 the driver of the German ambulance which was to have driven wounded to a local first-aid-post was surprised, when on his way through Merville in Normandy he was stopped by British troops. He was even more surprised when he realised that the British were pleased to see him. They, too, had had casualties and their evacuation had caused them problems. They needed urgent help and what both British and Germans required was the attentions of a doctor.
>
> One of the British wounded, a lance-corporal, sat himself next to the driver and told him how he should drive to a new, but essentially similar destination, the British first-aid post at Le Plein. Communication was no problem for his new guide spoke German with a Bavarian accent. The driver, who at this stage was no longer surprised at anything, asked where the other came from and was told he was from Munich. He was with the British, he said, because he was against Hitler. Whether the two of them said any more to each other whilst the journey went on, we do not know. But it seems probable and perhaps they even got on with each other better than one might expect.
>
> A few kilometres before Le Plein they ran into another roadblock. This time the soldiers wore German uniforms. They took care of the wounded of both sides. The British lance-corporal was taken prisoner. For him the discovery of where he

came from would have had serious consequences. But the ambulance driver kept quiet.

The British lance-corporal was Saunders. On that occasion he did not remain a prisoner for long, but managed to escape. He returned to 45 Commando before the day was out. However, two days later he was taken prisoner for a second time and it seems that, following an abortive attempt at escape from a train in France, he spent the rest of the war in a prisoner of war camp near Sagan-on-Oder.

Later the same day 45 Commando was cut off from the British main body and hemmed in at Merville. Samain wrote:

> Throughout the afternoon the Germans surrounding the village gave us no respite whatsoever. They mortared our positions and sniped us continually. Just before three o'clock a small party of the enemy succeeded in working their way into Merville from the east, bringing up extra machine guns and snipers. However, two Sergeants attached to us from 10 Commando – Sergeants Shelley and Stewart – put a stop to this ruse. Unknown to the enemy they succeeded in crawling up to the side of the barn, on the other side of which the newly arrived party of Germans were hastily setting up their machine-gun post, and lobbed grenades over the roof. These fell right amongst them, wounding two (who were captured) and putting the remainder to flight.

Shortly afterwards 45 Commando succeeded in breaking out of Merville and getting back to the brigade at Le Plein. For their part in this action Shelley and Stewart were commissioned in the field a short time later.

In addition to Nichols and Masters, Fletcher and Drew were also with 6 Commando. Masters was attached to the bicycle troop commanded by a Captain Robinson. According to his own report he was almost disappointed, when on landing they were not even fired at. 'We had,' he told Ian Dear, 'what was called a very good beach. The people before us got cut up and those behind us had an artillery barrage put down on them, but we were O.K.'

Later they took some prisoners and Lord Lovat asked Masters to find out where the German artillery was located. The man Masters chose to ask, however, was a Pole, who understood no German at all. Thinking that Poles often know French, Masters switched to that language, but it turned out that Lord Lovat, who had been watching Masters's efforts with interest, knew French a lot better. So he took over the interrogation himself and Masters just caught a phrase or two of the animated conversation which developed.

Drew's first interrogation also was not 100 per cent successful. He wanted to impress his prisoner by showing him what liars Goebbels and the crew of his propaganda ministry were. 'Do you realise,' he asked 'that the Allies are just a few miles from Rome?' 'No, no,' came the answer, 'our radio has just announced that the city has fallen.'

Following these more amusing incidents Masters's next experience was a lot more unpleasant. On the outskirts of Bénouville the bicycle troop was held up by enemy machine gun fire. Robinson ordered Masters to walk along the road on foot, to see where the fire was coming from. It was perfectly clear to Masters that he was expected to draw the enemies' fire upon himself, so that Robinson could see where it came from. He knew that Robinson was playing with his life and thought about how he could improve his chances of survival. He remembered an old Cary Grant film, set in the Khyber Pass or somewhere like that, in which the hero, in a similar position, walked straight into a rebel stronghold, calling 'You're all under arrest.' He had thought that very funny at the time but decided to act similarly. He walked down the centre of the road, visible to everyone, and shouted, in German, 'Everybody out with your hands above your heads. You are totally surrounded. For you the war is over. Come on and give yourselves up.' Of course, no one came out, but he was not fired at either. At last some one took a pot shot at him, but missed, and Masters's Tommy gun packed up after he had fired a single round in reply. Fortunately he found a little cover by the side of the road, where he waited until a bayonet attack by the rest of the troop released him from his predicament.

Drew was wounded some time later.

The X troopers with 41 Commando did not have a much easier time than those with No.4. Although already in the first few days both O'Neill and Gray had been mentioned for their bravery in the war diary of the commando, all four from the X Troop were out of action at an early date. O'Neill and Swinton were wounded and sent back to Britain. They did not return to the X Troop. Latimer also was wounded, but his wound did not seem serious and at first he was not going to take notice of it. During hand-to-hand fighting he had wanted to make as little noise as possible and used his pistol to hit an enemy soldier on the head. In doing so he injured his finger. This turned into blood poisoning, so that he too had to be sent back to Britain. However, he returned very soon.

With regard to Gray, Ian Dear wrote that on 6 June he was wounded five times, but none of these had been serious enough to make an evacuation necessary. Under the date 1 July the war diary of 41 Commando contains the following entry:

> On afternoon of July 1st as a result of exchange of fire between a patrol and the enemy FDLs Cpl. F. Gray (10 IA Cdo) became detached from patrol. As he had not returned at dusk a search party was sent out to locate him, without success. Cpl. Gray returned early in the morning of 2nd July, uninjured, having lain up close to the enemy and having gained much useful information.

47 Commando had as its objective the capture of Port-en-Bressin. In this they had the support of Sergeant Fuller, Webster, Terry, Andrews and Davies, all of the X Troop. But although, according to Dear, Thornton was with 46 Commando, he also was present with the 47th on the evening of 6 June. They also suffered heavy losses. As mentioned previously, Webster fell during the landing. He drowned as his landing craft went down. Andrews was wounded in the first hours after the landing. Fuller, always described as an extrovert, is said to have succeeded in talking the men of a hostile battery into surrender, so that the undamaged guns could be used against their former owners. The sector of 47 Commando does not seem to have been defended by the enemy with the same ferocity as some of the others. After they had established themselves on land Terry, together with a small group of men, entered the village of La Rosière, where some 20 Poles in German uniform awaited them with their hands above their heads. The Poles immediately offered to help the British, and this was taken up without delay.

In the afternoon of the same day a cyclist was sighted near La Rosière, who appeared to be an enemy officer. Fuller and Terry were sent to find out what was going on. Terry's story deserves to be quoted verbatim:

> I waited hidden in a ditch beside the road. He was riding quite slowly with his heels on the pedals and his toes pointing outwards. He appeared to be an officer and evidently felt quite safe. He was after all several miles from the beachhead and the road seemed quiet. Just as he passed me I jumped from cover, pointed my Tommy gun at him and called in German: 'Halt, hands up!'
>
> For an instant I felt very silly. The man calmly dismounted, carefully placed his bike on the ground, raised his hands and said, also of course, in German: 'I am a *Regimentsstabsfeldwebel*. I am

entitled to be treated according to the rules of the Geneva Convention.'

My first reaction was one of pride. I had been told at a course in England that this was a very rare rank in the *Wehrmacht* and that we were unlikely to come across it. And here we had one on the very first day. We questioned him and it appeared that he had been on the Russian Front, had suffered from frostbite and had been given a medical discharge. Then, when things began to go really badly for Germany, he was called up again for light occupation duties in France. He was put in charge of a camp for Spanish republican refugees, who had come to France across the Pyrenees after Franco's victory in the civil war. That morning he had been woken early by one of the guards who had seen the Allied fleet on the horizon. Seeing literally thousands of ships from the edge of the camp, he decided that he had had enough and told his men either to surrender or to make their way inland. He himself was now on the way to his favourite brothel in Ouistreham, after which he intended to give himself up to the first Allied troops, so as to spend the rest of the war in a prisoner of war camp. He had heard that prisoners were sent to Canada and that was where he wanted to settle after the war, anyway.

He was quite a character and we took him along, because of his knowledge of the locality. Fuller asked him for the address of the brothel and made a note of it in his paybook.

In the evening the commandos occupied a hill between Port-en-Bessin and Commes. From this position they demanded the surrender of Port-en-Bessin. Then the mayor of Commes came and told them that a wounded RAF fighter pilot was lying hidden in his village. So Terry and some other commandos accompanied the mayor to Commes, where the inhabitants were pleased to see them. Right in the middle of the festivities a shot was fired at them from a window. Terry ran up the village street and into the house, where the shot appeared to have come from. A few minutes later he came back with four prisoners. Apparently he had just had to talk to them.

In the meantime the situation around the hill, which was held by the commandos, had got rather worse. Enemy parachutists had attacked the position, so that the commanding officer of the 47th had been forced to order the retreat. When Terry and his companions got back, this was well under way. A shot grazed Terry's thigh, but Thornton managed to bandage him up. Later they got into an ambush, from which they saved themselves only by everybody disappearing in a different direction.

Terry was able to reach a nearby house, where the inhabitants hid him and saw to his wound.

Next day, 7 June, his host drove him into Port-en-Bessin with his horse and cart. The place had in the meantime been occupied successfully. On the way they ran into a group of enemy sailors, who wanted to surrender and marched behind them. Fuller was amongst those who welcomed Terry. He had got into enemy captivity the night before but in the general chaos had managed to escape. Although Terry did not want to be sent back to England, he was evacuated the same day, so that he was back home with his parents already on 8 June. At that time he was still less than 20 years old.

However, a short time later he was back again with 47 Commando. On the night of 24 June during an attack on Sallenelles he was again wounded. A shot went through his arm. Another X trooper, Harris, found him and brought him back to the British positions. He survived. Fuller fell on 16 June. Mistakenly, Allied aircraft attacked the position of his unit. He was one of several who were killed. Having come back cured from his wound, Andrews was killed on 19 August. He trod on a landmine near Grande Ferme de Buisson.

Harris, who was with 46 Commando, was injured by a hand grenade at the breakthrough at Troarn. He had fallen into an enemy-held trench and landed on top of a soldier, who had taken cover there. Later he told Ian Dear: 'The man asked me, "*Hans, bist das du?*" and I said "*Nein*," and then he said that he was not German and wanted to surrender. He really did want to, for after that he practically carried me to our lines. I took him to our HQ and handed him over. Before he left he said to me in German, "You gave me my life, I want to give you my watch." As he insisted, I took it. The next day I was on my way back to the rear when I saw him in the road. He was dead.'

At the landing Peter Moody had a special job to do. This was to observe the fall of shot from the supporting naval vessels and to direct it to its objectives. Together with a Royal Navy signaller he had to get through the hostile positions and to establish himself in a position in the immediate vicinity of the targets.

After the landing and until 18 August it was the aim of the Allied armies to extend and consolidate their positions. On 12 June 4 Commando Brigade came under the command of 6 Airborne Division and was deployed in the bridgehead over the river Orne. From then on until the Allied breakout from Normandy the activities of the opposing forces were confined largely to fighting between patrols. This did not exclude a few more large-scale actions and one of these occurred immediately after the Commando Brigade had joined up with the

Airborne Division on 12 June. Here, too, men of the X Troop were involved. Under the direction of Hilton-Jones, Nichols, Drew and Masters from the 6th and Stewart and Shelly from 45th Commando infiltrated a village with the object of giving an attack an initial impetus. From this they got back without a scratch.

Three nights later the same people were given the job of getting three French civilians across the enemy lines. Until then their information had been that the enemy had not dug in everywhere and they hoped that they might find some place where the trench was not continuous. However, the Germans had been busy and when they actually got up to their lines they could not find any gap. Searching for a suitable place took time and effort. The civilians were not up to this and declared they were exhausted and could not go on. After this the patrol split into two parts and started to withdraw. Then both groups came under hostile fire. Hilton-Jones was shot through the stomach and was taken prisoner. Presumably it was due to his extraordinary physical condition that he was still alive when eventually he reached a German field hospital. There he had the great good fortune that one of the surgeons was a specialist on injuries to the abdomen. He operated on Hilton-Jones and saved his life. In August, when the British overran this hospital, they found him well on the way to recovery. After the shooting when Hilton-Jones was injured, the patrol dispersed in all directions. Each man thought he was the only survivor, but eventually all except Hilton-Jones got back to the British lines. Despite that, one of the French was shot dead when he was challenged by a sentry of the Free French Commando and apparently could not remember the password. After Hilton-Jones's involuntary exit the command of the X Troop was taken over by James Griffiths, the first OC who had come up through the ranks of the Troop. On 6 June he had still been at OCTU.

Two days before the events described above, that is, on 13 June, Lord Lovat had also been badly wounded. He was watching an attack of the 1st Canadian Parachute Battalion on Bréville, when he was hit. Nichols, who was one of the X troopers in the immediate vicinity, got him out of the firing line and called a doctor to him. As a result Nichols later had to stand up to a lot of leg-pulling by his friends. It certainly was amazing, they said, what some people got up to merely for the sake of getting promotion.

On the day when Lovat was wounded, but not in the same action, two X troopers lost their lives. Peter Moody, Ernest Norton, Envers and Broadman were together when a high-explosive shell detonated between them. Moody and Norton were killed, Broadman was injured and only Envers remained unscathed.

X troopers Lawrence, Turner and Tom Spencer, as well as Sergeant Ken Bartlett, were with No.3 Commando. Lawrence seems to have been a man who was prepared to take an awful lot upon himself, but had little confidence in others. Whenever volunteers were asked for to get close up to the enemy, he asked to go. However, he always preferred to go on his own and as he had been successful before on several occasions, permission was normally granted. On the night of 23 June he again went forward on his own with the object of finding out what enemy unit or units were in front of the Commando. About half an hour after he had gone, Bartlett heard shots and voices from the direction where he thought Lawrence would be. He was never seen again.

At that time Bartlett had received permission to hang up some loudspeakers in nearby trees. Through these he passed on news and information to the enemy soldiers and called upon them to surrender. This drew fire upon the loudspeakers, but a few of the enemy decided to give themselves up and came over. One of them reported that a British soldier had been captured and taken behind the lines at the time when Lawrence disappeared. It seems probable that Lawrence was recognised as a German and summarily executed. On the other hand it is not impossible that he was killed accidentally as a result of Allied bombing or artillery fire during his transport to the rear.

Another member of the X Troop detachment with 4th Commando who was made prisoner by the enemy was Sergeant Thompson. He accompanied a Lieutenant Littlejohn on patrol, when they ran into an enemy ambush. Both tried to get away as quickly as possible, but Littlejohn was wounded and could not run. He pretended to be dead and some enemy troops who found him fell for it. He heard one of them say: 'This one is dead and we've got the other.' Littlejohn managed to get back to the British positions. Thompson's true identity must have remained his secret, however, for he survived his imprisonment and returned to Britain after the war was over.

In a clash between hostile patrols near Grande Ferme du Boisson on 19 August Ronnie Gilbert was wounded in the leg. He had to be sent back to England.

After the Allies had broken out of Normandy the majority of the X troopers remained attached to the units which they had accompanied since D-day.

After Antwerp had fallen on 4 September, British troops had reached the mouth of the river Scheldt. However, the island of Walcheren remained in enemy hands and this prevented Allied shipping from using the port. It therefore became essential to clear the island and this task was given to the 4th Commando Brigade. The attack began on 1 November. 4 Commando, together with the Free French Troop of 10 Inter-Allied Commando, attacked Flushing, 41, 47 and 48 Commandos moved against Westkapelle. Some Belgian and Norwegian Commandos were attached to 41, the Dutch Troop of 10 Commando was split up between 4 and 47 Commandos. A detachment of X troopers consisting of Sergeants Farr and Gray, Corporals Keith Douglas, Hamilton and Latimer and Private Watson, was directly under command of brigade HQ. Whilst the attack on Flushing was successful and British and French losses there were relatively low, the attack on Westkapelle met with strong resistance. The X Troop detachment which went ashore there with Brigade Headquarters was decimated. Hamilton was killed whilst still in the water, Watson wounded. He was taken back to Ostend.

At that time Gray and Latimer were attached to 41 Commando. When they were fired on from a tower on the east side of Westkapelle, Gray handed his arms to Latimer so that he could be seen by the enemy to be unarmed and walked down the road to the hostile position. A German NCO came out and the two began to negotiate. In the meantime Latimer, who was a Bohemian socialist and had always maintained that one must talk to the ordinary people, went round the back of the tower and managed to persuade the men inside to surrender. He led them out without being seen by the two NCOs, who were still negotiating. Then he went over to the German and told him, he might as well give up, he had not got any more men anyway.

The next few days were marked by heavy fighting. Nevertheless by 7 November the end seemed near. Gray and Latimer were again involved. At 3am they got into the enemy positions opposite 41 Commando and succeeded in taking prisoner some soldiers who were carrying a large pot of coffee. Of course they wanted to know who this was for. Whilst the prisoners were still refusing to answer, an officer came out of a dugout and called angrily asking what had happened to his coffee. Latimer tackled him immediately with a flying rugby stop and landed on top of him. It turned out that he was the officer commanding this particular position and it did not take long before he was ready to hand it over. It was one of the last to resist and the final surrender of the enemy came before the evening of the same day.

Belle Isle is an island in the river Maas near Linne, south of Roermond in Holland. In January 1945 an attack there by 45 Commando was beaten back by the defenders. Two X troopers, Howarth and Griffiths, the latter by that time a captain, were involved. About this business we have the report of a British member of the Commando:

It was decided at this stage that, whatever loss of dignity we might incur in German eyes, we should make every possible attempt to recover our dead and wounded from Belle Isle. Accordingly, that very afternoon a small party under Captain Griffiths and Sergeant Major Howarth (of 10th Commando) set out for the river bank bearing a flag of truce.

Sergeant Major Howarth, who spoke fluent German, set the flag up on the bank, then shouted to the Germans to hand us back our wounded and surrender the dead. Minutes passed before he received an answer, which was finally supplied by a young cadet officer, who emerged from a slit trench carrying a white flag. He told Howarth to come back the following morning, when he would give the answer of his commander, Hauptmann Muller.

At nine o'clock on the 29th Howarth, Captain Griffiths and the remainder of the party went down to the river's edge again. The cadet officer again came forward with his white flag, bearing Muller's answer. We could have our dead, but not the wounded.

The grisly business of ferrying the corpses across the Maas by boat lasted the entire morning. Most of them were unrecognisable, due to exposure in the snow ...

The truce continued for another 24 hours, during which time both Captain Griffiths and Sergeant Major Howarth tried very hard to convince the German cadet officer that it would be better to surrender whilst there was still a chance of coming out of the war alive. The young German replied, however, that much as he and his comrades would like to go to England as prisoners of war, neither their honour nor Hauptmann Muller would permit them to do so.

By midnight on 31 January the truce had ended. We were again at war with Number 10 Company, Regiment Muller, on Belle Isle.

For his part in this action Howarth was commissioned in the field.

Even in the last remaining weeks of the war various members of the X Troop participated in further actions, which again caused losses. Thus on 4 April Corporal K.E. Clarke was with the Dutch Troop of 10 Commando in front of Osnabrück. It is not known definitely that he was a member of the X Troop. He may, possibly, have belonged to the Dutch Troop anyway. The story goes that two officers and a corporal of the Dutch troop were in a jeep, which was ambushed. The corporal was badly wounded and the party trapped in a ditch. Clarke grabbed the bicycle of a passing German civilian and pedalled away to get help. He found a British officer who arranged for artillery fire to be put down on the German position, so the trapped party could extricate themselves. After that Clarke, 'now wearing civilian clothes', cycled on towards Osnabrück, where he spoke to German civilians and ascertained the exact positions of the enemy. As a result no more of the Dutch were killed or wounded and Clarke himself remained unscathed. He was recommended for a mention in despatches.

Before this Villiers and Seymour, both of the X Troop, had been killed during the crossing of the Rhine at Wesel. Howarth and Griffiths also died in the last days of the war. Harris lost an eye at the crossing of the river Aller. For his bravery he received the Military Medal. Wilmers and Kingsley, both of whom had been comissioned by that time, were transferred to other regiments, Kingsley having been commended for bravery. Sergeant Nelson found important documents including the entire order of battle of the enemy east of the river Elbe when searching the command post of Major General Brunning at Buchhorst. Drew was in the last advance to Hamburg. He wrote:

> At the crossing of the Aller we were involved in heavy fighting, but this was the last time that we had to deal with any resistance. Shortly afterwards we entered Luneburg victoriously and the first house which I entered there was the home of the Richthofen family. The old lady, who was introduced to me there was the mother of the 'Red Baron'. I kissed her hand.
>
> Shortly afterwards we crossed the river Elbe at Lauenburg without any difficulty. The road to Hamburg and Schleswig-Holstein lay open before us.
>
> In the Hamburg district of Blankenese the men of the 3rd Troop, 10th Commando, now used mainly as interpreters, found themselves quarters in the home of the governor, Kaufmann …

A major party of the X Troop consisting of three officers and 26 men came under command of 1 Commando on 26 April 1945. They, too, entered Hamburg and were still there, in the district of Niendorf, when fighting ceased on 8 May. After that they took over the military government in the southern half of the district of Eutin in Schleswig-Holstein.

Shortly afterwards many of the X troopers were posted to newly created units of the Field Security Service, mainly to Section Nos. 446, 447 and 448. These were commanded by Captains Dwelly, of Walcheren, Scott, of Lissa, and Nichols, who had looked after Lord

Lovat after he had been wounded. The job of these sections was to find the hiding places of leading Nazis, a task in which they had some successes.

Altogether 18 of the men of No. 3 Troop, 10 Commando were commissioned. Almost all the remainder finished the war as NCOs. At a later stage, when everything was over, Lord Mountbatten, who in the meantime had been Supreme Commander, Allied Forces in the Far East and had become Lord Mountbatten of Burma, wrote in the Jewish Chronicle: 'In the Inter-Allied Commando there was also a group of Germans who believed in freedom and democracy in their country and were good soldiers. None of them let us down. Half of them lost their lives'.

8

Fighting Units of the Army, Royal Navy and RAF

After 1943 and excepting only those who had remained pioneers or joined the X Troop, the Germans and Austrians who served in the British forces were distributed over the whole range of regiments, corps and other branches of the services. For this reason their history is identical with the history of the services as a whole. It may be that at some time there was some action in which British troops were involved, where no enemy alien took part on the British side, but there cannot have been many. It is no exaggeration to say that after 1943, wheresover there were British troops, Germans and Austrians were there with them.

When, following their transfers, they got to their new units they often caused surprise. Officers, NCOs and men had to digest the idea that nationals of the principal enemy country were there, in their own ranks, partaking in the war on their side. It was a new situation. They had to consider the consequences. Something that no one had ever thought about had occurred and everyone was forced to define his attitude and take a stance in the light of circumstances. It is, therefore, remarkable that no single instance is known where any of the transferees were met with hostility or were even made to feel suspicion against them. From the first, wherever they went, at unit level they were made as welcome as any other new members and where they were made to feel different, it was in order to protect rather than to disadvantage them.

After they had been there for even a short while, however, their new officers and comrades realised that they were most useful in all sorts of different ways. Many joined the intelligence sections of their units, but even where they did not, they were useful as interpreters, they knew the enemy intimately and understood his mentality. In addition they were good, even enthusiastic soldiers, who wanted nothing more than to get at the enemy. They were intelligent, disciplined and gave little trouble. Many indeed were promoted at an early stage and hardly anyone was allowed to feel that his talents were wasted, as had been the case when they were pioneers.

Even if the story of every one of them were known, which is not the case by any means, it would not be possible to tell each. It is entirely coincidental who and whose story is mentioned here. In the same way as Bentwich had appealed to the public for facts concerning non-British members of the forces in 1948, I did so again in 1995. Neither then nor now did these appeals reach everyone; of those whom they did reach only a limited number replied. Muchitsch got his stories from notes and publications which he found searching in various archives. He, too, turned to individuals, but was able to use other sources to a greater extent. Thus it is absolutely fortuitous, whether the deeds or the fate of one or other person has become known.

As a result the only way to deal with the problem of reporting on the whole of the group, is to tell as many stories as possible concerning individuals, who by that time had no more in common than their British uniforms and their nationality, on the assumption that, taken together, these may give a picture representative of the whole.

Altogether 174 men were transferred from the pioneers to the various regiments of infantry. They were joined by others, who had never served in the Pioneer Corps, but who used the opportunity now presenting itself to get into fighting units direct. Let me begin with them – the footsloggers in the eyes of some, the backbone of the army for others.

One of the most distinguished military careers among them was that of Walter Eberstadt, from 1944 to 1961 also known as Walter Everitt, born in Frankfurt in 1921. He had served in 220 Company PC. He was commissioned in the pioneers and on 31 December 1942 his name appeared in the officers list of 88 Company. In 1943 he transferred to the Oxfordshire and Buckinghamshire Light Infantry. In action in Normandy attached to the 2nd Worcesters he was wounded. When fighting ceased he was in Psychological Warfare, with Radio Hamburg (NWDR), where he advanced to major.

Another was Rudolf Ehrenberg, nicknamed Rolli. Having studied at St Andrews University, interned 1940 and shipped to Canada and back, he joined up in 1941 and served in 251 and 229 Companies, Pioneer Corps. In 1943 he transferred to the infantry, the Queen's Royal Regiment, then to the Leicestershire Regiment. He was sent to OCTU at the Royal Military College Sandhurst. There he was senior under-officer and awarded the Sword of Honour, which is given only to the most exceptional cadets. He was badly wounded in the Teutoburg Forest in the last days of the war and prematurely demobilised as lieutenant in 1946.

Albert Edwards, born in Vienna as Adalbert Eisner on 7 March 1924, joined the Loyal North Lancashire Regiment in 1943. He joined them direct from 'civvy street', without having been a pioneer first. Following his basic training in Yorkshire and Norfolk, he reported to his unit, then in the neighbourhood of Bayeux in northern France, on the sixth day after the Normandy landings had begun. Having explained to his commanding officer that he understood and spoke German fluently, a major and an RSM came down from 2nd Army HQ to interview him. He wrote:

> When they found that I was bilingual, an infantry signaller and that I could write shorthand and type, they told me to get my kitbag and took me with them straight away. I joined the General Staff Intelligence (GSI) section of 2nd Army HQ somewhere in Normandy and stayed with them in Normandy, the Falaise gap, Belgium and Holland.
>
> At that time I discovered the existence of the 21st Army Group Interpreters' Pool and applied to join them. I had to go back to Brussels to be interviewed and was accepted. I stayed with them for six months, checking documentation of German medical personnel, working on automatic arrest categories, etc. [At that time I] became a full corporal.
>
> In the spring of 1945 I was transferred to the intelligence section of the 5th Paras of the 6th Airborne Division. They had not yet dropped. I went to Bethune, northern France, to join the land element of the 6th Airborne Division. I travelled with them through France to Wesel on the Rhine, saw them actually jump into the dropping zone (DZ) at Wesel and was in the DZ. On finding the intelligence section I found one of the NCOs dead and the other two evacuated to field hospital, so I was the intelligence section. My job was field interrogation.
>
> The division advanced from Wesel in the general direction of Berlin, but turned half left to finish off in Wismar, where we met the Russians and got blind drunk. That is now known as VE-day.
>
> Incidentally, there were quite a few Jews in the Division of German and Austrian origin...

Later Edwards was stationed at Bad Oeynhausen, Neustadt in Holstein, Pinneberg and lastly in Kiel. There he acted as interpreter at the local military court until 1949.

At Richborough in 1939 the newly recruited pioneers had been amused, when they found that the suitcase of one of the new arrivals was marked 'Major Schnabel'. Schnabel had held this rank as a member of the *Heimwehr*, a paramilitary political organisation in Styria, where he came from. His experience there did him no harm in his new surroundings where he was promoted to sergeant at an early stage. In 1942 he was commissioned in the pioneers and a year later transferred to the Cameronians of the 52nd Lowland Division. There he became divisional ski-instructor and later intelligence officer of his battalion. In August 1944 he was sent to SHAEF to form units of information control. Starting in Belgium, he went on to Germany, where he edited a newspaper in Hannover. His last job in the army, once again as major, was assistant controller of the information services branch of the Allied commission for Austria. He was released from the service in Vienna. He remained there and became well known as an odd character. As he frequently wore Scots trews, he was generally known as MacSchnabel. His obituary in the *Presse* newspaper referred to him as 'Royal British Major'.

Captain Leyser had also been a pioneer. He was commissioned in the Black Watch, was with them throughout the fighting in Holland and the crossing of the Rhine. There his unit claims to have been first across the river. Like Schnabel he became his battalion's intelligence officer. Amongst the men serving under Leyser in the Black Watch may well have been Wolfgang Litwornik. He came from Vienna and was one of those who, some time before 15 January 1944, were recruited into the Black Watch from Glasgow where he had lived. The same bunch of recruits to the Black Watch undoubtedly also included Kurt Schwarz, another Viennese. Following his emigration he had been an agricultural trainee like so many others; then he had been interned and sent to Canada. There he enrolled himself at McGill University. In spite of this he was returned to Britain and was employed in an aircraft factory in Glasgow. The information concerning his recruitment tallies with what is known concerning Litwornik. He was commissioned in 1945 and advanced rapidly to the rank of captain. He was attached to the British headquarters in Germany, but ended his army service as interpreter to the British High Commissioner in Vienna.

Ronald B. Walters was another honorary Scotsman. Having emigrated from Breslau in June 1939 and after being employed on war work in Glasgow, he volunteered for the army in 1943. He served in the Argyll and Sutherland Highlanders and fought in Belgium, Holland and eventually Germany with the 15th Scottish Division. He was wounded crossing the river Elbe at Lauenburg a few days before the end of the war and spent VE-day in a military hospital. After the end of the war he was promoted to staff sergeant and served as an interpreter at a prisoner of war camp in South Wales.

No.14442059 Private Geoffrey Phillips had come to England as Gunter Phillip. He had been born at Wanne (now Herne), Westphalia, on

19 April 1925. He left Germany with a *Kindertransport* in December 1938, got to Dovercourt, Westgate-on-Sea and to Bradford, where he worked in a textile mill. He volunteered for service in 1943. He was posted to the King's Own Yorkshire Light Infantry. After training as a signaller he was transferred to the Seaforth Highlanders of the 51st Scottish Division. In December 1944 he saw action in Belgium and again before the end of hostilities in 1945 in Holland and Germany. After that he was posted to the Control Commission, Germany, but having been a textile worker he was, quite unexpectedly, released before his proper demob group.

Francis George Sutton was born in Vienna. About him Bentwich wrote:

> He volunteered for the army at the outbreak of war, having been rejected after a previous attempt at the time of Munich. In August 1940 he was accepted for the Pioneer Corps...Within a month he was Lance-Corporal in a company working with an Australian forestry unit in Northumberland (probably 219 Coy PC). A month later he was a Corporal, in March 1941 a Sergeant in command of a detachment in Derby. He was the first of the enemy aliens to be sent to a War Office selection board (and) was sent to the Pioneer OCTU at Bradford...
>
> [After he was commissioned] he was posted...to an alien company of the Pioneer Corps...Repeatedly he applied for a transfer to the infantry...[and] the special services. He was sent for courses of commando and parachute training...He was posted overseas in April 1943 to a British pioneer company and sent to Algiers...
>
> He joined the Bedfordshire and Hertfordshire Regiment as Lieutenant...[and] became commander of his battalion's pioneer platoon, which distinguished itself in the Italian campaign...He [was] wounded at Cassino. In December 1944 his battalion was rushed to Greece...He became town major of Thebes...In June 1945 he was sent to Capri to interrogate V.I.P.s, some of whom had just been liberated from the concentration camps. They included the Austrian ex-chancellor Schuschnigg, the son of Hungary's dictator Horthy, Pastor Niemoeller, Prince Friedrich of Prussia, Fritz Thyssen, and the wives of Generals Halder, Schroeder and Lindemann...

As from 1946 he was in charge of the paper, leather and textiles division of the British Control Commission for Austria. Sutton was awarded the Military Cross.

After the Victoria Cross the Distinguished Conduct Medal (DCM) is the highest award for bravery available to all below commissioned rank. Johann Schneider, later Taylor, had been deported to Australia in 1940 and stayed there for two years, after which he came back to Britain. He volunteered for the Leicestershire Regiment, where as corporal in charge of a section he won the DCM. Later he was promoted to sergeant and put in charge of the intelligence section of his battalion.

Manfred Herzog was a member of the 4th Battalion of the Welch Regiment. He was killed on 8 April 1945. He has been buried in the Canadian war cemetery at Groesbeek in the Reichswald.

Peter Maxwell came from Vienna. He had gone to the same school there as myself, the Elisabeth *Gymnasium*. He served in the Pioneer Corps and, after he had been transferred to the infantry, was sent to India as an officer cadet. He completed his training at an OCTU in India, was commissioned and eventually became adjutant of the 3rd Battalion, 14th Punjab Regiment, Indian army. During an operation for the protection of the then prime minister of All India, Jawaharlal Nehru, at Razmak, Waziristan, in 1946 I was attached to that very battalion as an artillery observer. We discovered the fact that we had been to the same school, though in different years, in the course of an idle conversation during the battalion's withdrawal back to its Razmak quarters.

Manfred Alweiss had been born in Berlin in 1925. He emigrated to Britain with a Youth Aliyah *Kindertransport* on 1 September 1939. In the summer of 1943, on completing his schooling at age 18, he volunteered for the army. He was called up in January 1944, did his primary training at Maryhill Barracks in Glasgow after which he served with the Essex Regiment, later with the Buffs. In January 1945 he was posted to a unit at Louvain in Belgium. From there he was transferred to 21st Army Group Main HQ in Brussels. In May 1945 he moved with them to Suechteln, on to Buende and finally to Bad Oeynhausen. After various interim postings he arrived in Berlin in 1946 and served with Information Control.

Alan Bright, originally Horst Guenther Breitbart, was also a Berliner. In 1939 a *Kindertransport* brought him to Sheffield, where he was able to continue his interrupted schooling. His army career commenced in January 1944, when he joined the Duke of Wellington's Regiment. After training in Durham he was posted to India, where he joined the 2nd Battalion the King's Own Scottish Borderers, part of the 7th Indian Division at Kohima. Having been in action in Burma he was regraded, joined the RAOC and became a sergeant in the Army Kinema Corps. Then he served in India, Ceylon, Malaya, Thailand and Singapore before being discharged in 1948.

Dr Gerhard Oertel came from Chemnitz. Having volunteered in 1943 he joined the Essex Regiment. Previously he had been a member of the Free German Youth movement and even after he had become a soldier he was still one of the organisers of the World Youth Congress in London, 1944. He was discharged in Germany in 1947.

Georg-Dieter Engel of Mannheim comes from a military family. His grandfather served in the army of the Grand Duke of Baden, his father in that of the Kaiser. He himself served with the Royal West Kents, with the 2nd Jewish Brigade in Palestine and with the 2nd Battalion the Royal Scots.

The King's Royal Rifle Corps was the regiment in which Lieutenant Hachenburg, a member of the well-known Mannheim lawyers' family, became an officer, whilst his father remained in 249 Company, PC, where until then they had been together. Sergeant Oliver Fisher also was in the KRRC.

Another rifleman was Benno Block, originally Bloch, from Breslau. He had been born there in 1925. After his flight from home in 1939 he worked in a Northampton leather factory. He must have been one of the youngest there. Four years later, as soon as he was 18, he volunteered for service. With the KRRC he saw action in Holland and in Germany. After that he was first at Hannover, then in Tripoli and elsewhere in North Africa.

Martin Glenville, originally Gerechter, also joined the Rifles. A Berliner, he was born on 6 October 1919. There also he had attended school, in his case the Königstädtische *Oberrealschule*. In view of his father having been in the Kaiser's army in the First World War, when he gained the Iron Cross, he was permitted to remain at this school in spite of being a Jew until August 1939. He departed from Germany literally at the last minute. His mother remained behind and was murdered in a concentration camp. Having served in 229 Company, Pioneer Corps, until 1943, he also was transferred to the Royal Rifles. The stations of his further military progress are those of his battalion: Normandy, Bayeux, Belgium, the Ardennes, Holland, Munster, Osnabrück. After the end of hostilities he was attached to the REs as an interpreter. There he played his part in the de-Nazification of the German railways.

The King's Own Yorkshire Light Infantry was the regiment in which Harry Weiss, an Austrian, served from 1944 onwards. About him it is said that as a result of a telephone conversation with an enemy officer he was able to cause a hostile field HQ to be destroyed. Although he is credibly reported to have died of wounds in Belgium, his name does not appear on either Bentwich's list or in the Ex-Service NB Association's roll of honour.

The story of Erich Clement, originally Klementschitz, does not follow the usual pattern. He was born at Graz in 1911, the youngest member of a family which described itself as politically active socialists. Already after the failure of the socialist uprising in Austria in February 1934 the whole family was subjected to constant police harassment and imprisonment. In 1937 he had had enough of this and followed his elder brother to Spain to serve in the International Brigade in the civil war, although, as he states, 'he knew that it was a lost cause'. After the defeat of the republicans in February 1939 he escaped to France, where he was interned at Gurs until he obtained permission to visit Britain. He was very lucky indeed to be able to sail on the last ship before war was declared. He made his way to Merseyside to stay with his sister, who had married into a Jewish family there. He was interned in May 1940 and was one of those who were shipped to Canada. Released from internment in 1942 he was shipped back to Britain. In 1944 he enlisted, along with a group of Austrian friends, to find himself a private soldier in the Suffolk Regiment. After six weeks training he was sent to France. Mrs Joyce Clement wrote:

> My husband wishes you to know that his treatment by his officers and acceptance by his fellow comrades was commendable, particularly having in mind that he was considerably older than those he was serving with. Having suffered the privations of the Spanish civil war he found life in the British army beyond his expectations.
>
> In 1945 he learned that his mother had died in Ravensbruck concentration camp, but that his father was believed to be alive in Buchenwald. He asked for permission to visit his father, but since the war was still on his commanding officer could not grant him leave of absence. He hinted, however, that he would not make any inquiries about him, should Erich decide to go. Should he be discovered to be absent without official leave, he would, however, have to bear the consequences. Erich consulted his padre, who after some thought, offered to take him in his jeep. This meant journeying from the north-west of Germany to the south-east, but all went well. The Americans had overrun most of this territory and willingly gave assistance with food and petrol.
>
> ...His father did not immediately recognise Erich, since he was in British uniform, but in spite of the awful garb and physical changes brought about by over five years' imprisonment Erich immediately knew him.

Later Clement was interpreter and clerk of the court at a military court in Germany. For his work there he was highly commended. Asked whether he had approached the two conflicts in which he was involved, the Spanish civil war and the Second World War, with the same commitment, he said: 'Yes. In each case I was fighting for democracy. When the Republican army was defeated, I was devastated, but when I joined the British army I knew I was on the winning side'. At the end of hostilities Clement had fully intended to return to Graz, where employment had been lined up for him. But he found that there were still too many Nazis around. He remained in England and, as he says, 'eschewed politics'. He did whatever work came his way. He drove taxis and lorries and ended up as a progress chaser in industry. He retired in 1976.

Eric M. Beecham was also in the Suffolk Regiment. He was originally Bischheim and his family has been traced back to the fifteenth century, living in Frankfurt am Main. His older brother Bernard and he himself served in the British army. Bernard was a sergeant in the Engineers, mainly in Italy. Eric was in the infantry. After a spell with the Suffolks he was posted to the Lincolnshire Regiment attached to the 3rd Army Corps. He got as far as Bremen. From there, due to an injury to his knee, he had to be flown back to Britain, where he landed on VE-day.

Rothbart, who showed exceptional talent at Cambridge – and also played hockey for the university – worked with Lord Keynes until he was interned in 1940. He was released to continue his research, but joined the army as soon as he could serve in a fighting unit. He died of wounds received at Arnhem.

George Baer, born 25 July 1921 in Munich, changed his name only inasmuch as he added an 'e' to the end of his forename. Having suffered internment on the Isle of Man in June 1940, he joined 246 Company PC in October of the same year. Early in 1944 he was transferred to the gunners and, after a short period of training, was retained in training camp as instructor on Bofors guns. This, too, did not last long. He was sent to OCTU and commissioned, by then a six-pounder anti-tank specialist, into the Queen's Own Royal West Kents still in December of the same year. In August 1945 he joined the 4th Battalion of this regiment, then on anti-insurgency duties in support of the civil power in Rangoon, became its transport officer and put up his third pip. In February 1946, following the disbandment of his battalion, he became commandant of the British transit camp, Rangoon, with the rank of major, a rank he retained until his release from the service in September 1946.

93 Company PC contained amongst its men a distinguished German doctor, Karewski, for whom his company commander endeavoured in vain to obtain a commission in the Royal Army Medical Corps. A year or two later he was commissioned in the infantry. After he had advanced to captain the RAMC changed its mind and offered him the commission in that corps, which previously he would have liked to have, but he chose to stay in his combatant unit.

Professor Keith Spalding of Bangor University, one of the leading German scholars in Britain, was Karl-Heinz Spalt when his birth was registered at Darmstadt in 1913. Already in 1931 at the age of 18 and whilst studying he became the target of unwelcome attentions by the police of his home town, where he published a 'Handbook of Pacifism'. As a result he realised very early on what would be his fate when the Nazis came to power. In March 1933 he fled to Vienna. But the Nazis pursued and pestered him even there, and to escape their unwelcome attentions he walked – all the way on foot – from Vienna through Switzerland to Paris. Later he returned to Vienna via Italy. Still knowing himself to be under observation he went to Poland and, in 1934, to Britain. In Birmingham he could at last continue his studies. He was still there in 1940, when he was interned. Professor Roy Pascal, however, intervened on his behalf and secured his early release. At that time his convictions underwent a change and he realised that what he had advocated hitherto could not be sustained when people like Hitler and his minions were in power. He became a pioneer in November 1940, joining 246 Company. In 1943 he obtained a transfer to the Border Regiment. Some time later he was transferred to Psychological Warfare. Following the end of the fighting he became editor of the *Mitteilungen*, one of the first papers to be published in Germany after the war, and after he had been able to hand over this job to a German civilian, he was still active in the control of films for a time. Spalding has written a number of books including his *magnum opus*, a historical dictionary of German figurative language. This represents the work of some 40 years.

What happened to Max Schneider has been graphically described by Muchitsch. Schneider was born in Vienna in 1921, joined the communists and eventually fled to Britain in 1939. In 1940 he was interned and deported to Canada. During the following year he was brought back and put on work of national importance, as a turner in a Birmingham armaments factory. In 1943 he volunteered for service, adopting the name Peter Shelley. He was posted to the 7th Battalion of the Cameronians. With this unit he got to Belgium in December 1944. As from January 1945 they were in continuous action in Belgium,

1 Badge of the Pioneer Corps, later Royal Pioneer Corps

2 5th Battalion Coldstream Guards entering Arras, *Daily Sketch*, 1945. Second man: E. Goodman (Ernst Gutmann) from Breslau; fourth man: Archie Newman (Adolf Neuberger) from Walduern (courtesy Professor E. Goodman)

3 The first of the many: No. 1 Section, 69 Company PC at Kitchener Camp (courtesy Royal Pioneer Corps Association)

4 No. 3 Section, 88 Company PC before embarkation for France, 1940 (courtesy Heinz Schmoll)

5 Nominal Roll of 74 Company PC with the British Expeditionary Force in France, 1940 (courtesy Royal Pioneer Corps Association)

6 An Alien Pioneer with the Iron Cross won in the war of 1914–18 when serving in the German
  Army (courtesy Royal Pioneer Corps Association)

7 74 Company PC returning from France, 1940 (courtesy Royal Pioneer Corps Association)

8 Alien Pioneers clearing up after German air raids on the East End of London
(courtesy Royal Pioneer Corps Association)

9 74 Company PC in France, 1940 (courtesy Royal Pioneer Corps Association)

10 Footballers of 74 Company PC (courtesy Royal Pioneer Corps Association)

11 Lunch break in the forest (courtesy Royal Pioneer Corps Association)

12 Small arms training, 1942

13 The Fonthill Gifford Band (courtesy Royal Pioneer Corps Association)

14 Every company had its own band (courtesy Royal Pioneer Corps Association)

Holland, France and Germany. Shelley, as he then was, received the Military Medal for gallantry. His citation tells of the cold courage and the high degree of initiative which he showed at Alpon and at Rheine. Then, on the night of 16 April 1945, along the river Weser a patrol led by him encountered an enemy position held by 15 men. Whilst calling to his men to give him covering fire Schneider ran towards the enemy, firing his Sten continually. Having reached a hollow some five yards from the enemy position he threw hand grenades at them, which led to some of them running away. Schneider continued to advance and after an exchange of fire at closest range he took the rest of them prisoner. By his exceptional leadership and great gallantry he not only overwhelmed a superior enemy, but also set his comrades a first-class example of quick thinking, initiative and daring. In the last action of his unit he was wounded and had to be brought back to Britain. Having been restored to health and before his release at Villach in February 1947, he was employed as interpreter at a prisoner of war camp in the South of England.

The Cameronians were a lowland regiment. A highland regiment with a very similar name were the Cameron Highlanders. They had amongst them Richard Feiweles, later Fairfax, born in Breslau on 7 February 1924. Before transferring to them he had been a pioneer. He was in action at Monte Cassino and at Salonika. After the end of hostilities he served at Travemuende.

Dr Ernest J. Goodman, originally Ernst Guttmann from Breslau, was born in 1925. Having reached Britain by *Kindertransport* he volunteered for service in December 1943. At first he was in the Northamptonshire Regiment, later in the 5th Battalion Coldstream Guards. A patrol of this battalion, in which he was the number two on the Bren gun, was photographed as it entered Arras in September 1944. This photo was published in the *Daily Sketch*. It is the only picture showing enemy aliens in HM Forces in action. Later during 1944 the 5th Coldstreamers were in action against General Student's SS, on which occasion Goodman was wounded. After seven months in Bromsgrove Hospital he was restored to health sufficiently to take his place in the line along the processional route at the VE-day parade on 8 May 1945.

On this photo, on which Goodman appears as the second man of the patrol the number four is Archie Newman, originally Adolf Neuberger. He, too, was wounded at a later stage. He suffered an injury to the head, from which it was not possible to remove every single shell splinter. He and Goodman appear to have been the first Jews in the Coldstream Guards since the regiment was founded in 1650. In these circumstances there was no provision in the regimental rules for Guardsmen to attend Jewish religious services. With all others whose religion was difficult to classify they were sent to church parade at the Salvation Army.

Another comrade of Goodman's, though not in the Guards, but in the Northamptonshire Regiment, was Walter Brian, who got that name by leaving out the 'u' in his original name Burian. He had been born in Vienna on 21 October 1922, left Vienna with a *Kindertransport* on 10 December 1938 and arrived in Britain two days later. After two months' agricultural training in Buckinghamshire, he was placed on a farm at Newbury, Berkshire. There he lived and worked until he was interned in June 1940. He was sent to Canada, but came back to Britain in the summer of 1942. He returned to the same farm at Newbury and remained there until he joined the army in January 1944. In the Northamptonshire Regiment he was in the 1st Battalion, which was part of the 20th Indian Division in Burma. He was in action against the Japanese from November 1944 until May 1945. After a short stay in India the battalion went to Singapore as part of the occupation forces there and in Malaya. He was returned to Britain in 1947 and released from the services later that year. Both of Brian's parents died in Theresienstadt. His eldest sister and his brother made it from Vienna to Yugoslavia, but Hitler caught up with them there and they were not heard from again.

Little is known about Staff Captain Colin Brooks, an ex-pioneer. He was commissioned in the infantry and in the last stages of his service time he was in East Africa where he was responsible for the transport of 200,000 African soldiers back to their homes.

The Royal Armoured Corps appears to have been more popular amongst ex-pioneers than the infantry. In 1943 216 men went from the Pioneer Corps to the RAC. Their experience in their new units was uniformly good. They were accepted by their new comrades and by their officers without question. After a short period of training each one became part of the crew of an armoured vehicle or was given a task in another part of his unit. Almost 50 were posted to the 8th Irish Hussars (8IH), who by that time were equipped with light armour and no longer had horses. Following the new intake it was rumoured that the 'I' in 8IH might be thought to mean 'International' rather than Irish. The newcomers there were not entirely German and Austrian. Hollos, a Hungarian, and a Turkish Jew by the name of Albala helped to make the group a little more international. By and by about half of the ex-pioneers in the 8IH were commissioned. Six were killed. In the last stages of the war the unit was in the van of the British advance on Hamburg. Their tanks were the first to enter the city. During the negotiations for the surrender of the German forces under Admiral Doenitz, German-born soldiers of the 8IH acted both as guards and as interpreters.

Harold Becker from Berlin also got to an Irish cavalry regiment, but his was the 5th Royal Inniskilling Dragoons. This regiment had also been converted to armour. The following is his own story, entitled 'My War':

> On learning from the Berlin evening papers that Messrs. Molotov and Ribbentrop had signed a non-aggression pact, I hastily returned home from a good-bye visit to friends, telephoned my mother (who was also visiting) to meet me at Zoo station, put my bags which had been packed for several days into a taxi – and was just in time to catch the evening train to Holland. That was the last time I ever saw my mother.
>
> In due course a xenophobic British government put me, together with 4,000 others, behind barbed wire and within six months I had joined the Pioneer Corps (No. 249 Company). Later on I transferred to the cavalry who, to the chagrin of their regular officers, had had their horses exchanged for tanks of which they (the officers, not the horses) were wholly ignorant. Eventually, in March 1945, I found myself back on German soil, my unit having crossed the Rhine at Wesel. I will not and cannot pretend that I had any feelings of anger or hatred for the ordinary German soldier or civilian with whom I came into contact. Of course, I never encountered anyone who admitted to having committed a crime – or even to having been a party member!
>
> I had some remarkably lucky escapes from injury or worse during the campaign. Once, when driving the leading tank of my troop, the tank behind me blew up on a mine which I must have missed by a fraction of an inch. On another occasion, we were halted in order to allow the sergeant major to deal with a mine in an adjoining field. We took cover behind our tank; he pulled the string attached to the mine – and the chap standing next to me fell to the ground, peppered with shrapnel. I did not receive a scratch.
>
> In the closing days of the war, we got word from regimental headquarters that in the woods on the right of the road along which we were advancing, there were a large number of German soldiers. We halted, I jumped from the tank, ran towards the woods and shouted in my best German something to the effect that the war was as good as over and that anyone hearing me should come out with their hands up. Alas, nothing happened, so we had no choice but to go in and clear the wood. Among the

prisoners we took was one who, on surrendering his rifle to me, said that he had had me in his telescopic sight all the while I was shouting my head off! I kept that sight for some years; eventually I exchanged it for something more useful.

When the ceasefire came into operation we were ordered to take up billets in a tiny hamlet near Itzehoe, consisting of no more than a couple of dozen houses. The largest was the burgomaster's, so we turfed him and his family out and made ourselves comfortable. Since there were not enough tables and chairs, I was told to commandeer some. I set off and did just that in the first two or three houses. When I knocked on the door of the next house, it was opened by a middle-aged woman who took one look at me and said quite matter-of-factly: 'You are Herr Becker who lived with his mother in the Danziger Strasse – *nein*?' Just imagine – there I was in British army uniform encountering, among the millions on the move at that time, someone who had known me five years earlier!

A few days afterwards my application to be transferred to Berlin was granted – to my great surprise, because it was almost axiomatic in the British army that such a request should have been followed by a posting to anywhere except the requested destination. Thus I returned to Berlin in that beautiful summer of 1945. Miraculously, several relatives had survived; two had spent the war in the Jewish hospital; two had returned from Theresienstadt, and two were still living in their Charlottenburg flat.

Being young and fancy free, I decided before long to sample Berlin's reviving nightlife. Several nightclubs had sprung up on and around the Ku-damm. In the first one I visited, I spotted a beautiful blonde – who became my wife for 34 years.

The army in its wisdom decided to attach me to the Intelligence branch, and very interesting it was, too. I met, amongst others, Schumacher, Grotewohl and Luft. Security, as we know it today, was non-existent. Our office block, an apartment house near the Reichskanzler Platz, was not guarded. Anyone could walk in and wander about.

In due course the Allies decided to hold local elections. Intelligence branch was ordered to show the flag in the Soviet sector. A convoy of vehicles with flags flying set out one morning, with yours truly as guide. I thought I knew East Berlin! Suffice it to say I didn't know it well enough. Had we not beaten a hasty retreat, Intelligence branch might have been in for some nasty surprises at the hands of our Soviet allies.

When the time for my demob arrived, I reported to Zoo station one bitterly cold December evening – only to find myself appointed guard commander of the military train to Helmstedt. So on my second departure from Berlin I held the Soviet army at bay on my way back to civilian life.

One of the men who were transferred to the heavy tanks of the first Royal Tank Regiment (1 RTR) was Henry Mortimer, previously Heinrich Mosenthal from Rheine. He had emigrated in 1933, because as a Jew he had not been allowed to study medicine. In England he had a variety of jobs which enabled him to survive, but of course, he too was interned in 1940. From internment he volunteered for the pioneers. He also got into 249 Company. Later he changed to 69 Company. No. 1 RTR was known as Monty's Own, because Montgomery always wanted to have the regiment under his direct control. There Mortimer became a tank-driver. With his tank he drove from Normandy through Belgium and Holland to northern Germany, taking part in a number of battles and other actions on the way. He was in the Nijmegen corridor during the battle of Arnhem. Then the regiment was taken out of the line and was in Brussels, when on Christmas Day 1944 they were attacked from the air. In the front line again they saw action in the Reichswald and at the Rhine crossing at Wesel. His last action was a strategically unimportant one, but one which was fought most bitterly. At Jarlingen, a village to the north-west of Fallingbostel, there was an SS training establishment, whose men put up strong resistance. None of them survived. When fighting ended 1 RTR was still in Luneburg Heath. Then they moved to Hamburg.

Bryan Fisher came from Vienna. There he was known as Bruno Fischer. Having served in 229 Company PC he also went to the RTR. He, too, was in the whole of the northern European campaign from Normandy to Germany. His unit was right at the front all the way. At one stage he lost his tank and spent several days hiding up in no man's land. After it was all over, he got a job in the Control Commission for Germany. He was in Field Security.

Martin Amson, formerly Abrahamsohn, was from Hamburg. He was born there on 27 June 1923 and there he went to school, at the Jewish Talmud-Thora-School. At the end of 1943 he volunteered for service with the British army and eventually joined the 4th Battalion of the RTR. With them he landed on the Normandy beaches on 8 June 1944 (D+2). In November 1944, however, he was sent to the interpreters' school at Brussels and a few months later attached to the 6th Airborne Division. Since the Rhine crossing at Wesel on 24 March

1945, where the 6th Airborne was in action, he has been posted as 'missing, believed killed'.

Originally Garry Rogers was called Gunther Baumgart. He had been born on 8 December 1923 in Breslau. There he attended the Jewish school on the Rhediger Platz until 8 November 1938, the day before all the synagogues and other Jewish institutions in Germany were destroyed. He was another one of those who got to Britain by *Kindertransport*. He arrived on 30 March 1939 and was accommodated in hostels, first at Westgate, later in Croydon. Interned on the Isle of Man in 1940 he joined the pioneers from there. He was in Pembroke with 87 Company, before transferring to the RAC at Farnborough in 1943. Already with the pioneers he had been a physical training instructor. The RAC employed him in a similar way. He was sent to PT training courses at Warwick and Chester, but at the same time received instruction as a wireless operator and tank driver. Eventually he too joined 1 RTR. With them he landed in Normandy on 7 June 1944 (D+1) and was in action from then in France, Belgium, Holland and Germany until the regiment reached Hamburg. Only after all this was over was he transferred to interpreter duties in a camp for war criminals. He was released from service in Germany in April 1947.

Henry H. Seaman, originally Schueftan, was arrested by the Gestapo on *Kristallnacht* (9 November 1938) and, together with his father and brother, taken to Buchenwald concentration camp. He stayed there for six weeks and was released to go to Britain with a *Kindertransport*. After a sojourn in Dovercourt he was assigned to the assistant camp commander in Kitchener Camp to act as interpreter for the many refugees that arrived at Dover. Having been interned in Huyton he was sent to Australia on the HMT Dunera. The guards on the ship he describes as 'miserable, not very bright members of the Pioneer Corps, commanded by a Lt. O'Neill, VC, who also was a miserable bastard, drunk on most occasions'. He came back to Britain in 1941, joined 229 Company, Pioneer Corps, and became driver to the officer commanding. In 1943 he was transferred to the 5th Battalion RTR and with them he was in action from Normandy to Berlin.

Peter Harry Leopold Gayduschek changed his name to Gayward in 1943. He had been born in Vienna in 1925, where he attended the Goethe School. Having come to Britain he went on to St Christopher School in Letchworth. He joined up in 1943 and was sent to RAC OCTU Sandhurst direct from 58 Training Regiment RAC. After being commissioned in 1945 he first joined the Reconnaissance Corps, then the RTR and from there was posted to the Yorkshire Hussars all within the year. For the next four years he was at GHQ 2nd Echelon, for a time as deputy assistant adjutant general with the rank of major.

He was released in 1949.

Another member of the Royal Tank Regiment is Henry R. Brook, originally Brod. He wrote:

> I was a Czech citizen, volunteered for war service in May 1940 and after training in Westward Ho! was posted to 87 Company, Pioneer Corps. In spring 1943 I transferred to the Royal Armoured Corps and after completion of training in Farnborough, Hants, was posted to the 5th Royal Tank Regiment, part of the 7th Armoured Division (Desert Rats).
>
> I 'travelled' in my tank from Portsmouth to Arromanches–Bayeux–Caen–Falaise to Ghent (on the first British tank to enter the town after some fierce street fighting), continued into Holland and the Ardennes to stem the German breakthrough in the winter of 1944–45, eventually crossed the Rhine near Xanten and continued via Westphalia, Rethem-on-Aller to Hamburg. I was stationed in the *Rathaus* (the city hall) when the armistice was signed. It all sounds like a travelogue but it was not a particularly smooth run; actually I am the only survivor of the crew with whom I crossed the Channel.
>
> After attending a Field Security (Intelligence Corps) course at Bad Drieburg in February 1946 I acted as intelligence person of the 5th RTR in Schleswig-Holstein until my release in June 1946.

Kenneth Robert Ward, alias Karl Robert Wuerzburger, born on 29 November 1922, is one of the sons of the then organist of the West End Synagogue in Frankfurt on Main. Having attended school in his home town he reached Britain by *Kindertransport* on 26 August 1939. He served in 87 Company PC. In August 1943 he was transferred to the RAC and joined the 1st RTR as a driver/wireless operator. He was with the battalion when it landed at Arromanches on D+1. He had intended not to take any prisoners, but when first confronted with a surrendering German hastened to make him a cup of tea. He, too, was with 1 RTR at Caen, Falaise and Brussels. There he met his brother Paul, who had joined the Jewish Brigade in Palestine, had been with them throughout the entire campaign in Italy from Calabria to Friaul and had also finished up in Brussels eventually. Following this, Ward was at Arnhem and at Ahaus. There his tank received a direct hit and was destroyed. With a new vehicle he reached Hamburg in May 1945 and finally to Meldorf. There he actually saw and found Himmler in his hideout, but did not recognise him. From July 1945 until his release in 1948 he served with the military police in Berlin.

Ward has written the following story concerning an actual happening in the last days of the war:

> The briefing by the Squadron Leader was short, to the point and very unpleasant. My stomach turned into a solid ball. Charlie, our driver used some of the foulest language possible, using innumerable four-letter words. Eric, the gunner, muttered something not very complimentary under his breath. Stan, the tank commander, quite new to the game, was very keen and, with shining eyes, willing to go anywhere in his ignorance. I made up the fourth member of the crew, the wireless operator, gun-loader and second in command.
>
> I shall never forget that day, Wednesday 18 April 1945.
>
> We had only just rejoined the regiment in a brand new tank (a 'Firefly', with the most powerful British tank gun at that time, but still no match for the feared German 88), as our previous tank had been badly damaged in battle. We had just taken delivery of the tank, had had sufficient time to load our gear, but had not had a chance to test and check out our new acquisition.
>
> We were deep inside Germany, and the tank column had been held up by a dense impenetrable forest, which was looming only a short distance ahead of us, black and uninviting. Three attempts had been made to get through the German defences, without much success and with very heavy losses.
>
> We, No. 7 troop, had been chosen from 'A' Squadron of the 1st Royal Tank Regiment, 7th Armoured Division, for one last attempt. We were told to try and get through before dusk. Only one infantry platoon was available to cover our flank during the advance. The major, with his bristling moustache and carefully knotted desert scarf, was not very happy about sending us down the road either. So we cracked jokes that weren't funny and tried to appear as unconcerned as possible. I was as scared as always when I knew that battle was about to commence.
>
> I nipped inside the tank, checked the wireless and made sure I was still 'on net', our lifeline to the regiment, after having listened to the BBC all morning. I put one of the high-powered armour-piercing shells into the breech of the 17-pounder gun and fed a new belt into the Browning machine gun. I loaded my Sten gun and put some grenades in easy reach round the top of the turret. Dusk was approaching fast and we did not have much time left.
>
> The troop leader started up and we followed like lambs being led to slaughter. About eight infantry boys from the Rifle Brigade

crouched on the back of the tank until we reached the wood. The trees suddenly started closing in on us. The infantry boys jumped off the tanks and formed up on either side. The undergrowth was so thick that they had to keep to the ditch on either side of the road. Passing two of our burned out tanks on the road did nothing to boost our morale.

The troop of four tanks, three Cromwells and our Sherman, moved along the road at walking pace. We sat on top of the tanks, earphones clipped tightly to the head, with one ear uncovered, trying to listen to any unusual sounds over the din made by the tanks. We were sitting ducks. They could hear us coming for miles. We couldn't even see them.

As the tanks rumbled on, the tension mounted. The infantry boys practically crawled in the ditches by now. We slowed down still further, travelling with our long gun pointing over to the right, eyes strained for any suspicious movement, any suspicious reflections. All I could see were trees and shrubs. No movement anywhere.

Suddenly, a blinding flash. I could just see a tree being cut in half in front of me. The blast threw me onto the turret floor of the tank before I could hear the bang. The earphones were still tightly on my spinning head. I could hear a voice coming through the crackle: '. . . being fired upon. Seven Charlie has been knocked out. Only one man bailed out. The rest of the crew must have bought it.'

I recognised the voice of our troop leader. He was talking about us. Our code name was Seven Charlie. Well, I wasn't dead. I was still all there. I looked to my right where Stan should have been. There was only an empty hatch through which I could see a now dark sky. Stan must have got out all right. That meant they got Eric and Charlie. Eric and Charlie! Well, they were not going to get away with it.

I looked through the telescope and saw the stump of the tree that had been cut in half right in front of me. That must be it, that's where the Jerries are. The Browning was right in front of me. I just squeezed the trigger and watched the bullets rip into the dense shrub.

Above the din I heard Eric's familiar voice: 'Here, Buzz, what are you firing at?' So they had not got him after all. 'It's the Jerries,' I shouted back, 'go on, traverse the turret, if you can, spray the bastards, go on let them have it.' I happily carried on squeezing the trigger. I had not felt so happy for a long time. Now the other tanks joined in. Concentrated fire from all the tanks followed my tracer bullets. A beautiful sight. Nothing could survive this hail of bullets.

I looked down into the driver's compartment and Charlie was grinning back at me. I shouted over the intercom: 'Is the tank all right?' and got a curt reply: 'You bet it is.'

I reported over the air to the troop leader that we were alright and fit for action. A shadow over the tank commander's hatch announced the return of a sheepish Stan, who had been lying in an uncomfortable wet ditch for the last few minutes. The radio crackled into life and the troop was ordered back to the squadron. We all pumped a few more belts into the shrub for good measure, collected our infantry boys and moved at top speed back down the road we had come.

A young cockney had seen it all happen. He was full of it. 'Cor, matey, you were dead lucky. I sor it all. One of them there bazookas 'it the tree in front of your tank. I sor it being fired. Cor, you would 'ave 'ad it, if it 'ad 'it yer. I fink you got 'im alright though, matey. I wouldn't be in one of them there coffins fer anything.'

I was pleased with myself. That was the appreciation we deserved. I settled back in the tank as we were rumbling back along the road.

Suddenly I sat up with a jerk. The breech block was open. But that was impossible. I had loaded our 17-pounder with one of our new, high-powered, armour-piercing shells before we started out and now there was its empty shell case on the turret floor. I touched it and burned my hand. Impossible, we had not fired the big gun, since we had taken delivery of the tank – or had we?

I looked across at Eric, nudged him and pointed to the empty shell case. He shouted across the din: 'Keep quiet and get rid of that shell case as quick as you can, and don't let anyone see it.'

Then it all clicked into place. We had not been fired on at all. Our gun had fired, the shell had hit the tree and cut it down, and the blast from the muzzle had blown me down into the turret.

As always the explanation was simple. When the tank was delivered the cables to the firing buttons were incorrectly connected; the Browning trigger to the big gun and the trigger for the big gun to the Browning. When Eric had thought he had spotted some movement, he wanted to fire a burst with the machine gun, but the big gun went off instead.

That night an artillery barrage was laid onto the forest, which continued all through the night. The Royal Air Force supported it with a bombardment. A lot of noise, a beautiful sight and an uneasy conscience.

Next morning, on Thursday the 19th, we moved in again. We drove down the road at full speed. In the light of the bright sunny morning the forest looked less forbidding. A quiet calm now hung over everything. There was not a soul in sight as the advance continued.

Several units of the Royal Armoured Corps used former pioneers for what was called phantom communication. This was a method of misleading the enemy by interfering with his wireless. Both sides used wireless to control the movements of its armour. This meant that the vehicles of each unit were in constant contact with each other by short-wave radio. One only had to find the frequency on which a unit was operating in order to be able to interfere with its communications. Naturally, the operators within such a network all knew each other and each other's accents, and anyone trying to break into an enemy network in German with an English accent would not have been able to convince the radio operators of a German panzer formation that he was one of them. But the British had quite a few men who were German themselves, and so were able to cause confusion in many an opposing unit.

Ernest and John Lennard, originally Ernst and Hans Loevy, were able to do quite a bit of this. They were brothers who had served with 77 Company PC before, as officers, they were transferred to the Inns of Court Regiment, a former cavalry regiment of the Territorial Army. This had been equipped with light armoured vehicles. Via Belgium, Holland and Germany they got as far as Denmark by the end of hostilities. They were amongst the first to cross the Danish frontier at Niebull and Tondern, coming from the south. Having been put in charge of controlling the traffic across the Rendsburg bridge over the Kiel Canal, they actually had to issue the permits allowing Admiral Doenitz's plenipotentiaries to cross that bridge, in order to get to Montgomery's headquarters at Luneburg, where the final capitulation took place. Before they were discharged, both were engaged with the prosecution of Nazi war criminals and with de-Nazification generally in the Hamburg area.

Frank Geoffrey Turner, formerly Franz-Guenter Trier, was a Hessian. Although born in Berlin on 26 November 1918 he always considered himself to be a Darmstadt man. His parents having returned to their native city, he attended school there and from there he emigrated to Britain in 1938. He was one of the first volunteers who joined up at Richborough, was in 87 Company and with them he went through all their adventures in France in 1940. In 1943 he was transferred to the RAC and served in the 7th Armoured Division. Commissioned in the autumn of 1944, he returned to his former division and was with them throughout the campaign in north-western Europe. From 1946 to 1947 he was divisional intelligence officer. Having been released from active service, he joined the Territorial Army. There he was promoted to major.

Harry Curtis, originally Helmut Cahn, was born at Dusseldorf on 25 August 1923. He attended the Jewish school there and after he had left at age 14 he worked in a liqueur factory for six months. Together with his brother Gunther (see below) he arrived in England on a *Kindertransport* on 19 June 1939. Their parents were left behind and in due course were murdered, like 64 other relatives of theirs. Harry served with the pioneers. He, too, was transferred to the RAC in 1943. He trained as a tank driver. Then he joined the Reconnaissance Regiment in the 6th Airborne Division. In Holland he and his armoured vehicle were landed by glider, after which he fought his way through to the river Elbe. When the war in Europe ended he was already on a ship in the Mediterranean on the way to the Far East. Then the war ended there, too, and the 6th Airborne Division was landed in Palestine. He found himself in an invidious position as, being Jewish, he was not trusted by the British and had trouble with the Jews, as he wore his red Airborne beret when visiting relatives in Tel-Aviv. He refused to obey orders and demanded a court martial. It was then that he heard of the fate of his family. He was transferred to the Pay Corps in Cairo and worked in a prisoner of war camp. There he refused to speak German. As a result, he was allocated a German interpreter from amongst the prisoners. This was a man from Recklinghausen, not far from Harry's home town of Dusseldorf. They became good friends. Their friendship lasted for many years and eventually included also their families.

According to Rudolf H. Hellmann, who for a time was called Robin Hilary, the details of his service are very 'humdrum'. He wrote:

> I joined in February 1940 and went to Richborough, where I was posted to 87th Company. We went to France and worked on the docks at Le Havre. As the Germans came nearer, we were sent to a depot outside Rennes, which we left in rather a hurry to return to England. We were greeted like heroes! We actually had rifles for some time! Fortunately, we never used them, being quite untrained, and handed them back before returning home.

We went to North Devon and worked from there. Thence to West Wales, where we laid many miles of pipes to bring running water to people who had never had it. We also dug out many unexploded German bombs. The local people prayed for us in the churches. After that, believe it or not, we were allowed to join the army at large. I chose the Royal Armoured Corps, was trained and sent to India, to my fury. I had no personal quarrel with the Japanese. I went to Imphal on the Burma border and joined the 3rd Carabiniers (Prince of Wales Dragoon Guards). With them all the way to Rangoon and then to Madras and up all the way to the Khyber country. I fell ill with tuberculosis.

I was in action mainly across the Irrawady. I was discharged with a 100 per cent disability pension and two pints of gold cap milk a day. I was also given a very pretty medal with the King's head on it.

I saw more of India than most Indians ever do. The King Emperor paid the fares...

When I was interviewed for naturalisation the junior officer said to his senior: 'A very distinguished career, sir!' I nearly fell off my chair laughing.

H. Peter Sinclair wrote:

I volunteered (as Hans Peter Siegel) to join HM Forces and started in Westward Ho! in the 219 Company, Pioneer Corps, section 8, Sergeant Aptowitzer, I believe. We moved to Ilfracombe – more basic training, Seahouses – working with Australian lumberjacks, Derby – loading huge cheeses into and out of railway trucks, Leamington Spa, Whittlebury Lodge/ Stony Stratford – building armoured car emplacements for the KRRC, and Matlock. To kill the boredom I also volunteered at one time to go on an army catering course in Bedford and qualified as a class 1 cook. I have hardly touched a saucepan since.

My record of service card tells the following story: AMPC: from 22 August 1940 to 13 July 1943; RAC: from 14 July 1943 to 11 July 1945 and finally RASC from 12 July 1945 to 23 September 1946.

During December 1943 I embarked in Greenock on the S.S. *Strathmore*. It took six weeks via the Mediterranean to reach Bombay. First stop Poona, then Deolali, Hyderabad, Karachi – a brief spell as driving instructor with the Intelligence Corps. After a lengthy and severe episode of infective hepatitis my medical

classification was downgraded to category C in 1944. I spent the
next two and a half years working in the adjutant general's branch,
GHQ Delhi as Chief Clerk (Sergeant) in Org. 7(d). I was
demobilised in September 1946.

The name Walter Horn is as English as it is German, and so the man
who had been born with this name in Breslau on 29 December 1923 saw
no reason to change it at any time. Nevertheless, when he was in Italy
with the 56th Reconnaissance Regiment, RAC, this did not save him
from being called Ted – short for 'Tedesco', the German. Like so many
others he, too, had come to Britain with a *Kindertransport*, had been sent
to Flint Hall Farm at Fingest in Buckinghamshire to learn which end of
a cow was which, and hired out as a farm labourer. For a time he and I
shared lodgings in Little Missenden. In 1942 Walter volunteered for the
army and got to 219 Company, Pioneer Corps. In 1943 he was
transferred to the RAC and posted to the Reconnaissance Regiment
mentioned above, whose members, he says, were a very rough lot. It was
useful that he knew how to handle animals, for his skills in this respect
came in useful on many occasions, both legitimate and otherwise.

During the winter of 1944–45 his unit was used in an infantry role
in the front line in the Apennines, which meant that they were in slit
trenches, out in the open, in close contact with the enemy, for months
on end. The losses of both sides in that theatre during that period were
high and the 56th Recce were no exception. Horn, however, was
fortunate. He survived unscathed.

When the snows melted, the enemy resistance did so, too. Horn's
unit resumed its proper station at the head of the division's advance
and his armoured vehicle was the first across the Ploecken Pass into
Carinthia. The frontier guards had left their offices, including all their
official paraphernalia, and so Horn, by then a sergeant, was able to
amuse himself stamping official German entry visas into his pals'
soldier's service books.

Later on the 56th were in Lienz, in eastern Tyrol. When the
Cossacks and other Russians, who had fought for the Nazis and
surrendered to the British, were handed over, together with their
womenfolk and children, some 70,000 people in all, to the Soviets at
Graz, the regiment was part of the British escort. The Soviets shot the
lot still within earshot of the British. The memory of the scenes of
desperation – and of bravery – which occurred during this handover
haunts Horn to this day. The Cossack horses remained with the
British. With them the regiment took part in inter-Allied horse races
at Vienna and on this occasion Horn's agricultural training proved

useful. It was his job to take care of the horses. As a result he was also able to render an unforgotten kindness to my mother. Having spent several years at Theresienstadt concentration camp she had returned to Vienna a short time before. Horn visited her, brought her chocolates and corned beef and other goodies which were then unknown for ordinary people there, and told her about me, then in India, whom she had not seen since 1938. After his release Horn continued his studies. Later he had a senior position with a leading oil company in Holland. He lives in Buckinghamshire, not very far from where he and I shared lodgings way back in 1941.

Clive Teddern, formerly Kurt Tebrich, from Hamburg has written several most interesting stories about what happened to him. Others who served in the RAC and about whom more may be found in the register were:

Beadle, A.
Bernard, Kelly
Carter, Charles P., from Austria
Dreifuss (Dreyfuss?), alias P.C. Denby
Eberstadt, Ernst Carl Eduard, from Frankfurt, alias David Edward
    Charles Eversley
Eimerl, Siegfried, from Vienna, alias Sidney Edwards
Farnborough, Robert F., from Austria
Gaensler, Friedrich, alias Frederick Gordon
Golding, Frank P.
Goldstein, Franz, from Wiesbaden.
Goodman, Dennis
Harvey, from Austria?
Herold, Wolfgang, alias Ian Herold
Hughes, W.
Jung, Otto, from Vienna, alias Thomas Young
Kohn, PAL/3453
Krivine, J.D.
Ladewig, Jochen, from Hamburg, alias J. Lawrie
Liebel, Peter, from Vienna, alias Peter Leigh-Bell
Linford
Loewenstein, Max, alias Mark Lynton
Nagler, Kurt, from Austria, alias Michael Norville
Pollak, Sigi, from Vienna, alias Sidney Pollard
Prager, Hans, from Vienna
Samaragd
Reutner, from Germany, alias Robert Rodney

Spies, Horst, from Biblis, alias Harry Spiers
Stein
Stephens, Freddie, from Vienna
Wolf, Gerhard Victor, from Steinau in Hesse

With a total of 221 the number of alien pioneers who applied for transfer to the Royal Artillery was slightly greater than the number who joined the RAC. However, relatively little is known about them. A reason for this may be found in the fact that so many of them were sent to India and did not therefore participate directly in the fighting in Europe.

I was the first enemy alien to have been commissioned in the gunners. That was in October 1944. Although I had been at the 123 OCTU RA in Catterick, Yorkshire, and had asked for a posting to Italy, I also was sent to India. There I was posted to 201 Indian Independent Medium Battery on the north-west frontier. At that time the headquarters and one troop of this unit were in Peshawar, the other troop at Razmak, in the hills of Waziristan, 6,000 feet up, 200 miles to the south. The eight 5.5 inch gun-howitzers of the battery were the heaviest pieces of artillery in the vast area between the Turkish–Persian border, the southern border of the Soviet Union, the Indus river and the Arab Sea. The objective of having them there was mainly to impress. When they were used it was almost always for the purpose of showing someone the might of the British Raj. The only time the guns of my troop were used operationally was during a punishment action against a Mahsud tribe, which had tried to hold the government to ransom. In a way it is a fascinating thought that, within months after my arrival and then for nearly two years more the four guns at Razmak were entrusted to me – an enemy alien! It was only at the end of 1946 that 201 Battery was withdrawn from the north-west frontier. I remained there, however, and was posted to the 8th Field Regiment, Royal Indian Artillery, at Nowshera. There I became battery captain of No.19 Battery.

The only other one of the 221 transferees to the Royal Artillery of whom it is known that he was commissioned at Catterick was Stephen Nelson, originally Netter, a native of Berlin who had attended the Grunewald Gymnasium there. He had served in 251 and 69 Companies, PC. But he, too, was promptly sent to India, to become motor transport officer of the School of Artillery at Deolali.

Several Germans and Austrians who had become gunners were commissioned after having attended the RA OCTU at Deolali near Bombay. One of them – I think he was called Adler, but, getting older, I cannot be sure – later became adjutant of the 28th Mountain Regiment of the Indian Artillery. This unit had been in action at the battles of Kohima and Imphal in the Burma campaign, after which it was moved to the north-west frontier. As the commanding officer of the regiment was then the senior gunner in the Waziristan District he was also the commandant, Royal Artillery, and thus my direct superior.

To my certain knowledge there were several others who were commissioned from the RA OCTU in Deolali. However, only one of them, Eric A. Kirby, whose original name had been Erich Alfons Klappholz, has been so kind as to give me his name and details of his service.

The fact that so many, in fact probably all of us, who had commissions in the Royal Artillery, eventually ended up in India and that no case is known of any enemy alien gunner officer being employed in the European theatre of war, leads me to the assumption that this was no accident. The decision to which unit within a regiment an officer would be posted was the prerogative of the colonel of the regiment, in the RA just the same as anywhere else. In the years before war ended this was Field Marshal the Lord Milne, a very distinguished and wise, but also very cautious and conservative officer, who would have retired years earlier, had he not held this highest rank in the British army. It may be thought in character with what is known about him, that he might have said to himself something on the lines of: 'These chaps are white Europeans and deserve our full confidence in any action against the Japs, but against their own people...? I would rather not take the risk.' Had he thought so, he would not have been alone. It is no insult whatever to his memory that one believes this to have been possible. After all, he was a cautious old bird. For this there is no shadow of proof, but the fact remains – even the two of us who were commissioned at 123 OCTU at Catterick, finished up in India.

In further defence of Lord Milne it should also be explained, that in the days of the Second World War senior gunners were by no means as confident that the shells which their guns fired would really hit the intended targets, as might appear – justifiably or not – to be the case nowadays. The risk that projectiles fired from behind the lines might hit men of one's own side was never great, but also the possibility was never to be excluded. Usually when this happened there was a court of inquiry which led to some officer being accused of carelessness and reprimanded. This officer could however be sure of the sympathy of his colleagues, because they all knew that it could have happened to them just as easily. But whether this would have applied also, if the man who was careless had been an enemy alien, one may be entitled to doubt. Perhaps this was one of the considerations taken into account.

Although not an officer of any kind Ronald George Norton also arrived in India at the end of his service time. He was the elder brother of Group Captain Hans Neubroch and had volunteered for service in January 1940. He was posted to 87 Company PC, went to Le Havre and Rennes with them and was evacuated from France via St Malo. In the autumn of 1940 he was in London clearing unexploded bombs. Later, with the Royal Artillery, he was in India, Burma and Malaya. In his spare time he calculated mathematical tables, which were accepted by the School of Artillery and adopted for use in the whole of the Royal Regiment. Despite this he received no promotion and was released, still with the rank of gunner, in 1945.

The story told by H. Hoffmann is remarkable. He was born in Vienna on 27 November 1922. He was at school there until 1938. He maintains that he was accepted by the Royal Artillery in 1940 and received his initial training with this regiment at Sennybridge in Wales. He goes on to say that for a time he had been a motorcycle courier in the Royal Horse Artillery, to have been in India in 1941 and with the 144 Airborne Division in 1942. After that, he says, he was in Burma. As proof of this he has supplied me with a post-war newspaper article and photos which show him wearing the gunner badge. That all this need not be completely incredible is borne out by the experiences of Hans Neubroch and Klaus Adam, both of whom were accepted by the RAF in 1941. Nevertheless, Peter Block writes that Hoffmann had served together with him in 246 Company, PC and as Sennybridge was a training unit of the Pioneer Corps, doubts as to the timing of Hoffmann's transfer to the gunners may be justified.

Artillerymen who were not commissioned did get to other theatres of war. Ernest Morton, whom we have met as Helmut Moser of 77 Company PC, was transferred to the RA in 1943 and trained as an anti-tank gunner. In 1944 he was sent to Italy. He was posted to 81 Anti-tank Regiment. There he was on the guns and also radio operator. He was in action in Italy from Anzio to the Gothic Line, taking part in the liberation of Rome and of Florence. In 1945 his division (the 1st British Infantry Division) was sent to the Middle East to train for action in Burma. The following is his own story:

> On 1 March 1944 I found myself in Algiers waiting for the troopship to take us to Naples. While in our transit camp, which was also used for men recuperating, our party of eight former refugees was discovered and we were asked to give talks about our experiences in Germany, Austria and Hungary. We told them our story with such success that the commanding officer wanted to

keep us there. GHQ of CMF decided that they could not afford to keep us away from the front.

After a few days in Naples, one night we were awaiting our next move to Anzio. Looking from the landing barge towards Vesuvius, I was fascinated by the incredible display of gigantic flames erupting from the volcano. Little did I realize this was a happening that had not occurred on such a scale for over 1900 years.

Moving slowly from the harbour we were allowed to settle anywhere we liked on the craft. Exploring the boat was a new experience. We were now under new management, the Americans, the Fifth Army. I encountered comforts not known in Britain at that time. Delicious coffee from the latest machines, comfortable bunks and showers.

It was soon morning, and we were landing gently close on the beaches. The Anzio beachhead had been established at the end of January and now in March after heavy losses we had been sent in as replacements.

Our first surprise was the complete silence. It was difficult to believe that this was supposed to be the hottest spot apart from Cassino.

We were soon allocated to our Regiment, the 81st Anti-tank, RA, in the 1st British Infantry Division. This division had taken part in the evacuation of Dunkirk under General Alexander, had later participated in Tunisia and had led the landings at Anzio. Our battery 'BB' had been in all these actions and had suffered heavy losses. Their function had been to support the 24th Guards' Brigade. The German counter-attack had decimated the brigade and our battery. Now we were here to take their place. The adjutant who received us was horrified suddenly to find eight refugees in his unit. His first question was, were we naturalised? He was most astonished to hear that this was not the case, especially since only a few days earlier a number of his men had been taken prisoner. After this interview I joined my new unit and very soon felt completely at home. The German forces who surrounded us could see us very comfortably from the hills they occupied. The silence which I experienced in the first hours after our arrival soon changed and we were often under heavy artillery bombardment. One of my little jobs happened to be to occupy a position between the Allies and the Germans in no man's land, where we had the interesting experience of watching not only the German positions but also our own. Our observation post happened to be a ruin in which we stayed two to three days at a time armed with binoculars, radio contact and telephones, by which we communicated. It was always quite touching to watch the British sector, where one could see men moving about making tea. The German sector seemed deserted and very rarely showed any movement.

Often we were bombarded by both sides and when we moved from our hide-out we were sniped at. Our provisions were brought to us during the night. One late evening I was brought a big parcel. I was a little uneasy because there was nobody in existence who could have given me this surprise. It turned out to be two cartons of Mazzot for Pessach. In view of our position being just a couple of hundred yards from the Hermann Goering Regiment, I politely declined the present. I am not aware of what happened to it finally. As I discovered later on, it had been sent by the Jewish community in New York.

Whenever we returned to our unit, which was situated nearer the beach, we were taken to an underground cinema and shown the latest films specially flown in from Hollywood. We also had a shower and delicious cakes. When we changed our underwear and shirts we were always given brand new ones in replacement.

At the end of May everything changed when we were informed that it had been decided that we should break out from the beachhead. This happened and succeeded much faster than anticipated because the German command had decided after initial skirmishes to withdraw and leave Rome to the Allies.

We entered Rome on June the 4th...

Concerning the Allied entry into Rome, Morton sent the following account to a friend in Germany:

The guns are quiet, the peasants return to their fields and we, the soldiers in our armoured vehicles, follow the enemy, follow the war. For months we have waited for this moment and now it has come. In a few minutes we shall be in the city. As in the books we sing, for we believe that the eyes of the world are upon us. Soon we shall see the city, so we increase our speed. It is 4 June 1944. Perhaps it is the greatest day of our lives and the last, for today we shall liberate Rome.

Thousands of people around us. They laugh, applaud and throw flowers at us. I feel like an actor after a successful first performance. Friends shake my hand and invite me to come to their houses. Wine, jubilation, ear-splitting noise, sunshine and girls' smiles. This is life, life to the full, after all that time of isolation in our beachhead. It is a happening, unreal as a dream. Geoffrey was killed yesterday. He was only 18 and last week he had said, he thought he was too young to die. Was he fey? – I drink the wine and forget – Sergio asks me whether I've got any chocolate. We are hungry, he says, and you've come to help us, yes? We are greeted with clenched fists, guns are carried proudly and many have tied on red armbands. Banners ask us to give their greetings to Stalin, Roosevelt and Churchill. A car passes carrying a captured German officer. Everyone hisses and he looks very arrogant. – Everybody runs towards the Vatican. The Pope wants to bless us, the Italians, the Allies and the whole world. The beauty of St Peter's is overwhelming. In the audience chamber one of our officers calls for three cheers for His Holiness. We join in hesitantly and the Pope looks astonished. – First impressions of the city are disappointing. Perhaps one expects too much. There are historical ruins in all parts of the town. They look as if they had been put there for the tourists' entertainment. – Street urchins follow us everywhere. They sense the sympathy, which soldiers everywhere feel for children. Who can withstand the hungry glances of their big, dark eyes, without giving him some of his rations? – I take a bath in a proper bathroom and enjoy every moment. The whole irony of my experiences comes back to me time and again. As a boy in Germany I had read the novel *The Battle for Rome* and it had seemed to me the most wonderful and exciting book ever written. I had been full of the deeds of the Goths and had suffered with them in their final defeat. How odd to experience it all now in reality! Did the Goths perhaps have a Gestapo? – Sandra looks at me through a haze of tears. Her father was killed yesterday, run over by fleeing Germans. How beautiful she is! I try to make a date with her. – Mario proudly shows me his Iron Cross, which he has got from the *Luftwaffe* for his services as a pilot and asks whether maybe the Royal Air Force might employ him now? Morals in Rome? Yes, he says, after lunch maybe we have morals.

From a distance comes the sound of Scottish bagpipes, oddly out of place in these surroundings. Again we must move. I return to my regiment, the advance continues.

Morton's story continues:

moving through Italy in a Bren gun carrier we occupied one side of the river Arno, watching our Italian allies fighting the Fascists in the streets of Florence. We supplied the arms and equipment.

The Germans did their bit by blowing up most of the bridges, which were later replaced by our Bailey bridges.

Eventually we were allowed to liberate Florence and then we moved north as part of the 8th Army in the 13th British Corps.

A very unnerving operation was the reconnaissance of a market town with the name of Borgo San Lorenzo. This place had just been evacuated when we were ordered to find out if it was safe to enter. A senior officer with a sergeant and myself plus radio set off in a jeep on this mission. We drove very cautiously through the town which had not been destroyed. It was during the middle of the day with nobody in sight, a deathly stillness, no dogs or cats nor any other living creature. We went round and round, watching and listening carefully, expecting at any moment to be blown up by a booby trap or mine. Eventually we decided that everything seemed clear and I was ordered to send a message to that effect.

Within a few hours Borgo San Lorenzo became a busy place again and our headquarters for quite a few months.

We continued our advance and participated in the battle of the Gothic Line, which became the last line of defence for the Germans in Italy. Our share of this action lasted from early December 1944 until the end of January 1945. Usually I spent many days in observation posts on the top of various mountains, looking from deserted chalets and churches in the direction of the enemy. We had given up our anti-tank guns and replaced them with mortars. It became very cold with lots and lots of rain. Mud everywhere, the scenery looked gloomy because the trees and bushes, actually the whole landscape reminded one of the pictures of Flanders in the First World War. Usually we recuperated either in San Lorenzo, which had become a proper garrison town, or if enough time was available, in Florence.

For me personally this was always an exciting experience, because I had been able to make contact with the Psychological Warfare Unit stationed there. The man who was in charge of the unit was Klaus Mann, the son of Thomas Mann and author of *Mephisto*. He was always interested to see me and to hear about the effect (or non-effect) of German propaganda on our troops. We would have lunch together and I would look at the latest specimens of our leaflets (some brilliant) to be distributed over the German lines. Eventually Mann offered me a job in his office and applied for my transfer, but nothing came of it, because my activities in our battery were considered more important.

At the end of January we were told that we should move to the Middle East to be trained for new ventures ...

In fact Morton's battery left Italy in February, was amalgamated with another battery which belonged to the Argyll and Sutherland Highlanders and the lot were taken to Haifa to train for use in Burma. From Haifa Morton was able to move freely around the whole area, including Egypt to the south and Lebanon and Syria to the north, and he used this freedom to the full, hitchhiking everywhere. However, with the end of the war and the changed situation in Palestine he began to feel very uneasy. He was offered a posting to a prisoner of war camp for the SS. He declined and was demobbed in due course.

Frederick Hogan, formerly Fritz Hofstaedter, was born in Vienna on 17 January 1921. There he attended grammar school for seven years before emigrating to Britain. He volunteered for service in the army in August 1940, was posted in turn to 165, 137 and lastly 229 Companies in the pioneers. In 1943 he was transferred to the gunners, where he served with the Queen's Own Royal Glasgow Yeomanry (Qorgy), an air-portable anti-tank regiment in the 52nd Lowland Division. He was in action in Belgium, Holland and Germany, after which he continued in the 41st Intelligence Unit until his discharge in July 1946.

Ian Lowit, originally Hans Loewit, a Viennese Jew, wrote:

I joined 77 Company, Pioneer Corps, when they were in Longmarston near Stratford-on-Avon in October 1943. As far as I recall we later moved to Hereford. I was transferred from there to anti-tank training. In spite of the combatant feel of 'anti-tank' I saw little action. We were slow-moving, having a tracked heavy towing vehicle. Therefore we were left behind in advances. My troop had been decimated at Colombelles losing all four guns, but that was before I joined them or I might not be here. For a time we played at being infantry, but again we were given quiet assignments, being not trained for more.

To sum up – I did my job and was lucky. It was a cushy one assigned to me by fate. – My war was good enough, too!

To join the Royal Horse Artillery, the poshest part of the artillery, was the fate of George Jacob Rosney, previously Rosenfeld. Of course, even the RHA no longer had horses in the Second World War, but was equipped with self-propelled guns. It is only since then that they have been allowed to have a few horses again, in order to be able to look right when firing a royal salute in Hyde Park. Rosney was from Karlsruhe. His father was a veteran of the First World War, in which he had lost a leg and won the Iron Cross. He was convinced that the Nazis would leave him in peace, as a result of which he returned to Germany after having been to Britain in 1938 to make arrangements for his son's emigration. He was mistaken. Both he and his wife, Rosney's mother, ended their days in Auschwitz. At first Rosney worked in a factory. He was 19 when he was interned in 1940. He joined the pioneers from internment camp in 1940, was transferred to the REME in 1943 and got to the RHA from there. He landed in Normandy on 14 June 1944 (D+8). Eventually he got as far as Hamburg. From there he managed to ride to Theresienstadt on a motorbike in an attempt to find his parents. On the way he was stopped by Soviet troops, who locked him up, thinking he was a spy. After three days of questioning they believed his story, let him go and even gave him food and petrol. Following his return to Hamburg he was employed as an interpreter. At the time of his release he was a sergeant.

Others who are known to have served as gunners and whose details may be read in the register are:

Auerbach, W.H., alias Michael Gordon Ashley
Baer, Georg, from Munich, alias George Baer
Bass, Ernst, from Vienna, alias Ernest Elie Bass
Blau, alias Blair
Elkan, Walter, from Hamburg.
Felton, J., from Austria
Fleischmann, Kurt 13803486, alias Kenneth D. Fraser 13116161
Friedmann, Peter, alias Peter Frean
Goldwasser, A.
Groser, Dr Franz, 13804734, from Vienna, alias Frank Gregg
    13051415
Jellinek, Hans, from Austria
Keynes, from Austria
Klaar, Georg, from Vienna, alias George Claire
Ladewig, Jochen, from Hamburg, alias J. Lawrie
Landau, Norbert, from Vienna, alias Norman Landon 13053560
Ordynanz, Sigmund
Reiss, from Bratislava, alias Reisz
Rhoades
Sichrovsky, Harry, from Vienna
Sims, Alfred E.
Simonson, Alfred Georg, from Berlin, alias Alfred George Simms

Teweles, Hans, from Vienna, alias Henry Trevor
Wallich, Walter, from Berlin

Only about 80 men succeeded in joining the Royal Navy from the pioneers. Most of them were accepted in early 1944 and became wireless operators. Generally their job was to listen in on enemy radio communications. They were on ships of all kinds, wherever these might be on their normal stations. Thus they were on convoy escort duty, on coastal watch and wherever else the navy was in action. They were on cruisers, destroyers and on the little ships.

Most were given the rank of leading writer within a short time of joining, but before the end of the war almost all had risen to petty officer. To start with they met with quite a bit of prejudice, but after a relatively short while their officers realised that they were absolutely reliable and had only one object in life, to beat Hitler and his Nazis. As a result many were used in other ways than as radio operators only. However, the prejudices in the Admiralty, particularly against the Germans from the Reich, were never overcome. As a result two Austrians and one Czechoslovak were given commissions in the navy, but although several were proposed, no German from the Reich actually got that far.

One of the two Austrians was Harry George Stevens, originally Heinz Georg Steiner. He joined the Royal Naval Volunteer Reserve (RNVR) in 1944. He trained as an electrical officer, became midshipman, then sub-lieutenant on a minesweeper. Then he was transferred to a royal marine commando. Later he took part in technical and scientific investigations. In the last year of his service, from 1946 to 1947, he worked in the Admiralty. The second Austrian was Peter Sieber, who eventually rose to the rank of commander. The Czechoslovak was John Winterburgh, previously Winterberg. In spite of his passport, however, and his birth in Prague he had been to school in Vienna. He was actually a Royal Navy officer, which – for the information of those who are not terribly familiar with naval affairs – means much more than mere RNVR rank.

On joining the navy, R. Karo, a former pioneer, was given technical training in a former Butlin's Camp at Skegness (which had become HMS *Royal Arthur*). He was posted to a destroyer, HMS *Cottesmore*, and stayed with that ship till the end of hostilities. Part of the time they were fighting the E-boats in home waters and on the Antwerp run. On D-day and for months thereafter they took part in the bombardment of the Normandy coast. Later the ship was engaged in the assault on Walcheren. Karo remained in the navy until December 1945 and for the last six months was translating German documents for the Admiralty.

Another of the naval radio experts was Petty Officer Vernon.

Originally he had been Kurt Werner, from Vienna. Having been in the pioneers he was posted to a destroyer, HMS *Westminster*. For the D-day operation he was on HMS *Volunteer* and later transferred to a French destroyer, *Le Combatant*, which was doing duty in the war against the German E-boats. With this ship he took part in the Walcheren expedition, where she was torpedoed. Vernon was in the water for one night before he was picked up. He was decorated by the French with the *Croix de Guerre* in recognition, as he says, of the gallantry displayed by the British contingent.

Julius Carlebach was in the Home Fleet. His first ship was HMS *Blencathra*. His stay there was brief, however, and even before D-day he was transferred to HMS *Strule*. This was in action off the American beaches in the invasion and Carlebach made 25 crossings to ferry Americans. There he also watched the sinking of HMS *Quorn*, when his friend and comrade Russel, formerly Landsberg, went down with his ship. Later Carlebach took part in the battle of Antwerp and was on board the British ship which was the first to enter the port of Rotterdam.

Petty Officer Buchanan served in a Canadian destroyer which was in action in the Adriatic in aid of Yugoslav partisans. Subsequently his ship escorted the convoy for the invasion of the south of France. Another of the non-British volunteers who were posted to Canadian ships, Petty Officer Heaton, previously Heymann, was lost with his ship, when this went down.

Allan Jackson had come to England as a schoolboy in April 1934. He matriculated in 1936 and subsequently studied economics and languages in London. His mother, brother and two sisters remained in Germany. Until 1938 he went home during his holidays. As on his mother's side he was not Jewish he was liable for military service in Germany and, so as not to endanger his family, he reported to the German embassy in London for a medical. Found fit he was given leave to continue his studies with the proviso that he must return to Germany on mobilisation. As he did not comply with this in 1939, he was in fact a deserter from the German army from the day before war was declared. In April 1940 he joined the Pioneer Corps and in January 1944 he transferred to the Royal Navy. He served on destroyers on convoy work in the Western Approaches and took part in the Normandy landings on D-day. Later, his destroyer was the first British ship into Wilhelmshaven, to 'show the flag'. He was petty officer by the time he was discharged at the end of 1945.

One enterprising Pioneer, Sigmund Ordynanz, who, having transferred to the Royal Artillery, answered a circular asking for volunteers for the navy, was accepted and saw active service for 18 months on a landing craft in the Channel.

Hans Hartmuth Weil served on HMS Royalist in the Mediterranean. Later he was transferred to a destroyer on the Murmansk run. Before joining up in the British forces he had been in Paris as a refugee. From there he had joined the French foreign legion, concerning which he later wrote a most interesting and moving account. After the Allied occupation of North Africa he was in 338 Company PC and it was from there that he was able to transfer to the navy.

Rudy Verney had been a cocoa merchant in Hamburg before the war, when his name had been Vogel. He served in 246 and 220 Companies for three years, after which he also transferred to the navy. His first ship was HMS *Melbreak*. Rudy was on this destroyer at the Normandy landings. Then he was posted to HMS *Rutherford*, another destroyer, which took him to Murmansk and back several times. The enemy fought desperately to stop supplies getting to the Soviets and the *Rutherford* came under attack sometimes two or three times a day, altogether about 80 times. As everybody on a ship of that size had to lend a hand wherever it was necessary, Rudy had to help in the cookhouse and man the ack-ack guns, as well as decoding the admiral's orders. Being rather older than the average, he was one of the first to be released when hostilities ended.

W.A. Howard, originally A.H. Herzberg, had been in 88 Company PC from the beginning. In 1940 he was with them in France and in London during the air attacks, clearing up the mess after the bombs had fallen. In 1941 he tried to get into the RAF, but his application was turned down. A year later he tried the RAC and this time he managed to get accepted, but before his transfer came through, he saw a notice in the mess hall asking for volunteers for the Royal Navy, who had fluent German. He applied and was accepted there also. To stop the services quarrelling about him, he invented a rule that the senior service had priority and apparently managed to convince the RAC people that this was so. As a result of this, in 1943 he became a naval rating. He had a month of intensive training as an interpreter, concentrating on instant translation from German to English, and the use of secret codes, used by the enemy in combat situations. He wrote:

> I joined a Hunt class destroyer, HMS *Tanatside*, in February 1944. We were on anti-E-boat patrol in the Channel. In May 1944 I had to report to HMS *Bellona*, a light cruiser. She was commissioned at the end of 1943. Consequently she was the most up-to-date ship of her class at that time.

My brief was to intercept enemy RT [radio transmissions] at sea, mostly coded information, which I had to translate instantly and pass to the bridge. The VHF [very high frequency] receiver had a range of approximately 15 miles, hence any intelligence received was within combat strike facility and range.

HMS *Bellona* was attached to the Home Fleet at Scapa Flow and was engaged in various operations in the western Channel and off north-west France. We were allocated for the Normandy invasion as a reserve bombarding ship in the western task force – the only British ship alongside the US Navy.

The Normandy invasion, having been put back by 24 hours, was preceded by air strikes of unprecedented proportions. Naval bombardment commenced very early in the morning of 6 June and continued for several hours. The noise level was such that I could not hear any radio activity except during momentary lulls.

For the first three days we experienced only sporadic enemy activity. However on the third day enemy aircraft carried out a concerted bombing raid on our position. All hell broke loose, but *Bellona* was truly blessed and came out of it unscathed.

During the enemy attack I felt claustrophobic cooped up in the plotting office, with bombs dropping all round us. It was not until the navigator, one of our senior officers, in his heavy duffel coat and a pair of binoculars round his neck, popped his head inside and exclaimed in a very relaxed drawl: 'Don't worry, chaps. I'm here!' that we all relaxed and burst out laughing. The comment was so delightfully British.

After about ten days off Normandy beach, we joined the 10th Cruiser Squadron, Home Fleet, for the rest of the war. In July 1944 we escorted carriers for an air strike on the Tirpitz off Alton Fjord in Norway. We engaged in attacks on enemy shipping off Norway with numerous successes close inshore off the south-west coast of Norway.

I managed to intercept and pass useful information to the bridge on several occasions. After one particularly successful night I was personally thanked by the captain next morning. I was also promoted to petty officer and was recommended for a commission. However, because of my place of birth, i.e. Berlin, the admiralty turned down the captain's recommendation.

Towards the end of 1944 and early in 1945 the ship took part in the escort of convoys to Russia – destination Kola Bay – and dodged enemy U-boats and air attacks. According to Lord Haw-Haw *Bellona* was sunk by German U-boats, an announcement which my father heard on the wireless in London. He was none too pleased, but withheld the information from my mother. What actually happened was that we were pursued by a U-boat, but took evasive action. The torpedo must have missed us by inches. My father was happy to hear my voice, when I phoned him from Scapa Flow.

When hostilities ceased Howard was sent to Chatham and finally released in November 1945. Others who are known to have served in the navy were Werner Lampel from Leipzig, Charles Brook from somewhere in Germany, and Sydney Graham formerly Gumpricht.

Dr Peter E. Trier, born at Darmstadt on 12 September 1919, comes from a Jewish family, six generations of which were born and bred, and had died in that city. During his childhood holidays in the nearby town of Heppenheim he stayed with the chief of the electricity generating station there. This, he says, awakened his interest in electro-technology. He arrived in Britain in 1935, continued his schooling and received an engineering degree from Cambridge in 1941. From there he went directly to the Admiralty, where he remained until 1950. He was one of the 'boffins' in the Royal Naval Scientific Service. In his later career he became Pro-Chancellor of Brunel University and from 1982 to 1984 was scientific adviser of the House of Lords.

The later professor of radio-biology at the Sutton Institute for Cancer Research, Peter Alexander, should also be mentioned here. He was born on 27 January 1922 in Munich, the son of a Jewish father and a Protestant mother. He emigrated from Germany in 1933 and in the same year joined London University School. During the war he, too, was research assistant at the Admiralty.

Paul Husserl, a Viennese, served on HMS *Nancy* and HMS *Nile*. Previously he had been in Egypt and in Palestine and had been one of those who were sent to Australia on HMT Dunera.

According to Muchitsch there exists a list of Austrian soldiers who volunteered for service in Tito's army in Yugoslavia. Amongst these are said to have been 'seven drivers [?] and helmsmen of the British mine-sweeping flotilla stationed in Alexandria'. Some of them also are said to have been pioneers recruited in North Africa.

Almost all those who had expressed the wish to be transferred to the RAF from the pioneers had to prove that they had no near relatives living in the territories occupied by the enemy, so that the number of those who eventually were transferred was relatively small. Only some 25 or thereabouts actually managed to change their khaki denims for the light blue uniform of the RAF. They were joined by an unknown number of direct entries at a later stage. Nevertheless quite a few names are known and where there is additional information concerning these people this, too, is generally of some interest.

Hans Neubroch's story is quite remarkable. His father, an Austrian, is said to have been managing director of BMW at Eisenach in Thuringia. Neubroch attended elementary school there, after which, somehow, he got to England via Karlsbad and Vienna. In May 1941 he volunteered for service in the RAF. Although the only document in his possession with which he could prove his identity was a German passport complete with swastika, this was accepted by the recruiting officer. Concerning this he wrote: 'Some 40 years later, an old friend who in the meantime had become Director of RAF Security, told me that it was simply impossible for someone not born of British parents to have had the sort of career which I enjoyed ... So, it must all have been an administrative error'. It may, however, be permitted to mention that there is another story concerning this incident. According to this Neubroch was staying with a friend whose father was an air marshal. To him Neubroch revealed his desire to join the RAF, upon which a recruiting officer, a flight sergeant, was called and in the air marshal's all-sanctioning presence Neubroch was sworn in. If indeed this story were to be true, it would offer a perfectly credible explanation for such an 'administrative error'. Neubroch completed his training in Canada, where he remained until late in 1944. After this he saw action as navigator of a Mosquito bomber in north-western Europe. He remained in the RAF as a professional officer after the war, studied at the RAF Staff College and in due course became commanding officer of a squadron, station commander of an airfield in Cyprus, strategic planner in the London Air Ministry and finally adviser to the UNO Armaments Control Commission in Vienna. He left with the rank of group captain, which, even though well after the end of the war, makes him the highest ranking of all the Germans and Austrians who served with the British Forces. He was also awarded the OBE for his services.

Richard Levente, another Austrian who became an RAF officer by profession, was born in 1912. An engineering apprentice in Vienna, he became an aircraft mechanic, then an engineering officer. He made it to wing commander, was a member of the Royal Aeronautical Society and an OBE.

The story told by Klaus Adam, the later production designer of the James Bond films, of how he got into the RAF, is almost more surprising than Neubroch's. He, a Berliner, who had been at St Paul's School OTC and had studied architecture in London, says that he joined up 1940, was posted to 3 PCTC where he became a corporal, that he applied through the normal channels to join the RAF in April 1941 and was accepted. He also maintains that nobody pulled any strings! He, too, went to Canada for some of his training. In May 1942 he was back in Scotland. Then he was posted to 609 Fighter Squadron as a pilot. Later this unit was equipped with rocket firing Typhoons. In Normandy they flew in support of the Canadians, especially at the battle of the Falaise gap. Adam became known as 'Heinie, the tank buster'. Later, in Germany he was at Wunsdorf air base. There he was in charge of some 10,000 prisoners of war reconstructing the base to British requirements. He was demobilised late in 1946 as flight lieutenant. For five years afterwards he was in the RAFVR.

Flight Lieutenant Adler was from Bohemia. His father had been a leading social democrat journalist in Prague. He gained the Distinguished Flying Cross.

Bentwich wrote that Flying Officer Ziegler had been one of the scientists who had been dismissed from their academic positions in Germany following the Nazis' assumption of power. The British Academic Assistance Council was able to procure a position for him at an equivalent British institution. He served with the pioneers and was able to get a transfer to the RAF in 1943. He was killed in action.

Alfred Lammer from Zell-am-See in Austria had studied at Munich and Innsbruck. Having been an active member of a political strong-arm group in Austria – which one it was is not certain – he was able to secure a job at the Austrian Tourist Office in London in 1934. There he remained until the *Anschluss*. By 1939, having been in England the requisite five years, he was one of the last to be naturalised. As a result he was accepted by the RAF. He was observer in a fighter squadron in North Africa. He shot down five enemy planes, for which he received the Distinguished Flying Cross and bar, and became a squadron leader.

The same rank was reached by Michael Salzer, a former London correspondent of the *Wiener Journal*, one of the leading Vienna newspapers. After he had joined the RAF as a mechanic, his past occupation became known. He was appointed an official war correspondent and reported on the war from North Africa, Pantellaria, Italy and Yugoslavia. Later he was in India and Burma. At the end he reached Germany via Denmark and was one of the reporters at the Nuremberg Trials.

The Warburgs, the well-known Hamburg banking family, also appear to have been represented in the RAF. Edmund P. Kohn-Speyer, a Warburg descendant, is said to have been in RAF intelligence and, at some stage, 'to have been employed in the Control Commission for Germany, drafting legislation for use there after the war'.

The final rank of squadron leader is known to have been reached by

Silverman, previously Silbermann, and by Schlossberg. Amongst those who ended their service as flight lieutenants were Lichte, Deventer, Newman, formerly Neumann, and Robertson. Newman is known to have been an Austrian. Schlossberg is said to have fought in the Spanish civil war and Robertson to have been an interpreter for Russian.

Sascha and Peter Manierka were from Leipzig. Although neither could speak a word of Polish, they were Polish nationals, having had a Polish father. Sascha had been born on 1 October 1920, Peter in 1923. The family had lived in the centre of Leipzig, in the immediate neighbourhood of the *Gewandhaus*, the famous concert hall. The RAF accepted them on the basis that they were neither enemy aliens, nor could they serve with the Poles, because they could not communicate with them. Both wanted to become pilots. During training Sascha crashed a Tiger Moth, after which the RAF did not want him as a pilot any more and reclassified him as a bomb aimer. As such he was posted to Bomber Command and served with 428 and 405 Canadian Squadrons. Having flown altogether 56 missions, including 45 as pathfinder and ten in daylight and after surviving two belly landings he was given the Distinguished Flying Medal and posted to the British Bombing Survey Unit. After that and before his release from the service he still acted as technical interpreter in Paris and various locations in Germany and Austria. His brother Peter Manierka became a fighter pilot, flying Typhoons. After the war he was transferred to a Polish squadron, but as he was still completely unable to understand anything that was said to him there, he was returned to the RAF rapidly. He lives in Canada. Others in the RAF were:

Abrahamsohn, Kurt, from Stettin, alias Ken Ambrose
Bluh, A., 775983, from Austria
Bondi, Fritz, 775320, from Austria
Cahn, Gunther, from Dusseldorf
Deutsch, Arthur, 775951, from Austria
Drechsler, Fritz, 775211, from Austria
Dresner, Rolf Hermann, 1798068, from Leipzig
Eisenfeld, Leo
Fischhof, Georg, 769461, from Vienna
Fischhof, Kurt Peter, from Vienna
Frankfurt, Eduard, 775826, from Austria
Gaertner, alias H. Gardner
Goldberg, Sidney
Gruder, Erwin, 775930, from Austria
Gruener, Gerhard, 775446, from Austria

Heilig, G., from Vienna
Katz
Katz, Manfred, 75833, from Austria
Kraus
Lauber, S., 771738, from Austria
Lifschitz, T., 775995, from Austria
Lowy, Otto, from Prague
Mautner, Karl, 77426, from Austria
Meysels, Lucian, 769526, from Vienna
Moser, C.A.
Neumann, Hans Georg, 1882507, from Vienna, alias George
    Newman
Reismann, K., 774485, from Austria, alias Joseph Raanan
Reitzner, Almar, from Czechoslovakia
Rezek, G., 775843, from Austria
Riesenfeld (Reisenfeld?), from Austria, alias Ernst Rivin
Robinsohn, Rudolph, 774906, from Austria
Rosenthal, Philip
Rubin, David, 775832, from Austria
Rubner, Wenzel, from Czechoslovakia
Schueller, Peter, 774660, from Austria
Schwarz, Erich, 774194
Seinfeld, Hugo, 769412, from Austria
Semenowsky, Konstantin, 775575, from Austria
Spiegel, Peter, from Austria
Starer, Robert, 775943, from Austria
Sternfeld, Albert, 775953, from Vienna
Szper, Marcello, 774635, from Austria
Taglicht, Oswald, 775439, from Austria
Wieselmann
Wilpred, David, from Nuremberg, alias David J. Morrison-Wilpred

An airman, who was in British service only during the last months of the war was Hans Amoser from Linz in Upper Austria. At the time of the *Anschluss* he had been in the Austrian air force. Subsequently this was incorporated into the *Luftwaffe*. He continued his service there, but in 1943 he was court-martialled for disobedience to orders and sentenced to eight months' detention. He deserted and fled to Italy. In Verona he was caught by the Germans, court-martialled for a second time and sentenced to death. He shared the death cell with a British officer, Lieutenant John Morris, and together with him he broke out of prison again. The escape was successful and they managed to reach the British lines. After this Amoser joined the special services for the rest of the war. In August 1945 he was released to Austria having previously been under treatment in the British Military Hospital at Castelnuovo Monti.

Lewis Haig, MM, originally Louis Hagen, became a pilot without serving in the RAF, for he flew gliders. Born on 30 May 1916 as son of the chief general manager of the Berlin Bank Hagen & Co., he served with the pioneers of 165 Company, after which he was transferred in quick succession first to the REME, then to the RAOC and from there to the gunners, where he was in the Artillery Assault Corps, a unit which was equipped with tanks that carried explosives to blow up bridges and such like. Then he was trained as a glider pilot. In this capacity he took part in the battle of Arnhem. He got his Military Medal for bravery in the field during that action. Before the end of hostilities he was sent to South East Asia as a war correspondent. In Calcutta he wrote for a paper published by South-East Asia Command and the *Phoenix* magazine. At the same time he wrote a book which was published under the title *Arnhem Lift*. It was well received. He wrote another book concerning his experiences in India, called *Indian Route March*. In this he thought he detected similarities between the mental state of those who called for 'Quit India' and those who had called '*Juda verrecke*' (death to the Jews) in Germany a few years earlier. *Arnhem Lift* was illustrated by George V. De Liss, previously Delitz, who had also been a sergeant glider pilot and a friend of Hagen at Arnhem. An Austrian, nicknamed 'Pepi', he was with the 6th Airborne Division.

Headquarter staffs also were not without their share of enemy aliens. Werner Emanuel Abrahams hails from Duisburg. He was interned on the Isle of Man in 1940. From there he volunteered for the pioneers and got to 248 Company in Catterick. Three years later he was commissioned and should have gone to Normandy. During manoeuvres shortly before the invasion, however, he broke a leg. As a result he was not sent to France, but was put on board ship bound for India. Once there he was appointed staff captain at GHQ India in Delhi.

Regrettably it has to said that the late Robert Maxwell was also a member of this group, despite the fact that throughout his life he had tried to deny it. He was born Jan Ludvik Hoch in what was known as the Carpatho-Ukraine, then a part of Czechoslovakia. He, too, volunteered for service with the pioneers and served in 88 and 251 Companies. The branch of the service to which he was later transferred is not known, but he was commissioned and distinguished himself by his bravery. He was awarded the Military Cross, which he received from Field Marshal Montgomery personally. It would appear that he became a staff officer at an early stage. He is said to have told a story that his general had suggested to him that as an officer in His Majesty's service he could not possibly be called Jan Hoch and would he kindly change his name. Without doubt this is another way of saying that in 1943 he changed his name under the same Army Order as everybody else. It has been said that after the end of hostilities he was involved in secret missions and perhaps not only in the British interest, but there is no evidence to this effect. However, the origin of some of the monies he was able to use may well have been doubtful. His later career as head of Pergamon Press, as Labour MP for Buckingham and as chief executive and chairman of the *Daily Mirror* group, which made him one of the most influential people in Britain, is too well known for it to be enlarged on here. Macmillan spoke of his way of doing business as the 'the ugly face of capitalism'. In the end he misappropriated several hundred million pounds from the pension funds of his employees, before he disappeared from his yacht in the middle of the Mediterranean. His body was found at sea. It is generally assumed that he committed suicide.

These are just a few stories, which have become known almost accidentally.

9

The Special Services

Special operations were no part of the secret service. Nevertheless, some of the activities performed by members of special operations were not in a completely different class. Usually they were actions behind the enemy lines. They were not always covered by the conventions of the Geneva Declaration. Sometimes their object was reconnaissance, sometimes it was sabotage and sometimes it was the fomenting or support of subversive activities. Sometimes those involved wore uniform and sometimes they did not. Germans and Austrians were involved in these activities in large numbers.

There were two principal centres of activity from which special operations were controlled, the SOM in respect of the Mediterranean area and the SOE concerned with Europe. Although everything concerning both these organisations was strictly secret then and some of it still is, many a London taxi driver knew very well, even at the height of the war, that the SOE headquarters were in the Baker Street head office of Marks & Spencer. It says much for the discretion which was exercised by everybody in those days that this information did not become known generally. Also the fact that the SOE, doubtless in a fit of carelessness, got most of its agents commissioned in the Royal Fusiliers did not remain a complete secret. The real fusiliers, the ones who were intent on maintaining the traditions of the regiment, were by no means enamoured of the fact that they were expected to welcome a large number of very doubtful characters in their ranks, and that their public image was in the hands of people over whom they could exercise no control. They protested loudly and who could blame them?

The man who organised all the foreigners in the SOE was a British officer who remains anonymous, but who was generally known as 'Father Christmas'. In the years 1940–42 this gentleman had been able to select his men from over a thousand pioneers, all of whom had volunteered for specially dangerous assignments. He saw and spoke to each one of them and in the course of time he selected about 200. In 1943, when some of the alien companies of the Pioneer Corps were disbanded or converted to other uses, another 116 were added to his crew, so that the total number of Germans and Austrians in special operations would appear to have been over 300. This is not including later additions who, however, seem to have been recruited largely from amongst deserters of the *Wehrmacht* and 'turned' prisoners of war.

In some cases these men are described as 'Twelve Force'. This, however, is no official title, but is the result of the fact that several training units and other installations connected with special operations had the number 12 in their designations.

The training which the selected men received was thorough, hard and sometimes exceedingly unpleasant. Not only did they have to do everything which was normal training for the commandos and suchlike, they were also given a taste of what might happen to them if ever they should be careless enough to let the Gestapo lay hands on them. One particular case of such training is documented. A group of four men were given the task of carrying out sabotage in Birmingham. They were given everything that was necessary for this, tools, coded orders and so on. They were told that the object was to test the efficiency of the police. Without the knowledge of the men, however, the police for their part were warned and given information, which enabled them to pick up the 'saboteurs' without a great deal of difficulty. What they were not told was that it was an SOE exercise and that the men, though of German origin, were British soldiers. The result was that the SOE men were treated in the way the police would have treated any German saboteurs, who might have fallen into their hands, that is, not very kindly. It took several days before anyone bothered to inform the Birmingham Constabulary of the true state of affairs and several more before the bobbies believed it. The intervening period was held to be good experience for the SOE men.

In view of the fact that special operations were surrounded by a cloud of secrecy it is obvious that by no means everything that was done by these organisations can be known. Also it is possible that some of the stories told in this chapter were the result of actions by people who had no connection with the official special operations organisation.

For many of those involved in such operations it was absolutely essential that nobody other than themselves and others directly involved should know about what they were doing. Their lives depended on absolute secrecy then, and for all they know, this may still apply now. What holds good for them also holds good for their colleagues, whom they had to trust and who had to trust them. Very many, therefore, are not prepared to say anything at all about their adventures, and those who are will not involve their comrades even today, 50 years and more after the event.

In view of the passage of time, however, I do not take the view that I am under an equal obligation. I am under no obligation to maintain secrecy, except as far as is necessary to safeguard the security of living persons. I feel that I may also try to reconstruct past events by connecting one story with another in order to give a better picture of what went on. Moreover I hold that, after all, the motives of all involved were most honourable and that their efforts should be remembered, their memory honoured.

It should also be said that in some cases the names of persons involved in some of the actions are not known. It is known what they did, but not what they were called. But this is quite a lot compared to the many about whom nothing is known, although they, too, went out and did what they had been trained for and commanded to do.

A further peculiarity of the special services organisation must be mentioned. Unless they were commissioned already at the time of their transfer to special services, the members of SOE and SOM did not hold commissions until they went into action. Having completed their training they were treated with respect and enjoyed many privileges, which are normally accorded to commissioned officers only. But if for any reason they were returned to their original units they went as other ranks and, where they had been NCOs, they resumed their original ranks only if they were lucky. When going into action, however, they went in officer's uniform with proper badges of rank. This ensured that were treated as officers if captured. When they came back they remained officers. This practice also meant that in some cases at least they could virtually choose their own ranks. In the case of the Zeltweg party, of whom more below, the participants elected their own leader, which resulted in Bryant wearing a lieutenant colonel's badges of rank, whilst all the others went in as lieutenants.

A story by Ralph Wand, which has been published in Vienna, gives a picture of how things were done in the special services. Actually Wand was in the US forces, but the unit with which he served eventually was a joint British–US organisation, so it may be held to apply equally to the way things were done in Britain. According to him he had not finished his normal army training when he was posted to a unit which he had not heard of previously. On arrival there he was interviewed by a senior officer and a civilian, quite informally, and asked about his past in Europe. At the same time, he thought his knowledge of languages and of geography might have been tested. Then he was asked whether he might be prepared to join a new type of intelligence service. He was told that entry was voluntary, but that it might be quite dangerous. At the end of the interview he signed a document that he was prepared to accept such a transfer. After this the atmosphere changed immediately. He was treated quite differently. He was ordered to go to Washington, where he was told to report to a Major Arthur Goldberg. On arrival he was led into a waiting room where he was most astonished to meet an old acquaintance from Vienna, Heinz Soffner.

> I greeted him enthusiastically, 'Hallo, Heinz!' But he turned on me furiously and hissed, 'Don't you know where you are? You don't know me, you've never heard of me and you've never seen me before.' Of course, I had no idea about secrecy and was very astonished...
>
> That evening I phoned my wife in New York and she told me that the FBI had been and had asked questions about me and my family from everybody in the block from the porter to the newest tenant ...

It was only then that he discovered that he had been posted to the Office of Strategic Services. Although he remained a soldier he was issued with civilian clothes. Nevertheless he had to undergo a further six-week period of training, which seems to have been very similar to what the commandos had to do. He wrote: 'This training was very hard. Fortunately I had always done a lot of sport, skiing, mountaineering and suchlike, so that I was in reasonable condition, but it was gruesome'.

He was sent to London and posted to the BACH unit. The commander of this outfit was a member of the scientific staff of an American trade union, who held the rank of private first class (equivalent to lance corporal). His deputy was Corporal Henry Sutton, which was the cover name for the Heinz Soffner mentioned above, and the No. 3 was Wand. They were authorised to draw on personnel from everywhere, because their first job was to build up the unit to a strength of 40 men. The people who eventually joined them were all very different and came from different countries, and between them all were fluent in 18 different languages.

The BACH unit was used to train people 'as liaison officers, organisers or leaders in underground organisations in countries under Nazi occupation. They were sent to France, Belgium, Holland, Yugoslavia, Germany and Austria'. The trainees came from prisoner of war and internment camps as well as from amongst the many political refugees who at that time lived in Britain. 'The selected candidates were given a new identity... We made up a cover story for them, they got new names and a completely new life history...new parents and a new family. As some were supposed to go as foreign workers we had to re-educate, inform and equip them according to that also'. As far as possible the cover story had to be supported by authentic documents, which would stand up to official inspection even when suspicion had been roused. Particularly if the agent were arrested his story had to be sound, his family must have been real people and his address had to be a place which really existed: 'let us say he was supposed to be from Mainz, Joseph Schmidt from Mainz. We had to give him a real Mainz address, but the house must not be there any more...So we took the addresses of houses which had been bombed and the names of families which had been wiped out...'. Then the agents were given money and encoding equipment and taken into enemy territory. That was Wand's job. At the end of the war Wand himself reached Denmark and played a part in the hand-over to the Allies.

A German deserter, who may well have been recruited by the BACH unit, was dropped into Germany in the autumn of 1944. His mission came to an early end, because he was caught by the Gestapo. His cover story appears to have held, however. He was not treated as a spy or as a saboteur, but was sent to a concentration camp; which one is unknown. There he is supposed to have had some influence on the camp commander, whom he is said to have caused to improve the conditions for the inmates. Unfortunately no details are known, but the story is well supported.

A really odd story is taken from records in the *Dokumentationsarchiv des österreichischen Widerstands* in Vienna. Richard Oppenheim, Austrian, born on 20 August 1903, had emigrated to Palestine before the war began. There he joined the British army on 15 November 1940. He was released from the service on 30 April 1946. He served in Africa and his conduct whilst serving was very good. These details are taken from a British Confirmation of Period of Service document contained in a file at the archives of the Austrian Resistance in Vienna relating to him. The same file contains an order by the investigating judge of the people's court for Austria, dated 26 November 1941, releasing him from prison where he had been held under suspicion of espionage. There is no indication in the file how all this might fit together.

The next two stories originate from the same archive. Paul Poemerl, born 30 October 1923 in Vienna, was admitted as a medical student at the university of his native city before he reached 18. He was called up for service in the *Wehrmacht* in 1941 and taken prisoner by the British in May 1943. After a period of imprisonment he appears to have decided to throw in his lot with his captors and joined the Intelligence Corps of the British army. There he was a wireless operator with the rank of sergeant. In May 1944 he parachuted into Carinthia in the neighbourhood of Klagenfurt. In July he was arrested by the SS. Concerning the next six months no information is available, but on 28 January 1945 he was taken to Gestapo headquarters on the Morzinplatz in Vienna, where pressure was put on him to act as a counter-espionage agent. He refused. From 1 to 23 February 1945 he was held at Mauthausen concentration camp. According to his own report he was then returned to Vienna, kept under lock and key in the Rossauer Laende barracks, and freed by the Russians during the battle of Vienna. Another report in the same file states that he was liberated by the Americans from Dachau concentration camp.

Another Viennese was Hans Prager, who, as far as I know, may still live in Vienna. He was a parachutist and not quite 20 years old when he was dropped somewhere into Austria on 17 February 1945. Nothing is known about his instructions. He was arrested by the Gestapo on the day after his arrival. He spent the time between then and May of that year in various Gestapo cells and in Mauthausen concentration camp. Immediately after being liberated he was released from the service because of a nervous disorder. In August 1945 he was a guest of the British army at Klagenfurt, where clearly an attempt was made to compensate him for some of what he had gone through just previously. His excellent conduct and his loyalty to the Allied cause were certified by F.W. Barber, at a later stage officer in charge of the British secret services in Austria.

The following story has not been confirmed in detail, but could well be true, at least in outline. Its hero is Fritz Becker, a native of the Rhineland. He was born 1921 or 1922. The only other thing that is known about his background is that his parents are said to have been deported to and murdered in Poland, which was no unusual fate in those days. It is quite certain that he was in the SOE and that his cover name was Frederick Benson.

He is said to have parachuted into enemy-held territory altogether three times, always wearing SS uniform. His trick was to pretend to have toothache and visit a dentist in a military camp, so that he could spend a night there. He came back twice. The third time he parachuted into Polish territory, possibly near the city of Pinsk or maybe near Warsaw. On this occasion he is supposed to have led Polish partisans, also wearing German uniform, in an attempt to free an important resistance leader who had been captured by the Germans. In this action he is said to have been killed. After the war he was awarded the King's Commendation for Brave Conduct posthumously. His papers were destroyed, why is not known.

Fritz Becker cannot be the same person as Robert Becker, who has been mentioned by Stephen Dale (see below). Of Robert Baker, alias R.P. Baker-Byrne and nicknamed Butch, it is also reported that he parachuted into enemy territory and he is said to have done so twice. But his first jump appears to have been carried out at the end of November 1944, by which time Poland was largely in Russian hands already and, whilst it is fairly immaterial whether the story about a man of this kind tells of two or three jumps, it is really only the original surname of the two men which is the same.

In 1944 a group of men were sent on a journey, which led them via Gibraltar and Algiers to Bari in Italy, where in a nearby place called Monopoli the SOE had established a headquarters. There they were directly behind the advancing Allied armies in Italy, but also in a convenient position to take a hand in Yugoslavia, Albania and Greece. However, despite the chances offered by the geographical position of the headquarters, they were not used as had, clearly, been envisaged. This led to a not inconsiderable part of the group either not being used operationally at all or being used at a very late stage of the war.

Nevertheless some of the men from Bari did undertake an operation into the Tramontina Valley in the neighbourhood of Udine. Towards the end of the war some of these played a part in an operation to save a number of Americans who had got themselves into trouble in the hinterland of Trieste. Their main job, however, was to carry out sabotage and to support local partisans. A party which jumped into the Tramontina valley on 13 August 1944 was under the command of Otto Karminski, alias Simon, nicknamed Putzi. Like so many other SOE men, he was officially a member of the Royal Fusiliers.

A man who was dropped into the same area at a later stage became well known as Stephen Dale in his later years. However, in the course of his adventurous earlier life he had so many names that he called his autobiography *Spanglet, or by any other name*. Spanglet, indeed, was the name by which his birth was registered. This was in Berlin, where he was born on 17 February 1917. As he had dark hair and was of generally rather sinister appearance, his friends nicknamed him 'the *Zigeunerbaron*' (the Gipsy Baron). This was duly shortened to 'Ziba'. Stephen Dale he became in 1943, but as the SOE insisted that he had to have a different name whilst serving in that organisation, he became Stephen Turner for as long as he with them. All these names refer to the same man, however.

In Berlin he was a pupil of three different schools in short succession. The frequent changes of school suggest that he might have been an intelligent pupil who got himself into frequent trouble on account of high spirits or similar pranks. In 1934, at the age of 17, he was arrested for activities hostile to the Nazi regime and kept under lock and key for some time. After his release he signed on with a German freighter and went to sea. He stuck to this until in 1938 he was again arrested and this time sent to Sachsenhausen concentration camp. Released in early 1939 he got himself to England as quickly as possible, together with his sister. His parents were later deported to Poland. He joined the Pioneer Corps on 2 January 1942 and was posted to 87 Company. During his time there he again got himself into trouble. He was sentenced to two weeks detention for disobedience to orders. Despite this the SOE took him, when he volunteered. They sent him on one of the parachute courses in Ringway. Then he was sent to Monopoli.

On 13 October 1944 he was supposed to drop into the Tramontina valley by parachute. As the result of a navigational error, however, he did not come down there, but in the valley of the river Butt between Tolmezzo and the Ploecken Pass. He was taken prisoner by Italian fascist forces and taken first to Tolmezzo, then to Udine and finally to Trieste. There he spent some time in the death cell of the Coroneo jail. In the end, however, it was decided that he should not be shot, but that he should be treated as an ordinary prisoner of war. He was handed over to the Germans, who sent him first to the officers' camp at Kaisersteinbruch in eastern Austria and eventually to Oflag 79 at Brunswick. From there he was liberated by advancing US troops on 12 April 1945. Before his release from the service and after the end of hostilities he still had some controlling function in the German railways based on Bielefeld.

Peter Priestley, originally Egon Lindenbaum, came from somewhere in Germany. Apparently he was a member of the same group as Dale, for he, too, parachuted into action on 12 October 1944. The story goes that he jumped directly into an enemy camp, where, of course, he was taken prisoner immediately. He, too, was sentenced to death by the Italians, but survived in the death cell of the Coroneo. He was liberated from there in April 1945. In his later life he is said to have suffered from severe depression, which eventually led to his suicide.

Erhard Wolf Wilhelm Saar also was a man of many names. His SOE name was E. (presumably Edward) Cheney. In his later life he was known as Edward Lees and the Italians of the Tramontina valley knew him as 'Teddy *il dinamitardo*'. He came from Stettin, where he had been born on 12 June 1921. Having had a son from a first wife, his father, a communist, had married again and Erhard was a son of this second marriage. The family moved to Berlin when he was still a child. Some time before the war he was sent to Britain and was taken in by a Jewish family in Manchester. From there he volunteered for service in the army. He was posted first to 220 Company, Pioneer Corps, and then to 88 Company. In 1943 he was transferred to the SOE.

He jumped into the Tramontina valley, probably on 13 August 1944. Unlike many of his colleagues he escaped capture and established himself with a group of partisans, some of whom are even known. During a visit to Udine in the course of an official town twinning in 1964, Lees was welcomed by Don Ascanio de Luca, Candido Grassi, Manlio Cencig and Faustino Barbina, his former colleagues. As his nickname implied his task had been the sabotage of bridges and transports, but in the last stages of the war he also was involved with the stranded Americans in the Trieste hinterland already mentioned. Later on he managed to get back to the Allied lines by boat from Trieste. After all these adventures he was posted to a 'cushy job' as interpreter in a prisoner of war camp at Bridgend in Wales, where he was amazed to find his father amongst the prisoners.

Noe Czupper changed his name to Alan A.R. Grant, but when he was in the SOE he was known as A. McCabe. On 13 August 1944 he appears to have parachuted into the Tramontina valley, although some will have it that he actually jumped into Yugoslav territory where he may have assisted the partisans.

As the war was drawing to its close a group of six men was sent to Styria. Their primary objective was sabotage, but they were also told that the airfield at Zeltweg might be very useful as a supply base for British troops in Austria, if it could be preserved from destruction. If they could do something in that direction, they would be doing a very good job for the British in the long run. At the time they were dropped into the area where they were supposed to operate, this was still many miles behind the lines and at least outwardly the Nazi regime there showed no signs of breaking up. Despite this they were successful. The group consisted of Germans and Austrians only. Their leader was a Viennese lawyer, Dr Georg Braeuer, who had chosen to be called George Bryant. For the jump he wore the insignia of a lieutenant colonel on his shoulder straps. With him were the Lieutenants Warner, Kelly, Rhodes, Stevens and Freud. Bryant had been a lawyer in pre-war Vienna. In Britain he had been a member of the Free Austria Movement. In the army he was in 88 Company PC. Having transferred to SOE, he served in North Africa and Italy. Frederick Michael Warner had been born Manfred Werner in Hamburg on 6 December 1919. He has written an autobiographical report, 'Don't you know there is a war on? A very personal account', on the earlier part of his life, which is why more is known about him than anyone else in the group. Having gone to a technical school in his home town he was apprenticed to a corn merchant in 1936. He worked there till shortly before the war, then went to Britain. He joined the pioneers in January 1940, was posted to 88 Company and went to France with that unit. He was with them at Harfleur, when the men of the 88th did not allow themselves to be disarmed in an orderly fashion, but threw their rifles to the ground. Frank Kelly had been born Franz Koenig, somewhere in Germany. Like Warner, Eric Rhodes came from Hamburg. He had originally been Erich Rohde. Harry Stevens had previously been Hans Schweiger and came from Vienna. He had been a pioneer before he joined the SOE. Anton Freud is Sigmund Freud's grandson.

The following account of the action is based on Muchitsch's report in *Mit Spaten, Waffen und Worten*, except for the details of Warner's adventures. These are taken from his own very detailed and descriptive report.

> The whole group assembled at Rossignano. After a good dinner on the evening of 24 April 1945 they were entrusted to the crew of an American Liberator. After a four-hour flight across the front lines and over the peaks of the Alps they parachuted into the valley of the river Mur in two groups of three at 2am the following morning. Whilst the first group apparently came down more or less where they should have done and were able to remain together, the second group were allowed to jump from too great a height and therefore got badly dispersed. One man from the second group did find his way to the members of the first group and joined up with them. The other two were left on their own. They were Warner and Freud and we shall come back to them later.
>
> The crew of the aircraft had been instructed to drop the group's arms and equipment into the dropping zone on a third run, but made a complete hash of this rather important operation and dropped everything right into the centre of the village of Niederwoelz, where the inhabitants did not really know what to do with all the explosives and other dangerous stores, with which the group should have carried out sabotage behind the enemy lines. In the event everything finished up in the hands of the Gestapo.
>
> Being now completely unable to carry out their primary task, the main group of four, who had remained together, decided to see what they could do about the airport at Zeltweg. Having come down near Niederwoelz, they marched across the mountains to the village of Pusterwald, taking care not to be seen, as there were SS troops in the neighbourhood, whom they had no wish to encounter. Having

arrived there they made contact with a number of local people, who had been named as reliable anti-Nazis by Austrian prisoners taken in Italy. When they heard of the capitulation of the German army group under the command of General Vietinghoff in Italy they felt that the time was ripe to appear in public and marched into the village openly. They received an enthusiastic welcome from the village folk. As the telephone service was working normally, Bryant was able to call the *Wehrmacht* headquarters at Judenburg and demand that a car should be placed at their disposal. Next day the car duly arrived with two German officers and an escort. They informed Bryant that the area around Judenburg was not under Vietinghoff's command, but under that of General Rendulic, who at that time had not yet capitulated. As the Germans were in the majority Bryant and his group had to comply with an invitation to accompany them to Thalheim castle, where they had not really wanted to go. However, during the trip it became obvious that the German officers considered the war to be over and were prepared to help the British. The upshot was that still on the same day Bryant was taken to Altaussee for a conference with a Dr Werner, formerly a senior member of the Austrian Social Democratic Party, who was trying to form a free Austrian government of the political centre. On the following day he was taken to Klagenfurt to discuss the surrender of General Loehr's Army Group South-East with one of his officers.

On 7 May the commanding officer of the *Luftwaffe* at Zeltweg declared his readiness to surrender the airport to the British. The actual hand-over took place the following day. In the meantime Bryant drove over to Wolfsberg on the Styrian–Carinthian border, to make contact with a group of air force officers, who had been dropped, also by parachute, to prepare for the evacuation of British prisoners of war in the area. On 10 May, however, Bryant had to hand over control of the Zeltweg airport to the Soviets, who had arrived whilst he was away. As a preliminary measure an agreement between the Allies had allocated all territory north of the river Mur to them. The river having become the line of demarcation, the airport, being north of it, was in territory temporarily to be occupied by the Soviets. Bryant therefore decided to withdraw across the river...

Anton Freud had come down near the village of Oberzeiring. Being independent and also unable to do anything else, he is said to have made an attempt to occupy Zeltweg airport on his own, before the main group decided to do so. He asked the burgo-master of the village of Scheifling to drive him to Zeltweg. The village fire engine was the only vehicle available for this purpose and so in the fire engine they went. Although in these circumstances his entry into the airport must have been impressive enough, the commanding officer there was not yet sufficiently convinced of the seriousness of the situation to conform to Freud's demand for surrender. Nevertheless he did not clap Freud in chains, as he could undoubtedly have done, but treated him as a guest of honour. After a night in Zeltweg Freud, accompanied by an escort of *Luftwaffe* officers, was driven to Linz to meet Rendulic. There he was taken prisoner, but he managed to get away in a westerly direction and was very glad to be picked up by advancing US troops.

It is quite possible that Freud's early endeavours softened the ground for the later appearance of the main group at Zeltweg.

Warner had come down alongside a farm almost in the village of Niederwoelz. He was extremely fortunate not to be discovered, particularly as the nearness to human habitation made it necessary for him to hide his now useless but very obvious parachute actually in the farm's barn. Being on his own, however, decided him not to stay where he was, but to seek shelter in the woods covering the mountains to the north of the village.

After several hours' climb in the dark he gained the top of the ridge, where he managed to find an unoccupied woodfellers' hut, in which he promptly established himself. During his climb he had had to cross a mountain stream and in doing so had got himself soaking wet right up to his chest. The loneliness of his retreat was very useful for the drying of his clothes and other gear. His iron rations kept him going. During the second night at the hut he was wakened by voices outside and an attempt to open the door, which he had secured. His call (in German) as to who was there, was answered by firing, to which he replied in kind. He wrote, 'The shots echoed all round the mountain . . . and with each shot fired a large flame shot out of the short barrel of my Colt. For a moment everyone kept quiet, giving me time to reload . . . Whilst doing this I heard . . . running feet and . . . thought my adversaries were going to rush me. To my great relief, however, they . . . were running away'.

Much later Warner found out that the attacking party had consisted of an elderly and unarmed local farmer, acting as guide to two young, inexperienced, but keen and heavily armed members of the Nazi labour service. They had been told to search for enemy paratroops. When the farmer realised that the firing of his companions was being answered, he first of all threw himself down and then ran for it, having no intention of being killed at that late stage of the war. When his companions saw him run they followed suit. Maybe, without their guide, they would have been lost in the thickly wooded mountains.

Warner also left his hideout immediately. He ran and marched through the woods for about six hours until he found an open hayloft where again he found shelter. As it started to snow at about that time he stayed there for several days. When the weather changed again, he commenced offensive activity. In the nearby village of Weissenbach, he approached an outlying farm, where the owners, an old couple, their daughter and a woman evacuee with her two children, were delighted to look after him. He was fed, washed and taken care of. Then they put him in touch with the local 'resistance', who in turn secured for him the help of the police. They spread the glad news that a British officer had arrived.

The Russians having in the meantime crossed the border into Styria, leaving a trail of shot civilians, raped women and burnt down houses, the entire population, including the Nazi bosses, were praying for the early arrival of the British. Everyone was keen to help Warner, as the only British officer in sight. The police of Murau, the nearest town, put itself under his orders and informed him of all that was going on, including the news that a party of British officers had taken over at Zeltweg.

With a car put at his disposal by the local Nazi boss and accompanied by a British prisoner of war and two of the locals, Warner travelled to Zeltweg, passing through the retreating German army and through groups of Yugoslav partisans, who were trying to gather as much loot as possible before the return of more settled conditions. In one case he actually had to brandish his gun, before a group of such bandits felt it advisable to let him and his companions pass. By the time he got to the airport the Soviets were there already, but Bryant and the other three of the group had not yet withdrawn. The group's withdrawal to the southern shore of the river Mur took place shortly afterwards. There they found shelter in Authal castle, which at that time was the residence of Prince Croy, a generally respected Styrian noble. As he was involved in the reconstitution of a Styrian provincial government, the group also took a hand in this. They remained at Authal until after the arrival of a more substantial British unit. In the process of the reallocation of occupied zones in Austria, Zeltweg was reoccupied by the British some time later.

In his capacity as an Austrian lawyer Bryant joined the British Army Legal Unit (BALU) in Vienna. Warner was posted to the War Crimes Group of the British Army of the Rhine, where he remained for three years. After his release he remained in British service in a confidential position. He lives in Hamburg. Later Harry Stevens, alias Schweiger, again distinguished himself by arresting a man, who turned out to be Himmler's deputy Oswald Pohl.

Paul Yogi Mayer is a Frankfurter by birth. He served in 87 Company, Pioneer Corps. From there he was transferred to the SOE. He was together with Dale at No.1 Training School at Stodham Park, in Arisaig House, in Ringway, Brockhall and at Anderson Manor. Although he acted as trainer, he was not actually used against the enemy direct at any time.

When he was with the pioneers Karl Kaiser seems certain to have been in 74 Company. The name of 'Kaiser' without a forename appears in the nominal roll of 74 Company, when this company was in France with the BEF in 1940, but nobody else by the name of Kaiser has ever been heard of. Later he was trained for the SOE. He was in action in the last weeks of the war. Whilst Dale was not certain of his facts in this respect this is confirmed by another source. Harry Williams, previously Wunder, was another SOE trainee. He parachuted into action in the last weeks of April 1945. Otherwise nothing is known about him.

A number of people were trained in the SOE, but did not get into action whilst hostilities were still in progress. Amongst these there were three men who had served in 87 or 88 Company, PC. One of them was Eric F. Bowes, previously Erich Franz Brauer from Breslau. He had been trained as a parachutist, but broke an ankle on his second jump. Hugh Peter Falton, previously Faltitschek, born in 1901, was even more unlucky for he broke his back in training, but was still commissioned in the Royal Fusiliers later on. F. Layton, originally Alfred Leschziner from Beuthen, was the third man in this group. Other SOE men who were not called upon to go into action despite their readiness to do so were Heinz Aufrecht alias Michael Alford, R. Beatty, Peter Berger alias Barry, Lothar Ettlinger alias Roger Elliott, Herbert Fein from Leipzig, Georg Huelsmann, H. Pincus alias H.J.R. Peters, Pojur Palmer, Sepp Rasborscheg, Eric Sanders and Ron Stewart.

Stephan Wirlander was in quite a different category. Before the war he had been secretary of the Vienna Chamber of Labour, an official body representing working-class interests in the legislative process. In London he was a member of the Austrian Socialist Party's representative office. In the first two years of the war he was very active there as a journalist. He volunteered to join the pioneers in 1941 and at a later date turned into Captain John Miller. He was transferred to one of the special operations executives, presumably the SOM and was sent to North Africa, Turkey and Italy. His activities there are still shrouded in secrecy. The post-war Austrian Socialists asked for his return to Vienna almost immediately after the end of hostilities. This was agreed to and he was reinstated in his pre-war job with the Chamber of Labour on the day of his arrival.

Whilst Wirlander was a representative of the Austrian left in politics, Hans Hladnik, a Styrian, was very much to the right. Coming from a strictly Catholic background he had been secretary of the Styrian farmers' and smallholders' association. He, too, was in special operations and at one time served in the same team as Wirlander, Theo Neumann and Sanders.

The Distinguished Conduct Medal, for other ranks in the services the second highest award for bravery, was awarded posthumously to Sergeant Robert Lodge, who had been born as Rudolph Friedlaender at Fuerth in Bavaria. He was in the 2nd Special Air Service Regiment (SAS). On 12 July 1943, that is, before the allied invasion of Sicily, he was number nine in the jumping order when his unit parachuted into that island, near Nicosia, a small town north of the city of Enna. The unit was dispersed over a wide area. Lodge was able to team up with a few of his companions, but too few to resist a considerably greater number of Carabinieri who discovered them on the following day. They had no choice but to surrender. They were taken to the Italian mainland, but during the transfer by ship from Messina they tried to get away. However, the small boat in which they were making their escape was fired upon and sank beneath them. They were picked up and returned to captivity.

At the beginning of September they were taken to the Italian prisoner of war camp No. 73 at Carpi, north of Modena. They were there at the time of the Italian armistice. Although in this agreement the Italians undertook to release all their Allied prisoners at once and the camp commander received orders to do so, he did not open the camp gates and refused to arm the prisoners. They were handed over to German troops, who immediately proceeded to march all the inmates to Carpi railway station. During this march Lodge succeeded in getting away a second time and this time he was more successful. Whilst still within the town he found refuge with an Italian woman, who hid him until it was safe for him to get away. From there he walked in a southerly direction.

Over two months later, on 2 December, he walked into the lines of a 25-pounder battery of the 5th British Division near Bari. He had covered the entire distance, some 600 kilometres as the crow flies, in all weathers, including snow, on foot. He was suffering from jaundice, had frostbite on the toes of both feet and a festering sore on a finger of the right hand. He was covered in lice. Following his recovery he wrote a report concerning his experiences for the War Office, who thanked him for a valuable contribution.

On 13 August 1944 he and a small group of men again got behind enemy lines. This time it was the Alsatian Vosges mountains, where they were dropped into action. Their story appeared in the London *Evening Standard* of 28 May 1945. At that time their area of operations was still a long way behind the enemy front line. The report says that their job was to make the area unsafe for the enemy. 'They hid alongside the roads and fired upon [enemy] columns. With their jeeps they were able to escape all attempts to take them captive'.

On 19 August Lodge, leading a group of four men, was surrounded by a larger enemy unit. An intensive exchange of fire ensued. In the course of this Lodge came out of cover and fired his machine gun from a standing position at the enemy from a distance of about 30 yards. This allowed him and his comrades to get away to safety. Later the same day a similar situation arose again and again Lodge fired at the enemy without cover. As a result his group was enabled to free itself from a difficult situation. They got away with the loss of only one man. For this action Lodge was awarded the decoration mentioned above. The citation states that his action had been in the best tradition of the service. He would appear to have been killed the following day.

The name Friedlaender is mentioned also by Ernest Winter, a man who 'for important personal reasons' refuses to give any information about himself. Most probably he means the same person. According to him Friedlaender had been in 137 Company, PC. He writes that, during his extremely dangerous mission Friedlaender had been 'together with Kugler', had completed his task successfully, but had subsequently been captured, tortured and killed. Curiously enough, neither the name of Friedlaender nor that of Lodge appear in Bentwich's Roll of Honour, nor in the list of dead of the Ex-Service NB Association. Kugler has disappeared. He is said to have been an Austrian and, like Friedlaender, to have served in 137 Company.

The following story is taken from Bentwich's *I understand the risks*. There the actions described are attributed to a Sergeant X, MM, an enemy alien. Like Sergeant X, Sergeant Gilbert also was an enemy alien and he, too, was awarded the Military Medal. So there is some justification for thinking that the story may refer to him. However, this is mere conjecture and it is quite possible that yet another enemy alien sergeant may also have been decorated similarly.

In March 1945 Sergeant X and a comrade crossed the river Rhine by canoe. At that time the left shore of the river was occupied by the

British, the right by the Germans. Both men wore the uniform of the *Wehrmacht*. After walking 200 kilometres in four days through the German lines they made their way to the barracks at Essen purporting to collect spare parts for a tank. They were arrested and brought before a formidable high officer, who wore all possible German decorations including the Knight's Cross of the Iron Cross with diamonds, swords and oak leaves. They were subjected, each separately, to a horrific grilling and, miraculously, passed it. Their movement order was in fact home-made, but they succeeded in satisfying the major that it was correct and got his stamp on it: 'This man's identity has been checked and proved correct. He is to be instructed on his return on the regulations concerning movement orders'. Having passed these trials, they still had to make their way back to the British lines, which meant re-crossing the Rhine by night.

It took them two days to get to the crossing which they had selected. They had to hide near the dyke till complete darkness. They sat in a haystack watching like hawks. Luck was with them; heavy mists began to rise from the river. With their luminous compass they found their way through the sentries to the riverbank. They found a boat, but it was without oars. They paddled with the seat. At that point the Rhine was 500 yards wide and they took over two hours to cover half the distance. Then an aircraft crashed into the river near them. Mortars opened up; they had to swim for their lives in heavy shellfire. They reached the west bank and picked their way across the dykes for 500 yards. Challenged by a Scottish sentry, they established their identity and were taken to the intelligence officer. After two hours' sleep they gave their report for 18 hours on the dispositions of the German army units facing the 21st Army Group across the Rhine.

Some time before all this had taken place a listening service had been installed within 21st Army Group with the object of controlling wireless communications between enemy formations. To start it off six men were designated for this job. They were Corporals John Goodman and Paton, Privates Heckssher and Lister, and two others, all from various companies of the Pioneer Corps. They were divided up into two groups of three, of which one worked for the British, the other for the Americans. At a later stage Lance Corporal Rolf James from the X Troop also joined this unit. They commenced their work in the neighbourhood of Bayeux shortly after the Normandy landings. They continued their work as the Allies continued their advance eastwards and when it was all over they were reunited at the British headquarters in Germany. Goodman received a Certificate of Good Service. James, who was a journalist, was posted to Keith Spalding's newspaper *Die Mitteilungen*. Later he was commissioned and worked in the British press and newspaper section in Berlin, before, with the rank of major, he became chief of information services in Schleswig-Holstein and deputy to Hugh Carlton-Greene at the end of his military career. He had a very interesting background, being related to the Siemens family. Before the war in Germany he had been called up for the *Wehrmacht* and had got as far as corporal. In 1939 he was in Britain because he was a Rhodes scholar.

CSDIC was a unit engaged in detailed interrogation of captured Nazis and important prisoners. F. Lustig, whom we have met in a previous chapter as a musician in the Southern Command Pioneer Corps Orchestra, was later transferred to this organisation. According to him he is not permitted, even today, to say more than 'I was promoted sergeant and was in Buckinghamshire with CSDIC UK. In the autumn [of 1945?] I was sent to CSDIC WEA, where I was first company and later regimental sergeant major. In the summer of 1946 I was demobilised from there'.

Before his emigration from Vienna Sergeant, later Captain Theo Neumann had been an important member of the Austrian Social Democratic Party. According to both Bentwich and Muchitsch he returned to his native city shortly before the Russians took it in the spring of 1945. It is not clear what his task there was supposed to have been. However, after the Russians had occupied the town he is said to have made himself known to them as a British officer. According to Dale, however, Neumann did not reach Vienna until after the end of hostilities. All three sources agree that Neumann was a lawyer, that he was in the British-Austrian Legal Unit and that he rejoined the Austrian Socialists in a leading function after he had left the army.

Manfred Czernin, of ancient Bohemian noble lineage, was a major in special operations in Algiers. It is probable that he had held that rank in the *Wehrmacht*, had changed sides and, in accordance with ancient practice, had been confirmed in this rank in the British service. He is also said to have held the rank of squadron leader in the RAF. From North Africa he went to Italy. Later, when the British marched into Florence, he was there already. He seems to have had excellent connections with the Italian partisans. The only other thing that is known about him is that he played table tennis really well.

Also about Major Cayzer and Lieutenant Williams, originally Wunder, little more is known than that they existed. Both are said to have been with the republicans in the Spanish civil war, then with the *Maquis* in France. Both somehow arrived in Britain and both finished up in special operations.

Ronnie Gilbert, originally Hans-Julius Guttmann and a member of

3/10 Commando, of whom we have heard at Grande Ferme du Boisson, where he was injured, transferred to the Intelligence Corps and remained with them for several years after the war was over. His efforts to find and arrest members of the Nazi Party who had gone underground are said to have been very successful and according to a former colleague he was highly respected in the corps. He was awarded the MBE. The name Schnek or Schneck is mentioned several times. With regard to Drs Johannes and Friedrich Schneck there has been some confusion which has, however, been cleared up recently. This we have dealt with already in a previous chapter. Walter Schnek, however, had no connection with either of the two mentioned above. He too seems to have had an adventurous life. There is documentary evidence for the following story. He was born in Vienna on 12 June 1919. On 18 March 1938 he reached Amsterdam from a place called Bielitz, probably in Czechoslovakia. In July 1941 he was working near Eindhoven (Netherlands) as a farm labourer. A year later the Gestapo arrested him and took him away on a charge of espionage. As nothing was proved against him, he was again released. From that time onwards he wore the yellow Star of David on his clothing, signifying that he was a Jew. On 27 July 1942 he was again arrested in order to be deported to Poland. He succeeded in getting away and from August 1942 on he lived in hiding in The Hague, in Eindhoven and in Valkenwaard. In September 1944 Holland was occupied by British troops. In a letter dated 15 September 1965 Schnek's former employer at Eindhoven, J.N. Seulijn, confirms that 'from September 1944 until the end of the war he was an officer in the British army'. Perhaps the Gestapo were not unjustified when they arrested him on suspicion of espionage?

A group of 25, which was remarkable for the fact that all its members had some knowledge of wireless, was established within the framework of the special services in 1943. During the next two years all of them were taken, somehow, to locations within enemy-occupied territory. Their job was to observe and report. It is almost incredible that only three appear to have been discovered. They paid for their daring with their lives.

A group of Austrians, who were parachuted into Austria at Tolmein, south of the city of Salzburg, were all killed. Their leader, Wolfgang Treichl, had been in the German Africa Corps as an officer. He had taken his entire platoon across the lines. Like Czernin he was commissioned in the British service in the rank he had held in the *Wehrmacht*. He and his men jumped right into a German military camp at Tolmein and were shot after an intensive engagement.

Sergeant P. Weiss, an Austrian, who had parachuted into Germany towards the end of 1944, was captured and taken to Dachau, where he was executed.

Ernst Perthain, who later changed his forename to John, was the son of an Austrian judge. Before 1938 he had held a commission in the Austrian federal army. It seems that he was in the British army during the war, but that he was transferred to the US forces at some stage. They made him a captain in counter-intelligence. He was at the Nuremberg trials and eventually left the service of the Allies with the rank of major.

Two other officers whose names are unknown were liaison officers in the Balkans. One, a German, maintained contacts with Tito's partisans. After the end of hostilities he was in Berlin, where he found employment in British Army Headquarters. The other was an Austrian, who first served in Albania, only to be transferred to 8th Army Headquarters at a later stage.

Friedrich Traenkler's field of action was in Styria. Born on 18 July 1910 in Vienna his communist beliefs led him to become an officer of the republican army in the Spanish civil war. He was there from May 1937 until February 1939. After the republican collapse he fled to France. There he was interned in the camps at St Cyprien, Gurs and Le Vernet. Then he was taken to North Africa. It is to be assumed that he was one of those released from French internment by the intervention of Harold Macmillan and the people who were with him at the beginning of 1943, for he served in the British army from that time on. Clearly, he must have been in one of the 'A' companies formed in Algiers at that time. In June 1944, however, he returned to Austria to take his part in a 'fighting unit Styria' and he remained with them until May 1945.

The most mysterious of all these men, however, is Captain J. Kennedy. There can be no doubt at all that he has been known under at least five, but probably more, different names in the course of his chequered career. According to an SOE document his original name was Hillman, but he also used the pseudonyms Hofer and Gerber. Hillman, however, is not in any way a German name. The German equivalent would be Bergmann and indeed there was a Dr Bergmann, a lawyer, said to have been born in 1903 at Lissa (Leszno today) in Prussia. He is supposed to have practised at Sonthofen, a small town in the Bavarian Alps. It should however be said that no trace of a Dr Bergmann has been found at the Sonthofen town hall. Warner, who knew him personally as they were together on a course of parachute training, says he called himself Baron Schnitzelberger. He seems to have taken a positive delight in laying false trails about his identity. Martin Sugarman, archivist of the Jewish Ex-Servicemen's' Association in London, suspects him of having been identical with Peter Liebelt, alias Leigh-Bell.

He was twice decorated for bravery in the face of the enemy. When still an NCO he was awarded the Military Medal. After he was commissioned he also received the Military Cross. With his two decorations for bravery he was one of the three Germans and Austrians with the highest number of awards. His appearance was peculiar. Warner describes him as 'small and fat, wearing gold framed glasses and looking like a professor, but always smelled of garlic. Certainly, no-one looked less like a parachutist'. Dr Bergmann, if indeed he was Dr Bergmann, almost certainly emigrated to France in 1933. In 1939 he joined the French foreign legion and this tallies with what is thought to be known about Hillman alias Kennedy. He was sent to North Africa. After the fall of France he was discharged and interned. He is known to have been an inmate of Colomb-Bechar, Abadlah and Hadjerat M'Guil concentration camps. After the British landing he served in 338 Company PC, but was soon transferred to the SOM. He is said to have been in charge of a commando undertaking against Tobruk from which only four men including himself returned. That was probably where he got his MM and may be when he was commissioned.

Towards the end of the war, during the night of 23–24 March 1945, he was dropped by parachute in the area north of Tulln near Vienna. For this operation he called himself Kennedy. The name is typical for the man. Undoubtedly, it is a pun on the Austrian dialect question '*Kenn i' di?*' – 'do I know you?'. He is said to have got in touch with men of the Austrian resistance and to have been the chief of a group of 130 of them for a time. They were mainly deserters from the *Wehrmacht*. At the beginning of April 1945 he commenced intensive sabotage and propaganda activities. Later, in Vienna he co-operated with the Soviets and assisted them in rounding up prominent Nazis. After the cessation of hostilities he commanded a prisoner of war camp in Austria. Dr Elisabeth Lebensaft of he Austrian Academy of Sciences is quite certain that later he emigrated to Australia where he became Vice-President of the Blue Mountains Historical Society, wrote books (*The Blue Mountains* and *Gustav Weindorfer, the hermit of Cradle Mountain*), and eventually died at Vila, New Hebrides, on 21 October 1979. Nevertheless, there is also a suggestion that having been released from the army he went to Canada. I may be excused for doubting whether any of the stories about him can be proved beyond doubt, but what is true and what is a product of the imagination I would hesitate to determine.

Somewhat less endangered than these men of the SOE were those who became involved with psychological warfare. Four Austrian pioneers of 337 and 338 Companies formed a team which broadcast to Austria on behalf of the Allies from locations first in Algiers, then in Bari and lastly in Rome. Apart from Erich Denman, whose story follows, these were Sergeant Stappler, a former musical agent, and Privates Glaserfeld and Hoppe. These two remained in broadcasting also after the war. Originally the broadcasts went out from a station generally known as 'Radio Swindle', a part of 'United Nations Radio Algier'. They were directed both at the Austrian civilian population and at Austrian soldiers with the fighting units of the *Wehrmacht* in the Mediterranean area. Derman, born 1909 and previous to the war feature editor of the *Wiener Tagblatt*, the *Pester Lloyd* and the *Neue Zurcher Zeitung*, wrote:

> One day an English major turned up at the company headquarters (of 338 Company). That was a few days after the Moscow Declaration. There they had decided to start up a broadcasting service which should go out to Austria and especially to the Austrian soldiers along the southern front. This English major, his name was Colby, knew Vienna very well, he had been there as a student. He came into the orderly room and said he needed a few journalists, who should make these broadcasts. He looked at the nominal roll and I was the first one he came across. I might even have been the only one. Four days later I was the chief of the radio station, without any kind of test. Indeed, Colby did say, 'Ah yes, do me a favour and write an article, in German, on any subject you choose and let me see it.' I sat down and wrote an article with the headline 'Democracy for democrats only'. He was very satisfied with that.
>
> I was posted into the town, into Eisenhower's headquarters. There were a lot of very important offices there, including those of the various broadcasting services. They were broadcasting in French, English, Italian, Serbo-Croat and German. There was no office space for us at all. All the rooms were occupied. So they put in a door at the end of one of the corridors and said to us, 'That's your office.'
>
> I created the broadcasts out of thin air. For a long time I was the only broadcaster, without any check on me of any kind. I could have called 'Heil Hitler' over the air. They just trusted me.
>
> Eventually I got two more people from the company and an elderly gentleman from London also joined us. I had the political say-so. We were on the air twice a day, at five and at nine in the evening.

[After the Normandy landings] we were relocated at Bari.
Then we went on to Rome. For me personally that was not only
the time I worked hardest, but also, somehow, the time when I
was at my most creative in my whole life. The thought that now
there was a common enemy against whom all of us were fighting
together, really made me go.

When I had left Vienna I was rather young and whilst I had
worked in newspapers, I had never had anything to do with the
political part. That began in Algiers out of nothing ...

After the end of hostilities, at which time he was in Rome, Derman
went to Klagenfurt and eventually joined the *Weltpresse* in Vienna.

Herbert S. also contributed an article on his own experiences to
Jüdische Schicksale. He was born in Vienna in 1920, the son of a Jewish
horse dealer and a Catholic mother. In 1938 he fled to France, was
interned there at the commencement of the war, joined the foreign
legion and, after the French collapse, was again interned, but this time
in the Sahara. There he worked in a coal mine. After the Allied
landings in North Africa he escaped and after an adventurous trek of
more than 1,000 kilometres reached Oran.

On arrival there I reported to the Allies (with a view to joining
up). The first thing they did was for an American colonel and a
British lieutenant colonel to give me a thorough grilling. I told
them my story and when I had finished they both got up and
shook my hand. After that I worked for the Yankee army as an
interpreter. But I wanted to fight and volunteered for a special
mission with the British...

I had to do training courses for almost a year. Hand-to-hand
fighting, sabotage, motorcycling, parachuting, recognition,
physical and mental, always another course, one after the other.
At last I was sent to Bari. I was scheduled to go into action behind
the enemy lines in Austria, in Carinthia. But I was supposed to go
in uniform, not as a spy...Instead of all that, however, I
eventually had to parachute into Yugoslavia together with six
other British officers.

There I was received by partisans. The next morning I was
introduced to Tito personally, and to his number two, General
Popovic...Tito wanted to get to know me. He must have known
that I was Austrian and he wanted to see, what that was all about.

For breakfast the three of us had scrambled eggs. There was a
big frying pan with scrambled eggs in it and we all ate out of this,

Tito and Popovic and I. Each of us had a spoon and there was only the one pan and that's how we had our breakfast...

My job was logistics. I had to co-ordinate the Allied supplies, but not in Bosnia, where we were, but along the border between Slovenia and Carinthia. I marched all the way along mountain trails – all that was occupied territory – to Slovenia, or, to be more correct, to the border with Germany. It was very dangerous, there were Germans everywhere.

I got there and I did my job as well as I could. I also had to collect what news there was and pass it to HQ in Rome. In a way we were constantly running away. We hid in the woods and in the mountains, but every time we got new supplies, these came by plane and had to be parachuted in. We had to set markers for the planes, so that they should know where they had to jettison their loads. And that was our dilemma. The moment we set our markers we had to expect that the German army would notice and get on to us. That was the 13th SS brigade and every time they tried to surround us and then we had to get out of that somehow. God knows, this happened dozens of times.

In 1944 at last I was replaced. I got orders to return. They sent a plane for me, which could land in a meadow. I got in quickly and flew back.

After I had had a good leave in Italy I was used as editor for broadcasts to Austria...

Other members of 337 Company also distinguished themselves. Robert Feigl, who had been one of those who had negotiated with British Army HQ in Algiers for the formation of this company, was sent on a secret mission. Hans Cohn became editor of a newspaper directed at enemy soldiers in the south of France. Two brothers by the name of Wertheim parachuted into Germany, were taken prisoner and executed in Alsace in 1944. Concerning Wilhelm Kirsten, Bentwich wrote that he 'had a miraculous escape. Sent to Germany to organise a resistance movement in the Ruhr, he was caught by the Gestapo, tortured and sentenced to death by a military court, but rescued by partisans. Later he was appointed director of police in the Saar region. Before this exploit he and a refugee comrade, posing as German deserters, rounded up a Nazi spy gang among the Arabs'. However there is no other evidence to support this story.

All the details concerning Ernst Rosenstein of Bensheim in der Bergstrasse will probably never be known. At first sight he could be identical with the Ernst Rosenstein of 74 Company mentioned earlier.

However, according to documentary evidence in his home town he did not emigrate to Britain in 1938, but to Palestine. It is, therefore, unlikely that he should have been in France with 74 Company. Later evidence points to his having been a member of SOM. An old friend of his is quite certain that he saw him in a hospital in Benghazi at some point. He is said to have parachuted into Albania. His body lies in a British cemetery in Greece. What happened in between is not known.

Peter Johnson is a man with good connections and some interesting stories. He maintains that an Austrian by the name of Warndorfer was a nephew of Admiral Lord Cunningham. His mother, Cunningham's sister, is said to have married in Austria before the outbreak of the war of 1914. Johnson also says that Warndorfer had been an officer cadet in the Austrian navy in the First World War. Having joined the pioneers in 1940 he is said to have been posted to 220 Company, where his abilities with the axe were unsurpassed. Johnson believes that Warndorfer was sent to Austria by the SOE, but that he did not return.

What Sergeant E. Conrad did is not known. Nor is it clear whether he and E. Conradi were two people or whether the two names refer to the same person. As both Conrad and Conradi sport the initial E. the second possibility seems the more likely. In any case, Sergeant E. Conrad, a Viennese lawyer, was in the Psychological Warfare Group and was decorated with the Bronze Star by the Americans. E. Conradi received a Certificate of Gallantry from the British.

Gerhard Hermann Carl Cossmann is a native of Potsdam and lived variously in Biedenkopf, Schleswig and Freiburg before he emigrated. In the British army he served first in 165, later in 219 and 220 Companies, Pioneer Corps. In 1943 he changed his name, since when he has been known as Peter Crawford. He was transferred to the Intelligence Corps and took part in a course of parachute training at Ringway. He finished his service in Hamburg and Hannover.

A story which does not refer to activities initiated by the Allies, but which nevertheless has some of their cloak and dagger flavour, is told by Alfred George Simms, formerly Simonson. Having served in 137 Company PC and, from 1943 onwards, in the anti-tank regiment of the 4th Indian Division in Italy and Greece, he was at Salonika when he was contacted by a *Wehrmacht* officer, a Major Ebers, the son of a one-time prominent German socialist journalist. Ebers suggested to Simms that he (Ebers) was the right man to organise German deserters against the Nazis. Duty-bound, Simms passed Ebers along to his superior officers, but nothing came of his efforts.

Although Edita Zukermanova wrote her name the Czech way and was a Czechoslovak citizen, she actually came from Vienna, where she had been known as Edith Zuckermann. In later life she married and became Mme Katona. For four years during the war, however, the Free French knew her simply as 'Marianne'. She worked in both the German and Italian High Commands and throughout that time she passed on information from there to the people around de Gaulle. In acknowledgement of her services she was appointed member of the *Ordre de l'Armee de Mer avec le Croix de Guerre avec Palmes*. The citation tells of her having executed her tasks bravely, coolly and intelligently. In the meantime, whilst she was doing this, her mother was arrested by the OVRA, Mussolini's secret police, in Genoa. She was subjected to torture, as a result of which she committed suicide by hanging herself in her cell. Edita was informed of what had happened by a French colonel with the words, '*Pas neccessaire, que tu t'en vas a Genua, ta mère s'a pendu pour ne pas trahir.*' She is said never quite to have recovered from the shock caused by these words. She died in London at the beginning of the 1990s.

An activity totally different from those hitherto described was that carried on by Sergeant William George Fort. Although seemingly unspectacular, what he did was of the highest importance to the war effort and in the end he was honoured by King George VI, who paid him a personal visit, and by the government of the United States, from whom he received a Certificate of Merit. Before his emigration from Vienna Wilhelm Fortgang, as was his name then, had been a master tailor and had numbered amongst his customers such famous people as the singer Richard Tauber, actress Diana Napier, her colleague Anton Walbrook, the composers Oskar Strauss and Emmerich Kalman and many others. Having been born on 10 June 1893 he was one of the oldest amongst the Germans and Austrians in the army. He was 47 years old when he volunteered for service from Huyton internment camp near Liverpool in the summer of 1940. Despite his age he felt perfectly fit and so, when the opportunity arose, he applied for transfer to the commandos. However, they would not have him. But his application directed attention towards him. He was called to the War Office, was interviewed at length and after his absolute *bona fide* had been established, he was told that he was just the right man to make clothes of proper continental cut for all allied secret agents operating on the continent.

Until that time a number of British agents who had been able to speak German fluently had been discovered and taken by the Gestapo, only because the clothes which they wore had clearly been made in England. Although Savile Row, the street where the best and most expensive London tailors were to be found, was positively crawling with Bohemian tailors, these people had become so assimilated that they were unable to produce gentlemen's clothing in the style of

Vienna and other Central European locations. From the time of Fort's interview onwards, however, every British agent, and after the entry of the United States into the war, every American agent also, was fitted out with clothing produced in Sergeant Fort's workshop in the London Natural History Museum in South Kensington. From then on, no agent was ever caught again because the cut of his clothing had given him away.

10

Elsewhere in the Empire

In writing this I have taken the view that I cannot write about all the parts of the British Empire as it was then. I personally was a member of the British forces recruited in the United Kingdom and the majority of the refugees were in the same or similar position to myself. These and the very few who were recruited in India are the men and women to whom I refer when I say that there were 10,000 of us. I am aware of the fact that I cannot limit myself completely to those who were recruited in Britain because there are borderline cases. But on the whole I feel that when I write about those from Britain I am writing about 'us', about something which I know.

There were refugees in other parts of the Empire. In Australia some 2,500 of them are thought to have been in the forces, in South Africa probably there were several hundred and in Palestine the estimates vary, but some are as high as 30,000. I personally doubt that this figure is right, but I have no intention of checking it. I do not know about what went on in Australia, South Africa or Palestine. There were enough people who served in each of those countries for one of them in each to use his spare time after retirement from an active job to tell the story of what happened where he served. It has been suggested to me that I might well use my time on this – 'you do it so well' – but I have no intention of doing so.

However, in the course of my researches concerning the refugees to Britain (and India) I have heard from or about people, who were in the Australian or South African forces or in the British forces based on Palestine. In many cases they had interesting stories to tell and it may well be that in reproducing them here I might encourage someone else to make himself and his comrades the subject of his further researches.

Emigration to South Africa seems to have started immediately after Hitler came to power in 1933, and apparently quite a few of the refugees who went there then were able to establish themselves in the period before the war began. South Africa was the last of the British dominions to enter the war. It did so against the opposition of a part of the Boer population. As a result there was no conscription in the country and every member of the South African services was a genuine volunteer –

not only the enemy aliens as in Britain. Presumably because of the number of different nationalities which went in to making up the white population of the country, there does not really appear to have been a great deal of prejudice against people of German and Austrian, or those of Jewish, origin, and no doubt this had something to do with the fact that South Africa did permit enemy aliens to be naturalised even during the war. The South African forces, being where they were, were used largely in the fighting in Africa, but appear to have remained largely separate from those from other parts of the empire. The most detailed story of any of the refugee members of the South African forces comes from Staff Sergeant Ludwig Fried. Born in Berlin on 7 September 1919, he emigrated to South Africa, where he was employed at a large department store. In the autumn of 1939 he volunteered for service in the Union Defence Force.

Whilst the distance from South Africa to Ethiopia is by no means inconsiderable, South African troops were nevertheless nearer to the Abyssinian theatre of war than to any other, which led to them being used there in the first place. To get there they had to travel all the way over good roads and bad, from one end of the country to the other, through Rhodesia, Nyasaland, Tanganyika and Kenya. Despite this they still reached Ethiopia to be able to take part in the battle of Amba Alagi, where their presence had a decisive effect.

Following this episode they were ordered further north yet and this time Fried was with the advance guard. Their arrival at the Suez Canal coincided with a major attack by hostile aircraft. That was the South Africans' first action against the Nazis. Some time later Fried was able to get some leave. This he spent in Palestine where he was reunited with his mother and five of his six sisters, the sixth having in the meantime been sent to Auschwitz with the whole of her family. As Fried had been a resident of South Africa where the laws were different, he was able to apply for naturalisation, which he was granted on 20 November 1942. The whole of the South African Corps was put under command of the 8th Army. At that time Fried was in charge of 12 water supply vehicles and he took these all the way from Egypt to Tripoli.

H.G. Wolf's history is similar to Fried's in some respects. He was born in Berlin in 1911. A lawyer with Swiss and German qualifications he was not permitted to continue in his profession in Germany. He emigrated to South Africa where he married a Swiss girl and qualified as a chartered accountant. Then he joined the army. Concerning the situation in South Africa at the time when war began, he wrote: 'The army in South Africa (was) a voluntary organisation, because the Prime Minister, General Smuts, had to consider the sentiments of the

Afrikaners, who were friendly towards the Germans. In actual fact, however, these Boers also joined the army...'. Like Fried he was posted to the South African Service Corps and trained at Zonderwater. Then,

> all of a sudden, a fear of aliens arose, and whilst the enlisted men were retained and had to participate in drill and on parades, they were no longer allowed to carry arms...I applied for office work ...I was put in charge of the orderly room with three provisional stripes, followed much later by the pay due to the rank... Because of medical reasons I was not sent up north...I could arrange my discharge from the army after almost four years service.

Walter L. Bock was from Frankfurt, where he had been born on 11 January 1915. Already in December 1933 he emigrated to South Africa, where he became naturalised. As a South African citizen he volunteered for service in 1939 and became a tank driver. Having been sent to North Africa he was taken prisoner by the Germans at Tobruk in 1941. He was treated correctly. Having first been taken to Brindisi, he was later sent to Silesia. In the chaos of 1945 he managed to get to Prague on foot. There he met up with the advancing Americans.

Kurt Land, originally Landenberger, served in the South African Air Force from November 1940 until August 1945, having previously been in the army for nearly a year. During that period he rose from private to WO1 to lieutenant and served in a variety of places between Cape Town and Udine.

At the capture of Tobruk by Rommel's Africa Corps and Italian units a German refugee named Schuster became a prisoner of the Italians. He was transported to Italy where he was treated correctly, although his captors must have known about his origins, for he gave German lessons to his fellow prisoners. When Mussolini was deposed he and a friend were able to reach Switzerland where they were interned until the end of the war. Apart from this nothing is known about him, but he may well have been in Tobruk with the South Africans.

This is also the right place to tell the unusual story of Sabina Flesch, later – after her stepfather – Sabina Landsberg, now the Hon. Mrs David Gibson. She was born in Berlin in 1920. When she was 13, her mother emigrated to South Africa taking her daughter with her. Sabina studied sociology at Cape Town University. She joined up in 1941, served first with the British military mission in Cairo as a sergeant, then in Italy. She was commissioned in 1943. After hostilities had ceased she was promoted to captain WAAS, South African Forces, and was seconded to the British military mission in Austria, working in CSDIC and in the de-Nazification in Vienna. Her 'clients' there included Admiral Kaltenbrunner, SS General Wolff, Mrs Himmler and T. Gudrun alias 'Sweet Sally', British radio reporter in Nazi services.

Many of the Germans and Austrians who joined up in Palestine became pioneers. Ari Dick from Vienna tells the following story:

> In December 1939 I joined the British Army as a volunteer. There was a central training camp at the Palestine Harbour Centre (Sarafand) where we got our training. Then we were shipped from Haifa to Marseilles in a big trooper. After that we were taken to camp in Normandy. There we were used like navvies. We built a railway line and loaded and unloaded freight trains until the German attack on France came. Then they used us as a rear guard. That's the people who fought the Germans so that the others could get away. I was with that lot...
>
> First we saw the big cars with suitcases and then came the lorries with suitcases and after them the horse drawn carts with suitcases and then came the people on foot and with bicycles, with little carts, with children. Those were the people who were running away from the Germans. These are pictures I can't forget to this day.
>
> We reached Britain on a collier. At first they sent us to Wales and then we went by rail, first to a camp near London and then on to Glasgow. In a convoy of 40 ships we travelled to Cape Town, including a landing at Freetown where they did not allow us to go on land...
>
> At the Cape the Jewish people made us very welcome. Every night we were invited for dinner and to all sorts of performances. They were mainly old residents and a few emigrants from Germany who had left in 1933 or 1934. We didn't find any Austrians. We asked whether there were any, but we didn't find any. You must not forget, it was 1940...
>
> In Cape Town we stayed for two months and then we were taken via Suez to the Middle East. There I was in the western desert, that is the whole area between Alexandria and Tripoli. Twice I was in Tobruk, half a year each time, under bombardment from the first to the last day. [When it fell] we were evacuated in an English freighter, which was carrying ammunition...
>
> I was a corporal in the pioneers...

Hans Paul Weiner is the author of a hitherto unpublished book, *They lost their freedom fighting for yours*, concerning the fate of 608 Company PC, a unit which had been formed at Sarafand in Palestine. Although he himself had come from Trautenau in Bohemia he was rather proud of being officially domiciled in Vienna and an Austrian citizen. His father, a burgher of Vienna, had wanted to retain this status when, after the First World War it had been open to citizens of the old Austria-Hungary to opt for the country of their choice amongst the successor states. In 1939 Weiner had fled to Palestine, but could not get in legally. He got in just the same, but had to be careful not to get caught by the British.

When war broke out the army took everybody, whether they were legally in Palestine or not. Obviously Weiner was amongst the first to report and was taken for the RASC. However, after a very short period it was made clear to him that, really, he ought to be a pioneer and he actually consented to have himself transferred. He was posted to 608 Company, which consisted entirely of Jews from Germany, Austria and Czechoslovakia. At first the company was sent to Egypt, then to Tobruk whilst this town was besieged. In 1941 they were taken to Greece.

There they helped the Greeks to get rid of the Italians, but were still there when the Germans intervened. Before the German advance they withdrew nearly the whole length of Greece, until they reached Kalamata at the southern tip of the Peloponnese. They were supposed to be evacuated from there, but there were not enough ships to get them all off. Some of the men found boats and escaped to North Africa only to be taken prisoner there by the Italians, but the great majority of the men were taken prisoner by the Germans in and around Kalamata. Having been held for a time in Greece and elsewhere in the Balkans, they were eventually taken to Carinthia and Weiner spent some time building roads near Lienz in East Tyrol. Then he and his mates were taken to Stalag 8b at Lambsdorf near Oppeln, not all that far from his home at Trautenau.

These men posed a problem for the Germans. They had realised at an early stage that their prisoners were emigrants from Germany, but, through the intermediary of the Swiss government, the British authorities made it very clear that these men enjoyed the full protection of the British government and if they were not treated as prisoners of war under the rules of the Geneva Convention, the British would take it out on German prisoners in their hands. Goering himself is said to have signed the necessary instruction that these men were to be treated as 'British Palestinians' and that their status should be the same as any other British prisoners.

Like all other prisoners of war except officers they were used for various kinds of work. As they were in the neighbourhood of Auschwitz, some apparently even had contacts with the inmates of that camp. Weiner himself was not in that position, for he and about a dozen others were taken to a large farm near Lubowitz alongside the frontier to Poland. Weiner worked as driver of a tractor. In Lubowitz all the men of the village had been conscripted into the *Wehrmacht*. The women, however, gave the glad eye to the handsome British Palestinians and it is not surprising that in due course this had all the normal consequences. It appears that even the local Nazi Party fully understood.

At the end of 1944, however, something occurred which did not please the local Gestapo, for Weiner was arrested and locked up by them. This was reported to the senior British warrant officer at Stalag 8b whereupon he and two other warrant officers, including a Scotsman, donned their best uniforms and marched to the camp gate. These were opened to them by an overawed sentry, who saluted them. They commandeered a vehicle including its driver and had themselves driven to Gestapo headquarters. Led by the Scotsman in kilt and plaid they marched into the boss's office and demanded that Weiner should be handed over to them. This was done without delay and they took him back with them to Stalag 8b. The incident is said to have caused a great deal of amusement on both sides.

Only a few weeks later, however, all the prisoners were forced to take part in a march through the deep snows of the winter of 1944–45. It took two months and brought many of the men near to death. They marched as far as Thuringia. From there they were taken to Fallingbostel in Lower Saxony by rail. There they were liberated by Allied troops on 4 April 1945.

Paul Graetzer's story is similar to Weiner's. He was from Austria, of Jewish ancestry. He had been taken into 'protective custody' in 1938, after which from November 1938 to April 1939 he was in a concentration camp. Then he fled to Palestine. From then on his adventures were similar to Weiner's, except that he was forced to work in a coal mine near Beuthen. Later he somehow got to a place called Ziegenheim near Kassel in central Germany, where eventually he was picked up by advancing US troops.

According to Weiner the following were amongst his comrades at Lubowitz. Ludwig (Vicky) Bleicher from Vienna had been one of those who had escaped to North Africa from Kalamata, but had been taken prisoner there. The Italians had handed him over to the Germans. At first these treated him as a spy and sent him to Vienna, where he spent ten months in a cell in the central court building. Only after nothing could be proved against him was he treated as prisoner of war. I. Elkind died of cancer whilst a prisoner. The Germans buried him with military honours. Franz Meyer had been a master painter and decorator in Vienna. He was only about four feet tall. He had gone to Palestine despite the fact that he had not been a Jew by religion. As master of his trade he was greatly esteemed by his captors. Alfred Palmai, about 40 years of age, had been trainer in the Vienna Jewish sports club Hakoah. The three Sachs brothers had come from Prague originally. There were also two medical orderlies. One was Popper, forename unknown. He is said to have given medical advice and to have treated the German inhabitants of Lubowitz, as well as his fellow prisoners. The other was called Zucker, but has since changed his name to Sukari.

A man whose fate was a similar one was J. Loebl, later Jehoshua Arieli, born in 1916 in Karlsbad, Bohemia. In 1939 he had been on a course for future officers of the Israeli army. Whilst a prisoner he was on forestry work. Having tried to organise a strike he was going to be shot, but his special status saved him. Instead he was sent to a punishment camp in eastern Poland. From there he got to an NCOs' camp, from which he was freed by advancing Soviet troops.

Amongst those who joined the RAF from Palestine were Flight Sergeant Heinrich Fialla, an Austrian, and AC2 Kurt Peter Fischhof, a lecturer of psychology at Vienna University. A man who worked in the Control Commission in Hamburg was Ernest Spielmann. He was from Graz, where he had worked as a tailor. He had emigrated to Palestine, where he became a diamond cutter. In the army he was with the Jewish Brigade in Italy. In 1945 he was sent to Britain for further training. He was demobilised in Hamburg.

The Jewish Brigade was only formed in 1944. It would appear that the great majority of its members came from Palestine. However, Heinz Hirschberg of Berlin, later, as Harry M. Jacobi rabbi of the South Bucks Jewish Community, had arrived in Britain in 1940 via Holland. He joined up in Britain in 1945 and was posted to the Jewish Brigade direct. Quite a few women joined the women's services from Palestine. More about them will be found in the next chapter.

A number of German and Austrian refugees had got as far as Australia before the war began. In 1940 they were reinforced by the men deported from Britain on HMT *Dunera*. Eventually many from both groups joined up. The Australian forces were divided into the Australian Military Forces (AMF) and the Australian Imperial Forces (AIF). Only the latter were allowed to be used outside Australia. Germans and Austrians were generally not allowed in the AIF. They had to join the AMF and many were posted to so-called employment companies, which were similar to the British pioneers. It is said that about 2,500 men served in this way. However, at least one man, Willy Maas, succeeded in joining the AIF. He is known to have been in action against the Japanese on the Solomon Islands.

11

The Ladies

Many of the German and Austrian women who lived and worked in Britain wanted to join the women's services during the war. At first, however, no one other than themselves had thought that this might be a desirable course of action, and so, whilst German and Austrian men were able at least to join the pioneers, there was no similar opportunity for the women. This state of affairs continued throughout the first two years of the war.

However, the fact that German and Austrian women had more good reasons to join up and serve in the women's organisations than most British women was the subject of a discussion, which Colonel Josiah Wedgwood MP had at the House of Commons with an unknown lady in the winter of 1940–41. Most probably the lady was a potential recruit herself and an article by Leonore Bendit in the *Ex-Serviceman* of November 1948 displays such detailed knowledge about what went on, that the question must be asked whether the authoress herself was not Wedgwood's partner. According to this article the lady succeeded in convincing Wedgwood that it was most unfair to expect German and Austrian women to act as spectators only, when their menfolk, in furtherance of their common objective, were permitted to don uniform.

Wedgwood had always given support to the cause of the refugees from Nazi oppression. On this occasion, too, he promised to do what he could. He was so successful that it took less than two months for the War Office and the Ministry of Labour to agree to permit female enemy aliens to join the ATS. The 1st Allied Volunteer Platoon was formed on 11 April 1941, when some 50 young and not quite so young ladies met at Euston Station in order to take the train to Lancaster, where their training began. By a fortunate coincidence a list of the members of this first platoon was discovered by Mrs Erica Prean, daughter of Mrs Ilse Barrington-Stiefel, née Bernstein, when she went through papers belonging to her mother some years ago. Realising how important this was to me, she kindly put it at my disposal. The list includes 51 names. I assume that the remarks in brackets refer, at least in part, to later changes. It reads:

Susi Birnbaum
Antonie Valerie Seltz (Toni)
Eva Oppenheimer (Towse)
Renate Wolfes
Felicia Neumann
Pit Masur
Loni Herrnstedt (Louise?)
Margot Schindler (Morcombe)
Eva Elkiner
Liesel Goetze (US)
Kaethe Beckmann
Lotti Loewenstein
Marianne Rosenthal (South Africa)
Louise Hauer (now Peiser, Germany)
Hedi Niederer
Gerda Samuel
Dr Miriam Racker (Phil.)
Leonore Bendit (Gruenderin, founder)
Gisela Pordes
Joan V. Claer
Ilse Lachmann
Edith Palishaut (Palestine)
Else Abraham
Norma del Mar (Italy, possibly Nella)
Margot Loewie (Smith, Morcombe)
Ilse Marianne Ehrlich (US)
Else Cohn (Palestine)
Susanne Rosert
Doris Hirschfeld (Scotland)
Ruth Feldheim
Mary Pallany
Marianne Gruenbaum (Greenwood?, Mexico City)
Dr Ann Taussig-Bittner (Vienna)
Ellen Wechselmann
Erna Zirker
Trudi Salomon
Hanna Silbiger
Dita Keller (Lawson, Stockholm)
Otti Prochnick
Gertrud Jaffe
Ellen Bergmann
Lilly Kudelka

Billie Kuh
Trudie Reid
Anneliese Erlanger
Hilde Kassel
Lilo Berger
Irmgard Loewenstein
Ilse Stiefel (Barrington)
Eva Stadthagen

At Lancaster they were kitted out and given basic training. Despite the fact that as far as is known all of them came from what might be termed a middle-class background, the experiences which had immediately preceded their date of joining were often very different. Some had been in proper employment, a few even in positions to which their education and training had befitted them, but others had been in situations in which they considered themselves to have been subjected to exploitation. For those who had stood on their own feet, who had been respected by their colleagues and had been treated as ladies in their previous environment, military manners may well have been a shock. But for the others the ATS meant liberation from thraldom.

Eva Oppenheim, later Mrs Gillatt, was not amongst the first batch. She joined later, becoming a member of the 4th Allied Volunteer Platoon. However, her feelings may be typical for those for whom military life was a release from bondage. She wrote:

> my service time was wonderfully happy!
>
> Previous to joining, I had lived with an aunt and uncle in London. I had arrived a few weeks before the outbreak of war, supposedly to live as a family member. I did not have a work permit. Well, – I can only say that I lived a slave-like existence, worked in the home, scrubbing, cleaning, cooking, 12 hours every day, for which I did get the grand sum of 2s 6d per week...I wanted to get away, of course, but I was an enemy alien without a work permit.
>
> In January 1941 I learned that an ATS platoon was about to be formed. For me there was at last a light at the end of the tunnel! The relatives would not let this cheap and efficient slave go, but in May 1941 I was 21 years old and legally could not be held.
>
> I remember posting my application form and seeing big notices to the effect that Hess had arrived in Britain. That was 10 May 1941. I had my medical on 20 May, a day before my 21st birthday. 13 June I was on a train to Lancaster, to be trained as a

cook. Putting on the uniform, learning to march, being somebody, after years of persecution – it was wonderful! On the first Saturday some of us went to Morecambe, woollen gloves (khaki, of course) and saluting officers and being saluted by them – ordinary people will never understand the elation we felt.

I was in Lancaster, learning mass cooking for hundreds of soldiers, for about four weeks.

The 4th AV Platoon...now moved to Huyton, where the 1st had been installed a little while before. Standing in line I was very shy and was the last in the line. The sergeant allocated us into houses – this was a housing estate – two in here, three in here, another two in here...until she came to the end, me. I did not realise that my whole future life was about to be decided. I was allocated into the last house, which really was the ATS sergeants' mess. The occupants were the ATS cook, a corporal, who later showed us how to light a fire, and another girl, Ruth. All belonged to the 1st Platoon.

During the evening Ruth asked me if I wanted to be a cook in the men's mess where she was employed. Why not – I had to cook somewhere. The ATS sergeant came the following morning and I was marched, left, right, left, right, to the male sergeants' cookhouse. The mess sergeant was just ladling out some custard onto a boiled pudding when we got there. 'I suppose she'll soon be gone,' he grumbled about my arrival.

Well, I didn't! I enjoyed all I was doing, it was wonderful and I stayed. In fact, I was still there after almost 38 years of marriage, when he died just 16 years ago. We had three children...

All of us were still enemy aliens, mostly from Germany and Austria, and a few Czechs and Italians...

Some of the others, however, suffered disappointment. At the time of registration the forms used for these women were those in general use. They were the same forms as were used for all the British girls who volunteered as well, and therefore they contained questions which were not applicable to the German and Austrian girls and mentioned employment possibilities which were not available to them. Having been given these forms, however, the women were under the impression that what was contained in them was what was meant. Naturally they were very disappointed when, in Lancaster, they were told that they could work only as cooks or mess orderlies. All their dreams of being drivers, radar operators, secretaries and so on were just pie in the sky.

In these circumstances it would be quite surprising if at that time the number of volunteers should have been as high as about 700, which it must have been, if the number of Allied volunteer platoons in the ATS should really have been 14. But this is the figure given by Bentwich. Against this it should be said that I have not had contact with any lady who belonged to a platoon with a number higher than '4'. It is difficult to believe that Professor Bentwich, writing as he did shortly after the end of hostilities, should have made a mistake of this magnitude. But until ladies come forward who served in Allied volunteer platoons numbered 5 to 14, the existence of units bearing these numbers and with them the figure of 700 for the number of volunteers at that time must be questioned.

However, whether there were four platoons with about 200 or 14 with some 700 members, at the beginning they were kept quite separate from the normal British ATS units. This, together with the restrictions to which they were subjected, gave them the feeling that they were not appreciated. To compensate for this many took an active part in external activities, such as sport, education and in discussion groups, activities in which they were able to meet with their British comrades on an equal footing or better. In all these units, also, strong feelings of solidarity developed.

The period of isolation does not appear to have been too long, however. Hannelore Gumpel, later Laura Selo, who was a member of 3 AV Platoon, says that they were on their own only in their very first location. After that they were always together with British units. Hannelore Gumpel had been one of those who had had a fairly tough time before joining up. Born 1923 in Berlin she had first emigrated to Czechoslovakia, but came to Britain when that country was occupied in 1938. She and her two sisters were taken in by the owner of a small tobacconist's in north London. This lady's motive in taking the three girls appears to have been that she wanted to accomplish a really good deed before she died. Unfortunately she passed away fairly soon afterwards, which left the three children completely on their own in a strange country. Hannelore accepted the responsibility of looking after her sisters and found a job as a maidservant. She did this until 1942, when she was able to join up. After the initial period of segregation she was first attached to the Royal Artillery, then to the RAMC and lastly to the REME. As she moved from regiment to regiment so her job changed. Having started as a mess orderly she became a courier and eventually finished up as a translator. After the war she got married. She has written an autobiography.

Following the fall of Singapore the members of an ATS platoon consisting of Austrian women only made several attempts to get the War Office to send them out to either the Middle or the Far East. Their request was turned down, however, as at that time foreign women were not permitted to be used outside Britain.

As in the case of their male counterparts the restrictions governing the employment of the enemy alien women in the ATS were lifted in 1943. After this they were able to do more interesting jobs. As a result a further contingent of such women, who until that time had worked in industry and in other jobs, reported for service. In December 1944 there were 861 female enemy aliens in the British forces. This figure does not include the many nurses, and perhaps this is also the right place to mention that quite a few did their bit as land girls. The great majority of female enemy aliens in the forces undoubtedly were Germans or Austrians. For the younger ones it was perfectly normal to wear uniform at that time. But also amongst those who continued to wear civilian clothes, there were many who would have wished to wear uniform, but were stopped from doing so by their parents' wishes. In those days the older generation still had more authority than it has today.

The end of the restrictions also meant that the AV Platoons were disbanded. After that both the old and the new ATS girls were treated in the same way as British members of that service. They were given equal rights and equal duties and, with one exception only, no one bothered about their different nationality any more. The exception was that they were not allowed to be used in signalling and communications. Despite this implied distrust, however, they were used as guards, as couriers, as drivers and motor mechanics, to man searchlights and radar apparatus, and a whole lot were called to positions for which a higher education than the average was considered necessary, for the educational level of many of the German and Austrian women also was higher than that of a lot of their British colleagues. Thus Mrs Kenneth, wife of Eric Kenneth, previously storekeeper in the ATS, was transferred to a position of such secrecy that she was not allowed even to tell her husband where she was working, never mind what she was doing there.

Like the men many of the women also were very successful in their further employment. Following the occupation of Austria Major Hess became head of the gynaecological department of the British military hospital in Vienna. Another lady doctor, Major Hamlin, was in the same hospital as her husband at a time when he had just been promoted to lieutenant. Toni Seltz (see nominal roll of 1 AV Platoon above), a sister of Major Sely, was commissioned in the ATS. Mrs Buchanan, wife of Petty Officer Buchanan of the Royal Navy, was a nurse and Sergeant Fleischmann of No.4 AV Platoon was in the

Hamburg HQ of the Allied Control Commission before she completed her service in Vienna.

Lore Sulzbacher changed her name to Sulby. Then she got married and today she is Lorraine Allard. She was born in Fuerth on 8 December 1924. She went to school there and at nearby Nuremberg. Her parents were murdered at Auschwitz. She volunteered for the ATS in June 1943 and after training at Pontefract she was posted to an ack-ack battery in Knightsbridge. There she became driver to the ATS OC of 902 Company, RASC. She remained in this capacity until September 1945, when she was demobilised.

Helga Relation, née Bernstein is a Berliner. She was born in 1923 and there she went to school. In 1941, when still 17, her guardian permitted her to volunteer for the ATS. She joined the E Group and was attached to the Suffolk Regiment in Bury St Edmunds as a cook. Her platoon consisted largely of German, Austrian and Hungarian girls. There were also two Italians. She was a little careless, for in 1942 her pregnancy made it necessary for her to quit the service.

Frankfurt-am-Main is the town where Lieselotte Bier, née Bock, originally came from. In 1927 her family moved to Berlin, where she went to school. She was not allowed to sit her final exam at grammar school, but when she arrived in Britain she was admitted to the examination for school certificate and passed this successfully. As from July 1943 she served in the WAAF, where she was employed as a secretary. Her first job was with Bomber Command, No.5 Group, in Coningsby. She volunteered for service overseas, but as her brother had by that time been made a prisoner of war by the Germans, her request was not granted. However, when in December 1944 she received a posting to HQ 2nd Tactical Air Force in Brussels, this was disregarded, as it was when eventually she was transferred to the SHAEF mission in Paris. In Coningsby she worked, amongst others, for Guy Gibson, OC 617 Squadron, RAF, and for Wing Commander Woodroffe, both of whom had rendered distinguished service. With the senior officer in HQ 5 Group on the other hand, she did have some trouble. He wanted to get rid of her because she was of German origin, but officers with whom she had worked and who had liked working with her persuaded him to leave her where she was. For a while during her time there she was entrusted with the onerous and responsible task of looking after and disposing of the property of officers who had been killed in action.

Alice H. Gross, who in later life became Mrs. Anson, was born in Vienna on 22 September 1924. She became a WAAF in March 1943. In Farnborough she received her training as a photographer. Then she worked at RAF Bomber Command HQ in High Wycombe, where she developed the first photos of V1 firing ramps. Later she was sent to Lincolnshire and finally to Egypt, where she served for ten months. When she joined the WAAF she was one of a group of five. The four others were two Germans, a Czechoslovak girl and a Hungarian.

Though born in Berlin in 1920 Trudi Ornstein was Austrian, being the daughter of Colonel Hans Ornstein, CBE, later to be managing director of the German subsidary of British Petroleum. Having emigrated to Paris in 1933, she reached Algiers in 1941, whither her father had preceded her. She was still there when the Allies landed in North Africa and took Algiers in 1942. As soon as possible after this she reported to British headquarters and was able to join the First Aid Nursing Yeomanry (FANY), which was a unit generally reserved for young ladies of distinction. Despite its name it had very little to do with nursing. She became secretary to Major Ronald Searle of the intelligence service and in this capacity she followed the British troops from Algiers to Siena and eventually to Florence. As the entire FANY was returned to Britain for discharge she was released from the service there on 25 June 1945. Later she married a British officer, who had had a distinguished career with Greek and Yugoslav partisans. Today she is Mrs King, mother of two and lives in Wales.

Elisabeth Mortimer, née Koessler, comes from Miesbach, a small town in Bavaria. She was trained as a nurse. The same applies to Frances Ashley, born as Franzi D. Renner, granddaughter of Dr Karl Renner, twice chancellor and first president of Austria's second republic. She had emigrated to London in 1938, but returned to Vienna, her home town, after the end of hostilities. Having married Eric Ashley, formerly Erich Ascher, a Viennese who had served in the US army, she eventually moved to San Francisco, where she still lives. Klara Ester Graetz, born on 1 March 1921 in Berlin, also belonged to this group. Her father had been an army doctor with the Germans in the First World War.

Irene Lazarowicz, born 28 June 1921 in Vienna, lived there until she emigrated. In 1943 she volunteered for service in the ATS. At that time she changed her name to Lennert. At a psychological test it was found that she had mathematical abilities well beyond the average, after which she was attached to a radar unit, where she became a corporal. Her unit was under command of an anti-aircraft battery stationed in the immediate neighbourhood of Wormwood Scrubs prison in West London. There her job was to locate hostile aircraft and V1 rockets and to pass their positions to the guns.

Susanne Kohn came to Britain from Breslau. At home she had been trained as a nursery nurse. In Britain she first worked as a housemaid.

In March 1943 she reported to the ATS and was given the job of dentist's assistant. However, in December of the same year she was transferred to secret intelligence. She got to CSDIC UK, where she met Sergeant F. Lustig (see above). They married shortly afterwards. Before her discharge in October 1945 she had been promoted to company sergeant major.

Ruth Feldheim, who had been in the 1st AV Platoon, served in Wales as member of an anti-aircraft battery. An excellent violinist, she took part in an Eisteddfod and won first prize. Another WAAF, G. Novelli, was mentioned in despatches. Regrettably the reason for this is not known. Mrs Joan Holden, née Ephraimson, also in the WAAF, was sergeant interpreter. She served from 1943 until 1947 and quit the service having been awarded a Certificate of Merit. A considerable number of other women were employed as interpreters by the WAAF.

Some of the WAAFs were given a special job. In order to confuse German fighter pilots the RAF had early on started using German-speaking wireless operators to pass misleading orders to them. This was countered by the *Luftwaffe* by employing women wireless operators. The Allies again responded by employing German-speaking members of the Women's Auxiliary Air Force. This was known as the double cross (XX) service. Amongst those employed in this way was Edith Perutz, born 1918 in Vienna, who later, by marriage, became Edith Smith.

Until her retirement in 1981 Mrs Anna E.C. Harvey, was in charge of the Dutch section of the British Library. She still is an acknowledged expert on the subject of Dutch literature from the seventeenth century onwards and has published books and articles on this subject. However, she is not Dutch herself. In 1916 she was born in Leipzig as Anna E.C. Simoni and under this name she served in the WAAF during the war. She wrote:

> I had come to the UK as a refugee in 1939. I had not come directly from Leipzig... but (had) spent nearly four years in Italy first. Thence I was kicked out by Mussolini after his agreement with Hitler. I had nearly completed my studies there... London University then demanded an entrance examination including maths, which I had not done since leaving school...
>
> Glasgow University turned out trumps; my German *Abitur* [matriculation exam] was allowed as sufficient for entrance, my three completed years in Italy were allowed as two and I could take an Honours degree in two years... I entered Glasgow University that autumn and graduated in 1941. I took the equivalent of an Honours degree in Greek.

At that time nobody wanted to engage a so-called enemy alien and I continued at Glasgow as a postgraduate student. When I completed my course of studies in the summer of 1943 the situation had changed and refugees were able to join the forces.

After unsuccessful attempts at joining the ATS – where I would have been restricted to the job of storekeeper, whereas I wanted to join only if on equal terms with any other volunteers – and the WRNS – where my status as refugee prevented my acceptance to the regret of the recruiting officer who said my qualifications would otherwise have been most welcome – I was at last lucky with the WAAF. Here no obstacles were raised. The fact that there was a very limited choice of trades, i.e. those of chiropodist, waitress in the sergeants' mess, and flight mechanic, was at least the same for all entrants at that time...I opted for flight mech which seemed to me at least an active way of fighting Hitler. I passed the test...went through basic training at Winslow in Cheshire and through flight mechanic training at Locking in Somerset, being then posted to Training Command at South Cerney, near Cirencester in Gloucestershire. I shared the joys and miseries of other flight mechanics attached to this station and its much happier 'satellites' and my refugee status seemed to make no difference. I applied on one occasion for training as a met officer, when this had been solicited, but the WAAF officer delayed forwarding my application until it was too late; I cannot tell whether this was a deliberate act to frustrate me or just due to her general stupidity and incompetence. A later application for a job as interpreter got me as far as an interview in London. I was given several tests, which I passed, but was then regretfully turned down on the grounds that King's Regulations objected to a downward movement and unfortunately an interpreter ranked lower in the eyes of the RAF than a flight mechanic. When the opportunity arose to be moved to a smaller airfield I grabbed it. There the women's huts were so far from the actual airfield, where we did between-flight inspections and the like, that we were issued with bicycles and were also allowed to use them outside working hours. Bliss in that lovely area of the Cotswolds.

I was finally successful in achieving work more suited to my academic education when, with the end of the war imminent, the Educational and Vocational Training Scheme (EVT) was instituted. I received a fortnight's teaching training and spent the remainder of my service life as a peripatetic EVT instructor, teaching Latin, French, Italian and German at various airfields to highly motivated and hardworking men and women. [This was] at South Cerney, Watchfield near Oxford and Beaulieu Heath in Hampshire. I had been translated for this purpose from a humble LACW to the dizzy heights of sergeant, acting, paid. The greatest advantage of this position was the entitlement to a single room.

I had much fun at Watchfield. It was a station for men only and I could therefore not stay there overnight. I had absolutely charming pupils there, eager to learn and very keen, in addition to being very nice. One afternoon they told me they would all be going by coach to Oxford that evening to go to the theatre. I answered that I wished them a wonderful evening, but would they spare a thought for me as they left their coach at 8 o'clock when I would be standing on the dark and draughty station at Eastleigh, after a long, dark journey from Swindon, with not even a cup of tea to be had. They were flabbergasted that I had to make the journey to Beaulieu by train, or rather three trains, for I had to change once more in Southampton, then get out at Brockenhurst and wait for a car to come from the airfield to collect me . . .

There was a murmur and then they said: 'Wait.' A couple of them ran off and returned a little later with permission to fly me to Beaulieu that Thursday and every coming Thursday.

These flights were often adventurous in themselves . . . Two [other] satellite stations in which I served were called Southrop and Moreton Valence. Especially Southrop was a lovely place to be in . . . [There] there were opportunities to join training flights – in planes with dual controls – and, if the instructor felt generous, he allowed one to take over for a while, which was of course thrilling.

The same instructors also occasionally took one quite illegally to Denham where it was easy to get out of the station with or without a pass and make one's way home to London, to return the next day by train, if one had a pass, by hitch hiking if one hadn't . . .

I once hitch hiked from South Cerney . . . and when the car I had waved to drew near I saw to my horror that its occupant was a RAF officer. He allowed me in, but very soon asked me sternly whether I had a pass. I timidly answered: 'No, sir.' Whereupon he replied: 'Nor have I.' After this we were the best of companions and he took me all the way to Windsor, which was his home town and from where I could get home quite easily.

In general, colleagues and students treated me with great courtesy and kindness. The boorishness of the Education Officer at South Cerney had nothing to do with my refugee status, but was native to him. I was demobilised in May 1946.

Did I have fun...? Yes, a lot. The worst of service life was the feeling that it might never end. It was of course uncomfortable, often pointless, and the job I did was certainly not one I fancied doing for the rest of my life. One was also always afraid for one's family in parts of the country which were being bombed.

I do not think that I greatly contributed to victory. But if by my efforts a few pilots were trained a little sooner, who then helped to defeat Hitler and maybe to save even one Jewish life, I shall be satisfied with those three years of mine.

My WAAF number was 2148120.

A large number of young women joined up in Palestine. All of them started their service at Sarafand, near Haifa. There they received their basic training, which took between six and eight weeks. From the beginning a wider range of jobs was open to them than to the women who joined in Britain. They were wireless and radar operators, lorry drivers and at least one was sent on a secret mission. This was Hannah Szenes, from Hungary. She parachuted into her homeland. However, she was captured, tried and executed. In Israel today she is considered to be a poetess and heroine and there is what almost amounts to a cult about her. Before she died she wrote a poem: 'Blessed is the match that is consumed in the kindled flame'. This has been translated into other languages.

Others had an easier time. One of them was Lilly Gottlieb from Vienna. She was in 508 Company ATS and was attached to a RAOC unit in Cairo. There she served for four years. She was discharged in Jerusalem. Others who served with her were Susan Mizner and Brigitte Sutton, who may well have had other names at the time of their service. Irma Levy, formerly Buer, née Holzer was also in 508 Company. She got to North Africa. Her adventures are recorded in her autobiography, which she published under the title of *Barbara*.

Renate Rothschild was born in Vienna, though her father was a native of Alsfeld in Hesse. She emigrated in 1939 and went to Palestine. She joined up on 5 July 1942 and became a cook. She served at Sarafand for two years. She and her colleagues spoke either Hebrew or German with each other. This was followed by two years at Tel-el-Kebir in Egypt, where her colleagues were Egyptians and Sudanese. She ended her service with six months at Ismailia. After her demob in 1946 she worked as a nursery nurse in Jerusalem. A girl who had emigrated to Palestine from Austria and joined the WAAF from there was M. Biegeleisen, who became an LACW, working on the equipment side of the RAF.

Two sisters who joined the ATS only shortly before the end of hostilities were Frieda and Martha Herzfeld. However, both of them had served in the Northern Ireland Fire Brigade before that. They had come from Kelsterbach near Frankfurt. They emigrated to Britain in 1939. Frieda found work in a London hospital, but after having given satisfactory service for a year she was suddenly dismissed without notice because she was an enemy alien. Martha had by that time got to Ulster, where she worked as a housemaid. In 1940 she was interned, but released shortly afterwards. At this point Frieda joined her. Both then joined the National Fire Service. After joining up both came to the ATS. They were given clerical jobs with the RASC. After her release Frieda became a secretary at Edinburgh University. In 1958 she took a translator's job at Darmstadt. There she married and there she lives until today. Martha trained as a hotel manageress and now works at Edinburgh.

The last report concerns Sergeant Berczi. She was an Austrian meteorologist. The WAAF employed her in her proper profession. She was chief meteorologist at an airfield near London. She is said to have been familiar with most of the languages of the old Austro-Hungarian monarchy. As the airfield was used by Czech and Polish units, as well as British and Norwegian ones, she was certainly a most useful person in her job. Others who are known to have served are:

Anderson, Rose
Beare, Evelyn
Beuger, Lilo
Boehm, Ettie
Biegeleisen, M., 2992399, from Austria, alias Saunders
Braun, Therese, from Vienna, alias Therese Bornstein
Cohn, Susanne, from Breslau, married Lustig
Cohn, Suse (Susan), from Breslau and Mannheim, married Foot
Czempin, R., from Austria
Czerny-Gruenbaum, M., from Austria
Davies, Leonore
Deutsch, L., married Talbot
Dukat, Tilly
Ephraimson, Joan, married Holden
Fleischmann
Friedlaender, Ilse
Gottfried, Lilly, 2992372, from Austria
Haberfeld, Helen, from Vienna, alias Harper
Hirschfeld, Margot
Hulsen, Beate G.
Kalman, Ann
Kalman, Edith

Kalman, Lilo
Kernek, from Linz, married Jones
Koenigsberger, Margaret, from Heidelberg
Koppel, Blanka
Kosteletzky, N.N.J., from Czechoslovakia
Kraemer, Marga
Krassototzky, S., from Austria
Krell, Rosemarie
Kronfeld, Renée, 2992341, from Austria
Lampeitl, V.
Lampert, Lilly, from Vienna
Lange, Helene
Levy, Henny
Lustig, Franziska, No.W/118218, from Vienna, married Frances
    Waldek
Lustig, Lisl, from Austria, married Lustig
Malik, M., from Vienna
Markovicz, Helen, 2992596, from Austria
Mengen, Friedl, married Tauber
Meyer, married Norville
Neumann, Ilse, married Klein
Neumann, Steffi, married Nussbaum
Pach, Sonia, from Berlin and Israel
Peschel, Ruth, from Breslau, married Garland
Redlich, Hedda, from Austria
Rosat, Susanne
Rosen, Lore, from Mannheim
Rosenbaum, Gerti, from Austria
Rosenbaum, Ilse, from Vienna, married Walters
Rosenberg, from Vienna
Rosenrauch, Alice, 2992162, from Austria
Samaskewitz, Lore
Schlesinger, Marianne, from Vienna, married Egtman
Schreiber, Irene, from Berlin
Schulz, Margaret
Simmons, Helga, from Berlin
Spears, Lotte Lorraine
Taus, Hilde, from Austria
Theimer, Mimi, from Austria
Tuerkl, H., 2992235, from Austria
Wachtel, Blanka, 2992780, from Austria
Weiss, Edith
Wurzl, Gertrude

12

Afterwards

The reports of the conditions which Allied troops found in the Nazi concentration camps which they liberated seemed just as incredible to the British soldiers of enemy nationality as they appeared to the public in Britain and other countries. When everything that one might have feared about them turned out to have been a mere nothing when contrasted with reality, the shock to those who knew their near and dear ones to have been the victims was terrible. The realisation of what had happened, and the stories of how it had been done, left those whose families had been exterminated like vermin in a state of trauma which in many cases left permanent marks. One had been afraid for those left behind, but now it was clear that what had really happened was much worse than what anyone in his wildest nightmares might have dreamt. Most of those affected, however, were not in a position to do anything about it, other than to grieve. It was too late and everyone had a job to do in the forces and this had to be given priority.

Only few were able to give direct assistance to the victims. One such was Captain Horwell, who long before he had been commissioned had been quartermaster of 93 Company PC. Following the liberation of Bergen-Belsen concentration camp he was appointed deputy to the officer commanding there. In this position he was able to help many of the survivors. Also at Belsen were Staff Sergeant Schreiber and Sergeant Keith Enoch. Schreiber was there as Lord Janner's assistant and did a great job clearing up the concentration camp. Enoch, having been a pioneer had transferred to the Royal Fusiliers. Probably he was a member of SOE. He had to interrogate Kramer, 'the butcher of Bergen-Belsen', and his fellow jailers.

A few were able to visit camps in which they suspected that their own relatives were being held, and some of them even succeeded in finding the people they sought, but the vast majority had no such opportunity. However, their bitterness did not deter them from participating in the jobs which were necessary to cleanse Germany and Austria of those who had built up this engine of destruction. They did not even refuse in the chaos of the days following the Nazi surrender to lend a hand in the work of restoring to the defeated a working administration. They ignored that substantial numbers amongst the enemy population had given active support to the Nazis and worked hard at giving them the opportunity to recognise and turn from their error. They even helped the German and Austrian people to form and order their lives anew. Those who took part in this work were many, and the few names which are mentioned in this chapter are only a fraction of those who were involved. Some who took part in this have already been mentioned in previous chapters, but even when these are added, what can be told here is but a minute part of what was done. Most of those who were in Germany and Austria immediately following the end of hostilities remained there only until they were demobilised. Only a few remained longer. Not all had an easy time and some did not get a lot of sympathy.

Some did not get to Germany or Austria, but were used in the British Empire and even in countries outside this, wherever British troops were stationed after the war had ended. They might indeed have been better employed in the countries where they had originally come from, but, apart from the general contribution they made in the jobs for which they were used, they also contributed to the regeneration of Germany and Austria by releasing others to be employed there.

In the first few months after hostilities had ceased a great deal of the official contacts between the British forces of occupation and the population of the newly occupied countries was handled by the Germans and Austrians who were serving with the British. Besides those who had remained pioneers until they had been sent to the interpreter schools in Brussels and elsewhere, many of those who had served in combatant units also joined the Allied military government for Germany and Austria. As a result of their ability to communicate easily with both sides, victors and defeated, they became essential to all, and as most of them were not only good communicators, but intelligent and capable people to boot, they were used in positions in which one would not normally expect to find men holding the ranks which they held. In some cases this anomaly was recognised and they received rapid promotion, whereas others remained in their lowly ranks, and received rates of pay which stood in no relationship to the responsibilities with which they were burdened and the jobs they undertook.

Amongst those who had especially important positions within the Control Commission for Germany was Ulrich Hollander, alias Michael Alexander Thomas, the son of Felix Hollander, a well-known author. He had been born in Berlin in 1915 and had studied at the University of Tübingen. But although he had been allowed to finish his course of studies there, he had not been allowed to receive the degree to which by virtue of his exam results he was entitled. He had been a member of 88 Company PC. Later he became British liaison officer with a Polish division in Normandy. Amongst his direct subordinates he became known as 'the Prussian baron', because he required them to clean their teeth and have a shower every day. Having been appointed a political officer upon his arrival in Germany he made early contacts with German politicians, such as Petersen in Hamburg and Karl Severing. Then he became liaison officer to the burgomaster of Cologne, at that time Konrad Adenauer. It was he who first of all warned his superiors of the consequences of Adenauer's dismissal from office by General Barraclough. Later he also warned General Templer concerning the wisdom of his order stopping male German civilians from wearing parts of old military uniforms, for he knew that many had nothing else to wear. Templer is said to have resented this and to have ceased to support him, as he had done until then. Some time later his direct superior, a Lieutenant Colonel Pearson, called him a 'Jew boy'. As a result Hollander withdrew his application to remain in the army as a professional officer and was demobilised with his proper group. Nevertheless he continued in his employment with the military government for some time afterwards as a civilian. In the end he remained in Germany, where he wrote a German-language book, the title of which is a skit on the opening lines of the old German national anthem – *Deutschland, England Über Alles*.

Major Lynton, who had first been a pioneer, after which he had been in a RAC unit during the advance from Normandy to the Rhine, became chief of the political section of the British army in Schleswig-Holstein. At the same time the British army's information section in Austria was staffed by Majors Calmon, who had been in the action on the island of Lissa before he had become head of the 8th Army's mobile intelligence service, and Kendal, previously Knobloch. These two were instrumental in the discovery and arrest of various war criminals.

Major Linford, who had been a pioneer officer and was later transferred to the RAC, became second secretary of the Allied Control Commission for Austria. This meant that he was the British liaison officer to the other member states in the commission. His Berlin counterpart was Captain Lederer.

A Berliner, Walter Wallich, brother of the later US Federal Reserve governor Henry Wallich, served in the Pioneer Corps and with the Royal Artillery, before he became responsible for the *Reichskulturkammer* in Berlin in 1945. Later he was controller of broadcasting in the British zone.

The Information Services Intelligence Control Sections in both

Berlin and Hamburg had as their officer commanding Major Kaye Wolve Frederick Sely, previously Kurt Wolfgand Friedrich Seltz, a Pioneer officer, who had been born in Munich. His job was the de-Nazification of actors, musicians, writers and other artists and people in cultural life, a job, which, apparently he undertook with a great deal of humour and understanding. Sely was assisted by Sergeants Oliver, a German, and George Clare, previously Klaar, of Vienna. The latter, who had previously been in 77 Company PC and 157 Field Regiment, Royal Artillery, became chief representative of the Axel Springer publishing empire and got this position as the direct result of being introduced to Axel Springer personally by Sely in his (Sely's) office.

A handbook about Germany for the use of the military government generally had been written by Francis L. Carsten, previously Franz L. Carsten from Berlin. Having volunteered for the services in October 1940 he first served as orderly room clerk in No. 3 PCTC. From there he was transferred to the Political Warfare Executive at the War Office.

Even the reoccupation of the Channel Islands, the only part of the empire to have been occupied by German forces during the war, did not happen without the services of a German member of HM Forces. On 9 May 1945, on board HMS *Beagle*, Sergeant Sheldon, in civilian life a German lawyer, translated for the British commanders, Brigadier Snow and Rear Admiral Stuart, the surrender terms for the German troops on the islands to their commander General Wolff. Afterwards Sheldon remained there and became chief investigator concerning the crimes committed on the island of Alderney by the Nazis against Russian prisoners who had been sent there as forced labourers.

British soldiers from Germany and Austria took a leading part in the re-establishment of trustworthy newspapers and other media in the occupied countries. Thus Captain Prince Franz Weikersheim was in charge of Sub-Section 3, No.2 Information Control Unit in 1945. This position qualified him to become the founder and first editor-in-chief of the *Ruhrzeitung*, the forerunner of today's *Neue Ruhr Zeitung – Neue Rhein Zeitung* of Essen, one of the leading newspapers in western Germany. On this subject the owner of the paper, the late Professor Dietrich Oppenberg, wrote:

> After the Americans had handed over the Ruhr area to the British, a number of Germans, Austrians and ethnic Germans from Czechoslovakia turned up. Captain Prince Franz Weikersheim's family originated from the famous Castle Weikersheim in southern Germany. When he arrived I was able to obtain for him a copy of the *Gotha* [the German equivalent of *Debrett's*] in which,

fortunately, he himself figured. He was a London banker. After he had ended his activities in Essen and Oelde he returned there.

I also well remember Colonel Eric Mosbacher, who had an important position in the Press Control Section.

At the British headquarters in Benrath, Leo Felix and Heinrich Kisch, from Prague, were active and showed themselves fair in their relationship with our undertaking.

Peter de Mendelsohn, the well-known author, was in the Berlin headquarters. I am especially grateful to him, as he was the man who enabled me and my staff to remain in the building in Essen, which we ourselves had restored, although the British had proposed to accommodate there their own paper *Die Welt* only.

Other names which occur to me are Bernhard Menne, later on the first editor-in-chief of the *Welt am Sonntag*, and Erich Brost, who worked as a journalist at the *Kölnische Kurier* and the *Ruhrzeitung*, before I was able to engage him as editor-in-chief for my own NRZ...

E.H. Pollitzer, alias Pollitt, was Viennese and had been a teacher before he became a journalist. He was at Harfleur and later in Herefordshire and in Catterick with 88 Company PC. Because of his journalistic background he was transferred to a propaganda unit in 1943. Many of the leaflets which were distributed in France were written by him. During the advance through France, Belgium and Holland it was usually his voice which was broadcast to soldiers of the *Wehrmacht* to give them news of the true state of affairs. For a time after 1945 he acted as editor of the *Lübecker Post*. After the war the parliamentary constituency of Limehouse in the East End of London elected a communist by the name of Pollitt several times as its member to the House of Commons. However, I have been assured that this was not the same man.

Leonard Felix Field had been born Leo Felix at Karlsbad in northern Bohemia on 16 November 1902. He had been a journalist in his homeland. He joined the pioneers in March 1940. Later he was transferred to the Intelligence Corps, where he served in several different units. He was in Sicily, Greece, Italy, Corsica and North Africa, before he was transferred to the Control Commission for Germany. There at first he was in No. 12 Field Security Section, then in No. 428. In the Benrath HQ BAOR he was in newspaper control and helped to found the *Neue Rhein Zeitung*. For a time he also ran the Hamburg office of the Information Services Intelligence Control Section under Major Sely. Having become a warrant officer class III he was discharged in May 1948.

Very little is known about W. Blum. He served in 249 Company PC, which he left to attend OCTU. He was commissioned, for his name appears in the officers' list of 88 Company PC for 31st August 1943. Most probably he, too, had originally been a journalist, for he was asked for by the Press and Publicity Service of 21 Army Group to join them for a job in Information Control. Other members of the publicity and psychological warfare sections also made themselves felt in the newly revived press and in other media. Several names are known. Also the Publicity and Psychological Warfare Group of 21 Army Group gave employment to quite a number.

According to a source which wishes to remain unnamed, but which had connections to information control, L.E. Jellinek was a member of a family of 'Viennese boffins'. He was in a publicity and psychological warfare section in 1944. His name appears in a list of personnel who were posted from Le Tronquay to Amiens between 3 and 11 September 1944. H. Landsberg who had previously been with 220 Company PC was in the same unit.

E. Guttmann, who had also been with the pioneers before, was in a unit where he worked with Heckssher, James (alias Jessen) and Patton. He is not to be confused with Ernest Goodman alias Ernst Guttmann of Breslau, who was in the Coldstream Guards.

Another Priestley, not the Peter Priestley alias Egon Lindenbaum mentioned above, had been a pioneer before he was transferred to the interpreters pool in Brussels in 1944. From there he was posted to the publicity and psychological warfare section to fulfil a task in information control.

Rothmann from Vienna, son of a Jewish father and an Irish mother, called himself O'Rourke at that time and had the army number 13117466. He also served in this section. On 17 January 1945 he was transferred from its 11 Amplifier Unit to its No.18 Leaflet Unit.

Henry D. Ormond, originally Hans Oettinger from Kassel, was one of the older ones. He was born in 1901. Having studied law, in 1930 he had been appointed a public prosecutor and later a judge in Mannheim. In 1933 he was dismissed from office. He worked as an advocate until 1939, then he fled to Britain via Switzerland. It seems that he joined the pioneers in 1942 and that he had several postings before he was transferred to the 12th Amplifier Unit. In April 1945 he was the author of a proclamation to the citizens of Oldenburg, a copy of which forms part of the collection of the *Gedenkstätte Deutscher Widerstand* in Berlin.

In 1944 E. Knapp was one of the members of 10 Psychological Warfare Group in the Allied Information Service. In the same year C.

Schreiber, who appears to have been a pioneer, A. Goldwasser, a gunner, and F. Stockner were in No.1 Psychological Warfare Group, SHAEF. J.D. Krivine, who had served in the RAC, was OC No.10 Amplifier Unit, 21 Army Group in 1944–45. M. Martin served in the same unit. There he was responsible for information control. Eric Heller, a former pioneer in 137 Company PC became a film censor at the rank of major. He died on active service. The cause is unknown.

Any number were interpreters. A few of their names are known. Major Reitlinger was an Austrian. He served in the SOE. Later he was personal interpreter of the British High Commissioner and commander-in-chief of the British Forces in Austria. Sergeant Rawdon from Vienna was interpreter for the Military Police unit, which marched into Berlin at the head of the British troops when they entered the city. Richard Burnett, formerly Behrendt, a Berliner born in 1910, had served in four Pioneer Companies, Nos.246, 249, 229 and 93. He became an interpreter with the Allied Coal Commission at Wetter-on-Ruhr. Modestly he wrote, 'My service was neither interesting nor unusual'. Ernest Brown, born Ernst Braun, was from Penkum, a village in Pomerania. He had gone to school in Schwedt-on-Oder, after which he got an apprenticeship at a jeweller's in Breslau. In the pioneers he belonged in turn to 248, 69 and 74 Companies. Towards the end of hostilities he entered the interpreters' college at Brussels. He finally ended his military service as a corporal in the military government at Moenchengladbach and at Loehne. The Reverend Eric Cahn, now a rabbi in Australia, had served in 248 and 69 Companies PC and was in France with the last named of these units in 1944. He, too, was at the Brussels interpreters' college. From there he was posted to the 18th Canadian Field Security Section in East Friesia. Alfred Spier was with the British military government in Lippstadt, Munster and Bielefeld. Having been born in a village near Marburg in Hesse, he had gone to school there and at Nauheim. He joined up in 1943 and was taken by the REME. Shortly before the end of hostilities he went to Brussels and thence to Germany.

E.J. Studley, formerly Studinsky, came from Berlin. He had been born there on 19 November 1916 and there he had gone to school. He joined the pioneers on 4 December 1940 and served in 69 and 137 Companies. As from the middle of 1945 he worked as an interpreter in Berlin, where he met several members of his family, some of whom had survived the war in concentration camps, whilst others had lived undercover and been looked after by people who had taken pity on them. He was demobilised in October 1946. Herbert P. Goldsmith, originally Goldschmidt, arrived in Britain from Delmenhorst in 1936.

On 10 July 1940 he signed up at a Yorkshire recruiting office and was posted to 69 Company PC. He was still with that company when it landed on the Normandy coast at Arromanches on 5 August 1944 (D+60) and later at Caen, Brugge and Antwerp. Then he, too, was sent to the interpreters' college at Brussels. He finished his service at Oldenburg. Peter W. Johnson was born Wolfgang Joseps. He came from Berlin, where he had been born in 1916. After joining up on 23 December 1941, he was sent to 220 Company PC, which landed at Arromanches one day after the 69th. He was still with this company when it was involved in the fighting to stop Rundstedt's offensive at St Hubert in the Ardennes at the beginning of 1945. Having been trained as an interpreter in Brussels, he finished up in Hildesheim, where he stayed until being demobilised in December 1946. An interesting example for the close co-operation between the British and US armies is what happened to George T. Duffhaus. Having served in 219 Company PC, he worked as interpreter in the censorship department of the US army in their zone of occupation.

The pursuit of war criminals was the job of a group of teams most of which consisted wholly or in part of former refugees. Captain Peter A. Alexander, who had been a bank clerk in Vienna before the war and who had been commissioned in the pioneers, where he served in 69 Company, was one of the first to be entrusted with this task. We have come across Frederick Michael Warner, formerly Manfred Werner from Hamburg, as one of the officers who jumped into Upper Styria with the object of securing for the British the airport at Zeltweg. At a later stage of his career, having in the meantime been promoted to the rank of major, he was a member of one of these investigating teams in the British zone of Germany. This consisted of some 80 officers and men, many of whom were former pioneers, but it also included Canadians, Poles and several other nationalities. The group succeeded in arresting several war criminals. Warner tells the story of how he had to take Dr Schweder, the former head of the Bremen Gestapo, to prison in Hamburg. On the way he stopped at an RAF station and, whilst he had to attend to other matters, left his prisoner in what he thought were the safe hands of a group of RAF officers. He was delayed and when he got back after some time he found that these officers had used the opportunity to stage a Gestapo-type trial with Dr Schweder. It must have been extremely realistic for Warner says his prisoner was greatly relieved to see him (Warner) again. Schweder had thought his last hour had come. In the same team were Captain Joe Leniewski and Sergeants Ullmann and Jellinek. Bentwich refers to a Captain Lewianski but I think it is fair to assume that he means the same man. Another ex-member of the Zeltweg group, Anton Freud, was similarly engaged in the pursuit of leading Nazis. Having become officer commanding his team he was able to arrest Dr Tesch, who had been responsible for the production of the killer gases used at Auschwitz. It may be that he was together with Stevens (Schweiger) for both claim to have captured Himmler's deputy Oswald Pohl.

Fred Pelican, who had merely had to change the 'k' in his original name to 'c', was in yet another such team. Born on 8 January 1918 at Miastezko near Kattowitz, Upper Silesia, he was a thwarted medical student, who, as a Jew, had not been allowed to complete his studies by the Nazis. Having been an active sportsman and a member of the Gleiwitz Makkabi football team as well as a chorister in the synagogue, he was particularly suspect to them, for which reason he had also spent some time at Dachau. He left for Britain shortly after his release. He was in Richborough and volunteered for the army from there. With 74 Company PC he went to France twice, in 1940 and again in 1944. In his book, *From Dachau to Dunkirk*, he describes the devious ways he had to pursue to be able to arrest Hans Esser, a leading Nazi in Essen.

One of the X troopers, Peter Jackson formerly Jacobus, was a member of another, similar team. It was he who succeeded in arresting Rudolf Hoess, who had been in charge of the Auschwitz concentration camp. The arrest took place in the kitchen of a farmhouse where Hoess had hidden. Although his superiors were aware of the fact that Jackson's mother had been at Auschwitz and had been gassed there, they nevertheless left the job of questioning Hoess to him. Jackson could not overcome the disgust he felt when in close contact with that man, other than by dosing himself with what spirits were to hand. He is said to have been completely drunk during the entire week which the interrogation lasted. Three other former X troopers were in security sections. John Envers was at Poppendorf near Lubeck, where he, too, pursued war criminals. However, he did not stay with them for long. Eventually he was in Egypt, where he was given the job of re-educating prisoners of war. Gerald (Jerry) Nichols, who in Normandy had led the X-troop detachment with No.6 Commando, ended up in information control in Schleswig-Holstein after he, too, had been in an investigating team. Geoffrey Dickson (Dobriner) was in 98 Field Security Section. When Stalag Luft 3 at Sagan was disbanded, Flight Sergeant Wieselmann, a former pioneer, was charged with investigating the murder of some 50 RAF officers at that camp.

An interesting observation concerning the attitude of individual Germans to the regime comes from Reginald Pringle, formerly Paul Rosenzweig. His mother had been a Jewess, who remained in

Germany and was sent to her death in Auschwitz in 1942. He had been brought up as a Protestant. Although his father had not been a Jew, he had been made to work on the land in a village called Altleiningen, as early as 1933. In 1938 he was taken to Dachau concentration camp. He was a pioneer as from 18 February 1940 and was at Le Havre with 88 Company. Later he was posted to 229 Company, where he served in the same section as myself. Having done the usual term at the interpreters' school at Brussels he was sent to a security unit at Bad Oeynhausen and at Minden. He wrote to say that he took part in many searches of suspected houses and flats, but wheresoever there was a bible in the house, there was never any sign of any Nazi literature.

There is some doubt concerning the number of the pioneer company which was Henry Lewis Morland's first unit after he had joined the army. He maintains that it was 339 Company, but with the greatest respect to his powers of recollection it must be said that 339 Company was a very ordinary British company of the Pioneer Corps and, as Morland's name at that time was Heinz Ludwig Merlaender and he hailed from Hannover, it seems more than unlikely that he should have been there. Perhaps he has turned two 2s into two 3s and it was 229 Company, which had the honour of being his first home from home, or maybe it was another one altogether. But whichever it was, he did not stay there for long, because he was posted to 220 Company and then, in 1944, transferred to the Intelligence Corps, where he became a sergeant and later even sergeant major. He, too, was with a security section after the war. In the end, however, he was an intelligence officer with the Control Commission for Germany.

The end of hostilities and the occupation of Germany meant that German law was temporarily invalidated and German courts ceased to function. Their places, in the British zone of occupation, were taken by military courts in which British officers acted as judges. As is usual in British courts they were advised by suitably qualified personnel. Outside the ranks of the enemy aliens in British service such people were extremely scarce, however, with the result that not a single one of these courts managed without at least one such person as interpreter, clerk of the court or even as general administrator.

Having reached Schleswig-Holstein by a tank of the 1st Royal Tank Regiment Henry Mortimer, originally Heinrich Mosenthal, whom we have met before, was first transferred to the 2nd Fyfe and Forfars, at that time stationed in and around Itzehoe. Then a call went out for a suitably qualified person to act as interpreter at the military court at Rendsburg. Trooper Mortimer applied and was welcomed. In view of the fact, however, that he not only spoke and understood the local language, but also knew how a court of law should operate, he was entrusted with the job of administrator within the space of a few days only. He remained at Rendsburg in this capacity until his discharge on 16 January 1946. In the meantime his commanding officer had proposed him for an immediate commission, but nevertheless his discharge certificate shows his rank as 'Trooper RAC' to the last day of his service.

A somewhat similar job was done by Alfred Summerfield (Sommerfeld), who came from Taplow in East Prussia and had been a sergeant in 137 Company PC. After the end of hostilities he had first of all been transferred to the military police of the Coldstream Guards, after which he found employment at the headquarters of No.1 Army Corps. There he was entrusted with the examination of war criminals and acted as court interpreter.

Peter H. Wayne had originally been Dieter Wolff. He was born in Berlin on 8 May 1920. Having served in 251 and 93 Companies, PC, he became chief interpreter at the war crimes court in Minden. Later he was charged with examining the activities during the war of German financial institutions. He was discharged in 1946.

Walter Fast, the secretary of the Anglo-Austrian Society, whom we have met earlier, did not go to the Brussels college to be an interpreter. He attended a course in Kensington instead. Having completed this he got to the military government at Munster. There he was employed not as an interpreter at all but in the interrogation of war criminals. This way he got to Bueckeburg. Next thing he became deputy chief of the legal department, again at Munster. One of his jobs was, together with his boss, to inspect the Westphalian jails – a terrible job, as he says. His last task was to look after a group of former concentration camp internees who had survived the rigours of imprisonment at Stutthof in Estonia. His discharge came in October 1946.

The work of the British-Austrian Legal Unit (BALU) was of considerable importance for the re-establishment of a separate body of law in Austria and for the reintroduction of an Austrian legal system. The need for this was realised already in 1943, but the proposal to call a number of Austrian lawyers into the War Office to make the necessary plans was thwarted by a regulation which did not allow foreigners of any kind to work in the legal department there. This was circumvented by the establishment of a separate unit to which this regulation did not apply. It was formed under the command of Lord Schuster, an English lawyer who was descended from a German-Jewish family. Apart from him all members were Austrian lawyers serving in the forces.

In 1945 they moved to Vienna. There they became part of the

British military government for Austria and were instrumental not only in the formulation of all the ordinances and legal provisions of the Allied Control Commission, but also for the vetting of all the legislation of the Austrian parliament, whose decisions had to be sanctioned by the Allied governors before they attained legal force. They were also able to exert some influence on the appointment of Austrian judges and were able to ensure that those tainted by undue co-operation with the Nazis were not reappointed.

The deputy to Lord Schuster and the man who actually ran the unit was Lieutenant Colonel Wolf Lasky, a Viennese, who had studied at Vienna and Heidelberg. Before his emigration to Britain he had worked in the legal department of the Vienna city government and had written a treatise concerning the Austrian law of civil administration. His activities as a ski instructor in the British army and his transfer from the pioneers to the RASC have already been mentioned in previous chapters. The order that he should report to the War Office to be used in BALU reached him just as he was about to go aboard ship to go to India, where he had been drafted. Eric Saunders, formerly Schwarz, who worked with Lasky, wrote:

> Wolf Lasky was a remarkable person. When he got to Vienna, he discovered that his books, which he had written before the war, had continued to earn royalties, so that he had a certain amount of money at his disposal. As soon as his arrival became known the provisional Austrian government appointed him a judge of the court of administration. Thus he was in the unique position of being an Austrian judge and a British officer simultaneously. However, he never actually exercised any Austrian judicial function. He did not want to remain in Austria. After BALU had been disbanded [in 1948] he became legal adviser to the British Control Commission for Germany. When this also came to an end, he was supposed to become legal adviser to the British forces in Germany. However, the British government did not agree to this appointment. According to the rules this post could only go to a British-born person whose ancestors had been British for at least two generations. The position remained open for over a year during which a search was made for such a person, who could do the job as well as Lasky. It was only when it became clear that no one else could be found that the rules were changed so that Lasky could get the job after all. After his retirement he received the OBE. He remained in Germany. By that time he no longer had a home to go to anywhere else.

Another member of BALU, if only for a limited period, was Major Dr Friedrich Schneck, whose adventures in North Africa have been the subject matter of reports in an earlier chapter. He, too, had been a lawyer in Vienna. His other qualification was that he had been a prominent member of the Social Democratic Party. He had joined Lasky at the War Office at an early stage. Recently his life has been the subject of intensive research by the Austrian Academy of Science.

Captain Blair, formerly Blau, of the Royal Artillery was another BALU member. Apparently he had been in the Normandy landing as regimental intelligence officer, after which, somehow, he had reached Vienna via Rome and Klagenfurt. Major Norvill also joined BALU in Vienna. Having been in the RAC for as long as hostilities lasted, he became legal adviser to the military government in Lubeck, where, incidentally, he also got married, his bride being an ATS member who, like him, still had enemy alien status. Until her marriage her surname had been Meyer. After that it was discovered that his legal qualifications were Austrian, rather than German. This explains his transfer to Vienna. He also has been mentioned earlier.

Amongst these good people Eric Sanders, originally Erich Schwarz of Vienna, must have stuck out like a sore thumb. He commented that he hated school and was enormously grateful to Hitler for liberating him from all that nonsense in 1938. Having come to London that year he worked for the German-Jewish Aid Committee, Woburn and Bloomsbury House. Then he was a dairy hand at Basingstoke. He went to France with 88 Company PC in 1940, was at Harfleur, Le Havre, Rennes and St Malo. Having returned to Britain he took a correspondence course for his intermediate B.Sc., after which he was transferred to SOE. In Bari, together wirth Hladnik and Wirlander he was employed questioning Austrian prisoners of war. Then he was given training for a job in Styria, which never came off, because the war ended first. After all of which, as WO1, he too was in BALU.

German jurists, unlike the Austrians, were not organised in a separate unit. However, some of them also had some influence on events. A few names which are mentioned by Bentwich are Lieutenant Colonel Farnborough, legal adviser to military government HQ, Lieutenant Colonel Wilhelm Cohn, a judge at Hannover, Major Romberg, responsible for liaison with the German judiciary, Captain Renow, who supervised the trials of war criminals, and Captain Fleming. Dr. Ernest Cohen had been a gunner. After the war was over he was commissioned and eventually became first legal assistant to the Control Commission. He completed his service as deputy judge advocate in BAOR. Major Dr Hermann Strauss came from Weiden in Upper Palatinate. He had served

15 Bobby Spuner (Spooner), former Bantam weight champion of Europe, who had both hands crushed in Dachau concentration camp, with Sgt Dr Baer, both 74 Company PC.

16 Kit inspection, 74 Company PC, after their return from France, 1940 (courtesy Royal Pioneer Corps Association)

17 A normal scene in the Pioneer Corps: one man is working, the other watching (courtesy Royal Pioneer Corps Association)

18 Work on defence positions (courtesy Royal Pioneer Corps Association)

19 'Allied Volunteer Platoon' of the ATS, probably No. 1 Platoon (courtesy Mrs L. Bray)

20 British War Cemetery, St Laurent-sur-Mer, the grave of R. Leonard (Lehniger) bears witness to his socialist beliefs (courtesy Franz Gockel)

21 No. 3 Troop, 10th Inter-Allied Commando, the X Troop (courtesy John Envers)

Key to the X Troop photo

1 Graham	13 Scott	25 Lewis	37 Seymour	49 Mason
2 Aitcheson	14 Sayers	26 Anderson	38 Arlen	50 O'Neil
3 Masters	15 Laddy	27 Merton	39 Drew	51 Streets
4 Hamilton	16 Gilbert	28 Saunders	40 Grey	52 McGregor
5 Tenant	17 Franklin	29 Griffith	41 Barnes	53 Davis
6 Hepworth W.	18 Farr	30 Envers	42 Fenton	54 Hilton-Jones
7 Garvin	19 Long	31 Bentley	43 Nichols	55 Emmett
8 Naughton	20 Ross	32 Harris	44 Bartlet	60 Kendall
9 Streeten	21 Nelson	33 ?	45 Miles	61 Villiers
10 Douglas	22 Anson	34 Marshal	46 ?	62 Wells
11 Carson	23 Hudson	35 Kingsley	47 Wallen	
12 Andrews	24 Shelley	36 Stewart	48 Turner	

22 Second Lieutenant Steve
Nelson, Royal Artilllery after
commissioning at 123
OCTU, RA, Catterick, 1944
(courtesy Steve Nelson)

23 Erich Klementschitz, in
Belgium, 1945 (courtesy
Eric Clement)

24 The author as Second Lieutenant, London, 1944

25 The author (right)
with a colleague,
Waziristan, 1945

26 The author; a recent photo at his birthday party

his articles as a lawyer in Bingen-on-Rhine, after which he started to practise in Kenya. He joined up there and was accepted immediately for the army's legal department. Before the end of the war he was transferred to South-East Asia Command at Jhansi, India, in a similar capacity, but as soon as hostilities were over he, too, came to the Control Commission for Germany. Sergeant Lazarus, a pioneer who had served in one of the North African Companies, was judge at a German labour court in 1950. A former X trooper, Captain Michael Merton, previously Blumenfeld, became public prosecutor at the military court in Dusseldorf. Later he was transferred to Kiel. Sergeant Dr H. Hachenburg, together with his son, was in 249 Company, PC. He had been one of the leading lawyers in the city of Mannheim before the war. He worked with the military government for Germany after the war. He asked to be released in Germany and made his home there again. At a later stage he was a member of the German commission for the restitution of Jewish property, in addition to which he was appointed a judge at the ordinary court at Heidelberg. He was awarded the Federal Cross of Merit, 1st class, by the German government.

A considerable number of German lawyers were also involved in some way with the Nuremberg trials. Amongst them were Captains W. Frank, Forest and Palmer (Peyer), and Sergeant Stern, who had previously been quartermaster of 251 Company, PC. Others, lay people as it were, acted as interpreters and in various other capacities, both at Nuremberg and in other similar trials elsewhere. In a trial of 15 members of the board of Volkswagen, Herbert Anderson, formerly Helmut Fuerst, was the chief interpreter. Born in Vienna in 1916 Anderson was a man of many talents. He had studied both musicology and economics. From 1936 to 1939 he worked in Istanbul. Then the Turks wanted him out of their country because he had an Austrian passport, which at that time they no longer recognised as valid. As a result of his employers' intervention he was able to go to Britain. Here he first worked on a farm in Dorset, but volunteered for the army as soon as he could. He appears to have joined 93 Company PC, and went to France with them in 1940. In 1943 he was transferred to the SOE, but was not actually used on a mission. After the end of hostilities he was posted to the Civil Affairs Directorate of the British Army on the Rhine. From there he got the job described above.

Germans and Austrians in the British forces, however, did a lot of other things too. An Austrian, Robert Kennard, was a corporal in 220 Company, PC. He volunteered to be an interpreter and was attached to a railway company in the Royal Engineers. With them he reached Magdeburg, where he was the only man who could communicate with equal ease with everybody and soon found himself in the position of stationmaster. Moreover he was responsible, eventually, for the control of all trains and their passengers which crossed the zonal border, for the British guards and for the German personnel of the station. Throughout this period he remained a corporal. Reports say that Richard Urban had been in the Desert Long Range Group, that he had taken part in the liberation of a concentration camp and eventually that he was instrumental in the transport of released prisoners from concentration camps to Palestine.

After the war, what remained of the *Wehrmacht* found itself largely in prisoner of war camps. In the British ones very frequently much of the communication between prisoners and guards took place through the medium of German and Austrian members of HM Forces. But in most cases their services did not stop at enabling communication; they took an active part in the re-education of the prisoners, and thus helped enormously in the re-democratisation of the Germans and Austrians at large.

Probably the best known amongst these men is Herbert Sulzbach. In the First World War he had been an officer in the 69th Prussian (Frankfurt) Regiment of Artillery and had been awarded the Iron Cross for gallantry. At that time he wrote a book concerning the technical aspects of trench warfare, which remained a standard work of reference for a long time afterwards. Having been imprisoned in a concentration camp by the Nazis he emigrated to Britain. He joined up in 1940 and became a pioneer. He served in Britain until 1944, when he became one of the many interpreters. In January 1945 he was posted as a sergeant to Comrie prisoner of war camp, where a clique of unyielding Nazis had achieved a dominant position. They enforced rigid discipline in the worst Nazi manner upon their fellow prisoners, indulging in all the most unpleasant aspects of Nazi behaviour. Shortly before Sulzbach's arrival one of the prisoners had been 'executed' by them. He had been careless enough to allow his diary, in which he had noted his doubts concerning Germany's eventual victory, to fall into the wrong hands. He was brought before a mock court and murdered. The camp was in a state of fear and terror.

Sulzbach spoke to each of the prisoners separately. By intelligent questioning and patient listening he gained the confidence of the greater number of the prisoners and was able to identify and isolate the murderers. Whilst these were taken away, brought to trial and, having been found guilty, hanged, he could convince the rest of the prisoners of their errors. In due course the International Red Cross became aware of Sulzbach's work and recommended that his methods should be copied elsewhere.

This led to Sulzbach being commissioned, after which he was transferred to the prisoner of war camp at Haltwhistle, where he continued his work. Haltwhistle became the most prestigious of the many camps and eventually had its own newspaper, an orchestra, theatre, art exhibition and, finally, a university of its own. Many of the prisoners of both camps, Comrie and Haltwhistle, remained in friendly contact with Sulzbach after their release. Concerning Sulzbach the *Manchester Guardian* wrote:

> All the prisoners like and trust him. He receives letters from ex-prisoners, who have returned to their homes and have nothing to gain by keeping good friends with him. Reading them there can be no doubt of his influence as an apostle of political ideas and as father confessor to his charges.

After his discharge Sulzbach was put in charge of logistics in the Berlin Airlift. After 1947 he was sent to the German embassy in London as a secretary. There he was concerned with the foundation of the European Economic Community, in which connection he received several decorations. His diary and other records are preserved in the military section of the German Federal Archives, now either at Freiburg or at Potsdam.

The *Manchester Guardian* article quoted above went on to say:

> In the South of England there is another camp in which a German Jew exercises a similar influence on several hundred somewhat recalcitrant German Nazis. He looks like a caricature from the 'Stuermer' newspaper. Only as a result of his firmness of character he has gained the affections of the whole camp and the prisoners treat him like a raw egg.

The subject of this song of praise was Captain Starbroke, another ex-pioneer, who got similar results at the Cambridge prisoner of war camp as Sulzbach had achieved at Comrie and Haltwhistle.

Already in the winter of 1942–43 Lieutenant F. Gross had been entrusted with the interrogation of prisoners of war. After the end of hostilities he rose rapidly to the rank of lieutenant colonel, having been appointed to a responsible position in the field of intelligence control and censorship in Germany. Major Gumble also took part in the interrogation of prisoners of war. Major Piblich, who had been second-in-command of one of the alien companies, ended his military career as officer commanding the prisoner of war camp at Bicester.

A former member of the French foreign legion who eventually served in a prisoner of war camp was Paul Hollander. Having been born in Cologne in 1906 he started on his travels early. After 1927 he lived variously in London, Amsterdam and Paris. When war started he joined the foreign legion for the duration of the war. However, by the spring of 1942 he was in Algeria, but no longer a legionnaire. After the British occupied North Africa he joined 338 Company PC, and was with that unit from Hussein Dey to Caserta. Then came a short interlude at GHQ 2nd Echelon in Maddaloni, after which he was posted to the pioneer depot at Prestatyn. His activities in No.157 prisoner of war camp at Bourton-on-the-Hill marked the end of his military career. He was released in August 1946.

Watton in Caithness was one of the major camps for prisoners of war. It contained some 2,000 men. Staff Sergeant Henry Platt, formerly Platzer, a Viennese born in 1921, worked there. Before that he had been in 249 Company PC. Lieutenant Farnham was transferred to military intelligence in North Africa from the Pioneer Corps. After the war had ended he was responsible for the re-education of prisoners on all airfields in Cyrenaica. Having been in charge of No. 6 prisoner of war camp at Brent in 1947 and afterwards of similar camps at Cattistock, Tiverton, Moreton-in-the-Marsh and Cheltenham, Captain Grenville's responsibilities included the release of some 1,000 prisoners of war per week, as well the logistics of getting 7,500 men from southern England to Scotland and back again to help with the potato harvest there. Henry William Grenville had been born Heinz Wilhelm Greilsamer at Stuttgart in 1926. He joined in 1944, when he was 18. He entered the infantry, but was soon transferred to the interpreters' college in Brussels. From there he was sent to the military government at Buende. He was commissioned in 1946. His activities in connection with prisoners of war took place after that.

All the foregoing refers to people and events which have or had some connection with Germany or the defeated enemies. There were, however, also Germans and Austrians in HM Forces who were used in totally different capacities, largely within the empire, which at that time was still very much in existence and showed no noticeable outward signs of disappearing. In the wide spaces of this empire quite a number of enemy aliens were used in various ways. One of these was Peter Masters, formerly Arany, whom we have met before as a member of the X Troop and who has more recently become an author, publishing his wartime experiences. Masters was sent to OCTU towards the end of the war, was commissioned into the Oxfordshire and Buckinghamshire Light Infantry and sent to West Africa. There he was attached to the Gold Coast Regiment.

As mentioned previously I myself was entrusted with the command of B Troop, 201 Indian Independent Medium Battery, Royal Indian Artillery, which lay in Razmak, a fortified camp in Waziristan, in the late summer of 1945. I remained there until the winter of 1946–47. Then I became battery captain of 19 Battery of the 8th Indian Field Regiment in Nowshera, in the North-West Frontier Province. In the troubles which accompanied the division of British India into two separate states, Pakistan and the Union of India, the 8th Field Regiment was used in support of the civil government in the Punjab. I had been very seriously ill just before all this began and was still in a rather weak condition. Therefore I was the obvious man to be left behind at Nowshera to look after the regimental barracks. On 3 September 1947, two days after the regiment had moved out of the town, where order had previously been preserved by its presence, fighting broke out. Some 500 Sikhs and Hindus were murdered by Pathan tribesmen and the remainder, some 2,000 men, women and children, fled into the barracks, which I was looking after. This resulted in my becoming responsible for their safety during the remaining period of my stay in what had then become Pakistan. As a British officer attached to the Indian army I received an offer from the Pakistanis, who were very short of commissioned officers, to remain there as an advisor. Having turned this down, I received orders to return to Britain in late autumn 1947. Having got back I withdrew my application to become a regular officer and was released from the service at the end of that year.

A totally different story was that of Sergeant Peter Meyer. At the end of the war the Greek army added modern wireless sets of British manufacture to its equipment. Meyer was expert on matters of this kind and was given the responsibility for the successful implementation of the relevant programme. Meyer had previously been in Egypt with the Royal Fusiliers, after which he had also served in Iraq and Iran. He was demobilised in 1948.

The question whether, after it was all over, one should return to Germany or Austria did not pose itself for everyone and certainly not to the same degree. In the six years the war lasted and the years following, many had made their homes in Britain or other parts outside their original homelands. For them the question of a return never arose. For a very much smaller number, mainly people who were not Jews and who had made no roots anywhere else, there was never any doubt that they would return to their original homes. But quite a few were uncertain and where eventually they finished up depended to quite an extent on where they could see opportunities for their future lives. Some of those who did go to Germany or Austria did not have entirely pleasant experiences, particularly those who decided to reside in the German Democratic Republic.

One who thought about it quite a lot before he made up his mind was Harry Nomburg, who had been Harry Drew when he served in the X Troop. He wrote:

> A few months after the occupation of Hamburg I was transferred to Berlin. As a sergeant in the British occupation forces I ended up in the very same neighbourhood as that which I had had to leave in a hurry as a young Jewish refugee in a *Kindertransport* in May 1939. Since then my parents had been transported eastwards, where they may either have starved to death in the ghetto of Litzmannstadt (Lodz) or were gassed in the nearby death camp of Chelmo. I have had their names entered in the roll of those who met their deaths as a result of persecution in my native city of Coburg.
>
> Having got to Berlin, which I had known so well, I first of all visited my old teacher, who had taught me to read and write, and the next thing that happened was that I met the mother of one of the boys of the 3rd Troop, No. 10 Commando, who had lost his young life on a Normandy beach on 6 June 1944, whilst she had survived in Berlin. Fortunately I was able to help the woman to obtain a pension.

From Berlin he was transferred to military government in the Eifel mountains, all the time looking for opportunities to settle in Germany, where he felt that his command of the language was better than elsewhere. It was only when he found that no such opportunities offered themselves that he eventually decided to try his luck in the United States, where he started a new life in 1948.

George Clare has been mentioned above. In his case the opposite took place. Whilst Clare had no great intentions to make his home in Germany, the offer of a top job by the publisher Axel Springer persuaded him to try his luck in Berlin and he went back there immediately after his discharge from the army. That this decision was not taken because of any great love for the city, where he remained for the rest of his working life, is borne out by the fact that after his retirement he took up residence in England at once and has been there ever since.

Ken Bartlett, originally Billmann, moved to Munich, where he originally came from. He had been born in 1912 and emigrated to Britain in 1938, having studied musicology at Munich and Tubingen universities. After his arrival in London he continued with his studies at the Royal College of Music. In the army he joined the 3rd Troop, 10th Commando, in Normandy and soon received his commission for outstanding bravery in the field. After this he was sent to Italy, first to Monopoli near Bari and then to Minervino near Ancona. Eventually he assumed command of the X Troop and was the last officer commanding it before it was disbanded. Following the end of hostilities he was sent to Germany. He became music controller of the newly founded NWDR, the North West German Broadcasting organisation. Then he went to Berlin, but ended up in Hamburg with the job of music controller for the whole of the British zone. Later, he was for a time secretary of the Sheffield Philharmonic Society, but as a result of the contacts he had made was soon appointed chief dramatic adviser to the Hamburg Opera. His last full-time job was with the musical publishers B. Schott's Soehne in Mainz. Having retired he remained active as a translator of operas and other works of art, working from his home in Munich.

Ken Levy, who had also served in the X Troop, remained in Germany after his discharge and did so from conviction and because of his sympathy for the people of Elmshorn, a town to which he had come quite accidentally in the last days of the war. In the chaotic days which preceded the arrival of Allied troops the citizens of most German towns, however much they may in some cases have hoped for their early arrival, did little to rid themselves of the Nazis, whose rule had become more and more unbearable. The people of Elmshorn were an honourable exception. There a group of workers seized power by throwing the Nazis out of their offices and into prison. When the British arrived red flags were flying from the town hall, and a workers' committee welcomed the occupiers. Levy, a lifelong communist, immediately fraternised with them and in the circumstances was allowed to do so by his officers. It seems that he remained at Elmshorn until the time of his discharge. After this he studied and eventually became a schoolmaster in this town, which he seems to have regarded as his spiritual home. Some of the locals indeed were not at all happy to have him around and there was quite a bit of hostility towards him. This may have had something to do with his decision to go to South America to teach there for a while, but he returned to Elmshorn and finished his working life as headmaster of the local comprehensive school. For his efforts the British government awarded him the BEM. He died in 1998 as a result of a sudden illness.

Eberhard Zamory also returned to Germany. He was from Breslau. A man of high ideals he became a founder member of the Free German Youth movement in Manchester in the autumn of 1939. In accordance with the instructions of this organisation Zamory did factory work until, in 1943, the decision was taken that all members who were able to do so should join the forces. However, although he would have liked to join another regiment, he was posted to the pioneers even at that late stage. Like so many other in this corps, however, he soon found himself an interpreter, in his case in No.9 prisoner of war camp on the racecourse at Kempton Park. There he was in his element, as he thought that this was an ideal opportunity to put his socialist principles into practice by ensuring that former trade unionists and socialists would take over the leadership amongst the prisoners. He wrote:

> From then on there was chaos. As low ranking NCOs, which most of them were, they simply did not have the necessary authority. But I did not want to give up. Although my British comrades urged me to change my ways, I stuck to what I thought was right until a British lance-corporal, a friend of mine, said to me: 'You are a real bloody German, you never know when you are beaten.'

From Kempton Park Zamory was sent to Norway. His reports from there highlighted the scandalous conditions which continued to exist in that country even after the German surrender. Apparently the British policy of allowing the German army there to continue to administer its own affairs had been due to the British forces who occupied Norway having been initially numerically very much inferior to the surrendering Germans. Having been promoted, Staff Sergeant Zamory arrived there together with five other former refugees from Hitler's Germany. Their job was to supervise the return to Germany of the German troops there. On a visit to Gjernes, one of the *Wehrmacht* camps, he came across a regular German prison in which a sailor by the name of Gerhard Werth was serving a prison sentence. When he investigated the circumstances of Werth's imprisonment, Zamory found that this man had deserted in the spring of 1945, relying on instructions contained in a British leaflet. He had, however, been arrested by the Germans and on 25 May, 17 days after the German surrender, had been sentenced to four years' imprisonment by a German naval court on the west coast of Norway. Thus Werth was being punished quite legally by German authorities under German law in a German camp, which, almost *pro forma*, had become a British prisoner of war camp, for obeying British instructions several months after hostilities had ended. Zamory ensured Werth's immediate release and saw to it that he was returned to his home in Germany at once. From the end of the year until his release Zamory returned to no.9 prisoner of war camp, which had been relocated at Quorn in the meantime.

Despite his experiences Zamory continued to regard himself as a German. Wanting to be an ordinary German amongst Germans he went to Hamburg and matriculated at the university there. He did everything he could not to draw attention to the fact that he had been a British soldier, but found this a very difficult task. The fact that, lacking other clothing, he had to wear his British battledress dyed deep brown did not help. One of his teachers, Professor Hans Wolffheim, told him the truth: 'All want to be on the side of the victors,' he said, 'but you have changed to the side of the losers. You are just absolutely crazy.' Both Levy and Zamory remained in the Federal Republic of Germany and both ended their connection with the communists in the course of time.

The military part of Artur Bratu's life is the one about which least is known. He served in the British army from 1940 until 1945 and during part of this time he was called George Bennett. It is known that in 1940 he was in the pioneers, at some time transferred to the sappers, and before his discharge he had made it to warrant officer class II in the Personnel Research Branch of the Intelligence Corps. This is what he told his friend Willy Usher and this is virtually all that is known.

His history as a civilian is much better documented. He was born in Offenbach in 1910, was an early member of the *Reichsbanner*, a socialist paramilitary organisation, and fled to Belgium in 1933. The Nazis tried to get him even there, but fortunately they were unsuccessful. When they marched into Belgium in 1940, he was still there. He fled to Britain by fishing boat. There he was imprisoned, but let out so as to be able to join up. After the war he returned to Germany as a civilian. He settled at Darmstadt, where at first he was chief prosecutor at the de-Nazification trials. Although he met with quite some enmity he remained active in the public life of the town. At a later stage he became director of the town's education system and before he died he was in charge of the Centre for Political Education for the Land of Hessen. He was awarded the Federal Order of Merit by the German government. He died at Darmstadt in December 1993.

Walter Beck was a Viennese born in 1897. During the First World War he had served in the Austro-Hungarian army and was awarded the Gold Medal for Bravery in the battle of Caporetto. In the Second World War he served in 77 Company PC, and in 1944 got as far as Normandy with them. Then he became an interpreter and worked in the military government at Schleswig. He must have extended his service in the army, because he was discharged only in 1947, and men of his age group were normally demobilised no later than the end of 1945. He went back to Vienna, where he died in August 1955.

Largely for ideological reasons a number of people went to the Soviet zone of Germany, which later became the German Democratic Republic. One of them was David Rummelsburg, who had joined up in 1943. He was commissioned and became a captain before he was discharged. At the beginning of 1953 he was employed in the press information office of the Leipzig Fair. For no known reason one of the Leipzig party organisations of the Socialist Unity Party (SED) denounced him as unreliable. This denunciation finished up on the desk of H. Matern, who at that time was a member of the Politburo of the SED and chairman of the party's central commission of control. He made a marginal note to ask what sort of nonsense this was and sent it back to where it came from. However, the denunciator's reaction was merely to repeat the original accusation and add a new one to it. Rummelsburg continues to live in Berlin.

Goetz Berger, first a judge and later a lawyer in the former German Democratic Republic, died in court whilst giving evidence at the notorious Havemann trial. He had been in the British army for six months during the war. Before the war he was a junior partner in the law office of Hilde Benjamin, a well-known communist lawyer in Berlin-Wedding. In 1936 he left for Spain to take part in the civil war. He was in the International Brigade. He did not, however, see any fighting himself. Later, after the defeat of the republicans he fled to France, where he was interned at Argelés, Guis, Vernes and lastly at Djelfa. In April 1943 he was able to get out and join the pioneers in Algiers. He did so after consultation with the communist party. He was in either 337 or 338 Company. During his time of service in the British army he was given the opportunity to lecture about conditions inside Germany. This, as well as all the other circumstances, made him think very highly of his service with the British, a point of view which later on he was to state in at least one public interview. Despite this, however, he asked to be sent to the Soviet Union and, with the assistance of the Soviet consul at Algiers, he was actually transferred there in the autumn of 1943. He reached the Soviet Union, all the time wearing the uniform of a private in the Pioneer Corps, by ship, rail and bus via Alexandria, Cairo, Haifa, Baghdad and Teheran. The British released him from the service only after his safe arrival in Crasnowodsk in the USSR. Whilst he had thought that he would be welcomed and used immediately against the Nazis, he was actually met with deep suspicion. He was subjected to a most intensive interrogation, after which, completely against his own ideas of what he should be doing, he was sent to a silk factory in

Turkmenistan. There he was employed as an ordinary factory worker. It was only after the end of hostilities that he was allowed to return to the Soviet Zone of Occupation of Germany. Berger always refused to answer questions concerning his activities as a judge in the early days of the GDR. However, it is to be assumed that he remained true to the ideals of his youth. There is no doubt that in the case of Havemann he showed courage by taking a strong line in favour of his client and against those who held the reins of power in the GDR. However, there is also no doubt at all that the leadership of the German Communist Party entertained neither respect nor personal regard for him.

The fate of Klaus Walter Rosenthal was different. He was from Berlin. Having been interned in Canada for about a year he joined up together with a lot of other communists and members of fellow-travelling associations at the behest of the German Communist Party organisation in Manchester in 1944. He joined under the name of Walter Rogers, becoming a sapper and serving in India. In 1947 he went back to Germany. At first he worked in East Berlin training and getting work for young people. Then he was supposed to get a senior job in the GDR government in the same field. This was stopped by the Soviets and he even had to resign the job he was doing. He then became editor of a daily paper. In 1953 the state prosecutor started inquiries against him as a suspected Western agent. This is thought to have been in preparation for a show trial against a number of people who had emigrated to Western countries. At that time the communists gave better treatment to ex-Nazis than they gave to people who had returned to Germany after having spent time in any of the Western countries. This continued persecution, first by the Nazis and then by the communists, broke Rosenthal mentally and physically. He died of heart failure in 1957, aged 36, whilst acting as press representative of the Chamber of Foreign Trade of the GDR at the Leipzig Fair.

13

Reticence Can Go Too Far

Ten thousand is quite a lot of people. One can form nearly two divisions from ten thousand men. As there were that many one would have thought that their existence would be better known. After all, a great many were well educated, able to express themselves and to tell their tales. Emigrants who were not in the forces have written about their adventures, about the fate that befell them when they left their homes, and as one or other of them even showed some literary talent, some of these tales have become well known. The experiences of thousands who were British servicemen, however, have remained almost a secret. Why are they so reticent?

Their reticence is such that the whole story concerning their participation in the war is in real danger of being forgotten. This is not for lack of interest. There are many other groups, far fewer in numbers, who have managed to impress the historically interested public with the fact of their having played a part in the defeat of Hitler, the Nazis and the Third Reich, so what is it that makes these men and women hide their lights under the proverbial bushel?

The public ignorance concerning the part played by Germans and Austrians in the prosecution of the war by the British Forces is not limited to any one country. But there are certain differences between the countries concerned. In Britain, *I Understand the Risks* by Norman Bentwich was published in 1950. The book sold out within a year or two and no second edition was issued. Old copies are still around and are treasured by those who own them. The odd library may still have a copy. But by and large the public has forgotten and, every now and then, when the facts are referred to in a newspaper article, as does happen occasionally, they cause a minor sensation. A lot of information is available at The National Archives, but this suffers from being extremely detailed. It is hidden in amongst a tremendous amount of other detail, and to access it is like looking for a needle in a haystack. To present what is there in a readable form, a lot of work would still be required.

In Austria the Archives of Austrian Resistance contain evidence of the participation of several hundred Austrians in the British services. This information is available to anyone who bothers to look for it and some of it has even been presented in readable form and is available in publications of the Archive. A book by Wolfgang Muchitsch, *Mit Spaten, Waffen und Worten* (With Spades, Weapons and Words), which tells a great deal of the story from the point of view of Austrian participants, was published in 1992, but its sales have been disappointing. At the time of writing copies are still available from the Archive's bookstall at a reduced price.

In Germany not even that much exists. Individual members of the German public who are interested in what happened to emigrants from the localities where they themselves live may occasionally be aware of the fact that one or other of those who left Germany before the war served in the British forces. But they believe them to have been exceptions, not members of a group numbering 10,000. Even those who are supposed to know such things, the federal archives in Coblence, the military archives at Potsdam and Freiburg, the German Historical Society in London and the Memorial to German Resistance in Berlin, knew nothing until in recent years I managed to draw their attention to the facts. The military archives indeed had some records concerning Major Sulzbach, but somehow these led them to believe that he had been 'chief of staff to the officer in charge of the prisoner-of-war administration in the British War Office' already in 1940, a time when Sulzbach was a private soldier in the Auxiliary Military Pioneer Corps. When I asked the German Historical Society in London what records it might have about Germans in the British army the reply was that 'it is to be assumed that a considerable number of refugees did enter war service'. All of which goes to show that up until now no one in or connected with Germany knows even the rudiments of the story.

However, all this ignorance does not necessarily have to be the result of malevolence, nor of lack of interest. It may be that the story of the existence of a German contingent in an Allied army does not conform to the general picture concerning the nature of the war or the nature of its participants. It may well be that the idea that all Germans were guilty is so prevalent that the very idea that there might have been Germans, even non-Jewish Germans, who were so strongly opposed to the Nazi concepts that they took up arms against them appears incredible. And, after all that has been written, this is not by any means surprising.

Patriotism is basic to most people's political thinking. From an early age children are brought up with patriotic symbols. They are fed with information – true or otherwise – about the countries in which they grow up and learn very little about any others. They support their national sides in sporting events and are upset when the other side wins. The people we love and support may be the biggest idiots or the most evil crooks, but provided they share our nationality they are 'ours' and the others are 'they'. For the average person, whatever his or her nationality, to be patriotic is normal and anything else is inconceivable, unacceptable and treasonable.

At the basis of everybody's patriotism – at least in Europe – is the feeling of security conveyed by the knowledge of the institutions, traditions and habits of the country to which one belongs. One knows more or less what to do in any situation. When one is in trouble one knows whom to turn to. One is familiar with the way things are done. One relies on the probity of the authorities, on the justice of the judges. One knows how to communicate and one expects a fair hearing. When this feeling of security is removed, however, patriotism very soon disappears and turns into its opposite – a deep disappointment with one's country and a desire to remove those who have caused this reversal of feeling. This is the point which the great majority of the Germans and Austrians who were in Britain at the beginning of the war had reached.

However, not having had this experience themselves, the vast majority of people everywhere were and are still virtually incapable of believing that patriotism may not always govern everybody's allegiance. As a result, the idea that the Second World War may not have been just another war between nations also finds but few adherents. Yet Germans – and Austrians – fought against the state to which, legally, they belonged. For them the Second World War was a civil war, even though they wore British uniforms and had taken an oath of obedience to the officers of His Britannic Majesty.

It is, of course, so very much easier to use terms like 'the Germans', 'the British', 'the Americans', 'the Italians' and 'the French' than to try to define exactly whom one means. If one did not simplify in this way it would be boring to have to define one's meaning every time, and this is much too complicated in normal speech. Therefore it is not done. But because this results in a woolly use of language, thoughts based on it are equally woolly. The muddle which this causes merely serves to strengthen the nationalist view of the world, concerning which every child is taught that it is the natural way of thinking. And this again prevents people from understanding that the Second World War included a civil war for almost every nation that took part in it.

The required accuracy has certainly caused problems also in the writing of this book. As the subject matter of this book is the story of the Germans and Austrians in British service, I have used the words 'Germans' or 'Germans and Austrians' in general only to describe those who served in the British forces.

As I have emphasised already, a very large number of these were Jews or somehow connected with Jewry. Those who had no connection with Jewry at all were certainly no more than 15 per cent and probably less. But the fact that there were some precludes the use of the word 'Jewish' to describe the lot. The use of this word is further precluded by the fact that we were not treated as we were because we were Jewish, but our treatment was the result of our being of German or other enemy nationality.

The word 'Jew' is another one of these words which escape exact definition. Does it mean the member of a religion or are the Jews a people? What is a people? Modern historians imply that anyone is a Jew who was in any way disadvantaged by the 1935 Nuremberg Laws, the anti-Jewish laws of the Nazis. But amongst those disadvantaged were even people who had no more than one Jewish grandparent. The Nazis called them 'second-degree hybrids'; those with two grandparents of each variety were 'first-degree hybrids'. But is it seriously suggested that someone who has one grandparent of one kind and three of another is to be classed with the one rather than the three? Is the person who is half and half to be denied his or her free choice? This goes further than even the Nazis did, for on the whole they classed as Jews only those who had at least three Jewish grandparents. Religious Jews themselves do not recognise anyone as Jewish born unless he is the circumcised son of a Jewish mother. That cuts out an awful lot of people whom modern slovenliness thoughtlessly classes as Jews, and therefore this also has helped to preclude me from describing us as 'Jews'.

In fact, it left me with no choice but to speak of us, as I have done, as Germans and Austrians, for that is how we were treated and that is the one characteristic which almost all of us had in common. Therefore the Germans on the other side had to be described as 'the enemy', 'the *Wehrmacht*', 'the Nazis' or as 'Hitler and his gang', or suchlike. At times this has not been easy. In quotations from other authors, regrettably, it would not have been right to make changes to conform with this practice. As a result the practice I have followed does not appear as obvious as otherwise it would be. Furthermore, I have not used the word 'fascists' in place of 'Nazis', which, again, is the usual practice today. I strongly suspect that the reason why such a lot of people prefer to call themselves anti-fascist, rather than anti-Nazi, is the fact that the full name of the Nazi party was the 'German National-Socialist Workers' Party'. Including, as it does, the word 'Socialist', many have looked for a way of not having to be anti something that includes this designation. As I have been a member of the Labour Party myself for many years and know such feelings from personal experience, I agree that this is a real difficulty. However, I refuse to call myself an 'anti-fascist' because the Fascists were the party of Mussolini and limited to Italy. They were unpleasant, dictatorial and none too gentle in their methods, but by comparison with Hitler's gang of murderers they were ineffective petty bourgeois. I also have not used the word 'National Socialists', but 'Nazis' is an abbreviation which was already used to describe them in Vienna in the 1920s and it was not considered polite.

On the whole the soldiers, and especially those of German nationality on both sides, knew very well that the war was about ideologies. After all, one really cannot believe that any soldier of the *Wehrmacht* did not appreciate that on his uniform he wore the swastika. It was there on his cap and in most cases also in a prominent position on his tunic or blouse. It is equally unlikely that any member of the *Wehrmacht* was so ignorant as not to know that this was the symbol of the Nazi Party. The symbol of the German state was the eagle – as it is to this day. The eagle carrying the swastika was meant not only to symbolise the fact that the German state had been taken over by the Nazis, but also that everyone who displayed this symbol on his person was in their service. This was the way the Nazis understood it and this was the way the other Germans understood it, too. When we fought against German soldiers, who might have been relatives, old school friends or others whom, perhaps, we would not have wanted to hurt, we did so in the full appreciation that anyone who displays a symbol on himself must be identified with it.

The governments of most of the countries which at one time or another opposed Hitler generally realised that the fight against him was a war against the Nazi ideology, but there was no single ideology which could have had the support of all of Hitler's opponents. There was no basis for this. Indeed, all involved declared themselves in favour of democracy, but even the major protagonists would have had tremendous difficulties agreeing on a definition of this, acceptable to all. The only thing on which the Allies were able to agree was their opposition to and detestation of the Nazi idea of the 'master race' and, in consequence, that this should allow the 'Aryan' Germans to dominate all others. All, indeed, had deep feelings of dislike for the Nazi ideology, which they rejected unconditionally, but equally there were none who were able to formulate their rejection in such a way that it could have been substituted for the old, accepted and well-tried motivation by patriotism. Therefore the appeal to patriotism was the simplest method of motivating people and it was used and accepted everywhere. There was no discussion about it, there was no practical alternative and everyone had other worries. Those who took part for ideological reasons accepted that this was the only practicable way to motivate the mass of the Allied armies and considered it right that any discussion – even of common war aims – should be postponed until after the war had been won. If it had been lost, there would have been nothing to discuss, and for something as immediately useless as finding a common positive ideology, the unity of the Allies could not be jeopardised, as it would have been had the subject been generally discussed.

A further factor which may well militate against an acceptance of the facts as stated here is the real need which some people have to avoid admitting that not all Germans had fought for Hitler. Even today many propagandists live by avoiding this admission. If it was generally accepted that there were many exceptions, they might find themselves unemployed. Therefore it comes as a surprise that the patriotism of many Germans who fought against the Nazis was of very much greater intensity – at least at the beginning – than that of many of those in other countries who accepted Hitler's grasp of power in Germany.

It is after all so much more simple to understand a war between nations and to believe that love of one's country must include the acceptance of its government. Even historians do not like civil wars. The explanations are so complicated. Wars between nations are much easier to explain.

All this is not new, by any means. During the war many officers of the British forces and with them the War Office and the secret services were completely unable to imagine that Germans and Austrians, nationals of the principal enemy state, might really wish to fight against Hitler. The great majority just could not believe that any motivation other than the simple patriotic one could make anyone wish to join up. Some, indeed, changed their minds as a result of experience, but it was no more than some. Therefore the decisions in those circles led to the German and Austrian soldiers changing their allegiance bit by bit until finally most of them saw themselves as British, rather than German and Austrians wearing British uniforms. These decisions were not made according to any plan. They were made in the circumstances of the time and by persons who had to consider only the prosecution of the war and had nothing to guide them other than what average citizens of Britain are taught and what they consider to be normal and generally acceptable. The fact that a lot of this is based on half-truths and prejudices did not worry them in any way. After all, their expertise lay in the prosecution of the war and not in the areas of politics or – God forbid – of philosophy!

Because of their decisions, however, the desire of many of the Germans and Austrians who were in Britain in 1939 to take an active part in the fighting was frustrated until the Austro-German companies of the Pioneer Corps were broken up to yield a large number of highly motivated and absolutely reliable individuals who could not be regarded as a national grouping. It might be worth speculating what would have happened had the War Office decided to reorganise those companies as fighting units. What might have been the effect on the situation in post-war Germany if a larger formation, perhaps a brigade of Germans and Austrians, had been in existence as part of the British army? But this is idle speculation, because the British government decided otherwise. The Germans and Austrians in the British army were given the opportunity to transfer to fighting units as individuals only, and the changes of name to which they were encouraged turned out to be a major step in the process of changing their national adherence. It seems unlikely that a large number would have opposed a conversion of the Alien Pioneer companies into fighting units. On the contrary, it is probable that they would have welcomed this just as much as the permission to transfer to other branches of the service.

The view that the war was just a war between nations is a simplification. One says that the Germans, Italians and Japanese were on one side, the British, Russians, Americans, French and all the other nations which made up the Allies, were on the other. Quite simple! But it was not like that. Throughout the war, but especially at its beginning, there were people of every nation who were opposed to the side which their government had chosen. And the governments changed sides or were replaced by other governments, which then took the other side. The best examples are France and Italy, but at the beginning of the war even the Soviet Union was not exactly inimical towards Hitler, and all the efforts of so-called historians who try to explain that in reality Stalin's policy was always directed towards containing Hitler cannot change the fact that the two co-operated very effectively in the rape and division of Poland.

Of course it was a war between states, between nations. But in each of these states there was also internal dissent. In some cases this was of minor importance, but in other cases it became a full-scale civil war. The British authorities did not appreciate this situation and in many cases took a narrow legalistic view. In the case of the Germans and Austrians who had taken up arms against their government, their policy was to further their Anglicisation. The character of the German and Austrian engagement as a fight against an enemy of their own nationality receded as the protagonists identified themselves with the

British more and more closely. As the memories which the emigrants retained of their countries of origin were by no means pleasant, and as the difficulties which the British authorities had made earlier largely disappeared after the war, one cannot be surprised that much was forgotten or suppressed. Nevertheless, for the great majority of the Germans and Austrians who were in Britain at the beginning of the war, the Second World War was never anything other than a war for freedom and justice and against racism, injustice and inhumanity. They were fully justified in believing that this was also the aim of the British. This was the reason why so many of them joined the British forces. But British patriotism was not amongst the reasons for their actions.

It is not fashionable today to believe that idealism might have had anything to do with the British engagement in the war. The British action of guaranteeing the Polish frontier with Germany in 1939 is seen as an expression of the traditional British policy of maintaining the European balance of power. Eventually this guarantee was the legal reason for British intervention when German troops attacked Poland, but it could never have been given by the British government had there not been strong political forces who opposed Hitler and his Nazis for idealistic and humanitarian reasons. From its beginning it was not only those who had fled from Nazi oppression, but also many, many others, who saw the war as a fight for freedom and against the horrors of Nazi dictatorship. Thus the war contained the characteristics of a civil war within it and there is hardly a country which took part, except only Germany and Austria, in which the two sides did not have a bloody reckoning with each other either during or afterwards.

An additional factor is that in all the Allied countries there were people who sympathised with the Nazis. Of course, the vast majority of them changed their minds when it became clear that the Nazis would lose. In the aftermath, however, people like that have always relied on being members of a nation which fought against Hitler. It has made it so easy for them to appear personally blameless. For them it is essential that their nationality and not their personal history is taken as the criterion for their decency. Their influence and their way of looking at things also help to deny that there were internal divisions in every nation. So there are lots of reasons why facts, which do not fit into the story of the war between nations, do not enter the minds of those who have to rely on others to tell them what went on.

Another factor is that in many cases the feelings of the men from Germany and Austria changed during the time of their service. Six years is a long time and, by the time they were released, men who had joined at 18 had spent a quarter of their lives in the British services.

However strong their loyalties to their homelands might have been at first, after six years in a British environment they had absorbed much of the British spirit and of British traditions. They had every reason to be grateful to the British and they looked on events largely through British eyes. So they became more British with every day of their service. In the above chapters I have tried to describe just how some of this occurred, but at this stage one can only say that at some time or other – and everyone at a different time – the vast majority had come to the conclusion that they wanted to apply for British nationality. Having been granted this, they assimilated further and became British not only by their passports, but with their hearts. They did all they could to become just like those who had been born in Britain, to think, to live, to be like those of British birth. They wanted to continue their lives in the pattern of the country, which they had adopted and which had accepted them.

It was not always easy. The pages of the *Ex-Serviceman*, the journal of the Ex-Service NB Association, were full of complaints about the discrimination with which these men had to cope after their release from the services. However, this discrimination did not put them off, but made them even keener to shed all characteristics of their previous nationality and to become even more British, if this were possible. In this frame of mind they did not wish to draw attention to their different origins and upbringing.

As has been mentioned earlier, Norman Bentwich wrote *I Understand the Risks* at the behest of former pioneers. But he did not write it merely to preserve the memory of the deeds of the Germans and Austrians in the British services, he wrote it mainly to make the British public aware of the fact that the men who had just become naturalised were good, decent and reliable. As a result the book was aimed at the British reader, and a considerable part of it tells of all the native Brits who had realised this already and acted accordingly. The whole tenor of the book is directed towards showing that those who were the subject of the book's report had rendered great services to Britain, and not that they had taken part in the war because they had wanted to fight against the Nazis. It came to the same thing in the end, but the motives were made to appear slightly different.

Most of them did indeed undergo a change. Having arrived in the United Kingdom as refugees from Nazi oppression, as Germans and Austrians fleeing from the countries of their birth, but still very much as Germans and Austrians, they became loyal citizens of Britain and members of the British nation. But this too did not encourage them in any way to tell about what they had done and how it all happened.

In a way a change of nationality is like a religious conversion. Every nation has certain ideas about itself and about other nations. To change one's nationality means that one changes one's ideas, which have hitherto formed the background of one's thinking, and adopts new ideas in conformity with one's new environment. One gets rid of old beliefs and prejudices and adopts new ones. When one turns into a Briton, this includes, *inter alia*, the acceptance of the 'We are British' feeling and all that this implies.

In the second act of *HMS Pinafore*, Sir W.S. Gilbert wrote 'and it's greatly to his credit that he is an Englishman...'. This expresses a feeling, which is not in any way unknown to everyone born in the British Isles. The British – the English – are not arrogant or overbearing, but they are very satisfied, sometimes almost smug, concerning their nationality. Also, most English people have a very fine ear for their own language and are very good at recognising accents, particularly foreign ones. The certainty with which they can distinguish between an accent acquired in another part of Britain and that of a foreigner, however slight, is sometimes positively amazing, as is their ability to differentiate between the oddities of a British eccentric and the peculiarities caused by a foreign education. Being thus able virtually to smell a foreign origin, they tend to ask, in the nicest possible way, where the foreigner comes from. This is followed by 'How do you like it here?' and finally by 'When are you going back?'

For a former refugee, who is trying to become 100 per cent British, such questions are exceedingly painful. They make it obvious to him that he has not achieved his objective of becoming 'one of us'. He remains 'one of them'. It implies defeat. Therefore he tries to forestall such questions. He tries to convince his opposite number of his Britishness by denying his foreign origins. In due course this becomes a habit and, of course, with the passage of time it does become easier and ever more credible. Thus a former foreigner – now British – tends to feel accepted by his fellows only if he hides from them the ghastly truth, and as he goes on hiding it from his fellows he eventually begins to hide it from himself. The more he believes that he is indistinguishable from a real Brit, the more certain he becomes that he is telling the truth about himself. His days when he was a German or an Austrian fade from his memory and become just a bad dream, of which he does not want to be reminded.

Not wishing to be reminded of his foreign origins includes, of course, not wishing to be reminded of his service in the Pioneer Corps. After all, why should anyone, who is neither a former criminal nor soft in the head, have been a member of this Corps, particularly in its early days, unless he had been an alien? Having lived as a Briton amongst British people for any length of time it becomes impossible also to admit to membership of the pioneers. There cannot be a satisfactory explanation. It would be an admission that, after all, he is not what he pretends to be, not British born, and not the same as his fellows. It would mean that he would have to come clean about his past, that one's foreignness is not imagined but real. To acknowledge himself as a native German or Austrian, however, is the last thing he wants and so he does and says nothing to connect him with the country of his birth.

Clearly this does not apply to everyone. This book was written with the help of several hundred people who wanted to tell of their adventures during the war and of their previous lives. Today, however, all those who took part in the events described in this book are getting on. No one who was born later than 1927 can possibly have had any part in what has been described herein, and that means that it is most unlikely that he is doing anything much other than drawing his old age pension and whatever else he may be able to draw on. It may well be that even amongst those who have contributed to this book there may be some who would have been more reticent before their retirement. The aged enjoy greater freedom than those who have to earn their living.

There are further reasons. Many had relatives who remained behind. Parents, grandparents, brothers and sisters, even husbands and wives and children had not been able to emigrate and had remained in the hands of the Nazis. They were humiliated, locked up, tortured and murdered. As long as the war lasted little in the way of news got through, but afterwards everything that one had worried about, what one had feared in one's worst dreams, was shown to have been exceeded. Then it became clear to everyone that whatever he had been through, however unpleasant his own experiences had been, it was as nothing in comparison to what mother and father, brother and sister and all the others had suffered.

We had survived, when the others were slaughtered. We had had a good time, whilst others had to wear the yellow Star of David on their clothing, were spat on, mobbed and ill-treated and eventually – naked like animals – driven into the gas chambers. Some of us, very few indeed, had at one time or other had the ability to do something about that, but for most of the time the great majority, even those who fought in the front line or participated in the air attacks on Germany, were occupied with the usual routine jobs which servicemen do or try to get out of, dodged the rules, went on leave, messed about with girls and did nothing to help their families. All the time we should have been right there at the front, behind the enemy lines, in the headquarters of the *Wehrmacht*! But what did we do? We were soldiers! Only if all of us had died in the attempt to keep our loved ones out of the gas chambers could we be satisfied with ourselves. This is not rational thinking, but it is an additional reason why many of us do not wish to revive the memories of that time and refuse to mention it.

Some have not overcome the feeling of inferiority which was the result of being a pioneer. Certainly when we were in it, this was no more than a labour corps, and the alien companies were denied the right to carry arms for nearly three years. *Esprit de corps* is the basis upon which military units have always built up their efficiency. This spirit is not engendered by the mere fact that one is a member of a body of men dressed alike and capable of moving like marionettes when commanded to do so. It has to include pride in oneself and in the group, as well as respect for its symbols.

I have experienced this myself. My friendship with the members of the various units of the Royal Regiment of Artillery, in which I served, was rarely as close as that with members of 229 Company, Pioneer Corps. When I was in this company I really did try to be proud of it. I pressed my uniform, polished my badges and buttons and had really shiny boots. But when I had done all that and more I was still just Private Peter Langer, a member of a unit which thought of itself as 'this shower'. To begin with we were unarmed. Our badge was pick and shovel crossed under the crown and above the motto *labor omnia vincit* – which reminds one a little of *arbeit macht frei* over the entrance to Auschwitz concentration camp. We had no colours. The only symbol of our military identity we were allowed to have was a brightly coloured red and green cap for off-duty wear. Our drill was quite good and we were not bad at building camps and roads, we produced wonderful wall newspapers and in the sum of our intelligence we were streets ahead of all other units in all the services. We knew all this, but we also knew that we were considered inferior to all the others by everybody, including ourselves. We were short on tradition and we lacked *esprit de corps*. Our womenfolk did indeed wear our badge as an ornament – at least when we were together with them – but when asked by others what regiment that was, which their loved ones belonged to, they tended to shrug their shoulders and say, 'Well, he's just a pioneer'.

All this was very different when I joined the Royal Artillery. I was not terribly impressed by many of my new comrades, but our 25-pounders certainly were some of the best guns which existed anywhere in the world. And did we know how to handle them! Admittedly, the gunners also had no colours, but this did not matter at all for 'when on parade with their guns the Artillery will stand at the right of the line', in other words in the position of honour. When my then girlfriend (now my wife of more than 50 years' standing) was asked about the artillery badge which she wore as a brooch, she was pleased and would say, 'Oh yes, Peter is a gunner!' Even today I still wear the gunner tie and I do not think that I ever had to explain its meaning to any English person.

All this, of course, is quite childish and I am fully aware of this. Nevertheless it is something I cannot ignore. These feelings are a part of myself and they are just as real as the experiences I have had through my five senses. I am proud of having been a gunner. I still try to persuade myself that I should also be proud of having been a pioneer and, having written the foregoing, I am much more successful nowadays than I ever used to be before I started on this job, but this is because I have discovered what interesting and even remarkable people they were, with whom I had the honour to serve.

There is a last point which I should still like to mention in my list of reasons why the story of the Germans and Austrians in British service is so unknown. Countries do demand more of their citizens than mere patriotism, mere feeling. They also demand service, and they certainly call it a crime when its citizens make common cause with a foreign power. This is high treason and in this respect German and British law books agree.

From 1939 until at least 1941 all the Germans and Austrians in the British forces were in the situation of being traitors to Germany, the country whose nationals they were. Even after 1941, when the German government deprived the Jewish emigrants unilaterally of their German citizenship, there is evidence that some German authorities did not take any notice of this, for they treated such people who had become their captives as traitors. Germans and British thus agreed that, by carrying arms against the country which, as a result of our nationality we should have served, legally we were committing high treason.

Today Germany is very proud of being a *Rechtsstaat*, a country in which the law and its rule are absolute. However, Germany also sees itself as the legal successor of the Third Reich. Germany has accepted the guilt of that Reich, but, as far as I know, it has never taken the steps necessary to eliminate the legal consequences of treasonable acts against it. Without going into the question of any statutory limitations, it might, therefore, be feasible that pioneers, who were German citizens before 1938, could still be accused of treason. There is even an outside possibility that the same might apply to persons of Austrian origin, but the Moscow declaration, in which a separate Austrian nationality was re-created, has become part of German law. Those who, according to the Nuremberg Laws, were not held to be Jews and therefore remained German citizens even after 1941 are almost certainly in that position. I have not the slightest doubt that there are people in Germany, and even elsewhere, who think that this is as it should be.

On the other hand the question is not of immediate interest. None of us has been actually accused of high treason. But I correspond with people whose approach to dealings with German authorities has been coloured by the fear that this might still be the situation, and that as a result they might be disadvantaged. And certainly, all of us were convinced that legally we were German nationals throughout the whole of the war.

14

To Sum Up

I began my researches into the King's Own Loyal Enemy Aliens in 1994. At that time I knew but the bare outlines of the story, our story, and since then I have learnt a lot. I have been in touch with a large number of individuals and many have told me things which maybe they have not told anyone else. I believe that this may well have given me a better insight into what made us tick than many another.

It may not therefore be inappropriate if, in addition to the facts of the case which I have given above, I also add a summary of some conclusions which I have formed. If some of these are politically not quite correct, I am very sorry, but they are based on the facts as they have presented themselves to me.

First, to our motives. These were simple and very much the same for everyone. We were against Hitler and the Nazis and wanted to do what we could to stop that gang of criminals in their tracks. Some of us would have said that we found it incompatible with our honour not to do so. We had reached this attitude for different reasons. Most had been persecuted. Some had political reasons. A few were emotionally affected. But all of us were united in our rejection of everything the Nazis stood for. We wanted them defeated, destroyed and obliterated. It was as simple as that.

Not everyone was a hero. Not everyone even had the opportunity to do anything heroic. But in choosing to be a soldier or a member of the women's services each one did the only sensible thing open to him or her in order to oppose the Nazis effectively. Dictatorships have never been removed except by force. In a country ruled other than on democratic lines, it is idle to suppose that one can remove the government by any other method and in Hitler's Germany, in which everyone spied on everyone else, such force could not be organised from the inside. The only possible way to get rid of the Nazis was the way it was actually done – by defeating Germany from the outside. Joining an army opposed to Germany was the only sensible way in which any German opposed to Hitler could proceed with some hope of succeeding.

Yet in joining His Majesty's Forces each individual took the full risk that being an enemy alien member of these forces constituted, not only the risk of being killed or maimed, but also that of being taken prisoner and, being recognised, held to be a traitor, and finally, the risk that Britain might have lost the war with all the unthinkable consequences such a contingency would have brought about. Having taken the oath of obedience there was little any of us could do to minimise any of these risks. A soldier – and a member of the women's services – has to go where he or she is told. One can protest, one can volunteer, one can try to steer one's fate, but in the end one obeys orders, one goes where one is sent, into danger or away from it, and always with one's eyes open. None who joined up could ignore them, none was not afraid of them and everyone knew these risks. Yet all took them upon themselves. In the end, whether an individual covered himself in glory or remained an obscure member of an obscure unit, whether he or she was an officer or a private soldier, whether he or she was a commando, a pioneer or an ATS orderly, at the time one joined and throughout one's period of service, the risk which one took, knowingly and voluntarily, was the same.

Due partly to the historical background of the Jews in Germany and Austria and partly to the restrictive policy of the British government as to who might be admitted into Britain, a larger number of us than might otherwise be expected had a middle-class background. A considerable number, however, lost all they had materially when they emigrated. They arrived in Britain with a good education but without a penny to their name. Their social position was in accordance. There is little doubt that the services helped many to regain their self-confidence, but it is still amazing how many managed to regain the social status they had lost, and have ended their careers in more or less the sorts of positions which they might have been expected to have held had all this never happened. It sounds elitist, but it is, I think, based on facts – we were brought up to be an elite and have proved ourselves one, despite all vicissitudes.

As a last thought, however, it may be worth pointing out that no one can be gainsaid who points to the fact that a small but not insignificant number of Germans volunteered to carry arms against Hitler. By comparison to those who fought on the side of wrong and of injustice, we were but a few, and even fewer retained their German nationality after it was all over. But every one of us had received a German education, or at least an education in the German language, and according to the laws of Britain and partly also of Germany, we were German nationals. There is nothing to stop the German government or individual Germans from being proud of the fact that some Germans successfully opposed the Nazis.

Equally, there is nothing to stop those who are anxious to prove that not all Jews allowed themselves to be led to slaughter unresistingly, from pointing to the many Jews amongst us who carried arms and used them – to good effect.

The Register of Germans, Austrians and other 'enemy aliens', who served in HM Forces in the Second World War

As known in January 2005. Additions and amendments are still being made. The University of Freiburg, under Professor Wolfgang Hochbruck, will include on its internet home page an up-to-date version of this register: http:www.anglistik.uni-freiburg.de/institut/amerikanistik/leightondata.htm.

Abraham, alias Graham, served in 246 Coy PC

Abraham, enlisted at Richborough 1940; served in 74 Coy PC and was with BEF in France

Abraham, G., later Atkins, G., served in 77 Coy PC

Abraham, Heinz

Abraham, Ilse, served in 1 Allied Volunteer Platoon ATS, at Ripley Hospital, Lancaster, then in Huyton, Llandudno, Cowley, Rhyl, Denbigh and Colchester

Abraham, L.L., 13804777, served in PC and RASC

Abraham, P., Cpl, RASC; died on active service, apparently leaving no next-of-kin; he left £42.19.9

Abraham, Werner Emanuel, pupil at Duisburg Gymnasium; interned on Isle of Man 1940; joined 248 Coy PC Nov. 1940; transferred to RASC, served in UK and India; commissioned 1943, Staff Capt. GHQ Delhi

Abrahamovicz, generally shortened to Abramowicz, Richard, 13807122, alias 13118719 Arlen, R.G. (Samain calls him Arnold); born 4 Jan. 1923, boxer, SS deported him from Germany by taking him to Belgian border and leaving him there; Pte in 77 Coy PC; RWK; and 3/10 Cdo; aimed at getting VC; in afternoon 7 June 1944 with 45 RM Cdo in Franceville-Plage, shot at whilst carrying white flag in effort to get enemy to surrender, went back to get his Tommy gun and was killed in ensuing exchange of fire

Abrahams, Dudley, Capt.; post war: prominent in Ex-Service NB Association

Abrahamsohn, Kurt, later Ambrose, Ken; born Stettin 1919, to Britain 1934, at King's College Taunton 1935–38, then business studies; interned 1940, by HMT *Dunera* to Australia, back 1941; volunteered for RAF 1943, trained as pilot but pranged a plane; interpreter in Bombing Survey Unit; served in France, Germany and finally Whitehall; demob as Sgt Feb. 1947; post-war: manager with Marks & Spencer, then lecturer at polytechnic and UNO consultant on management training

Abrahamsohn, Martin, later Amson, Martin Leslie; born Hamburg 27 June

1923, pupil at Talmud Thora Schule, to England 1939, as labourer; enlisted 1943; to 4 RTR, landed in Normandy on D-Day + 2; transferred to interpreters' college Brussels 1944; interpreter to 6 Airborne Div. from Dec. 1944, took part in Rhine crossing at Wesel; posted as missing, probably killed in action 24 Mar. 1945

Abrahamson, Peter, alias Abbey, Peter, served in 229 Coy PC

Ackermann, W., served in 77 Coy PC; his name is known because he acted in the company's Christmas pantomime *A Midsummer Night's Scream* (probably 1941)

Adam, Klaus, later Adam, Ken; born Berlin 1921, pupil at Französische Gymnasium, emigrated to UK 1934, first to Scotland, later in OTC at St Paul's School, London, studied architecture; enlisted 1940; Cpl in 3 PCTC; applied to join RAF Apr. 1941 and was accepted; training at 11 ITW Scarborough, Jan. 1942 to 1 EFTS flying Tiger Moths, then to Canada and US on Arnold Training Scheme; May 1942 back to Scotland, as pilot to 609 Sqdn (fighters), Oct. 1943 at Lympne, equipped with rocket firing Typhoons; in Normandy in support of Canadians, particularly at Falaise Gap; known as 'Heinie the tank buster'; in Germany at Wunsdorf air base, there i/c 10,000 PoWs reconstructing base to British requirements; demob late 1946 as Flight Lt, then 5 years in RAFVR; post-war: 53 years in film design, production designer for James Bond films, OBE, hon. Dr Royal College of Arts

Adam, brother of above (?), said to have been amongst the first alien pioneer officers before transfer to RAF

Adler, H.

Adler, Gabriel, 13806053, Pte, may have been commissioned; served in 253 Coy PC; killed in action

Adler, Heinrich, Jewish member of Young Austria, lived in Essex; enlisted end 1943, beginning 1944; Cpl

Adler, Robert, probably Czechoslovak citizen who had lived in Vienna, father was social democratic journalist and had connections with foreign ministry, pupil at Sperl Gymnasium, Vienna; served in 220 Coy PC; transferred to RAF, commissioned, Flt Lt; awarded DFC; post-war: to Israel, became pilot of El-Al, eventually maintenance manager there

Albala, Jack, from Turkey, Jewish, served in PC; transferred to 8th Irish Hussars; later 1 RTR; killed during the advance of this regiment in France 1944

Alban, Ernest

Alberti, had been stationery manufacturer in Germany, imprisoned at Dachau; served in PC; transferred to RASC, commissioned; post-war: in Germany, controlling German printing shops, British Army periodical *Soldier* printed in one of his works, greatest moment when German general, von Blaskowitz, knocked at his office door before coming in, stood to attention, saluted and requested permission to have something printed

Alexander, Hans

Alexander, L.

Alexander, Paul

Alexander, Peter; born Munich 27 Jan. 1922, father Jewish, mother Protestant, to UK Oct. 1933, pupil at London University School; scientific assistant at Admiralty; post-war: Professor of Radiobiology, Institute for Cancer Research, Sutton

Alexander, Peter A., 13800986, bank clerk from Vienna; joined 69 Coy PC, to which he returned after having been commissioned on 5 Mar. 1943; after end of hostilities involved with search for Nazis; demob as Capt.; post-war: member, history committee, Ex-Service NB Association

Allan, F.L., served in 249 Coy PC

Alweiss, Manfred, also temporarily Wildman; born Berlin 1925, to UK with *Kindertransport* of Youth Aliyah 1 Sept. 1939; enlisted1943; posted to Essex Regt; later Buffs, in Belgium during Rundstedt Offensive, then 21 Army Gp Main HQ Brussels; May 1945 as Sgt RF to Süchteln, then Bünde and later Bad Öynhausen; 1946 at Information Control in Berlin, Schluterstrasse offices of the former Reichskulturkammer; after discharge, chartered accountant, to Germany 1961, Frankfurt, qualified as German Wirtschaftsprüfer, then Munich and finally Hamburg, after retirement to London, mentioned in George Clare's *Berlin Days* as Sgt Wildman

Amoser, Hans, from Linz, Upper Austria, served in Austrian air force (joined 1 Oct. 1937, taken over into *Wehrmacht* 1938); 1943 sentenced to eight months' detention for disobeying orders; deserted to Italy, arrested in Verona and sentenced to death; fled from death cell with British officer, Lt Morris; joined British Army 1944, served in special forces; after Aug. 1945 was at British military hospital Castelnuovo Monti; post-war: returned to Linz

Andermann-Engelart, H., later Anderman, H.B., served in 229, 137 and 362 Coy PC; Cpl 229 Coy; to PC OCTU 2 June 1942, 31 July 1942 on officers' list of 137 Coy, on 30 May 1943 in 362; demob as Capt.; died Mar. 1995

Anderson, Duff, served in 220 Coy PC

Anderson, K., served in 137 Coy PC; post-war: became insurance broker.

Anderson, Rose, served in one of the Allied Volunteer Platoons ATS from 1943

Andexser, F.W., 7 Oct. 1940 to 74 Coy PC as Lt, 13 Jan. 1942 Capt. and Coy 2 i/c; 15 Jan. 1943 to 4 Coy; demob as Maj..

Anschel, Klaus, V., 377772; born Duesseldorf 11 Jan. 1921, pupil at Gymnasium Duesseldorf, emigrated to Australia 1938, confectioner; joined 6th Australian Employment Coy, AMF, 9 Mar. 1942, in Melbourne, Victoria; demob 1 Feb. 1946; Australian Service Medal and General Service Medal; post-war: confectioner in Sydney, 1961 art dealer in Chelsea

Anson, H.

Anzbock, Fritz Peter, alias Horak, German soldier, PoW; taken into British service; joined SOE

Apsley, Henry

Aptowitzer, Sgt in 219 Coy PC (8 Sect.)

Arany (father of Peter Arany – below), from Vienna, served in Austrian Army WWI; Pte in PC WWII

Arany, Peter F., 13804450, later Masters, Peter F. 13118720 and 6387025; born Vienna 5 Feb. 1922, pupil at Robert-Hamerling-RG until Apr. 1938, after emigration lived in Maida Vale and worked as messenger boy in Polish publishing house; joined 246 Coy PC 3 Sept. 1940; later 77 Coy PC;

transferred 3/10 Cdo (QORWK), was attached to bicycle troop of 6 Cdo on D-Day; noted in action at Breville on 11 June 1944, and along River Maas Jan. 1945; in Rhine crossing at Wesel; later Lt in Ox. & Bucks. LI, Gold Coast Regt in West Africa; post-war: to US, studied at Central School of Art & Design, Fulbright scholar, artistic director of a TV station, later in Office of Economic Opportunity and finally in US General Services Admin, author of *Striking Back*, a history of 3/10 Cdo

Arenstein, Hans Richard, 13804450 (also Arnstein), later Andrews, Harry, 13118502 and 6436352; born Erfurt 18 Feb. 1922, father owned dept. store Zum römischen Kaiser, after emigration agricultural trainee at Wallingford 1939/40; joined 87 Coy PC; transferred to Hamps. Regt; then 3/10 Cdo Aug. 1942, but trained with 12 Cdo, took part in action 'Forfar'; on D-Day with 47 RM Cdo, wounded on landing and evacuated; killed by landmine on 17 or 19 Aug. 1944 near Grande Ferme du Boisson

Arnhold, George Gerald, later Arnold, Jerry, served in 88 & 249 Coy PC; later pioneer officer

Arnold, Jerry, commissioned in PC

Arnsdorf, Alfred, later Arnott, Alfred, from Friedland, East Prussia; born 1921, twin to Max, brother to Selmar Frank Arnsdorf (see below), father was horse dealer, both parents perished at Auschwitz, pupil at Bartenstein Gymnasium and Agnes Miegel Schule, Friedland, to UK 9 Mar. 1939, agricultural trainee; interned 3 July 1940, to Australia on HMT *Dunera*, back 1942; enlisted Feb. 1942; served in 248, 249, 220 and 88 Coy PC; then Interpreters' Pool; in military government at Alhorn near Oldenburg, looked after displaced persons; demob May 1947 as Sgt; post-war: to Australia 1948, retailer

Arnsdorf, Max, later Arnott, M.V., twin brother of Alfred Arnsdorf (see above), whose fate he shared from birth until the end of the fighting, brother of Selmar Frank (see below); after 1945 in Field Security at Nienburg near Hannover; post-war: to Australia like Alfred 1948, textiles manufacturer until 1987

Arnsdorf, Selmar, later Arnott, Stanley Frank, younger brother of Alfred and Max (see above); born Friedland 1923; shared fate of both brothers until 1945; then interpreter; demob as Sgt; post-war: to Australia 1949

Arnstein

Arnstein, Alfred Valentine, 13802282, later Anderson, 13118501; born 11 Jan. 1919; served in PC; 3/10 Cdo; RWK

Aronheim, joined 74 Coy PC from Richborough 1940 and was with BEF in France

Aronowitz, C., served in No. 3 PCTC and 229 Coy PC; first violin in Southern Command Continental Orchestra; also solo violinist

Aronsohn, joined 74 Coy PC from Richborough 1940 and was with BEF in France

Artman, E., kosher butcher; served in 249 and 93 Coy PC

Ascher, Claus Leopold Octavio, 13805191, later Anson, Colin E., 13118503 and 6436355; born Berlin 13 Feb. 1922, father perished in Dachau 1937, pupil at Bad Homburg RG, then Vegesack Gymnasium near Bremen, and

Woehlerschule, Frankfurt, after leaving became apprentice at asbestos works, to UK 7 Feb. 1939 with *Kindertransport* of Society of Friends, worked as agricultural trainee; enlisted Dec. 1940; served in 87 Coy PC and 6 PCTC; transferred 3/10 Cdo Aug. 1942; with 40 Cdo at Sicily landing 9–10 June 1943, received head wound before landing in Catania; after return to unit in action in Yugoslavia, Albania and northern Italy; on Lissa (Vis) until Aug. 1944; later in CCG, Field Intelligence Agency, translated important documents found in German ministries; found his mother, who had survived in Frankfurt; demob Aug. 1946 as Sgt; post-war: active glider pilot

Askenazy, Karol Maksymilian; born Vienna 18 May 1920; 2/Lt in 1 Indep. Polish Para. Bde; served at Arnhem

Aszner, (Miss) Tony

Atkin, E., served in 137 Coy PC

Atlas, joined 74 Coy PC from Richborough 1940 and was with BEF in France

Aubrey, Peter

Auer, L., 13804561, served in 93 Coy PC; selected for service in Cdos, but appears to have been returned to original unit

Auer, 'Mish', from Czechoslovakia, having served in 310 Sqn Czech Air Force; transferred to 101 Sqn RAF; referred to as a 'special operator'

Auerbach, served in 87 Coy PC

Auerbach, W.H., later Ashley, Michael Gordon; born 1921; enlisted 6 May 1940; served in 93 Coy PC; later RA; demob 1946; died 1954

Auerhahn, Werner, 13802608 (in PC records 13802068 also appears), later Wells, Peter Vernon Allen, 13118504; born 1917 or 1918, with family to UK when father moved with his export and import firm; served in 165 Coy PC; later L/Cpl in 3/10 Cdo; in Sicily landing; killed in action whilst attached 40 Cdo by treading on mine crossing the Garigliano river near Ninturno on 21 or 22 Jan. 1944

Aufrecht, Heinz, later Alford, Michael, served in RF; later in SOE, member of group with Eversley, Frazer, Ettlinger, did not get into action; post-war: lives in US

Aufwerber, Otto, later Ashley, Austrian; post-war: lives in Canada

Austin, R.

Babin, M., 13807884, served in PC; later probably SOE

Bach, H.I.

Bachrach, Philipp; born Vienna about 1918

Bachwitz, 13805440, later Blakeley, Chris, served in PC; transferred to 21 Indep. Para. Coy after participating in 61b and 62nd parachute training course, may have been discharged to go to US before the company saw action in North Africa; or may have been at Arnhem

Back, Siegbert

Badt, H., later Benson, Harry

Baer, Dr, joined PC from Richborough 1940; Sgt in 74 Coy PC and was with BEF in France

Baer, Frank, served in 246 Coy PC

Baer, Georg (George); born Munich 27 May 1921, emigrated to Italy 1938, to

UK Mar. 1939; interned 1940; enlisted 22 Oct. 1940; served in 246 Coy PC; transferred to RA Ack-Ack 1944, instructor on Bofors gun; 15 Dec. 1944 commissioned in QORWK, 1945 to Burma, 1946 Maj., OC British transit camp, Rangoon; demob in UK 22 Sept. 1946; post-war: chemical industry, director of Croda International

Baerblinger, Nicholas, 13807673, later Allington, Nicky, said to be Russian, but doubtful, fought in Spanish Civil War; interned in Oran; served in PC; transferred to 21 Indep. Para. Coy after participation in 61b and 62nd parachute training course; served in North Africa and Italy; Sgt

Baerwald, Ernst, alias Charleroi, Pierre, 13807861, son of the Munich liberal Rabbi; served in 229 Coy PC; REME; and probably in SOE; married a Belgian at Lessine near Charleroi, wife converted to Judaism

Balaschov, Russian, Capt. in 337 Coy PC, Russian translator at HQ SHAEF, later in Vienna

Balaz, L.

Ball, Benno, served in 93 Coy PC

Ballin, K., joined PC from Richborough 1940; Sgt in 74 Coy PC and was with BEF in France; died shortly after demob

Balling, E., 13806024, Pte in 253 Coy PC; later probably SOE

Baloun, Franz, Austrian, served in French Foreign Legion 29 Nov. 1939–30 Nov. 1940; interned at Colomb-Bechar until 23 Apr. 1943; joined 337 or 338 Coy PC 23 Apr. 1943; demob as Sgt 10 Jan. 1947

Bamberger, served in 246 Coy PC; post-war: owner of British Artid Plastics, Slough

Bandler, George, served in 137 Coy PC (6 Sect.); post-war: to US

Bandman, H.K. (Ken), served in 87 Coy PC; transferred to RN; post-war: to Melbourne, Australia

Banks, M.J.

Barany, K.H., shown as 2/Lt in officers' list of 251 Coy PC on 28 Apr. 1943

Barbasch, Julius, joined PC from Richborough 1940; Sgt in 74 Coy PC and was with BEF in France; still in 74 Coy 1943

Barbier, Paul, name appears on list of social democratic Sudeten Germans in British Army, maintained by Central Committee of German Socialist Unity Party

Barford, H., awarded Military Medal

Barsaw, joined PC from Richborough 1940; Sgt in 74 Coy PC and was with BEF in France

Bartfeld, A.

Barth, Georg Alexander, 13802051, later Streets, George Bryan, 16118505, Austrian; born 5 Feb. 1917; Sgt in PC; R. Sussex Regt; later in 3/10 Cdo; posted to OCTU on 6 June 1944; killed in accident at OCTU

Barthel, Kurt, served in PC North Africa

Baruch, joined PC from Richborough 1940; Sgt in 74 Coy PC and was with BEF in France

Baruch, Lothar, later Brent, Leslie Baruch; born Koeslin 1925, to Berlin 1937, to UK by *Kindertransport* 1 Dec. 1938; enlisted 1943; commissioned in R. War. R; later seconded to Worcs. Regt, in N. Ireland, Italy, Germany;

demob as Capt. 1947; post-war: PhD, FInstBiol, Hon MRCP, Professor of Immunology, St Mary's Hospital Medical School, renowned in field of transplantation medicine

Baruch, Siegfried Josef, later Brook, Sidney Edward; born Krefeld 3 Oct. 1920, pupil at Volks- and Realschule Krefeld, probably the very first enemy alien to volunteer for the army, reported to the recruiting office at Thirsk in N. Yorks. 4 Sept. 1939: 'I did not join until Nov. 1940, as I was too young and the people in Thirsk did not know what to do with an enemy alien'; posted to 249 Coy PC; owing to severe asthma transferred to RAPayC

Bass, joined PC from Richborough 1940; Sgt in 74 Coy PC and was with BEF in France

Bass, Ernst, later Bass, Ernest Elie; born Vienna-Ottakring 19 Dec. 1919, after parents' death to orphanage in Doebling, in concentration camp 10 Nov. 1938, active in organising *Kindertransporte*, at Hachshara Bruderhof 17 Aug. 1939, Cotswolds; interned Isle of Man 1940; enlisted 10 Dec. 1940; posted to 249 and 93 Coy PC, at Arromanches July 1944, wounded in Normandy; transferred to 3 Btn Jewish Brde in Italy, wounded again; A/Z Reserve RA; Cpl

Batkin, Stephen

Bauer, Georg, later Bower, Austrian, in 3/10 Cdo

Bauer, Hans, Styrian, took part in suppression of attempted Nazi revolt in Austria July 1934, fled to France on day of *Anschluss*; served with French Army and interned at Kenadsa; served in British Army (337 Coy) from 6 Feb. 1943

Baum, Ernst, 13804847, later Brown, Ernest, 13051500; born Penkun, Pomerania, 30 Mar. 1916, pupil at Schwedt-on-Oder Gymnasium, jeweller's apprentice in Breslau, emigrated to UK 1937; enlisted 19 Nov. 1940; served in 248, 69 and 74 Coy PC; in PoW camp Otley instigated latrine inscription '*dass wir hier scheissen, danken wir dem Führer*' (we shit here thanks to Hitler); landed at Arromanches D-Day + 59; at Caen and Antwerp; interpreter training at Brussels, then Moenchen-Gladbach and Loehne; demob Aug. 1946; post-war: upholsterer, then rep for family factory

Baum, Hans, 13805027, later Trevor, C. Leslie; born 14 July 1922; served in 249 Coy PC; transferred to 3/10 Cdo; post-war: fashion retailer, organiser of old boy meetings of X Troop; said to have drowned in 1995

Baumann, chef in Hotel Kaiserhof, Berlin; Sgt in 88 Coy PC, cookhouse chief

Baumfeld, later Hamley, A., 13041807, Austrian, Cpl; died 11 Apr. 1945

Baumgart, Gunther, later Rogers, Garry; born Breslau, 8 Dec. 1923, pupil at Jewish school am Rhediger Platz, Breslau, until 9 Nov. 1938, *Kindertransport* to UK 30 Mar. 1939; interned Isle of Man 1940; joined 87 Coy PC, Sgt PE Instructor; transferred to 1 RTR as member of Army PT Corps, also driver/wireless operator, landed in Normandy on D-Day + 1, then through to Hamburg; interpreter and investigator in camp for war criminals; demob in Germany Apr. 1947; post-war: married there, worked in Halver and Wipperfürth, Westphalia, returned to Britain June 1949, emigrated to Australia 1964, still there 1997

Baumgarten, joined PC from Richborough 1940; Sgt in 74 Coy PC and was with BEF in France

Baumgarten, Horst Norbert, 13807029, later Barrett, Norbert, 16001311, enlisted 29 Nov. 1941; served in 246 and 249 Coy PC; transferred to REME Donnington, later Egypt, Tel el Kebir; Staff Sgt; demob Dec. 1946.

Baumwollspinner, Gotthard, 13807400, later Barnes, Robert Gerald, 13118507; born Vienna 4 Dec. 1918, Polish citizen who spoke no Polish, public school in UK, then Manchester University; L/Cpl in 69 Coy PC; transferred 3/10 Cdo, in Sicily and Italy, wounded by mortar bomb in attack with 9 Cdo over open ground at Monte Ornito, survived but badly handicapped; awarded BEM; post-war: Treasurer of Cdo Association

Beadle, A., 2/Lt in 248 Coy, attached 69 Coy; 19 June 1943 to 28th Armd Bde

Beare, Evelyn, served in 10 Isle of Man Platoon ATS

Beatty, R.M.H., served in SOE

Beck, Walter, from Vienna; born 1897, served in Austrian Army as Lt in WWI, awarded gold medal for bravery in battle of the Isonzo (Caporetto); served in 77 Coy PC, crossed to Normandy 1944; later interpreter with 298 Military Government, Schleswig; demob 1947; post-war: returned to Vienna; died Aug. 1955

Becker, joined PC from Richborough 1940; Sgt in 74 Coy PC and was with BEF in France

Becker, Fritz, later Benson, Frederic, 13053511; born Rhineland 1921 or 1922, parents taken to Poland, from where they did not return, by *Kindertransport* to UK 1938 or 1939; in hostel in Sutton, Surrey, Mar. 1939–June 1940; then interned; popular as imitator of Prussian military manners; Sgt in PC; transferred to SOE, in 3 Coy IG, IC, parachuted into Poland three times in SS uniform, his trick was to visit dentist in a German military camp and spend night there; on his third trip, 1944 (into Pinsk or possibly Warsaw), was supposed to liberate Polish resistance leader, for which purpose he was to command group of Polish partisans, also in German uniform, but mission unsuccessful; it is thought he perished on this occasion; however, there is a record which says he was killed in western Europe 29 Oct. 1944; posthumous King's Commendation for Brave Conduct

Becker, Harold, from Berlin, emigrated to UK Aug. 1939; interned Isle of Man; served in 229 and 249 Coy PC; transferred to 5 R. Inniskilling Dragoon Guards, at Rhine crossing at Wesel; at end of hostilities near Itzehoe, where he met former neighbour from Berlin; in Berlin summer 1945; met Grotewohl, Schumacher and Luft; post-war: industrial chemist and company secretary, author of *My War*

Becker, Heinz, later Blake, Harry, 13051547; born Berlin 15 July 1920; served in PC; later RAC, 1st Corps, in France, Belgium, Netherlands and Germany

Becker, Robert, later Baker-Byrne, R.P. (Butch), said to have served in *Wehrmacht* – Pasewalker Cuirassiers; served in SOE, completed two missions into enemy territory after Nov. 1944, in first he pretended to be a sergeant in the German Labour Corps, second led to his arrest and detention in a concentration camp, which he survived

Beckmann, Kaethe, served in 1 Allied Volunteer Platoon ATS

Begich, G., 13807892 (WO166/13954 also quotes the name Beh), later Begic, 13122247, Cpl in 69 Coy PC; interview with Gp Cdr 25 Jan. 1943, may have had connection with transfer to SOE

Behr, Dr, from Berlin, had been in concentration camp; gave lectures about his experiences there to British troops; Sgt

Behrendt, Günter, temp. Gene O'Brian, later (in Israel) Gideon Behrendt, from a Berlin orphanage; parachutist in Normandy landing; later, despite small stature, in Scots Guards; post-war: author of *The Long Road Home*

Behrendt, Richard, later Burnett, Richard; born Berlin 15 Jan. 1910; served in 246, 249, 229 and 93 Coy PC; 1944 with 93 Coy in Bayeux, Dieppe and Brussels; Feb. 1945 in interpreters' college at Brussels; then interpreter with coal commission in Wetter/Ruhr; demob 24 Dec. 1945; post-war: accountant

Beier, Anna, from Frankfurt, a member of an international socialist fighting organisation, was scheduled to parachute into Frankfurt to foment unrest, but this went wrong and she actually jumped into Switzerland; as a result she got to Frankfurt only after the fighting had ended

Bein, E., Austrian, appears to have acted as driver in connection with HMS *Stag* at Suez

Bein, Julius

Bellak, Geri, member of Young Austria, living in London; enlisted around Dec. 1943–Jan. 1944

Bendit, Ernst, 220741, joined PC from Richborough 1940; served in 74 Coy PC and was with BEF in France; commissioned in PC 23 Dec. 1941, 31 Dec. 1942 in list of officers of 249; 19 Nov. 1943 as Capt and 2 i/c of 137 Coy PC; may also have been in 246 Coy; OC of PC at end of war; Daniel Cohn-Bendit, leader of French Green Party and City Senator of Frankfurt, denies any relationship

Bendit, K., served in 74 Coy PC

Bendit, Leonore, W/53517, in all probability, as a result of an interview with Col. Wedgewood at the House of Commons either she or her mother was instrumental in the founding of alien platoons in the ATS; served in 1 Allied Volunteer Platoon ATS as from 11 Apr. 1941

Bendix, Peter, of Leipzig

Benecke, C.E., Staff Sgt in Intelligence, 1945 in No.1 Infm Control Unit, 21 Army Gp

Benjamin, R.T.; died on active service

Bennett, served in 137 Coy PC and SOE; post-war: prominent in Ex-Service NB Association

Berczi (Miss), Austrian, Sgt in WAAF; meteorologist, for five years meteorological section chief on airfield near London used by British, Canadian, Norwegian, Czech and Polish planes; able to speak most languages of the Austro-Hungarian monarchy

Berger, Goetz, German; born 1905, partner in lawyer's office of Hilde Benjamin in Berlin-Wedding, volunteer in International Brigade in Spanish Civil War, but did not see action; interned for four years by French at Argelès, Gurs, Le Vernet and Djelfa on the Transsahara railway; joined 337 or 338 Coy PC at Algiers 1943, lectured British units on events in Germany; asked for transfer to Soviet Union, which was granted; released from British service after arrival in Russia; after thorough investigation there was forced to work in silk factory in Turkmenistan; post-war: returned to Berlin, became judge in GDR, later again lawyer, defence counsel in Havemann trial; died 1996 whilst giving evidence at reopening of this case

Berger, I., later Bennett J., served in 93 Coy PC

Berger, Lilo, served in 1 AV Platoon ATS

Berger, Oskar, served in Austro-Hungarian army in WWI; in French Foreign Legion 1940–42; also in British service in North Africa

Berger, Peter (Putz), later Barry, Peter, served in SOE, but not used in action

Berger-Waldenegg, Baron Heinrich, alias Baum, Henry, alias Burleigh, Henry Oswald, alias Boccafurni, son of Heinrich B.-W., Austrian minister and ambassador in Rome; *Wehrmacht* deserter; continued in rank in British Army; served in SOE, in June 1945 in operation 'Big Bug' in Austria; demob as Lt in Austria

Bergmann, Dr Georg F.J. or G.M. or F.G.M., 13810003, alias Butler, F.G., 5550125, alias Hillman(n?), Leo, or F., or Charles, alias Kennedy, Charles Victor, or J., alias Gerber, Leopold, alias Hofer, nicknamed Baron Schnitzelberger; might have been born in Lissa (Leszno), Prussia, lawyer, writer, mountaineer, described as 'small and fat, wearing gold framed glasses and looking like a professor, always smelled of garlick. Certainly, no one looked less like a parachutist', said to have studied economics and law, may have practised as lawyer at Sonthofen, Bavaria and Munich, 1933 to France; interned there 1939; joined Foreign Legion Dec. 1939, to North Africa, again interned, at Colomb-Bechar, Abadlah, Hadjerat M'Guil; after British landing in 1942 to 338 Coy PC; then Pte in RHamps., said to have been one of 4 survivors of a commando raid on Tobruk and to have been in action in Romania (!?); on 61b and 62nd parachute training course; Capt., Special Services, 1944 in Villa Rossa, Monopoli; parachuted into Austria north of Krems 23 Apr. 1945, said to have infiltrated Gestapo and to have raised a squad of 130 partisans; later contact to Soviets; participated in arrest of prominent Nazis; reported missing in June 1945; but was interrogator in Wolfsberg, Carinthia, later in 1945; discharged at Klagenfur 1947; awarded Military Cross and Military Medal (but see also Liebel, Peter, below); post-war: said to have gone to Canada, thence to Australia, prominent in Ex-Service NB Association there, Vice-President Blue Mountains Historical Society (author of *The Blue Mountains* and *Gustav Weindorfer, the Hermit of Cradle Mountain*); died at Vila, New Hebrides, 21 Oct. 1979; all of which the author of these lines takes with several grains of salt

Bergmann, Ellen, Cpl in 1 Allied Volunteer Platoon ATS

Berk, served in 137 Coy PC

Berkeley, J.

Berkovics, served in 74 Coy PC

Berkowitz, S.; died on active service

Berliner, F.M., later O'Hara, F. Michael, alias F.M. Chirgwin, also F. Knoll, also F. Hofer, father Viennese Jew, mother Irish, he himself Austrian, served in

SOE, parachuted into northern Italy and returned to Monopoli after completed mission 1944; later that year in Operation 'Evansville' in which he jumped onto Koralpe, Austria, very successful at first; escaped capture and got to Yugoslavia, betrayed by partisans and captured by Gestapo, taken to Graz, tortured and murdered there, shortly before Soviet troops arrived; Gestapo officer responsible, a man named Hess (or Herz?) later tried and hanged; Dale thought he had been contact man to Operation 'Historian' (Zeltweg group), which seems impossible, however

Berliner, Kurt, later Berliner, Peter, served in 246 Coy PC

Berman, Rudolph, served in PC; later RASC; lastly Intelligence, Maj. in charge of translators' office at British Control Commission for Germany

Bernadelli, Professor of Economics at Oxford; was field cashier officer, Pay Corps; later transferred to staff of Ministry of Information; in Burma 1942–43; at end of war radio commentator New Delhi

Bernaert, Willy Gustave (H.?) Clement, 13806045, Pte in 253 Coy PC, mentioned in dispatches; killed on active service 19 Apr. 1944; name on Brookwoods Memorial, Surrey, panel 20, col.3

Bernard, E., 13806015, served in 253 Coy PC

Bernard, Kelly, enlisted Oct. 1944; PC; Para. Regt; demob Mar. 1948; post-war: later in Israeli Army

Bernard, R.P., Cpl; letter from him written whilst serving in France 1944 is preserved in the Vienna archives

Bernheim, served in 137 Coy PC; mentioned by Bandler, who did cookhouse fatigue with him

Bernstein, joined 74 Coy PC from Richborough 1940 and was with BEF in France

Bernstein, Fritz; died on active service

Bernstein, Helga, married relation; born Berlin, 1923, pupil at St Franciscus Ober-Lyzeum, Nollendorf Pl., then in Jewish school, Regensburger Str., Berlin, to Britain by *Kindertransport* June 1939, then Purley Sec. Grammar and Barrett Street Tech, tailor's apprentice; enlisted 1941; ATS E Group; demob 1942 because of pregnancy

Bernzweig, J., joined 74 Coy PC from Richborough 1940 and was with BEF in France

Bertschi, W., 13805635

Bettelheim, Wilhelm, from Vienna

Beuger, Lilo, served in 1 Allied Volunteer Platoon ATS

Bianchi, served in 229 Coy PC

Biebermann, Lt in Sharpshooters, BAOR War Crimes Gp

Biegeleisen, Miss M., 2992399, Austrian, emigrated to Palestine; was LACW in WAAF

Bielschowski, Wilhelm, 13801201, later Blake, William, 13041470; born Bochum 5 Jan. 1907, pupil at Oberrealschule Bochum, studied at Karlsruhe and Goettingen, active member of Alemannia student corps, studied law, started judicial career, additional studies at London University and Sorbonne, dismissed from legal service 1933, then commercial apprentice in Bornum and Berlin, 1938 to UK, land worker in Lincs; enlisted 1 Feb.

1940 at Lincoln; served in PC; 31 Oct. 1943 to RF (SOE); 13 June 1944 Intelligence; in Norway at end of war, then interpreter No. 300 German PoW camp; Sgt; released 31 Jan. 1946; had to report to police as enemy alien on day after release – very disappointed; post-war: export merchant

Bier, Herbert N., 13106759; born Frankfurt 17 Jan. 1905 pupil at Hirsch Realschule (orthodox), Frankfurt, moved to Berlin 1918–19, joined his uncle's art business 1922–23 (Z.M.Hackenbroch, Frankfurt), apprentice in Munich and Paris, 1928 back to Frankfurt, to London 1935, art dealer in St James Street; interned 1940, but released because of business connections with US; enlisted Mar. 1942; Sgt in 93 and 165 Coy PC; transferred RASC, with them in Belgium; in HQ 21 Army Gp, Mar. 1945 EPW Documentation Unit, 2218 PWC BAOR; demob 10 Apr. 1946; post-war: again in art business; died 9 Oct. 1981

Bierer, F., 13802155, later Bentley, Frederick, 13046572 and 6387013, Sgt 3/10 Cdo; appears that he was one of few who returned from a raid carried out by '62 Cdo', part of the Small Scale Raiding Force, on 30 Mar. 1943; not clear whether this was the attack on the isle of Herm on 27–28 Feb. 1943 or another subsequent action

Biesenthal, George

Bilisic, Alois, Austrian, alias Brenner, served in IC; in June 1945 in No.6 Special Force Staff Section in Austria

Billmann, Karl Walter, 13801297, later Bartlett, Kenneth Walter, 13118508; born Munich 21 Apr. 1912, pupil at Munich Gymnasium, studied musicology at Munich and Tuebingen, and after emigration at Royal College of Music, London; served in 87 Coy PC; transferred to RHamps.; then 3/10 Cdo; in Normandy and Italy, commissioned for bravery in the field; instrumental in getting many enemy soldiers to surrender by judicious use of loudspeakers; later at HQ 2 Cdo Bde at Monopoli near Bari and at Minervino near Ancona; from Jan. 1945 OC 3 Troop 10 Cdo until disbandment; after end of hostilities music control officer with Radio Cologne, then for whole of British zone of Germany; post-war: Secretary Sheffield Philharmonic Society, then Chief Dramatic Advisor Hamburg State Opera House, lastly with German music publisher B. Schotts Soehne in Mainz, last heard of working as translator in Munich

Bindel, Jakob, Austrian; born 14 Nov. 1901, Secretary of the Friends of the Children Society for Lower Austria until 1934; served in British Army Oct. 1942–May 1946; post-war: Secretary of the Austrian Federal Socialist Party

Bingham, Walter, served in PC; later in RASC as driver, awarded Military Medal for bravery whilst evacuating wounded under heavy fire June 1944

Birnbaum, Susi, later Saunders, served in 1 Allied Volunteer Platoon ATS

Bischburg, Leo, joined 74 Coy PC from Richborough 1940 and was with BEF in France; died on active service

Bischheim, Bernhard, later Beecham, Bernard, member of a Frankfurt Jewish family that can trace its roots there back to the 15th century, older brother of Erich Bischheim; Sgt with RE in Italy; post-war: emigrated to Israel; died 1988

Bischheim, Erich, later Beecham, Eric M. from Frankfurt; younger brother of

Bernhard Bischheim (see above), served in Suffolk Regt and Lincs. Regt, with these in 3rd Army Corps advance to Bremen, wounded in knee and returned to UK 8 May 1945

Bischitz, E., holder of Iron Cross from WWI; Cpl in 229 Coy PC; commissioned 1942, as Lt with 251 Coy PC Jan. 1943; 2 i/c 93 Coy PC whilst at Bicester

Blackie, served in 137 Coy PC

Blake, Arthur

Blake, Peter, served in SOE; same man as Blau, P., later Blake?

Blank, E.

Blau, later Blair, served in PC; transferred to RA, in Normandy landing, commissioned and became artillery intelligence officer; in British Austrian Legal Unit; demob as Capt.; post-war: legal adviser to British embassy in Vienna, married his general's daughter

Blau, P., later Blake, served in 87 Coy PC

Blaywas, joined 74 Coy PC from Richborough 1940 and was with BEF in France

Bleicher, Ludwig (Vicky); born Vienna 1919, son of a jeweller, student at Italian navy school, to Haifa 1938; Cpl in 608 Coy PC, served in North Africa and Greece; after disbandment of 608 Coy on beach at Kalamata fled to North Africa in open boat, captured there by Italians and handed over to German Army, imprisoned at Criminal Court in Vienna for 10 months before being recognised as PoW

Bleichroeder, Adolf, 13807288, later Bleach, Timothy, 14623928; born Hamburg 7 Jan. 1922, scion of Berlin banking family, to England 1936; interned 1940, to Australia on HMT *Dunera*, returned end 1941; volunteered PC, to 229 Coy 28 Jan. 1942; transferred to 21 Indep. Para. Coy, took part in 61b and 62nd parachute training course; fought in North Africa, Italy and at Arnhem; killed in action

Bloch, joined 74 Coy PC from Richborough 1940 and was with BEF in France

Bloch, later Block, Benno; born Breslau 1925, pupil at Jewish RG, Breslau to UK 1939, worked in leather factory, Northampton; enlisted 1943 or later; Rifleman in 12 KRRC, in action in Holland and Germany as from Feb. 1945, May 1945 in Hannover, then Tripoli, North Africa; post-war: lives in US

Bloch, H.E., later Bryan, H.E., served in 87 Coy PC

Block, Peter, 13804512 and 14623936, from Frankfurt, family originated from Bechhofen (Abenberg), south of Nuremberg, where resident since 15th century, school in England; interned June–Oct. 1940; served in PC in 246, 251 and 248 Coy; transferred to 21 Indep. Para. Coy, was on 61b and 62nd parachute training course; in action at Taranto, Foggia, operations 'Hasty' near Rome and 'Dragoon' on south coast of France; after 1st Airborne Div. became Anglo-American formation to 1 Indep. Para. Platoon; action in Greece, occupation of Athens, fighting against EAM and ELAS; post-war: BSc.Econ., LSE, manager Beechams, mainly in GDR, CSSR, Bulgaria and Romania

Bluh, A., 775983, Austrian, emigrated to Palestine; joined RAF, LAC

Blum, Rupert, brother of Blum, Walter

Blum, W. (Walter?), probably in 246 Coy PC; 2/Lt on officers' list of 88 Coy PC 31 Aug. 1943; asked for by Press and Publicity, 21 Army Gp, for information control

Blumberg, Dr Erich, interpreter in Psychological Warfare, Bari, 1945

Blumenau, M., later Barring; died on active service

Blumenberg, Alex, served in Sudan Defence Force

Blumenfeld, Ludwig Georg, 13801895, later Merton, Michael James, 13118509; born Berlin 21 June 1920, pupil at Fichte *Gymnasium*, Berlin; joined 93 Coy PC from Richborough 1940 and in France with BEF, at St Malo; transferred to 3/10 Cdo, attached to 2 Cdo Bde in Sicily, attached to Polish troop of 10 Cdo, at Pescopennataro and at Monte Cassino; later in landing on Lissa (Vis); after end of hostilities in legal service, prosecutor in military court Dusseldorf, intelligence service Kiel

Blumenfeld, W., served in 77 Coy PC; acted in that company's Christmas panto *A Midsummer Night's Scream*, probably 1941

Blunz, joined 74 Coy PC from Richborough 1940 and was with BEF in France

Blutstein, Feb. 43 on officers' list 251 Coy PC as Lt, war diary there shows him to have been posted to 6 PCTC Bradford 23 Apr. 1943

Bluweis, Davidl, emigrated to Palestine, bus driver in Tel Aviv; joined 608 Coy PC, served in North Africa and Greece, taken prisoner by Germans at Kalamata 1941

Bock, Lieselotte, married Bier; born Frankfurt 21 Sept. 1919, moved to Berlin 1927, pupil at Fuerstin Bismark Schule, Goldschmidt Schule, after emigration in Sept. 1938, school certificate in England, worked as nanny in London and Leicester until 1941, then in armaments factory; volunteered July 1943; LACW clerk in WAAF; RAF Coningsby, Base HQ No.5 Gp Bomber Command, there worked for Guy Gibson, OC 617 Sqn and W/Cdr Woodroffe; volunteered for overseas posting, was refused because brother was PoW; from Dec. 44 HQ 2 TAF, Brussels; Mar. 45 SHAEF Mission Paris, then RAF Mission in France

Bock, Max

Bock, Walter L.; born Frankfurt 11 Jan. 1915, emigrated Dec. 1933 to South Africa, became SA citizen; enlisted 1939; SA forces, tank driver, taken prisoner near Tobruk 1941, taken first to Brindisi, then Silesia, June 1945 after end of hostilities on foot to Prague; post-war: returned to SA, later to California

Bohm, Etty, from Frankfurt, father was editor of *Frankfurter Zeitung*, emigrated to Palestine; joined ATS at Sarafand, then Egypt; post-war: pianist, standard bearer of AJEX ladies

Boehm, Rudolph Walter, later Boam, Rudolph Walter; born Breslau 1916, lived in Berlin 1922–Nov. 1938, pupil at Prinz Heinrich Gymnasium, then with Bleichroeder Bank, emigrated to Holland Nov. 38, to UK Apr. 1939, worked in City of London; interned at Huyton 1940; enlisted Sept. 1940; to 246 Coy PC, later 249; transferred RASC; then RAOC; 1943 to HQ 21 Army Gp, appointed S/Sgt 1945, served in Rome, Klagenfurt, there contact with Yugoslav partisans; demob at Villach 31 Oct. 1946; post-war: senior financial appointment with Control Commission for Austria, highly decorated by Carinthian government, trader on London metal exchange and bullion market

Boelskov, E., 13806065, served in PC, later commissioned

Bohm, G.

Bondi, Fritz, 775320, Austrian, emigrated to Palestine; joined RAF, Sgt in accounts dept; later officer in Israeli air force

Bonnard, Sgt Maj. in PC; later in IC, Psychological Warfare; demob as Maj.

Borchard, joined 74 Coy PC from Richborough 1940 and was with BEF in France

Borchard, Ulrich, later Bourne, Eric, 360569; born Berlin 1924, father well-known Social Democrat, pupil at Schmargendorf Volksschule, emigrated 1933, attended Bunce Court School, Otterden, Kent, until 1940, then agricultural worker; volunteered 1943; training in Glasgow and Colchester; then 4th Ox. & Bucks. LI, 3in. mortar training, Wrotham, then India, OTS Mhow, commissioned 20 Oct. 1945; then with 2nd Berks Regt in Burma, there minor skirmishes with Burmese veterans of both sides; after return to UK in No.300 PoW camp, Wilton Park, Beaconsfield; released 16 Oct. 1947; post-war: studied at London University, in socialist youth movement in Essex, Sussex and Derbyshire, inspector adult education ILEA until 1986.

Borger; post-war: in welfare committee, Ex Service NB Association, to US 1948

Braeuer (Breuer?), Dr Georg, also known as Bryant, George Herbert, Viennese lawyer pre-war, in Britain member of Free Austria Movement; served in 88 Coy PC; transferred to SOE (RF), in North Africa and Italy; parachuted into Styria as Lt Col. and leader of group that took over German military airport at Zeltweg (Operation 'Historian') in Apr. 1945; took active part in reconstituting democratic government in Styria; June 1945 in No.6 Special Force Staff Section; later 2 i/c British Austrian Legal Unit, Vienna; married a BALU secretary; post-war: to Canada

Brandes, C., joined 74 Coy PC from Richborough 1940 and was with BEF in France

Brann, R.H., Cpl in 69 Coy PC

Bratu, Artur E., temp. Bennett, George; born Offenbach 30 Mar. 1910, active member of SPD and Reichsbanner, studied philosophy at Frankfurt, fled to Brussels 1933, where he worked as court interpreter and continued studies, Germany asked for his extradition on political charges, fled to England by fishing boat 1940, imprisoned in Pentonville 5 months; enlisted later that year; served in PC; transferred RE; then Psychological Warfare dept, IC, there WO II; to Control Commission for Germany, prosecutor in denazification court Darmstadt; demob Dec. 45, but remained in Darmstadt and continued previous work; post-war: active there in public life, prosecutor at court of appeal, education officer, political education, highly decorated

Brauer, Erich Franz, later Bowes, Eric F., from Breslau; served in 87 Coy PC; transferred to SOE, broke ankle during parachute training and did not get into action; both parents sent to Theresienstadt, but found father alive at Auschwitz

Braun, Ernst, later Brown Ernest, from Penkum, Pomerania, pupil at Schwedt Gymnasium, then jeweller's apprentice in Breslau; Cpl in 248, 69 and 74 Coy PC; later in Control Commission in Mönchengladbach and Loehne

Braun, Kurt, Austrian, served in 337 or 338 Coy PC

Braun, Therese, married Bornstein, from Vienna; served in ATS, mess orderly in Bury St Edmunds; post-war: writes essays etc.

Braunsberg, H.

Breitbart, later Bright, Geoffrey, from Berlin

Breitbart, Horst Guenther, later Bright, Alan; born Berlin-Charlottenburg, 23 July 1925, family from Breslau, pupil at Kaliski Waldschule, Berlin, *Kindertransport* to Britain 21 May 1939, attended Sheffield Technical School until 1943; enlisted Jan. 1944; to Duke of Wellington's Regt; then 2 Scottish Borderers, RAOC, Army Kinema Corps; with 7 Ind. Div. in Kohima, then India, Ceylon, Malaya, Thailand and Singapore; demob 1948; post-war: manager in several companies and fellow or member of various professional institutes; lives in Bucks.

Breitfeld, Austrian, served in 337 or 338 Coy PC

Bremmler, A., one of first six alien sergeants in 69 Coy PC

Brent, Bern G., from Berlin, came to England 1939; interned 1940, sent to Australia on HMT *Dunera*; there volunteered for Australian military forces and served in 8 Australian Employment Coy; demob Jan. 1946

Brent, G.R., Capt. in 77 and 93 Coy PC

Brett, David (Bertie), from Berlin; served in 219 Coy PC

Brettell, H., served in 69 Coy PC, commissioned 1943

Brettschneider, served in 337 or 338 Coy PC

Brian, Harry

Brichta, Friedrich; died on active service

Bright, Berliner, emigrated from Germany 1933 and went to Gibraltar, qualified there as engineer, 1939 volunteered for UK armed services, at that time Japan was neutral and as fares on Japanese ships were cheaper, he decided to travel to UK by such a vessel, but ship went via Casablanca and when it docked there French security officers discovered he had a German passport and arrested him, interned for three months, when released was able to board boat for Britain in June 1940; interned on landing, sent to Isle of Man, then shipped to Australia on HMT *Dunera*, some time later received permission to join Australian military forces, but at medical was found unfit for service, asked to be returned to Britain; there at last accepted into PC; posted to 165 Coy; 1943 transferred to REME and immediately sent to India, 25th Ind. Div., entrusted with command of divisional REME workshop and became WO Class 1, finishing up in Malaya; released from service there

Brill, Hans, submarine officer RN; presumably a regular as still serving in late 1950s

Brings, Erich, 13809102, Austrian from Friedeck (in Czechoslovakia?); served in North Africa and Italy; 25 May 1940 reported for service in the French army at Montpellier; released again 6 Nov. 1941 at Gerryville; somehow got to Algiers, where accepted for service in British Army 31 Dec. 1942, in either 337 or 338 Coy PC, remained in North Africa until 20 Jan. 1945, got to Italy, but returned to North Africa on 10 Jan. 1946; demob 6 Aug. 1946 as WO Class II

Brod, E., PAL/726, Austrian, enlisted in Palestine; S/Sgt, instrument maker and driver/mechanic, served in MEF

Brod, H.R., later Brook, Henry R., Czechoslovakian citizen; served in 87 Coy PC; later 5 RTR; with 7 Armd Div. in Portsmouth, Arromanches, Bayeux, Caen, Falaise, Ghent, tank led British advance into Ghent during the street fighting, then Holland, Ardennes, Rhine crossing at Xanten, into Hamburg May 1945, occupied town hall, only survivor of original tank crew; after cessation of fighting in Control Commission; demob June 1946

Brook, Charles, from Germany; served in PC and RN.

Brooks, Colin, served in PC; transferred to infantry; Staff Capt. in East Africa and responsible for repatriation of 200,000 African soldiers

Brost, Erich, after end of fighting became editor of *Kölnischer Kurier* and *Ruhrzeitung*, then first editor-in-chief of *Neue Ruhr Zeitung*

Brown, C., served in 77 Coy PC

Bruell, Egon, 14442497, Austrian, craftsman in 14 AFV Depot REME at Kegworth

Brunner, Hans; born at Tulln, Lower Austria, 6 Dec. 1921, pupil at Tullner Gymnasium, emigrated to London Sept. 1938; served in British Army; post-war: lived in Prague

Buchanan, PO in the RCN, served in Adriatic in support of Tito's partisans, later in escort to landing force for south coast of France

Buchanan (Mrs), wife of above, medical orderly, RAMC; transferred to Intelligence, Northern Command

Buchdahl, Werner, from Wiesbaden, one of P.Y. Mayer's 'Pimpfs' in the *Schwarzes Faehnlein* (Black Flag Movement); served in PC; transferred to SOE; killed in action in Yugoslavia

Buchholz, Adolf

Buchsbaum, S., 13800112, Austrian, Pte in PC; killed in action during Blitz London 29 Dec. 1940

Buchwalder, Austrian, served in 338 Coy PC in North Africa

Bukofzer, Gert

Bume, M., Austrian, L/Cpl in 405 Coy RASC (WT) MEF

Bun, Walter, 13800008; born Vienna 5 Apr. 1914; reported for service 16 Nov. 1939, service number shows him to have been in first batch to have been enrolled, after reaching France in spring 1940 he fell ill with a renal disease, sent to the military hospital at Alton, where one of his kidneys was removed; released from military service in 1942; on 25 Aug. 1945 he died of tuberculosis; brother, conscripted into *Wehrmacht*, killed at Stalingrad

Bunzl, Georg, later Beaumont, from Vienna

Bunzl, P.F., Austrian, Pte HQ AAIA A 7 CLT, CMF

Burger, Dr F., served in 69 Coy PC

Burger, Steffie, married Wahle, served in one of the women's services; post-war: prominent in Ex-Service NB Association

Burgess, R.E.

Burian, Walter, 14442327, later Brian, Walter; born in Vienna 21 Oct. 1922, both parents killed in Theresienstadt, older sister went to Yugoslavia with husband, neither heard of again, two sisters went to US, to UK on *Kindertransport* 10 Dec. 1938, agricultural training; interned May 1940, to Canada, brought back summer 1942, member of Young Austria; volunteered 11 Apr. 1943, called up 6 Jan. 1944; with 1 Btn Northants Regt in 20 Indian Div. in Burma Nov. 1944–May 45, then India, Singapore and Malaya; demob 17 Dec. 1947; post-war: in travel trade, 1952 in US

Burnell, F. from Berlin, to UK with 90 Berlin students on day before war commenced, found work in factory in Birmingham; volunteered for PC, but not permitted to join as his work was of national importance; interned and sent to Isle of Man; on 18th birthday received letter from the recruiting office where he had previously been refused and was told to report for duty; released from internment, reported to PC and joined 248 Coy; as a result of intervention of a Jewish officer, Colonel Levey, who knew him, Burnell was first transferred to the RASC in 1941; later, on the basis of his completed engineering apprenticeship, to the REME; demob 1946

Burnett, W. 13117462, Pte RF; then with 3/10 Cdo in Italy

Busse, Guenther

Bustin, F. (E.R.A.4), HHX 594984, Austrian served in HMS *Nile*, Alexandria

Butcher, Max, served in 137 and 69 Coy PC

Buttner, CQMS 229 Coy PC; on 30 Apr. 1942 to PC OCTU, would appear not to have been commissioned, for his name appears as CQMS 137 Coy on 2 Sept. 1942

Buxton, served in 137 Coy PC

Cahn, Erich; born Hamburg 31 May 1922, to UK on *Kindertransport* 14 Dec.1938; interned 1940; volunteered for service Dec. 1940, served in 248 & 69 Coy PC; later in IC and Canadian Army IC (18th Canadian Field Security Section); demob 1946; post-war: Rabbi, Moorabbin Hebrew Congregation, Australia

Cahn, Gunther; born Dusseldorf 17 Aug. 1925, brother of Helmut Cahn (see below, also details of family), to England by *Kindertransport* Mar. 1939; joined RAF on reaching age 18 in 1943; known to have been stationed at RAF Wunsdorf (Germany) at one time and to have voluntarily extended his service so that he was still in the service at the time of the Berlin airlift

Cahn, Helmut, later Curtis, Harry; born Dusseldorf 25 Aug. 1923, brother of Gunther Cahn (above), pupil at Jewish school, Dusseldorf, lost his parents and 64 family members in Holocaust, to England by *Kindertransport* 19 June 1939, worked in handbag factory in London; served in PC; transferred to RAC (Recce, 6th Airborne Div.), landed from glider in Holland and drove his tank right through to the Elbe river, in May 1945 on way to Far East but regiment diverted to Palestine, refused orders and asked for court martial, which was denied, then posted to a PoW camp at Cairo, where he refused to speak German and was given an interpreter (Kuno Mueller of Recklinghausen, who became his friend); transferred to Pay Corps; demob 1947; post-war: store manager with Marks & Spencer, active in community affairs, retired on health grounds 1980, died 1990

Caley, served in 137 Coy PC

Calman, C., also Calmon, C.; Berlin lawyer according to one source, Viennese according to another; served in 248 & 69 Coy PC; later in 2 Cdo Bde and Field Security Service; 24 Oct. 1942 to 69 Coy as 2/Lt; 31 Dec. 1942 on officers' list of 248 Coy; on 15 Feb.1943 in charge of draft of 52 men on posting from 69 to 249 Coy PC; in Lissa (Vis) landing, acted as editor of forces paper *Vis-a-vis* there; later head of 8th Army Intelligence, investigated war crimes in Austria; last posting as political observer; discharged as Maj.

Calman, J.F., on officers' list of 363 Coy PC 1 Aug. 1943; ditto 362 Coy. 31 Dec. 1943

Cane, H.J.

Cappel, Franz Erwin, later Francis; born Cologne 2 June 1916, pupil at RG Lindenthal school, father lawyer, emigrated to France 1933, then Switzerland, then Czechoslovakia, to UK 1938; enlisted Richborough 10 Jan. 1940; Cpl in 93 Coy PC, with BEF in France, evacuated via Brest; served in bomb disposal unit in Windsor Great Park; clerk; electrician; interpreter for German and English, used in communication with French resistance; was in team at first start of V2 rocket under British supervision Oct. 1945; orderly room Cpl 736 Coy PC (PW Coy); demob 26 Apr. 1946; post-war: Golders Green, importer of briar wood for 'Permalon' pipes, 1947 to San Francisco, philatelist

Carlebach, Julius; born Hamburg 28 Dec. 1922, son of Chief Rabbi Joseph Carlebach, family from SW Germany, parents and 3 siblings perished in Holocaust, to England 1938; served in 248 and 69 Coy PC; transferred to RN, Leading Writer, later Petty Officer/Captain's secretary on HMS *Blencastra* and HMS *Strule*; on escort for landing craft in Normandy landing; then in 21 Flotilla, Skegness, saw explosion and sinking of HMS *Quorn*; in escort group of Liverpool/Azores convoys; in E-boat alley (east coast); post-war: lecturer in sociology at Sussex University 1988–98 rector of High School for Jewish Studies at Heidelberg University, author

Carlebach, Peter, 13805994, later Carson, Peter Andrew, 13118801; born Berlin 27 Oct. 1919, family had come from Frankfurt, father lawyer, mother singer, pupil at Grunewald Gymnasium, to UK 1935; interned 1940, to Australia on HMT *Dunera*; on return to UK joined 93 Coy PC; transferred 3/10 Cdo, involved in preparations for attack on V2 launching ramps in France, badly wounded during cliff climbing 1944

Carlton, Sgt in 69 Coy PC

Caro, a Viennese, served in 338 Coy PC, N.Africa; post-war: editor Weltpresse, Vienna

Carruthers, served in 137 Coy PC

Carsten, Franz (Francis) L. from Berlin, father medical practitioner, through his mother descended from a well-known Berlin banking family, studied at Wadham College Oxford; enlisted Oct. 1940; Pte 3PCTC (orderly room); later in Political Warfare Executive, War Office, wrote handbook for AMGOT – for use in Germany; post-war: Professor, FBA

Carter, Charles P., Austrian; born 1921, emigrated to England 1938, draughtsman; interned 1940; enlisted 1 Jan. 1941; L/Cpl 229 Coy PC; transferred to 2/8 Bn Essex Regt; later to RAC, 5 Inniskilling Dragoon Gds; cartoonist of 'Foresight', wall newspaper of 229 Coy; saw action in Normandy against Goering Panzer Grenadiers, took part in advance through Belgium, Holland and Germany, finally at Itzehoe

Casabayo, F., 13803004

Cayzer veteran of Spanish civil war; then French resistance; PC, SOE, Maj.

Charles (surname not known), led a group of three who parachuted into Styria in Apr./May 1945 near Knittelfeld, presented with statuette by people of Knittelfeld, the base of which was inscribed 'To our liberator'

Cemach, Harry (Hans), to England as journalist from Vienna; interned 1940; Cpl in all-Viennese No. 4 section, 229 Coy PC, editor of that company's wall newspaper 'Foresight'; transferred to RAOC in 1943, commissioned shortly afterwards, first job as officer was to organise German PoWs to work in British ammunition depot; later sent to Burma, to Singapore and finally to Java, where he was attached to a division of the Indian Army (while in Batavia – now Jakarta, Java's chief city – ran across Captain Pollack, MC, formerly of 88 Coy PC, who had got there with an Airborne division; post-war: ACA; prominent in Ex-Service NB Association

Chalaupa, Manfred, alias Achatz, Alfred, also Kaulaut, Anton, Austrian, German soldier, PoW; taken into British service; joined SOE, in op DUCIMER near Klagenfurt; June 1945 in Nr 6 Special Force Staff Section in Austria, was intended to remain there

Christensen, A.E.E., 13806026

Christensen, A.M., 6598695

Christensen, K., 6298612

Christensen, K.F.A., 13806047

Christiansen G., 13806027

Chutuk, E.J., 13807893 and 13122224

Cibronski, S., served in 74 Coy PC

Claer, Joan von, served in 1 Allied Volunteer Platoon ATS

Cleaver, R.; post-war: prominent in Ex-Service NB Association

Cohen, served in French Foreign Legion; then 246 Coy PC

Cohen, Dr Ernst, served in RA; then Legal Research Branch; later legal advisor to Control Commission in Germany; lastly deputy controller, legal division for British Zone of Germany; Lt Col

Cohn, CQMS in 69 & 270 Coy PC

Cohn, Sgt in 246 Coy PC

Cohn, joined 74 Coy PC from Richborough 1940 and was with BEF in France

Cohn, later Horley (or Harley?), R.; died on active service

Cohn, David, later Smith, Henry, joined 74 Coy PC from Richborough 1940 and was with BEF in France. (Pelican writes that there had been a David Cohen in 74 Coy, the nominal roll, however, shows two men by name of Cohn and no Cohen.)

Cohn, Else, served in 1 Allied Volunteer Platoon ATS

Cohn, Hans, later Carson, John; born Wolfenbuettel 1921, pupil at Fichte Gymnasium, Berlin and Bodenbach CSR technical school 1936–38, to UK

1938; NCO in 251 Coy PC; transferred to 4 REME workshop in Donnington, also in Cairo; post-war: 3 years LSE, then town planner, to Canada 1959, then to USA, Indonesia, Thailand, China, India, Kenya, Ghana, Nigeria, Bahamas, Trinidad, retired to Dominica

Cohn, Hans, served in 337 Coy PC, North Africa, then France; edited newspaper addressed to German soldiers; post-war: prominent in Ex-Service NB Association

Cohn, Hans Joseph; born Hannover 22 Sept. 1913; interned 1940; enlisted same year; served in 219 Coy PC, released after one year's service for important war work in metal recycling

Cohn, Heinz

Cohn, Hugo

Cohn, K., served in 77 Coy PC, acted in Xmas panto *A Midsummer Night's Scream*, presumably 1941

Cohn, Susanne, married Lustig; born Breslau 1921, pupil at Jewish school there until 1937, became nursery nurse, emigrated 1939, worked as housemaid; enlisted 1943; ATS, Sgt; then WO II (SQMS) attached to RAMC and IC (CSDIC UK); demob Oct. 1945; post- war: worked for the UN refugee organisation; mother of two sons, but after they had left home she went back to work and became secretary of a London college

Cohn, Wilhelm, from Hannover, judge, served in PC; later Lt Col Army Legal Research Branch

Collins, E.

Collins, R; post-war: prominent in Ex-Service NB Association

Colman, A.H., served in 219 & 248 Coy PC; post-war: painter and decorator

Conradi, M. 13800694, from Dresden, joined 74 Coy PC from Richborough 1940 and was with BEF in France; one of three from PC who rescued two ladies from a bombed building at Weymouth 1942

Conradt, later Curtis, Richard

Conway, M.

Cooper, Jack

Cooper, Ronald, served in 69 Coy PC

Coot, M., 13807888

Corfield, William, bandsman in 3 PCTC

Cossmann, Gerhard Hermann Carl, 13807090, later Crawford, Peter 13053571, had lived in Potsdam, Biedenkopf, Schleswig, Freiburg i.B; born 1922, pupil at Freiburg Gymnasium, emigrated Nov. 1938 to Brentwood, Essex; interned 1940, to Australia by HMT *Dunera*, returned 1941; enlisted 29 Nov. 1941; served in 165, 219 & 220 Coy PC; then transferred to Intelligence; on parachute course at Ringway, also courses in morse and coding; demob as Sgt; post-war: theology studies, clergyman 1952, various parishes in North of England, Rural Dean at Ripon and St Edmundsbury, retired in 1987

Costello, C.H., 2/Lt in 69 Coy PC

Cover, L., 13807927

Cramer, Robert

Craven, served in SOE

Crofton, W.A.

Czempin, Miss R., Austrian, served as driver in 511 Coy ATS TEK Gp

Czernin, Austrian, presumed to have been *Wehrmacht* defector; was Maj. in SOE, ISSU 6 in North Africa and Italy, worked behind *Wehrmacht* lines, had line of communication to Italian partisans; in Florence 1945 when allied troops marched in; SOE chief in Friaul

Czerninski, M., 13810014, later Curtis, F.M. or F.H., 6305489, Pte, served in PC; then in the Buffs; returned to PC in autumn 1944

Czerny-Gruenbaum, Miss M., Austrian, was driver in 511 Coy ATS TEK Gp

Czupper, Noe, alias Grant, Alan Norman Ronald, alias McCabe, A., served with SOE and RF; parachuted into Tramontina Valley 13 Aug. 1944; also in Yugoslavia; post-war: with Unilever

Daikes, joined 74 Coy PC from Richborough 1940 and was with BEF in France; later Cpl in 3/10 Cdo, in action at Walcheren

Dantowitz, Gerhard

Danziger, Dr Heinz G., later Dunn, Dr Henry; born Leipzig around 1917, pupil at Nikolai Gymnasium, studied medicine at Leipzig, went to India about 1935; was Maj. IAMC

Danziger, Walter, later Dunn, Walter; born Leipzig around 1918(?) brother of Heinz Danziger (Dunn) above, pupil at Nikolai Gymnasium, studied medicine at Leipzig

Daubrawsky, O.

Davantro, A., 13806125

Davico, E., served in 229 Coy PC; killed in motor accident on active service 1 July 1942

David, joined 74 Coy PC from Richborough 1940 and was with BEF in France

David, Walter

Davies, Leonore, served in WAAF

Davis; emigrated to Manchester, where he had connections with German communists; joined British (or possibly US) service

De Jonge, joined 74 Coy PC from Richborough 1940 and was with BEF in France

Delitz, Josef (or Georg?), later de Liss, George V., known as Peppi, Austrian, was Sgt in PC; then glider pilot in 6th Airborne Div; illustrated Louis Hagen's book about Arnhem

Delitz, T.C., was L/Cpl in 248 Coy PC; exhibited paintings at Darlington Society Exhibition on or about 20 Aug. 1942

Denes, a Hungarian, was Sgt in 246 Coy PC

Denman, E., was Maj. in Special Services; awarded MC

Dent, R.E.

Dermann, Erich, later Derman; born Vienna 14 June 1909, journalist, from 13 Nov. 1938–June 1939 at Dachau, fled to Italy, then by freighter to Antibes, thence to Grasse; interned in France, in various camps, then Prestataire in Rennes; fled to Morocco, interned again, this time in Boghari; spring 1943 to 338 Coy PC; appointed chief of Austrian broadcasts from Algiers, later Bari, then Rome; post-war: editor in Klagenfurt, then Weltpresse, Vienna

Dessauer, Franz, later Davenport; born Vienna 7 May 1921, attended Albert

Gymnasium (G8) 1931–35, then textile school till 1938, to England, 2 years at Notts University (textile technology); interned on Isle of Man 1940; volunteered for army service Oct. 1940, enlisted at Ilfracombe; posted to 219 Coy PC; transferred to RA 1943, L/Bdr instructor to 123 OCTU RA at RAPC Shoeburyness; commissioned May 1945 as Lt in Fd. Regt RA in 5 Div. stationed at Duderstedt; demob 1946; post-war: 2 years with ICI textile development, Terylene, then 1948–83 with Bunzl Pulp & Paper; plays violin

Desser, served in 87 Coy PC

Deutsch, Arthur, 775951, Austrian, emigrated to Palestine; joined RAF, was LAC; post-war: worked in Israeli post office

Deutsch, Heinz, member of Young Austria; enlisted Dec. 1943 or Jan. 1944, from Manchester

Deutsch, J., was orderly Sgt of 74 Coy on 9 June 1943

Deutsch, L, married Talbot, enlisted 1943; Sgt ATS attached to Ordnance Depot Feltham; later in Education Dept; then in ABCA Current Affairs

Deutsch-Renner, Franzi, married Ashley, Frances, from Vienna, granddaughter of Austrian president Dr Renner; was VAD; post-war: to Vienna, later USA

Deutschkron, J.H., died on active service

Deventer, was Flight Lt, RAF

Diamant, S. P., (AL)/6137, Austrian, served in Ordnance Depot Benghazi

Dick, Ari; born Vienna 6 Mar. 1922, parents from Galicia, grammar school pupil till 1938, emigrated to Palestine, mother, who followed him, was killed by attack on SS *Patria* in Haifa harbour; enlisted Dec. 1939 at Sarafand; with PC in France building railways, also transport duties; 1940 in rearguard of BEF, then by collier to UK; drafted to North Africa, journey round Cape; in Tobruk; then Greece; transferred RASC; post-war: in charge of Israeli immigration camp Atlith, later with Israel Hypobank

Dicklich, G.P. (or possibly D.), 13806066

Dienemann, Alfred, 13805322; born Krotoschin, Prussian Poland, 5 Nov. 1888, father had been in Prussian army 1866 & 1870 as 'Feldwebel', pupil at Krotoschin Gymnasium, Dr of Law, Breslau University, served 4 years in German Army in WW1, judge at Myslowitz, then Cottbus, 1931 in Court of Chambers in Berlin, prematurely retired 1935, emigrated to England Apr.1939; interned 1940; joined 3 PCTC 16 Jan. 1941, was officer's batman but released on grounds of bad eyesight 5 May 1941; employed for remainder of war in Oxford Co-op Accounts Dept; post-war: reinstated as President of the Senate of the Court of Chambers in Berlin; died Oxford 1957

Dietrichstein, J., later Dickson J., was 2/Lt in 69 Coy PC

Dobriner, H., 13801397, Pte

Dobriner, Max, 13805976 and 13810026, later Dickson, Geoffrey, 6387042; born Deutschkron, West Prussia, 16 Mar. 1926, pupil at normal school there, forced to leave under racial law 1936, then attended Jewish Schneidemuehl school, to England 4 July 1939, apprentice baker; enlisted 1944; to 6 PCTC (Buxton) and 93 Coy PC; then 3/10 Cdo; lastly 98 FSS, Sgt; demob Dec. 1947

Dobson, G.J.

Dolnica, A. 13805774, later Jones, P.A. 13111566, Pte, released before Nov. 1944

Dombey, C.H; post-war: prominent in Ex-Service NB Association

Dossmar, (Bernhard?), later Descarr, Bernard, 13814390, also Dawson, Bernard Kenneth, 14623924; born Vienna 1915; served in PC; transferred to 21 Indep. Para. Coy, 1 Indep. Para. Platoon, on 61b & 62nd parachute training course at Ringwood; wounded in Italy, did not return to Para.

Douglas, P.M.

Drake, Francis

Drechsler, Fritz, 775211, Austrian, emigrated to Palestine; served with RAF, Sgt navigator

Dreifuss, P.C. (Dreyfuss?), later Denby, a student; joined 74 Coy PC from Richborough 1940 and was with BEF in France that year; transferred to Para. Regt; was in Normandy landing, killed in action on D-Day

Dresner, Helga, German communist in Manchester; joined British (or US) forces 1944

Dresner, Rolf, Polish citizen (spoke German only), from Leipzig; with RAFVR, Sgt, served in Nassau, Bahamas and in W. Europe; interpreter in Germany; demob 27 Dec. 1947; post-war: bank manager in Germany, died Bramhall nr Manchester 23 May 1991

Druzick, M.N., 13806067 (possibly Druzzick), Pte., 253 Coy PC

Drucker, Austrian cavalryman, joined 74 Coy PC from Richborough 1940 and was with BEF in France that year

Duffhaus, George T., 13802786, was in 219 Coy PC; at end of hostilities transferred to US army censorship dept

Duich, S., 13807894 and 13122239 (possibly Duic)

Dukat, Tilly, served in No. 1 or No. 4 AVP ATS

Dungler, Kurt, 13802948, later Douglas, Keith, 13118510 and 6308482, Cpl in PC, the Buffs and 3/10 Cdo; with another Cdo unit at Walcheren

Dunn, F.M.

Durovecz, A., 13807976 and 13122237, served in PC and probably SOE

Duschenes, L., 13810028, later Dudley, L.A., 6387043, was Pte in PC and SOE

Duschinski, Ernst, member of Young Austria; enlisted in Dec. 1943 or Jan. 1944, from Preston

Dutka, Harry, probably member of Young Austria; served with British forces in Italy

Dzialoszinski (Ziechzwinski?), joined 74 Coy PC from Richborough 1940 and was with BEF in France that year

E. 'Captain E.', pseudonym used by Bentwich for a man about whom we know quite a bit; interned and sent to Australia aboard HMT *Dunera*, returned 1941, interned again, released after protests; volunteered for PC; 3 months later transferred to RASC as lorry driver; sent to OCTU and commissioned; then rejected by RASC so returned to PC; after 6 months rejoined RASC, posted to troop transport company, in battle of Falaise and advance through Northern France, Belgium and Holland to Bremen; after

German surrender to Far East, where he served as 2 i/c of an RASC company in Ceylon (Sri Lanka) until his release in 1946

Eaton, Henry, Austrian, served in PC

Ebenster, A., served in 74 Coy PC

Eberstadt, Ernst Carl Eduard, later Eversley, David Edward Charles; born Frankfurt 1922, pupil at Goethe *Gymnasium*, emigrated England 1937, attended Leighton Park School, studied at LSE; volunteered 1940, served in 219 or 249 Coy PC; on 30 June 1943 on officers' list of 87 Coy PC; transferred to 3/10 Cdo, later SOE, but saw no action there; demob 1945; post-war: B.Sc.(Econ.) at LSE, Ph.D. 1960, later Professor of Population and Associated Studies at the universities of Birmingham, California and Sussex, Chief Planner (strategy) to the Greater London Council 1969, held several research posts in social policy, and appointments at various universities in Europe and the USA, died 3 July 1995

Eberstadt, Walter A., from 1944 to 1961 aka Everitt; born Frankfurt 1921, pupil at Johanneum, Hamburg, then at Tonbridge School in England, studied at Christ Church Oxford; served in 220 Coy PC; on 31 Dec. 1942 on officers' list of 88 Coy as 2/Lt; 1943 transferred to Ox & Bucks. L I, attached to 2 Bn Worcs. Regt, wounded in action in Normandy; later in Psycho Warfare; with Radio Hamburg (NWDR), Maj.; post-war: editorial staff of *The Economist*, to New York 1951 with Lehman Bros., lastly partner Lazard Freres, trustee New School of Social Research, Treasurer American Council for Germany, Chairman Martha's Vineyard Preservation Trust, President Northvill Centre for Child Development (Harlem), awarded both OBE and German Cross of Merit

Eckstein, Andor, killed in action in Normandy

Eckstein, Eric, from Düsseldorf, interned 1940, to Australia on HMT *Dunera*; served in Australian Employment Coy; post-war: Professor of English, Melbourne University

Ehrenberg, Gottfried, later Sir Geoffrey Elton, Kt., Fellow British Academy; born in Prague, came to England 1938, taught in North Wales, studied through correspondence course at London University; served in PC; post-war: historian, expert on Henry VIII and his times, Fellow Clare College Cambridge, Regius Professor of Modern History, President Royal Historical Society, various publications

Ehrenberg, Rudolf Wolfgang Hans Victor, nicknamed Rolli, later Elliott, Ralph Warren Victor; born Berlin Aug. 1921, lived at Karlsruhe, descendant of Luther and relative of Goethe, Sir Geoffrey Elton (above) and Olivia Newton-John, studied at St Andrews University; interned 1940, shipped to Canada, returned 1941; enlisted 1941, 251 and 229 Coy PC; transferred to infantry 1943, Queen's R. Regt, Leics. Regt Sword of Honour at RMC OCTU; wounded in Teutoburg Forest in last days of the war; demob as W/S Lt 1946; post-war: lecturer at St Andrews University, professor at Adelaide University, returned St Andrews 1949–52, founding Professor of English at Flinders University of South Australia, was also at National University of Australia, many publications

Ehrenfeld, A.H, was officer in 246 & 77 Coy PC, killed on active service

Ehrlich, Charlie, had been professional footballer in Vienna, playing for Vienna FC; served in 74 Coy PC

Ehrlich, George, served in 220 & 88 Coy PC

Ehrlich, Ilse Marianne, served in 1 Allied Volunteer Platoon ATS

Ehrlich, Jakob, died on active service

Ehrlich, Max; post-war: prominent in Ex-Service NB Association

Ehrlich, Oscar

Ehrlich, William

Eiffeler, A., 13800894, L/Cpl in 74 Coy

Eimerl, Siegfried, later Edwards, Sidney; born Vienna 15 May 1925; enlisted 1943, trained as glider pilot; transferred to Para. Regt, with 13 Bn 5 Para. Bde in Ardennes Jan. 1945, Parachuted into action at Rhine crossing at Wesel, present when British troops met Soviets at Wismar; later in India, Singapore, Java, Sumatra, Malaysia, then Near East and West Africa

Eisenberg, Dr Elmar, studied at St Andrews University; joined 74 Coy PC from Richborough 1940 and was with BEF in France

Eisenberg, K., later Allington, Ken, was active in Free German Youth before enlisting

Eisenfeld, Leo, was Sgt in RAF

Eisenmayer, Paul, member of Young Austria; joined Dec. 1943/Jan. 1944 from Oxford

Eisenstein, Robert (Bobby), later Evans, Robert; born Vienna 8 Oct. 1920, pupil at Federal Gymnasium at Baden bei Wien, emigrated to London 1938 worked as clerk in stockbroker's office; enlisted 14 June 1940 at Westward Ho!, posted to 219 Coy; Aug. 1943 to 69 Coy at Darlington; autumn 1943 to 93 Coy at Southampton, landed in Normandy 19 July 1944, then to Bayeux and Caen, Sept. 1944 in Brussels; Nov. 1945 Bruges, clerk in office of town major, 1946 similar capacity Ghent; demob July 1946; post-war: worked for Britannia Electric Bulbs, after which he studied electronics, restaurant owner since 1968

Eisinger, Heinz, member of Young Austria; joined Dec. 1943/Jan. 1944 from Leeds

Eisinger, Oskar; born Tulln, Lower Austria, 15 June 1908, held at Dachau and Buchenwald 25 June 1938–18 Feb. 1939, fled to Jerusalem via Romania and Yugoslavia autumn 1939; served in British Army during the war; post-war: returned to Tulln 1947, in 'Tulln ist judenrein' by P. Schwarz, which tells his story, he appears as Otto Rosenberger

Eisner, Adalbert, 14436727, later Edwards, Albert; born Vienna 7 Mar. 1924; enlisted 1943, trained as wireless operator; Cpl in Royal N. Lancs. Inf.; later Colour Sgt, in Normandy on D-Day + 6, Falaise Gap, posted to GSI, interpreter, dealt with lists of German medical doctors; transferred to 5 Para. Bn., 6 Airborne Div., in action at Bethune, in advance party on foot in landing zone at Wesel, sole survivor of intelligence section there; present when British troops met Soviets at Wismar; in CCG Bad Oeynhausen, Neustadt, Pinneberg, Kiel; demob Aug. 1949

Eisner, K.J.H., 13800980, possibly K.J.M., later Belgrave, R.H., 6387021, also Grant, R.H., 13116381, Cpl in 93 Coy PC; later in SOE

Ekstein, Andor, Hungarian, killed in action, Normandy 1944

Eldon, J.H; post-war: prominent in Ex-Service NB Association

Eldone, J.

Elkan, Walter; born Hamburg 1923, pupil at the Goethe Schule, to England 1938, atttended Frensham Heights School till 1940, trained at Selfridges, but became prep school master 1941–43; served in 87 Coy PC, played violin in Coy orchestra; later in 1943 transferred to RA, attached to East African Artillery, served in Kenya, then at Imphal, in 128 Base Hospital, back via Secunderabad, Kenya, Nyasaland; demob 1947; post-war: studied economics at LSE, taught at Makere University, Kenya 1953––60, professor at Durham 1960–78, since then Brunel University

Elkind, I., emigrated to Palestine; joined 608 Coy PC, at Tobruk and in Greece, taken prisoner 1941; died of cancer in Silesian prison camp and buried with military honours by the Germans

Elkiner, Eva, served in 1 Allied Volunteer Platoon ATS

Elting, Guenther, 13807082, later Elting, John Gordon; born Berlin-Wilmersdorf 1921, pupil at Rheingauschule Friedenau, started toolmakers apprenticeship 1936, to UK 1939, employed at Longbridge works, Birmingham, at Lord Austin's behest; dismissed on outbreak of war; interned 1940, to Australia by HMT *Dunera*; volunteered for service in Australia, but sent back to UK and served in 93 Coy PC until May 42; then transferred to reserve and worked as toolmaker for war industry; 1944 instructor Coventry Technical College; post-war: 1953 MIProd.Eng., 1967 Fellow, later MD of aerospace company, retired 1988

Elwyn, served in 87 Coy PC

Emden, Ralph, served in 220 Coy PC; post-war: prominent in Ex-Service NB Association in Birmingham

Emer, came from France to serve in 337 Coy PC; later back to Paris via Italy

Emmett, Bunny, officer in 3/10 Cdo, where he wore RTR badge and RAF pilot's wings, national status not at all clear, but seems to have fitted in and was 'a good egg'; later adjutant 4 Cdo at Walcheren, wounded there

Enemstein, joined 74 Coy PC from Richborough 1940 and was with BEF in France that year

Engel, Georg-Dieter; born Mannheim 1924, grandfather had been in Badensian, father in German imperial army; served in Royal West Kents, 2 Bn Jewish Bde, 1 Bn Royal Scots, northwestern Europe and India; post-war: in Aliya B and Israeli Air Force, eldest son served with Israeli helicopters, daughter is Israeli parachutist, 2nd son is sergeant in Swiss army

Engel, Hanns-Guenter, 13803417, later Envers, John; born Breslau 7 Apr. 1922, father lawyer, family moved to Berlin shortly after birth, pupil at Fichte Gymnasium, later at Clifton House School, Cliftonville, Kent; served in 249 Coy PC, 3/10 Cdo, IC, Field Security in Normandy, Germany and Egypt; with 4 Cdo Bde HQ on D-Day, patrol activity in Normandy, wounded 19 Aug. 1944; later in FSS at Poeppendorf near Lubeck examining prominent Nazis; then re-education of German PoWs in Egypt; demob 1946, Sgt, in Germany held temporary officer's rank; post-war: in Foreign Office London, then to Canada as Editor CBC Radio, ran own airline for a time, after retirement worked part time with YMCA

Engel, R.H., as Lt on officers' list 77 Coy PC 31 Dec. 1942; also in 88 Coy PC 31 Aug. 1943

Engel, Werner, later Eden, Peter W., interned 1940, to Australia by HMT *Dunera*, back to UK 1941; enlisted in 249 Coy PC; transferred to RE explosives unit, in North Africa and Palestine; in FSS in Germany; delayed demob Apr. 1947; post-war: owned hotels and restaurants in London and elsewhere, prominent in Ex-Service NB Association, etc.

Engelhard, Alfred, Austrian, L/Cpl, in British Army June 1944–Oct. 1945, unit unknown

Engelhardt, Wolf Hermann, 1895899; born Leipzig 9 Nov. 1920; enlisted 24 May 1943; Sgt in 101 Sqn RAF (previously 310 Sqn Czech airforce); killed in action in Lancaster during air attack on Stuttgart 28 July 1944

Engetschwiler, was in French Foreign Legion; then served in 246 Coy PC

Enoch, Keith, Sgt in PC; transferred to Royal Fusiliers (SOE) and served in France and Germany; was at Belsen, where he conducted examination of Commandant Kramer and other SS men

Ephraimson, Joan, married Holden, enlisted1943; Sgt Interpreter in WAAF; demob 1947, awarded Certificate of Merit

Eppenstein, Andrew H.H., later Elliott, Andrew, interned 1940, to Australia on HMT *Dunera*, camp leader in Australia, then returned to UK; joined 87 Coy PC; On 5 Mar. 1943 Lt in 74 Coy PC; transferred 4 Oct. 1943 to RASC

Epstein, joined 74 Coy PC from Richborough 1940 and was with BEF in France

Epstein, H.G., Sgt in 77 Coy PC, acted in their Xmas panto *A Midsummer Night's Scream*

Eric, whose surname is not known, served in 88 Coy PC and was a friend of Warner's; post- war: lived in Carmarthen

Erlanger, Anneliese, served in 1 Allied Volunteer Platoon ATS

Ernst, joined 74 Coy PC from Richborough 1940 and was with BEF in France

Ervin, Kurt Felix, PAL/3009, Austrian; born 10 Aug. 1920, emigrated to Palestine; served in British Army

Escher, Hans, 13809254; born Vienna 16 Feb. 1918, attended grammar school there but expelled for socialist activities, to Paris 1937; *prestataire* May–July 1940; joined British Army 337 or 338 Coy PC at Algiers, was in North African and Italian campaigns 4 Apr. 1943–17 July 1945; transferred to Psychological Warfare Section in Austria on 18 July 1945; demob as Cpl in Vienna on 17 Dec. 1946, discharge certificate mentions his exemplary service; post-war: draughtsman in Vienna, extraordinary professor at Secession Vienna 1975; died there 23 Dec. 1993

Ettinger, Gerry S., served in 165 Coy PC; transferred RASC and Airborne; later in No. 1 Information Control Unit, 21 Army Group; post-war: said to have been boss of UFA film company for a time

Ettlinger, Lothar, later Elliott, Roger, from Karlsruhe, was with RF in SOE group with Eversley, Frazer and Alford, but did not see action

Etzdorf, Ruediger Otto Ulrich, Baron von, later Ellerman R., 13111286; born Berlin 30 Apr. 1920, of ancient Saxon nobility, nephew of Hasso v.E.,

German ambassador in London, was Sgt in *Wehrmacht* and participated in march into Bohemia in autumn 1938, after release fled to France, then in 1940 to England; served with PC; later with 1 Cdo on Dieppe raid, where he was badly wounded; said to have married Audrey Cattens, daughter of Basil C. deputy governor of Bank of England, but other source says his wife was Jewess without any such interesting connection

Exler, served in SOE

Eyck, son of a German historian; served in PC and in FSS in CCG

F., Maj., RE, highly qualified engineer, served in PC; later transferred to RE and was posted to Gibraltar

Fabian, Ken, served in PC

Fabisch, Walter, from Breslau; in India at outbreak of war, interned there; joined Indian Medical Service; Maj.

Faith, H.E., an Austrian

Fafalois, Paul, 13807639

Falck, Rudolph (Rudy) Julian, studied at Balliol College, Oxford; served in 88 Coy PC, commissioned, then in 93, 165, 251 & 337 Coy PC; later in Para. Regt, 1st Airborne Div., Provost Corps, CMP; killed in action at Arnhem 26 Sept. 1944

Falk, driver in 88 Coy PC

Falk, served in 88 Coy PC (There is definite evidence that two men named Falk served in 88 Coy PC.)

Falk 1, served in 87 Coy PC

Falk 2, served in 87 Coy PC (There is definite evidence that two men named Falk served in 87 Coy PC.)

Falk, Dr F.E.

Falk, M., died on active service (Could be identical with one of the Falks named above.)

Faltitschek, Hermann, later Falton, Hugh Peter; born Vienna Jan. 1901, railwayman; served in 88 Coy PC (No. 9 Sect.), commissioned; then in RF (SOE), broke his back in training, therefore not used in action; later in Italy and Austria

Fantl, K., later Flynn, Charles, served in 229 Coy PC

Farago, V. (Ladislas?), 13807652, later Ford, V., 13118803 and 6305468, a Hungarian communist, enlisted Feb. 1943; served in 77 Coy PC at Long Marston; supposed to transfer to SOE, but finished up in 3/10 Cdo instead; returned to 77 Coy after collapsing on route march; post-war: author of *Patton, ordeal and triumph* (Arthur Barker Ltd. 1966) and *The Game of the Foxes* (McKay 1971); is said to have returned to Budapest and become an important functionary there

Farber, E.

Farley, was in 3/10 Cdo

Farnborough, Robert F., Austrian, appears to have been lawyer in Vienna; served in PC, RAC, Legal Research Branch, was interpreter for French and German, acted as such in Brit. military court in Germany; also legal adviser to military government in Germany; Lt Col; post-war: lecturer at Herriot-

Watt University Edinburgh

Farnham, served in PC and Political Intelligence, commissioned; responsible for re-education of PoWs in Cyrenaica

Fassbaender, later Ferguson, E., served in 87 Coy PC

Fast, Walter, later Foster; born Vienna June 1923, pupil at RG7 (Kandlgasse), and boy scout; interned 1940, to Australia on HMT *Dunera*, returned 1942; served in 251 Coy PC; later Craftsman in REME, Darlington, then Sgt; in CCG Westphalia; looked after DPs from Stutthof concentration camp in Estonia; post-war: Secretary of Anglo-Austrian Society, awarded OBE and high Austrian honours

Feder, E. Wolfgang, later Fenton, Bryan L. born Berlin 20 Apr. 1921, active footballer; served in 249 Coy PC; later 3/10 Cdo, was Sgt unarmed combat instructor; then 347 & 348 FSS, IC; in action Jan. 1945 at Maas river, Troop Sgt Maj. of X-Troop; later promoted to WO1; post-war: in Intelligence Unit in Hamburg

Federbusch, E.H., Austrian, served in 64th Field Section RAMC

Feger, Reinhard; born 1896; enlisted Feb. 1940; served in 88 Coy PC; demob July 1945

Feigl, Robert, from Vienna; served in 337 Coy PC, played major part in Algiers negotiations to persuade British Army to permit recruitment of Germans and Austrians held by Vichy French in North African internment camps; later said to have been employed on secret mission

Feilmann, George, joined 74 Coy PC from Richborough 1940 and was with BEF in France

Fein, Heinrich; born Ober-Laa, Lower Austria, 10 Sept. 1906, a Jew; is said to have served in Foreign Legion from 7 Nov. 1939 until 13 Apr. 1943, but is also said to have been interned at Bel-Abbes and at Kenadsa; his British service commenced on 14 Apr 1943, but was wounded in bombing raid and was unfit for service for 6 months; demob 9 May 1946, but having been injured spent 6 months in hospital

Fein, Herbert, also Frazer, from Leipzig; served in RF, in SOE group with Eversley, Alford and Ettlinger, but did not see action as he had asked for naturalisation first

Feiner, Austrian, served in 338 Coy PC

Feiweles, Richard, later Fairfax; born Breslau, 7 Feb. 1924; served in PC; transferred to Queen's Own Cameron Highlanders, in action at Monte Cassino and Salonika, after end of hostilities at Travemuende

Feldbauer, Peter, a member of Young Austria; enlisted from London between 15 Jan. and 25 Mar. 1944

Feldheim, joined 74 Coy PC from Richborough 1940 and was with BEF in France

Feldheim, Dr Heinz Dietrich, 13804320; born Dortmund 1908, brother of Ruth (below), Ph.D. of Munich University, held at Dachau and Buchenwald for 3 years, including 14 months in darkness in attempt to make him confess to having committed high treason, but as his aunt played the piano with Frau Papen, wife of Hitler's predecessor as German chancellor, he was eventually arraigned before an ordinary court and found not guilty on 2

Aug. 1938, emigrated to England; interned 1940, but appealed to Churchill personally and was released immediately; enlisted 1940; served in 249 Coy PC, RAOC, REME, was member of REME orchestra that performed for the BBC's Home Service on 8 May 1945; demob 1945; post-war: author of controversial article in *Ex-Serviceman* (Oct. 1948), in which he advocated restraint in dealing with Germany and was remarkable for its humanity; he was attacked vehemently in subsequent issues, these attacks in turn calling forth a good deal of support for his views, and the debate lasted several months; he taught maths at technical college in Acton until 1966, then Fachhochschule Munich

Feldheim, Ruth; born 1911, sister of above; served in 1 Allied Volunteer Platoon ATS; played violin at eisteddfod and took first prize, attached to RA ack-ack; died 1996

Feldman, Eric, extended service several years whilst in CCG

Feldmann, Austrian, brother of Kurt Feldmann (see below)

Feldmann, Kurt, Austrian, amongst the first in Brussels, took 4 prisoners and 'captured' Mercedes staff car

Feldschreiber, 13800336, Pte in 69 Coy PC, explained at interview with Col. C.F.T. Swan, MC, 28 Mar. 1942 he had conscientious objection to carrying deadly weapons

Felix, Dr Alfred, Austrian journalist and diplomat, served in 137 Coy PC; wrote a book on future of Europe whilst on active service; died on active service 1942

Felix, Leo, 13801835, later Field, Leonard; born Karlsbad, Bohemia, 16 Nov. 1902, to London with parents in Apr. 1939; enlisted 26 Mar. 1940; served in PC, temporarily attached to RAF 329 Wing Wireless Unit in Italy, North Africa and Greece; later in 12 FSS, IC, then 428 FSS; was WO III in CCG until 8 May 1948, in Benrath HQ, BAOR newspaper control, helped to found *Neue Rhein Zeitung*, Chief of ISC Bureau in Hamburg, continued with CCG after demob; post-war: worked as correspondent of various newspapers in Germany, prominent in Ex-Service NB Association

Fellner, Austrian, served in 338 Coy PC

Felton, J., Austrian, served as Gnr. RA, in CMF; met former friends amongst PoWs in Italy and gave them the London *Zeitspiegel* to read

Fenner, served in 229 Coy PC; was court-martialled for unknown crime on 26 Jan. 1943, attempted suicide 27 Jan., went on hunger strike 29 Jan., and was taken to detention centre on 1 Feb.

Fenner, Juergen, 13804402 and 14623920, served in PC, could be identical with above; later in 21 Ind. Para. Coy, was on 61b & 62nd parachute training course of at Ringwood, said to have been at Arnhem

Fenucci. E., 13806114

Fenyce, 13805878, later Fenton, was L/Cpl in 69 Coy PC; later 21 Ind. Para. Coy and 1 Indep. Para. Platoon, took part in 61b & 62nd parachute training course

Feri, Franz Paul, name appears on a list kept in the German Unity Party archives, of Sudeten-Germans who served in the British Army

Fernley, Henry Steven

Ferraro, E., 13806120, Pte. in 253 Coy PC; later commissioned in SOE

Fettner, Ernst (Ernest); born 29 May 1921 Vienna, held by Gestapo 10 Nov.–23 Dec. 1938, to UK Mar. 1939, agriculturalist in Scotland; interned 1940, to Isle of Man; after release factory worker and Civil Defence, member Young Austria; enlisted from Glasgow 2 Dec. 1943; served with Gordon Highlanders, NW Europe 31 July 1944–18 Feb. 1946, CMF 19 Feb. 1946–15 Oct. 1946; saw frontline service July 1944–May 1945, in Ardennes winter 1944/45 company assisted Americans and suffered heavy losses, in Rhine crossing at Rees; at end of war in Bremerhaven, then Neustadt am Ruebenberg; A/Sgt; demob Klagenfurt 18 Aug. 1947; post-war: journalist, first in Klagenfurt, then Volksstimme, Vienna, member of Austrian Journalists' Union for 50 years

Fialla, Heinrich, 775721, Austrian, Flt Sgt/pilot in RAF; post-war: in Israeli Air force, then senior pilot, Austrian Airlines

Fields, A.

Finch, Ernest; born 1903; served in 93 Coy PC, incurred 50% disability as a result of war service

Finckelstein, changed name to Ferguson, then to Findlay, is said to have done this so that he could answer truthfully that his name had been Ferguson before he had changed to Finlay (probably apocryphal)

Fink, K., 13806115, Pte in 253 Coy PC; later commissioned in SOE

Finkelstein, joined 74 Coy PC from Richborough 1940 and was with BEF in France

Finkelstein, Kurt, a member of Young Austria; enlisted from Manchester Dec. 1943 or Jan. 1944

Finkeltaub, Morris

Fischer, Bruno, later Fisher, Bryan; born Vienna 1921, pupil at Vienna Commercial Academy, to England Jan. 1939, having previously been in Holland 3 months; interned 1940; enlisted Jan. 1941; served in 229 Coy PC; transferred to RTR 1943, in Normandy landing on D-Day, also saw action throughout France, and in Belgium, Holland and Germany; transferred to IC, Field Security, Berlin, after end of hostilities; Sgt; post-war: in publishing

Fischer, Dr, Austrian psychiatrist, served with RAMC in Indian mental hospital

Fischer, Egon, member of Young Austria; enlisted from Stroud Dec. 1943 or Jan. 1944

Fischer, nicknamed 'Katowice'

Fischer, Heinrich R. (Harry); born Vienna 30 Aug. 1903, father lawyer; apprenticed to bookseller, friend of Robert Musil, Hermann Broch and Walther Neurath, to UK 1938; joined 74 Coy PC from Richborough 1940 and was with BEF in France; post-war: with *Financial Times*, founder of Marlborough Fine Arts, noted art dealer (Kokoschka, Henry Moore, etc.); died 12 Apr. 1977

Fischhof, Dr Georg, 769461; born Vienna 23 May 1922, Nov. 1938 via France to Palestine; enlisted 2 Apr. 1944; trained as motor mechanic in Egypt; then further training as meteorologist, in which capacity served in Beirut, Baghdad, Mossul; Cpl in RAFVR; demob 15 Sept. 1946; post-war: studied in Vienna 1947–51, Dr (psychology), wrote several books, 1960 founded

Institute of Industrial Psychology – still director in 2000

Fischhof, Kurt Peter, 769490; born Vienna 18 Apr. 1927, 1938 with parents to Palestine; enlisted 1944; served in 107 Maintenance Unit RAF as aircraft mechanic, repaired and maintained Spitfires & other fighter planes, then in admin; later interpreter in PoW camp; demob 1946; post-war: 1947 to Austria, adviser in US enterprise, 1966 pilot, 1974 MU Dr (psychiatrist), habil. 1994, 1998 professor at Vienna University

Fisher, Oliver, pupil at Charterhouse School, later student at Balliol College, Oxford; served in 137 Coy PC; later in King's Royal Rifle Corps; Sgt

Fisher, W., served in 137 Coy PC

Flach, Robert; born Vienna 1 Feb. 1923, pupil at Theresianum 1933–38, to Italy July 1938, to Australia Dec. 1938, matriculated in Tasmania Dec. 1940; tried to join French Foreign Legion in New Caledonia, but turned down because of residence in Australia; joined 6 Empl. Coy Australian CMF, interpreter for Italian PoWs in Tasmania; volunteered for AIF 12 July 1945; demob 13 Feb. 1946; post-war: barrister in Tasmania till 1957, then UK, Labour candidate for Eastleigh 1970

Fleischer, F., later Fletcher, Austrian, served in 3/10 Cdo, attached to 6 Cdo, in Normandy; killed in action at Le Plain 11 June 1944

Fleischmann (Miss), Sgt in 4 AV Platoon (?) ATS, after end of hostilities stationed at British HQ Hamburg, then Allied Control Commission Vienna

Fleischmann, Kurt, 13803486, later Fraser, Kenneth D., 13116161, L/Bdr RA in 1st Airborne Div., in action at Arnhem

Fleischmann, P., 13804126, L/Cpl in 165 Coy PC, volunteered for commandos, but appears to have been refused

Fleming, served in PC; later Capt. in Legal Research Branch

Flesch, Sabina, took her stepfather's name of Landsberg, married Gibson (Bina); born Berlin 1920, pupil at Schlachtensee Gymnasium Berlin, later educated privately at St Gallen, Switzerland, father murdered at Auschwitz, emigrated with mother to South Africa 1933, studied sociology at Cape Town University; enlisted 1941; served as Sgt with British Military Mission Cairo, then Italy; commissioned 1943, Capt. WAAS, South African Forces, seconded to British Military Mission Austria, CSDIC, denazification in Vienna, clients included Adm. Kaltenbrunner, SS Gen. Wolff, Mrs Himmler and T. Gudrun aka 'Sweet Sally', British radio reporter in Nazi services; post-war: married Hon. David Gibson

Flescher, Heinrich, Austrian, PO on HMS *Toneline* at Port Tewfik

Fleschner, L., later Fletcher, Louis, Sgt PC

Fletcher, Harry (perhaps identical with Flescher, Heinrich, above?)

Flinn, Peter

Floro, Alessandro, 13807796

Forbes, P.P.

Forest, a Viennese actor, served in PC and was interpreter at Nuremberg trials; Maj.

Forrest, H.G., received Commendation in the Field

Forschaner, served in 229 Coy PC, on 19 July 1942 a wound on his finger was subject of a Court of Inquiry

Fortgang, Wilhelm Georg, 13804290, later Fort, William George; born Vienna 10 June 1893, had been master tailor in Vienna, fled to England in spring 1938; interned 1940; joined PC in same year (tried to join commandos but was refused on grounds of age), became Sgt i/c tailors' shop in Natural History Museum, South Kensington, manufacturing clothing to continental standards for all British and US agents who were clothed and equipped in England; demob 1945, received personal congratulations from King George VI, and US Certificate of Merit

Foster, H., served in 220 Coy PC; drowned 11 Aug. 1943 boating on River Avon near Tewkesbury

Foster, R., 16001269, REME; transferred to 3/10 Cdo in Italy

Fraenkel, E., later Foster; died on active service

Fraenkel, Max, joined 74 Coy PC from Richborough 1940 and was with BEF in France

Fraeser, Kurt

Fraeyhan, R., served in PC; then in AEC

Frank, Austrian from Klagenfurt, served in 337 or 338 Coy PC

Frank, Guenter Max, 13807365, later Franklyn, George Mack, 13118512; born 30 Apr. 1923; served in 69 Coy PC; then in 3/10 Cdo, survived serious climbing accident, attached to 41 Cdo in Sicily landing; killed in action at Normandy landing 10 June 1944

Frank, H.K., 2/Lt, name appears on officers' list of 248 Coy PC on 31 Dec. 1942

Frank, W., Capt. in PC, was interpreter at Nuremberg trials

Frankel, Ernest

Frankel, Leopold, 220747, commissioned in PC 23 Dec. 1941

Frankel, Theo; born Vienna1898; served in 219 Coy PC; died London 1986

Franken, joined 74 Coy PC from Richborough 1940 and was with BEF in France

Frankenstein, Kurt, 13800012, later Franklyn, Ken, volunteered 14 Nov. 1939; served in 69, 229 & 87 Coy PC, was one of the first six alien sergeants in the British forces, on 31 Dec. 1942 on officers' list of 87 Coy PC

Frankfurt, Eduard, 775826, Austrian, emigrated to Palestine; joined RAF, became Cpl; post-war: General Manager of TWA Israel

Fraser, Leslie

Frazer, H.M., was mentioned in dispatches

Freeden, Herbert

Freedman, H.J.; died on active service

Freeland; post-war: prominent in Ex-Service NB Association, Birmingham

Freeman, R., served in 137 Coy PC, received Royal Humane Society Testimonial for Gallantry

Freud, joined 74 Coy PC from Richborough 1940 and was with BEF in France

Freud, Clement Raphael, later raised to Freud, Sir Clement; born Vienna 24 Apr. 1924, brother of Lucian (below), grandson of Sigmund Freud; served in RUR, BAOR War Crimes Group Liaison Officer at Nuremberg trials; post-war: caterer, journalist (sports and cooking), radio and TV star, prominent Liberal, rector Dundee University, author

Freud, Ernst, son of Sigmund Freud, had been Lt in Austrian Artillery in WW1; served in PC with son Walter Anton

Freud, Lucian, Austrian; born Vienna 8 Dec. 1922, brother of Sir Clement (above), grandson of Sigmund Freud, painter; served in merchant navy, ordinary seaman on SS *Baltrover* 1942

Freud, Walter Anton, grandson of Sigmund Freud; interned 1940, to Australia on HMT *Dunera*; later in 87 Coy PC, at Pembroke when exploding hand granade caused death of five men; transferred to RF, SOE, Lt, parachuted into Styria in Apr. 1945 to attempt take-over of Zeltweg airfield (Operatian HISTORIAN), became separated from main group, but reached Zeltweg before them, after adventurous journey to HQ Gen. Rendulic at Linz was taken prisoner, then picked up by advancing US troops; later member of FSS which dealt with Rudolf Hoess (commander of Auschwitz) and Oswald Pohl (Himmler deputy), also arrested Dr Tesch, Auschwitz chief chemist; post-war: author of *Before the anticlimax*

Freudenberg, Conrad, 13805292; born 27 Nov. 1911, to UK to install Freudenberg patents at Litherland Tanning Co. Ltd (part of Freudenberg group.); served in 69 Coy PC, transferred to reserve 29 July 1941 to continue previous work; post-war: built up market orchard at Taunton

Freudenthal, Dr, from Schluechtern in Hesse, a dentist; joined French *Prestataires*, not evacuated from Dunkirk, fled on foot and by boat, picked up by HMS *Imogen* and brought to Plymouth; interned; then 69 Coy PC

Freund, Julius, had been editor of *Kleines Blatt*, Vienna; served with CMF Italy

Freundlich, Salo, served in PC, at Kitchener Camp; discharged on health grounds; died 1954

Frey, H.C.,13805167, later Fraser; born 23 Mar. 1920; served in 3/10 Cdo, injured in climbing accident, discharged as unfit for service

Frey, Peter Hans, later Fry, Peter Howard, 13116167; born Berlin 26 June 1922, pupil at College Français, Berlin, to UK Feb. 1939, worked in furniture factory; interned 1940, to Australia on HMT *Dunera*, back to England 1941; volunteered 10 Dec. 1941; served in 229 Coy PC; transferred REME 8 June 1943; to RF 26 Oct. 1944; then East Surrey Regt 25 May 1945; after end of hostilities with Intelligence at Bergen, interviews with PoWs; then interpreter in 54 PoW camp Droitwich, re-education of prisoners; post-war: manager and director of leather goods firm

Freytag, Ernst Herbert, 13801057, later Farr, Ernest Herbert (Tommy), 13118514; born Berlin 26 Feb. 1919; Sgt in 77 Coy PC; also in 3/10 Cdo, in Operation PREMIUM against Wassenaar 27 Feb. 1944, under command 47 Cdo at Walcheren Nov. 1944

Fried, Kurt, member of Young Austria; enlisted from London between 15 Jan. 1944 and 25 Mar. 1944

Fried, Ludwig; born Berlin 7 Sept. 1919, pupil at Askanisches & Tempelhofer Gymnasium 1929–33, Jewish Mittelschule till 1935, emigrated to South Africa by SS *Stuttgart*, became floorwalker, manager, central buyer at 'Ackermans' general stores; enlisted autumn 1939; with Union Defence Force in Abyssinia, Egypt, Near East, Libya, training at Zonderwater, long march to Abyssinia, battle of Amba Alagi, in advance party to Egypt, Geneifa, met mother and five sisters in Palestine (6th sister killed in Auschwitz), in charge of 12 water supply vehicles in Western Desert, then Tripoli; became South African citizen 20 Nov. 1942; post-war: return to Ackermans, to Switzerland 1962

Friedenstein, Walter, later Foster, also Foster-Friedenstein, Viennese banker; L/Cpl in company police 229 Coy PC; post-war: founded London banking company

Friedlaender, served in 137 Coy PC; appears to have been in SOE, in company with Kugler was sent on dangerous mission, which is said to have been successful, but Friedlaender is said to have been captured, tortured and killed; but see also Friedlaender Rudolph – the same man?

Friedlaender, Dr H.A., Capt. in RAMC and IAMS

Friedlaender, Hans, later Forest, H.J.; born 1906; enlisted Nov. 1939 ; served in 3 PCTC., released on account of illness Apr. 1942

Friedlaender, Ilse, served in 1 Allied Volunteer Platoon ATS

Friedlaender, Rudolph, 13801992, later Lodge, Robert, 8550151, Sgt in 2nd SAS, taken prisoner in Sicily, escaped, recaptured, after Italian armistice escaped again just before Italians tried to hand him over to Germans, after six months' trek to Southern Italy picked up by British troops, recuperation in Belgium (Vosges); awarded DCM for outstanding courage on 19 Aug. 1944 when, in action behind German lines, he twice exposed himself to enemy fire in order to cover the withdrawal of his unit; killed in action near end of 1944

Friedland, joined 74 Coy PC from Richborough 1940 and was with BEF in France

Friedmann, Peter, later Frean, Peter, served in 77 Coy PC and in RA

Frisch, Erich, member of Young Austria; enlisted from Leicestershire between 15 Jan. 1944 and 25 Mar. 1944; served in PC and 8 Royal Scots

Frischmann, joined 74 Coy PC from Richborough 1940 and was with BEF in France

Froehling, (Miss) J.F.

Frohwein, later Frewen, a Berliner, Cpl in 77 Coy PC, in Berlin 1945

Fromm, Edgar, served in PC

Frucht, L/Cpl in 229 Coy PC

Fry, Jack, served in 338 Coy PC

Fuchs, Dr G., had been X-ray assistant at Rothschild Hospital in Vienna; Maj. in RAMC and surgeon in 8th Army

Fuchs, E.; died on active service.

Fuchs, Emil, alias Blaha, Emil, alias Straker, Emil, Austrian, German conscript, PoW; taken into British service; joined SOE, together with Hemetsberger in Operation DUVAL near Salzburg; June 1945 in No. 6 Special Force Staff Section in Austria, was intended to remain there

Fuchs, Karl, Austrian, mechanic at naval camp in Haifa

Fuhrmann, P., joined 74 Coy PC from Richborough 1940 and was with BEF in France

Fuerst, Helmut Herbert, later Anderson, Herbert, nickname Lofty; born Berlin 16 Apr. 1913, family moved to Vienna 1914, finished school 1932, studied music and economics, to Istanbul 1936, deported 1939 as he had an Austrian passport, to England, worked on farm in Dorset; enlisted Feb. 1940; with 87 Coy PC in BEF France; transferred to SOE (RF) but did not see action; to CCG, was interpreter *inter alia* at trial of VW works board of directors; post-war: in travel industry

Fuerth, Hans G., 13807080, later Firth, Anthony, 13118515; born Halle, 7 Sept. 1918, in school hockey team, engineer in his home town, after emigration to UK worked in films; interned 1940, to Australia on HMT *Dunera*, pretended to be butcher by trade and so got enough to eat, returned to England; enlisted 1941; served in 87 Coy PC, acted in various plays; transferred to 3/10 Cdo, badly injured in climbing accident during training; transferred to CCG in Duesseldorf, involved with German film industry, especially logistics; Editor *Neue Westfaelische Zeitung*; then film controller in Berlin; post-war: in Rank Organisation, author, later to Canada where he became owner of publicity agency, active skier all his life, won ski contest at age 75

Fuss, Hans, served in 77 Coy PC; post-war: prominent in Ex-Service NB Association

Gaiswinkler, Albrecht, alias Schumacher, Karl Hans, alias Winkler, Alfred, Austrian, German conscript, PoW; taken into British service; joined SOE, in Operation EBENSBURG near Bad Aussee; June 1945 in No. 6 Special Force Staff Section in Austria, was intended to remain there

Galler, Johann, alias Shell, Fritz, alias Kleinschuster, Fritz, Austrian, June 1945 in No. 6 Special Force Staff Section in Austria

Gaensler, Friedrich, later Gordon, Frederick, served in 220 Coy PC; then RSF; later Para. Regt, in Normandy, during night of 5–6 June 1944 was one of first 60 men parachuted into France ahead of D-Day landings, later Norway; lastly with CCG

Gaertner, H., later Gardner, served as instrument maker and mechanic in RAF

Gang, Hans, a member of Young Austria; enlisted from London shortly before 15 Jan. 1944

Gans, Manfred, 13805014, in some documents H. or N.L., later Gray, Frederick (Freddie), 13118516 and 6387019, from Borken, Dutch family background (father had been politically active, lost a leg in WW1, a brother emigrated to Palestine 1935), sent to school in England; served in 249 Coy PC, RWK, and 3/10 Cdo, in Italy, then Normandy, on 1 July 1944 separated from his patrol, lay up near enemy lines all night, returned next morning with valuable information, wounded five times he remained with his unit; then Walcheren attached to 41 Marine Cdo, at Westkapelle (Walcheren) succeeded twice in obtaining surrender of enemy units of superior strength, also succeeded in capturing a high enemy officer, commissioned in field for bravery; after 8 May 1945 first British serviceman by jeep into Theresienstadt, where he found his parents

Garai, Otto, later Garry, O., thought to have been Austrian, but spoke with distinct Hungarian accent, joined 229 Coy PC as Lt 6 July 1942

Garfield, H.S.

Garston (Garson?), served in137 Coy PC

Garton, C.H.K., served in PC and IC, commissioned and promoted to Capt. 1945

Gassman, Johannes, also Gassman, John; born Breslau 1906, emigrated Apr. 1939, worked on rabbit farm; enlisted Dec. 1939; L/Cpl in 69 Coy PC, was in France spring 1940; wounded in air raid on London 1941, in hospital for 15 months, discharged on 27 Mar. 1942

Gayduschek, Peter Harry Leopold, later Gayward, Peter Harry; born Vienna 14 Mar. 1925, pupil at Goethe-Realschule 1936–39, to UK, atttended St Christopher School, Letchworth, member of Young Austria; enlisted end of 1943; served in RTR and Yorks. Hussars; commissioned in Recon. Corps 1945, became DAAG GHQ 2nd Echelon CMF, Stats. Centre HQ BAOR, served in Italy and Germany; discharged as Maj.; post-war: Colonial Service, 3rd Secretary to Minister of Finance, Uganda, then Financial Director University of Warwick, Registrar Liverpool University, retired 1990, in addition has held considerable number of other offices in educational, administrative and charitable fields

Geber, Heinz, member of Young Austria; enlisted in London between Jan. and Mar. 1944

Geiger, Sgt, an artist, worked for the BBC

Geiser, H.E.A.,13801168, later Gordon, Henry; born 3 Apr. 1915, great-grandson of Wilhelm Liebknecht one of the great names in German socialism, lived in Dresden, Berlin, Vienna, Silesia and Bruenn, played football, centre forward for Dresden-Sued, worked in Spanish Embassy, Paris, enabled to come to England through intervention of senior members of Labour Party; served in 77 Coy PC, RHamps. Regt, and 3/10 Cdo; post-war: with BA

Geisler, O.C.S. or H.?, 13806041, Pte in 253 Coy PC; later commissioned in SOE

Gelband, Israel; born 1905; enlisted from Kitchener Camp 5 Dec. 1939; served in 77 Coy PC; discharged on medical grounds Oct. 1941; died 20 June 1956

Gellert, from Miastecko near Kattowitz, joined 74 Coy PC from Richborough 1940 and was with BEF in France as L/Cpl; later transferred to Cdos.

Gelles, Bertschi, member of Young Austria; enlisted from Leeds between Dec. 1943 and Feb. 1944

Geppner, served in 137 Coy PC

Gerber, J.H., Dr, was Maj. RAMC in India and Burma; later in Colonial Service in Sierra Leone; post-war: worked on tropical diseases and received Langley Memorial Prize 1951

Gerechter, Martin, later Glenville, Martin G.; born Berlin 6 Oct. 1919, pupil at Koenigstaedtische Schule (as father had been awarded Iron Cross in WW1, he was allowed to attend a normal school until Aug. 1939), mother killed in concentration camp; reached UK 16 Aug. 1939; interned May 1940; enlisted Oct. 1940; served in 229 Coy PC; then 1 RRC; lastly with RE; interpreter in railway control, Germany, worked on de-nazification of German railways

Gerson, joined 74 Coy PC from Richborough 1940 and was with BEF in France

Geta, Josef, Austrian, prisoner at Dachau and Buchenwald; was one of first volunteers at Richborough.

Gilbert, Sgt, joined 74 Coy PC from Richborough 1940 and was with BEF in France

Gilbert, E., Sgt, wireless communications expert

Gilbert, R., 13118805, Pte

Gildener, joined 74 Coy PC from Richborough 1940 and was with BEF in France

Gillard, G.W., joined 74 Coy PC from Richborough 1940 and was with BEF in France

Gilly, volunteered from Richborough, served in 74 coy PC and was in France with BEF 1940

Gimpel, served in 5 Training Centre PC and ACC

Gimpel, joined 74 Coy PC from Richborough 1940 and was with BEF in France

Glas, later Glass, CQMS in 249 Coy PC, awarded Certificate of Good Service for building up contacts to civilian population in Scotland

Glaser, Kurt J., 13802030, later Griffiths, Keith James, 13118519; born 3 Sept. 1918, medical student, accompanied father to Spain, where latter was medical officer with International Brigade; served in 137 Coy PC; then 3/10 Cdo, at OCTU 6 June 1944; rose to Capt, was with patrol of 45 RM Cdo at Belle Isle (River Maas) 28 Jan. 1945, negotiated two-day armistice to exchange dead; officer commanding 3/10 Cdo, fought at Maas, Rhine and Aller crossings; killed by sniper fire 11 Apr. 1945

Glaser, P., 13801188 and 3613070, Pte, Dvr; 2/Lt; served in PC, RASC and probably SOE

Glaserfeld, H.J., a Viennese, served in 338 Coy PC; seconded to Intelligence, wireless editor and broadcaster to Austrian soldiers and civilians from Algiers, Bari and Rome

Glatter, J.

Glatter, Paul

Glauber, Kurt E.; died on active service.

Gluecksmann, Heinrich, said to have served in 339 (229?) Coy PC

Gobetz, H.

Goerke, Ernst Werner, 13805832; born Breslau 2 Aug. 1918; enlisted at Ilfracombe 12 July 1941; served in 77 Coy PC; discharged on medical grounds 31 Jan. 1942; Home Guard service 12 Dec. 1943–31 Dec. 1944

Goetze, Liesel, served in 1 Allied Volunteer Platoon ATS

Gold, Israel, 13801205, alias Gardner, Charles, alias Lt Goodwin, alias Gumley, Charles, Lt in PC and IC; June 1945 in No. 6 Special Force Staff Section in Austria

Goldberg, David, 13807457; born Kiel 23 Nov. 1923, to UK with *Kindertransport*; enlisted spring 1942; Cpl in 69 Coy PC

Goldberg, F., joined 74 Coy PC from Richborough 1940 and was with BEF in France

Goldberg, Jakob, appears on list in German Unity Party archives of comrades who were members of allied armies

Goldberg, Sidney, from Poland, RAF listening service

Goldberger de Buda, 13802043, served in PC and RASC

Goldberger, Laszy, was member of Young Austria; enlisted from Birmingham at year end 1943

Golden, M; post-war: prominent in Ex-Service NB Association

Goldenthal, Aldo

Goldhammer, Erich, alias Gordon, Eric, 14443291; born Vienna 10 Feb. 1924, pupil at grammar school, Vienna, to UK Jan 1939, attended secondary school, Marylebone, at brickworks in Loughborough May 1939, later trainee waiter in Bristol, clerk in Cheltenham; enlisted from London between 15 Jan. 1944 and 25 Mar. 1944; served in Suffolk Regt (2nd Bn), wore 'Austria' shoulder flashes, saw action in France, Belgium, Netherlands, at Albert Canal crossing covering retreat of forces from Arnhem, wounded Oct. 1944; after hospitalisation, interpreter in Rome Jan. 1945; at Maniago May 1945; in Allied Control Commission for Austria, Vienna June 1945; demob as S/Sgt Nov. 1947; post-war: in oil industry in Vienna till Aug. 1959, then independent supplier of plants etc. to oil and chemical industry, Vienna, retired 1981.

Goldin, served in 137 Coy PC

Golding, Frank P., served in PC and RTR, Sgt

Goldner, Charles; born 1901; served with 3 PCTC and was member of the theatre group there: 'Although he became famous on the British stage and in films only very much later, he was the admired star of the Ilfracombe theatre group already in the early stages of the war'

Goldscheider, F., Austrian, was in Cairo shortly before 18 Mar. 1944

Goldschlaeger, K.T., 13801160, later Clarke, K.E., 13118804 and 5550135, served in PC and No. 10 Cdo, but possibly in Dutch rather than German troop, distinguished himself in attack on Osnabruck 4 Apr. 1945, mentioned in dispatches.

Goldschmidt, Cpl in 88 Coy PC; on 10 Nov. 1940 during air raid on London 'Cpl Goldschmidt and Pte Wolfram helped the wounded until the arrival of ARP aid detachments'

Goldschmidt, B., 13800564 (Goldschmitt?), from Schneidemuehl (now Poland), joined 74 Coy PC from Richborough 1940 and was with BEF in France; took part in rescue of two ladies at Weymouth in air raid, he received considerable praise

Goldschmidt, F., appears on officers' list of 246 Coy PC on 31 Dec. 1942 as 2/Lt; also on officers' list of 69 Coy PC on 30 Apr. 1943 as arrival from MOTC Scarborough

Goldschmidt, H.F., later Goldsmith, Herbert P., from Delmenhorst, to England 1936; interned 1940, by HMT *Dunera* to Australia, there 20 months, then return to England; enlisted Feb. 1942; posted to 69 Coy PC, stationed in Yorks., then Sussex, on D-Day + 60 to France, then Caen, Bruges and Antwerp; worked on development of ultraviolet binoculars; interpreter in Oldenburg

Goldschmidt, J.P., later Goldsmith, J.P., from Frankfurt, served in 69 Coy PC; was amongst first 80 volunteers at Richborough; amongst first aliens to be commissioned 1941; served in 74 Coy PC as 2/Lt in Jan. 1942; posted to 846 Coy PC on 6 Aug. 1942., CO of African Pioneer Dispersion Centre; demob as Lt Col; post-war: prominent in Ex-Service NB Association

Goldschmidt, V.L. or K.L., 13805610, Pte in PC, RAOC and RWK; apparently also in SOE

Goldschmidt, Werner,13807299, later Dwelly, Vernon (Ducky), 13118517, interned 1940, to Australia by HMT *Dunera*, returned to UK; joined 165 Coy PC; transferred to R. Sussex Regt, 3/10 Cdo attached to 41 Cdo; unarmed combat instructor in 10 Interallied Cdo, specifically for German, French and Dutch troops; commissioned, in HQ Cdo Brigade, took part in Walcheren expedition as intelligence officer of 4 Cdo, there his landing craft sunk by mine; later Capt. OC FSS at Burgsteinfurt, in Germany, chasing Nazis in hiding; post-war: to USA, eventually general manager American Express for Latin America

Goldsmith, O.A., Dvr, RASC; died on active service and left no known next-of-kin

Goldstein, Dr, was Maj., RAMC, and served in Nigeria, India and Burma

Goldstein, Ernest, 220751, commissioned in PC 23 Dec. 1941, 2/Lt on officers' list 219 Coy PC on 31 Dec. 1941

Goldstein, Franz, from Wiesbaden, member of 'Schwarzes Faehnlein' youth resistance group there; served in PC and RAC as Sgt tank commander; post-war: in Australia, farming

Goldstein, H.M., 13800016, volunteered for service 14 Nov. 1939; L/Cpl in 69 Coy PC; killed in action during air raid on London 29 Dec. 1940

Goldstein, J., later Stewart, Joe, volunteered in Kitchener Camp; posted to 69 Coy PC; died 25 Jan. 1950 of illness contracted while on active service

Goldstein, Len, Sgt, glider pilot, was at Arnhem

Goldstern, Konstantin, 13800982, later Garvin, Robert Kenneth, 13118518; born 11 Jan. 1917; served in 87 Coy PC; then 3/10 Cdo

Goldwasser, A., served in PC, RA and Intelligence, where he was commissioned and promoted to Capt.; also in No. 1 Psycho. Warfare Gp and 4 Inform. Control Unit, 21 Army Gp A

Gondos, P.C., name appears as 2/Lt on officers' list of 93 Coy PC 30 June 1942; transferred 6 Feb. 1943 to 2/5 Welch Regt

Gonzenhauser, winner of sprint event at 93 Coy PC sports event

Goodman, Dennis, Cpl. in 246 Coy PC; then in RAC; eventually in monitoring unit in 21 Army Gp, in Normandy July 1944, probably member of a listening unit; also record of him in Bayeux; and in British HQ in Germany; awarded Certificate of Merit

Goodwyn, John, served in 220 Coy PC

Gordon, Charles

Gordon, H.

Gordon, Helmut, L/Cpl crane driver in PC and RE, awarded Certificate of Merit by C. in C. Home Forces for risking own life to save life of comrade on crane

Gordon, L.J.

Gorman, Sgt in 69 Coy PC

Gottesmann, later Hastings, Alex

Gottfeld, served in 74 Coy PC; joined at Richborough 1940 and was with BEF in France

Gottfried, Lilly, 2992372, Austrian, emigrated to Palestine; joined WAAF, ACW1, secretary; post-war: well-known painter

Gottheimer, served in 74 Coy PC; joined at Richborough 1940 and was with BEF in France

Gottlieb, L.

Gottlieb, Lilly, married Laker; born Vienna 1919, pupil at RG Albertgasse, emigrated to Palestine 1938, illegal immigrant; volunteered for ATS at Sarafand 1942; posted to 508 Coy Cairo; demob as Staff Sgt Jerusalem 1946; post-war: married British soldier, still Mrs Laker today, lives in England, has several grandchildren

Gottschalk, served in 74 Coy PC; joined at Richborough 1940 and was with BEF in France

Gould, E.L.M; post-war: prominent in Ex-Service NB Association, active in Liberal Party

Grabowsky, served in 229 Coy PC

Graetz, Marianne Klara Ester, married Fried; born Berlin 1 Mar. 1921, father medical officer in German Army in WW1, emigrated to England; served as nurse; post-war: lives in Basel, Switzerland

Graetzer, E.F.

Graetzer, Paul, PAL/23139, Austrian, in protective custody from Nov. 1938 to Apr. 1939, to Palestine 1939; served with British Army; taken prisoner at Kalamata 1941, forced labour in coalmine at Beuthen, liberated at Ziegenheim near Kassel 4 Apr. 1945

Graf, later Grant, Gary, interned 1940, sent to Canada, returned to UK; joined PC; acted as interpreter in Germany

Grafl, alias Green, John, alias Boenisch, Johann, Austrian, German conscript, PoW; taken into British service; joined SOE, in Operation EBENSBURG near Bad Aussee; June 1945 in No. 6 Special Force Staff Section in Austria, was intended to remain there; described as missing

Graham, served in 137 Coy PC

Graham, Anthony, CQMS in 69 Coy PC from its formation until its dissolution; mentioned in dispatches

Graham, Henry E.

Graham, K.G.J., Lt in PC; in 1945 served in 2 Inform. Control Unit, 21 Army Gp

Grange, Thomas, commissioned in Black Watch

Grant, A.N.R., 13802335, Pte in 253 Coy PC; then RF; presumably also in SOE, commissioned

Grant, H. served in 93 Coy PC

Grauer, served in 137 Coy PC

Graupe, served in 87 Coy PC

Gray, F., 13041024, Pte, served in Italy; recruited into 3/10 Cdo by Bartlett; transferred to RWK

Greilsamer, Heinz Willy, later Grenville, Henry William; born Stuttgart 1926, pupil at schools in Ludwigsburg and Stuttgart, left Germany by *Kindertransport* July 1939, attended Camelford Grammar School 1939–41, worked in biochemistry lab at Hammersmith Hospital 1942–44; enlisted Dec. 1944; L/Cpl interpreter at Buende; commissioned June 1946; promoted Capt. Sept. 1947, served at five different PoW camps all over southern England, responsible for checking political reliability and release of some 1000 PoWs per week; after discharge from army studied biology at King's College London; post-war: after college for next twenty-three years taught biology at Repton School, during this time also elected vice-chairman of Institute of Biology, lives at Dorchester

Griessman, 249461, later Grierson, Sir Ronald; born Nuremberg 1921; served in 251 Coy PC; later 21 Indep. Para. Coy and 1 SAS, in Italy, France, Belgium, Holland and Germany; wounded in Italy and again (1945) in Germany; mentioned in dispatches; post-war: worked for *Economist*, S.G.Warburg, Orion Bank, Director GEC, member of South Bank Board

Griffel, served in 74 Coy PC; joined at Richborough 1940 and with BEF in France

Griminger, P., Austrian, Pte, fitter at 2BW L-Camp , MEF

Grohs, St, 241413, Austrian, Sgt, instructor at Durban, Natal

Groschnitz, Austrian, served in 338 Coy PC

Groser, Dr Franz, 13804734, later Gregg, Frank, 13051415; born Vienna 10 May 1914, studied law at Vienna University; served in 248 Coy PC; then 550 A/Tk Regt RA; finally Interrogation Section, No. 5 Civilian Internment camp, IC, in Germany; Sgt; post-war: chartered accountant and treasurer of the Liberal Party Home Counties Region

Groshut, S.V.

Gross, served in 74 Coy PC; joined at Richborough 1940 and was with BEF in France

Gross, Alice H., 2149735, married Anson; born Vienna 22 Sept. 1924, apprentice tailoress; joined WAAF Mar. 1943; LACW, worked as photographer at Farnborough RAF HQ, at Croydon, and at Bomber Cmd HQ, High Wycombe where she developed first photos of V1 firing ramps; also served in Egypt; demob Jan. 1947

Gross, Friedrich Herbert (Freddy), Austrian, educated England; handed over CQMS 137 Coy PC on posting to OCTU 6 Nov. 1941; commissioned in PC 23 Dec. 1941, name appears in officers' list of 77 Coy PC 30 June 1942; winter 1942–43 to interrogation of PoWs; later intelligence control Germany; censor; final rank Lt Col; post-war: owner of Wentworth Park Country Club in Nairobi 1967

Gross, L., later Cross, L., served in PC (220 Coy?); died on active service

Gross, Willy; died on active service.

Grossfield, Karl

Grossmann, Czibi; born Vienna, active in Young Metal Workers' Union; enlisted from London between 15 Jan. 1944 and 25 Mar. 1944

Gruebel, served in 74 Coy PC; joined at Richborough 1940 and was with BEF in France.

Gruber, S.H. (Schani), as he says 'a member of the Austrian Herzstark calculating machines family', reached England by *Kindertransport* 1939, continued to go to school (father died 1939, mother murdered 1941), leading member of Young Austria; enlisted from London 1943; served in REME 6th Airborne Div. workshop in England, Egypt, Italy and Austria, wore 'Austria' flash on battledress blouse; with War Crimes Commission for SE Europe at Ferlach, Carinthia; extended service till 1952; S/Sgt; released in Austria

Gruder, Erwin, 775930, Austrian, emigrated to Palestine; joined RAF there and became LAC, concerned with equipment; post-war: medical practitioner in Stockholm

Gruhn, served in 74 Coy PC; joined at Richborough 1940 and was with BEF in France

Gruenbaum, Marianne, later Greenwood, served in 1 Allied Volunteer Platoon ATS

Gruenbaum, Robert, later Greenwood, served in 248 & 69 Coy PC

Gruenberg, Joe, served in 74 Coy PC; joined at Richborough 1940 and was with BEF in France

Grueneberg, Hans, scientist, emigrated to UK 1933; became Capt. RAMC; worked in War Office with Solly Zuckermann on bulletproof vests for soldiers in the field, talked War Office out of idea; later in blood reserve depot Bristol; then pathologist at military hospital Italy; also coroner; post-war: geneticist at London University, professor

Grunen, later Green, served in 3 Bn Para.; in action at Arnhem

Gruener, Gerhard, 775446, Austrian, emigrated to Palestine; joined RAF there and became Sgt electrician

Gruenfeld, Fritz, member of Young Austria; enlisted from London between 15 Jan. 1944 and 25 Mar. 1944

Gruenfeld, Leo

Gruenwald, Oskar, 13809112, served in 337 Coy PC; accidental death whilst on active service 3 May 1943

Gruich, B., 13807895

Guggenheimer, F., served in 74 Coy PC; joined at Richborough 1940 and was with BEF in France

Gumbel, Maj., member of CSDIC

Gumpel, Hannelore, married Selo, Laura; born Berlin, 1923, to England (with two sisters) 1939 (all taken in by London Archway tobacconist, who died soon after), worked as housemaid; joined 3 Allied Volunteer Platoon, ATS 1942; attached RA; later RAMC (in Abergelly); then REME as mess orderly, courier, secretary and interpreter; post-war: authoress of *Three Lives in Transit* (Excalibur Press, 1992)

Gumpert, E, one of oldest to volunteer; died 11 Dec. 1948

Gumpertz, Kurt Wilhelm, 13804337, later Graham, Kenneth Wakefield; born 27 June 1919; served in 69 & 77 Coy PC; later in Normandy with 3/10 Cdo; with 4 Cdo on D-Day; killed in action 13 June 1944

Gumpricht, later Graham, Sidney, served 4 years in RN

Guenz, served in 74 Coy PC; joined at Richborough 1940 and was with BEF in France

Gutmann, Egon, later Goodman, John E.; born Vienna 1916; served in PC and
    Intelligence
Guttentag, served in 74 Coy PC; joined at Richborough 1940 and was with
    BEF in France
Guttfeld, K.E.
Guttmann, 13805451 or 13807110, later Gordon, Tony, served in 69 Coy PC;
    transferred to 21 Indep. Para. Coy, Cpl; in North Africa, Italy and Arnhem;
    on 61b & 62nd parachute training course; commissioned, as Capt. adjutant
    to commanding Gen. in Norway 1944–45; afterwards in Airborne Div. in
    India
Guttmann, E., Cpl in Publicity and Psychological Warfare Unit, 21 Army Gp,
    1944
Guttmann, Ernst, later Goodman, Ernest J.; born Breslau 1925, to UK 21 Aug.
    1939 by *Kindertransport*, agricultural trainee at Park Hill (Derby) & Flint
    Hall (Fingest, Bucks.) farms, also at Barham House near Ipswich; enlisted
    Dec. 1943; Northants. Regt; transferred to Coldstream Guards, first Jew
    ever; posted to 5th Bat. (infantry of Guards Armd Brig., 30 Corps), in first
    patrol into Arras 1944 (photo in *Daily Sketch*); then in Belgium, saw action
    against General Student's SS, wounded, 7 months hospital; then at Victory
    Parade Westminster 8 May 1945; post-war: to USA, Professor of Political
    Science, taught at SUNY, then at Wuerzburg University Germany
Guttmann, Fritz G., had been officer in Austro-Hungarian army in WW1,
    wore Imperial Austrian decorations on battledress, lawyer in Vienna before
    1938, called to bar at Gray's Inn.
Guttmann, Hans-Julius, 13807042, later Gilbert, Ronnie; born Singen 28
    Sept. 1919; served in 3/10 Cdo, wounded in leg in fight with enemy patrol
    at Grande Ferme du Boisson, Normandy, 19 Aug. 1944; in fighting along
    the Rhine and at Essen; later in IC where, according to John Envers, he was
    'intelligence wallah' in Dusseldorf after hostilities ceased; post-war: well
    known in Intelligence circles in Germany, eminently successful in bringing
    war criminals to justice, awarded MBE

Haarhans, F.C., 2/Lt, name appears in officers' list of 165 Coy PC 31 Dec. 1942
Haas, J. de
Haberfeld, Helen, married Harper, from Vienna, served in 1 Allied Volunteer
    Platoon ATS
Habettler, Josef, alias Ervis, German conscript, PoW; taken into British
    service; joined SOE, June 1945 in No. 6 Special Force Staff Section in
    Austria
Hachenburg, son of Dr H. Hachenburg (below), Lt in 249 Coy PC; later in
    KRRC in Far East
Hachenburg, Dr H.; born Mannheim 1897, well-known company lawyer,
    practising certificate withdrawn 1938, sent to Dachau; served as Sgt in 249
    Coy PC; later interpreter at Nuremberg trials; post-war: Advocate of the
    German Restitution Commission, judge at Heidelberg 1948–63, awarded
    Federal Cross of Merit class 1 by German Federal Government
Hacker, Walter, alias Cpl Harris, Walter, Austrian socialist, Lt, served in the

SOE, in Operation BOBBY THREE at Innsbruck

Hagen, Louis, temporarily Haig, Lewis; born Potsdam 30 May 1916, pupil at Schulgemeinde Gut Marienau near Luneburg, to UK Jan. 1936, worked for Pressed Steel Co., Cowley, Oxford; served in 165 Coy PC, REME, RAOC, RA, in 'Artillery Assault Corps' – armoured vehicles with special destructive capacity; Sgt glider pilot 1943; 2nd pilot at Arnhem, awarded Military Medal for bravery in the field; later war correspondent in Calcutta for *SEAC* newspaper and *Phoenix* magazine; post-war: MD Primrose Film Productions Ltd, author of *Arnhem Lift*, *Indian Route-march*, *Follow my leader* and *The secret war for Europe*

Hahn, Gerhard, member of Young Austria; enlisted from London Dec. 1943/Jan. 1944

Hahn, Peter

Hahn, Walter

Hahn, Walter P., later Hanleigh, also Hanleigh-Hahn, served in 137 Coy PC

Hajos, Hans Ludwig, 13801533, later Harris, Ian Walter, MM, 13118601 and 6387036; born 1 Jan. 1920; Sgt in 3/10 Cdo, wounded in D-Day landing, returned to action within few days; wounded again at Troarn, Normandy, whilst attached to 46 Cdo; in action along Maas river, Jan. 1945; wounded again at Rhine crossing at Wesel; lost an eye at Aller crossing whilst attached to HQ 45 Cdo, awarded Military Medal; post-war: member of Reparations Commission, Berlin, chartered accountant

Halkett, served in 87 Coy PC

Hallerz, H.

Halpern, served in 74 Coy PC; joined at Richborough 1940 and was with BEF in France

Hamelin, Max; born 1895

Hamilton, Peter

Hamilton. L.

Hamlin, Dr, Maj. in RAMC; in military hospital together with husband (also medical officer)

Hammerich, P.M., 13806138, Pte in 253 Coy PC

Hammerlund, P.R.S., 13806028, Pte in SOE

Hammermann, PAL/6062, Austrian, appears to have served in REME as craftsman/driver/mechanic after joining from Palestine

Hanbury, Hans, German surgeon interned in India; joined Indian Army and became Col, IAMC; later Col in TA

Hansen, Einar Reska, 13802951, later Davies, Jack, 13118602, first and only Dane in 219 Coy PC; then in 3/10 Cdo; took part in operation TARBRUSH against Onival; mentioned in dispatches; with 47 RM Cdo on D-Day, only member of 3/10 Cdo detachment not wounded; Jan 1945 at Maas river

Hansen, P. 13806020, Pte in 253 Coy PC; not numbered among strength of company on 2 Nov. 1944

Harding, Ken M., served in 88 Coy PC

Harff, served in 137 Coy PC

Harris, a Viennese, Cpl in 69 Coy PC

Harris, Sgt at Arnhem

Harris, David

Harris, L.E; post-war: rominent in Ex-Service NB Association Birmingham

Hartmann, L/Cpl in 93 Coy PC; transferred to RAOC 24 Sept. 1941

Harvey, from Austria, served in RAC

Harwood, served in 137 Coy PC.

Harz, Samuel; born Berlin about 1901 or 1902; enlisted from Richborough late 1939 or early 1940; served in 69 Coy PC throughout war; in France 1940 and again 1944/45; demob 1945

Hauer, Luise, married Peiser, served in 1 Allied Volunteer Platoon ATS

Hauser, served in 74 Coy PC; joined at Richborough 1940 and was with BEF in France

Hauser, Emil, Austrian, got to Palestine illegally autumn 1938; worked for NAAFI; lent to British unit as cook; post-war: returned to Austria 1947

Hauser, Richard, Austrian, Cpl at HQ AES/UDF, served as education officer and nutrition expert

Hayden, R.R., served in 87 Coy PC

Hayek, one of those transferred to RAOC from PC in 1941; commissioned 1943; sent to India 1945; ended service as Maj. Commanding technical depot there

Hechinger, served in 74 Coy PC; joined at Richborough 1940 and was with BEF in France

Hecht, G.A., served as company tailor in 246 & 69 Coy PC

Heckscher, G., later Heckssher, G., Pte PC; from Apr. 1944 in Monitoring Unit, 21 Army Gp; in Normandy from July 1944; then Bayeux; finally British HQ Germany

Heilbronn, Dr, physicist and mathematician; served in PC and Royal Signals

Heilig, Gerhard; born Budapest 19 Apr. 1925, pupil at schools (Gymnasiums) in Berlin and Vienna, to UK 11 Dec. 1938, attended Quaker school in Yorks., trained as electrician, then telephone engineer in London; joined RAF 28 June 1943; after wireless training to Bomber Cmd, 214 Sqn at Scunthorpe and Oulton; 22 July 1944 to Bomber Cmd, 101 Sqn, was used in wireless countermeasures, Sgt later Flt Sgt; 5 Feb. 1945 to 105 Tpt OTU near Carlisle; to 215 & 48 Sqn, Transport Cmd, Singapore 28 Nov. 1945; demob 6 May 1947 as WO; post-war: in civil aviation, pilot 1954, from 1958 Capt., stopped flying 1974, then in business

Heimann, Joseph, served in 249 und 229 Coy PC

Heine, Peter, later Howard, K. Peter; born Berlin about 1908, to England 1938 or 1939; served in 88 Coy PC; said to have been Maj. at time of demob; post-war: in textile trade, returned to Berlin about 1980

Heinrich, Berthold, served in 137 & 69 Coy PC

Heinz, H.J., 13805963, later Ellern, or Ellery, H.J., Pte in PC; later RE(Fd)

Heldt, Dr H.R., ophthalmologist; Maj. in IAMS

Helfgott, Isaak, later Halford, Jack; born Vienna 1925, member of Young Austria; enlisted from Bradford Refugee Hostel end of 1943; served in India, Burma and Singapore; wounded

Helfgott, Walter, 13801853, later Harvey, W., 13053316, Pte in PC; name appears on German Unity Party list of Sudeten-Germans who served in British Army

Heller, Eric Gordon, served in 137 Coy PC; then in Intelligence, CSDIC; finally in No. 1 Inform. Control Unit, 21 Army Gp, in film censorship; Maj.; died on active service 3 Feb. 1946

Hellmann, R.H., some time Hilary, Robin, joined 87 Coy PC from Richborough; with them in Le Havre, Rennes, evacuated through St. Malo 1940; later at Carmarthen, Aberavon and Tenby; also bomb disposal; transferred to 3 Carabiniers; with them in India, Burma, battle of the Irrawady; after demob for some time in receipt of 100% disability pension

Hemetsberger, Josef, alias Ruzicka, Josef, alias Schmittbauer, Josef, from Salzburg, German conscript, PoW; taken into British service; joined SOE, in Operation DUVAL near Salzburg, was intended to remain in Austria; reported missing June 1945

Hendon, Jack, served in 74 Coy PC

Henley, Dr Keith S., joined 69 Coy PC 18 Nov. 1943, Cpl

Henoch, served in 74 Coy PC; joined at Richborough 1940 and was with BEF in France

Henschel, Sgt

Henschel, Oskar Oswald, 13800022, later O'Neill, Oscar Roy, 13118603; born Upper Silesia 1 Mar. 1913; joined PC 14 Nov. 1939; was Tp Sgt Maj. 3/10 Cdo; attached to 41 RM Cdo (4 Cdo Bde) D-Day, 'CSM O'Neill and his men broke through at 2 a.m.', was wounded and evacuated; returned to original unit because of disobedience to orders in the field

Herbst, served in 74 Coy PC; joined at Richborough 1940 and was with BEF in France

Hering, P., later Herring, P., served in unknown unit at Pontesbury near Shrewsbury 1940 and 1941.

Hermann, E.B., 13803398, later Howard; died on active service

Hermann, V.; died on active service

Herold, Wolfgang, later Ian, served in 249 Coy PC; then in RAC; finally interpreter in Hamburg

Herr, Ottfried, Austrian, served in either 337 or 338 Coy PC

Herrnstadt, Loni (Louise?), served in 1 Allied Volunteer Platoon ATS

Herrnstadt, T., later Halford, T.; died on active service

Herschdoerfer, Samuel, to England Aug. 1938, worked with GEC; said to have volunteered Sept. 1939; called up Nov. 1939; wounded in air raid on port of London; post-war: prominent in Ex-Service NB Association

Herschend, K., 13806129, Pte in 253 Coy PC; later commissioned, probably in SOE

Herschthal, Fritz, 13801503, later Hepworth, Freddy, 13118604; born 11 Feb. 1920; L/Cpl in 219 Coy PC; then in 3/10 Cdo; on D-Day with 45 Cdo, at Merville, Normandy, unsuccessfully attempted to persuade enemy troops to surrender; in patrol action with Lt J.E. Day; Jan. 1945 in action along Maas river

Herschthal, Walter, 13801397, later Hepworth, Walter Douglas, 13118605 and 5550145; born 16 Jan. 1918; served in PC; then RHamps. Regt, 3/10

Cdo; in action in Normandy; Jan. 1945 in action along Maas river

Hertz, worked on renovation of Richborough camp; served in PC; later Capt. RE in Home Command and architect NAAFI Germany

Hertzog, J. Heyman, 1869878, later Hereford, John Heymann, Sgt in 101 Sqn RAF (previously 310 Sqn Czech airforce)

Herz, R., 2/Lt, name appears in officers' list 219 Coy PC 31 Aug. 1942

Herzberg, A. H., later Howard, W.A., enlisted Feb. 1940; served in 88 Coy PC, in Le Havre, Rennes, evacuated through St Malo 1940; bomb disposal in London; then 220 Coy PC, forestry work in Wales; transferred RN 1943 as interpreter, decoding expert; Feb. 1944 on HMS *Tanatside* (Hunt class destroyer); May 1944 on HMS *Bellona* (cruiser), Scapa Flow; under command US fleet on D-Day; Jul. 1944 attack on *Tirpitz*; 1944–45 convoys to Russia; demob Nov. 1945

Herzberg, E., PAL/32404, Austrian, served as Dvr in 468 GT RASC CMF

Herzberg, Hans, name appears on German Unity Party list of 'comrades who served in Allied armies'

Herzfeld, Frieda, married Wollmerstedt; born Kelsterbach 1915, pupil at Westend Mittelschule Frankfurt, May 1939 to London, worked at Hounslow Hospital, dismissed May 1940, then Belfast; Sgt, National Fire Service (NI) 1943–45; then ATS attached to RASC; then RAEdC until 1948; post-war: secretary at Edinburgh University., then to Darmstadt

Herzfeld, Kurt, later Hutton, Ken, Austrian; born 1923, pupil at Theresianum School, Vienna; served in RAF (Air-Sea Rescue)

Herzfeld, Martha; born Kelsterbach 1910, May 1939 to London, then domestic service in Northern Ireland; interned May 1940, in Armagh prison, then Belfast; in National Fire Service (NI) 1943–45; then ATS attached to RASC until 1948; post-war: hotel manageress

Herzl, Erich, Austrian; born Vienna 1 Nov. 1920, pupil at Stuben Gymnasium and, from 1935, Maschinenbauschule; parents deported to Riga (killed there); 1939 to UK, agricultural tractor driver, member of Young Austria; volunteered for service 1941 but retained for civilian war work; called up 1 June 1944; joined REME; later interpreter in PoW camps in Scotland and lastly Swanscombe; S/Sgt; released in Vienna: post-war: engineer, lives in Vienna

Herzog, Manfred, served in 4 Welch Reg, in 53 Div, 21 Army Gp; killed in action 8 Apr. 1945

Hess, a lady Dr and Maj. RAMC, chief medical officer in gynaecological ward of British military hospital Vienna

Hess, Otto, 13802070, later Giles, Peter D., from Wiesbaden, member of 'Schwarzes Faehnlein', farmer's boy in England, artistic vein, drew pictures, wrote stories; served in 165 Coy PC; then in 3/10 Cdo; sent to Yugoslavia on special mission 1943, taken prisoner by enemy, tortured and killed

Hevesi, an Austrian in 338 Coy PC

Heyman, P., later Heaton, PO in RCN; lost at sea with his ship

Heymann, Richard, later Hyman, Richard, grew up in Breslau, imprisoned at Buchenwald 12 Nov. 1938–2 Jan. 1939, emigrated 1 Aug. 1939, at Kitchener Camp; served in 248 & 69 Coy PC, MP and Interpreters' Pool;

in Cherbourg, Rennes with 69 Coy PC, evacuated from St Malo in Dutch collier; then in Okehampton, Ilminster, London (Blitz), Darlington, Bolton, Bexhill, Newhaven, Arromanches (July 1944), Caen, Bruges, Brussels; then MP in 51 Highland Div., Hamburg, on anti-VD (venereal disease) duties; demob Mar. 1946; post-war: carpenter, then milkman, eventually owner of dairy company

Hibberd, Peter

Hill, Roland; born 1920, has roots in Vienna and Hamburg; served in PC; later HLI

Hillman, Peter John; born 1924; served in 87 Coy PC

Hilton, (Mrs); post-war: prominent in Ex-Service NB Association

Hilton, Paul

Hinrichsen, Klaus, served in PC; later in Home Guard

Hinrichsen, Robert, later Harris, Robert, from Leipzig

Hirsch (1), served in 74 Coy PC; joined at Richborough 1940 and was with BEF in France

Hirsch (2), served in 74 Coy PC; joined at Richborough in 1940 and was with BEF in France

Hirsch, Alfred, served in 77 Coy PC

Hirsch, Guenther P.; born Berlin 1907, pupil at Joachim-Friedrich Gymnasium; 2/Lt in 1 Berks Bn, Cumnor Place, Home Guard; later University of Oxford Platoon, Home Guard

Hirsch, Stephan, 13802194, later Hudson, Stephen Keith, 13118606; born 5 June 1918; served in 165 Coy PC; then 3/10 Cdo, suffered serious climbing accident during training

Hirschberg, Heinz, later Jacobi, Harry M., from Berlin, pupil at Theodor-Herzl-Schule, to Holland, from there with last ship to UK 1940; served in Jewish Bde; post-war: Rabbi of South Bucks Jewish Community

Hirschfeld, Sgt in 69 Coy PC

Hirschfeld, Doris, served in 1 Allied Volunteer Platoon ATS

Hirschfeld, Margot, served in 1 Allied Volunteer Platoon ATS

Hirschfeld, Otto

Hirschfeld, Willy, later Field, Willy, from Bonn, held at Dachau Oct. 1938–May 1939, to England May 1939; interned June 1940, to Australia by HMT *Dunera*, back 1941 by SS *Stirling Castle*; enlisted immediately on return; served in 165, 248 and 88 Coy PC; transferred to RAC; to 8 King's Royal Hussars as tank driver; landed in Normandy on D-Day, only survivor when tank hit by 88mm shell in Holland, wounded; with new tank on to Hamburg; demob as Sgt Dec. 46

Hirst, served in 137 Coy PC

Hladnik, Hans, Styrian, had been secretary of Styrian Farmers' and Smallholders' Association, strictly Catholic background; 1942 member of Austrian Committee for Post War Relief; served in SOE, though probably not in action, interrogated Austrian PoWs, was in same team as Wirlander, Theo Neumann and Sanders

Hoch, Jan Ludvik, later Maxwell (Ian) Robert; born Carpatho-Ukraine 10 June 1923; served in 88 & 251 Coy PC, CCG; enlisted1939; in 88 Coy football team; commissioned; received Military Cross for conspicuous bravery in the field from FM Montgomery; as Capt. was chief of press section, Berlin; post-war: publisher (Pergamon Press), owner of *Daily Mirror* and other newspapers, MP for Buckingham (Labour), connections with computer industry, Salzburg festival, USSR; committed suicide from own yacht at sea

Hochfelder, Hermann, may have come from Slovakia, name appears on German Unity Party list of members who served in British Army

Hoexter, Prof. Dr, from Hamburg, ear, nose and throat specialist; Maj. RAMC, having joined from Palestine

Hofbauer, Austrian, emigrated to Palestine; joined 608 Coy PC; served in Tobruk and Greece; fled Kalamata in open boat, but taken prisoner by Italians after landing in North Africa, handed over to Germans, treated as spy, spent 10 months in Vienna criminal court, eventually given PoW status

Hoffenberg, Max, Austrian

Hoffer, Abraham

Hoffmann, H.; born Vienna 27 Nov. 1922, pupil at textile college, Vienna, until 1938, emigrated first to Italy, then through Quaker mediation to UK, farmhand there; according to P. Block served in 246 Coy PC; according to own report joined RA in 1940; sent to India 1941, newspaper article states he was motorcycle courier in RHA; goes on to say he was transferred to 144 Airborne Div. in 1942; after which he was in Burma; holder of Burma Star

Hoffmann, Hans Guenther Josef, 13805451, later Compton, David Michael; born Hamburg 7 May 1921, pupil at Johanneum, to London through father's business connections 1934, attended Tonbridge School, started CA training; interned 1940, to Canada, returned to England; enlisted 1942; served in 249 Coy PC; 1943 to 21 Indep. Para. Coy, took part in 61b & 62nd parachute training course; then in 1st Indep. Para. Platoon, served in North Africa, Taranto landing and advance to Foggia, landing in Southern France, then Greece; later Sgt chief interpreter at military court at Lubeck; demob 18 Dec. 1946; post-war: chartered accountant

Hofstaedter, Fritz, later Hogan, Frederick; born Vienna 17 Jan. 1921, pupil at RG8, Vienna; served in 165, 137 & 229 Coy PC; then QORGY; then RA Anti Tank; then No. 41 Intelligence Unit in Belgium, Holland and Germany; post-war: quantity surveyor, lives in London

Hollaender, Paul; born Cologne 17 Sept. 1906, lived in London, Amsterdam and Paris 1927–31, emigrated to France 1933, worked as journalist; joined French Foreign Legion 1939, got to Algiers 1943; served in 338 Coy PC as Colour Sgt; then GHQ 2nd Echelon Maddaloni CMF; later Prestatyn; finally at 157 PoW camp Bourton-on-the-Hill; demob Aug 1946; post-war: prominent in Ex-Service NB Association

Hollaender, Ulrich, later Thomas, Michael Alexander; born Berlin 1915, studied in Tuebingen, but not admitted to final exams; served in 88 Coy PC; then Cdos; commissioned; liaison officer to Polish Div. in Normandy; known as 'the Prussian baron' because he insisted that his men should clean their teeth and take showers regularly; after end of hostilities on staff of Gen. Templer, with contacts to German politicians, including Adenauer; asked for and got discharge, having been called 'Jew boy' by senior officer;

post-war: author of *Deutschland, England ueber Alles*

Hollander, J., Cpl in 74 Coy PC; joined at Richborough 1940 and was with BEF in France

Hollander, V.A. (Miss), married Hibberd

Hollitscher, Dr Gerti; born Vienna 1906, father Markus H. attorney to the Imperial Court; said to have served in RAMC in Egypt, Malaya and Belize

Hollos (Holos?), Paul, Austrian born in Hungary, member of Austrian Centre; served in PC; then 8th Irish Hussars; killed in action Normandy 10 June 1944

Holm, Hans, Austrian, enlisted from Birmingham between 15 Jan. 1944 and 25 Mar. 1944

Holmes, served in 137 Coy PC

Holt, Arthur, served in 165 Coy PC

Holzer, Irma, married Buer, now Levy, emigrated to Palestine; Sgt in 508 Coy ATS; served in North Africa; post-war: lives in Frankfurt, authoress of: *Barbara* (autobiography)

Holzhacker, K., PAL/6879, Austrian, enlisted at Sarafand; served as Craftsman in HQ 3 BW, REME, MEF

Hoppe, from Vienna, served in 338 Coy PC; member of team that broadcast to Austrian soldiers and to civilian population, first from Algiers (Radio Swindle), then from Bari, then from Rome and lastly from inside Austria

Hopwood, Ernest, served in 74 Coy PC, joined at Richborough 1940 and was with BEF in France

Horn, G., served in 74 Coy PC in 1943

Horn, Walter; born Breslau 29 Dec. 1923, pupil at Elisabet Gymnasium, Aug 1939 to England, atttended Whitgift School, Croydon, farmer's boy in Little Missenden 1941, later Hitchin; enlisted 1942; served in 219 Coy PC; then 55 RTR Training Unit RAC; 56 Recce; 12th Lancers; Derbyshire Yeomanry; in Italy, Austria, Egypt, Libya and Greece; not sent to France because of sickness; later with 56 Recce in Italy, in infantry role throughout winter 1944–45; in first armoured vehicle over Ploecken Pass into Austria; at handover of captive Cossacks to Soviets; later with Cossack horses at Vienna races; then Libya protecting Italian colonists against Senussi; finally with military mission to Greek Army, demob summer 1947; post-war: ontinued studies, later senior executive Dow Chemicals and Conoco, Holland

Horne; post-war: prominent in Ex-Service NB Association Birmingham

Horne, J.K., served in 137 & 246 Coy PC

Hornig, Paul, 13805606, later Streeten, Paul; born Vienna 18 July 1917, member Red Falcon socialist youth movement, studied at Vienna University, before moving to UK to continue at Aberdeen and Oxford; interned 1940, to Canada by SS *Ettrick*, returned 1941; enlisted same year; served in 248 and 251 Coy PC; later in 3/10 Cdo; attached to 41 Marine Cdo in Sicily landing 9/10 June 1943, seriously wounded at Catania; hospitalised in Egypt and UK for several months (disabilities remain in left arm and foot); post-war: studied PPE at Aberdeen and Oxford, Warden Queen Elisabeth House, Director Institute of Commonwealth Studies, Fellow of Balliol College Oxford, professor at Boston University, Senior Consultant of World Bank, other appointments at universities in Britain, USA, etc., with Unesco and various British ministries and international institutions, author of large number of publications on economics and related sciences

Horoschovsky, Austrian, served in 337 or 338 Coy PC

Horowitz, Georg, later Hampton, George, from Vienna, a grandson of court painter to Emperor Franz Joseph; served in RAF

Horsetzky, from Klagenfurt, served in 337 or 338 Coy PC

Horvath, Heinz, member of Young Austria; enlisted from Leeds Dec.1943 or Jan. 1944

Horwell, A.R., CQMS of 93 Coy PC; after liberation of Belsen concentration camp became 2 i/c there, by then with rank of Capt, rendered assistance to inmates; later acted as interpreter at surrender of *Wehrmacht* in Northern Germany

Howard, Eric (could be same person as Howarth, see below), TpSM; later officer in 3/10 Cdo; followed Hilton-Jones as OC; killed in action Reichswald 1945

Howard, J.

Howard, J.P.

Howard-Fisher, Barrie, served in PC at Buxton

Howritz, A. R., name appears in officers' list of 88 Coy PC as 2/Lt on 31 Aug. 1943

Hubak, Gerhart, member of Young Austria; enlisted from Coventry between 15 Jan. 1944 and 25 Mar. 1944

Huber, O., 13809084, Austrian, served in PC; killed in accident on active service 3 July 1944

Huetz, Nikolas, alias Hauber, alias Hammer, Johann, alias Heger, Alois, Austrian, 2nd Lt in SOE; June 1945 in No. 6 Special Force Staff Section in Austria

Hughes, Harold (Kirk?), commissioned probably 30 Oct. 1942; Capt. 1 May 1944; SOE instructor

Hulsen, Beate G., served in ATS

Huelsmann, Georg, later Hulsman, George, served in SOE, but did not see action; Cpl with German railways after end of hostilities; post-war: with British Rail

Husserl, Paul, Austrian, might have had connections with Young Austria; interned 1940, to Australia by HMT *Dunera*, returned to UK; Coxswain in RN, served on HMS *Nancy*, HMS *Nile*, HMS *Stag*; post-war: Suez

Husserl, U.F., Austrian, served on HMS *Prometheus*

Inlander, R.; post-war: prominent in Ex-Service NB Association

Isaack, H.; born 27 Feb.1892; post-war: prominent in Ex-Service NB Association

Isaack, K., later Kay, C., served in No. 3 PCT and 251 Coy PC, appears to have been in charge of officers mess cookhouse in Ilfracombe; post-war: restaurant manager

Israel, L. later Linton, L

Jackson; died on active service

Jackson, Allan, to UK 1934, matric. 1936, studied economics and languages in London, was registered at German embassy and called up to *Wehrmacht* 1938, did not respond and held to be a deserter; enlisted Apr. 1940; served in PC; transferred RN Jan 1944, PO on destroyer in Western Approaches and in support of D-Day landing; ship was first Allied vessel into Wilhelmshaven

Jackson, Eric J.

Jackson, Harold

Jacob, Ernst M., also Ernest M.; born Aldekerk 5 July 1903, 1919 at school in Dinslaken, 1922 apprentice at M. Lissauer & Co. Cologne, founded own metal company, 1938 via Brussels to London, there founded Metallo Chemical Refining Co.; enlisted Jan. 1941; served in 248 and 87 Coy PC, Cpl; transferred RASC 1943, in Italy; demob 1945; post-war: VIP in metal industry

Jacobius, James

Jacobs, B., Col, OBE, MC; post-war: prominent in Ex-Service NB Association

Jacobsberg (1), served in 74 Coy PC; joined at Richborough 1940 and was with BEF in France

Jacobsberg (2), served in 74 Coy PC; joined at Richborough 1940 and was with BEF in France

Jacobus, Hans, served in 8 AEC (Australia)

Jacobus, Peter, later Jackson, Fred, German communist, served in 3/10 Cdo, found and interrogated Hoess, commandant of Auschwitz where his (Jackson's) mother had been killed, is said to have got himself completely drunk throughout interrogation, as otherwise he would have been unable to go through with it; went to Germany after discharge from army, but returned to England later on

Jacoby, served in 74 Coy PC; joined at Richborough 1940 and was with BEF in France.

Jacoby, E.H., CQMS in turn of 87 & 77 Coy PC; died on active service

Jacoby, Jack, served in 219 Coy PC (8 Sect.), one of the youngest in this company (he and three others, who stuck together, were known as 'the nursery')

Jacoby, Manfred, name appears on list in German Unity Party archives of party members who served in British Army

Jacoby, Prof., brought to England by Lord Wedgwood; Sgt in 88 Coy PC, although not admitted as medical practitioner in UK, with the support of OC he took the sick parade in 88 Coy and his instructions were carried out; demob 1944; post-war: worked at Newcastle hospital

Jaffe, Carl, had been actor and producer in London; original organiser of the entertainment side at Ilfracombe, actor in theatre group there; got to BBC directly from 3 PCTC 1942, broadcasts to continental Europe

Jaffe, Gertrud, served in 1 Allied Volunteer Platoon ATS

Jaretzki, K.S., 13802733, later Jarrett C. S., enlisted at 3 PCTC at Westward Ho! 1940; posted to 165 Coy PC, when company moved to Bridestow, Devon, he was attached to CRE Devon district at Lydford as draughtsman, well qualified for this, having studied architecture for three years before enlisting; CRE applied for Jaretzki to be transferred to RE, resulted in transfer to RASC in Edinburgh, from there he passed a War Office Selection Board and after attending OCTU was commissioned into RE June 1943; posted to India and appointed SO RE, class III, at GHQ India, New Delhi, Feb. 1944; returned to England with rank of Capt. and was discharged in Sept. 1946; post-war: completed studies at Regent Polytechnic School of Architecture

Jaslowitz, H.; post-war: prominent in Ex-Service NB Association

Jasper, Harry

Jellinek, Ernst H. (Ernest); born Vienna 1922, pupil at Schottengymnasium, emigrated to UK 1938, attended St Edmund's College, Ware; interned on 18th birthday June 1940; volunteered same year; served in 220 Coy PC till 1943; to RTR; at OCTU Sandhurst, commissioned 1944, 15 Scots Recce Regt, NW Europe 1944–45, wounded Feb. 1945 near Cleves and again Apr. 1945 (loss of one eye) whilst in lead vehicle of 2nd Army advance on Belsen, which his Regt. reached later that day; post-war: studied medicine at Oxford, consultant neurologist Edinburgh from 1966

Jellinek, Hans, member of Young Austria; served in Yorks. Regt and RA.

Jellinek, Kurt A., Viennese; born 1919, pupil at Schottengymnasium, served as officer cadet in Austrian Artillery 1937–38, studied at Queen's College Oxford until 1940; interned 1940; volunteered same year; posted to 220 Coy PC till 1941; on officers' list of 251 Coy PC, Mar. 1943, fell ill whilst on embarkation leave for North Africa; died of abdominal TB, Axbridge, Somerset, 1944

Jellinek, L.E., from Vienna, was S/Sgt, later commissioned, served in PC; later Legal Research Branch, in Publicity and Psycho Warfare, 21 Army Gp, name appears on 'Nominal Roll of P & PW personnel who moved from Le Tronquay to Amiens 3–11 Sept.' (1944), war crimes investigator in Germany, 'Was one of the refugees in information control'

Jellinek, M.; died on active service

Jenauth, Austrian, served in either 337 or 338 Coy PC, was with 'Radio Swindle' – Austrian broadcasts out of Algiers and Bari, in cooperation with Dermann and Stappler

Jenk, J.R. 13806135

Jensen, J., or B.A. or J.W., 13804482 or 6298697, commissioned in SOE

Jensen, J., 13806058, served as Pte in 253 Coy PC; no longer in this company on 2 Nov. 1944

Jensen, K.K., 13806018

Jess, Rudolf, operatic tenor, Sgt in No. 3 PCTC; later at BBC, programme director for European broadcasts

Jessen, J.F., 13806030, served as Pte in 253 Coy PC; no longer in this company on 2 Nov. 1944

Jessen (Ralph ?) (possibly Jensen), later James, Rolf; born Hamburg, close connections with Siemens family and firm, conscripted into *Wehrmacht* pre-war, L/Cpl, Rhodes scholar; served in PC and commandos, as NCO from L/Cpl to Sgt Maj., then commissioned; transferred to monitoring unit, 21

Army Gp, Normandy, monitoring enemy wireless traffic in France and Germany; journalist with *die Mitteilungen*, officer in press department Berlin, chief of intelligence service in Schleswig-Holstein, deputy to Hugh Carlton-Greene; post-war: with CBC Toronto

Joachim, Dr, Capt. in RAMC

Joachimsthal, served in 74 Coy PC; joined at Richborough 1940 and was with BEF in France

Johansen, H.R.F., 6298667

Jonansen, V., 6298613

Jonas, volunteered from Richborough 1939/40; was in 74 Coy PC and was with BEF in France

Jorgensen, O., 13806034

Jorns, C.H.L.A., 13810019, later Clay, J.C., 6436378, is said to have fled from France to North Africa, interned there by French; joined 337 Coy PC after British occupation; then R. Sussex Regt; returned to PC autumn 1944; eventually back to Paris (in author's opinion this account cannot be absolutely right, as personal number does not agree with facts given and should commence with 13809)

Joseph, fled to North Africa from France; served in 337 Coy PC; got back to Paris via Italy

Josephsberg, N., served in 74 Coy PC; joined at Richborough 1940 and was with BEF in France; post-war: owner of Bentley Travel Bureau, London

Joseps, Wolfgang, later Johnson, Peter W.; born Berlin 1916; interned 1940, to Australia by HMT *Dunera*, returned 1941; enlisted 23 Dec.1941; served in 220 Coy PC, landed at Arromanches 6 June1944, in action with 220 at St Hubert; in Interpreters' Pool at UCCLE; then interpreter at Hildesheim; demob Dec.46

Juliusberg, H., L/Cpl in 77 Coy PC, acted in that company's Xmas panto *A Midsummer Night's Scream*, probably 1941

Jung, Austrian architect, came to England several years before beginning of war; volunteered for service at beginning of 1940; enlisted at Richborough; served in 74 Coy PC and was with BEF in France; according to Muchitsch, was first enemy alien to be commissioned in PC, after which his qualifications were taken notice of, resulting in his being transferred to the RAOC

Jung, Otto, later Young, Thomas; born Vienna 11 June 1921, carpenter's apprentice, then farmer's boy at Schwadorf 1938, emigrated to England same year; interned Isle of Man; enlisted Nov. 1940; served in 248 Coy PC; later in RAC, Recce Regt 6th Airborne Div, in Ardennes winter 1944/45, tank was landed by glider at Wesel; interpreter at Leer, East Friesia; demob Sept. 1946; post-war: in toy industry, before retirement London taxi driver

Jung, Werner, his name appears on list in German Unity Party archives of party members who served in British Army

Jurman, M., 13807896, served in PC and possibly in SOE

K., did not agree to publication of his full name; served in PC and RHamps in France (Normandy) and Germany (Rhine crossing); finished as Capt. in

War Crimes Group, arrested last Gauleiter of Schleswig-Holstein

Kaempfner, Arpad; died on active service

Kafka, Otto, member of Young Austria; enlisted from Nottingham between 15 Jan. and 25 Mar. 1944

Kagan, C.

Kagerer-Stein, E. von, 13801130, later Fuller, Didi; born Vienna 19 Dec. 1913; Sgt 87 Coy PC; then in 3/10 Cdo, John Wayne type, about whom any number of stories are told, full of blah, but fearless; in Normandy landing attached to 47 RM Cdo; accidentally killed in action by splinter from Allied bomb

Kahane, R., served in 229 Coy PC; post-war: prominent in Ex-Service NB Association

Kahn, Josef; died on active service

Kainz, W. R., later Cainz, W.R.; post-war: prominent in Ex-Service NB Association

Kaiser, Karl, served in 74 Coy PC; joined from Richborough Camp and was with BEF in France 1940; probably same man who, having joined the SOE, took part in Operation HAMSTER near Zeltweg in Apr. 1945; may also have been in Vienna after that; in June 1945 he was in No. 6 Special Force Staff Section; later Maj. in BAOR war crimes group

Kaiser, M., 13800540, CQMS, mentioned in dispatches

Kajdic (or Kajdich), I., 13807897 and 13122226, Cpl in PC

Kaldor

Kalisch, later Gray, from Berlin, Sgt of No. 10 Sect., 229 Coy PC, 1941–43

Kallir, E.; post-war: prominent in Ex-Service NB Association

Kallmann, Jaques; born Neisse, Upper Silesia, 1895; served in 74 Coy PC; joined from Richborough Camp and was with BEF in France 1940

Kalman, A, later Colman, A.H., served in 248 & 219 Coy PC

Kalman, Ann, served in Allied Volunteer Platoon ATS

Kalman, Edith, served in Allied Volunteer Platoon ATS

Kalman, Lilo, served in Allied Volunteer Platoon ATS

Kalmar, P., served in 77 Coy PC, acted in that company's Xmas panto *A Midsummer Night's Scream* 1941.

Kalmus, Ernst George

Kalmus, Hans Marcus

Kammerling, Walter, member of Young Austria; enlisted from London between 15 Jan. and 25 Mar. 1944; served in Suffolk Regt

Kampfer, Fritz, member Young Austria; enlisted at Cheltenham Dec. 1943 or Jan. 1944

Kanders, Martin, later Kind, joined army at the behest of the Free German Youth Movement; post-war: journalist with *Neues Deutschland*, Berlin

Kanders, R. O., Austrian

Kanfer, F., temporarily King, Frederick; born Vienna 13 June 1925, emigrated to England July 1939, worked in building trade, in agriculture, and as lacquerer and in aircraft factory; served 4 years, highest rank Cpl, with Gloucester Regt, Royal Scots Fusiliers and IC, in Normandy and NW Europe; attached to US intelligence in Frankfurt; lastly in London; post-war: returned to Vienna 1947, employee till 1965, then self-employed in connection with banking

Kanin, served in 74 Coy PC; joined from Richborough Camp and was with BEF in France 1940

Kanitz, Fritz, alias Jonson, Alan, Austrian, Cpl in PC; in June 1945 in Intelligence Pool, Austria

Kann, Kurt, name appears in German Unity Party's list of members who served in Allied armies; his loyalty to the Communists may have been greater than that to the British

Kantor, Friedrich, alias Kirby, Frederick G., from Vienna, grandfather was founder of Kantor Bank in Vienna; served in PC; later RA

Karewski, Dr, well-known medical practitioner, denied entry to RAMC; served in 93 Coy PC; then infantry, commissioned, promoted Capt., refused transfer to RAMC when offered

Karg Babenburg, H., well-known actor, served in No. 3 PCTC

Karminski, Otto (Putzi), 13801455, served as Pte in 253 Coy PC, but must have been in older PC Coy previously; Lt in SOE, known as Simon, led group of men who parachuted into Tramontima Valley 13 Aug. 1944; co-operated also with Yugoslav partisans; involved with recovery of US officer group shot down at the back of Trieste; post-war: photographer on Col Hunt's Mount Everest expedition

Karo, R, served in RN, on HMS *Royal Arthur*, and on HMS *Cottesmore* (destroyer) at the Normandy landings, against German E-boats in the Channel, at Antwerp and at Walcheren; interpreter in Admiralty 1945

Karpe, F.J., 13800363, served in PC and RASC

Karpeles, R., 13802072, later Kent, R.K., 5550157, served as Pte in PC; later RHamps; returned to PC autumn 1944

Kasparovitch, Boris, alias King, B., served in SOE or SAS; killed in action.

Kassel, Hilde, served in 1 Allied Volunteer Platoon ATS

Kassner, served in 74 Coy PC; joined from Richborough Camp and was with BEF in France 1940

Katz, a Fellow of Trinity College, Cambridge, medical officer in both Australian Air Force and RAF

Katz, a gifted pianist, served in 87 Coy PC

Katz, Emanuel, served in 74 Coy PC; joined from Richborough Camp and was with BEF in France 1940

Katz, Ernest, served in 8 AEC in Australia

Katz, Frederick G., 13801002; born Hannover 23 June 1918, pupil at Grunewald Gymnasium, Berlin; enlisted 21 Jan. 1940 at Richborough; posted to 87 Coy PC, was at Le Havre 1940, then Rennes, evacuated from St Malo; later in 3 PCTC; then IC, became CSM

Katz, Manfred, PAL75833, Austrian, emigrated to Palestine; became Sgt in RAF

Katz, Meinhardt Paul Oscar, 13805511, later Heathcote, Michael Paul, 13118605 and 6387029, served in 3/10 Cdo

Katz, Rudi, later Karrell, Rudi, 13046367; born Berlin 12 May 1922 pupil at Werner Siemens RG and Lesser Schule, Grunewald, emigrated 1938,

Kindertransport, became upholsterer; enlisted from Liverpool 30 Nov. 1941; posted to 74 Coy PC; transferred to Interpreters' Pool, Brussels; later at HQ 2 AIO Stade Aug. 1946 to Jan. 1947; transferred to Kinema Corps, entertainments organiser; A/Sgt; demob 8 Oct. 1947

Katzin, Alfred, Lt Col in South African UDF, led advance party from Abyssinia to Egypt; post-war: worked at UNO, awarded OBE

Kauders, Martin A., also Kent, Alexander; born Hannover-Ahlem 21 Dec. 1920, father murdered at Auschwitz, emigrated to England with mother 1939, gardener; interned 1940, to Canada, after return worked in armaments factory Cambridge, founder member FDJ; enlisted 1943/44; RA, training in Glasgow, then Wales; in 20 Mobile Disarmament Unit, disarming German troops in Norway 1945, then Germany till 1947; lastly 34 Light AA Regt RA; discharged as Bty QMS; name appears on German Unity Party's list of members who served in Allied armies; post-war: returned to Germany, first to Thuringia, then East Berlin, news editor of *Neues Deutschland* (ND), suspected of having connections to British Secret Service and dismissed 1953, studied at Leipzig till 1961, then editor *Die Wirtschaft*; died Berlin 17 Mar. 2002

Kauders, Rudi, member of Young Austria; enlisted from Leicester before 15 Jan. 1944; Cpl

Kaufmann, served in 74 Coy PC; joined from Richborough Camp and was with BEF in France 1940

Kaufmann, Dr, Maj. in RAMC, served as specialist in military hospital in British zone of Germany

Kaufmann, Leo, from Frankfurt, served with French *Prestataires*, unit under British command was in retreat to Dunkirk, but not evacuated from there. Fled with other Hessian *prestataires*, got fishing vessel to take him from area of Nantes to unoccupied France, vessel captured by HMS *Imogen*; interned UK recognised for what he was and permitted to join PC

Kay, Bobby, served in 69 Coy PC

Kay, C.; post-war: prominent in Ex-Service NB Association; manager Kay Restaurants

Kay, Charles

Keith, served in PC and RE; Capt.; in HQ Canadian Army, responsible for repatriation of Canadian PoWs; later auditor for *Wehrmacht* accounts

Keller, Dita, married Laursen, served in 1 Allied Volunteer Platoon ATS

Keller, Steven Fred, served in 137 Coy PC

Kellmann (or Wellmann?), M. (or possibly H.H.?), 13800170, later Kirby, M. J. (Ernest), 13118608 and 6436357; born 26 Dec. 1903; served in PC, R. Sussex and 3/10 Cdo (Exceptionally, not even PC records, otherwise a mine of exceedingy accurate information, was able to determine what exactly he was called.)

Kellner, Austrian, served in R. Signals

Kelly, Ernest Michael

Kemp

Kemp, Roy, CQMS of 220 Coy PC

Kendrick, George A

Kendrick, John Gerald

Kennard, Robert, Austrian, Cpl in 220 Coy PC; later interpreter with RE; eventually in charge of Magdeburg railway station, as only person who could communicate with British military and German railway personnel

Kennedy, A.D., joined 229 Coy PC as 2/Lt on 13 Nov. 1943; posted to 167 Coy on 15 Dec. 1943

Kenneth, Mrs, served in one of the Allied Volunteer Platoons, ATS, at first stockroom admin; later in secret job

Kent, H.S., served in 137 Coy PC

Kent, P.O.

Kerbel, served in 69 Coy PC

Kern, Leo, member of Young Austria; enlisted from Birmingham, Dec. 1943/Jan. 1944

Kernek, Miss, married Jones, from Linz, Austria, Catholic with three Jewish grandparents, served in one of the Allied Volunteer Platoons ATS, first as orderly; later as dentist's assistant

Kerner, L., Austrian

Kerpen, Ludwig, later Kerpen, Lewis

Kerr, Frederick

Kerr, Michael Robert Emanuel, later Rt. Hon. Sir Michael Kerr; born 1 Mar. 1921 Berlin, schools in Switzerland and France, then Aldenham School, studied at Clare College Cambridge; interned Isle of Man 1940; served as Ft Lt in RAF1941–46, pilot flying Wellingtons in Coastal Command; post-war: QC, Lord Justice of Appeal, Treasurer of Lincoln's Inn and President British–German Jurists' Association as well as many other legal appointments; high British and German distinctions; died 14 April 2002

Kessler, Hans (Wrucki?), member of Young Austria; enlisted shortly before 29 July 1944

Kesten, Georg, served in 74 Coy PC; died on active service

Kester, served in 74 Coy PC; joined from Richborough Camp and was with BEF in France 1940

Keynes, Austrian lawyer, served in PC, which he joined at Richborough; later RA, lastly in British Austrian Legal Unit; Maj.

Kindermann, Max, served in 69 Coy PC

King, Felix, Sgt in 101 Sqn RAF (previously 310 Sqn Czech airforce); killed in action 28 Dec. 1944, buried in Rheinberg cemetery

King, L.G.T., from Berlin

Kirschner, André G., 13805755, later Kershaw, Andrew, Hungarian, swimmer and water polo player, served in 77 Coy PC; later 3/10 Cdo, commissioned; post-war: President of Ogilvy & Mather, USA

Kirstein, Wilhelm, is said to have tried to start trouble for Nazis in Saarland, arrested and sentenced to death, liberated by resistance (?); served in 337 Coy PC; later SOE, capture of Nazi spies in North Africa under pretence of being deserter; post-war: after end of hostilities police chief in Saarland (unconfirmed)

Kisch, Heinrich, from Prague, press control officer at HQ BAOR, Benrath

Kiwi, Heinz, 13803339, served in 69 Coy PC; killed in action during air attack on London 29 Dec. 1940

Klaar, Georg, later Clare, George; born Vienna 21 Dec. 1920; served in 77 Coy PC; then 157 Fd Regt RA; then Intelligence, Bdr/Interpreter with Control Commission in Berlin, assistant to Maj. Sely, offered job on *Die Welt* newspaper whilst still in service; post-war: became chief representative of Axel Springer publishing group (having been introduced to Springer himself by Sely in his (Sely's) office), author of the best selling stories *Last Waltz in Vienna* and *Berlin Days 1946–47*

Klajn, A. (Klain ?), served in 74 Coy PC

Klamper, Hans, member of Young Austria; enlisted from Birmingham Dec. 1943/Jan. 1944

Klappholz, Erich Alfons, later Kirby, Dr Eric Alfons; born Vienna 19 May 1926, went to school there in the 2nd and 20th districts, which adjoin, to England 1938, parents later fled to Yugoslavia, where they were killed by the Nazis; joined the army on 2 Nov. 1944; at first in GSC; after initial training transferred to Green Howards, first to 11th and then to 2nd Bat; at war's end sent to India, attended infantry OCTU at Bangalore, commissioned into RHamps.; returned to England 1947 and as RHamps. had too many officers, finished up with 43rd SL Regt, RA; released Oct. 1948; never saw action, which, as he says, was unfortunate, because 'the only reason I enlisted was to fight the Germans'; post-war: dentist, qualified 1958, practised until his retirement in March 1992; lives in Sussex

Klaryn, served in 74 Coy PC; joined from Richborough Camp and was with BEF in France 1940

Kleedorfer, T., 13805806, Austrian, served in 220 Coy PC; Kklled on active service in accident, loading ashes on to a lorry 20 Mar. 1942

Klein, served in 74 Coy PC; joined from Richborough Camp and was with BEF in France 1940

Klein, Alfred, 220760, commissioned in PC

Klein, Dr M. V., Maj. in IAMS

Klein, Robert, later Clyne, Robert

Klein, Robert, served in 165 & 74 Coy PC

Kleinberg, engineer, bridging expert, served in PC; transferred to RAOC; later RE, commissioned as Capt., in War Office planning and construction of Mulberry harbours

Kleingericht, J., served in 74 Coy PC

Klementschitz, Erich, later Clement, Eric; born Graz 24 June 1911, was in trouble with Austrian police as active socialist from Feb. 1934 onwards, served in International Brigade in Spanish Civil War, fled to France 1939, interned, sailed on last ship to UK; interned again, sent to Canada 1940, returned 1942; enlisted Feb. 1944; served in Suffolk Regt, informed of mother's death at Ravensbruck, but found father alive at Buchenwald 1945; interpreter from Oct. 1945; clerk of military court; demob 2 Mar. 1947; post-war: taxi and lorry driver, progress chaser in factory, thought there were too many Nazis in Graz for him to return there

Klinger, a Viennese, served in 229 Coy PC

Klinghofer, A., Austrian, Pte welder/fitter at 2BW B-Camp, MEF

Knapp, Bernhard, from Graz

Knapp, Charles Percy, served in 88 Coy PC

Knapp, E. served in PC; was in No. 10 Psycho Warfare Team, Allied Information Service 1944

Knie, A. or M.K.P.O., 13800841, later Kay, A., 6387012, served in 74 Coy PC, where he signed a round robin to the OC concerning Jewish holidays; may have been commissioned later in SOE

Knoblach, Austrian, served in 337 or 338 Coy PC

Knobloch, Gunther Hans, 13800841, later Kendal, George Harold (Nobby), 13118610, Austrian; born 9 Dec. 1907; Sgt in 87 Coy PC; then in 3/10 Cdo; later in Field Security Service, in Near East, then Sicily landing 30 Dec. 1943, attached to Belgian Troop 10 Cdo as muleteer; with Polish troop at Montenero (left flank of 8th Army opposite Monte Cassino); formed ski patrol – first in 8th Army; with 2 Cdo in landing on Lissa (Vis), commissioned 18 Dec. 1944; later chief of mobile intelligence, 8th Army, investigated war crimes in Austria, reported on political matters; Maj; post-war: publications on legal themes, lawyer, Vancouver, Canada

Knox, served in 137 Coy PC

Knudsen, A. ,13806017, Pte in 253 Coy PC; later commissioned, in SOE

Koban, Blasius, alias Kent, Bernard, alias Loeffler, Bernard, alias Kezeker, Austrian, German conscript, PoW; taken into British service, SOE, in Operation DINTYLAKE near Klagenfurt; June 1945 in No. 6 Special Force Staff Section in Austria, was intended to remain there

Koch, R.M.

Kochmann, Wolfgang Rudolf, 220761, Lt in 229 Coy PC; transferred RE, DCRE Home Command

Koelz, Mathaeus Johannes, 1380591, later Kelts, John Matthew; born Muelldorf 5 Apr. 1895, well-known painter, had been Capt. in German Army in WW1, joined Munich police and was involved in action against Nazis in *Bierhallenputsch* 1923, refused to paint portrait of Hitler when requested to do so, in last hours before his flight from Germany he cut up his masterpiece, a triptych, into several parts which he hid in various places (his daughter, who tried to restore this at the time, now owns a few of the pieces, others she is still looking for), fled to Prague 1937, then Rotterdam, 1939 to England where, as a German, he met considerable hostility at Oxted (daughter was subject of assault, in which she suffered grievous bodily harm); interned 1940, to Australia by HMT *Dunera*, returned 1941; enlisted; served in 248 & 74 Coy PC; transferred to16 Bn RAOC, Sgt as of 15 July 1944; demob 18 Aug. 1945; painted portraits of colleagues, officers and wives during war, exhibited at Darlington June 1942 and received highest praise; died 1971; see biography *Three Point Perspective* (AMF, Heather, Leics.; ISBN 0952545403)

Koenig, Franz Josef, later Kelly (Kelley?), Frank John, from Frankfurt, but apparently born in Innsbruck, served in PC; then RF (SOE), Lt, with Bryant (Breuer), Warner (Werner) and Rhodes (Rohde) parachuted into Styria 25 Apr. 1945, Operation HISTORIAN, to take over Zeltweg air base, in subsequent withdrawal to Authal Castle, concerned with re-establishment of Styrian government; June 45 in No. 2 Special Force Staff Section in Austria

Koenigsberg, Peter, later Kinghill, Peter, served in 229 Coy PC

Koenigsberger, later King, F.; born 1901; enlisted Mar. 1940; served in 220 Coy PC; demob 10 Aug. 1945

Koenigsberger, E.R., later Kingsley, Edward Roger, served in 229 & 69 Coy PC; Cheshire Regt; and lastly Field Security, name appears on officers' list 69 Coy PC as 2/Lt June 1943; by war's end with Cheshires; then OC Field Security Section in Germany

Koenigsberger, Margaret, from Heidelberg, served in 3 Allied Volunteer Platoons ATS; post-war: to Kenya, then Japan

Koenigshut, Manfred, later Kingsley, Michael, served in 87 Coy PC

Koenigstein, served in 74 Coy PC; joined from Richborough Camp and was with BEF in France 1940

Koessler, Egon, Austrian, imprisoned Dachau 14 Nov. 1938–15 July 1939, emigrated; served in French Army 11 May 1940–20 Dec. 1942; thereafter in 337 Coy PC 2 Apr. 1943– 1 Nov. 1946

Koessler, Elisabeth, married Mortimer, from Miesbach, Bavaria, served as VAD

Koestler, Arthur, 13805661; born Budapest 5 Sept. 1905, studied in Vienna, originally a communist, after experience in Paris turned round completely, journalist in Near East, Paris, Berlin and Russia; interned in France 1939; joined French Foreign Legion; to England 1940; enlisted 1941; served in 251 (possibly 248) Coy PC; discharged on health grounds (nervous breakdown) 1942; author of *Scum of the earth*, *The Yogi and the Commissar*, *Thieves in the night* and many others; wrote script of Ministry of Information film *Lift up your head, comrade*, official film about enemy aliens in PC; post-war: Vice-President of EXIT, voluntary euthanasia society, awarded CBE; died Mar. 1983

Kohlberg, P., served in 77 Coy PC, acted in that company's Xmas panto *A Midsummer Night's Scream*, probably 1941

Kohn, served in 74 Coy PC; joined from Richborough Camp and was with BEF in France 1940

Kohn, Erich, later Walters-Kohn, Eric; born Vienna 1907, imprisoned Dachau and Buchenwald, to England Mar. 1939; enlisted 19 Aug. 1940; Sgt in 248, 69 & 703 PW Coy PC; in battle of Caen; in action at Breteville, Belgium; interpreter in PoW camp; post-war: published articles, lectured on subject of enemy aliens in British forces, member Institute of Directors

Kohn, Felix, member of Young Austria; enlisted from Cambridge Dec. 1943/Jan. 1944

Kohn, Heinz, member of Young Austria; enlisted from London between 15 Jan. and 25 Mar. 1944

Kohn, PAL/3453, served in PC; was on 61b & 62nd parachute training course; later in Para. Regt

Kohn, Walter, later Clayton, Walter; born Hamburg 28 Feb. 1921, pupil at Wahnschaff Schule, emigrated to England 1938; says he served in 216 Coy PC, but as this was not an A-company he was probably in 219; transferred to West Yorks Regt Dec. 1943; Feb. 1944 to South Staffs Regt; in France with 30 Corps on 16 June 1944, in action at Caen and Falaise; with Field Intelligence at Brussels; 1945 to First Canadian Army, 46 US Army Group; 1946 to SHAEF and 62 Division; demob 1946; post-war: Collins Fur Co. Birmingham, then Christian Dior London, 1953–75 restaurant owner, 1952– 63 with AFS, London Fire Brigade

Kohn, Walter, later Keats, Walter, to Australia on HMT *Dunera*; was on active service

Kohn, Walter, Austrian, served in International Brigade in Spanish Civil War; in PC in North Africa

Kohn-Speyer, Edmund P.; born 1904, a grandson of Moritz M.Warburg, banker in Hamburg, served in RAF Intelligence; '[Is said to have] drafted laws for use in Germany after the war ...'

Koller, R., 13800157, served in 74 Coy PC; joined from Richborough Camp and was with BEF in France 1940; L/Cpl

Kolmer, Herbert, Austrian, said to have enlisted on 25 June 1943, but was civilian in 1944

Komaromi, Hans, PAL/1401, Austrian; born 3 Jan. 1922; enlisted Sarafand 15 May 1941; driver RASC, wounded in action at Benghazi, severe burns on both legs 21 Apr. 1943, after which he was classified unfit for service abroad; demob 12 July 1947

Konikoff, served in 74 Coy PC; joined from Richborough Camp and was with BEF in France 1940

Konrad, Erich, later Conrad, Eric, Viennese lawyer, served in 74 Coy PC; later in Psychological Warfare; awarded Certificate of Gallantry and US Bronze Star; Sgt

Koppel, Blanka, enlisted in Oxford 3 July 1942; served in 1 Allied Volunteer Platoon ATS

Korn, Frank, Berliner, enlisted winter 1939–40; with 87 Coy PC in France, evacuated through St Malo; later in RAOC; post-war: Director Trafalgar Investments, OBE

Korn, Konrad Paul, later Douglas, Paul Michael; born Berlin 14 Apr. 1917; enlisted 21 Jan. 1940 Richborough; Cpl with 87 Coy, 1940 at Le Havre, Rennes, evacuated through St Malo; to IC, there Sgt; post-war: chartered accountant

Kornhaeuser, name appears in German Unity Party's list of members who served in Allied armies

Kornitzer, served in 74 Coy PC; joined from Richborough Camp and was with BEF in France 1940

Korolany, Peter, member of Young Austria; enlisted from Cambridge Dec. 1943/Jan. 1944

Korytowski, Ludwig; born Treuen, Saxony, 1903, left his home in Silesia for Berlin 1934, England 1935; enlisted from Richborough 13 Feb. 1940; served in 77 Coy PC; severely wounded in foot whilst building bridge at Stratford-upon-Avon, found unfit for further service; discharged 1943

Kosteletzky, N.N.J., Czechoslovak citizen, enlisted in Oxford; served in 1 Allied Volunteer Platoon ATS, was one of its older members

Kotek, Leo, later Kaye, Leo, served in 77 Coy PC

Kottka, Vladimir, 13802873, later Jones, 13118611, said to have been a Russian, Cpl in 219 Coy PC; later 3/10 Cdo, in Op HARDTACK opposite Graveline, taken prisoner there, liberated at end of war

Kottkowski, Willi, later King, R.S.; born 1906, had been in concentration camp prior to emigration; served in 74 Coy PC; joined from Richborough Camp and was with BEF in France 1940

Kouloukas, J., 13807698, served in PC and probably in SOE

Kowalski, J., later Kowalsky, I., served in 74 Coy PC; joined from Richborough Camp and was with BEF in France 1940; died on active service

Krainz, W.R.; post-war: prominent in Ex-Service NB Association

Krakenberger, F., later Kenber, Fred, Lt in 15 Scots Recce Regt RA, served in Mediterranean area; post-war: studied at Oxford, then worked in City of London

Krall, Austrian, served in 338 Coy PC

Kraemer, Marga, enlisted from Oxford 3 July 1942; served in 1 Allied Volunteer Platoon ATS

Kraemer, Max, name appears in German Unity Party's list of Sudeten Germans who served in British forces

Kramer, Maria, from Vienna, later Selby, was VAD nurse; eldest son is present Bishop of Worcester

Krassototzky, S., Austrian, served as wireless technician with 520 Coy ATS in TEK Gp

Kraus, a pupil at Charterhouse School, student at Balliol College Oxford; killed on active service with RAF

Kraus, served in 74 Coy PC; joined from Richborough Camp and was with BEF in France 1940

Kraus, 13804344, later Kendall, Bob, came from Bohemia or Moravia, served in PC; was on 61b & 62nd parachute training course; then with 21 Ind. Para. Coy in North Africa, Italy, Norway and Palestine; may have been at Arnhem

Kraus, W.A.

Krausen (in some documents: Klausen), Heinz (or Hans), 13805629, later Aitcheson, Harry, 13118612, served in 251 Coy PC and 3/10 Cdo; post-war: to USA, worked in US post office

Kraw, M., 13807898

Krebs, Leopold, 13801308; born 1892 or 93, had been judge at the German Supreme Court; served Feb. 1940–June 1945; died Apr. 1952

Krell, Rosemarie, served in 4 AV Platoon ATS, went on leave single and came back married

Krivine, J.D., served in RAC; was OC No. 10 Amplifier Unit, 21 Army Gp 1944/45

Kriwaczeck, served in 74 Coy PC; joined from Richborough Camp and was with BEF in France 1940

Kronfeld, Renée, 2992341, Austrian, served as LACW in WAAF in Palestine

Kronfeld, Robert, champion glider pilot from Vienna, held world height and speed records, first to cross Channel by glider, glider aircraft designer, was close relative of Dr Karl Renner, Austrian Chancellor and later President of

Austria, emigrated to England 1934; Col in Glider Regt, Squadron Leader in RAF, planned and organised glider landings in Normandy that took place the night before D-Day; killed in accident flying a wing-only glider of own design 12 Feb. 1948

Kronheim, Jochen, later Whittinghame, Tony (Icke), Berliner, proud of his proletarian background, with *Kindertransport* to England, Lord Balfour's estate at Whittingham (nickname is Berlin slang for 'I'); joined from Manchester on orders of German Unity Party there, volunteered for commandos, but was refused, wounded in leg, which had to be amputated; post-war: returned to Germany

Krossmayr, alias Kennedy, Austrian, German conscript, PoW; taken into British service; SOE; June 1945 in No. 6 Special Force Staff Section in Austria

Krotzky, V.; 13806113, served in 253 Coy PC; later SOE; missing since 8 Jan. 1944

Krumbein, K., 13810012, later MacAllister, C.S., 6305492, Pte in PC; then the Buffs; returned to PC unit autumn 1944

Kubach, V., 13807171, Pte in 165 Coy PC; volunteered for transfer to commandos, application refused

Kuc, Roman

Kudelka, Lilly, served in 1 Allied Volunteer Platoon ATS

Kudernatsch, Otto, 13809263, Austrian; born 13 May 1918; enlisted at Hussein Dey; served in PC North Africa; demob 20 Nov. 1946

Kugelmann, H.J., later Coleman; killed on active service

Kugler, Joseph, 13801945, later Smith, J., 6305456, Austrian, served in 137 Coy PC; then the Buffs, on dangerous mission in company with Friedlaender, since when nothing has been heard from him

Kuh, Billy, served in 1 Allied Volunteer Platoon ATS

Kuh, Leopold (Poldi), later Kew, member of German-Jewish youth movement, acted as trainer in emigrants' training establishment at Gross Breesen, continued this work in UK after emigration; enlisted at Richborough; CQMS in 219 Coy PC, commissioned, 6 July 1942 as 2/Lt to 74 Coy PC; 15 Jan. 1943 as Capt. 2 i/c same company; post-war: prominent in Ex-Service NB Association in Birmingham

Kuhn Otto; born Vienna 1924; joined PC Coy at Taunton 1942 (either 87 or 137 Coy)

Kuhnel, L/Cpl in 93 Coy PC; 24 Sept. 1941 transferred to RAOC

Kupler, Cpl in 69 Coy PC

Kury, Manfred H., 13804473, later McGregor, Jack F. (Jock), 13118613; born 18 Sept. 1903 on board ship in German territorial waters, to England aged 3, spoke no German; interned June 1940; served in 229, 246 and 337 Coy PC and 3/10 Cdo, name appears in officers' list 337 Coy PC 31 Aug. 1944; died either on active service or shortly after war's end

Kurzweil, E., 13810024, later Fairbanks, G., 6387044, Pte

Kush, Dr G.M.; post-war: prominent in Ex-Service NB Association

Kustera, F., 13806068

Kutschka, K. (or W.?), 13802299, Pte

Labe, served in 74 Coy PC; joined from Richborough Camp and was with BEF
    in France 1940

Lachmann, Ilse, served in 1 Allied Volunteer Platoon ATS

Ladewig, Erwin, from Hamburg; post-war: became clergyman

Ladewig, Jochen, later Lawrie, J.; born Hamburg 1923; served in PC;
    transferred RAC; killed in action near Hamburg in last days of the war

Lambert, C.L.

Lammel, served in 74 Coy PC; joined from Richborough Camp and was with
    BEF in France 1940

Lammer, Alfred (Ritter von); born Linz 28 Nov. 1909, lived first at Braunau,
    then Zell am See, studied at Munich and Innsbruck, was member of
    'Schutzkorps der Heimwehr', in Austrian tourist office, London, 1934,
    connections to Guinness Bank; observer in RAF night fighter squadron,
    accounted for five enemy planes, 3 German, 2 Italian; rose to Sqn Ldr;
    awarded DFC and Bar; said in BBC interview: 'Whoever fights on the side
    of Hitler is an enemy of all right thinking people'; post-war: photographer,
    stamp designer; died 4 Oct. 2000

Lampeitl, V., Cpl in one of the Allied Volunteer Platoons ATS

Lampel, Werner, alias Langford, Herbert, nicknamed 'The Duke'; born
    Leipzig 20 Feb. 1919, son of Samuel Lampel, cantor at liberal synagogue,
    wanted to become a rabbi, mother née Grueneberg from Hannover, pupil
    at Jewish primary school and Koenig Albrecht *Gymnasium*, both parents
    murdered in concentration camp, to England 20 Mar. 1939; volunteered
    probably 1939; served 4 years in PC, orderly room Sgt; to RN 1943(?),
    Writer Special RN, served on HMS *Westminster*, HMS *Wanderer*, HMS
    Curzon, interpreted enemy radio traffic at sea, translated captured material,
    wrote comrades love letters; was in D-Day landing; converted to C. of E.
    before end of war, married Molly Hughes, a devout Ulster woman, and
    became clergyman in Church of England; post-war: studied history at
    London University, 1st Class Hons., then theology at Wells College, later
    vice-principal St Chad's, Durham, then registrar exams at Church House,
    Westminster, finally Rector of Winthorpe; deceased

Lampert, Lilly, from Vienna, served in 1 Allied Volunteer Platoon ATS

Lampl, Fritz, member of Young Austria; enlisted shortly before 29 July 1944

Land, Peter, served in No. 3 PCTC, in entertainment sect.

Landau, served in 74 Coy PC; joined from Richborough Camp and was with
    BEF in France 1940

Landau, E., later Langley, E.R.F.; born.18 Sept. 1903; orderly room Sgt in 3/10
    Cdo; died on active service in UK

Landau, Kurt, served in 137 Coy PC

Landau, Norbert, later Landon, Norman, 13053560; born Vienna 24 Aug.
    1919, came to England 1938; enlisted 12 Nov. 1940; served in PC; later Bdr
    in Anti Tank Artillery; interpreter in Austria; demob 3 Oct. 1946; post-war:
    chartered accountant in London

Landauer, Walter, later Landon, from Munich, served in 229 Coy PC; killed in
    action, posthumous Certificate of Gallantry

Landenberger, K.J., later Land, Kurt Jakob; born Nuremberg 18 Mar. 1914, emigrated Apr. 1933, to South Africa 1936; joined SA Air Force 4 Nov. 1940, Cpl; later Flt Sgt, 12 Bomber Squadron, SAAF WO1, commissioned 1 Nov. 1944, in Chief Inspectorate Stores & Accounts Air, as Stores Inspector and Technical Stores Officer; landed at Baria at end of war in Udine; post-war: back to SA, then Kenya, 1961 to England, co-owner 'Medikus' Shoes, Nuremberg

Landsberg, later Russell, served in PC; transferred RN, PO on HMS *Quorn* (Hunt class destroyer); killed in action when ship exploded off Normandy on D-Day

Landsberg, H., Cpl in 220 Coy PC; 1945 in Publicity and Psychological Warfare, 21 Army Gp

Landsberg, Rolf, Prof. Dr; born Berlin 1920. industrial chemist, came to England 1935; in HM forces 3 years, name appears in German Unity Party's list of members who served in Allied armies

Lang, Austrian, served in 338 Coy PC

Lang, Bruce; born 1891 served in 220 Coy PC

Langdon, P.E.

Lange, Helene, served in 1 Allied Volunteer Platoon ATS

Langer, Hans Peter, a Langer of Hareth, changed forename Hans to Henry, served in 87, 165 and 251 Coy PC.; 91 Group PC; 17 Aug. 1942 as 2/Lt to 165 Coy PC; name appears on officers' list of 251 Coy PC Feb. 1943; posted to 6 PCTC Bradford 23 Apr. 1943; 7 June 1943 to 337 Coy in Hussein Dey, Algeria; 1 Sept. 1943 to civilian labour force; 4 Jan. 1946 to 91 Group PC as Maj.; post-war: married Canadian ENSA artist, ives in Toronto

Langer, Peter Paul Wilhelm, a Langer of Hareth, later Leighton, William Peter, also Leighton-Langer, Peter; born Vienna 3 Aug. 1923, father (senior civil servant in Austrian Ministry of Finance) killed at Auschwitz, pupil at Elisabeth-*Gymnasium*, Vienna, to England 4 Sept. 1938 by *Kindertransport* of Society of Friends, agricultural trainee; enlisted 21 Dec. 1941; to 229 Coy PC; transferred RA Sept. 1943, 123 OCTU RA, commissioned Nov. 1944; to India Jan. 1945; in 201 Indian Indep. Med. Bty, RIA, till Dec. 1946, Capt. commanding A Troop and OC Waziristan Indian Medium Frontier Post, RIA, Razmak; then 8th Field Regt, RIA, battery Capt. 19 Battery, Nowshera, NWFP; in charge Hindu refugee camp after Nowshera massacre Sept./Oct. 1947; demob Dec. 1947; post-war: with Singer & Friedlander, merchant bankers, then Marks & Spencer, Tesco, Co-op, then CFO Bata Schuhe in Germany, active in Labour Party and in politics concerning foreigners in Germany, author of this book

Langfaer, served in 74 Coy PC; joined from Richborough Camp and was with BEF in France 1940

Langford, Peter

Langley, E.L. or E.E., officer in PC, mentioned in dispatches in connection with Rhine crossing 1945; commanded civilian work force at HQ BAOR: Maj.

Langley, Max, joined 87 Coy PC from Richborough Camp, with them in France 1940, Le Havre, Rennes, evacuated from St Malo; later in IC

Lanyi, Djury (Georg) H., 13802870, later Lane, George; born Hungary 18 Jan. 1915, Capt. of Hungarian water polo team at Olympic Games 1936, student at Christ Church Oxford, and at London University, journalist, expulsion from UK 1939 countermanded after intervention by Eden, Margesson and Jim Thomas; enlisted 1939; Grenadier Guards threw him out; served in PC; then SOE; transferred to 3/10 Cdo, there first troop Sgt, commissioned 1943; commanded Operation TARBRUSH at Onival 17/18 May 1944, taken prisoner, interviewed by Rommel, held in Oflag 9; awarded Military Cross, Military Medal

Lanzmann, served in 74 Coy PC; joined from Richborough Camp and was with BEF in France 1940

Lapide, Pinchas; born Vienna 28 Nov. 1922, spent time in concentration camp, fled to Palestine 1940; served in Jewish Bde; post-war: Israeli Consul at Milan, theologian

Larson, Eric; born 1896, served in 137 Coy PC

Lasky, Johann Wolfgang; born Vienna 31 July1902, studied law at Vienna and Heidelberg and was legal advisor Vienna City Council, wrote commentary on admin law in Austria, active in Boy Scout Association, taught Edward, Prince of Wales, how to ski, emigrated to Belgium 1938, then UK; Cpl in 77 Coy PC; ski instructor 52 Lowland Div., transferred RASC; then translator at HQ SHAEF; involved with legal planning for Austria, Lt Col 2 i/c British Austrian Legal Unit; appointed administrative judge by Austrian government whilst officer in HM forces; post-war: legal advisor to British Control Commission for Germany, then to NATO, for which purpose the rules had to be changed, OBE, after retirement in law firm at Bonn; died Cologne 28 July 1987

Larsen, A.T., 13806049, served in 253 Coy PC; later commissioned in SOE

Larsen, H.H.P., 13806042, served in 253 Coy PC; later commissioned in SOE

Last, Dr, Viennese psychiatrist, Maj. in RAMC

Latzer, N.

Lauber, S., 771738, Austrian from the Burgenland, served as AC in RAF, based in Palestine

Laufer, Uli

Lauffer (also Laufer), Guenther, 13801331, later Lawton, B.R., 13118806 and 6436365, Pte in 87 Coy PC, probably also 3/10 Cdo; died on active service

Lavezzari, E., CQMS in 188 & 229 Coy PC

Law, served in PC; later in Army Education Corps, 21st Army Group; CSM; lectured on Germany, also acted as commentator in BBC German broadcasts

Lawrence, K.P.

Lawton, H.

Layton, Julian, served in PC

Lazarowicz, Irene, later Lennert, married Carter; born Vienna 28 June 1921, emigrated 1939; joined ATS 1941; due to above average mathematical abilities, radar operator attached RA AA, Wormwood Scrubs; on aircraft locating V1 and V2; post-war: in exhibition studio, then statistician for Hounslow Borough Council; died 1991

Lazarus, Sgt in 337 Coy PC; post-war: judge at labour court in Germany

Lechner, Austrian, served in 229 Coy PC

Leder, alias Leach, Austrian, German conscript, PoW; taken into British service; SOE; June 45 in No. 6 Special Force Staff Section in Austria

Lederer, served in PC; later IC, Capt., was personal interpreter to British High Commissioner and C. in C. in Germany

Lederer, E., served in 220 Coy PC; later REME; post-war: watchmaker

Leeser, H., served in 74 Coy PC; joined from Richborough Camp and was with BEF in France 1940

Lehmann, served in 137 Coy PC

Lehmann, served in 229 Coy PC; had connections with Russia

Lehmann, served in 74 Coy PC; joined from Richborough Camp and was with BEF in France 1940

Lehmann, Elias Ernst; born Nuremberg 14 June 1914, pupil at Bensheim Gymnasium, studied at Heidelberg and Berne, MD, emigrated to Palestine 1938; Maj. in RAMC, attached to 52 general hospital, Polish artillery; with 8th Army Benghazi, Tripoli, Sicily, at Syracuse, Porte Caddiano, Cassino, Lago Statomeno, Rimini; finally British base hospital Vienna-Schoenbrunn; demob 1947; post-war: from 1948 with Israeli Army, department head Jerusalem Hospital, professor at Beersheba University

Lehmann, Klaus, name appears in German Unity Party's list of members who served in Allied armies

Lehniger, Richard, 13801849, later Leonard, R., Sudeten German communist from Aussig (Usti-nad-Labem), Bohemia, served in Czechoslovak PC Coy, probably 226; took part in Operation AQUATINT as interpreter; killed in action, buried in war grave at back of Omaha Beach, tombstone quotes Marx in German *'Die Internationale wird die Menschheit sein'*, name appears in German Unity Party's list of members who served in Allied armies

Leicht, Norbert, member of Young Austria; enlisted from Leeds Dec. 1943/Jan. 1944

Leighton, Eric

Lemberger, Hans Karl, 1441666, later Lee, J.C.; born Vienna 1923, pupil at Wr. Neustadt Gymnasium, to UK Dec. 1938 by *Kindertransport*, worked as motor mechanic Belfast 1939–40; interned in Crumlin Rd jail, Belfast, then Huyton, then Isle of Man 1940– 42; tried to join RAF, Czech Army; accepted for RASC 28 Oct. 1943, in 753 Coy, ambulance driver in Normandy as from 11 July 1944; then 1 Petrol Station Coy, 21 Army Gp; finally 2 years interpreter in Germany; demob 18 May 1947

Lemberger, Kurt, member of Young Austria; enlisted from Preston Dec. 1943/Jan. 1944

Lenel, Ernst R., 13801313, later Lawrence, Ernest R.; born Darmstadt 26 Oct. 1918, though some reports make him the scion of a Darmstadt Jewish family, F.G.Katz says, he was not a Jew; served in 87 Coy PC, member of hockey team; later Sgt in 3/10 Cdo, distrusted others and relied on himself, taken prisoner while on patrol 22 June 1944; killed after capture

Lenel, Victor; born Darmstadt, older brother of Ernest (above), enthusiastic sportsman, Cpl in 77 Coy PC

Leniewsky, Joe, from Poland, served in Field Security Service, Germany, arrested Dr Schweder in Bremen; returned to Poland after demob, but returned to UK rapidly

Leonard, John Howard

Lercher, H., served in 74 Coy PC; joined from Richborough Camp and was with BEF in France 1940; L/Cpl

Lerse, Albert, from Stuttgart, served in 249 Coy PC, commissioned

Lerse, Randolph, from Stuttgart, brother of Albert (above), served in 249 Coy PC; Capt.; post-war: solicitor

Leschziner, Alfred, later Layton, Freddie, from Beuthen, served in 87 Coy PC; later RF (SOE); not sent into action

Leser, Hans, 13800085, was at Buchenwald, after release from there to York 19 Jan. 1939; served in 74 Coy PC; joined from Richborough Camp 12 Nov. 1939, was with BEF in France 1940 transferring military supplies from ship to rail, evacuated from Brest; 1942 to RASC, remained a driver, until someone noticed he was capable of speaking German rather well and transferred him to staff of General Eisenhower (G2) as translator; promoted Sgt; eventually discharged from Iserlohn in Germany 26 Feb. 1946; post-war: lives at Stanmore

Lesheim, Ingeborg, cook in A-Coy in Bury St Edmunds

Lesser, Kurt, served in 246 Coy PC

Lessig, Herbert

Lester, Peter

Leven, Peter Guenther ,13805333, later Long, Peter, 13118616 and 3436348, Pte in PC, Sussex Regt, 3/10 Cdo

Levente, Dick; born Austria 8 Dec. 1912, completed apprenticeship as engineering mechanic in Vienna; enlisted 1940; motor mechanic, then flight engineer, RAF; did 2 tours of duty in Bomber Command, commissioned, became professional engineering officer, last rank Wing Cdr, M.R.Ae.S., awarded OBE, retired 21 Jan. 1968

Levi, served in 74 Coy PC; joined from Richborough Camp and was with BEF in France 1940

Levin, Hubertus, 13801467, later Miles, Patrick Hugh, 13118617, Austrian; born 22 Jan. 1920; Cpl in 137 Coy PC; later Sgt in 3/10 Cdo; member of 62 Cdo SSRF in raid on Herm 27/28 Feb. 1943; with 40 Cdo in Sicily landing 9/10 June 1943; with 2 Cdo Bde in landing on Lissa (Vis), Sgt Maj., then commissioned; post-war: with Cadbury, then vice-president J. Walter Thompson publicity agency

Levin, Hans; born about 1895, had been judge in Germany, imprisoned at Dachau Nov. 1938; interned on Isle of Man 1940; served in 77 Coy PC, reports say he was the most useless soldier, but British NCO, who knew his background, protected him and got him through all the scrapes into which he got himself

Levin, Ludwig, from Munich, later Lawrence, K. Peter, Sgt in 8th Irish Hussars

Levinsohn, served in 74 Coy PC

Levkovich, member of Young Austria; enlisted from Leeds Dec. 1943/Jan. 1944

Levy 1, served in 74 Coy PC; joined from Richborough and was with BEF in France 1940

Levy 2, served in 74 Coy PC; joined from Richborough and was with BEF in France 1940

Levy 3, served in 74 Coy PC; joined from Richborough and was with BEF in France 1940

Levy, Guenter, served in 87 Coy PC

Levy, Hans Werner, later Laurant, Henry W.

Levy, Henny, served in 1 Allied Volunteer Platoon ATS, in Oxford 3 July 1942

Levy, Inge, was at Manchester before joining British forces at behest of FDJ or other communist party organisation; returned to Germany after demob

Levy, Karl Ernst, 13810017, temporarily Lincoln, Ken, 6436377; born Grabow, Mecklenburg, 24 Sept. 1920, moved to Berlin-Kreuzberg 1930, apprentice technical, then sanitary engineer, 1939 to Liverpool; interned 1940, released 1941; joined British forces at behest of FDJ or other communist party organisation summer 1944; in 3/10 Cdo; but returned to original unit in PC autumn 1944; got to Elmshorn in last week of war, participated in workers' council there; Field Security Section, Disbandment Control (interrogation of Germans released from service in *Wehrmacht*) till Jan. 1946; then political supervision in and near Elmshorn; awarded BEM July 1947; after demob again to Elmshorn, teacher, eventually director of secondary school there, also spent some time in S. America; died 1998

Lewiansky, a communist, member of FDJ, interned from May 1940–Dec. 1941; Capt. in PC; later in Legal Research Branch

Lewin 1, served in 74 Coy PC; joined from Richborough Camp and was with BEF in France 1940

Lewin 2, served in 74 Coy PC; joined from Richborough Camp and was with BEF in France 1940

Lewin, 13804344, later Lewis, Martin David, 13805077; born Tempelburg, Pomerania, 2 Jan. 1922, later Berlin, held at Sachsenhausen 1938, family murdered by Nazis, by *Kindertransport* to England Feb 1939; interned Isle of Man 1940; enlisted Dec. 1940; served in 248 Coy PC; participated in 61b & 62nd parachute training course; in 21 Indep. Para. Coy (Pathfinders), North Africa, Italy, lastly Arnhem, where he received severe chest wound; parachuted into Norway to support resistance 1945; refused to go to Palestine

Lewin, J., served in 74 Coy PC; joined from Richborough Camp and was with BEF in France 1940

Lewin, Siegfried, 13800645, later Louis, Frederick Mac, 13118618 and 6305458, Pte in 87 Coy PC; then 3/10 Cdo

Lewin-Goldschmidt, von, Konrad L., 13805610; born 5 Aug. 1917, 1943 changed name to (Hubert) Brian Groves after a friend, but family objected, changed name again to Grant, had studied at Trinity College Cambridge; interned 1940; served in PC; later 3/10 Cdo; had one foot blown off at Cassino 29 Dec. 1944 when with 9 Cdo (2 Cdo Bde) at Garigliano river; post-war: QC, county court judge, then Circuit Judge for Sussex and Kent, expert in family law, known for his work with the National Marriage Guidance Council

Lewine, Frank, served in PC in North Africa

Lewinsky, Max, 13807180, later Laddy, Max; born Vienna 19 Aug. 1911, grandson of actor Josef L., said to have been outstanding step-dancer; joined PC late 1941, medical orderly in 251 Coy PC; and again in 3/10 Cdo; killed in action on beach at Normandy landing 10 June 1944

Lewinsohn 1, served in 74 Coy PC; joined from Richborough Camp and was with BEF in France 1940

Lewinsohn 2, served in 74 Coy PC; joined from Richborough Camp and was with BEF in France 1940

Lewis, served in 3/10 Cdo

Lewis, Walter, L/Cpl in 248 & 69 Coy PC

Lewkonja, CQMS in 88 Coy PC

Lewy, Albert

Lewy-Lingen, Walter, 13803244, later Langdon, Louis, 14623912; born 1920, son of Richard L-L., judge of the German Supreme Court, studied chemistry at Balliol College Oxford; Sgt in 93 Coy PC, participated in 61b & 62nd parachute training course; joined 21 Indep. Para. Coy (Pathfinders), in North Africa, Italy, lastly Arnhem; killed in action there whilst attacking enemy armour with a PIAT 20 Sept. 1944, awarded Posthumous Certificate of Gallantry

Leyens, M.; post-war: prominent in Ex-Service NB Association

Leyser, served in PC; later Capt. in Black Watch, in action in Holland, along the Rhine; post-war: Fellow, Oxford University

Leyser, Herbert, member of Young Austria; enlisted from Birmingham Dec. 1943/Jan. 1944

Libowski, served in 74 Coy PC; joined from Richborough Camp and was with BEF in France 1940

Librowski, served in 74 Coy PC; joined from Richborough Camp and was with BEF in France 1940

Lichte, served as Flt Lt in RAF

Liebel (also Libell), H. Peter, 13803145 and 6387024, later Leigh-Bell, Peter, Austrian (?), served in 220 Coy PC, RAC, 3/10 Cdo (It has been suggested that this is yet another guise of Bergmann, alias Hillman, alias Kennedy, alias Gerber, alias Hofer (q.v.); however, PC records confirm that on 11 Nov. 1942 Liebel's papers were then in the possession of the War Office and Envers mentions him as member of 3/10 Cdo, all of which makes it rather unlikely that the above suggestion is true; it does not, however, exclude the possibility that Bergmann used Libell or Leigh-Bell as additional pseudonyms.)

Lieben, Herbert, later Lytton, Nicholas; born Vienna 1922, pupil at school Schotten Gymnasium; served in Scottish regiment as Capt.; ran around Vienna after the war sporting the kilt

Lieber, Erwin, from Berlin, served in 74 Coy PC; joined from Richborough Camp and was with BEF in France 1940; Sgt, is said to have been most punctilious in the performance of his duties; in France again 1944, distinguished himself whilst clearing enemy mines at Dieppe

Liebermann, served in 74 Coy PC; joined from Richborough Camp and was with BEF in France 1940

Liebmann, H., served in 6 Australian Empl Coy at Albury, loading war materials from Victoria to NSW railway, said to have been orderly room clerk

Lifschitz, T., 775995, Austrian, emigrated to Palestine, where he joined the RAF; Cpl in charge of equipment

Liftschitz, later Lee, Lt in 608 Coy PC, Tobruk, Greece

Lilienfeld, H., later Loder; died on active service

Lindenbaum, Egon, later Priestley, Peter, also Stockner, Michael, served in PC; later in RF (SOE), in Operation SEATHRIFT in Northern Italy, parachuted directly into enemy camp 12 Oct. 1944, captured, sentenced to death by Italians and spent some months in death cell of Trieste prison, liberated by Allied troops on 12 Apr. 1945; Maj. in BAOR War Crimes Group

Lindenberg, Walter, name appears in German Unity Party's list of members who served in Allied armies

Lindner, Paul, name appears in German Unity Party's list of members who served in Allied armies

Linford, Austrian, studied at Oxford, served in PC; in Algeria, there transferred to RAC, commissioned, intelligence officer of armoured brigade; then second secretary to Control Commission for Austria, responsible for liaison with other Allies; Maj.

Lintern, R., 13800220, Sgt in PC, served in northwestern Europe, mentioned in dispatches

Linz, winner of sprint event at 93 Coy PC sports event

Lion, Ernest

Lippmann, served in 74 Coy PC; joined from Richborough Camp and was with BEF in France 1940

Lister, served in PC; then monitoring unit, 21 Army Gp as from Apr. 1944, in spearhead of invasion force in Normandy, Bayeux

Littwack, served in 74 Coy PC; joined from Richborough Camp and was with BEF in France 1940

Littwitz, W., Sgt in 69 Coy PC, one of first six alien sergeants; 22 Jan. 1940, CQMS when 69 Coy embarked for France

Litvak, Eugen, later Dale, Leslie, served in 249 Coy PC; later in 3/10 Cdo

Litvinoff, E., in 69 Coy 24 Oct. 1942; 16 Feb. 1943 accompanied 17 ORs from 137 Coy, commanded Hawes detachment of 69 Coy; on 31 May 1945 Lt on officers' list of 363 Coy PC

Litwornik, Wolfgang, member of Young Austria; enlisted from Glasgow Dec. 1943/Jan. 1944

Lizza, P., 13806131, Pte in 253 Coy PC; later in SOE

Lloyd, F.K., co-founder of Marlborough Fine Arts, art dealers

Lobbenberg, G.; died on active service

Lobel, M., later Laughton, Austrian, served in 220 Coy PC; died by drowning in boating accident on River Avon near Tewkesbury 11 Aug. 1943

Lobl, Irma, joined British forces at behest of FDJ or other communist party organisation; post-war: to Germany

Locker, Fritz, member of Young Austria; enlisted from Guildford before 15 Jan. 1944

Loeb, 2/Lt, on officers' list of 137 Coy PC 31 Dec. 1943

Loebl, J., later Arieli, Jehoshua; born Karlsbad, Bohemia,1916, went to Palestine 1931, agricultural worker on Kibbutz, took part in officers' training for Jewish Army (Dochnut); joined PC 1939, Sgt in 608 Coy PC, in Tobruk, Greece, taken prisoner by Germans at Kalamata; sent to Stalag 8b, Upper Silesia, Forestry work, organised strike, sentenced to death, but status as British Palestinian saved his life; transferred to punishment camp in Eastern Poland; then NCO camp, liberated by Soviets; post-war: officer in Haganah, University don in Israel, author (philosophy, history)

Loeser, served in 74 Coy PC; joined from Richborough Camp and was with BEF in France 1940

Loevy, Ernst, later Lennard, Ernest G.; born Breslau 24 July 1918, in Berlin 1922–37, pupil at Reform RG Zehlendorf, to London 1 Apr. 1937, attended Pitmans College; enlisted Dec. 1939; served in 77 Coy PC; transferred RAC, Inns of Court Regt 1942; OCTU at RMA Sandhurst, commissioned 1944; same year in Holland; in 'Phantom' radio operations; in spearhead into Denmark at Niebull and Tondern; Regimental IO in Hamburg; movement control at Rendsburg canal bridge; war crimes tribunals; demob as Capt. Apr. 1946

Loevy, Hans, later Lennard, John Howard; born Oderberg, Berlin, 2 Aug. 1919, brother of Ernst (above), in Berlin 1922– 37, pupil at Reform RG Zehlendorf, to London 1 Apr. 1937, attended Pitmans College; enlisted Dec. 1939; served in 77 Coy PC, acted in that company's Xmas panto *A Midsummer Night's Scream*, probably 1941; transferred RAC, Inns of Court Regt 1942; OCTU at RMA Sandhurst, commissioned 1944; same year in Holland; in 'Phantom' radio operations; in spearhead into Denmark at Niebull and Tondern; Regimental IO in Hamburg; movement control at Rendsburg canal bridge. war crimes tribunals; demob as Lt Nov. 1946

Loewie, Margot, married Smith, served in 1 Allied Volunteer Platoon ATS

Loevy, H., L/Cpl in 77 Coy PC

Loewenberg, Dr Alfred; born 1902; musical expert, worked on *Grove's Dictionary* and other academic works after emigration to UK and whilst serving in 219 Coy PC; author *Annals of Opera* 1943; died 1950

Loewenstein, served in 338 Coy PC in North Africa

Loewenstein, served in 74 Coy PC; joined from Richborough Camp and was with BEF in France 1940

Loewenstein, Irmgard (Irma), (Little Loew), served in 1 Allied Volunteer Platoon ATS, cook in sergeants mess, Huyton; committed suicide after the war, when she discovered that her boyfriend, who had remained in Germany, had married another

Loewenstein, Lotte (Pip), married Bray; born Halle 13 Nov. 1921, came to England Jan. 1939, lived with English family and helped in café; enlisted Apr. 1941; L/Cpl in 1 and 4 Allied Volunteer Platoons, 1 Coy ATS, cook,

PT instructress; married Sgt G. Bray, Ox. & Bucks. LI 44; demob June 1945

Loewenstein, Max-Otto Ludwig, from Stuttgart, later Lynton, Mark, father was director-general of Horch motor car company, pupil at Franzoesisches Gymnasium, Berlin, Lycee Pasteur, Neuilly, lastly Cheltenham, studied law at Cambridge from 1938; interned 1940, Huyton and Isle of Man to Canada by *Ettrick*, return to UK; enlisted 1941; served in 251 Coy PC; transferred RAC; commissioned at Sandhurst 1944, to 3 RTR, at Normandy, Battle of the Bulge, Antwerp, Ardennes, Rhine crossing at Wesel, Aller, Elbe; chief of political department Schleswig-Holstein at Eutin; post-war: CEO of major company in New York, author of *A Cambridge Internee's Memoir of World War II* and *Accidental Journey* (Overlook Press, Woodstock, NY)

Loewenstein, O.J., later Kingsley, Roger James; born Stuttgart, 22 Feb. 1922, to UK 1936, pupil at Manchester Grammar School; although father had important job in war industry, was interned 1940; served in 229 and 69 Coy PC; transferred 3/10 Cdo 1943; commissioned 1945, attached to 45 Cdo, mentioned in dispatches; later in civilian internment camp, responsible for re-education; Capt.; post-war: assisted Bentwich with research for *I Understand the Risks*, studied technology at Manchester University, worked for petro-chemical company there and taught at the Manchester University Technical Institute, President of the Institute of Chemical Engineering, has made a significant contribution to the furtherance of technical education in Britain, OBE

Loewenthal, A., served in ATS; died on active service

Loewenthal, M., served in 77 Coy PC, acted in that company's Xmas panto *A Midsummer Night's Scream*, probably 1941

Loewit, Hans, later Lowit, Ian; born Vienna 6 Aug. 1919; enlisted 28 May 1942; served in 77 Coy PC; transferred to 247 Bty 62 A/Tk Regt RA (under command 1st Corps), guns were self-propelled, but slow; served in Normandy, at Falaise, Belgium in infantry role; along Maas river as A/Tk, on Tholen island in Maas delta; post-war: psychiatrist

Loewy, served in 74 Coy PC; joined from Richborough and was with BEF in France 1940

Loewy, Alfred Thomas, later Lane, Alfred Thomas; born Vienna 31 Mar. 1912, to UK July 1939; interned 1940, to Canada, there for 2 years; served in 220 Coy PC, forestry work; transferred RAOC, statistical section, worked on statistics for war cabinet; demob July 1946; post-war: ACMA

Loewy, Max, name appears in German Unity Party's list of Sudeten Germans who served in British Army

Loewy, also Levy, Lowy or Lowry, Moritz, 13801850, 550134 and 13810000, later Latimer, Maurice, 13118701 and 6436346, Czechoslovak citizen; born 13 Sept. 1921, in International Brigade in Spanish Civil War; served in 3/10 Cdo, at Dieppe 19 Aug. 1942 (one of two known survivors); Normandy (with 41 RM Cdo), wounded on D-Day, evacuated to UK; took leading part in capitulation of enemy on Walcheren, Nov. 1944; on list of Social Democrat Sudeten Germans who served in British forces

Lok-Lindblad, P., 13806035, Pte in 253 Coy PC; later commissioned in SOE

Lomnitzer, served in 74 Coy PC; joined from Richborough Camp and was with

BEF in France 1940

Long, served in 137 Coy PC

Long, served in 3/10 Cdo

Long, M.H.; post-war: prominent in Ex-Service NB Association

Longley, Max, served in 87 Coy PC

Loning, Fred Edward

Loose, Dr Charlotte

Lowy, Arthur F., served in 3/10 Cdo

Lowy, Otto, from Prague, served in RAF

Lubak G., member of Young Austria before enlisting

Luchtenstein, later Ludlow, served in 249 Coy PC; later in 3/10 Cdo

Lundin, Bengt, served in 137 Coy PC

Lustig, Eric

Lustig, F.; born Berlin 1919, pupil at staatl. Prinz Heinrich Gymnasium, Berlin-Schoeneberg, 1937–38 apprentice dental technician, emigrated 1939; interned 1940, Isle of Man; served in entertainment section at Ilfracombe and Southern Command Continental Orchestra; Sgt in CSDIC UK (Bucks.); then WO 1 in CSDIC (WEA), Bad Nenndorf; later in career became a chartered secretary, and as such had several different jobs before retirement in 1984

Lustig, Franziska, W/118218, married Waldek, Frances, from Vienna, dressmaker's apprentice, to England Dec. 1938 by *Kindertransport*; served in ATS, attached to 583 Coy RASC

Lustig, Lisl, married Lustig, from Vienna, sister of Franziska Waldek, to England Dec. 1938 by *Kindertransport*; served in ATS, attached to 583 Coy RASC

Lustig, J., L/Cpl in 77 Coy PC, acted in that company's Xmas panto *A Midsummer Night's Scream*, 1941

Luzia, served in 74 Coy PC; joined from Richborough Camp and was with BEF in France 1940

Lynder, Frank, got to UK from Germany just before the war; served in PC; from 1942 in Sefton Delmer's clandestine broadcasting unit; then NI17z (Naval Intelligence), broadcast to German U-boats by 'Kurzwellensender Atlantik'; post-war: returned to Germany, senior executive in Springer Verlag, married relative of Axel Springer; died 1984

Lzicar, Karl, this name is certainly incorrect, as there is no language in all of old Austria-Hungary, to which it could conceivably appertain; nevertheless, the relevant entry refers to a real person, an Austrian, who had been conscripted into the German Army and was taken prisoner; he was accepted into British service; in SOE, used as aliases Wallner, Franz Karl, and Fischer, Karl, was in Operation EBENSBURG near Bad Aussee; June 1945 in No. 6 Special Force Staff Section in Austria

Maas, Willy, served in NSW Empl Coy AMF; then attached to American Intelligence in New Guinea for some 2 years; later in Bougainville

MacKay, Charles S.

Mader, Gerszon; died on active service

Magyar, A., 13807977 and 13119537, Sgt in PC

Mahler, K., Austrian

Maimann, Martin, member of Young Austria; enlisted from London Dec.1943/Jan. 1944

Malik, M. (Mrs.), served in 1 Allied Volunteer Platoon ATS

Mamerow, E., Austrian, served in 337 or 338 Coy PC in North Africa

Mandel, O., Austrian, served as sapper/electrician in HQ Mov 81 Tn. MEF

Maneles, Henry, served in 248 & 69 Coy PC

Manhardt, Rudolf, alias Minter, Robert, alias Naumann, Alexander, alias Mrnka, Wenzel, Austrian, German conscript, PoW; taken into British service; SOE, in Operation DUCIMER near Klagenfurt; June 1945 in Austria

Manierka, Peter, from Leipzig, Polish national who spoke no Polish; born 1923, left Germany 1934; joined RAF 1942, fighter pilot on Typhoons; after end of hostilities briefly with Polish air force, but returned to RAF because of communication difficulties

Manierka, Sascha, from Leipzig, Polish national who spoke no Polish; born 1 Oct. 1920, left Germany 1934, brother of above, furrier's apprentice, to UK 23 Sept. 1932; joined RAF 1942; served in 2/42 RAF Tng Comd, crashed with Tiger Moth, therefore relegated from pilot training; became bomb aimer; in Aug. 1943 to 428 Sqn RCAF, 11 ops in Halifaxes, including raid on Mannheim 23 Sept. 1943; in Feb. 1944 to 405 Sqn RCAF, 45 ops as Pathfinder, generally as 'Blind Marker', including 10 daylight ops, suffered 2 belly landings; from Jan. 1945 in British Bombing Survey Unit, Paris; in Belsen day following liberation; last RAF job as technical translator with rank of WO, Bad Nenndorf, awarded DFM

Mannheimer, served in 74 Coy PC; joined from Richborough Camp and was with BEF in France 1940

Manning, George

Mar, Norma del (Nella?), Italian, served in 1 Allied Volunteer Platoon ATS

Marcus, served in 74 Coy PC; joined from Richborough Camp and was with BEF in France 1940

Marcus, Paul E., journalist, wrote as PEM; post-war: prominent in Ex-Service NB Association

Margitai, Peter, member of Young Austria; enlisted from Guildford Dec. 1943/Jan. 1944

Margulies, Fred, PAL 6194, Austrian, served as instrument maker, unit and service unknown, but probably RAF

Marischka, F. (nicknamed Zwetschi), son of well-known Viennese actor Hubert Marischka, served in 77 & 246 Coy PC, was one of Austrian ski instructors in Scotland, In 77 Coy's Xmas panto *A Midsummer Night's Scream*, probably 1941

Markovicz, Helen, 2992596, Austrian, emigrated to Palestine; became Sgt in WAAF, worked in education

Markstein, later Marshall, Paul, name in officers' list of 248 Coy PC as 2/Lt 31 Dec. 1942; 28 Jan. 1943 posted to 69 Coy PC

Marlow, Leo

Marmorek, R.S., Austrian, at the beginning of the war had studied technology at Cambridge; interned May 1940, sent to Canada, after return was asked to work as a civil engineer on important war work; in 1944 his job was incorporated into the army, as a result of which he was given an immediate commission in REME, responsible for waterproofing canvas covers of the lorries used in Normandy landings; later posted to Iraq; finished his service as deputy commander of the central repair shop at Benghazi, Cyrenaica

Marmorek, Walter H., a graduate of Vienna Technological University and architect, was at Richborough, where he was responsible for its conversion to refugee camp; served in the TR; then Cpl, later CQMS in 74 Coy PC; transferred to RE, commissioned; for a time in Psychological Warfare Unit; at end of war, as Maj. in Vienna, responsible for repairs to the palace of Schoenbrunn and British embassy; post-war: FRIBA, prominent in Ex-Service NB Association, senior partner W.H. Marmorek Culpin Partnership, Richmond

Marschkowski, served in 74 Coy PC; joined from Richborough Camp and was with BEF in France 1940

Marshall, P.

Martin, Ernest

Martin, F.,13806116, Pte in 253 Coy PC; later SOE

Martin, M., served in PC; 1945 S/Sgt in No.10 Amplifier Unit, 21 Army Gp; later in Information Control

Martin, Ray, composer and conductor, formed own band in 74 Coy PC; Cpl; post-war: Hollywood producer

Martin, W., 13053609, served in RWK; to 3/10 Cdo in Italy

Marx, served in 77 Coy PC, acted in that company's Xmas panto *A Midsummer Night's Scream*, probably 1941

Marx, F., 13301329, Austrian, Pte in 699 VAW, REME, CMF

Marx, U.F., on officers' list of 74 Coy PC as Lt 31 Dec. 1943

Mastbaum, A.D., 13810022, later Dunn, D., 6387046, served in PC, possibly also SOE

Masting, Dieter; killed in action, Normandy 1944

Masur, Pit, served in 1 Allied Volunteer Platoon ATS, commissioned in ATS

Matros, Max A.F., 220767, commissioned 23 Dec. 1941; Lt in 69 Coy PC 3 Dec. 1942–24 Apr. 1943; then posted to 6 PCTC

Mautner, H., 13801177 and 13041765, served in PC and RAC

Mautner, Karl, P 77426, Austrian, emigrated to Palestine; joined RAF, served as Cpl in accounts

Mautner, M., later Mortimer, Austrian; born 1921; served in 87 Coy PC

Maxton, Charles Henry

Maxwell, Peter; born Vienna 1922, pupil at Elisabeth Gymnasium; served in PC; later as Capt. adjutant of 20 Bat. Baluch Regt, Indian Army, served at Razmak, Waziristan, and took part in operation for the protection of Indian Prime Minister Jawaharlal Nehru 1946

Mayer; post-war: prominent in Ex-Service NB Association in Birmingham

Mayer, H. (Eden says Mayr, Hubert); died in action

Mayer, Paul Yogi, temporarily Frank, Michael; born Frankfurt, 8 Sept. 1912, but lived in Bad Kreuznach, teacher, leader of 'Schwarzes Faehnlein' 1934, silenced by Gestapo, at school in Wiesbaden, later Berlin University, to UK with wife and child 1939; enlisted Jan. 1940; served in 88 Coy PC (No. 9 Sect.); then SOE (RF), training organiser, should have been used in action against Rhine bridges, but action cancelled after Remagen; refused to serve in Germany, but lectured for Control Commission; post-war: youth worker with Jewish organisations, area youth officer ILEA, awarded MBE 1997, honorary Dr Potsdam University, publication: *Jewish Olympic Champions*

Mayer, Peter, served in SOE or Intelligence

Mayr, Hubert, alias Banks, alias Georgeau, Jean, alias Rimmel, Josef, served in SOE, in Operation BAKERSFIELD near Innsbruck; June 1945 in Austria on long-term posting

Meisel, Lucian, from Vienna, served in RAF

Meisels, Max, later Maxwell, Martin, Austrian, Sgt in Para. Regt; then glider pilot, Army Air Corps, wounded and posted as missing 20 Oct. 1944; PoW at Stalag 11, Fallingbostel

Meller, Erich, PAL/45758; born Vienna, 24 Feb. 1923, emigrated to Palestine, studied agriculture in Beer Tovia; enlisted Sarafand 17 Feb. 1943.; served in PC (Palestine); from 31 Mar. 1943 railwayman with RE; demob 21 Sept. 1946

Mellinger, Lucas

Melson, served in 137 Coy PC

Melzer, Kurt, member of Young Austria; enlisted from London between 15 Jan. 1944 and 25 Mar. 1944

Menasse, Kurt, temporarily Marshall, Ken; born Vienna 8 Feb. 1923, pupil at Vienna Gymnasium, to England Dec 1938, by *Kindertransport*, various jobs in London and Leeds, member Young Austria; enlisted Nov 1943; served in KOYLI, 1 and 2 Bn West Yorks. Inf., to Burma June 1944; in 1Bn WYI at Irrawady, Meiktila, Peen, Rangoon, then Moulmein, back to England; then with 2 Bn in Naples; lastly in British Forces Austria, interpreter; demob Oct. 1947

Mendelsohn, Heinz, 13805573, later Melford, John, 14623408; born Berlin, 13 Sept. 1922; served in 251 Coy PC; on 61b & 62nd parachute training course; to Para. Regt, 21 Indep. Para. Coy, served in North Africa, Italy and Holland, wounded by bullet through both cheeks; to OCTU 1945; commissioned in R. Sussex, with 2nd Bat. in Yugoslavia; then instructor BAOR college; demob 1946

Mendelsohn, Jacques, later Mendleson, John (Jack); born Berlin, communist, to England Aug. 1939; Capt. in Army Ed. Corps; post-war: Labour MP for Peniston

Mendelssohn, Peter de, US press officer in Germany; changed to British service, in British HQ Berlin, press control, stopped attempt by *Die Welt* to take over *NRZ* newspaper at Essen; married Hilde Spiel, feminist authoress

Mengen, Friedl, married Tauber (?), served in one of the Allied Volunteer Platoons ATS

Menne, Bernhard, served in British Army; first editor-in-chief of *Die Welt* newspaper

Mercer, F.S.

Merfield, J.P.

Merlaender, Heinz Ludwig, later Morland, Henry L., 17000031; born Hannover 28 May 1922, emigrated UK 1938; from 1941 in 220 & 339 Coy PC; from 1944 in Intelligence, WO II in Control Commission, Germany; discharge 1948; post-war: worked as personnel manager, after which he established himself as independent retailer of leather goods

Mertz, 13807470, later MacManus, John, 14623944, joined PC spring 1942; then 21 Indep. Para. Coy; on 61b & 62nd parachute training course; served in North Africa, Italy, Arnhem, Norway, Palestine

Merzbach, A.H., Lt in 74 Coy PC from before 1 Sept. to 26 Nov. 1942; then posted to 292 Coy PC

Mesner, Emil, 13800192, Cpl in 69 Coy PC; killed in action during air attack on London 29 Dec. 1940

Mesznik, served in 74 Coy PC; joined from Richborough Camp and was with BEF in France 1940

Metzer, Walter, Austrian, served on HMS *Mosquito* at Alexandria

Metzger, served in 74 Coy PC; joined from Richborough Camp and was with BEF in France 1940

Meyer, served in 74 Coy PC; joined from Richborough Camp and was with BEF in France 1940

Meyer, later Miles, Kenneth L., 13041863, served in PC; later Intelligence; in Berlin 1945 with Publicity and Psychological Warfare, 21 Army Gp, one of the first British soldiers in Berlin

Meyer, an ATS member at British Austrian Legal Unit; married Maj. Norville

Meyer, A., later Melville; died on active service

Meyer, H.P., 13810007, later Melvin, P.H., 5550137, Pte in PC; later RHamps

Meyer, H.U., 13810018, later Knight, K.W., 6305490, Pte in the Buffs; returned to original unit (most probably PC) autumn 1944

Meyer, Dr M. from Berlin; post-war: prominent in Ex-Service NB Association

Meyer, F.L., later Edwards, Fred H.; born Duesseldorf 1922, pupil at Comenius Gymnasium, later at Weymouth College; Sgt in 229 Coy PC; posted to 93 Coy when 229 was turned into purely Austrian unit, stressed German nationality, with 93 at Arromanches, Bayeux, then Dieppe and Brussels; interpreter with 30 Corps in Reichswald and at Bremen; attached to US Army Bremerhaven to help with DP problems, then interpreter at military court, Oldenburg; one of the first British soldiers in Berlin with Publicity and Psychological Warfare; then court interpreter at Oldenburg; post-war: active in British Legion

Meyer, Franz (Mayer?) Viennese, master painter and decorator, extremely small in stature, though recruited in Palestine, where he had gone in 1934, was not a believing Jew; Cpl in 608 Coy PC, North Africa and Greece, captured by Germans at Kalamata 1941, PoW in Stalag 9, as tradesman highly valued by German camp command

Meyer, Kurt, 13801092, later Moody, Peter; born Berlin 28 Sept. 1918, son of Dr F.M. Meyer, psychiatrist, middle distance runner with Makkabi Sports Club, to UK 1939; joined 77 Coy PC Jan. 1940, L/Cpl; then RHamps.; then

3/10 Cdo, tore muscle in parachute jump; with 4 Cdo Bde HQ on D-Day, tasked to direct fire of British battleships on selected targets, went forward with wireless operator to immediate vicinity of targets; killed in action (artillery fire) 13 June 1944; doctor at Birmingham Hospital, who treated him when wounded, wrote: 'I have never met a better soldier'

Meyer, Nathan; born 1903; joined 69 Coy PC from Richborough Camp 1 Dec. 1939, with 69 in France 1940; demob Oct. 1945

Meyer, P., B.Sc., Sgt in RF 1944–48; served in Egypt, Iraq, Iran, Greece; 1947–48 with British Military Mission Greece to introduce British wireless systems in Greek Army

Meyer, Peter, alias Morton, Peter John, 13053592, German; born 1920 or 1921; enlisted from Surrey; Sgt in PC; later on IC Extra Regimental list; killed in action Western Europe 10 Mar. 1945, posthumous King's Commendation for Brave Conduct

Meyerstein, later Marston, Eric, served with Irish Fusiliers, wounded at Caen 1944

Meysels, Lucian, 769526; born Laxenburg, Lower Austria, 14 May 1925, at school in Vienna, to Palestine 1938, attended St George's School Jerusalem, external BA London 1944; LAC/meteorologist at RAF HQ Levant, RAF Stations Amman, Heliopolis, No. 2 ME Met unit Wadi Halfa, RAF Station Lydda; post-war: MA London 1946, Wisconsin 1958, Ph.D. Vienna 1960, titular professor 1978, editor Pal, later Israeli Broadcasting Service, *Jerusalem Post*, in Information Department Jerusalem University, 1959–91 foreign policy editor Wochenpresse Vienna

Michaelis, George J.; born 4 May 1894; served in 69 Coy PC; post-war: Partner, Merton Insurance Brokers, Ltd

Michel, Leopold; born Niedaltdorf, Saar, 1908, moved to Weilheim, Bavaria, at age 1, member 'Jungbayern', until turfed out on account of being a Jew, pupil at Weilheim schools 1914–25, in protective custody 1933, emigrated to Egypt 1933, Palestine 1935, to UK 1938; L/Cpl in 249 Coy PC 1940; skiing instructor 52 Scots Lowland Div. 1942–44, Sgt 1943; with US division in Norway 1945 to document PoWs; post-war: director L. Kahn Mfg Co. & Caressa, London

Michelson, Paul Louis (in nominal roll of 74 Coy: Mickelsohn), served in 74 Coy PC; joined from Richborough Camp and was with BEF in France 1940; 2/Lt Michelson as per *London Gazette* 13 Feb. 1942.

Michelson 2 (in nominal roll of 74 Coy: Mickelsohn), served in 74 Coy PC; joined from Richborough Camp and was with BEF in France 1940; presumed to be relative of Lt Michelson above and carrying the same name

Mickel, served in 74 Coy PC; joined from Richborough Camp and was with BEF in France 1940

Midgley, Peter, served in PC; later with Control Commission

Miedzwinski, served in 74 Coy; joined at Richborough winter 1939/40 and was with BEF in France 1940 still in 74 Coy 1 May 1943

Milch, H., later Melvin; died on active service

Milch, I.S., as 2/Lt on officers' list of 249 Coy PC 31 Dec. 1942

Miller, F.K., served in 69 Coy PC

Mindel, David, served in 219 Coy PC

Mines, J., 14727794, Pte in RWK; joined 3/10 Cdo in Italy

Minuer, Mrs. H.

Miron, L.

Mirsky, Samuel, served in 74 Coy PC; joined from Richborough Camp and was with BEF in France 1940; died while on leave 13 Oct. 1941

Mizner, Susan, Czechoslovak citizen, served in 508 Coy, ATS

Mizzi, L.,13807928

Moldovan, T., 13807931

Molinari, A., 13807891

Monahan, served in 3/10 Cdo

Mondschein, F., served in 74 Coy PC; joined from Richborough Camp and was with BEF in France 1940

Montagni, served with French Foreign Legion; later in 246 Coy PC

Montgomery, M. A., served in 74 Coy PC; joined from Richborough Camp and was with BEF in France 1940; post-war: prominent in Ex-Service NB Association

Morgenstern, Henri A., was in French Foreign Legion; served in 362 & 678 GPWW Coy PC in North Africa 1943, examining PoWs in Tunisia, including General Thoma; post-war: translator in French element of Allied Command in Berlin 1951

Morley, Peter

Morley, Thomas

Mosbacher, Erich, Lt Col, in newspaper control of British zone of Germany

Mosenthal, Heinrich, later Mortimer, Henry; born Brussels 27 Feb. 1914, from Rheine, not permitted to study medicine by the Nazis, so went to UK 1933, had variety of jobs; interned Isle of Man 1940; enlisted 24 Oct. 1940; posted to 248 Coy PC, with them in Catterick, Darlington, promoted to Cpl; 1943 to 69 Coy PC; transferred RAC 9 Feb. 1944; posted to 1 RTR as tank and tank transporter driver, in Nijmegen corridor during Battle of Arnhem, in Brussels during German air attack 1 Jan. 1945, in action in Belgium, Holland, Reichswald, Rhine crossing at Wesel, and against SS at Jahrlingen, on Luneburg Heath at war's end; transferred 2nd Fyfe and Forfars, near Itzehoe; then court interpreter and administrator at Rendsburg; demob 16 Jan. 1946; post-war: sales management in glove and hosiery trade

Moser, C.A., served as instrument technician in RAF; interpreter Bomber Command; then Bombing Research Unit in W. Germany, whilst there used as interpreter for conversations between the Command and German industrial directors in the occupied areas, which had as their objective the assessment of effect of allied raids on industrial targets; post-war: Sir Claus Moser, KCB, CBE, FBA, created Lord Moser of Regents Park 2001, professor at LSE, chief statistician to the government, chairman of Covent Garden Opera, Warden of Wadham College Oxford

Moser, Helmut Ernst, 13801121, later Morton, Henry Ernest, 13046609, a Berliner, came to England after his brother Gerhard had emigrated to Moscow, where he was 'liquidated' under the Stalin regime, later, their mother was murdered at Auschwitz; enlisted 26 Jan. 1940 at Richborough;

posted to 77 Coy PC; transferred to RA 1943; posted to 81 Anti Tank Regt, in action at Anzio and Gothic Line as radio operator, took part in liberation of Rome and Florence; after end of hostilities refused posting to SS PoW camp; post-war: married 1957, became Quaker, trustee for 'Asylum Aid' (protection for asylum seekers in UK)

Moses, Erich, later Morris, Eric; died on active service

Moses, G., 13810004, alias Moss, Gerhard, Pte in RHamps, on German Unity Party's list of comrades who served in Allied Armies

Moses, M., 16001227, later Maynard, M.; born Alsfeld, Hesse, 4 Sept. 1922, pupil at Samson Raphael Hirsch school Frankfurt until 1938, then apprentice motor mechanic at Gambach, Hesse, in custody at Buchenwald Nov. 1938, after emigration again apprentice at Zipp Fastener Co. London, N18; interned 1940; enlisted Dec. 1940; served in PC; transferred to RAOC; later REME as gunwright, instrument mechanic and armaments technician; course at Military College of Science, as S/Sgt i/c several armaments workshops, including Dover during cross Channel artillery bombardment; in charge 30 Corps workshop in Holland and Germany 1945; then responsible for parts procurement for military vehicles from German industry, Hannover; awarded Certificate for Special Services by general officer commanding BAOR; demob 1947

Moss, Gerhard, name appears on German Unity Party's list of members who served in Allied armies

Mosse, Werner E., Capt.

Moszkowicz, S.

Muehlbauer, K., Sgt in 69 Coy PC, one of the first six enemy aliens to be promoted to Sgt

Mullard-Rodney, H.A.; born 1895; joined 88 Coy PC from Kitchener Camp; later in 251 and 229 Coy PC; demob 20 Aug. 1945; post-war: hotel owner Deal and Bournemouth, also part owner of Hotel Vienna, Maida Vale

Muller, Salomon, from Berlin, grew up in Jewish orphanage, to UK by *Kindertransport*; enlisted Feb. 1945; RCMP in India, Japan, Hong Kong, erroneously reported missing believed dead, in Japan; Sgt; post-war: regular service in RAF police, Germany, Cyprus, N. Ireland, awarded BEM 1962, with British Telecom, Littlewoods

Mueller, a clockmaker from the Black Forest, served in 74 Coy PC

Mueller, as Lt on officers' list of 93 Coy PC 31 Dec. 1943

Mueller, served as CQMS in 74 Coy PC; joined from Richborough Camp and was with BEF in France 1940

Mueller, Hans, 13116145, later Miles, John H.; born Berlin 5 Apr. 1907, emigrated to England; joined Richborough 26 Feb. 1940

Mueller, Johann, alias Malle, Johann, alias Morris, John, from Klagenfurt, German conscript, PoW; taken into British service; SOE, in Operation DUCIMER near Klagenfurt; June 1945 in Austria, was expected to remain there

Mueller, Sol, from Berlin, grew up in orphanage, to UK with Lothar Baruch (above)

Mueller-Schoen; died on active service

Muus, F.B., 13806063, Pte in 253 Coy PC; later commissioned in SOE

Muvrin, M. or N., 13807899

Nagel, P., seconded from PC to Airborne and took part in Bruneval raid, was in Section Hardy in Whitley aircraft under command of Lt Vernon, during that operation known as Pte Newman; said to have also taken part in raid on St Nazaire and been taken prisoner there; post-war: said to have become successful businessman

Nagel, P., 13801753, later Walker, Peter, 4272711, No. 2 Cdo and SOE; died on active service. (It may well be that there was only one Peter Nagel, that he called himself Newman on the Bruneval raid and changed his name to Walker later; however, Nagel/Newman is said to have survived the war, whilst Nagel/Walker did not; both versions seem well founded and, as both cannot be true of one person, it seems there were two men bearing the same name, as Nagel is neither a frequent, nor extremely rare, name.)

Nagler, Johann; born Czernowitz 25 Nov. 1902, Austrian; served in French Army 12 Feb. 1940–25 Feb. 1942, CAT Algier; in British Army 16 Dec. 1942–14 May 1946

Nagler, Kurt, later Norville, Michael, Austrian lawyer, served in 249 Coy PC; then RAC; later military government Luebeck, in same security section as Envers at Poeppendorf; then BALU Vienna; post-war: to Canada. Austrian honorary consul at Vancouver

Naidenhoff (also Naidenoff or Maidenoff), T., 13807930 and 13047930

Naphtalie, Manfred, 14457303, later Naftalie, Fred, served in 3 Bn C Coy Jewish Bde, Middlesex Regt; S/Sgt; after end of hostilities interpreter in Germany

Napier, Walter M.

Naschitz, later Nash, H., teacher from Vienna, Sgt in No. 4 Sect., 229 Coy PC; post-war: prominent in Ex-Service NB Association

Nathan, served in 74 Coy PC; joined from Richborough Camp and was with BEF in France 1940

Nathan, Erich, 13805632, later Howarth, Eric William; born Ulm 16 Oct. 1922, studied at London poly and King's College Cambridge; interned 1940, to Canada, returned 1941; served in 88 Coy PC; then 3/10 Cdo; in D-Day landing with 4 Cdo, wounded by mortar fire along Caen canal, saved by two German PoWs, who gave him morphium, operated on several times; returned to 3/10 Cdo as troop Sgt Maj., negotiated temporary armistice at Belle Isle (River Maas) Jan. 1945, commissioned for bravery in the field; killed in action at Osnabrueck 3 Apr. 1945 and buried where he fell

Nathan, Ernst (Eli), 13803316, later Norton (or Morton or Northon), Ernest, 13118703; born Hamburg 19 Aug. 1922; served in 69 & 77 Coy PC; RWK; and 3/10 Cdo, took part in Operation TARBRUSH (Onival); later attached to HQ 4 Cdo Bde; refused OCTU so as not to miss Normandy landing; killed in action by artillery fire on 13 June 1944

Nathan, K.A.

Nathan, M.H.

Naughton, served in 3/10 Cdo; died on active service

Nelken, served in 74 Coy PC; joined from Richborough Camp and was with BEF in France 1940

Nell, Heinz Herrman (also G.H.), 13807201, later Nichols, Gerald Peter (Jerry), 13118704; born 18 Oct. 1920; interned 1940, by HMT *Dunera* to Australia, back 1941; served in 69 Coy PC; then 3/10 Cdo; as Cpl i/c detachment with 6 Cdo at Normandy landing; later attached to 41 RM Cdo, saved Lord Lovat's life after Lovat had been wounded, was himself wounded on jaw by mortar bomb splinter shortly afterwards, commissioned in the field, Capt.; later in 447 Field Service Section chasing Nazi war criminals; lastly information control, British Control Commission in Germany

Nessler, Walter, artist

Netter, Hans Stefan, also Seligsohn-Netter, changed name to Nelson, Steve; born Berlin 9 Apr. 1920, pupil at Grunewald Gymnasium, family came from Baden, emigrated 1933, went to Repton School, 1938 to Pembroke College Cambridge; served in 251 & 69 Coy PC; transferred RA 1943; broke leg at Wrotham pre-OCTU, then to 123 OCTU Catterick Troop D47, commissioned, MTO School of Arty Deolali; demob 1946

Neubauer, Gottfried, from Czechoslovakia, would appear to have been conscripted into *Wehrmacht* and taken prisoner; transferred to SOE but found wanting; returned to PoW camp No. 207 with recommendation to join Czechoslovak Army

Neuberger, Adolf, later Newman, Archie; born Weinheim, from Wallduern, pupil at Jewish School Esslingen, deck boy on ship belonging to Jewish owners under German flag; interned 1940, sent to Canada, returned UK; served in PC; later transferred to 5 Bn Coldstream Guards, 30 Corps, in action Normandy, was in first patrol into Arras 1944 (photo in *Daily Sketch* 1944), later head wound (shrapnel)

Neubroch, Hans, Austrian; born 7 May 1923, at school in Eisenach, Karlsbad and Vienna (Stubengymn.), father director BMW works at Eisenach, in UK member Air Tng Corps; joined RAF 1941, recruiting Sgt accepted German passport with swastika as identification document, trained as flight observer in Canada, commissioned 1943; later navigator on Mosquito in 8 Group, Bomber Command; post-war: remained in RAF, commanded bomber squadron, British representative in British missions to Soviets and in SE Asia, commanded air base on Cyprus, staff officer in air ministry, SEATO, SHAPE & UKDEL Vienna, final rank Group Capt., awarded OBE

Neubroch, Rudolf, later Norton, Ronald George, Austrian, brother of Hans Neubroch (above), enlisted Jan 1940; served in 87 Coy PC, in France 1940; transferred RA, to India, Burma, Malaysia, designed artillery firing tables, which were accepted by School of Arty, but remained in rank of Gunner; demob 1945

Neufeld, Hans, alias Newman, Harry, alias Nuffield, alias Slade, W., IC, returned to UK (from Austria?) 4 May 1945

Neulaender, Fritz, later Newland; born Vienna 1896, pupil at Schottengymn, began studies at Vienna University before 1914, then Austrian Army in WW1, wounded on Russian front (loss of one eye), Senior Lt, held by Nazis, but released as old soldier after 9 Nov. 1938, to UK 1939; enlisted

1939; served in 69 (France 1940) and 248 Coy PC, Sgt with detachment which felled trees on Kentish coast to produce make-believe gun positions; later CQMS; portrayed by Johannes Koelz wearing uniform, with black eye shield and smoking pipe, but portrait has disappeared; arrested by British military police because he wrote diary on his private typewriter, in PoW camp, Keele, from 1944; lastly in civilian position in Cyrenaica with rank of Maj.; post-war: foreign correspondent for export firm, then in NHS, father of David N., violinist in Royal Philharmonic Orchestra

Neumann, later Newman, Austrian, Flt Lt in RAF, and had a function in public relations

Neumann, served in 74 Coy PC; joined from Richborough Camp and was with BEF in France 1940

Neumann, Berthold, served in 74 Coy PC (identical with above?)

Neumann, Bernhard Hermann; born Berlin-Charlottenburg, 15 Oct. 1909, pupil at Herder Schule, Berlin, studied at Freiburg University, D.Phil. Berlin, mathematician and physicist, lecturer at Cambridge 1935, Cardiff 1937; enlisted 1940; served in PC; later R. Signals; demob 1945; post-war: lecturer Hull University 1946, Manchester 1948, then professor at Canberra, Cambridge, Tata Institute Bombay, SUNY, Wisconsin, Illinois, etc., author of various books on algebra etc., FRS

Neumann, Felicia, served in 1 Allied Volunteer Platoon ATS

Neumann, Georg, Austrian from Wiener Neustadt, served in 337 Coy PC, North Africa; wrote most patriotic letter ever published in *Young Austria* newspaper

Neumann, Gerhard, 13800195, L/Cpl in 69 Coy PC; killed in action during air raid on London 29 Dec. 1940

Neumann, Gerhard; born Vienna 1922, mother's maiden name was Schnepp, to England by *Kindertransport*; served in PC; post-war: moved to Aarhus, Denmark

Neumann, Hans Georg, 1882507, later Newman, George; born 18 Jan. 1923, son of a Viennese lawyer and nephew of Julius Braunthal, long-standing secretary of the International Trades Union Congress; despite entirely pacific disposition he volunteered for RAF in Dec. 1943 and became an interpreter; Sgt; released in Mar. 1946; post-war: music publishing, teacher of music

Neumann, Ilse, married Klein, enlisted 1941; served in one of the Allied Volunteer Platoons ATS

Neumann, Karl, later Newman, Charles; born 26 Mar. 1919 Berlin, father was judge, dismissed 1933, emigrated that year, attended Ottersham School, studied history at Christ Church College Oxford; interned 1940; volunteered for PC; discharged 1942 on medical grounds; post-war: barrister 1946, took leading part in Britain's negotiations to enter EEC, drafted laws for this purpose, also engaged on other treaties, legal adviser to House of Lords, Fellow of Grays Inn, Hon. Fellow B.Inst. International and Comparative Law; Died 2001

Neumann, Kurt, member of Young Austria; enlisted from Oxford Dec. 1943/Jan. 1944

Neumann, Steffi, married Nussbaum, enlisted 1941; served in one of the Allied Volunteer Platoons ATS

Neumann, Theo, lawyer from Vienna, member Social Democratic Party; served in PC, Sgt; transferred to SOE (RF), with Sanders (radio operator), Wirlander and Hladek interviewed Austrian PoWs in Italy; as Capt., parachuted into neighbourhood of Vienna during night of 23 to 24 Mar. 1945, carried out sabotage and propaganda, also liaison with Soviets; concerned with arrest of known Nazis (according to Dale he did not get to Vienna until after end of hostilities; according to Sanders he should have gone to Styria, but never got there; however, everyone agrees that eventually he was in BALU.)

Neumark, Rudi, member of Young Austria; enlisted from London Dec. 1943/Jan. 1944

Neustadt, A.; post-war: prominent in Ex-Service NB Association in Yorkshire

Neunauer, Gottfried, alias Cijka, from Czechoslovakia, German conscript, PoW; taken into British service; SOE; returned to No. 207 PoW camp with suggestion to report to Czech Army

Newman, Isidor, served in SOE, after capture taken to Mauthausen concentration camp, murdered there

Newton, K.B., was in Kitchener Camp, enlisted early in 1940

Newton, Mickey

Newton, R., served in 93 Coy PC

Nickelsburg, served in 87 Coy PC

Niederer, Hedi, served in 1 Allied Volunteer Platoon ATS

Niggas, Paul, alias Norton, Paul, alias Windisch, Paul, Austrian, German conscript, PoW; taken into British service; SOE, in Operation DINTYLAKE near Klagenfurt; June 1945 in Austria, was expected to remain there

Nissels, Erich

Niven, David

Niwes, Austrian, served in either 337 or 338 Coy PC

Nomburg, Harry, 14216528, temporarily Drew, Harry, 6305461; born Coburg 17 Nov. 1923, grew up in Berlin, by *Kindertransport* to England May 1939, farmer's boy at Whittinghame (Lord Balfour's estate); interned May/Aug 1940; served in 137 Coy PC; later 3/10 Cdo; attached to 12, 6 & 3 Cdo, in 1943 in France on reconnaisance raid; attached to 3 Tp 6 Cdo on D-Day; wounded 19 Aug. 1944, returned from sick leave Jan. 1945; at Wesel Mar. 1945; in 5 river crossings 1945; during occupation of Luneburg at home of Richthofen family; 8 May 1945 in Oldenburg, Holstein; interpreter in Hamburg, Schleswig-Holstein, Berlin and Eiffel; post-war: to USA, from Jan. 1948 in 82nd Airborne Div. US Army, in US Federal Service for 42 years altogether, last job was with US Post Office; died in New York 1997

Norton, Edward F.

Novelli, G., served as Sgt in WAAF, mentioned in dispatches

Nuffield, H.J., served in 220 Coy PC

Nussbaum, served in 88 Coy PC, in Le Havre 1940 refused to go on cookhouse fatigue, for which he was sentenced to 28 days' detention, was not, therefore, with company when it was in the line before Harfleur

Nussbaum, 13800050, enlisted 17 Nov. 1939; CQMS in 69 Coy PC as from 23 Dec. 1941; to 52 Div HQ 1 Feb. 1943

Nussbaum, David, later Niven, Neville, 14442780; born Gelsenkirchen 16 July 1925, to UK by *Kindertransport*; served as Sgt in 9 Para. Regt, shot down in glider at Arnhem and badly wounded

Nutfield, H.I.

Oakley, A.

Odenheimer, Hans, later Oden, H., from Heidelberg, emigrated to Palestine and worked on kibbutz; joined RASC in 8th Army; also served in Near East and Italy

Oertel, Gerhard, from Chemnitz, emigrated 1934; enlisted 1943; Sgt in Essex Regt; whilst in the army was one of the organisers of 'World Youth Congress, London 1944'; demob 1947; post-war: returned to Saxony, where he graduated, name appears on list of comrades who served in Allied Armies, found in the archives of the SED (United Socialist Party) after unification of Germany 1990

Oettinger, Hans, later Ormond, Henry; born Kassel 1901, public prosecutor, later judge at Mannheim, dismissed 1933, 1939 to Switzerland, then UK, arrived there 11 Sept. 1939 and immediately interned, released, worked as butler; interned again May 1940, sent to Canada, returned 1942; enlisted; to PC; transferred to Intelligence, served in 12 Amplifier Unit as S/Sgt, in action Apr. 1945 at Oldenburg, where he appealed to the citizens to support the allies, text of the appeal is preserved in Berlin; then i/c ISC bureau in Hannover; post-war: acted as counsel in actions for restitution and for private prosecution in the 'Frankfurt Auschwitz trial'

Ojola, served in 69 Coy PC, on 23 Aug. 1943 sentenced to 28 days' detention for unknown crime

Oliver (Tolliver?), served in PC; later in Intelligence in Berlin; Sgt

Olsen, Olaf, film actor, served in 3 PCTC

Opoczynski (also Opocynski or Opoczymski), Abraham, 13801810, later Orr, Adam, 6387010; born 1921 or 1922; Sgt; may be relative of Michael Opoczynski, editor, 2nd German TV, and if so would be from Lenczyka, Silesia; clearly in PC and SOE; died (killed?) 12 Apr. 1945 at Duernbach near Bad Toelz, Bavaria

Oppelt, Gustav, later Bate, G., 5550123, might well be the Czechoslovak citizen named Bate, who was one of the first five members of 3/10 Cdo; in the Dieppe raid he had orders to take over Dieppe town hall; according to Bentwich, he was killed in the process; however, Oppelt seems to have survived the war and might have done so as prisoner in enemy hands; name appears in German Unity Party's list of Sudeten Germans who served in British Army, which suggests that at least for a time he was one of those who lived in the GDR

Oppenheim, Eva E., married Gillatt; born Berlin 21 May 1920, came to England summer 1939; served in 4 Allied Volunteer Platoon ATS

Oppenheim, Herbert; born Querfurt near Halle 6 Oct. 1913, completed his schooling at Halle, to London Dec 1933, motor mechanic at Chelsea 1934–36, then independent motor workshop and car leasing in WC1; enlisted 1940; driver to OC 137 Coy PC, then Cpl fitter; transferred to RASC, commissioned 8 Oct. 1943; June 1944 to Nigeria (WASC), promoted Capt. and OC workshop; demob July 1946

Oppenheim, Richard, PAL/11086, Austrian; born 20 Aug. 1903; served in British Army from 15 Nov. 1940, but documentary evidence shows that he was held in Germany under suspicion of espionage 1941; Peoples' Court ordered his release from custody 26 Nov. 1941, his release certificate, dated 30 Apr. 1946, shows him to have been a L/Cpl in PC and to have served in the army for 5 years and 166 days, his conduct is described as excellent

Oppenheim, Werner, later King, Ronald Michael; born Berlin 2 Dec. 1922, to UK May 1939; served in 249 Coy PC; transferred to East Yorks. Regt; then 22 Indep. Para. Coy, amongst first to parachute into Normandy on night preceding D-Day, in action there, also in Holland, Ardennes, Rhine crossing, Belsen, Java, Sarawak

Oppenheim, Werner, 13807055, later Oakfield, Bill, 13118807 and 638701; born Hamburg 7 Mar. 1922, pupil at Talmud Thora School; interned 1940, to Australia by HMT *Dunera*; after return to UK served in 165 Coy PC; eventually also in Jewish Bde; then War Crimes Executive; post-war: in Leicester, later in Israel

Oppenheimer, a Viennese, L/Cpl in PC; later in CCG, Knightsbridge office

Oppenheimer, B., served in 137 Coy PC

Oppenheimer, Eva M., married Towse, served in 1 Allied Volunteer Platoon ATS

Oppenheimer, R.

Oppenheimer, Rudolph, 13802972; born Fuerth 7 Mar. 1907; enlisted 10 Sept. 1940; posted to 3 PCTC; later 137 Coy PC; transferred RASC 13 May 1942, technical motor transport clerk, Doncaster and Gateshead, Sgt; transfer to Intelligence, 17 Mar. 1944, in CSDIC till 28 Dec. 1945; then demob

Orchudesch, Fred, served in PC, North Africa

Ordynanz, Sigmund, served in PC; later RA; transferred RN and served 18 months on landing craft in Channel

Ornstein, Gertrud, married King, Austrian; born Berlin 1920, daughter of Ornstein, Hans (see below), emigrated to Paris 1933, fled to Algiers 1940; enlisted there Nov. 1942; served in First Aid Nursing Yeomanry (FANY) in North Africa and Italy; secretary to Maj. Robert Searle, Intelligence, in Algiers, Siena and Florence; demob 26 June 1945 London; post-war: lives in Wales.

Ornstein, Hans; born Vienna 1892, Capt. in Austrian artillery 1914–18, on Russian and Italian fronts, worked for Olex Oil Co., later BP, Berlin and Cologne, to Paris 1933, in French fortress artillery at Algiers 1939–40, after dismissal back to BP there; after allied occupation of North Africa to British Military Government, Algiers; then to Free French, responsible for oil supplies there, in action Monte Cassino 1944; reverted to British service, full Col at Hamburg as custodian of German BP 1945; post-war: managing director Deutsche BP 1946 to 1957, CBE

Orton, P.K., awarded Certificate of Merit by Field Marshal Montgomery

Osborne, awarded Military Medal

Oschitzki, served in 74 Coy PC; joined from Richborough Camp and was with BEF in France 1940

Ostovich, S. 13807900

Otten, A, served in 137 Coy PC

Owen, R.

Pach, Sonia, served in ATS

Pahmer, Joseph, served in 337 or 338 Coy PC

Palishaut (Palishant?), Edith, served in 1 Allied Volunteer Platoon ATS

Pallany, Mary, served in 1 Allied Volunteer Platoon ATS

Palmai, Alfred, trainer at Hakoah Sports Club, Vienna; probably born around 1901, emigrated to Palestine; served in 608 Coy PC, North Africa and Greece, aken prisoner by Germans at Kalamata 1941

Panhofer, Ferdinand, alias Sokol, German conscript, PoW; taken into British service; SOE; posted to IS9 Jan. 1945

Panzenhofer, Walter, member of Young Austria; enlisted from London between 15 Jan. and 25 Mar. 1944.

Papes, E., 13807901

Parker, W.J., served in 137 Coy PC

Pascha, George E.

Paterson, T., 13041619, Austrian, L/Cpl in 220 Coy PC; killed in action by hostile artillery fire in Ardennes or Reichswald 31 Jan. 1945

Paton, served in PC; transferred to monitoring unit, 21 Army Gp; transferred to First American Army, Apr. 1944; Cpl

Patton, F.C., served in PC; later in Publicity and Psycho Warfare, 21 Army Gp

Paucker, Dr Arnold, German born, naturalised in Palestine 1938; in RE 1941–46; post-war: director, Leo Baeck Institute, London, author of many publications on Jewish resistance to Nazis

Paul, K. PAL/32733, driver in TD Holding Coy, 6 Pl. RASC

Pauli; born Vienna 1926, pupil at Sperl Gymnasium, fled to France; served in Foreign Legion till 1943; then in 220 Coy PC

Pearl, Walter

Pedersen, V.K., 13806050, Pte in 253 Coy PC; later commissioned in SOE

Pelikan, F., later Pelican, Fred; born Miastezko near Kattowitz 22 Jan. 1918, intended to study medicine, footballer with SC Makkabi, boxed and swam, sang in synagogue choir, pupil at Gleiwitz Gymnasium; served in 74 Coy PC; joined from Richborough Camp and was with BEF in France 1940, remained and was with BEF till end of hostilities; later Sgt in war crimes investigation, Germany, arrested Hans Esser, Nazi chief in Neuss; wrote autobiography

Perger, Gustav, of Horn, Lower Austria; interned 1940, to Australia by HMT *Dunera*, released in Australia; joined 6 Austr. Empl. Coy, AMF

Perl, served in 74 Coy PC; joined from Richborough Camp and was with BEF in France 1940

Perles, A., wrote best-selling book *Alien Corn* about life in PCs

Perlmann, T., 13106727, later Allen, Austrian, committed suicide 29 Apr. 1944

Perthain, Ernst, later Perthain, E. John, son of Austrian judge, officer in Austrian Army until 1938; served in 69 Coy PC; transferred to US Army, where he became Maj.

Perutz, Edith, married Smith; born Vienna 1918, to England 1938; Sgt in WAAF XX (double cross) service, passing misleading wireless instruction to Luftwaffe

Peschel, Ruth, married Garland, from Breslau, served in 1 or 4 Allied Volunteer Platoon ATS

Peters, H. 11316230, served in Black Watch, transferred to 3/10 Cdo in Italy.

Petzal, served in 137 Coy PC

Peyer, later Palmer, served in PC; then RAOC; later in 3/10 Cdo; finally Capt., interpreter at Nuremberg trials

Pezich, A., 13807902 and 13122243

Pfeffer, later Peters, Alan, served as Capt.in REME

Pfeffer, Richard, Czechoslovak citizen, served in 93 Coy PC, name appears in German Unity Party's list of Sudeten Germans who served in British Army

Pfeuffer, Ludwig, later Amichai, Jehuda; born Wuerzburg 1924, to Palestine 1935; served in Jewish Bde; post-war: teacher, university lecturer, lyricist and author, received Israel Prize 1982

Phillip, Guenter, 14442059, later Phillips, Geoffrey; born Wanne, Westphalia, 19 Apr. 1925., by *Kindertransport* to UK 15 Dec. 1938, in Bradford refugee hostel, worked in textile industry Sept 1939–late 1943; served with KOYLI in Berwick-upon-Tweed 1944, trained as wireless operator Richmond, Yorks., and Barnard Castle, to Belgium Dec. 1944; then Seaforth Highlanders (51 Div.), in action in Belgium, Holland and Germany; transferred to Control Commission Germany; early demob as textile worker; post-war: MD of textile works in Ireland, later independent

Phillips, H.

Phillipsohn, W., 13800803, or Phillipsen, W., served in 74 Coy PC; joined from Richborough Camp and was with BEF in France 1940; accidentally killed in lorry crash on active service 17 Sept. 1942

Piblich, having been 2 i/c of standard PC Coy, became OC PoW camp Bicester with rank of Maj..

Pichler, F., served in PC; post-war: owner of Beachbrow Hotel, Deal, Kent and Hotel Vienna, Maida Vale

Pick, served in 74 Coy PC; joined from Richborough Camp and was with BEF in France 1940

Pick, later Parker, Ralph

Pick, A., had been ski instructor in Austrian Army and designed the winter uniform of its Alpine Div.; served in PC, Sgt; ski instructor to 51 Highland Div.; killed in action 1942, presumably on Walcheren raid

Pick, Georg, 13116506, later 311174, Austrian; born 6 or 7 Dec. 1919, Jewish, sales representative in his home country; enlisted Richborough 13 Feb. 1940; Sgt in 88 Coy PC; later SOE, commissioned; demob 5 Jan. 1946

Pick, Max 13809161, Austrian; died on active service 17 Mar. 1944

Pimselstein, G., Austrian, served as fitter in 2BW D-Camp, MEF

Pinkus (also Pincus or Pineus), Ludwig (Lutz), 13810025, later Preston, L., 6387045, joined British forces at behest of FDJ or other communist party organisation from Manchester, name appears in German Unity Party's list of members who served in Allied armies; after demob returned to Germany

Pirquet, K., 13803195, Cpl in 165 Coy PC; appears to have volunteered for commandos, application refused

Pinschewer, Horst, later Perry, Geoffrey, H., 13804863, Maj., served in 248 Coy PC, editor *Pioneer News* at Catterick; in 'T' Force instrumental in takeover of Radio Hamburg; arrested British traitor Joyce (Lord Haw-Haw), whom he shot in the rear quarters while doing so; post-war: publisher

Pisano, G., 13806055, served in PC

Pisco, served in 87 Coy PC

Pistol, Harry, member of Young Austria; enlisted from Shrewsbury Dec. 1943/Jan. 1944

Pistori, J.A., Austrian, with British Army in France 1944

Plant, served in 137 Coy PC

Plapla, came to North Africa from France to serve in 337 Coy PC, returned to Paris via Italy

Plat, served in 74 Coy PC; joined from Richborough Camp and was with BEF in France 1940

Platek, Bruno, Czechoslovakian, name appears in German Unity Party's list of Sudeten German social democrats who served in British Army; might be same man as Platschek, alias Platt, below

Platschek (Plateck? Platek?), later Platt, Bubi, Czechoslovak citizen (Sudeten German), might be same man as Bruno Platek (above); served in PC, probably 226 Coy; later in 3/10 Cdo; in Dieppe raid 1942, which he survived with leg wound (one of two survivors, the other was Latimer), landed there with TLC 124 (HQ 4 Armoured Bde); returned to 3/10 Cdo as storekeeper; Latimer referred to him as 'Sudeten German traitor' – a phrase with several different meanings

Platzer, Heinrich, later Platt, Henry; born Vienna 27 Jan. 1921, B.Sc.(Econ.) of Glasgow University; served in 249 Coy PC from Sept. 1940–Aug. 1946, in France and Belgium; interpreter in PoW camp Watton, Caithness, with 2000 PoWs 1945–46

Plaut, Dr Ernst J., enlisted from Richborough; served in PC, early release because of bad health; post-war: helped emigrants to find their families

Pledge, S.L., name appears as Lt on officers' list of 69 Coy PC, July 1943

Pletschner, Dr, served in 74 Coy PC

Pleuse, Kurt, served in 338 Coy PC, according to order 445 of 338 Coy, on 12 May 1943, during an air attack when three petrol canisters in the middle of a large stack were ignited by shrapnel fire, he and two others pulled the burning canisters from the stack and thus prevented the fire from spreading with possibly untold damage

Poemerl, Paul; born Vienna 30 Oct. 1923, studied medicine at Vienna University, served in *Wehrmacht* 1941 until taken prisoner 1943; joined British Army from PoW camp; served in IC as Sgt/wireless operator, parachuted into Austria near Klagenfurt, middle of 1944, captured by Gestapo and held as British agent, held at Vienna Gestapo HQ Morzinplatz till 28 Jan. 1945, then Mauthausen concentration camp 1–23 Feb. 1945, back at barracks Rossauerlaende till Apr. 1945; he states that he was liberated from there by the Soviets during the battle for Vienna, but according to Austrian official report US troops freed him at Dachau

Pojur, later Palmer, served in RF (SOE), did not see action

Poliakow, Nikolai, OBE (Koko the Clown), Russian; born 5 Oct. 1900 in theatre at Besinuwitz, had been Cpl in 11th Siberian Regt, Russian infantry, under the Tsar, awarded Cross of St George, later in both white and red armies, had been in Busch's Circus in Berlin, 1929 in Bertram Mills' Circus; enlisted 20 Mar. 1940; served in 3PCTC entertainment section, ENSA; post-war: published autobiography 1950; died Peterborough 25 Sept. 1974

Polich, K., 13807903, served in PC

Pollack, served as Sgt in 74 Coy PC; joined from Richborough Camp and was with BEF in France 1940

Pollack (Pollak?) H.M., Cpl in PC; commissioned, served in 229 and 88 Coy PC; then 21 Indep. Para. Coy (Pathfinders) as Capt., at Arnhem, in Burma and at Singapore; awarded MC

Pollak, Franz; born 1901, had been employee of Berlin Jewish community; enlisted Jan. 1940 from Kitchener Camp; served in 3 PCTC and 349 Coy PC; early release Jan. 1945; died 1953 as consequence of service

Pollak, Oskar, Czechoslovak citizen, name appears in German Unity Party's list of Sudeten German social democrats who served in British Army

Pollak, Sigi, later Pollard, Sidney, 14441643; born Vienna 1925, came to England by *Kindertransport* 1939, in agriculture for 2 years, then gardener in Cambridge, took correspondence course on economics, member of Young Austria; enlisted on 26 Oct. 1943; served as Cpl in Recce Corps, also interpreter in Germany, was medical category B; demob 29 Jan. 1947; post-war: Ph.D. 1950 at LSE, member British Communist Party, Professor of History of Economics at Sheffield 1963, Berkeley University, 1980 Bielefeld, author of books on history of workers' movement and co-op, his book *Peaceful Conquest* demonstrates that nationalism leads to disaster; died Nov. 1998

Pollaschek (Polatschek?), O., 13801460, alias Turner, A.C., alias McCullough; born 13 May 1919, in Dachau and Buchenwald, released after Labour Party intervention, to England Aug. 1938, worked as bouncer in Soho nightclub; enlisted from Richborough 1939, in France with PC 1940, evacuated through St Malo; later in 251 Coy PC; served in 3/10 Cdo; on D-Day attached to 3 Cdo, Jan. 1945 at Maas river; seconded to Intelligence Bad Oeynhausen and briefly with Loewenstein (Lynton) at Eutin; post-war: meat trader in London

Pollitzer, later Pollitt, E.H., Viennese teacher and journalist, Ph.D., served in PC; in France 1940, Harfleur and St Malo, then at Catterick; later in Psycho Warfare Unit, prepared leaflets for distribution to *Wehrmacht*, in Belgium, then Germany 1944–45; editor *Luebecker Nachrichten*; post-war: teacher in Somerset (The question whether he is identical with Harry Pollitt,

Communist MP for Limehouse and editor *Daily Worker* is denied by other Austrian ex-Communists.)

Popower, served in 74 Coy PC; joined from Richborough Camp and was with BEF in France 1940

Popper, joined 608 Coy PC from Palestine, in North Africa and Greece as medical orderly, taken prisoner at Kalamata, held in Stalag 9, Silesia, at one stage of his captivity was only person with medical training in the area and helped German civilians in lieu of a doctor

Popper, Georg, later Pepper, George, a Viennese served in 229 Coy PC; post-war: teacher in England

Pordes, Gisela, served in 1 Allied Volunteer Platoon ATS

Portmann, a Viennese lawyer, served in PC in France, Belgium and Germany, control of civilian labour; later concerned in investigating murder of 7000 Jews, who were killed on transports between concentration camps; then in British Austrian Legal Unit; Sgt

Portner, W., later Porter, Viennese painter, served as Cpl in 229 Coy PC; died on active service

Posamentier, also Posamenpier, O., 13805817, later Parry or Parray, F., 6305462, Pte in 219 Coy PC

Pottlitzer, served in 74 Coy PC; joined from Richborough Camp and was with BEF in France 1940

Powell, R.C.

Prag, served in 74 Coy PC; joined from Richborough Camp and was with BEF in France 1940

Prager, Guenther, leading member of Young Austria; enlisted from London Dec. 1943/Jan. 1944; served in REME; published Austrian jingoistic letter in London *Zeitspiegel* 5 Aug. 1944

Prager, Guy, served in 337 or 338 Coy PC

Prager, 13807478 (..87?), later Bruce, George, Viennese, father was banker; enlisted spring 1942; served in PC; later 61b & 62nd parachute training course; then 21 Indep. Para. Coy; Capt.; post-war: accountant

Prager, Hans, alias Cihak, Hans, alias Mueller, Jakob; born Vienna 4 Mar. 1925, German conscript, PoW; taken into British service; in Para. Regt, SOE, in Operation DUVAL near Salzburg, parachuted into Austria 17 Feb. 1945, arrested 18 Feb. 1945, in various prisons and Mauthausen concentration camp until May 1945; after liberation discharged for medical reasons (depression); was guest of British Army at Klagenfurt Aug. 1945, certificate attesting to his excellent behaviour and loyalty to Allied cause signed by F.W. Barber, head of British secret services, can be found in Austrian archives

Pratt, served in 3/10 Cdo

Preminger, Ossi, Austrian, enlisted before 29 July 1944

Preston, Karl, Austrian, served in PC in France 1940 and again in 1944

Pretzner, Ejar(?), alias Blum, Harold, alias Berger Franz, Austrian, German conscript, PoW; taken into British service; SOE, in Operation DUCIMER near Klagenfurt; in Austria June 1945, was intended to remain there

Priester, took over as CQMS 69 Coy PC 12 May 1943

Priester, served in 74 Coy PC; joined from Richborough Camp and was with BEF in France 1940

Priestley, M.P., 13801984, served in PC; in Interpreters' Pool 1944; RF; was asked for by Publicity and Psycho Warfare for Information Control, commissioned

Probst, Hans, joined British forces at behest of Young Austria 25 June 1943

Prochnik, Otty, served in 1 Allied Volunteer Platoon ATS

Pronza, Victor, on German Unity Party's list of Sudeten Germans who served in the British Army

Propst, Friedrich; born Vienna 16 Feb. 1916, communist, served in British Army 12–20 June 1947, wounded in Germany.

Proskauer, served in 74 Coy PC; joined from Richborough Camp and was with BEF in France 1940

Prpich, P., 13807904 and 13122234

Przettecki, served in 74 Coy PC; joined from Richborough Camp and was with BEF in France 1940

Pulay, George, from Vienna, Sgt in Intelligence; post-war: city editor, *The Times*

Pulgram, Alois, Austrian, Pte, engineering draughtsman, 2BW D-Camp, MEF, served in British Army 11 June 1942–30 Aug. 1946

Quastler, Ernst, served in 74 Coy PC; joined from Richborough Camp and was with BEF in France 1940

Quetsch, served in 74 Coy PC; joined from Richborough Camp and was with BEF in France 1940

Raape, Freddie, later Austin, from Darmstadt, Cpl in 229 Coy PC

Raber, E., served in 219 Coy PC

Racker, Dr Miriam, Ph.D., served in 1 Allied Volunteer Platoon ATS

Radmesser, served in 74 Coy PC; joined from Richborough Camp and was with BEF in France 1940

Raduvany, Egon, member of Young Austria; enlisted from Guildford Dec. 1943/Jan. 1944

Rae, E.C.

Rafael, S.C., 13800320, L/Cpl in 69 Coy PC

Rahmer, later Rayner, John, Rabbi in Forces

Ranzenhofer, Walter, Austrian, Sgt in 69 Coy PC

Rares, Werner H.C.

Rasborscheg, Johann (Sepp), Austrian, veteran of Spanish Civil War; served in RF (SOE group) with Kaiser and Wunder, but was not used in action; returned to UK 4 May 1945; in TA, parachute instructor with more than 200 jumps

Rasp, Andy, from Heidelberg, interned 1940; enlisted from internment 1940; served in 88 Coy PC, on clearance work after air raids on London; released on medical grounds after 2 years' service

Rathe, R.; died on active service

Raudnitz, served in 74 Coy PC; joined from Richborough Camp and was with

BEF in France 1940

Rawdon, R., Austrian, Sgt in PC; later in Interpreters' Pool, interpreter with leading military police unit when British forces entered Berlin 1945

Rawock, Dr Kurt, served in 219 Coy PC

Rayant, L.M.

Redlich, Hedda, Austrian, joined ATS in 1941

Redlich, Leo, 13801995, Austrian, Pte in 137 Coy PC; killed in action during air attack on London 11 Jan. 1941

Redlich, Max

Reeves,W.

Regart, Alex Mast (?), alias Richards, Anthony, German conscript, PoW; taken into British service; in Para. Regt, IC, was in Bari Feb. 1945; posted to SI10

Regenbogen (also Regenboden), K., 13802074, later Reynolds, K., 3436362, L/Cpl in 88 Coy PC and in R. Sussex Regt

Richle, Joseph, alias Gilbert, Leslie Marius, alias Leonard, John Howard, said to have been from Switzerland but unlikely to have been a Swiss citizen; may have been sent to Australia with HMT *Dunera* and returned later; Sgt, wireless expert, together with Sgt Saunders crossed Rhine at Xanten on mission to discover German battle plan 1945, was arrested, but withstood questioning and again released, returned after two days with information of highest importance, awarded Military Medal, mentioned in dispatches

Rehfeld, served in 74 Coy PC; joined from Richborough Camp and was with BEF in France 1940

Reich, served in 137 Coy PC

Reich, S.R., 13700295 (Weil? Weich?) 13801207, later Hamilton, R.G. (or S.?); born 1 Aug. 1916; served in 3/10 Cdo, Cpl; killed in action at Westkapelle on Walcheren whilst attached to 41 RM Cdo during attempt to persuade hostile troops to surrender (The confusion about his original name is the result of the above action having been reported by four different witnesses, none of whom, apparently, knew anything about him personally.)

Reiche, C.E.L.H., name appears on officers' list of 219 Coy PC as 2/Lt on 31 Aug. 1942

Reichenberg, P.L., Cpl in RASC

Reichenfeld, Hans, Austrian, enlisted previous to 29 July 1944

Reid, served in 137 Coy PC

Reid, Trudie, served in 1 Allied Volunteer Platoon ATS

Reif, Dr Hans, Austrian, served with the French from 6 Oct. 1939 until 22 Sept. 1940; was interned immediately following his release and remained in a forced labour camp until 29 May 1943; went straight from internment into the British Army; released on 14 Jan. 1947

Reifenberg, Heinz, later Russell, Sgt in 5 Tng Centre PC and in Army Catering Corps, mentioned in dispatches

Reinefeld, Manfred, later Rayne, Fred, served in 87 Coy PC

Reinhardt, Max, member of Young Austria; enlisted from Leicester Dec. 1943/Jan. 1944

Reinharz, Max, Austrian

Reinisch, 13809617, Austrian, Pte in 699 VAW REME CMF

Reischer, Alfred, Viennese; post-war: active in Vienna Jewish community

Reismann, K., 774485, later Raanan, Joseph, Austrian, served as Flt Sgt in RAF, air gunner; post-war: Lt Col in Israeli air force, head of intelligence service, air attaché in London

Reiss, also Reisz, from Pressburg, then Czechoslovakia, served in 69 Coy PC, later RA

Reiss, served in 74 Coy PC; joined from Richborough Camp and was with BEF in France 1940

Reisz, Andor, 13800620, Austrian; accidentally killed on active service in lorry collision 7 Sept. 1942

Reiter, served in 74 Coy PC; joined from Richborough Camp and was with BEF in France 1940

Reitlinger, Friedrich, from the Tyrol, served in PC; transferred SOE (General List); parachute training at Ringway; intended for action in Yugoslavia with objective to get to Austria, but action was halted; later personal interpreter to British C-in-C and High Commissioner, Austria; post-war: author

Reitmann, Rudi, member of Young Austria; enlisted from London Dec. 1943/Jan. 1944

Reitzner, Almar, served in RAF, on German Unity Party's list of Sudeten German Social Democrats who served in the British Army

Renow, served as Capt. in PC; later in Legal Research Branch, observer of trials of Nazis in German courts

Retford, Henry, served in 249 Coy PC

Reutner, later Rodney, Robert, emigrated to France, served in French Army, to England from Dunkirk 1940; interned temporarily, as his claim to be Jewish was not believed; enlisted 1943 (?); served in PC; later RAC Recce, 6th Airborne Div., was in advance from Holland (after glider landing) as far as river Elbe; then to Far East; lastly in Palestine; post-war: in Israeli Army, served in reserve until age 56, married girl from Berlin and has two daughters and two sons, all of whom served in Israeli Army

Reynold, Henry

Rezek, G., PAL775843, Austrian, enlisted in Palestine and served as LAC, RAF; post-war: Canadian diplomat in Bonn

Rhoades, enlisted from Richborough; served in PC; later RA; then BALU; Maj.

Rice, probably Czechoslovak citizen, served in 3/10 Cdo; was in Dieppe raid attached to 40 RM Cdo, missing, said to have been taken prisoner in attempt to capture Dieppe town hall.

Richards, N.P., Austrian, BA Hons., L/Cpl in 69 Coy PC; later Sgt Army Education Corps; post-war: assistant probation officer Metropolitan Police courts

Richmond, J.; died on active service

Riemer, H.K., 13802245, later Roberts, H.K., 6436359, could be identical with Roberts, H.H.M.?, L/Cpl in PC and R. Sussex Regt; might well have been in SOE

Riesenfeld (Reisenfeld?), later Rivin, Ernst, Austrian; born 1919, went to Palestine; joined RAF; served in Sudan

Riester, W.F., served in 229 Coy PC

Rigby, Stephen, pseudonym of man said to have been in 3/10 Cdo (Hero of *Operation Nimrod* by James Leasor, which tells of Rigby having been successful in planting on Hitler false information concerning an intended invasion of the Pas de Calais in 1944. This is said to have made Hitler hold back his main forces in France after Normandy invasion. Leasor says his information stems from Louis Mountbatten, Sir L. Hollis and Sir R.Wingate.)

Ringel, H., 2/Lt on officers' list of 219 Coy PC on 31 Dec. 1942

Roberts, H.H.M.

Robertson, Austrian, Flt Lt in RAF; later Russian interpreter on Allied Air Force Council

Robinsohn, Rudolph, 774906, Austrian, went to Palestine; served as Sgt in RAF accounts department; died on active service.

Rodney, Peter W.

Roehr, Heinz Peter, later Rowe, Sir Henry, KCB QC, Sgt; post-war: first parliamentary counsel

Rohde, Erich, later Rhodes, Eric Douglas, from Hamburg, served in SOE (RF), said to have seen action in North Africa and Italy, in Operation HISTORIAN at Zeltweg, parachuted into Styria 25 Apr. 1945 and was in group occupying Zeltweg air base; Lt; later Maj.

Rohrlich, P., Austrian, Pte, fitter in VM, MEF

Romberg, served in PC; later in Legal Research Branch, liaison officer to German courts; Maj.

Rosat, Susanne, served in 1 Allied Volunteer Platoon ATS

Rose, H.K., awarded the Royal Humane Society Testimonial for Gallantry

Rosen, later Radwell, said to have served at Arnhem

Rosen, Lore; born Mannheim 1924, to England by *Kindertransport* 1 Feb. 1939; joined ATS Dec. 1942; attached to Royal Welch Fusiliers in Wales for 4 years

Rosen, Robert, on ship 'which was sunk with heavy losses after being torpedoed' (*Arandora Star*?), was rescued, but afterwards for some time in 'poor mental state'; attached to 8th Army, was in action in Italy and Austria

Rosenbach, K., served in 77 Coy PC, acted in that company's Xmas panto *A Midsummer Night's Scream*, 1941(?)

Rosenbaum, mentioned as Pte in war diary of 69 Coy PC on 4 Dec. 1943

Rosenbaum, Gerti, Austrian, served in ATS; married J. Frankel of the Dutch Army 1944

Rosenbaum, J., served in 69 Coy PC, one of the first six alien sergeants

Rosenbaum, L.R., later Reed, from Paderborn

Rosenbaum, Ilse, married Walters, from Vienna, emigrated 1939; served in ATS; orderly in Ilfracombe, probably attached to 3 PCTC

Rosenberg, served in 74 Coy PC; joined from Richborough Camp and was with BEF in France 1940

Rosenberg, from Vienna, sister of Lilly Lampert, served as S/Sgt in 1 Allied Volunteer Platoon ATS; lectured in BAOR college and to PoWs

Rosenberg, R., later Russell, R.; died on active service

Rosenberg, S.; died on active service (R. Rosenberg and S. Rosenberg are separate entries on Bentwich's Roll of Honour.)

Rosenblatt, Austrian, Cpl in 338 Coy PC

Rosenblum, served in 74 Coy PC; joined from Richborough Camp and was with BEF in France 1940

Rosenbluth, Eli, later Howell, M.A., nephew of Israel's first Minister of Justice, like his uncle he had studied technology; interned 1940, to Australia by HMT *Dunera*, returned 1942; served in PC, commissioned; transferred REME; died on active service at central workshops, Naples, cause unknown

Rosenbluth, Hans, later Ross, John C., served in 87 Coy PC; later Sgt in CMF; was a nephew of Israel's first Minister of Justice

Rosenfeld, served in 74 Coy PC; joined from Richborough Camp and was with BEF in France 1940

Rosenfeld, Georg Jakob, later Rosney, George Jakob; born Karlsruhe 23 Feb. 1921, pupil at Karlsruher Gymnasium, father won Iron Cross in WWI, but both he and Rosenfeld's mother were murdered at Auschwitz, emigrated 1939, factory worker in England; 1940 interned at Wormwood Scrubs and Preece Heath; served in 249 Coy PC; then REME,; lastly in RHamps, Sgt, landed in Normandy on D-Day + 8, after end of hostilities rode to Theresienstadt by motor bike, was arrested by Soviets and held for three days before being allowed to continue; interpreter in Hamburg; demob 1946; died 1991

Rosenfeld, Hans, 13804684, later Rodley, John Peter, 14623901, from Duesseldorf, to England 1939, mathematician; served in PC; later 21 Indep. Para. Coy, injured on 61b & 62nd parachute training course, in action in North Africa and Italy; killed in action at Arnhem 22 Sept. 1944, there are three versions concerning the circumstances of his death

Rosenfeld, Max, had lost several toes by frost in concentration camp; served in PC, but in view of his disability was released early on

Rosenfeld, Viktor, changed name to Ross, Victor; born 1919 Vienna, schools in Germany, France and Britain, studied at LSE 1937–40; joined 251 Coy PC 1942 at Arncott Camp; later in Hamilton, Scotland (probably in 137 Coy); 1943 RA, Catterick, L/Bdr; PC OCTU Wrotham & Newark, as Lt in PC to India 1944(?), transferred to General List, at Bombay, Calcutta, Burma, Hong Kong; defending officer at military courts, Capt. SO III; lastly Maj. i/c Formation College (all 3 services) Hong Kong; learned languages easily, could communicate in Urdu, Sinhalese, Karen, etc.; demob 1946; post-war: in advertising, publishing, finally chairman Readers Digest UK, retired 1984

Rosenkranz, Heinrich (Heini), 14448881, temporarily Robertson, Henry; born Vienna 21 Oct. 19, parents murdered in massacre of Stanislau, to UK 1938, intended to go on to USA but encountered difficulty, accommodated at Kitchener Camp; interned 1940, to Canada by SS *Ettrick*, returned 1941, then work in aircraft factory, member of Young Austria; enlisted 1942; served in REME, fitter class III Gp A; later Sgt Interpreter at Didcot PoW camp; demob in Austria 9 Jan. 1947, returned to Vienna

Rosenrauch, Alice, 2992162, Austrian, in Palestine; served as LACW, WAAF, as photographer

Rosenstein, Ernst, served in 74 Coy PC; joined from Richborough Camp and was with BEF in France 1940

Rosenstein, Ernst Zeno, PAL/1115; born Bensheim 11 Dec. 1922, 1935 to Amsterdam, then Palestine; served as L/Cpl RASC, CMF, in North Africa; transferred to Palestine Corps, survived sinking of torpedoed ship north of Tunis, in military hospital Benghazi; must have been in SOM or similar, for he parachuted into Albania and was killed in action 29 July 1944, buried in British war cemetery Voulamania near Athens

Rosenstiel, later Bryant, John, after training with 55 RTR at Aldershot to India by SS *Strathmore*, married an Anglo-Indian lady at New Delhi C. of E. cathedral whilst still serving there; post-war: with bakery machine manufacturer

Rosenthal, served in 74 Coy PC; joined from Richborough Camp and was with BEF in France 1940

Rosenthal, (Rosentall?), 13801214, later Redferne, Cpl in PC; transferred to 21 Indep. Para. Coy, on 61b & 62nd parachute training course, in action in North Africa, Italy, France, Arnhem

Rosenthal, Amnon, author, known as West, Arthur, Austrian, member of Young Austria; enlisted from London 13 Dec. 1943; in action in Italy 1944; went on writing poetry during his time in the service, won prize for literature; demob 4 Jan. 1947

Rosenthal, Dr Erwin Isaak Jacob, went to school at Heilbronn, studied at Heidelberg, Munich, Berlin, D.Litt., Ph.D., MA, lecturer in Semitic languages, Manchester University; served in PC; later RASC, Intelligence; lastly Army Education Corps; with IC in Near East, edited weekly newspaper, lectured to PoWs, headed organising group for re-education of PoWs; post-war: Lecturer for Hebrew and Oriental Studies, Cambridge, Fellow of Pembroke College, professor at Columbia and Mexico Universities, publications concerning Islam and Judaism

Rosenthal, Heinz, later Rodwell, H.; born Fuerth 20 Mar. 1919, school at Nuremberg and Annaberg (Ore Mts.), to England 1933, boarding school Brighton 1933–35; enlisted Sep. 1940, L/Cpl in 165 Coy PC; later RASC; then REME, responsible for reconditioning of motors returned to UK from 8th Army and later from NW Europe; post-war: MD various technological undertakings

Rosenthal, Klaus Walter, 14450334, temporarily Roberts, Walter; born Berlin 19 July 1921, nephew of Erich Nehlhans (chairman of Berlin Jewish community 1945–47, murdered by Soviets), taken into protective custody at Ulm, Stuttgart 10 Nov. 1938, 1 Mar. 1939 by *Kindertransport* of Society of Friends to UK, algricultural work near Leeds; interned 1940, to Canada, returned 1941; enlisted July 1944; served as Sgt in RE, 16 Feb. 1945–26 Nov. 1946 in India; demob Aug. 1947; on German Unity Party's list of comrades who served in Allied armies; post-war: to Berlin 1947, worked on usage of labour, but rejected by Soviets, then spokesman for Chamber of Foreign Trade, but fired because of 'associations with the West'; died of heart failure at Leipzig Fair 1957

Rosenthal, L.; died on active service

Rosenthal, Marianne, served in 1 Allied Volunteer Platoon ATS

Rosenthal, Philip, head of Rosenthal of Selb; born 1916; Flt Lt in RAF; also with Free French post-war: owner of Rosenthal porcelain, Secretary of State in German government

Rosenthal, R., served in 74 Coy PC; joined from Richborough Camp and was with BEF in France 1940

Rosenzweig, Paul, later Pringle, Reginald, 13051455; born Altleiningen, Palatinate 18 Feb. 1920, Protestant (mother was Jewish born, later murdered at Auschwitz), worked on the land from 1933 onwards, sent to Dachau Nov. 1938, to UK with help from Society of Friends, worked on farm near Louth, Lincs.; enlisted 18 Feb. 1940; became Cpl in 88 and 229 Coy PC, in France 1940, Le Havre, then St Malo; later interpreter in Brussels, Bad Oeynhausen, Minden, attached to 99 Heavy A.A.Regt RA, Hamburg, investigation of former Nazis; post-war: joiner and carpenter, wrote autobiography

Rosert, Susanne, served in 1 AV Platoon, ATS

Rosinski, served in 74 Coy PC; joined from Richborough Camp and was with BEF in France 1940

Ross, L. J., Austrian, Sgt in CMF, in Italy met Austrian PoWs whom he had known pre-war and passed to them copies of the London *Zeitspiegel* magazine

Rossi, A., 13807769

Rosskamm, Stephan, 13805787, later Ross, Steven; born Schwarza near Meiningen, arrested at Suhl together with father, who owned store there, Nov. 1938, 1939 to England; served as L/Cpl in 77 Coy PC; transferred to Buffs; then 3/10 Cdo; in Sicily, then Italy, attached to 9 Cdo, wounded by artillery fire in attack over open ground at Monte Ornito, in military hospital Pompeii; wounded again in bayonet attack at Anzio landing; wounded for third time by bomb on hospital

Roth, E. (E.R.A.), Austrian, served on HMS *Blenheim*, Alexandria

Roth, Josef, later Rodgers, Joseph, served in 220 Coy PC

Rothbarth, Erwin, later Rivers, Max, 14441856; born 1914, lecturer in economics at Cambridge, assistant of Lord Keynes; served in 1 Bn Suffolk Regt; died of wounds received at Arnhem, buried at Overloon; *The Review of Economic Studies*, Vol.XII, p. 122, quotes from his last letter: 'I was relieved to see that the knowledge of what one is fighting for helps, after all, to overcome the primitive feeling of outrage, which seizes natural man when he perceives the actuality of death behind the comforting mechanism of commands, dispositions, movements according to plan'

Rothenberg, Henry R., 13802670, served in PC; later RASC

Rothmann, later 13117466 O'Rourke, J., from Vienna, father Jewish, mother Irish, served in PC; later in Publicity and Psycho Warfare; on 17 Jan. 1945 posted from 11 Amplifier Unit to 18 Leaflet Unit, both part of 21st AGp Main HQ

Rothschild, Dr Paul, Lt Col in RAMC, India (Paiforce), also Persia

Rothschild, Renate, married Loewenheck, Viennese, 1939 to Palestine; served as Cpl in ATS in North Africa 5 July 1942–15 May 1946, at Sarafand, Tel-el-Kebir, Moascar near Ismalia; post-war: in Jerusalem, nursery nurse, then Switzerland

Rotner, served in 74 Coy PC; joined from Richborough Camp and was with BEF in France 1940

Rotschild, Freddy, served in 3/10 Cdo; post-war: painter and sculptor in Toronto

Rotstein, Oskar, senior member of Young Austria

Rottenberg, M.

Rotuch, S., served in 74 Coy PC

Rowley, F., served in 246 Coy PC

Rozengarten, served in 74 Coy PC; joined from Richborough Camp and was with BEF in France 1940

Rubensohn, served in 74 Coy PC; joined from Richborough Camp and was with BEF in France 1940

Rubin, David, PAL775832, Austrian, to Palestine; served as Cpl in RAF FMT; post-war: Capt. in Israeli Air Force

Rubin, Georg

Rubin, Hermann, enlisted shortly before 29 July 1944

Rubner, Wenzel, served in RAF, on German Unity Party's list of Sudeten German Social Democrats who served in the British Army

Rueman, T., 13046356 and 6387032, Pte in PC; RWK; probably SOE

Ruh, Toni (same as Sruh, alias G.Broadman?), on German Unity Party's list of comrades who served in Allied armies

Rummelsburg, David, Capt., on German Unity Party's list of comrades who served in Allied armies; post-war: in publicity office of Leipzig Fair, had difficulties with Communist Party, but appears to have enjoyed the protection of H. Matern

Rusikin, served in 74 Coy PC; joined from Richborough Camp and was with BEF in France 1940

Russ, Sgt in 93 Coy PC, camouflage expert

Russell, served in 137 Coy PC

Rutherford, Sgt in 69 Coy PC

Ryan, G.S.

Rychwalski, served in 74 Coy PC; joined from Richborough Camp and was with BEF in France 1940

Rywalski, served in 74 Coy PC; joined from Richborough Camp and was with BEF in France 1940 (NB: Rychwalski and Rywalski appear as separate entries on 74 Coy nominal roll.)

S., did not wish to give his full name, Sgt, later Maj.; served in PC, Military Police, SOM; Lt 1941, OC Arab labour unit in Algiers; Capt. in HQ African Force

S., von (name not revealed), served in PC, Military Police, SOM Algiers, Greece; whilst still interned in one of the desert camps in Algeria, was visited by his father, a naval officer in the German armistice commission at Algiers, who tried to persuade him to return to Germany, father unsuccessful; it is reported that Von S. later became an NCO in PC, other reports have it that he was commissioned, commanded an Arab unit in Algiers, became Capt. HQ Africa Force and lastly OC labour unit in Greece

S. Margaret (or Margaret S.?), surname not revealed, Austrian, Capt. in RAMC; contributed article to *Zeitspiegel* 25 Nov. 1944 about visit by FM Montgomery to military hospital

Saalkind, L., 13810021, later Macallister, A., 6436379, Pte in PC and R. Sussex Regt; returned to original unit (in PC) autumn 1944

Saar, Erhard Wolf Wilhelm, 13803191, later Lees, Edward (in SOE: Cheney, E., nicknamed 'Teddy il dinamitardo'); born Stettin 12 June 1921, but grew up with grandparents in Berlin, father was Sgt in German Army, parents divorced, stepbrother of Heinrich Saar, emigrated 1936, taken in by Jewish family in Manchester; enlisted Sept. 1940; served in 220, 88 and 251 Coy PC; then RF (SOE), in Operation DANBURY-SEATHRIFT (OC Capt. Karminski) parachuted into Tramontina Valley 12 Aug. 1944 to work with partisans there, contacts to Don Ascanio de Luca, Candido Grassi, Manlio Cencig, Faustino Barbina, carried out sabotage of bridges and transport, involved in rescue of three US officers who had crashed at the back of Trieste, escaped from Trieste by boat; finally in PoW camp Island Farm, Bridgend, where he found his father; Hon. Capt. 1949; post-war: served in Glamorgan Fire Brigade, chief officer Neath Fire Brigade, then personnel manager and official interpreter for German for Glamorgan County Council

Saar, Heinrich, stepbrother of above, on German Unity Party's list of comrades who served in Allied armies

Sabertschnig, A., CQMS in 137 and 229 Coy PC

Saborski, Harry, member of Young Austria; enlisted from Oxford, Dec. 1943/Jan. 1944

Sachs, one of three brothers from Prague, who all enlisted in Palestine; with 608 Coy PC in North Africa and Greece, taken prisoner by the Germans at Kalamata 1941, spent rest of war at Stalag 9 in Silesia

Sachs, second of the three brothers mentioned above

Sachs, third of the three brothers mentioned above

Sachs, H.P., 13805733, later Seymour, H.A.; born 1 Feb. 1918; served first in 77 Coy PC; then in 3/10 Cdo; renowned as locksmith; in action along Maas river Jan. 1945; at Rhine crossing attached to 46 RM Cdo; he and Villiers were killed in action simultaneously

Sachs, Walter, later Hughes, W., from Vienna, mother Gentile, fled to Switzerland, where he was at first permitted to stay, but was expelled after short time, returned to Vienna, to UK as student; enlisted 1940; served in PC; later in Para. Regt 6th Airborn Div., parachuted into Normandy on night preceding D-Day landings; taken prisoner 2 days later, spent 1 year in German prison camp, where British fellow prisoners distrusted him and on one occasion nearly caused disaster; after release interpreter in 1 Para. Bde; post-war: lives in Berks.

Sadowski, served in 74 Coy PC; joined from Richborough Camp and was with BEF in France 1940

Saenger, Sgt in 88 Coy PC; enlisted from Richborough, was in France (Le

Havre, Harfleur) 1940

Sagel, Herbert, in SOE, was used on special mission to Tito and partisans in Yugoslavia, operated in '4 zone' (Slovenia); post-war: lives in Vienna

Salinger, alias Saloschin (q.v.), later Saunders, L.

Salisbury, one of the ski instructors of the 52nd Lowland Div.; commissioned in PC; transferred to RASC and posted back to 52nd Div., this time as OC of one of last horsedrawn units in Corps

Saloman, M., 13117924, later Sheridan, M.R., 6305476, Pte in PC; later the Buffs

Salomon, served in 137 Coy PC

Salomon 1, served in 74 Coy PC; joined from Richborough Camp and was with BEF in France 1940

Salomon 2, served in 74 Coy PC; joined from Richborough Camp and was with BEF in France 1940

Salomon, Alfred; died on active service

Salomon, Kurt; died on active service

Salomon, M.F., later Martin, Frank M.; born 1890; enlisted 1 Apr. 1940; discharged for medical reasons 10 May 1942

Salomon, P., 13801833, Cpl, served in NW Europe, mentioned in dispatches

Salomon, Trude, served in 1 Allied Volunteer Platoon ATS

Saloschin, Count Georg V., alias Salinger, L. (q.v.), 13805183, later Saunders, George V.; born Munich 12 Feb. 1921, of ancient lineage, having been warned by a German general (or a prominent Gestapo man?) of their planned arrest, his family received help from high quarters to leave Germany, in UK was pupil at Gordonstoun with Prince Philip; interned 1940, sent to Canada; after return to UK served in 137 Coy PC as Sgt; transferred to 3/10 Cdo; attached to 45 Cdo in Normandy landing, wounded by shrapnel at Merville 7 June 1944, next day tried to lead party of wounded of both sides in captured German ambulance to British first-aid post Le Plein, but was in turn captured by Germans, though German ambulance driver had found out he was of German origin, he did not give him away, escaped, but was captured again 2 days later, spent rest of war in Stalag Sagan; awarded Military Medal; post-war: banker in London (There is some confusion about whether Saloschin and Salinger were the same person; Eden says Salinger had been killed in action.)

Salzer, Michael, from Zell-am-See, Austria, London correspondent of *Wiener Journal* newspaper; joined RAF as mechanic, was used as trainer, editor of an RAF journal, war correspondent in North Africa, Pantelleria, Italy, Yugoslavia, India and Burma; finally at Nuremberg trials; Sqn Ldr

Samaragd, 13802080, Pte in 69 Coy PC; applied for transfer to RAC on 12 Aug. 1941 (!); fate unknown

Samaskewitz, Lore, served in 1 or 4 AVP ATS

Samek, Bert

Samson, A.,13805613, later Shelley, A. Percy, from Hamburg, served in PC; later in 3/10 Cdo; attached to a Marine commando was, together with Stewart, in hand grenade attack on farm shed at Merville, Normandy, on 8 June 1944; in Italy Sept. 1944; post-war: banker in London

Samuel, served in 74 Coy PC; joined from Richborough Camp and was with BEF in France 1940

Samuel, Dr Anton G., from Germany, had been lecturer at Cambridge, served in PC as Cpl; later CSM in Intelligence; was released at request of FO, where he was installed in important position; at some stage worked on liaison with German church organisations

Samuel, Gerda, served in 1 Allied Volunteer Platoon ATS

Samuel, Herbert, later Samuel, John, served in 219 Coy PC (8 Sect.), one of youngest in that section, with three others he formed a group known as 'the nursery'

Sander, served in 74 Coy PC; joined from Richborough Camp and was with BEF in France 1940

Sander, Gus, later Saunders, said to have been refugee, but might also have been Belgian, Lt in RAMC with field ambulance at Arnhem; later with Intelligence; post-war: with Middx Regt in Korea

Sanders, G., 13806054, Pte in 253 Coy PC

Sanders, Steven Bert, served in 137 Coy PC

Sanderson, S.M., served in 87, 166 and 229 Coy PC

Saravolac, P., 13807905 and 13122231

Sarne, Herbert

Sarne, Th., served in 74 Coy PC; joined from Richborough Camp and was with BEF in France 1940

Satzmann, served in 74 Coy PC; joined from Richborough Camp and was with BEF in France 1940

Sauer, G.J. (Szauer?), 13807278, later Sayers, G.J., from Hungary, appears to have had French connections – spoke French fluently and is said to have been decorated with Croix de Guerre; joined British Army, Dec. 1941; served in PC, probably 229 Coy, as L/Cpl; transferred to 3/10 Cdo, took part in Operation PREMIUM against Wassenaar 27 Feb. 1944; attached to 4 Cdo on D-Day; on 14 June 1944 was with French Troop of 10 Cdo, when he was wounded in arm and chest; post-war: married to fashion designer, fashion retailer

Saul, served in 74 Coy PC; joined from Richborough Camp and was with BEF in France 1940

Saunders, Harry John, Sgt in SOE, carried out notable reconnaisance in Xanten area with Sgt L.M.Gilbert (see Richle above) prior to Rhine crossing, both fluent German-speakers, were disguised in *Wehrmacht* uniforms and spent several days behind enemy lines collecting intelligence, especially on artillery and troop movements; Sgt Saunders, a native anti-Nazi German, was arrested by *Feldgendarmerie* but managed to withstand interrogation and to make his way back to allied lines bringing with him information of highest military importance; awarded Military Medal

Saywood, E.A., Capt., commissioned 4 Dec, 1942, on officers' list of 77 Coy PC 31 Dec. 1942; also in 88 Coy on 30 June 1943

Schaechter, L. (PAL)/31453, served as driver in 468 GT RASC CMF

Schaefer, W.F.

Schaerf, served in 74 Coy PC; joined from Richborough Camp and was with

BEF in France 1940

Schaffer, Norbert, member of Young Austria; enlisted from Birmingham Dec. 1943/Jan. 1944

Schaerf, Bobby, member of Young Austria; enlisted from London Dec. 1943/Jan. 1944

Schapira, E.A., 13805780, later Shapire, E.A., served in PC

Scharf, K., later Scarfe, on officers' list of 88 Coy PC as Lt Scharf 30 June 1942 and again as Lt Scarfe 30 June 1943, as Capt. Scarfe and company 2 i/c 26 July 1943

Schatz, Hugo, alias Scott, William, German conscript, PoW; taken into British service; IC, posted to No.1 I (U) Apr. 1944; returned to 209 PoW camp Dec. 1944

Schatzberger, A., Austrian, fled to France; interned there; Sept. 1939–Apr. 1940 *Prestataire* under command of BEF, after Dunkirk via Rennes and Bordeaux to Bayonne and Casablanca, remained *Prestataire* till Apr. 1941; then discharged and interned as *travailleur étranger*; after Allied landing in North Africa joined British Army, 338 Coy PC, as Cpl, took part in liberation of internees in desert camps Kenadsa and Colomb-Bechor

Schechter 1, served in 74 Coy PC; joined from Richborough Camp and was with BEF in France 1940

Schechter 2, served in 74 Coy PC; joined from Richborough Camp and was with BEF in France 1940

Scheib, Erwin, Sgt in 69 Coy PC until 29 Apr. 1943

Scheib, Theo, served in 69 Coy PC

Scheinmann, Oscar G., alias Stephen, alias 2/Lt Perkins, J.G. IC, in UK June 1945

Schendel, served in 74 Coy PC; joined from Richborough Camp and was with BEF in France 1940

Scherchen, Wulff, later Woolford, John, son of then well-known conductor; post-war: to Australia.

Scheuer, H.E. (Heini), served in 87 Coy PC; post-war: flautist in Birmingham Symphony Orchestra, prominent in Ex-Service NB Association

Scheuermann, later Shermer, served in 77 Coy PC

Scheuermann, J.F, served in 74 Coy PC; joined from Richborough Camp and was with BEF in France 1940; Cpl

Schidlof, N.B.

Schiffermann, served in 74 Coy PC; joined from Richborough Camp and was with BEF in France 1940

Schiller, Norbert.

Schiller, PAL/17758, Austrian, craftsman/fitter in Palestine

Schilling, 13805947, later Bruce, Harold, 14623980, from Berlin, pupil at Franzoesisches Gymnasium, after emigration Gordonstoun School; served in 251 Coy PC; on 61b and 62nd parachute training course ; transferred to 21 Indep. Para. Coy, with them in North Africa, Italy and, as section leader, in Arnhem, lastly in Norway; transfer to Recce Unit RHKDF

Schimmelpfennig, served in 74 Coy PC; joined from Richborough Camp and was with BEF in France 1940

Schindler, served in 88 Coy PC; joined from Richborough Camp, in France 1940; post-war: waiter in Schmitt's Restaurant, London

Schindler, E., served in 74 Coy PC; joined from Richborough Camp and was with BEF in France 1940

Schindler, Margot, served in 1 Allied Volunteer Platoon ATS

Schirmer, or Schirner, K.K., 13810005, later Sanderson, J.K., 6305491, Pte in PC; later the Buffs; returned to PC autumn 1944

Schittkowski, served in 74 Coy PC; joined from Richborough Camp and was with BEF in France 1940

Schivern, 13807724, enlisted spring 1942; served in PC; on 61b and 62nd parachute training course; returned to unit because of ankle injury

Schlepps, R., trumpeter in 3 PCTC

Schlesinger 1, served in 74 Coy PC; joined from Richborough Camp and was with BEF in France 1940

Schlesinger 2, served in 74 Coy PC; joined from Richborough Camp and was with BEF in France 1940

Schlesinger 3, served in 74 Coy PC; joined from Richborough Camp and was with BEF in France 1940

Schlesinger 4, served in 74 Coy PC; joined from Richborough Camp and was with BEF in France 1940

Schlesinger, later Scott, served in PC; brother of Schlesinger, later Spencer

Schlesinger, later Spencer, served in PC; brother of Schlesinger, later Scott

Schlesinger, Eduard, later Stuart, alias Stuart-Schlesinger, Austrian; demob in Vienna

Schlesinger, Franz, later Sleigh, Frank James; born 1903; enlisted Dec. 1940, served in 249 Coy PC; demob Nov. 1945; died 1953

Schlesinger, John, had served in Czechoslovak Army, served in 88 Coy PC, France 1940, at Harfleur was able to show other members of company how to handle a rifle

Schlesinger, Kurt, later Mond, Frank (related to Mond family – Lord Melchett), had served in German Army in WW1, later boss of textile firm in England; Pte in 229 and 249 Coy PC; then RAMC, in various military hospitals on continent of Europe after Normandy landings

Schlesinger, M. O.; died shortly after release from service

Schlesinger, Marianne, married Egtman; born Vienna 19 Apr. 1926, to UK by *Kindertransport* 26 Apr. 1939, lived in Worthing; served in ATS 1944–47, attached to motorcycle training unit, shorthand typist in Keswick; then with BAOR Bueckeburg and Oyenhausen as interpreter; post-war: with Worthing solicitor, then Slaughter and May, London, lives in Denmark

Schlichter, served in 74 Coy PC; joined from Richborough Camp and was with BEF in France 1940

Schlonovien, 13887024, transferred from PC to 21 Indep. Para. Coy; on 61b and 62nd parachute training course, sustained knee injury on landing; as a result returned to his original unit

Schloss, Yarlow, 13041025, later Scott, Jack, Pte in 246 Coy PC; transferred to 3/10 Cdo and RWK, in action in Sicily, Italy and landing on Lissa (Vis); liaison with Tito and Yugoslav partisans

Schlossberg, veteran of Spanish Civil War, Sqn Ldr in RAF, chief interpreter there

Schmitt, served in 74 Coy PC; joined from Richborough Camp and was with BEF in France 1940

Schmoll, Heinz; born at Haynau, Silesia, 25 Feb. 1919, pupil at Gerhard Hauptmann Ober-Realschule, Breslau, then apprenticed to locksmith, conscripted into German Army 1935, discharged as Jew, Nov. 1938 at Buchenwald, emigrated to Scotland Apr. 1939, worked in sawmill; enlisted 6 Dec. 1939; served in 88 Coy PC, at Le Havre, Rennes, St Malo, then Mile End during blitz, autumn 1940, played clarinet and double-bass in military orchestra; later in RAOC; then REME, 1945 to Egypt; demob at Aldershot May 1946; post-war: sawyer, later rep., went to S. Rhodesia, there syndic at copper mine, wrote autobiography

Schnabel, A., Austrian, in CMF, met PoWs, with whom he had been at school

Schnabel, Peter J., Austrian; born 1900 or 1901, had been major in *Heimwehr*, a right-wing political militia pre-war; served in PC; seconded to 52 Lowland Div. as mountaineering and ski instructor, commissioned; first posting to 77 Coy PC 4 May 1942; later to Cameron Highlanders, with them in Belgium and Germany; intelligence officer; 1946 theatre and music officer of Allied Control Commission Austria; then asstistant controller British information service in Austria; known as MacSchnabel; post-war: was well-known figure in Vienna; died 17 Feb. 1983, his obituary in *die Presse*, the leading Austrian paper, described him as 'Royal British Major'

Schneditz, later Rockhill, Austrian, served in 337 or 338 Coy PC

Schnee, served in 74 Coy PC; joined from Richborough Camp and was with BEF in France 1940

Schneider, served in 74 Coy PC; joined from Richborough Camp and was with BEF in France 1940

Schneider, E.F., on officers' list of 88 Coy PC for 1942; Capt.

Schneider, Johann, later Taylor, John B; born Berlin 1923, came to UK July 1939; interned 1940, to Australia on HMT *Dunera*, returned UK 1942, on war work in Leicester; enlisted Sept. 1944, Cpl in Leics. Regt (other report says Sgt), awarded Distinguished Conduct Medal for bravery whilst commanding his section; died on active service

Schneider, Max, later Shelley, Peter, from Vienna, communist, member of Young Austria; enlisted from Birmingham Dec. 1943/Jan. 1944; with 7th Cameronians in Normandy, Belgium, Netherlands and Germany, in action at Alpon and Rheine, and at Rhine crossing, awarded Military Medal, wounded; interpreter in PoW camp in S. England; demob at Villach, Carinthia, 1947; post-war: lives in Vienna

Schnek, Dr Friedrich, 13809275; born in Vienna 6 Dec. 1900, attended Wasa Gymnasium, joined Austrian Army shortly before end of WWI, then returned to school at Piaristen Gymnasium, studied law in Vienna, Doctor of Law 1923, was leading lawyer, defended left-wing clients (Bentwich says he was in the Heimwehr, but this is highly improbable), fled to Yugoslavia 1938, then to Paris. From hereon he and Dr Johann Schnek (below) are mixed up with each other by several sources. According to E. Lebensaft, his biographer, he was *Prestataire* 1939, 1940 at Dunkirk, fled to North Africa; interned at Kenadsa, refused orders, transferred to Hadjerat M'Guil detention camp, after liberation witness in trial of camp officers; served in 337 Coy PC; later 362 Coy PC, awarded BEM for bravery at Maison Carrée for leading his section to put out a fire in an ammunition dump or, maybe, on a train; because of his presence of mind and qualities of leadership the fire remained under control and damage was limited, mentioned in dispatches, promoted Sgt in 362 Coy; in summer 1945 to BALU Vienna, then to Austrian Courts Section in Graz; commissioned 20 June 1946, used his influence to protect minor offenders in Austria and wanted to concentrate on the real criminals; died on active service at Klagenfurt 9 Jan. 1947

Schneck, Fritz, born Vienna 4 Apr. 1895, officer in Austro-Hungarian Army in WWI, served on Russian front, emigrated to England 1939; is thought to have served in France 1940, was stationed at Newbury and Gloucester later on; from these facts it appears probable he was with 93 Coy PC (in France 1940 and Newbury); then posted to either 220 or 229 Coy PC, both of which were at Gloucester supposedly to form nucleus of Austrian legion in 1941, might have been orderly room clerk there and had his family with him; post-war lived in London, worked as accountant; died 1955

Schnek or Schneck, Dr Johann, Viennese, had been secretary of Union of Stage and Cinema Workers, social democrat, fled to Paris, politically active there. From hereon he and Dr Friedrich Schnek (above) are mixed up with each other by several sources. According to some he was *Prestataire* 1939, fled to North Africa; interned at Kenadsa, refused orders, was transferred to Hadjerat M'Guil detention camp, after liberation witness in trial of camp officers there; joined 337 Coy PC in Algeria; then Cameronians, Intelligence, 1944 War Office London, SHAEF, BALU, mentioned in dispatches; died in Vienna 1947 of effects of treatment at Hadjerat M'Guil. Biographer of Friedrich Schnek maintains that all this happened to her subject, and that Johann, also called Jacques, was never in either the French or the British armies, but succeeded in getting to New York 1941, changed his name to John James Sheldon and died there 12 May 1973

Schnek, Walter; born Vienna 12 June 1919, on 18 Mar. 1938 moved from Bielitz to Amsterdam, is known to have been agricultural labourer at Eindhoven July 1941; arrested by Gestapo July 42 and charged with espionage, wore Jew's yellow star after release, was told he would be deported to Poland 27 July 1942, but hid and continued to live at the Hague, Eindhoven and Valkenwaard Aug. 1942–Sept. 1944; wore British officer's uniform after liberation of Netherlands

Schnitzer, served in 74 Coy PC; joined from Richborough Camp and was with BEF in France 1940

Schnitzer, Dr, Viennese, Maj. in RAMC, OC British military hospital, Vienna, 1945

Schnur, served in 74 Coy PC; joined from Richborough Camp and was with BEF in France 1940

Schoen, E.F., Austrian, driver in 4 Coy RASC BD MEF

Schoenberg, K.

Schoenfeld, Ernst A. (Ernest); born Vienna 23 Jan. 1921, to Prague summer 1938, UK Apr. 1939; interned, to Australia by HMT *Dunera*; joined 8 Empl. Coy CMF – AMF (Southern Command); L/Cpl; discharged 21 Aug. 1946; post-war: returned to Vienna 1947 to repossess parents' property

Schoenhorn, Max, Austrian, served in Near East

Schoissengeier, alias Georges, Henri Charles, alias Cosson, Pierre, alias Schwarz, Hugo, Austrian, Cpl in 362 Coy PC; BNAF; Operation DINTYLAKE near Klagenfurt; post-war: in intelligence service in Austria

Schonfeld, O.W., 13810008, later Shaw, P.M., 5550139, Pte in PC and RHamps

Schornstein, Fritz, PAL/30942, later Sharoni, S.; born Vienna 3 June 1920; enlisted at Sarafand; driver in RASC and RE; served in North Africa Mar. 1942–23. Oct. 1946

Schorr, L., Austrian, L/Cpl, at liberation of Rome

Schott, W.

Schotz, Dr, Austrian, Maj. in RAMC in Near East

Schramm, Martin; born 1896, served in 74 Coy PC; joined from Richborough Camp and was with BEF in France 1940; discharged on medical grounds Feb. 1944; died June 1955

Schreiber, C., Sgt in PC; 1944 in No. 1 Psycho Warfare Gp, Allied Information Service, SHAEF

Schreiber, Hermann, S/Sgt, Lord Janner's assistant in clearing up Bergen Belsen concentration camp.

Schreiber, Irene, from Berlin, served in ATS

Schreuer, Rudy, later Sherman, R.W.; born Berlin 10 May 1921, pupil at Zehlendorf Gymnasium till Oct. 1933, to UK same year, attended Leighton Park School, Reading, till 1938, then London University till 1940; interned, by HMT *Dunera* to Australia, returned 1941; enlisted end of 1941; served in 3 PCTC; then 229 Coy PC Jan. 1942; transferred to RAMC 1943, School of X-ray (Millbank), radiographer, London Hospital, to Belfast Feb.–Sept. 1944, then 24 General Hospital, Lagos, Nigeria, Oct. 1944 till demob Oct. 1946; post-war: export/import in London, Whitehaven and Eccles, then Stalybridge and Marlborough as sales manager, director and group MD

Schreyeck, J., Lt on officers' list of 406 Coy PC 16 Aug. and 31 Dec. 1944 at Casablanca; 30 Apr. 1945 to civilian labour

Schubert, Erich, later Stevens, Eric, Austrian, served in Dorset Regt; later in 21 Indep. Para. Coy, at Arnhem

Schueck, W., served in 77 Coy PC, acted in that company's Xmas panto *A Midsummer Night's Scream*, probably 1941.

Schueftan, H., later Seaman, Henry H., arrested with father and brother on night of 9 Nov. 1938 and taken to Buchenwald, held for 6 weeks, by *Kindertransport* to UK, accommodated at Butlin's Holiday Camp Dovercourt, then interpreter at Kitchener Camp; interned at Huyton, by HMT *Dunera* to Australia, there at Hay camp, returned to England; enlisted; served in 229 Coy PC as driver to OC; 1943 zu 5 RTR, with them from Normandy to Berlin; post-war: married and joined his family in

Seattle, with Boeing for 27 years, responsible for wiring diagrams and system schematics for 747 aircraft and AWACS

Schul, Pinkus, ear, nose and throat specialist, Maj. in RAMC; died on active service in Near East

Schueller, Peter, PAL774660, Austrian, went to Palestine; served as Sgt in RAF

Schulof, F.G., Lt, name appears in officers' list of 249 Coy PC 31 Dec. 1942

Schulz, Margaret, served in 3 Allied Vol. Platoon ATS

Schulze, R. 13807358; born 1922, seaman on German freighter, father communist and held at concentration camp, deserted at Boulogne Nov. 1941, fled through France, Spain and Portugal to England; served in 69 Coy PC from 21 Mar. 1942

Schumann, Martin, from Klagenfurt, served in 337 or 338 Coy PC

Schuster, fled to Switzerland from Germany, later to South Africa; enlisted there and served in 2nd S.A. Div., taken prisoner with whole of division at Tobruk and taken to Italy, like other Jewish prisoners was treated correctly, taught German in PoW camp; released after Italian armistice, fled to Switzerland, interned there for remainder of war

Schwalbe 1, served in 74 Coy PC; joined from Richborough Camp and was with BEF in France 1940

Schwalbe 2, served in 74 Coy PC; joined from Richborough Camp and was with BEF in France 1940

Schwartz, Austrian, served in 338 Coy PC

Schwartz, Hans, 1380162, later Stanleigh, John Hubert, 14623947; born near Posen (Poznan) 5 July 1919, lived in Brandenburg, pupil at Saldria, family had long military tradition going back to 1814, was boy scout and had pre-military training, emigrated UK Dec. 1938; served in 93 Coy PC as L/Cpl; later Bomb Disposal; then 21 Indep. Para. Coy; on 61b and 62nd parachute training course; in North Africa, Italy, south coast of France, Arnhem, Norway, survived jump when chute did not open; post-war: in fashion industry till 1959, then electrical engineer, after retirement 1982 active in CND, founder 'Ex-Service CND'

Schwarz (Schwartz?) Hans, 1876107, later Blake, Henry, son of Erich and Elli S. from Czechoslovakia, joined RAF 24 Apr. 1943, Sgt in 101 Sqn (previously 310 Sqn Czech Air Force), 'Special operator'; killed in action at age 19 in attack on Brunswick by Lancaster bomber, buried at Haverlee, Belgium

Schwartze, H.; died on active service

Schwarz 1, served in 74 Coy PC; joined from Richborough Camp and was with BEF in France 1940

Schwarz 2, served in 74 Coy PC; joined from Richborough Camp and was with BEF in France 1940

Schwarz, B., served in 246 Coy PC

Schwarz, Erich, later Sanders, Eric; born Vienna 1919, hated school and was glad when Hitler 'liberated him from that nonsense' in 1938, emigrated to London, stayed with relatives, pupil at Clarke's College, worked for German-Jewish Aid Committee, Woburn and Bloomsbury House, then together with father dairy hand at Basingstoke; enlisted Feb. 1940,

Richborough; with 88 Coy PC to France 1940, Harfleur, Le Havre, Rennes, St Malo, then Newport, Mon., Carmarthen, etc.; took correspondence course for intermediate B.Sc.; transferred to RF (SOE), in Bari, with Wirlander, Hladnik questioned Austrian PoWs, trained for use in Styria, but action did not take place; interpreter at PoW camp, Taunton; demob, but re-joined two days later; in Vienna WO 1 with Control Commission for 1 year, then London; released again; post-war: teacher and author, wrote books, plays and film scripts

Schwarz, Erich, PAL774194, served as Sgt in RAF, meteorologist; post-war: Capt. in Israeli Air Force, later CEO of World Meteorological Organisation

Schwarz, Felix, from Vienna, brother of S. Harry (below), member of Young Austria; enlisted from London Dec. 1943 or Jan. 1944; Leading Writer, RN, on destroyer in English Channel, encounter with enemy mine; Class B release 1945 to work in torpedo factory; post-war: degree at Manchester Institute of Technology, scientist with ICI, MA in Systems Engineering Lancaster University

Schwarz, Felix

Schwarz, Fredl, Austrian, enlisted shortly before 29 July 1944.

Schwarz, Gerhard, served in REME.

Schwarz, Harry, later Saunders; born Vienna 1923, brother of S. Felix, RN, (above), pupil at Theresianum 1933–38, emigrated to England with parents and brother 1938, graduated B.Sc.(Eng.) with 1st class hons. 1943; joined REME, commissioned 1944; in Middle East, seconded to PoW department as interpreter; later Judge Advocate Generals Dept. War Crimes Group NW Europe, Capt., observer at Loibl Pass and Stalag Luft 3 war crimes trials; post-war: joined Duke of Lancs. Own Yeo. (TA) as OR, again commissioned in REME 1948, Capt., 1952 to TARO, worked in engineering and chemical industries, 1962 chartered patent agent, 1970–84 own practice

Schwarz, Kurt, in agriculture after emigration to Canada, matriculated in McGill University, to UK, factory worker at Glasgow, active member of Young Austria; enlisted Dec. 1943/Jan. 1944; served in Black Watch, commissioned; demob, rank of Capt.

Schwarzschild, Paul, later Shields, Paul, Viennese, brother of Peter S., later Black

Schwarzschild, Peter, later Black, Peter, Viennese, brother of Paul S., later Shields; post-war: textile manufacturer, supplier of Marks and Spencer

Schwefel, Hans; born Vienna 31 Jan.1899, emigrated London 25 May 1938; when joining up on Boxing Day 1939, was looking forward to his 41st birthday; served in PC until 27 June 1941, told that his services were no longer required, as he was too old

Schweiger, Hans (Harry), alias Stevens, Harry, from Vienna, served in 88 Coy PC (9 Sect.) later in RF (SOE), Lt, saw service in North Africa, Italy, Styria, on Operation HISTORIAN at Zeltweg, at takeover of airfield there and in withdrawal to Castle Authal, there with Prince Croy, Andrassy, concerned with establishment of democratic government in Styria; in June 1945 in

Operation DUNCERY still at Zeltweg; after end of hostilities in Austria, arrested Himmler's deputy Oswald Pohl

Schwitzer J.G. (Schweizer? Schwytzer?), 13802309, later Swinton, Tommy G.; born somewhere in Hungary 8 Mar. 1920, attended City of London College; served in PC; transferred to 3/10 Cdo; in Normandy attached to 41 RM Cdo (4 Cdo Bde), wounded and evacuated on D-Day

Scott, H.

Sechestower, W., (E.R.A.), Austrian, served as Petty Officer on HMS *Stag*, at Suez

Seelig (Dr ?), served as Lt in Indian Medical Service

Seff, served in 74 Coy PC; joined from Richborough Camp and was with BEF in France 1940

Segal, Heinz, from Schwadorf, Austria, textile technician, served as commissioned officer with Free French, awarded Croix de Guerre by de Gaulle and became Chevalier de la Légion d'honneur

Seifert, Erwin, member of Young Austria; enlisted from Oxford Dec. 1943/Jan. 1944

Seilern, Count Antoine; born in England, dual national, British and Austrian, grew up in Vienna, studied history of art, left Austria after *Anschluss*; volunteered for service in PC 1939; post-war: well known art collector

Seinfeld, Hugo, PAL769412, Austrian, joined RAF in Palestine; at first LAC/medical orderly, reported to have been medical officer at a later stage

Sekler, Wolf Mesulem, Austrian; born Kolomea, Bukowina, 25 Dec. 1912: served in RAMC 20 Oct. 1944–27 Aug. 1946; discharge certificate describes him as an indifferent soldier

Selbiger, served in 74 Coy PC; joined from Richborough Camp and was with BEF in France 1940

Seligmann-Elsass, J.; post-war: prominent in Ex-Service NB Association

Seligsohn, Dr R., rabbi; died on active service

Seltz, Antonie Valerie (Tony), served in 1 Allied Volunteer Platoon ATS, commissioned; sister of Kurt Seltz (below)

Seltz, Kurt Wolfgang Friedrich, later Sely, Kaye Wolve Frederick, from Munich, served in PC, commissioned; transferred to Intelligence, CSDIC, then chief of information control, Hamburg, later Berlin; According to G. Clare in *Berlin Days* he was an exceedingly colourful personality

Selzer, E.; died on active service

Semenowsky, Konstantin, PAL775575, Austrian, joined RAF in Palestine; served as Sgt/wireless engineer; post-war: Maj. in Israeli Air Force

Seymour, Walter E., served in 229 Coy PC

Shabitch, B., 13806069, Pte in 253 Coy PC

Shearer, Kenneth, served in 220 Coy PC

Sheldon, had been lawyer in Germany, served in PC, Sgt/interpreter at surrender of German occupation forces of Channel Islands to combined British forces May 1945, translated surrender conditions, also at occupation of Alderney, investigated Nazi crimes there

Sheldon, Austrian, had been fire officer of his home town, served in PC; transferred to Army Fire Service and acted as trainer, teaching Austrian fire fighting methods; in Belgium 1944, at fire in Ostend harbour Dec. 1944

Sheldon, Walter, served in PC; transferred Military Police, in France, Belgium, Holland 1944/45, took part in search for Himmler; instructor to German police

Sheridan, Henry; post-war: prominent in Ex-Service NB Association

Sheridan, W., Austrian

Shilo, L., served in 74, 165 and 246 Coy PC; post-war: bespoke tailor

Short, served in 137 Coy PC

Shotts, A., served in 137 Coy PC; post-war: prominent in Ex-Service NB Association

Sichrovsky, Harry, Viennese, served in RA, India and Burma; member of 'Commission, Austrians in Exile'

Sieber, Peter, Austrian, served as Commander RNVR and RN

Siegel, Hans Peter, later Sinclair, H. Peter, from Munich, enlisted Westward Ho! 22 Aug. 1940; served in 219 Coy PC (forestry, railway work, building of defence works), boredom made him take cookery course, which he passed as army cook class 1; transferred RAC 14 July 1943, Dec. 1943 by SS *Strathmore* to Bombay, in Poona, medically re-graded, 30 months Sgt clerk in GHQ India Delhi; transferred to RASC 12 July 1945; demob 23 Sept. 1946; post-war: had polio 1947, chairman and CEO South American mining company

Siegelbaum, Rudi, member of Young Austria; enlisted from Wales Dec. 1943/Jan. 1944

Sieger, served in 74 Coy PC; joined from Richborough Camp and was with BEF in France 1940

Sielaff, Herbert, on German Unity Party's list of comrades who served in Allied armies

Silber, Willy, member of Young Austria; enlisted from Leeds Dec. 1943/Jan. 1944

Silberbusch, B., 13810009, later Stevens, B.T., 6305474, served in PC and Buffs

Silbermann, later Silverman, took over as CQMS 87 Coy PC on 25 Aug. 1943; transferred to RAF; demob as Sqn Ldr

Silbermann, H., Austrian, served as Pte/fitter VM in 2BW B-Camp, MEF, in action in Yugoslavia with Tito's partisans

Silbiger, Hanna, served in 1 Allied Volunteer Platoon ATS

Silvier, H. 13807686 or 13807686

Simicich, P.K., 13806070 Pte in 253 Coy PC

Simbuerger, Gerhardt, alias Stones, George, alias Huber, George, Austrian, German conscript, PoW; taken into British service; SOE, in Operation DINTYLAKE near Klagenfurt; in Austria June 1945; was expected to remain there

Simion, Ernst, 13803084, later Simeon; born Berlin 8 Aug. 1920, emigrated to UK 1939, worked as mechanic in Co. Down; interned 1940; served in PC; transferred to REME; then Army Air Corps, Sgt, glider pilot at Fargo, Wilts., flew glider into Arnhem, loaded with jeep, anti-tank gun and 2-man detachment 17 Sept. 1944; killed in action there 20 Sept. 1944

Simmenauer, Alfred, later Simenauer

Simmenauer, Kurt, served in 8 AEC (Australia); post-war: to USA

Simmenauer, brother of Alfred and Kurt (above), served in 8 AEC (Australia)

Simmons, Helga; born Berlin 1926, served in one of the Allied Volunteer Platoons ATS

Simon, served in 74 Coy PC; joined from Richborough Camp and was with BEF in France 1940

Simon, Stefan Helmut; born Berlin 16 Oct. 1920, pupil at Kaiser Friedrich Reform RG till Oct 1937, emigrated UK 3 Aug. 1938, worked as neon sign installer and clerical worker; enlisted 4 Oct. 1940; served in 248 and 88 Coy PC; transferred to RE 1943, with 4 EBW RE in Normandy (landed 15 July 1944), in action at Bayeux, then Haren near Brussels; 1945 interpreter in civilian internment camp at Hemer near Iserlohn; demob 4 Oct. 1946; post-war: electrical goods wholesaler, own company

Simoni, Anna E.C., married Harvey; born Leipzig 1916, to UK 1939, studied at Glasgow, graduated 1941, continued post graduate studies until able to join services in other capacity than cook or mess orderly; enlisted June 1943; in WAAF, there LACW, flight mechanic at South Cerne, Southrop and Moreton Valence, in educational and vocational training (languages instructress), South Cerney, Watchfield and Beaulieu Heath; permitted to fly with instructor from Watchfield; demob May 1946; post-war: language teacher at London girls school, 1950–81 assistant keeper British Museum Library, then i/c Dutch section, authoress various books and articles on Dutch subjects; awarded high Dutch honours

Simoni, H. L; post-war: prominent in Ex-Service NB Association

Simonovitch, Jean, served in 338 Coy PC; post-war: to Monrovia, Liberia

Simonson, Alfred, later Simms, Alfred George, enlisted 1940; served in 137 Coy PC; 1943 to RA anti-tank of 4th Ind. Div. in Italy and Greece, Bdr, at Saloniki had meeting with *Wehrmacht* Maj. Ebers (son of renowned German socialist journalist) who wanted to organise German deserters against Nazis; later interpreter at Judenburg and Eisenerz (Austria); demob 1946; post-war: MA (maths) at Nottingham University, telecommunications, lecturer at Woolwich, Leicester University and Cranfield

Sims, Alfred E., served in 251 Coy PC; then Sgt RA, airborne, No. 1 in gun detachment; later interpreter in Austria, where he helped to obtain evidence about murder of hundreds of Hungarian Jews

Sinai, served in 74 Coy PC; joined from Richborough Camp and was with BEF in France 1940

Sinclair, Jack

Sinclair, Peter

Singer, Fritz, member of Young Austria; enlisted from London Dec. 1943/Jan. 1944

Singer, George, served in PC

Singer, M.S.

Singleton, C.

Skalka, Erwin; born Vienna 14 Sept. 1903, communist, served in British Army 16 Dec. 1942–31 Aug. 1946

Skrein, Georg, member of Young Austria; enlisted from Guildford Dec.

1943/Jan. 1944

Slawyk, Johann; born Vienna 9 June 1918, fruiterer and greengrocer, communist., 1938 was wounded in Spanish Civil War, got to Paris, where he married in 1939, interned there and sent to Colomb-Bechar and Bou-Afra; served in British Army from 1943, in 337 or 338 Coy PC

Sleigh, F.J. served in 3/10 Cdo; in Dieppe raid attached to 40 RM Cdo, captured by enemy in attempt to occupy Dieppe town hall (enemy HQ); missing since then

Smith, J., 14437220, Pte in Ox. and Bucks. LI; taken into 3/10 Cdo by Bartlett in Italy

Smiles, Angela

Smith, Margot

Sobl, Willi, member of Young Austria; enlisted from Leeds Dec. 1943/Jan. 1944

Sobotka, 13804270, served in PC; then 21 Indep. Para. Coy; on 61b and 62nd parachute training course; in action at Arnhem

Sochaj, Witold, served in 338 Coy PC; post-war: to Canada

Soffner, Heinz, from Vienna, socialist, was i/c Bach Unit

Sokol, Alois, alias Sanger, German conscript, PoW; taken into British service; IC, posted to 1 I (U) Apr. 1944

Sollaender, served in 74 Coy PC; joined from Richborough Camp and was with BEF in France 1940

Sommerfeld, Alfred, later Summerfield, Steven Alfred; born Tapiau, East Prussia 1921, pupil at Deutsche Ordens Oberrealschule, Wehlau; served in 137 Coy PC; then Interpreters' Pool, BAOR; with intelligence section Coldstream Guards, Normandy, Belgium; then HQ 1 Army Corps, Germany, participated in search for Nazi war criminals, then court interpreter; Sgt; post war: lecturer in economics Teesside University

Sommerstein, T.

Sondheim, Mike, German, studied technology at Zurich, to Australia by HMT *Dunera*, interned and worked in orchard; in 8 Austral. Empl.Coy, Australian Mil.Forces, OC's driver

Sonnenschein, later Sunshine, served as Cpl in PC, at Caen 1944

Sonnenstein, served in 74 Coy PC; joined from Richborough Camp and was with BEF in France 1940

Sorda, Otto, Austrian; born 11 Sept. 1989, served in British Army 30 May 1941–16 Oct. 1946

Spalt, Karlheinz, later Spalding, Keith; born Darmstadt 1913, pupil at *Realgymnasium*, pacifist, published *Kultur oder Vernichtung. Ein Handbuch ueber den Pazifismus* (Civilisation or Destruction. Handbook of Pacifism) 1932, fled Germany 1933, to Vienna, but had to move from place to place for several years (in one attempt to get away, he walked from Vienna to Paris), continued studies in UK, then lecturer at Birmingham University; interned 1940, but released on intervention of senior university members; decided that Hitler had to be opposed by force of arms and volunteered for service; in 246 Coy PC; later Border Regt; finally Intelligence 1944, in psychological warfare section, OC leaflet section, then as S/Sgt editor *Die*

Mitteilungen, participated in schooling German journalists at Aachen, fired for exceeding authority, then film control; post-war: Professor of German at Swansea University, then Bangor, author *The long March* (autobiographical), *Historical Dictionary of German Figurative Usage* in 60 volumes, and many others, MA, Ph.D., D.Phil, awarded German Federal Cross of Merit

Spanglet, Guenter, later Dale, Stephen Patrick, 13807371, temporarily also Turner, Stephen, nicknamed Ziba, short for 'Zigeunerbaron' (gipsy baron); born Berlin 17 Feb. 1917, pupil at Fichte Gymnasium, Treitschke Schule, Goethe Gymnasium, then seaman on German freighter 1934–38, held at Sachsenhausen 1938–39, parents and brother murdered in Poland, to UK 1939, fellow seamen in Hamburg gave him big send-off, in UK John Cass Nautical Institute, London, not admitted to officers' exam; interned 1940, by HMT *Dunera* to Australia, returned after 19 months; enlisted 2 Jan. 1942; with 87 Coy PC at Pembroke, Aberaeron, Long Marston, 2 weeks detention for disobedience, Training School Nr 1 Stodham Park.; then to SOE (RF) in Arisaig House, Ringwood (parachute training), Brockhall, Anderson Manor and Heathrop Castle, in Italy at Monopoli, parachuted into Tramontina Valley 13 Oct. 1944, taken prisoner, to Tolmezzo, Udine, Trieste (Coroneo prison, death cell), then Kaisersteinbruch, finally Braunschweig, liberated by US Army 12 Apr. 1945, later with Reichsbahn at Bielefeld, Goettingen; demob as Capt. Sept. 1946; post-war: Author *Spanglet or by any other name* (autobiography), became specialist in international tungsten trade, consultant for UNCTAD and NATO, where his advice was highly valued, known as 'Mr Tungsten', also 'Prince of Tungsten'; died at Hyde Heath, Bucks., 1998

Spears, Lotte, served in 3 Allied Vol. Platoon ATS

Spencer, Frederick, Austrian, held at Buchenwald and Dachau; served as L/Cpl in 3/10 Cdo

Speyer, Dr Walter; born 1892; enlisted Jan. 1940; served in 87 Coy PC; released on medical grounds July 1942

Spiegel, A., later Spencer, A., brother of G. Spiegel (Spencer), served in 87 and 137 Coy PC; post-war: furrier, director Mirro Furs Ltd

Spiegel, G., later Spencer, G., brother of A. Spiegel (Spencer), above

Spiegel, Peter, Austrian, to Palestine; served in Jerusalem as Sgt in RAF

Spiegelglass, Mane, German; born 1923; Sgt when killed in action, awarded Distinguished Conduct Medal

Spieler, Franz, 13800920, Austrian, committed suicide 1 Oct. 1941

Spielman, E., driver in RASC in Italy, when Bartlett got him to volunteer for 3/10 Cdo

Spielmann, Ernst, native of Graz in Styria, had been apprentice tailor there, after emigration to Palestine he became a diamond cutter; served as a commando Jewish Brigade, coming to England for further training in 1945; demob in Hamburg; died 1992 in Australia

Spier, Alfred; born Rauisch Holzhausen (today Ebsdorfer Grund) Kreis Marburg, Hesse, 4 Jan. 1924, went to school at Holzhausen, Marburg and Bad Nauheim, emigrated 1939; enlisted 1943; served in REME, in Belgium and Germany; Sgt in 1946; demob Oct. 1947; post-war: worked himself up to management position with Dexion, then founded own company

Spier, John

Spies, Horst, later Spiers, Harry, 14435069; born Biblis, 25 June 1922, sent to Buchenwald, came to England by *Kindertransport* June 1939, farm labourer; enlisted 1943; served in RAC, Sgt; later interpreter at Bielefeld; demob June 1947

Spira, Heinz, member of Young Austria; enlisted from London Dec. 1943/Jan. 1944

Spira, Joseph, member of Young Austria; enlisted from London Dec. 1943/Jan. 1944

Spitzer, Rudi, leading member of Young Austria; enlisted from Coventry Dec. 1943/Jan. 1944

Sponer, Rudolf, served in RAOC; on German Unity Party's list of Sudeten Germans who served in the British Army

Spreitzhofer, Roman, alias Haas, Roman, alias Roschitz, Franz, alias Knabl, Andreas, alias Wieser, Hans, Austrian, German conscript, PoW; taken into British service; SOE, in Operation EVELETH near Muerzzuschlag; in Austria June 1945, was expected to remain there

Springer, CQMS in 219 Coy PC, mentioned in dispatches

Spuner, Bobby, later Spooner, Austrian, had been welterweight boxing champion of Europe, both his hands broken in Dachau; served in 74 Coy PC; joined from Richborough Camp and was with BEF in France 1940; his story is featured prominently in Ministry of Information film *Lift up your head, comrade*

Sruh, Gottfried Conrad (Friedl), 13804390, later Broadman, Geoffrey Max, 13118708; born Vienna 24 or 27 June 1917, both parents murdered in concentration camps, was judoka, mountaineer and skier, sent to relatives at Prague 1938, with aid of international trade unions to UK, taken in by Broadman family in Redhill, was PE instructor and played football for Redhill AC; interned June 1940 on Isle of Man; enlisted 1940; served in 220 Coy PC as unarmed combat instructor; then 3/10 Cdo, only survivor of attack on Vemork 1942; attached to 4 Cdo at D-Day landing in Normandy, wounded by gunfire 13 June 1944; lastly in Austria; participated in war crimes investigation and de-nazification in Styria and Carinthia, then ski instructor West Yorks. Regt; finally cliff assault trainer for Royal Marines; post-war: probation officer, then various jobs with Securicor, Rank Xerox, traded in sports goods, shone as sportsman, champion skier, well-known rock climber, founder member of Outward Bound Movement, last job was caretaker at Forest of Dean Grammar School; died 1997, funeral one of biggest ever in Lydbrook

Stadthagen, Eva, served in 1 Allied Volunteer Platoon ATS, was then between 30 and 40 years of age and one of oldest enemy alien members of ATS

Stambrooke, C., served in 88 Coy PC

Standhartiger, Karl, alias Roth, Josef Ludwig, alias Schmidt, Karl, Austrian, German conscript, PoW; taken into British service; SOE, in Operation EBENSBURG near Bad Aussee; in Austria June 1945, was expected to remain there

Stanley, served in 74 Coy PC

Stanley, Eric, well-known entertainer, served in PC; post-war: to Butlins, Bahamas

Stappler, Herbert; born Vienna 1920, father Jewish horse dealer, mother Catholic, music producer, fled to France 1938; interned near Dijon; joined French Foreign Legion, sent to Algeria, Sidi-bel-Abbes, in *Compagnie d'Instruction* (intelligence), discharged 1940; interned in Sahara, fled to Oran, then Algiers; joined 338 Coy PC, towards end of war concerned with production of broadcasts from Rome to Austria and Austrian soldiers in German Army; post-war: reverted to music, in broadcasting

Starbroke, Capt., OC of camp for young SS prisoners of war 1947

Starer, Robert, PAL775943, Austrian, served as AC1 in RAF; post-war: pianist, composer, Professor of Music at Juliard College

Stark, Fritz; died on active service

Staudt, K. 13805910, Pte in 219 Coy PC; volunteered for commandos, application refused

Steger, Erich, later Steger, Eric, served as Leading Writer in RN

Steigerwald, served in 229 Coy PC (10 Sect.)

Steigerwald, served in 338 Coy PC, North Africa

Stein, served in 74 Coy PC; joined from Richborough Camp and was with BEF in France 1940 as Cpl; later Para. Regt; according to Pelican 'one of the best'

Stein, A., 13800866, later Spencer, Tom; born Frankfurt 11 Dec. 1916, butcher; served in 74 Coy PC; joined from Richborough Camp and was with BEF in France 1940; received high praise for his part in saving two ladies in air attack on Weymouth; transferred 3/10 Cdo; on D-Day attached to 3 Cdo, took part in frequent patrols in Normandy, on Maas river Jan. 1945

Stein, Dr E.L., Austrian composer, served in 93 Coy PC; wrote articles concerning Austrian restitution

Stein, Erich, member of Young Austria; enlisted from Reading Dec. 1943/Jan. 1944

Steinberg, H. (probably Dr Hugo), Austrian violinist, served in 74 Coy PC; joined from Richborough Camp and was with BEF in France 1940; in Liverpool orchestra; died on active service

Steinberg, Rolf, later Stanton, Ralph, from Hamburg, served in 219 Coy PC

Steinberger, S. later Starmont (or Stormont?); died on active service

Steiner, Dr Ernst, Austrian medical doctor, appears to have served in PC; probably transferred to RAMC later on

Steiner, Friedrich, later Stanley, Frederick Allen; born Vienna 1921; PC; in infantry on D-Day; post-war: lives at Poettsching, Burgenland, Austria

Steiner, Heinz Georg, later Stevens, Harry George; born Vienna Nov 1924., pupil at R1, Vienna, to England Dec. 1938, studied at Manchester University, tried to join US Air Force 1943, but not accepted as foreigner not resident in USA; joined RN 1944, trained as electrical officer, commissioned, Sub-Lt; RNVR, on minesweeper; attached to RN Cdo, took part in technical and scientific investigations; then at Admiralty, evaluation of German armament systems; demob 1947; post-war: in Paris, later owner/director of engineering consulting firm in London

Steiner, Herbert, Austrian, enlisted shortly before 29 July 1944

Steiner, R.; died on active service

Steiner, Uli, 13801102, later Scott, Leslie, went to school in Switzerland, but had German nationality; served in 77 Coy PC; later in 3/10 Cdo, was in landing on Lissa (Vis), last OC of 3/10 Cdo; then CSDIC, took part in operations to find leading Nazis; finally information control of British zone of Germany; Capt.

Stensch, Rudolf, later Stent, Ronald; born Berlin 1914, law graduate of Bonn University 1932, to England 1935; interned Isle of Man, released Oct. 1940; served in 246 and 77 Coys PC; transferred RE; RE OCTU Newark, commissioned 1944; to India, there SORE 3 (S/Capt.) GHQ India; demob summer 1946; post-war: to New York, then Johannesburg, later BA and M.Phil. (hist) Birkbeck College, BA hons. 1970, lecturer in extramural department London University and University of the Third Age, author *A Bespattered Page* (Andre Deutsch, London, 1980)

Stephens, Freddie; born Vienna 1922; served in RAC, Airborne; died 1967

Stern, A.

Stern, Alfred, from Bad Mergentheim, served with French *Prestataires*, unit under British command, was in retreat to Dunkirk, but not evacuated from there, fled with other Hessian *Prestataires*, got fishing vessel to take him from area of Nantes to unoccupied France, captured by HMS *Imogen* interned UK; recognised for what he was and permitted to join PC

Stern, Bernhard, member of Young Austria; enlisted from Glasgow Dec. 1943/Jan. 1944

Stern, E.E. served in 77 Coy PC, acted in that company's Xmas panto *A Midsummer Night's Scream*, probably 1941

Stern, Erhard, 13801609; born Berlin 4 May 1918, emigrated to England July 1935, studied at Royal Dental Hospital, London from Sept. 1936; enlisted Feb. 1940; with 88 Coy PC in France from Apr. 1940, at Harfleur, evacuated from St Malo; released to continue studies Aug. 1942, graduated as LDS RCS June 1944; officer in Royal Dental Corps (pers. No.336883) 1 Jan. 1945, in Scot. Cmd. till Aug. 1945; Sept. 1945 to Beirut, 43 General Hospital, then Gaza; demob Jan. 1947 as Capt; post-war: LDS, RCS, dentist in Hampstead , London NW

Stern, H.M.

Stern, Hans, member of Young Austria; enlisted from Leicester Dec. 1943/Jan. 1944

Stern, Robert Eric, 16001118, later Stenham, R.E. (Bob), from Vienna, pupil at RG14, emigrated to England Aug. 1939; served in 220 Coy PC; then RASC; REME; 22 Indep. Para. Coy, was 8th man to reach ground in parachute attack preceding landing in Normandy during night of 5–6 June 1944; later in Ardennes and along Maas river; aircraft carrying his section into action at Rhine crossing at Wesel was fired at, as a result of which he lost his right arm

Stern, T., served in 88 Coy PC; post-war: prominent in Ex-Service NB Association

Stern, W. CQMS, later Sgt in 251 Coy PC; then interpreter at Nuremberg trial of major war criminals, was responsible for administration of documents for the prosecution; post-war: prominent in Ex-Service NB Association

Sternberg, served in 74 Coy PC; joined from Richborough Camp and was with BEF in France 1940

Sternberg, Dr Hans; born Austria 6 Nov. 1904, lawyer in Neuwald, Styria, and Arnoldstein, emigrated to Palestine Nov. 1938; served in British Army Nov. 1940–Nov. 1951

Sternfeld, Albert, PAL 775953, emigrated to Palestine; Cpl in RAF, equipment section; post-war: Capt. in Israeli Air Force reserve, later managing director Wiener Rueckvers. Ges., member of commission 'Austrians in Exile', author

Sternhell, Ernst, member of Young Austria; enlisted from North Morton Dec. 1943/Jan. 1944

Sternman, Jacques

Stevens, Martin, served in 220 Coy PC

Stevens, T., 13053600, served in RWK; joined 3/10 Cdo in Italy

Stewart, J. 13053667, served in RWK; joined 3/10 Cdo in Italy

Stewart, Ron, capable footballer, is known to have served in RF (SOE), but did not get into action

Stiassny, W., served in 3 PCTC and in 229 Coy PC; accompanied Southern Command Continental Orchestra as pianist

Stiebel, neé Bernstein, Ilse, later Barrington; born Aachen, 22 May 1908, helped others to leave Germany; enlisted 11 Apr. 1941; served in 1 Allied Volunteer Platoon ATS; released 15 Dec. 1942, was overweight; post-war: cook in West End hotels and clubs, later in civil service

Stillermann, J.E., served in 74 Coy PC, commissioned

Stock, Eduard

Stockner, F., served in PC; later in No. 1 Psycho Warfare Gp, Allied Information Service, SHAEF; Sgt

Stoessel (Ludwig?), from Vienna, soldier in Austrian Army, very religious, orthodox Jew; served in 74 Coy PC; joined from Richborough Camp and was with BEF in France 1940; whilst praying in Hebrew was arrested by MP, who assumed he was passing messages in unknown foreign language

Stoll, Peter

Stoppleman, G., served in 69 Coy PC

Stork, C., MBE, MC, served in 165 Coy PC; CSM; eventually Maj.; post-war: prominent in Ex-Service NB Association

Strauber, John

Strauss, D. 13801207, later Stewart, David, 13118710; born 19 Jan. 1914; served in 87 Coy PC; later 3/10 Cdo; in Normandy landing attached to 45 Marine Cdo, he and Sgt Shelley only survivors of group of 5 there; with Shelley in successful attack on enemy machine gun post at Merville, 8 June 1944; commissioned in the field; in Italy to recruit further men for 3/10 Cdo at beginning 1945; younger brother of Maj. Herman Strauss below

Strauss, Ernst, later Stevens, Ernest, from Bensheim, Hesse, served in British Army

Strauss, Dr (jur.) Herman; born Weiden, Upper Palatinate 25 Nov. 1906, studied at Munich and Wuerzburg, practised at Bingen, emigrated to Kenya 1933; served as Maj., Kenya Regt; then at HQ 2 Ech, E Afr Cmd, Chief of Legal Department; then at HQ SE Asia Cmd, Jhansi CP, Deputy Asst. Adj. Gen; post-war: called to bar at Lincoln's Inn, then advocate to Supreme Court, Kenya, moved to New Zealand 1962, there solicitor to Supreme Court till 1991

Strauss, Martin, served in RAMC

Strauss, Stefan, later Stewart, Stephen M, CBE QC LLD, Maj., prosecutor at war crime trials

Strauss, Ulrich (Steven); born Berlin-Charlottenburg 28 Apr. 1915, pupil at Grunewald *Gymnasium*, to London 1934, there in business; enlisted 1940; served in 165 Coy PC; then REME (11 Bn), promoted Sgt 1942; WO 1 1943 in charge of IEME workshop; post-war: manufacture and trading horological products

Striem, Hermann, 13800762, from Gross-Wartenburg (Sycow) near Breslau, family traded in agricultural products, imprisoned in Buchenwald, in Richborough; interned Isle of Man 1940; enlisted 18 June 1941; training at Ilfracombe, then with PC in Sandwich as lorry driver

Strietzel, M. later Streat, member of Vienna Symphony Orchestra; served as Sgt in No. 3 PCTC and 229 Coy PC; conductor Southern Command Continental Orchestra; post-war: leader, The New Band

Struewe, Walter, on German Unity Party's list of comrades who served in an allied army

Studinski, later Studley, E.J.; born Berlin 19 Nov. 1916, pupil at Kaiser Friedrich Realgymnasium, to UK 17 Jan. 1939, farming trainee; enlisted 4 Dec. 1940; served in 69 Coy PC; also one year with PC Gp HQ (Col Swan) in Boston Spa; then with 137 Coy PC in Scotland (Lockerbie, Dumfries, Castle Douglas) till 1944; 1945 interpreter; demob 21 Oct. 1946

Stukart, Robert, from Vienna, served 1 Sept. 1941–20 Nov. 1945

Stummer, Maximilian, served in PC in North Africa

Subak, Herbert, later Sharpe, John Herbert, in PC; later parachutist; post-war: Professor Subak-Sharpe, CBE, FRSE

Sulzbach, Herbert; born Frankfurt 8 Feb. 1894, Lt in German 69 Artillery Regt in WW1, awarded Iron Cross, wrote book on trench warfare, paper manufacturer; served in PC; later in Interpreters' Pool; then Sgt/interpreter in 21 POW camp Comrie, where Nazis had murdered a German warrant officer, who did not share their beliefs, was able to break Nazi hold on camp and re-educate prisoners, commissioned; transferred to Featherstone POW camp; Jan 1946 to PoW camp Haltwhistle, where he repeated his success, was highly praised and cited; post-war: chief of civilian labour at Berlin air-lift, later at German embassy, London, active at foundation of European Economic Community, awarded German Federal Cross of Merit and French Croix de Paix de l'Europe; died 5 July 1985

Sulzbacher, Lore, later Sulby, married Allard, Lorraine, from Fuerth/Bavaria;

born 8 Dec. 1924, schools at Fuerth and Canal Str. Nuremberg, to UK by *Kindertransport* Apr. 1939, to Lincoln; enlisted June 1943 at Pontefract; then Gresford Driver Training Centre, with AA Arty. 43, in London Knightsbridge as driver of deputy commander ATS, attached to 902 Coy RASC till demob Sept. 1945

Susman, F; post-war: prominent in Ex-Service NB Association

Suesskind, Herbert, later Sutton, Herbert, served in PC

Sussman, Lewis, served in 249 Coy PC

Sussmann, Hans, later Steward, John Gordon, 13046364; born Vienna 26 May 1917, L/Cpl in 251 Coy PC; then REME; lastly in RAMC, served in Egypt

Sutton, Francis George (Frank), from Vienna, joined at Westward Ho! 1940, Cpl in 219 Coy; officer in 249 Coy PC; in Special Services, Beds. and Herts.; served in Italy, wounded Cassino 1944, awarded Military Cross; then Greece, in major town of Thebes; 1945 on Capri questioning Schuschnigg, Horthy, Niemoeller, Frederick of Prussia; 1946 head of paper–leather–textile department of Economic Division in Austria

Sutton, Brigitte, served in 508 Coy ATS

Svetley

Szedo, Franz, later Seton, Francis; born Vienna 27 Jan. 1920, parents of Hungarian-Jewish origin converted to Catholicism, to England 1938, parents returned to Hungary, gained scholarship to Balliol 1938, studied PPE; interned 1940, to Canada, back to UK after 8 months; volunteered for PC 1941; changed name and transferred to Somerset LI 1943; then Intelligence; Sgt Maj.; demob 1946; post-war: continued to work with German PoWs till 1948, well-known economist, Fellow Nuffield College Oxford 1953, expert for USSR and other countries, spoke any number of languages, amateur pianist, died 7 Jan. 2002

Szenes, Hannah; born Budapest, 1921, daughter of Bela S, author and playwright, and Catherine S., Hungarian poetess, to Palestine; joined SOM, parachuted erroneously into Slovenia, was betrayed and captured crossing Hungarian frontier, arraigned before Hungarian civil court and sentenced to death for treason, executed 7 Nov. 1944; is considered one of the great heroines of Jewry in Israel

Szper, Marcello, PAL774635, Austrian, enlisted at Sarafand; served as Cpl in RAF, in accounts department in Vienna and Trieste

Tabori, George; born Budapest 1914, came to London as correspondent for Bulgarian and Turkish newspapers; served in HM Forces; post-war: well-known author and theatrical producer, USA and Austria, now in Berlin, subject of biography by Wend Kassen, Frankfurt 1989

Taglicht, Oswald, PAL775439, Austrian, emigrated to Palestine; Sgt in RAF, employed in public works; post-war: WO in Israeli Air Force

Tait, Bert, served in 137 Coy PC

Tandler, Henry R., served in 77 Coy PC

Tanne-Muenz, served in 74 Coy PC; joined from Richborough Camp and was with BEF in France 1940

Tauber, L/Cpl in 69 Coy PC

Tauber, a nephew of Richard Tauber, served in 74 Coy PC; joined from Richborough Camp and was with BEF in France 1940, was orderly to Lt H.F. Miller

Tauber, D., Austrian

Tauber, Joe, member of Young Austria; enlisted from Leicester Dec. 1943/Jan. 1944

Taufer, served in 74 Coy PC; joined from Richborough Camp and was with BEF in France 1940

Taus, Hilde, Austrian, served in ATS

Tausky, Fritz, member of Young Austria; enlisted from Princes Risborough Dec. 1943/Jan. 1944

Taussig, Ignac; died on active service

Taylor, B. deported to Australia, after return to UK became Sgt in Leics. Regt and intelligence chief of his battalion; DCM

Tebrich, Kurt, later Teddern, Clive, from Hamburg, came to England at early age; interned 1940, deported to Canada, but returned; enlisted 1941; served in 165, 87 and 74 Coy PC; then 8 RIH, military government Germany, and War Crimes Trial Centre, with 8 RIH at breakthrough at Caen, in action at St Pol, Albert Canal, Nijmegen corridor, Loon op Zand, Maastricht-Venlo, Antwerp and Rhine crossing, first into Hamburg; demob as Sgt; post-war: studied, 24 years' teaching in London, sociology and job advice, author

Tedrehin, J., 13806111, Pte in 253 Coy PC; SOE?

Teicher, J., served in 74 Coy PC

Teichert, Salomon; died on active service

Teichmann, Leo, leading member of Young Austria; enlisted from London Dec. 1943/Jan. 1944

Tell, W., served in 249 and 69 Coy PC

Tepper, W., Austrian, served as Pte welder/fitter in 2BW L-Camp, MEF

Terfus, Michael, served in 74 Coy PC; joined from Richborough Camp and was with BEF in France 1940

Teutzer, served in 74 Coy PC; was in France with BEF 1940

Teweles, Hans, later Trevor, Henry, from Vienna, served with RA in 53 Welsh Div.

Thausing, Dr Anny (aka Taussig-Bittner or Thaussing), from Vienna, served in 1 Allied Volunteer Platoon ATS

Theilinger, J., 13804028, later Taylor, J., Czechoslovak citizen; born 25 Sept. 1916; served in International Brigade in Spain; served in PC; then 3/10 Cdo; after accident with hand granade at Littlehampton was discharged from active service

Theimer, Mimi, Austrian, served in ATS; wrote poems in Viennese slang, were published in *Young Austria*

Thornton, served in 3/10 Cdo, in Normandy

Tichauer, W., served in 248 Coy PC; painter, whose pictures were exhibited at Darlington Society Exhibition 1942

Tickler, served in 74 Coy PC; joined from Richborough Camp and was with BEF in France 1940

Tirsan, served in 74 Coy PC; joined from Richborough Camp and was with

BEF in France 1940

Tischler, later Thompson, wanted to call himself 'Thistlethwaite', but was persuaded otherwise

Tischler, Peter J., 13807650, later Terry, Peter; born Vienna 21 June 1924, father was well-known doctor, whose patients included the Duke of Windsor, Seyss-Inquart and Richard Tauber, pupil at Frensham School; enlisted Feb. 1942; served in 77 Coy PC; later briefly in SO; temporarily also in SSRF, Anderson Manor; then transferred to 3/10 Cdo, sent to French coast to collect suitcase from French resistance; D-Day attached to 47 RM Cdo, wounded shortly after landing, evacuated to UK; back in Normandy 23 July 1944., took 4 prisoners at Commes, was himself captured but escaped, badly wounded in fighting near Buisson; post-war: in business, USA

Tobias, served in 74 Coy PC; joined from Richborough Camp and was with BEF in France 1940

Tobinski, A., later Tobert, A., served in PC

Toch, from Vienna, served in 229 Coy PC (Sect. 4)

Toch, Hans, member of Young Austria; enlisted from Birmingham Dec. 1943/Jan. 1944

Toch, Heinz; born Vienna 1924, to UK by *Kindertransport*; in Jewish Brigade,; then Sgt in Army Education Corps; post-war: inspector of taxes, politically active

Tonello, Harry, had run well-known restaurant in Vienna; enlisted from Kitchener Camp 17 Nov. 1939; Cpl cook in 93 Coy PC; discharged on health grounds 25 Feb. 1943; died 1955

Torok, Austrian, Cpl in 338 Coy PC, North Africa

Traenkler, Friedrich; born Vienna 18 July 1910, commissioned officer in Spanish Civil War May 1937–Feb 1939; interned by French at St Cyprien, Gurs, Le Vernet and in North Africa; served in British forces, member of fighting forces Styria (?) from 1944

Trauttmannsdorff, Count Norbert, Austrian noble, together with his batman defected to Allies from the *Wehrmacht*; served in SOE, known as Taggert (?); according to Dale, who knew him only by this name, he was in same aircraft as Dale and Priestley (Lindenbaum) on their Tramontina Valley mission, like them he parachuted into the valley, where he was shot, his batman, name unknown, survived and completed his task; also mentioned by Warner

Treichl, Wolfgang, alias Taggart, William, alias Martin, William, from Vienna, brother of Heinrich Treichl, later CEO of Creditanstalt, was Lt in German Afrika Korps, went over to British with all the men under his command, retained his *Wehrmacht* rank; served in SOE, in Operation SEAFRONT, with 5 men parachuted into Salzburg province near Tolmein, landed in *Wehrmacht* camp, shot and killed; some accounts have it that it was not at Tolmein but in the Tramontina Valley

Treitel, served in 74 Coy PC; joined from Richborough, was in France 1940

Trepel, Charles, from Odessa, Ukraine, moved to Germany with whole family, 1933 to Paris; joined French artillery at outbreak of war, Lt; released from service 1940, fled to Spain, interned at Barbastro; escaped to Gibraltar, thence to England; joined Free French Troop in 10 Cdo

Treuhaft, Gerd, 13800430, Austrian; born 10 Apr. 1918, had been Bonn correspondent of Austrian University publication and for *Bohemia* Prague, active in support of League of Nations, imprisoned at Dachau and Buchenwald until 3 May 1939; joined 69 and 251 Coy PC, in France 1940; stationed near London during blitz; wrote for army paper under the name 'Josef Geta'; post-war: journalist, associated with *Contemporary Review, UN News, Peace News* and *New Leader*, author

Trevelyan, Mrs J.

Trichter, Kurt, member of Young Austria; enlisted from Manchester Dec. 1943/Jan. 1944

Trier, Franz-Guenter, 13801132, later Turner, Frank Geoffrey; born Berlin 26 Nov. 1918, but lived in Darmstadt, pupil at Ludwig-Georgs-Gymnasium, emigrated to UK Nov. 1938; served in 87 Coy PC (2 Sect.); later in RAC, 7 Armoured Div.; served in France Mar. to June 1940 and again France, Belgium and Germany June 1944 to July 1946; after 1945 divisional intelligence officer; post-war: joined TA, Maj., was export manager WGI Ltd London; died 1990

Trier, Peter E., CBE, D.Tech. (hons.), MA, FEng, FIEE, FInstP, FIMA; born Darmstadt 12 Sept. 1919, pupil at Ludwig-Georgs-Gymnasium, emigrated 1935, attended Mill Hill School, Cambridge, civilian member of Royal Naval Scientific Service 1941–1950; post-war: with Mullard Research Labs 1969, R&D director of Philips Electronics, 1980 Pro-Chancellor Brunel University, 1982–84 scientific adviser to the House of Lords, author of various scientific treatises, retired to Tewkesbury, but there no longer

Trkulja, S., 13806072, served in PC; probably also in SOE

Trojan, Richard W., 13207275, later Tennant, Richard W., Austrian; born 14 May 1922; enlisted at Ilfracombe, Dec. 1941; served in 229 Coy PC; later 3/10 Cdo, commissioned; post-war: president of international tyre dealers, ran golf club near the Worthersee in Carinthia, at home both in London and in Austria

Tryger, Harry; born 1904

Tscherne, H.P., 45756, Austrian, served as driver HQ Mov. and Tn. MEF

Tsopke, served in 74 Coy PC; joined from Richborough Camp and was with BEF in France 1940

Tuechler, Erich, member of Young Austria; enlisted from Birmingham Dec. 1943/Jan. 1944

Tumiati, Paul, 220784., commissioned in PC 23 Dec. 1941, in one group of officers with Bendit, Frankel, Goldstein, Kochmann, Michelson and Stork, which allows one to assume that he too, was a KOLEA, though not necessarily German or Austrian

Turbin, Rolf (Ralph), from Berlin, enlisted from Richborough; served in 77 and 87 Coy PC, drummer in 87 Coy Band; post-war: football referee, prominent in Ex-Service NB Association

Turkl, Miss H., emigrated to Palestine; LACW in WAAF, responsible for equipment

Turkl, Siegfried, 13807810, Austrian, enlisted 1942; death by enemy action 12 Jan. 1945

Turner, served in PC; then 8th Irish Hussars, commissioned; after end of hostilities in intelligence

Turner, David, served in 69 Coy PC

Turner, Stephen Patrick, 2/Lt in PC; then General List, taken prisoner by Germans in Italy 13 Oct. 1944

Tuset, J., 13802425, CQMS in PC

Tutass, Samuel; died on active service

U.M., did not wish his name to be published, had been student at Balliol, became Capt. and served in PC; Infantry; and either SOE or IC

Ulanovsky, Peter Johann, alias Hall, Peter, alias Lt Brand, commissioned in IC; returned to UK 4 May 1945, presumably from Monopoli

Ullmann, S/Sgt, originally in PC; then to Legal Research Branch and war crimes investigation; post-war: Professor of Law, Cambridge University

Ullmann, Walter; born 29 Nov. 1910 at Paldau or Palfau, Styria, son of Jewish country doctor, studied law at Vienna and Innsbruck, lecturer at Vienna University and civil servant 1935, at Ratcliffe College Cambridge 1939; interned Isle of Man 1940; volunteered PC, but found to be useless as soldier, sanitary orderly, then clerk in orderly room; discharged 1943; post-war: Professor of Mediaeval Law at Cambridge, spoke Latin better than English; died 1983

Ullstein, interned on Isle of Man; served in PC; then SOE

Ulman, G., 13809063, Cpl in North Africa, mentioned in dispatches

Ulrich, Heinz, later Hulton, served in PC

Ulrich, Henryk, P1364; born Vienna 15 Aug. 1916.; 2/Lt in Ambulance Coy; 4 Cadre Rifle Bde; 3 and 1 Polish Paras, in action at Arnhem, awarded medal for bravery; post-war: Professor of Neuropathology, London Hospital, Whitechapel

Unger, E.E., joined 93 Coy PC from Kitchener Camp, Cpl/chief cook; post-war: owner of Florida Restaurant, Bournemouth

Unger, Jackie, member of Young Austria; enlisted shortly before 29 July 19 44; awarded Military Medal

Upton, served in 246 Coy PC; later in unit which landed in first wave in Normandy on D-Day, wounded immediately on landing by sniper's bullet, which nicked his lip

Urban, Richard, served in Long Range Desert Grp, participated in liberation of a concentration camp in Germany, organised transport for liberated prisoners to Italy for shipment to Palestine (this combination of circumstances suggests that he was in the Jewish Bde)

Urbanski, Arthur, joined British forces at behest of FDJ or other communist party organisation; post-war: appears to have returned to Germany

Uscherowitz, Artur; born Vienna 1921, fled Austria 1938 via Bruenn, Romania, to Palestine; served in PC, North Africa, Crete where he avoided capture; at Sfax, in marauder unit; later Jewish Bde; Cpl; met with brother Willi U. (below) at Venlo 1945; post-war: back to Palestine

Uscherowitz, Willi, later Usher; born Vienna 12 Nov. 1923, pupil at Sperl RG2, to England by *Kindertransport* Dec. 1938; interned 1940, to Canada, returned July 1941; in Home Guard, West Yorks. Regt, Leeds Bn, until Jan. 1943; then 219, 69 and 220 Coy PC, in St Hubert during Rundstedt offensive Jan. 1945; interpreter with Military Government of Germany; met brother Artur (above) at Venlo; demob 1946; post-war: inspector in Germany for Alexandre Ltd; cantor of new Darmstadt synagogue

Valfer, served in 74 Coy PC; joined from Richborough Camp and was with BEF in France 1940
Valfer, Mrs H.A.
Veters, R., 13806132, Pte in 253 Coy PC; probably in SOE
Vibeck, F., 13806124, later Vibert, F., 6305488, served as Pte in PC and Buffs
Viner, H.P., served in PC
Vivanti, A. 13807880, served in PC
Vivic, S., 13807906 and 13122259, Sgt in PC
Vogel, Egon, 13807326, later Villiers, Egon Ernest Robert (Robbie), 13118714; born 7 Sept. 1918; interned 1940, to Australia by HMT *Dunera*; after return to UK served in 87 Coy PC; then 3/10 Cdo, in Normandy; was very clever loscksmith – no lock could keep him out; attached to 46 RN Cdo at Rhine crossing; killed in action there
Vogel, Rudolph, later Verney, Randolph, from Hamburg, had been cocoa trader there; interned at Douglas and Huyton till 21 Oct. 1940; served in 246 and 220 Coy PC; on 2 Feb. 1944 transfer to RN, trained on HMS *Royal Arthur*, service on HMS *Melbreak* in North Sea, Normandy on D-Day, convoy duties in Arctic; 4 Dec. 1944 on HMS *Leeds*; 22 Dec. 1944 to HMS *Rutherford*, 26 Apr. 1945 *Rutherford* badly damaged; Leading Writer, then PO; demob 4 Dec. 1945; did not consult his wife on change of name, and she received War Office letter saying 'As from today you will be known as Mrs Verney'; post-war: went back to trading in cocoa, first in London, then in São Paolo; died there in 1950s
Volkmann, I.
Voss, Richard, served in 165 Coy PC
Vulkan, later Vincent, Frank, served in 137 Coy PC
Vulkan, Austrian, brother of above, served in 137 Coy PC; later RE

Wachenheimer, Sally; born Zwingenberg/Bergstrasse, 1912, had been bank clerk with District Savings Bank Bensheim, emigrated to France 1933; served with French *Prestataires*, unit under British command was in retreat to Dunkirk, but not evacuated from there, fled with other Hessian *Prestataires*, got fishing vessel to take him from near Nantes to unoccupied France, captured at sea by HMS *Imogen*; interned UK; recognised for what he was and permitted to join PC; discharged on medical grounds 1943; post-war: Professor of Modern Languages, Florida University
Wachs, Fritz; born Vienna 4 Sept. 1911, communist, detained at Woellersdorf Austrian detention camp; served in British Army
Wachs, Walter, Austrian, served in North Africa

Wachsmann, W.,13807531, later Hays (or Hayes), J.W., 13116420 and 6346358. Pte in 165 Coy PC; later probably commissioned in SOE

Wachtel, Blanka, 2992780, Austrian, emigrated to Palestine; served as Sgt in WAAF

Wachtel, Max, 13804100; born Vienna 1900, served in Austro-Hungarian Army in WW1, despite business connections in both Norway and Sweden and the fact that he was there at the time of the *Anschluss*, was refused asylum there, admitted to UK 1938 with family; interned on Isle of Man 1940; enlisted end of that year; served in 229 Coy PC; Cpl; early discharge May 1943

Wadenka, J., 13806044, Pte in 253 Coy PC; but released from service prior to Nov. 1944

Wagner, George, Austrian

Wahle, Gerd

Waldorf, Karl, Austrian, served in 337 Coy PC, was one of the two men, who chiefly negotiated with British HQ Algiers to obtain permission for inmates of French camps in Algeria to join PC

Wall, H.I.; post-war: prominent in Ex-Service NB Association

Wallace, Hugh

Wallich, Walter; born Berlin 1918, son of banker, brother of Henry Wallich, later governor of US Federal Reserve, Cambridge scholar; interned 1940, sent to Canada, returned; served in PC; later RA; then Intelligence Section ISC, commissioned 3 Apr. 1943, Maj., in Berlin 1945, responsible for *Reichskulturkammer*, then controller of broadcasting for the British zone; post-war: with BBC foreign service Bush House, then news editor, finally current affairs; died of cancer 30 Apr. 1980

Walters, Ronald B., from Breslau, came to UK June 1939, on work of national importance in Glasgow; enlisted 1943; served in Argyll and Sutherland Highlanders, S/Sgt; in Germany with 15th Scottish Div., wounded at Elbe crossing at Lauenburg shortly before end of hostilities; after return to duty, at PoW camp in Wales; post-war: CEng, FIMechE, engineering consultant

Walton, Kenneth

Wand, Otto

Wand, Raphael (Ralf); born 1907, originally from Cracow, then Vienna, active in (illegal) Austrian Social-Democratic Party after 1934, fled to USA via Czechoslovakia, Switzerland 1938; called up for service in US Army; in OSS, in charge of (Anglo-US) Bach unit in London (training etc. of secret agents), on secret mission to Denmark; demob Oct. 1945; later assistant to American prosecutor in Nuremberg

Wank, Robert, later Ward, Robert, Austrian; died on active service

Wapnitzki, C., later Wallace; died on active service

Warburg, K.S. (C.S.), Lt in PC, Name appears on officers' list of 87 Coy PC on 31 Dec. 1942, 363 Coy on 31 Dec. 1943, 406 Coy on 31 Dec. 1944

Ward, G., 14430010, served as Cfn. REME; joined 3/10 Cdo in Italy 1945

Warndorfer, August Jacques, a nephew of Admiral Lord Cunningham, whose sister had married Austrian before 1914; born Austria 1899 or 1900, officer cadet in Austrian Navy in WW1; enlisted from Inverness; served as Pte in

220 Coy PC, where he excelled at handling the axe; transferred to SOE, IC Extra Regimental List, it is thought he was used on mission in Austria; missing, believed killed in action on or after 14 Oct. 1944, posthumous King's Commendation for Brave Conduct

Warner, Arnold, enlisted 21 Dec. 1939; served in 93 and 251 Coy PC; discharged on medical grounds 23 Nov. 1942

Warren, H., 13041047, served as Pte in RWK; joined 3/10 Cdo in Italy in Mar. 1945

Warschauer, served in 74 Coy PC; joined from Richborough Camp and was with BEF in France 1940

Warwar, Hans Ludwig, 13051423, later Ward, Henry Louis; born Berlin 15 Jan. 1923, came to England 1938, apprentice electrician; enlisted 1942; Sennybridge and 5 PCTC Bradford; transferred to RE, further training as electrician, 6 months at Lucas, Birmingham; transfer to REME 1945, in Assam and Bihar, attached to Indian Army, Sub-Conductor, i/c IEME workshop 1945; demob 1947; post-war: chartered electrical engineer (MIEE), manager, Central Electricity Generating Board, author of *Power Station Practice*

Warwick, R., 13041045, served in Essex Regt; joined 3/10 Cdo in Italy 1945

Wasen, Emil, wine merchant from Hamburg, served in 88 Coy PC

Wassermann, G.A., served as Lt in 137 Coy PC

Wassermann, O., 13800419, later Watson, William J., 13118815; born Berlin 1 June 1914., Romanian national, after 9 Nov. 1938 on foot to Holland, there apprehended and returned to Germany, held at Dachau, with US visa Aug. 1939 to England, wife, children and brother killed by Nazis; enlisted from Richborough; served in 69 Coy PC, in France 1940; then 3/10 Cdo; at Walcheren with 41 Cdo Nov. 1944, wounded

Weber, later Webber, Jan, father had been President of *Staatspartei* (Democratic Party); interned 1940, sent to Australia by HMT *Dunera*, but returned; worked in BBC French service; then MI 19 – investigations with PoWs; naturalised British during the war; was given direct commission in IC; with 13 Corps; then 6 Armoured Div. in Italy, in action on Po river; OC FSS Italy

Webster, served in 137 Coy PC

Wechselmann, Ellen, served in 1 Allied Volunteer Platoon ATS

Wegner, 13805634, later Willert, Norman, 13053513, Austrian; born 1921 or 1922; volunteered 1940/41; made it to Sgt, served in 137 Coy PC; SOE; and after 1943 in IC for special duties; killed in action in Austria 1, 2 or 12 Sept. 1944, officially missing; name appears on Groesbeek Memorial

Weglein, Hans, later Walker, Henry, served in 87 Coy PC

Weidel, served in 74 Coy PC; joined from Richborough Camp and was with BEF in France 1940

Weikersheim, Franz, Prince of, Capt. in Intelligence, OC No. 2 Information Control Unit, Sub Section 3, 1945, acted as editor-in-chief of *Ruhrzeitung*

Weikersheimer, L., 13804308, later Wallen, L.; born 2 July 1920; served in PC; later in 3/10 Cdo

Weiksmann, served in 74 Coy PC; joined from Richborough Camp and was with BEF in France 1940

Weil, Austrian, served in 337 or 338 Coy PC

Weil 1, served in 74 Coy PC; joined from Richborough Camp and was with BEF in France 1940

Weil 2, served in 74 Coy PC; joined from Richborough Camp and was with BEF in France 1940

Weil, Hans Hardtmuth, served in French Foreign Legion; after 1940 interned in Sahara camp; freed by British 1943; served as Cpl in 338 Coy PC, transferred to RN, on HMS *Royalist* in Mediterranean, then on three different destroyers on Murmansk convoys; post-war: lecturer at Marburg University, head of German department University College London

Weil, Leo, member of Young Austria; enlisted from London Dec. 1943/Jan. 1944

Weil, M., later Winter (Winster ?); died on active service

Weiller; born 1903, served in PC (N Africa)

Weinberg, served in 74 Coy PC; joined from Richborough Camp and was with BEF in France 1940

Weinberg, K., 13803503, later Mason, Gary; born 2 Jan. 1920; served in PC; then 3/10 Cdo, in Jan. 1945 in action along River Maas, attack on Belle Isle 27 Jan. 1945; Sgt; later in Frontier Force, must have been commissioned as all except commissioned officers in that regiment were Indian.

Weinberger, 13802286, served as L/Cpl in 69 Coy PC; on fire-fighting course, Catterick, Sept. 1941

Weinberger, E.G., 13801574, later Webster, E.G.; born 11 Aug. 1916; served in PC; then 3/10 Cdo; temporarily also with SSRF in Anderson Manor, sent to French coast to collect suitcase from French resistance; D-Day attached to 47 RM Cdo; drowned at landing when LCA received direct hit

Weinberger, P., later Ritinitis; died on active service

Weiner, Ernst, 13800788, Austrian; died on active service 7 Aug. 1940

Weiner, Hans Paul, Austrian; born Trautenau, Bohemia, Feb. 1920 father burgher of Vienna, emigrated Palestine 1939, spent 6 months in jail as illegal immigrant; enlisted at Sarafand; served first in RASC; then (under pressure) 608 Coy PC, in Tobruk during siege; then Greece, taken prisoner by Germans at Kalamata 1941, taken to Saloniki, Belgrade, Wolfsberg, Lienz, Stalag 8b in Lambsdorf near Oppeln (Upper Silesia); in Lubowitz working party, arrested by Gestapo, but returned to prison camp after intervention by three British warrant officers; in two months march on foot through deep snow and on icy roads to Thuringia, there entrained for Fallingbostel; freed by Americans; wrote 'They lost their freedom fighting for yours'

Weiner, Harry (?), later Winant or Wynant

Weiner, Max; died on active service

Weiner, Rosi, on German Unity Party's list of comrades who served in Allied armies

Weingartner, Dr, Col in IAMS, in charge of Medical Services of the forces of the Maharajah of Bikaner

Weinstein-Rath, J., 13800077, later Rath, enlisted Richborough 17 Nov. 1939,

Sgt in 69 Coy PC.; commissioned1942, 2/Lt in 219 Coy PC; at end of war was Maj. and OC PC Coy consisting of Poles, Balts and other DPs; post-war: prominent in Ex-Service NB Association

Weintraub, Otto, later Montgomery, Cecil, said to have served in 74 Coy PC

Weisberger E.

Weiss, served in 137 Coy PC

Weiss, had studied economics at LSE, communist, served in 249 Coy PC; later RAOC; lastly RE, was RTO Brighton for a time; said to have been investigated by Military Police

Weiss, Austrian, served in 338 Coy PC

Weiss, Ali, 13106924, later White, A., served as Pte in RWK; 1945 in 3/10 Cdo, Italy

Weiss, E; post-war: prominent in Ex-Service NB Association

Weiss, Edith, served in 1 Allied Volunteer Platoon ATS

Weiss, Eduard; born Austria 14 Sept. 1912, jeweller, emigrated to Palestine; served as driver in RASC

Weiss, Harry, Austrian; born about 1920, member of Young Austria; enlisted from Leeds Dec. 1943/Jan. 1944; served in KOYLI, was able to cause hostile field HQ to be destroyed as result of telephone conversation with enemy officer; died of wounds in Belgium

Weiss, also Weisz, Peter, Austrian, 13053350, Sgt in IC, 3 Coy IC Depot, volunteered from Liverpool; parachuted into Germany, arrested, taken to Dachau and executed Apr. 1945, posthumous King's Commendation for Brave Conduct

Weissenberg, served in 74 Coy PC; joined from Richborough Camp and was with BEF in France 1940

Weissenberg, Werner, 13800300, served in PC and RAMC

Weissmann, served in 74 Coy PC; joined from Richborough Camp and was with BEF in France 1940

Weltmann, Lutz; born 15 Feb. 1901; served in 88 Coy PC

Weltsch, Robert, member of Young Austria; enlisted from Cambridge Dec. 1943/Jan. 1944

Welwert, probably from Klagenfurt, served in 337 or 338 Coy PC

Wenlock, Albert

Werner, George

Werner, Kurt, later Vernon, Austrian, was telephonist in Kitchener Camp; served in PC; transferred to RN, on HMS *Westminster*, then HMS *Volunteer* for D-Day; then to Free French, PO on French ship *Le Combatant* at Walcheren and on E-boat patrol, torpedoed and spent one night 'in the drink', awarded Croix de Guerre

Werner, Manfred, 13801637, later Warner Frederick Michael; born Hamburg 6 Dec. 1919, pupil at Thaer Oberrealschule vor dem Holstentor, to UK Feb. 1939; enlisted Jan. 1940; served in 88 Coy PC (7 Sect.), at Le Havre and Harfleur, in near mutiny when ordered to return arms and again when men of 88 Coy discovered that their families had been interned; transferred to RF (SOE), in Operation HISTORIAN at Zeltweg 25 Apr. 1945. but lost contact with main party after parachute landing near Teufenbach

(Weissenbach?), rejoined main party at Zeltweg airport and was in withdrawal of group to Authal Castle; then 3 years Maj. in BAOR War Crimes Gp, Bad Oeynhausen; demob Aug 1948; post-war: in Intelligence Div. of Control Commission for Germany, author of *Don't you know there is a war on? A very personal account*

Wertheim, H., enlisted in Algiers; served in 337 Coy PC, one of two brothers who parachuted into Alsace, were captured and executed 1944

Wertheim, enlisted in Algiers; served in 337 Coy PC, one of two brothers who parachuted into Alsace, were captured and executed 1944

Wertheimer, H., later Werth, Henry

Westford, Harvey; born Austria 18 Nov. 1926; S/Sgt in RASC; also GSC; served in British Army in UK 18 Oct. 1944–17 Oct. 1946

Wettenstein, J., served in 74 Coy PC; joined from Richborough Camp and was with BEF in France 1940

Wetterkann, served in 74 Coy PC; joined from Richborough Camp and was with BEF in France 1940

Weyl, served in 74 Coy PC; joined from Richborough Camp and was with BEF in France 1940

Weyler, served in 87 Coy PC

Wiant, Dr, Lt Col in RAMC

Wichmann, Robert, Austrian, served in 337 or 338 Coy PC

Wiener, L/Cpl, served in 74 Coy PC; joined from Richborough Camp and was with BEF in France 1940

Wiener, Edgar H., served in 219 Coy PC

Wiener, Heribert, on German Unity Party's list of Sudeten Germans who served in the British Army

Wieninger, served in 74 Coy PC; joined from Richborough Camp and was with BEF in France 1940

Wienskowitz, Hans, later Wheen; born 1894; served in 74 Coy PC; joined from Richborough Camp and was with BEF in France 1940; discharged on medical grounds Mar. 1943

Wieselmann, served in PC; later in RAF as Ft Sgt, engaged in investigations concerning the murder of 50 RAF officers at Stalag Luft 3 in Sagan

Wildmann, Austrian, served in 338 Coy PC in North Africa

Wilheim, served in 74 Coy PC; joined from Richborough Camp and was with BEF in France 1940

Wilk, M., later Higgins; died on active service

Wilmersdoerffer, H. J., 13807570, later Wilmers, John Geoffrey; born Munich 27 Dec. 1920; pupil at Leighton Park School, Reading, studied at St John's College Cambridge; interned 1940; enlisted beginning of 1942; served in 3/10 Cdo; also SAS, took part in Operation FORFAR against St Valéry-en-Caux; commissioned early 1945; post-war: QC, Judge of Appeal in Jersey and Guernsey

Wilmot, P., Austrian, appears to have served in RAC

Wilpred, David, later Morrison-Wilpred, David J., from Nuremberg, served in RAF; after demob went to New Zealand and served in NZ Air Force

Wiltzig, served in 74 Coy PC; joined from Richborough Camp and was with

BEF in France 1940

Winter, Ernest

Winter, Leopold, won prizes playing chess

Winterberg, Hans Karl, later Winterburgh, John Charles; born Prague, Czechoslovak citizen, lived in Vienna, pupil at Theresianum; served as Lt Comm. in RN

Winton, H., served in 88 Coy PC

Wirlander, Stephan, temporarily aka Miller, John, Austrian; born 11 Sept. 1905, member of foreign mission of Austrian Social Democratic Party, engineer, economist, financial expert, journalist, wrote for *Der Stempler* and *Der Strom*, in UK studied at Firecroft College, Bournville, near Birmingham; interned 1940, sent to Canada, after return was editor of radio station 'Sender Rotes Wien'; enlisted 1941; served in PC; also SOE, on special missions in North Africa, Turkey, Italy; together with Sanders, Theo Neumann and Hladnik in investigating team concerned with Austrian PoWs; in Operation BOBBIE ONE in Vorarlberg; post-war: Secretary of Vienna Chamber of Labour, connections with Creditanstalt

Wiseman, C.F.J., served as 2/Lt in 229 Coy PC 1942; later in 36 Gp PC

Wisloch, Harry, from Vienna, Cpl in 229 Coy PC; sent to PC OCTU 2 June 1942, 2/Lt in 69 Coy 31 Dec. 1942–24 Apr. 1943; then to 6 PCTC; named in officers' list of 362 Coy PC in Maison Carrée, Algeria, 30 May 1943

Wittkower, Dr, psychiatrist from Vienna, served as Maj. in RAMC; designed tests used by War Office for selection of officers

Wodak, Dr Walter, 13802754, from Vienna, lawyer and diplomat, member of foreign mission of Austrian Social Democratic Party, in England lecturer in Workers Education Association; enlisted 17 Aug. 1940; served in PC; also Army Education Corps; politically active throughout the war; lectured at BAOR College concerning international law, also British aims and methods; member of BALU; demob 26 Nov. 1945; post-war: Secretary of Austrian Embassy, London, 1948, Secretary General of Austrian Foreign Ministry

Wolf, served in 74 Coy PC; joined from Richborough Camp and was with BEF in France 1940

Wolf, Dr H.G.; born Berlin, Mar. 1911, went to school at Lankwitz, Steglitz district, studied law at Wuerzburg and Basle, doctor of law, emigrated to Johannesburg, chartered accountant; served as Sgt in South African Service Corps, was unfit for active service so was made orderly room Sgt; discharge on medical grounds after 4 years; post-war: lives in Zurich

Wolf, Erich A., 13810013, later Ward, E.A. 6436380, joined British forces at behest of FDJ or other communist party organisation; probably destined for SOE, but returned to (PC?) unit autumn 1944; post-war: returned to Germany

Wolf, Fritz, later Mason, Howard, from Breslau, studied architecture at Liverpool; interned 1940, to Canada; was in PC at Buxton

Wolf, Gerhard Victor, later Wolf, Gerald V., from Steinau a.d.Strasse, Hesse, where his ancestors had manufactured soap for 7 generations, firm was arianised 1934, after emigration pupil at Manchester Grammar School;

joined 87 Coy PC, with them in the line covering Le Havre and at Rennes in 1940, came out of France at St Malo; 1942 left PC to train as wireless operator for RAC; sent to Italy, posted to 1st Wilts. Yeo.; later to Queen's Bays, promoted Sgt; demobilised 1946; post-war: B.Sc.Chem., built up and eventually sold chemical factory, 1951 recovered 50% share of family enterprise in Steinau

Wolf, Leo, joined British forces at behest of Young Austria 1943

Wolf, Rita

Wolf, Victor

Wolf, Walter L., 13803539, later Marshall, Allan W.; born 2 Apr. 1922; served in 249 Coy PC; later in 3/10 Cdo; attached to Polish Troop, 10 Cdo in Cassino campaign, at Pescopennataro; though Jewish was nicknamed 'SS Wolf' because of his blue eyes, fair-hair and otherwise Aryan appearance and manner

Wolfe, Walter R., served in 93 Coy PC

Wolfes, Renate, served in 1 Allied Volunteer Platoon ATS; later commissioned

Wolff, served in 74 Coy PC; joined from Richborough Camp and was with BEF in France 1940

Wolff, Dieter, later Wayne, Peter H.; born Berlin 8 May 1920, schools in Germany, Switzerland and Friends' School, Great Ayton; enlisted 1941; served in 251 and 93 Coy PC; also Interpreters' Pool; 1944 in Normandy, Dieppe, Brussels; with 507 Military Government, Minden, chief translator at military court, investigation of German financial institutions; demob 1946; post-war: FCA, director of finance of various real estate companies in London

Wolff, Frank served in 137 Coy PC

Wolff, H.

Wolff, Margot, on German Unity Party's list of comrades who served in Allied armies; after demob returned to Germany

Wolff, Martin, served with 220 Coy PC at Lydbrooke; then in 2 SM Coy RASC, Bulford

Wolff, Victor; died on active service

Wolffberg, served in 74 Coy PC; joined from Richborough Camp and was with BEF in France 1940

Wolffsberg, served in 74 Coy PC; joined from Richborough Camp and was with BEF in France 1940

Wolfram, Pte in 88 Coy PC; during air attack on London 10 Nov. 1940 'Cpl. Goldschmidt and Pte. Wolfram helped the wounded until assistance could be obtained from ARP personnel' (War diary, 88 Coy)

Wolheim, Walter, later Wilson, Walter; born Vienna 9 May 1919, pupil at R9; served as Cpl in 87 Coy PC, Reconnaisance Corps and Interpreters' Pool

Wolken, Dr Peter, served in PC in North Africa

Wollstein, later Weldon, S.F.

Woolf, John E., in Brussels at beginning of 1945

Worel, Charles F.; born Vienna 3 Oct. 1910; enlisted from internment 1940; served in PC; was ski instructor for Black Watch; discharged 1944; then miner (Bevin Boy)

Wrecker, served in 74 Coy PC; joined from Richborough Camp and was with BEF in France 1940

Wreschner, Kurt; born 1903; served in 74 Coy PC

Wuerzburger, Karl Robert, later Ward, Kenneth Robert; born Frankfurt am Main 29 Nov. 1922, father organist at West End Synagogue there, pupil at Schwarzburg Schule 1929-33, Woehler Gymnasium 1933-36, Philanthropie 1936-38, By *Kindertransport* to London Aug. 1939, Worked as houseboy in boarding house, then apprenticed at uniform tailors; enlisted May 1942; served in 87 Coy from June 1942, Aug. 1943 transferred to RAC; after training to C Tp, A Sqn. 1 RTR, landed at Arromanches on D-Day + 1, said he would not take prisoners, but made cup of tea for first one; at Caen, Falaise, Brussels, Arnhem, survived destruction of tank at Ahaus, in Sherman with 17 pounder as gunner/wireless operator; at Hamburg, Meldorf May 1945; till June 1945 interpreter; July 1945 until 1948 in Military Police, Berlin, discovered Himmler's hide-out, but failed to recognise him; demob as SQMS

Wuerzburger, Paul (Daniel), from Frankfurt, brother of above and of Walter W., fled to Palestine, which he entered illegally 1939; served in Jewish Bde in Italy and Belgium; member of War Crimes Commission

Wuerzburger, Walter, from Frankfurt, brother of Karl and Paul W. (above), in Singapore at beginning of war; interned there and sent to Australia; served in AMF

Wunder, later Williams, Harry, veteran of Spanish Civil War; member of French Resistance; served in PC; later in RF (SOE group Kaiser and Rasborscheg), Lt, parachuted into action Apr. 1945

Wurmser, A.G., Pte in 248 Coy PC; painter whose pictures were exhibited by Darlington Society 20 Aug. 1942

Wurzl, Gertrude, served in WAAF; on German Unity Party's list of Sudeten Germans who served in the British Army

Young, Henry, served in 74 Coy PC

Young, Thomas, Austrian

Zacharias, served in 74 Coy PC; joined from Richborough Camp and was with BEF in France 1940

Zade, from Heidelberg, brother of Hanno Zade (q.v.), fought in Normandy from D-Day onwards

Zade, Hanno, from Heidelberg; born 1920, had completed an apprenticeship as locksmith at Heidelberg, to England by *Kindertransport* of Society of Friends, agricultural trainee; interned 1940, to Canada on Dutch (?) ship; after return enlisted 1941; served in 137 Coy PC at Lockerbie; transferred to REME, in Donnington 2 years, then India, at Deolali, Madras, promoted Sgt, offered commission but refused; post-war: returned to Germany, lives in retirement in village on borders of Hesse and Baden-Wuerttemberg

Zadik, Walter Gabriel, 13805471, later Thompson, Walter Gerald, 13118717; born 23 Aug. 1919, schoolteacher; served in 220 Coy PC; then 3/10 Cdo; landed in Normandy with 4 Cdo on D-Day, taken prisoner during night of

19/20 June 1944 near Gonneville-Longuemare; returned to England after release

Zamory, Eberhard; born Breslau 1922, pupil at Kaiser Wilhelm Gymnasium, 1939 to Manchester, founder member of Free German Youth (FDJ) in autumn 1939, apprenticeship as waiter, then worked in agriculture and gardening; tried to join RAC at behest of FDJ but was refused; joined PC; then interpreter in PoW camp No. 9 Kempton Park; June to Dec. 1945 in Norway to organise return of Germans to their homes, discovered German deserter in *Wehrmacht* prison months after end of war and secured his release; left British Army 1947 only after his German nationality had been satisfactorily established; post-war: studied history at Hamburg University, working student, later in book trade, editor (*Stern*) and publisher's reader, resigned from Communist Party 1968, active trade unionist, author of a biography *Das war mein Leben* (Verlag Neues Leben, 1996)

Zarek, Otto, author, served in 249 Coy PC, Pol. Int. Unit, African Force HQ, transferred to Pol. Int. Unit at request of FO, worked with Sir Robert (later Lord) Vansittart, wrote leaflets, acted as radio commentator, then involved in re-education of PoWs; post-war: film producer

Zattoni, A., 13806011

Zehetmeyer, served in 74 Coy PC; joined from Richborough Camp and was with BEF in France 1940

Zehngut, PAL/6530, Austrian, served as L/Cpl in RASC

Zeilinger, Hans, alias Linger, alias Lt Adams, G.H., Lt in IC, on list of intelligence agents in UK June 1945

Zeisler, served in 248 and 69 Coy PC

Zeisler, Siegmar, later Sanders, Ralph; born Berlin 28 Mar. 1920, left school 1934, in furnishing trade, then ladies' fashions, deprived of Polish and German citizenship, then stateless, emigrated to England 31 July 1939, to Kitchener Camp, there locksmith's apprentice, worked in comb manufacture, Bradford; interned at York and Isle of Man; enlisted from internment Nov. 1940; served in 246 and 69 Coy PC; Jan. 1943 transferred REME Central Workshop Donnington; 1945 attached to RAOC; lastly in 800 Workshop, Braunlage; demob Sept. 1946; post-war: locksmith, then bus conductor, trade union employee, 1959–60 TU scholarship to LSE, officer in municipal transport Leeds, administrator in College of Commerce, lastly admin assistant Leeds Polytechnic, 1971 MInstAM, 1969–90 JP

Zeissl, Stephan

Zeleckover, served in 74 Coy PC; joined from Richborough Camp and was with BEF in France 1940

Zelekovic, Jack

Zeles, Alex, served in 74 Coy PC

Zelinger, Peter P.

Zenker, E.

Zentner, served in 69 Coy PC

Zentner, Austrian, served in 337 or 338 Coy PC, North Africa

Zerner, Karl, enlisted at behest of Young Austria 25 June 1943.

Ziegler, scientist, lost his job in Germany when Nazis first came to power; served in PC; transferred to RAF, there FO; died on active service

Zirker, Erna, served in 1 Allied Volunteer Platoon ATS

Zivohlava, J., later Gautier, Jean, from Vienna, emigrated to Paris, then Angers, after French collapse twice shipwrecked on way to Canada, after second disaster landed at Oban and joined Free French; served in French Troop, 10 Cdo

Zobel, later Abingdon, Pte in 229 Coy PC

Zucker, later Sukari, enlisted from Palestine, Cpl in 608 Coy PC and medical orderly, in North Africa and Greece, taken prisoner by Germans at Kalamata

Zucker, from Kassel, served with French *Prestataires*, unit under British command was in retreat to Dunkirk, but not evacuated from there, fled with other Hessian *Prestataires*, got fishing vessel to take him from area of Nantes to unoccupied France, captured by HMS *Imogen*; interned UK; recognised for what he was and permitted to join PC

Zuckermann, Edit (Zukermanova, Edita), married Katona, *nom de guerre* 'Marianne', Czechoslovak citizen, had lived in Vienna; in Free French secret service, spied in German and Italian headquarters, 'She did her job courageously, coolly and intelligently', appointed member of *Ordre de l'Armée de Mer* with *Croix de Guerre avec Palmes* by de Gaulle

Zuntz, W., later Sandford; died on active service.

Zweig, Rudi, later Sanders, Ralph; born 4 Sept. 1918, from Breslau, later Berlin, should never have been allowed to pass his medical; joined 74 Coy AMPC, with them to France, also served in London during air raids of autumn 1940, then at Tisbury, Mere and Weymouth, after that, apparently, he could not stand up to normal duties any longer and so, for a time, became batman to a colonel, whose friend he remained later on; then a nervous complaint, the result of separation from his family caused him to be released 15 Dec. 1942; then worked peacefully as painter and decorator for many years, running his own business; manner of his death is symptomatic of state of his nerves, in May 1994 he was invited to Berlin as guest of the Mayor, the visit and seeing the places where he had spent his childhood excited him so much that he collapsed and had to be taken back to England in a coma; he died 13 days later without regaining consciousness

Zweig, Werner, 13805553, later Nelson, Vernon, 13118718; born Upper Silesia 5 Nov. 1922; served in 249 Coy PC; then 3/10 Cdo, broke leg in training; in Sicily and Italy attached to 40 RM Cdo, wounded in action; along River Maas in Jan. 1945; attached to 46 RN Cdo discovered order of battle of East Elbian forces when searching HQ of General Brunning in Buchhorst; after end of hostilities in Field Security Unit in Luebeck, awarded Certificate of Commendation, in charge of a Field Security Section 1949

Zwicker, Hans, member of Young Austria; enlisted from Reading Dec. 1943/Jan. 1944

The cookhouse team of 88 Coy consisted of Cpl Adolf who knew no English at all, and Harry. The latter had been chef in a Lyons Restaurant. According to Warner both were masters of their trade. Their surnames are not known.

Details concerning about 50 other persons are in the possession of the author, but as the persons concerned have asked to remain anonymous, they are not listed above.

Aliases

In the register above all persons are listed in order of their original names, where these are known. In many cases these are not the names by which they are known today or by which they have been known at other periods of their lives. This may be due to name changes under Army Council Instructions or as the result of marriage or for other reasons. Where such other names are known they have been listed in the left-hand column below in alphabetical order. The name under which they appear in the register is shown on the right.

Abbey, Peter	Abrahamson, Peter
Abingdon	Zobel
Achatz, Alfred	Chalaupa, Manfred
Adam, Ken	Adam, Klaus
Adams, G.H.	Zeilinger, Hans
Aitcheson, Harry	Krausen, Heinz
Alford, Michael	Aufrecht, Heinz
Allard, Lorraine	Sulzbacher, Lore
Allen	Perlmann, T.
Allington, Ken	Eisenberg, K.
Allington, Nicky	Baerblinger, Nicholas
Ambrose, Ken	Abrahamsohn, Kurt
Amichai, Jehuda	Pfeuffer, Ludwig
Amson, Martin Leslie	Abrahamsohn, Martin
Anderman, H.B.	Andermann-Engelart, H.
Anderson	Arnstein, A.V.
Anderson, Herbert (Lofty)	Fuerst, Helmut Herbert
Andrews, Harry	Arenstein, Hans
Anson, Alice H.	Gross, Alice H.
Anson, Colin E.,	Ascher, Claus Leopold Octavio
Anson, H.	Arnstein
Arieli, Jehoshua	Loebl, J.
Arlen	Abrahamowicz, Richard
Arnott, Alfred	Arnsdorf, Alfred
Arnott, M.V.	Arnsdorf, Max
Arnott, Stanley Frank	Arnsdorf, Selmar
Ascher, Franziska	Deutsch-Renner, Franzi
Ashley, Frances	Deutsch-Renner, Franzi
Ashley, Michael Gordon	Auerbach, W.H.
Ashley, Otto	Aufwerber, Otto
Atkins, G.	Abraham, G.
Austin, Freddie	Raape, Freddie
Baer, George	Baer, Georg
Baker-Byrne, R.P. (Butch)	Becker, Robert
Banks,	Mayr, Hubert
Barnes, Robert	Baumwollspinner, Gotthard
Barring	Blumenau, M.,
Barrington, Ilse	Stiebel, Ilse
Barry, Peter	Berger, Peter
Bartlett, Ken	Billmann
Bass, Ernest Eli	Bass, Ernst
Bate, G.	Oppelt, Gustav

Baum, Henry	Berger-Waldenegg, Baron Heinrich
Beaumont, George	Bunzl, Georg
Beecham, Bernard	Bischheim, Bernhard
Beecham, Eric M.	Bischheim, Erich
Begich	Beh
Behrendt, Gideon	Behrendt, Guenter
Belgrave, R.H.	Eisner, K.J.H.
Bennett J.	Berger, I.
Bennett, George	Bratu, Artur E.
Benson, Frederic	Becker, Fritz
Benson, Harry	Badt, H.
Bentley, Frederick	Bierer, F.
Berger, Franz	Pretzner, Ejar
Berliner, Peter	Berliner, Kurt
Bernstein, Ilse	Stiebel, Ilse
Bier, Lieselotte	Bock, Lieselotte
Bittner, Dr Anne	Thausing, Dr Anny
Black, Peter	Schwarzschild, Peter
Blaha, Emil	Fuchs, Emil
Blair	Blau
Blake	Blau, P.
Blake, Harry	Becker, Heinz
Blake, Henry	Schwarz, Hans
Blake, William	Bielschowski, Wilhelm
Blakeley, Chris	Bachwitz
Bleach, Timothy	Bleichroeder, Adolf
Block, Benno	Bloch
Blum, Harold	Pretzner, Ejar
Boccafurni	Berger-Waldenegg, Baron Heinrich
Boam, Rudolph Walter	Boehm, Rudolph Walter
Boenisch, Johann	Grafl, Josef
Bornstein, Therese	Braun, Therese
Bourne, Eric	Borchard, Ulrich
Bower	Bauer, Georg
Bowes, Eric F.	Brauer, Erich Franz
Brand	Ulanovsky, Peter Johann
Bray, Lotte	Loewenstein, Lotte (Pip)
Brenner	Bilisic, Alois
Brent, Leslie Baruch	Baruch, Lothar
Brian, Walter	Burian, Walter
Bright, Alan	Breitbart, Horst Guenther
Bright, Geof.	Breitbart
Broadman, Geoffrey M.	Sruh, Gottfried C. (Friedl)
Brook, Henry R.	Brod, H.R.
Brook, Sidney Edward	Baruch, Siegfried Josef
Brown, Ernest	Baum, Ernst
Bruce, George	Prager
Bruce, Harold	Schilling
Bryan, H.E.	Bloch, H.E.
Bryant, George	Braeuer, Dr Georg
Bryant, John	Rosenstiehl
Buer, Irma	Holzer, Irma
Burgleigh, Henry Oswald	Berger-Waldenegg, Baron Heinrich
Burnett, Richard	Behrendt, Richard

Cainz, W.R.   Kainz, W.R.
Calmon, C.   Calman, C.
Cappel, Francis Erwin   Cappel, Franz Erwin
Carson, John   Cohn, Hans
Carson, Peter Andrew   Carlebach, Peter
Carsten, Francis L.   Carsten, Franz L.
Carter, Irene   Lazarowicz, Irene
Charleroi, Pierre   Baerwald, Ernst
Cheney, E.   Saar, Erhard Wolf Wilhelm
Chirgwin, F. M.   Berliner, Friederich
Cihak, Hans   Prager, Hans
Cijka   Neunauer, Gottfried
Clay, J.C.   Jorns, C.H.L.A.
Clayton, Walter   Kohn, Walter
Claire, George   Klaar, Georg
Clarke, K.E.   Goldschlaeger, K.T.
Clement, Eric   Klementschitz, Erich
Clyne, Robert   Klein, Robert
Coleman   Kugelmann, H.J.,
Colman, A.H.   Kalman, A
Compton, David Michael   Hoffmann, Hans Guenther Josef
Conrad, Eric   Konrad, Erich
Cosson, Pierre   Schoissengeier
Crawford, Peter   Cossmann, Gerhard Hermann Carl
Cross, L.   Gross, L.
Curtis, F.M.   Czerninski, M.
Curtis, Harry   Cahn, Helmut
Curtis, Richard   Conradt

Dale, Leslie   Litvak, Eugen
Dale, Stephen Patrick   Spanglet, Guenter
Davenport, F.   Dessauer, Franz
Davies, Jack   Hansen, Einar Reska
Dawson, Bernard Kenneth   Dossmar, Bernhard
Dean   Deutschkron, J.H.,
Denby, P.C.   Dreifuss, P.C.
Derman   Dermann, Erich
Descarr, Bernard   Dossmar, Bernhard
Dickson J.   Dietrichstein, J.
Dickson, Geoffrey   Dobriner, Max
Dinamitardo, Teddy il   Saar, Erhard Wolf Wilhelm
Douglas, Keith   Dungler K.
Douglas, Paul Michael   Korn, Konrad Paul
Drew, Harry   Nomburg, Harry
Dudley, L.A.   Duschenes, L.
Dunn, Dr Henry   Danziger, Dr Heinz G.
Dunn, Walter   Danziger, Walter
Dwelly, Vernon (Ducky)   Goldschmidt, V.

Eden, Peter W.   Engel, Werner
Edwards, Albert   Eisner, Adalbert
Edwards, Fred H.   Meyer, F.L.
Edwards, Sidney   Eimerl, Siegfried
Egtman, Marianne   Schlesinger, Marianne

Ellerman, R. — Etzdorf, Baron Ruediger Otto Ulrich
Ellern, H.J. — Heinz, H.J.
Elliott, Andrew — Eppenstein, Andrew H.H.
Elliott, Ralph Warren Victor — Ehrenberg, Rudolf Wolfgang
    Hans Victor (Rolli)

Elliott, Roger — Ettlinger, Lothar
Elting, John Gordon — Elting, Guenther
Elton, Sir Geoffrey — Ehrenberg, Gottfried
Envers, John — Engel, Hanns-Guenter
Ervis — Habettler, Josef
Evans, Robert — Eisenstein, Bobby
Everitt, Walter A. — Eberstadt, Walter A.
Eversley, David Edward Charles — Eberstadt, Ernst Carl Eduard

Fairbanks, G. — Kurzweil, E.
Fairfax — Feiweles, Richard
Falton, Hugh Peter — Faltitschek, Hermann
Farr, Ernest Herbert (Tommy) — Freytag, Ernst Herbert
Farroll — Friedmann
Fenton — Fenyce
Fenton, Bryan L. — Feder, E. Wolfgang
Ferguson — Finckelstein
Ferguson, E. — Fassbaender
Field, Leonard — Felix, Leo
Field, Willy — Hirschfeld, Willy
Findlay — Finckelstein
Firth, Anthony — Fuerth, Hans G.
Fischer, Karl — Lzicar (?), Karl
Fisher, Bryan — Fischer, Bruno
Fletcher — Fleischer, F.,
Fletcher, Louis — Fleschner, L.
Flynn, Charles — Fantl, K
Foot, Susan — Cohn, Suse
Ford — Farago, Ladislas
Forest, H.J. — Friedlaender, Hans
Fort, William George — Fortgang, Wilhelm Georg
Foster — Fraenkel, E.,
Foster, Walter — Friedenstein, Walter
Foster, Walter, OBE — Fast, Walter
Foster-Friedenstein. Walter — Friedenstein, Walter
Frank, Michael — Mayer, Paul Yogi
Franklyn, George Mack — Frank, Guenter Max
Franklyn, Ken — Frankenstein, Kurt
Fraser — Frey, H.C.
Fraser, Kenneth D. — Fleischmann, Kurt
Frazer — Fein, Herbert
Frean, Peter — Friedmann, Peter
Frewen — Frohwein
Fried, Marianne Klara Ester — Graetz, Marianne Klara Ester
Fry, Peter Howard — Frey, Peter Hans
Fuller, Didi — Kargerer-Stein, E.von

Gardner, Charles — Gold, Israel
Gardner, H. — Gaertner, H.

Garland, Ruth
Garry, O.
Garvin, Robert Kenneth
Goodwin
Garvin, R.K.
Gassman, John
Gautier, Jean
Gayward, Peter Harry
Georgeau, Jean
Georges, Henri Charles
Gerber, Leopold
Gibson, Sabina (Bina)
Gilbert, Leslie Marius
Gilbert, Ronnie
Giles, Peter
Gillatt, Eva E.
Glass
Glenville, Martin G.
Goerke, Werner
Goldsmith, Herbert P.
Goldsmith, J. P.
Goodman, Dr Ernest J.
Goodman, John E.
Gordon, Eric
Gordon, Frederick
Gordon, Henry
Gordon, Tony
Graham
Graham, Kenneth Wakefield
Graham, Sidney
Grant, Alan R.N.
Grant, Gary
Grant, (Hubert) Brian
Gray
Gray, Frederick
Green
Green, John
Greenwood, Marianne
Greenwood, Robert
Gregg, Frank
Grenville, Henry Willam
Grierson, Sir Ronald
Griffiths, Keith James
Gross, Freddy H.
Groves, (Hubert) Brian
Gumley, Charles

Haas, Roman
Halford, T.
Hall, Peter
Hamilton, R.G.
Hamley, A.
Hammer, Johann
Hanleigh, Walter P.

Peschel, Ruth
Garai, Otto
Goldstern, Konstatin
Gold, Israel
Goldstern, K.
Gassman, Johannes
Zivohlava, J.
Gayduschek, Peter Harry Leopold
Mayr, Hubert
Schoissengeier
Bergmann, Dr Georg F.J.
Flesch, Sabina
Richle, Joseph
Guttmann, Hans-Julius
Hess, Otto
Oppenheim, Eva E.
Glas
Gerechter, Martin
Goerke, Ernst Werner,
Goldschmidt, H.F..
Goldschmidt, J.P.
Guttmann, Ernst
Gutmann, Egon
Goldhammer, Erich
Gaensler, Friedrich
Geiser, H.E.A.
Guttmann
Abraham
Gumpertz, Kurt Wilhelm
Gumpricht
Czupper, Noe
Graf
Lewin-Goldschmidt, Konrad L.
Kalisch
Gans, Manfred,
Grunen
Grafl, Josef
Gruenbaum, Marianne
Gruenbaum, Robert
Groser, Dr Franz
Greilsamer, Heinz Willy
Griessman,
Glaser, Kurt J.
Gross, Friedrich Herbert
Lewin-Goldschmidt, Konrad L.
Gold, Israel

Spreitzhofer, Roman
Herrnstadt, T.,
Ulanovsky, Peter Johann
Reich, S.R.
Baumfeld
Huetz, Nikolas
Hahn, Walter P.

Hanleigh-Hahn, Walter P.	Hahn, Walter P.
Harley R.	Cohn
Harper, Helen	Haberfeld, Helen
Harris, Ian Walter	Hajos, Hans Ludwig
Harris, Robert	Hinrichsen, Robert
Harris, Walter	Hacker, Walter
Harvey, Anna E.C.	Simoni, Anna E.C.
Harvey, Walter	Helfgott, Walter
Hastings, Alex	Gottesmann
Hauber	Huetz, Nikolas
Hays, J.W.	Wachsmann, W.
Heathcote, Michael Paul	Katz, Meinhard Paul Oscar
Heaton	Heyman, P.
Heckssher, G.	Heckscher, G.
Heger, Alois	Huetz, Nikolas
Hepworth, Freddy	Herschthal, Fritz
Hepworth, Walter Douglas	Herschthal, Walter
Hereford, John Heyman	Hertzog, J. Heyman
Herold, Ian	Herold, Wolfgang
Herring, P.	Hering, P.
Higgins	Wilk, M.,
Hilary, Robin	Hellmann, R.H.
Hillman(n), Leo, or F., or Charles	Bergmann, Dr Georg F.J.
Hofer	Bergmann, Dr Georg F.J.
Hofer, F.	Berliner, Friederich
Hogan, Frederick	Hofstaedter, Fritz
Holden, Joan	Ephraimson, Joan
Hollander, Paul	Hollaender, Paul
Horak	Anzbock, Fritz Peter
Horley, R.	Cohn
Howard	Hermann, E.B.
Howard, K. Peter	Heine, Peter
Howard, W.A.	Herzberg, A.H.
Howarth, Eric William	Nathan, Erich
Howell, M.A.	Rosenbluth, Eli
Huber, George	Simbuerger, Gerhard
Hudson, Stephen Keith	Hirsch, Stephan
Hughes, W.	Sachs, Walter
Hulsman, George	Huelsmann, Georg
Hulton	Ulrich, Heinz
Hutton, Ken	Herzfeld, Kurt
Hyman, Richard	Heymann, Richard
Jack Halford	Helfgott, Isaak
Jackson, Fred	Jacobus, Peter
Jacob, Ernest M.	Jacob, Ernst M.
Jacobi, Revd. Harry M.	Hirschberg, Heinz
James, Rolf	Jessen, Ralph
Jarrett C.S.	Jaretzki, K.S.
Jellinek, Ernest H.	Jellinek, Ernst
Johnson, Peter W.	Joseps, Wolfgang
Jones	Kottka, Vladimir
Jones, Mrs	Kernek
Jones, P.A.	Dolnica, A.
Jonson, Alan	Kanitz, Fritz

Karrell, Rudi
Katona, Edit
Kaulaut, Anton
Kay, A.
Kay, C.
Kaye, Leo
Keats, Walter
Kelly, Frank J.
Kelts, John Matthew
Kenber, Fred.
Kendal, George Harold (Nobby)
Kendall, Bob
Kennedy
Kennedy, Charles Victor
Kent, Bernard
Kent, R.K.
Kerpen, Lewis
Kershaw, Andrew
Kew, Leopold
Kezeker
Kind
King, B.
King, F.
King, Frederick
King, R.S.
King, Ronald Michael
King, Trudy
Kinghill, Peter
Kingsley, Edward R.
Kingsley, Michael
Kingsley, Roger James
Kirby, Eric Alfons
Kirby, Frederick G.
Kirby, M.J. (Ernest)
Klein, Ilse
Kleinschuster, Fritz
Knabl, Andreas
Knight, K.W.
Knoll, F.
Kowalsky, I.

Katz, Rudi
Zuckermann, Edit
Chalaupa, Manfred
Knie, A. or M.K.P.O.
Isaack, K.
Kotek, Leo
Kohn, Walter
Koenig, Franz
Koelz, Mathaeus Johannes
Krakenberger, F.
Knobloch, Gunther Hans
Kraus
Krossmayr
Bergmann, Dr Georg F.J.
Koban, Blasius
Karpeles, R.
Kerpen, Ludwig
Kirschner, André G.
Kuh, Leopold (Poldi)
Koban, Blasius
Kanders, Martin
Kasparovitch, Boris
Koenigsberger
Kanfer, Fritz
Kottkowski, Willi
Oppenheim, Werner
Ornstein, Gertrud
Koenigsberg, Peter
Koenigsberger, E.R.
Koenigshut, Manfred
Loewenstein, O.J.
Klappholz, Erich Alfons
Kantor, Friedrich
Kellmann, M.
Neumann, Ilse
Galler, Johann
Spreitzhofer, Roman
Meyer, H.U.
Berliner, Friederich
Kowalski, J.

Laddy, Max
Laker, Lilly
Land, Kurt Jakob
Landon
Landon, Norman
Landsberg, Sabina (Bina)
Lane, Alfred Thomas
Lane, George
Langdon, Lou,
Langford, Herbert
Langer, H. (Henry) Peter
Langley, E.R.F.
Latimer, Maurice

Lewinsky, Max
Gottlieb, Lilly
Landenberger, K.J.
Landauer, Walter
Landau, Norbert
Flesch, Sabina
Loewy, Alfred Thomas
Lanyi, Djury (Georg) H.
Lewy-Lingen, Walter
Lampel, Werner
Langer, Hans Peter
Landau, E.
Loewy, Moritz

Laughton	Lobel, M.
Laurant, Henry W.	Levy, Hans Werner
Laursen, Dita	Keller, Dita
Lawrence, Ernest R.	Lenel, Ernst R.
Lawrie, J.	Ladewig, Jochen
Lawton, B.R.	Lauffer, Guenther
Layton, Freddie	Leschziner, Alfred
Leach	Leder
Lee	Liftschitz
Lee, J.C.,	Lemberger, Hans Karl
Lees, Edward	Saar, Erhard Wolf Wilhelm
Leigh-Bell, Peter	Liebel, Peter
Leighton, William Peter	Langer, Peter Paul Wilhelm
Leighton-Langer, Peter	Langer, Peter Paul Wilhelm
Lennard, Ernest G.	Loevy, Ernst
Lennard, John Howard	Loevy, Hans
Lennert, Irene	Lazarowicz, Irene
Leonard	Richle, Joseph
Leonard R.	Lehniger, Richard
Levy, Irma	Holzer, Irma
Lewis Haig	Hagen, Louis, MM
Lewis, Martin David	Lewin
Lincoln, Ken	Levy, Karl Ernst, BEM
Linger	Zeilinger, Hans
Linton, L.	Israel, L.
Liss, George V. de (Peppi)	Delitz, Georg
Loder	Lilienfeld, H.
Lodge, Robert	Friedlaender, Rudolph
Loeffler, Bernard	Koban, Blasius
Loewenheck, Renate	Rothschild, Renate
Long, Peter	Leven, Peter Guenther
Louis, Frederick Mac	Lewin, Siegfried
Lowit, Ian	Loewit, Hans
Ludlow	Luchtenstein
Lustig, Susanne	Cohn, Susanne
Lynton, Mark	Loewenstein, Max
Lytton, Nicholas	Lieben, Herbert
MacAllister, A.	Saalkind, L.
MacAllister, C.S.	Krumbein, K.
MacManus, John	Mertz
Malle, Johann	Mueller, Johann
'Marianne'	Zuckermann, Edit
Marshall, Allan W.	Wolf, Walter L.
Marshall, Ken	Menasse, Kurt
Marshall, Paul	Markstein
Marston, Eric	Meyerstein
Martin, Frank M.	Salomon, M.F.
Martin, William	Treichl, Wolfgang
Mason, Gary	Weinberg, K.
Mason, Howard	Wolf, Fritz
Masters, Peter F.	Arany, Peter F.
Maxwell, (Ian) Robert	Hoch, Jan Ludvik
Maxwell, Martin	Meisels, Max

Maynard, M.

Moses, M.

McCabe, A.

Czupper, Noe

McCullough
    alias Turner, A.C.

Pollaschek (Polatschek?)

McGregor, Jack F. (Jock)

Kury, Manfred H.

Melford, John

Mendelsohn, Heinz

Melville

Meyer, A.,

Melvin

Milch, H.,

Melvin, P.H.

Meyer, H.P.

Mendleson, John (Jack)

Mendelsohn, Jacques

Merton, Michael

Blumenfeld, Ludwig

Miles, John H.

Mueller, Hans

Miles, Kenneth L.

Meyer

Miles, Patrick Hugh

Levin, Hubertus

Miller, John

Wirlander, Stephan

Minter, Robert

Manhardt, Rudolf

Mond, Frank

Schlesinger, Kurt

Montgomery, Cecil

Weintraub, Otto

Moody, Peter

Meyer, Kurt

Morland, Henry L.

Merlaender, Heinz Ludwig

Morris, Eric

Moses, Erich

Morris, John

Mueller, Johann

Morrison-Wilpred, David J.

Wilpred, David

Mortimer

Mautner, M.

Mortimer, Elisabeth

Koessler, Elisabeth

Mortimer, Henry

Mosenthal, Heinrich

Morton, Henry Ernest

Moser, Helmut Ernst

Morton, Peter John

Meyer, Peter

Moss, Gerhard

Moses, G.O.

Mrnka, Wenzel

Manhardt, Rudolf

Mueller, Jakob

Prager, Hans

Naftalie, Fred

Naphtalie, Manfred

Nash, H.

Naschitz

Naumann, Alexander

Manhardt, Rudolf

Nelson, Steve

Netter, H. Stefan

Nelson, Vernon

Zweig, Werner

Newland

Neulaender, Fritz

Newman

Nagel, P.

Newman

Neumann

Newman, Archie

Neuberger, Adolf

Newman, Charles

Neumann, Karl

Newman, George

Neumann, Hans Georg

Newman, Harry

Neufeld, Hans

Nichols, Gerald P. (Jerry)

Nell, G.H.H.

Niven, Neville

Nussbaum, David

Norton, Ernest

Nathan, Ernst (Eli)

Norton, Paul

Niggas, Paul

Norton, Ronald George

Neubroch, Rudolf

Norville, Michael

Nagler, Kurt

Norville, Mrs

Meyer, Miss

Nuffield

Neufeld, Hans

Nussbaum, Steff

Neumann, Steffi

O'Brian, Gene
O'Hara, F. Michael
O'Neill
O'Rourke, Jim
Oakfield, Bill
Oden, H.
Ormond, Henry
Orr, Adam

Behrendt, Guenter
Berliner, Friederich
Henschell, Oskar
Rothmann
Oppenheim, Werner
Odenheimer, Hans
Oettinger, Hans
Opoczynski, Abraham

Palmer
Palmer
Parker, Ralph
Parry, F.
Peiser, Luise
Pelican, Fred
Pepper, George
Perkins, J.G.
Perry
Perthain, E. John
Peters, Alan
Phillips, Geoffrey
Phillipsen, W.
Platt, Bubi
Platt, Henry
Pollard, Sidney
Pollitt, E.H.
Porter
Preston, L.
Priestley, Peter Michael
Pringle, Reginald

Peyer
Pojur
Pick
Posamentier, O.
Hauer, Luise
Pelikan, F.
Popper, Georg
Scheinmann, Oscar G.
Pinchever
Perthain, Ernst
Pfeffer
Phillip, Guenter
Phillipsohn, W.
Platschek
Platzer, Heinrich
Pollak, Sigi
Pollitzer
Portner, W.,
Pinkus, Ludwig
Lindenbaum, Egon
Rosenzweig, Paul

Raanan, Joseph
Radwell
Rath
Rayne, Fred
Rayner, John
Redferne
Reed
Relation, Helga
Reynolds, K.
Rhodes, Eric Douglas
Richards, Anthony
Rimmel, Josef
Ritinitis
Rivers, Max
Rivin, Ernst
Roberts, H.K.
Roberts, Walter
Robertson, Henry
Rockhill
Rodgers, Joseph
Rodley, John Peter
Rodney, Robert
Rodwell, H.

Reismann, K.
Rosen
Weinstein-Rath, J.
Reinefeld, Manfred
Rahmer
Rosenthal, (Rosentall?)
Rosenbaum, L.R.
Bernstein, Helga
Regenbogen, K.
Rohde, Erich
Regart, Alex Mast
Mayr, Hubert
Weinberger, P.
Rothbarth, Erwin,
Riesenfeld
Riemer, H.K.
Rosenthal, Klaus Walter
Rosenkranz, Heinrich (Heine)
Schneditz
Roth, Josef
Rosenfeld, Hans
Reutner
Rosenthal, Heinz

Rogers, Garry
Roschitz, Franz
Rosney, George Jakob
Ross, John C.
Ross, Steven
Ross, Victor
Roth, Josef Ludwig
Rowe, Sir Henry, KCB QC
Ruzicka, Josef
Russell
Russell
Russell, R.

Baumgart, Gunther
Spreitzhofer, Roman
Rosenfeld, Georg Jakob
Rosenblueth, Hans
Rosskamm, Stephan
Rosenfeld, Viktor
Standhartiger, Karl
Roehr, Heinz Peter
Hemetsberger, Josef
Landsberg
Reifenberg, Heinz
Rosenberg, R.

Samuel, John
Sanders, Eric
Sanders, Ralph
Sanders, Ralph
Sanderson, J.K.
Sandford
Sanger
Saunders, Susi
Saunders
Saunders, George V.
Saunders, Harry
Saunders, L.
Sayers, G.J.
Scarfe
Schmidt, Karl
Schmidtbauer, Josef
Schumacher, Karl Hans
Schwarz, Hugo
Scott
Scott, Jack
Scott, Leslie
Scott, William
Seaman, Henry H.
Selby, Maria
Selo, Laura
Sely, Kaye Wolve Frederick
Seymour, H.A.
Shapire, E.A.
Sharoni, S.
Sharpe, John Herbert
Shaw, P.M.
Shell, Fritz
Shelley, A. Percy
Shelley, Peter
Sheridan, M.R.
Sherman, R.W.
Shermer
Shields, Paul
Silverman
Simeon
Simms, Alfred George

Samuel, Herbert
Schwarz, Erich
Zweig, Rudi
Zeisler, Siegmar
Schirmer, K.K.
Zuntz, W.
Sokol, Alois
Birnbaum, Susi
Sander, Gus
Saloschin, Graf Georg V.
Schwarz, Harry
Salinger
Sauer, G.J. (Szauer?)
Scharf, K.
Standhartiger, Karl
Hemetsberger, Josef
Gaiswinkler, Albrecht
Schoissengeier
Schlesinger
Schloss, Yarlow
Steiner, Uli
Schatz, Hugo
Schueftan, H.
Kramer, Maria
Gumpel, Hannelore
Seltz, Kurt Wolfgang Friedrich
Sachs, H.P.
Schapira, E.A.
Schornstein, Fritz
Subak, Herbert
Schonfeld, O.W.
Galler, Johann
Samson, A.
Schneider, Max
Saloman, M.
Schreuer, Rudy
Scheuermann
Schwarzschild, Paul
Silbermann
Simion, Ernst
Simonson, Alfred Georg

Sinclair, H. Peter — Siegel, Hans Peter
Slade, W. — Neufeld, Hans
Sleigh, Frank James — Schlesinger, Franz
Smith, Edith — Perutz, Edith
Smith, Henry — Cohn, David
Smith, J. — Kugler, Joseph
Smith, Margot — Loewie, Margot
Sokol — Panhofer, Ferdinand
Spalding, Keith — Spalt, Karl-Heinz
Spencer — Schlesinger
Spencer, A. — Spiegel, A.
Spencer, G. — Spiegel, G.
Spencer, Tom — Stein, A.
Spiers, Harry — Spies, Horst
Spooner — Spuner, Bobby
Stanleigh, John Hubert — Schwartz, Hans
Stanley, Frederick Allen — Steiner, Friedrich
Stanton, Ralph — Steinberg, Rolf
Starmont — Steinberger, S.,
Steel, K. — Rosenstiel, K.
Stenham, R.E. (Bob) — Stern, Robert Eric
Stent, Ronald — Stensch, Rudolf
Stephen — Scheinmann, Oscar G,
Stevens, B.T. — Silberbusch, B.T.
Stevens, Eric — Schubert, Erich
Stevens, Ernest — Strauss, Ernst
Stevens, Harry — Schweiger, Hans (Harry)
Stevens, Harry George — Steiner, Heinz Georg
Steward, John Gordon — Sussmann, Hans
Stewart, David — Strauss, D.
Stewart, Joe — Goldstein, J
Stewart, Stephen M. — Strauss, Stefan
Stockner, Michael — Lindenbaum, Egon
Stones, George — Simbuerger, Gerhard
Straker, Emil — Fuchs, Emil
Strauss, Steven — Strauss, Ulrich
Streat — Strietzel, M.
Streeten, Paul — Hornig, Paul
Streets, George — Barth, Georg A.
Stuart (or Stuart-Schlesinger) — Schlesinger, Eduard
Studley, E.J. — Studinski
Sukari — Zucker
Sulby, Lorraine — Sulzbacher, Lore
Summerfield, Steven Alfred — Sommerfeld, Alfred
Sunshine — Sonnenschein
Sutton, Herbert — Suesskind, Herbert
Swinton, Tommy G. — Schwitzer J.G.

Taggart, William — Treichl, Wolfgang
Talbot, Mrs L. — Deutsch, L.
Tauber, Friedl — Mengen, Friedl
Taylor, J. — Theilinger, J.
Taylor, John — Schneider, Johann
Teddern, Clive — Tebrich, Kurt

Tennant, Richard W.

Terry, Peter J.

Thomas, Michael Alexander

Thompson

Thompson, Walter Gerald

Tobert, A

Tolliver

Towse, Eva M.

Trevor, C. Leslie

Trevor, Henry

Turner

Turner, A.C. also McCullough

Turner, Frank Geoffrey

Turner, Stephen

Usher, Artur

Usher, Willy

Verney, Randolph

Vernon

Vibert, F.

Villiers, Egon Ernest Robert

Vincent, Frank

Wahle, Steffie

Waldek, Frances

Walker, Henry

Walker, Peter

Wallace

Wallen, L.

Wallner, Franz Karl

Walters, Ilse

Walters-Kohn, Eric

Wand, Ralf

Ward, E.A.

Ward, Henry Louis

Ward, Kenneth Robert

Ward, Robert

Warner, Frederick Michael

Watson, William J.

Wayne, Peter H.

Webber, Jan

Webster, E.G.

Weldon, S.F.

Wells, Peter Vernon Allen

Werth, Henry

West, Arthur

Wheen

White, A.

Whittinghame, Tony (Ike)

Wieser, Hans

Wildman

Willert, Norman

Williams, Harry

Trojan, Richard W.

Tischler, Peter J.

Hollaender, Ulrich

Tischler

Zadik, Walter Gabriel

Tobinski, A.

Oliver

Oppenheimer, Eva M.

Baum, Hans

Teweles, Hans

Tabori, George

Pollaschek (Polatschek) O.

Trier, Franz-Guenter

Spanglet, Guenter

Uscherowitz, Artur

Uscherowitz, Willi

Vogel, Rudolph

Werner, Kurt

Vibeck, F.

Vogel, Egon

Vulkan

Burger, Steffie

Lustig, Franziska

Weglein, Hans

Nagel, Peter

Wapnitzki, C.,

Weikersheimer, L.

Lzicar (?), Karl

Rosenbaum, Ilse

Kohn, Erich

Wand, Raphael

Wolf, Erich

Warwar, Hans Ludwig

Wuerzburger, Karl Robert

Wank, Robert

Werner, Manfred

Wassermann, O.

Wolff, Dieter

Weber

Weinberger, E.G.

Wollstein

Auerhahn, W.

Wertheimer, H.

Rosenthal, Amnon or Arthur

Wienskowitz, Hans

Weiss, Ali

Kronheim, Jochen

Spreitzhofer, Roman

Alweiss, Manfred

Wegner

Wunder, Henrick

Wilmers, John Geoffrey | Wilmersdoerffer, H.J.
Wilson, Walter | Wolheim, Walter
Windisch, Paul | Niggas, Paul
Winkler, Alfred | Gaiswinkler, Albrecht
Winter | Weil, M.,
Winterburgh, John | Winterberg
Wolf, Gerald V. | Wolf, Gerhard Victor
Wollmerstedt, Frieda | Herzfeld, Frieda
Woolford, John | Scherchen, Wulff
Wuerzburger, Daniel | Wuerzburger, Paul

Young, Thomas | Jung, Otto

Ziba | Spanglet, Guenter
Zukermanova, Edita | Zuckermann, Edith

Units of HM Forces during the 1939–45 War, recruited either entirely or largely from amongst the then so-called enemy aliens of German or Austrian origin who enlisted in the United Kingdom or in Algeria

Units of the Pioneer Corps

3 Training Centre, PC – Richborough, Westward Ho!, Ilfracombe, disbanded 1942. Between 1939 and 1942 85% of German and Austrian recruits were trained in this unit.

69 Company, PC – Formed Richborough 27 Dec. 1939, Cherbourg, Rennes, 16 June 1940 evacuated from St Malo in Dutch collier, then Bideford, Ilminster, Okehampton, clearing up after air raids in Bexley, Erith and Welling, Doncaster, Darlington, Bolton; landed at Arromanches 4 Aug. 1944, disbanded at Caen 12 Dec. 1944.

74 Company, PC – Formed in Richborough 28 Jan. 1940, Cherbourg, Rennes, Vieux Marche, evacuated via Brest 17 June 1940, then Bideford, Llanvaches, London (in target area of air attacks), Tisbury, Mere (Wilts), Weymouth, Avonmouth Docks, Bicester, landed at Arromanches 6 Aug. 1944, Dieppe and Caen (attached to Canadians), Antwerp, disbanded there 30 Sept. 1945. Last OC Capt. Kew, previously Kuh.

77 Company, PC The 'Rachitenkompanie' (Rickets company) – Formed in Richborough Jan. 1940. Donnington, Trench, Long Marston (equipment depot for the invasion), Oakengates, Stratford-upon-Avon. All foreigners transferred to other companies 7 July 1943.

87 Company, PC – Formed Richborough 12 Feb. 1940, Le Havre, Rennes, evacuated from St Malo 17 June 1940, Chard, Taunton, Ilminster, then Bermondsey and Blackheath (in target area of air attacks), Velindre, Tenby, Pembroke Docks, Long Marston. All foreigners transferred to other companies 30 Sept. 1943.

88 Company, PC – Formed Richborough shortly after 21 Feb. 1940, Le Havre and Harfleur, Rennes, Betton, evacuated from St Malo 16 June 1940 with loss of all equipment, then Berrington, Bow, Poplar and Edmonton (in target area

of air attacks) Llanvaches, Mumbles, Carmarthen, Sennybridge, Abergavenny, Denbigh, disbanded at Oswestry 11 May 1944.

93 Company, PC – Formed Richborough Mar. 1940. Le Havre, Chateau Bray, Rennes, St Malo, evacuated 15 June 1940, Newbury, Cirencester, Calne, Codford, Watchet, Redruth, Weymouth, Portsmouth, Southampton, landed at Arromanches 20 July 1944, Bayeux, Dieppe, Brussels, disbanded there 30 June 1945.

137 Company, PC – Formed Westward Ho! 9 June 1940. Yeovil, then for clearing up work to Rotherhithe, Bermondsey and Deptford. 'The men of the Company who were medical doctors in civilian life, helped the victims of the air attacks'. Then Ilminster, Chard, Taunton, Dumfries, Peebles, Kirknewton, Douglas, Lockerbie and Dumfries again. Landed at Arromanches 2 Aug. 1944. Caen, Vaucelles, Le Bec Hellouin, Antwerp, from there the last foreigners were transferred to the Interpreters' Pool 19 July 1945.

165 Company, PC – Formed Bideford 23 July 1940. Then Cirencester, Newbury, Birdestow, Plymouth, Bicester, Thame, disbanded there 20 Feb. 1943.

219 Company, PC – Formed Ilfracombe 1 Oct. 1940, 'The men are drawn from 21 different nations'. Then Seahouses, Darlington, Long Eaton, Northampton, Wansford, Peterborough; all foreigners leave the company at Northampton 31 Jan. 1944.

220 Company, PC 'The British Foreign Legion' – Formed Ilfracombe 1 Oct. 1940. Forestry work in Forest of Dean, from 25 Feb. 19 41 Austrian company. Petersfield, Gloucester, Bourton-on-the-Water, Newhaven. Landed at Arromanches 1 Aug. 1944, Ryes, Montfiquet, Falaise till Oct. 1944, Hal, La Roche, Lembecque, St. Hubert during German Ardennes offensive, Schilde, Namur, Schinveld, Reichswald. In the end the Company had a Czech and a Baltic section, additional to the Austrian ones. Disbanded in Griethausen and Kellen near Kleve 11 Feb. 19 46.

229 Company, PC – Formed Bradford 18 Nov. 1940, 1941 temporarily Austrian company. Didcot, Gloucester, Codford (camp construction), Marlborough and Ogbourne (road construction), Southampton, Ogbourne again, Denmead, Wickham, Havant. From 14 July 1944 partly British. 21 July 19 44 landed in Normandy, then Bayeux, disbanded Englesqueville 18 Dec. 1944.

246 Company, PC – Formed Bradford 29 Nov. 1940. Then Saltney. all Austrians posted to 220 Company 28 Feb. 19 41. Stoke, Shrewsbury; disbanded there 20 June 1942.

248 Company, PC – Formed Ilfracombe Dec. 1940. Then Catterick. Turned into British company 26 Apr. 1943.

249 Company, PC 'The Jordan Highlanders' – Formed Ilfracombe 27 Dec. 1940. Catterick, Peebles, Hawick, Glasgow, Paisley. Turned into British company 5 Aug. 1943.

251 Company, PC – Formed Ilfracombe 19 Mar. 1941. Avonmouth, Cheltenham, Bicester, Thame, alien company until 22 June 1943, then British.

253 Company, PC – In existence in the United Kingdom on 13 Dec. 1943.

357 Company, PC – On 13 Dec. 1943 being formed overseas

358 Company, PC – On 13 Dec. 1943 being formed overseas

366 Company, PC – On 13 Dec. 1943 being formed overseas These four companies were SOE Special Companies formed to train personnel for infiltration into Germany and Nazi occupied territories. Their strength is unknown, but is unlikely to have exceeded 50 men at any time. They were recruited partly from amongst men of the *Wehrmacht* (prisoners and deserters, referred to as BONZOS) and partly from special groups of refugees, such as members of the German Communist Party and others. It is known that in 253 Coy there was a group of 34 men, all BONZOS, all paid as sergeants. Apart from this no information concerning these highly secret units is available.

337 Company, PC – Formed in Hussein Dey near Algiers 11 Dec. 1942, Maison Carrée (Algeria), Sessini, disbanded Algiers 31 Dec. 1944.

338 Company, PC – Formed in Ferne Souk Ali near Kolea (Algeria) 1 Apr. 1943. 'The formation of the company from 169 refugees from the camps of Colomb-Bechar, Kenadsa and Bidon was instructed by the Allied High Command. Many had served in the Foreign Legion. The majority were Germans and Austrians, but amongst them were also Czechoslovaks, Poles, Rumanians, Yugoslavs, Italians, Russians, Hungarians, Egyptians, Spaniards and Portuguese.' Then Maison Carrée, Algiers, Hussein Dey. Landed at Taranto 14 Sept. 1944, Naples, Caserta. Disbanded there 30 June 1945.

362 Company, PC – Formed Maison Carrée (Algeria) 16 May 1943. The ethnic composition of this company is not quite clear. There is no doubt that at least 60 men spoke German as their mother tongue. At Hussein Dey. 24 Oct. 1944 landed at Glasgow. Then at Penrith, Kirkham, Brampton, Carlisle, last entry in war diary is dated '31.12.45, Carnforth'.

Special units

3 Troop, No. 10 Interallied Commando, 'X-Troop'. – Formed Aberdovey, July 1942. 99% of the men were German speakers. Detachments were at Dieppe 1942, in various attacks on the French and Norwegian coasts, in the Sicily landings, various actions in Italy from Messina to Udine, Normandy, Walcheren, river Maas, Norway and in Germany. Finally stationed at Ploen, Schleswig-Holstein.

51 Middle East Commando – Most of the men were German and Austrian refugees to Palestine. In action in Ethiopia and Eritrea (battles of Amba Alagi and Keren), later in North Africa and Italy.

21 Indep. Para. Company – Pathfinder of 1st Airborne Div. Contained a significant German speaking element. In action at Bône (Algeria), in Sicily, Taranto, Bari, Foggia, Arnhem, Norway.

1 Indep. Para. Platoon – Pathfinder of 2nd Indep. Airborne Brigade, operation 'Hasty', Le Muy (South of France), Greece.

22 Indep. Para. Company – Pathfinder of 6th Airborne Div., had a number of German speakers. In action in Normandy and at the Rhine crossing at Wesel.

All Jewish Combatant Brigade – Formed in Palestine. In action in Northern Italy.

Numbers

Before the transfers to fighting units of the Army, Royal Navy and RAF in the middle of 1943 had taken place there were 15 German and Austrian Alien companies of the Pioneer Corps in the United Kingdom and two and part of one in Algeria, making a total of about seventeen and a half companies.

	Number of Men and Women
By the beginning of 1943 each company had 10 sections of 30 men making in each company. Each company also had 6 alien sergeants and about 10 HQ staffs.	300
	16
Not all the companies were at full strength, so let us take off	16
and take a company to have had about	300

There were seventeen and a half companies

So the total number of aliens in those companies was about	5,250

In the Pioneer Corps Training Centre there were some	150
The number of men, who by the end of 1941 had taken early discharge was about	100
The number of transfers to technical corps, which had already been actioned was	995
and those to Intelligence	220
Commissioned officers in the Pioneer Corps then were about	35
and in the ATS there were anything between 200 and 500 women, so let us take the middle	350

I therefore take the number who had joined before 1943 at	about 7,100

The number of these who have given me sufficient details to allow me to say with certainty that they had joined before 1943 is	115
which is equivalent to	1.62%
Those who have given me sufficient details to allow me to say with certainty that they had joined 1943 or later is	41
If they represent 1.62% of those who enlisted without having gone through the Pioneer Corps, they would represent	some 2,530
253 Coy PC might account for another	70

This would mean that altogether there were some	9,700

It is obvious that many of these figures are inexact and some are very inexact. One might say that an error of 600 or even more in either direction is absolutely possible. I therefore take it that we were anything between 9,000 and 10,300 and therefore feel justified to say 'we were about 10,000 men and women'.

I am encouraged by the fact that Norman Bentwich, making his calculation on quite a different, but even more approximate basis arrived at a total of 9,230, which is only 5 per cent different from my figure.

Sources

Individual reports (in writing or by word of mouth), from:

Werner E. Abraham, Mrs Lorraine Allard, Manfred Alweiss, Ken Ambrose, Martin Amson, Mrs Ruth Anderman, Herbert Anderson, Klaus Anschel, Alice and Colin Anson, Mr and Mrs M.V. Arnott, C.C. Aronsfeld, Mrs Isabelle Avetoom, George Baer, Horace Norbert Barrett, Ken W. Bartlett, Harold Becker, Eric M. Beecham, Mrs Lieselotte Bier, Mrs Marion Blin, Peter Block, Rudolph Walter Boam, Gerhard Boehm, Frau Ruth Bratu, Mrs Lotte S. Bray, Bern Brent, Walter Brian, Allan Bright, Henry R. Brook, Sidney Edward Brook, Ernest Brown, Harold Bruce, F. Burnell, Richard Burnett, The Revd Erich Cahn, Dr Julius Carlebach, John Carson, P.A. Carson, C.P. Carter, Mrs Ruth Cemach, Erich Clement, Hans Joseph Cohn, Prof. Patrick Collinson, D.M. Compton, Michael Conway, The Revd Peter Crawford, Mrs Rita Curtis, Stephen Dale, William W. Dieneman, Prof. Dr E.W. Duck, Peter Eden, Albert Edwards, F.H. Edwards, Sidney Edwards, Bernhard F. Eibner, Leo Eisenfeld, Prof. Walter Elkan, John Gordon Elting, Georg D. Engel, John Envers, Mrs Ava M. Farrington, Dr Heinz D. Feldheim, Mrs M.E. Felix, William Field, Herbert N. Frank, Bryan Fisher, Ralph G. Fort, Walter Foster OBE, Ludwig D. Fried, Peter Howard Fry, John Gassman, Peter Harry Gayward OBE, Mrs Eva E. Gillatt, Martin Glenville, Werner Goerke, Franz Gockel, Dr Bill Godsey, Sidney Goldberg, Herbert Goldsmith, Prof. Dr Ernest Goodman, Henry William Grenville, Sir Ronald Grierson, Ing. S.H. Gruber, Louis Hagen, Mrs Anna E.C. Harvey, Mrs Judith Headley, Howard Peter Hein, R.H. Hellmann, Ad Hermens, Her Royal Highness the Princess Margaret of Hesse and by Rhine, Richard Hyman, Guenther P. Hirsch, H. Hoffmann, Frederick Hogan, Ms Joan Holden, Mrs Eva Holland, Paul Hollander, Walter Horn, John Horton, W.A. Howard, Miss Beata Hulsen, Alan Jackson, Ernest M. Jacobs, C.S. Jarrett, Peter W. Johnson, HE the Canadian Ambassador at Bonn, Rudy Karrell, F.G. Katz, Eric J. Kennedy, Dr Eric Kenneth, Dr Eric A. Kirby, Mrs Trudi King, Mrs Ilse Klein, Heinz Klingler, Eric Koch, Manfred Kory, Mrs Lilly Laker, Kurt Land, Alfred Thomas Lane, Jack Charles Lee, Mrs Jennifer Langer, Martin Lawrence, Ernest Lennard, Hans Leser, Mrs Bertha Leverton, Frau Irma Levy, Karl-Ernst Levy, Frau Renate Loewenheck, Ian Lowit, F. Lustig, Lady McWilliam, Sascha Manierka, Walter Marmorek, Andrew Martin, Peter F. Masters, Peter Mayer, K.P. Mayer, Paul Yogi Mayer, M. Maynard, J.E. Melford, Peter Meyer, Leopold Michel, Mrs U. Miles, H.F. Miller, Frank Mond, Henry Lewis Morland, David J. Morrison-Wilpred, Henry P. Mortimer, Ernest Morton, Steve Nelson, S.K. Nelson, Group Captain Hans Neubroch OBE, George Newman, Harry Nomburg, H. Oden, Professor Dr Dietrich Oppenberg, Peter M. Oppenheimer, Dr Arnold Paucker, Manfred Pinz, Geoffrey Phillips, Henry Platt, Mrs Erica Prean, R. Pringle, Andy Rasp, Bob Reid, John D. Renner, Mrs Helga Relation, Henry Rodwell, Garry R. Rogers, Mrs Lore Rosen, Heinrich Rosenkranz, Dr Werner S. Rosenthal, Herbert Paul Rosinger, Mrs A. Rosney, Eric Sanders, Ralph Sanders JP, Mrs Sarah Sanders, Heinz Schmoll, Henry Seaman, John

Seaman, Mrs Laura Selo, R.W. Sherman, Avraham Shomroni, Stefan-Helmut Simon, H. Peter Sinclair, Mrs Margot Smith, Mike Sondheim, Prof. Keith Spalding, Alfred Spier, Ronald Stent, John Stanleigh, Frantisek Steiner, Bob Stenham, E. Stern, Frau Edith Stern, Dr Hans Sternberg, Harry Stevens, John Gordon Steward, Herman Straus, Steven Strauss, Ms Julia Stuart, E.J. Studley, Steven Summerfield, Ms L. Talbot, Hofrat Otto Talsky, C. Teddern, Gerd Treuhaft, Dr Peter E. Trier CBE, Hans George Tuchler, Willi Usher, Mrs Inge Lucy Verney, Ralf Wachtel, Ms Frances Waldek, Sighard Wahlhaus, Ron Walters, Eric Walters-Kohn, Mrs Irene Ward, Kenneth R. Ward, Fred M. Warner, Peter Wayne, Rolf Weinberg, Hans Paul Weiner, Konrad Weiss, HE the President of the State of Israel Ezer Weizmann, Walter Wilson, E. Winter, G.V. Wolf, Dr H.G. Wolff, Frau Friedl Wollmerstedt, Hanno Zade and Eberhard Zamory, as well as many others who have asked not to be named.

Archives

Public Records Office, Kew, London (PRO)
Imperial War Museum, London (ImpWarMus)
Dokumentationsarchiv des oesterreichischen Widerstands, Vienna (DoeW)
Bundesarchiv, Coblence
Bundesmilitaerarchiv, Freiburg im Breisgau (now Potsdam)
Gedenkstaette deutscher Widerstand, Berlin
Municipal archives, Darmstadt
Institut fuer personengeschichtliche Forschung, Bensheim
Archive of the parties and mass organisations of the GDR in the Bundesarchiv, Berlin
Archives of the Freudenberg Group, Weinheim.

Literature

I understand the Risks, Norman Bentwich, Victor Gollancz Ltd., London, 1950.
Mit Spaten, Waffen und Worten, Wolfgang Muchitsch, Ludwig Boltzmann Institut fuer Geschichte der Arbeiterbewegung, Materialien zur Arbeiterbewegung No.61, Europaverlag Wien * Zuerich 1992, ISBN 3-203-51176-2.
Ten Commando 1942–1945, Ian Dear, Leo Cooper, London, 1987, ISBN 0-85052-1211.
German- and Austrian-Jewish Volunteers in Britain's Armed Forces 1939–1945, Dr John P. Fox, Year Book XL, 1995, Leo Baeck Institute, London.
The Second World War, Winston S. Churchill, Cassell & Co, London * etc., 1948.
Both Sides of the Wire, The Fredericton Internment Camp, Vol. 1, Ted Jones, New Ireland Press, Fredericton, New Brunswick, ISBN 0-920483-21-6.
A bespattered page?, Ronald Stent, Andre Deutsch Ltd., London , 1980.
'Juedische Schicksale', Dokumentationsarchiv des oesterreichischen Widerstands, Vienna.
Commando Men, Bryan Samain, Stevens & Sons Ltd., London 1948.
Unternehmen Nimrod – Wie Hitler getaeuscht wurde, James Leasor, Paul Zsolnay Verlag GmbH, Vienna–Hamburg.

Geschichte der deutschen BP 1904–1979, Fren Foerster, Reuter & Kloeckner Verlags-Buchhandlung, Hamburg, 1979. ISBN 3-92 1174-05-8.

Berlin Days 1946–47, George Clare, Macmillan London Ltd. 1989, ISBN 0-333-60587-X.

Changing Enemies, Noel Annan, Harper Collins, London, ISBN 0-00-255629-4.

Die Warburgs, R. Chernow, Siedler Verlag, 1994.

The Fourth Estate, Jeffrey Archer, HarperCollins, London.

Palestinian PoWs in German Captivity, Yoav Gelber, Yad Vashem Studies XIV, Jerusalem 1981.

Three Lives in Transit, Laura Selo, Excalibur Press, 1992.

Der lange Marsch, Keith Spalding, Gunter Narr Verlag, Tuebingen, ISBN 3-8233-5161-3.

Das war unser Leben, Eberhard Zamory, Verlag Neues Leben, 1996.

International Biographical Dictionary of Central European emigrés 1933–45.

German Military Dictionary, Technical Manual TM 30-506, War Department, Washington, 1944.

'Naturalization of noncitizens serving in the Army of the United States', Circular No. 193, War Department, Washington 25, 17 Aug. 1943.

Report to the War Department. Naturalization of Members of the Armed Forces of the United States etc., etc.', Dr Henry B. Hazard, US Department of Justice, 30 June 19 1945.

'A well kept secret', Martin Sugarman, *Medal News*, Apr. 1996.

'List of Jewish servicemen at the battle of Arnhem', Martin Sugarman, 1999.

Who's Who.

Unpublished books and private documents

'All for the Best or the History of Young Walter', Walter Foster OBE, Bournemouth.

'Normandie – Die Invasion am 6. Juni 1944 ueberlebt', Franz Gockel, D 59069 Hamm-Rhynern, May 1994.

'Dachau to Dunkirk', Fred Pelican.

'Recollections of a Septuagenarian in the Twentieth Century', Heinz Lothar Schmoll, Perth, Western Australia, 1991, private.

'Spanglet, or by any other name', Stephen Dale, private.

Roll of Honour of Ex-Service NB Association, by courtesy of Peter Eden.

Excerpts from the war diaries of the A-companies, Pioneer Corps, from the working papers of Major Rhodes-Wood, by courtesy of Major John Starling.

'Before, during and after', Walters-Cohn, *Austria Today* Jan. 94

'Don't you know there is a war on? – A very personal account', F.M.Warner, private, Hamburg 1985

'They lost their freedom fighting for yours', Hans Paul Weiner, private.

Nominal roll of 1st Allied Volunteer Platoon, ATS, by courtesy of Erica Prean.

Nominal roll of Parachute Training School Ringway, report on Course No. 61B and 62, by courtesy of Peter Block.

Nominal roll of *Dunera* survivors, by courtesy of Mike Sondheim.

Nominal roll of the members of the Ex-Service NB Association at the time of its dissolution, by courtesy of Peter Eden.

War Diary of Auxiliary Military Pioneer Corps No. 3 (Alien) Centre, by courtesy of Major John Starling.

German Prisoner of War Companies, The Pioneer, 1946.

Letter of thanks from the men of 74 Company, Pioneer Corps, to their Officer Commanding, Shirehampton, 1 May 19 43.

Nominal roll of 74 Coy. AMPC with the BEF, by courtesy of Major John Starling.

Author's own records made between 1937 and 1996 and documents in the author's possession.

Newspapers, including wall newspapers, magazines

Bergstraesser Anzeiger, *Darmstaedter Echo*, Foresight (wall newspaper of 229 Company PC), *Frankfurter Allgemeine Zeitung*, *Free Austria* (by courtesy of Dokumentationsarchiv des oesterreichischen Widerstands, Vienna), *Juedische Rundschau*, *Evening Standard*, *The Ex-Serviceman*, *Renaissance*, *Journal of the Royal Pioneer Corps Association*, *Daily Telegraph*, *Telegraph Magazine*, *The Times*, *Watford Observer*, *Western Mail*, *Young Austria* and *Zeitspiegel* (the two last-named by courtesy of Dokumentationsarchiv des oesterreichischen Widerstands, Vienna).

Co-operation with and assistance from
Lt Col Tony Williams, MBE in respect of Intelligence Corps

We Will Remember Them
Henry Morris and Martin Sugarman

This highly illustrated edition, first published in 1989, comprises a comprehensive and indispensable history of the Jewish contribution to the British Armed Forces in the Second World War. Many were British-born or living in Britain, but large numbers of Jews in Palestine also volunteered. The Rolls of Honour contained in this book show that many more were wounded. The book is illustrated with photographs of individual servicemen and women. It also includes essays by Martin Sugarman on British Jews who served in the Spanish Civil War, Jews with the Chindits, Jewish servicemen in the Korean War, Canadian and Allied Jews at the raid on Dieppe, Jewish prisoners of war of the Germans and of the Japanese, and those who served in other units and in other theatres of war.

September 2006, 880 pages
ISBN 0 85303 621 7

War or Revolution
Russian Jews and Conscription in Britain, 1917
Harold Shukman

During the First World War, 30,000 Russian Jews of military age in Britain faced a terrible dilemma: to enlist for the carnage of the Western Front or risk everything by returning to Russia. Introducing conscription in 1916, the government had to decide whether the refugees should remain exempt. When Nicholas II was overthrown the picture changed – Russia was now seen as democratic, why not go back to defend it, and, if not, why not join the British army? That was the choice. Bolshevik agitation against compulsion added to the refugees' confusion. Some joined up in Britain. Nearly 4,000 – the author's father and uncle among them – chose to go back. They arrived in Archangel in the autumn of 1917 together with the Arctic winter and the chaos of the revolution, which soon descended into bloody civil war. How they fared and how they struggled to return to Britain is the story of *War or Revolution*.

May 2006, 150 pages
ISBN 0 85303 707 8, 0 85303 708 6

Jewish Resistance in Wartime Greece
Steven Bowman

While the murder of nearly 90 per cent of Greek Jews by the Nazis has begun to enter the Holocaust story, the participation of Greek Jews in the war against the Nazis is virtually unknown. Greek Jews actively fought in the war against Italian and German invaders. Veterans and young Jewish males and females went to the mountains to fight or serve in various ways in the *andartiko* among the several Greek Resistance movements. Other Jews remained in urban areas where they joined different Resistance cells, whether as saboteurs or in leadership roles. A number of Jews appear on the payrolls of Force 133. Additionally Greek Jews participated in the Sonderkommando revolt in the Auschwitz concentration camp in October 1944, while others fought in the Warsaw revolt from August to October 1944. Based on interviews and archival research the author has assembled a preliminary list of over 650 individuals who fought or served with the Greek Resistance forces. These include *andartes* and *andartissas*, interpreters, recruiters, doctors, spies, nurses, organizers and a number of non-Greek Jews who volunteered or were trapped in Greece during the war years.

January 2006, 136 pages
ISBN 0 85303 599 7, 0 85303 598 9